T0331398

Computable, Constructive and Behavioural Economic Dynamics

The book contains 30 original articles dealing with important aspects of theoretical as well as applied economic theory. The principal focus is on the computational and algorithmic nature of economic dynamics and on the individual as well as collective rational behaviour. Some contributions emphasize also the importance of classical recursion theory and constructive mathematics for dynamical systems, business cycles theories, growth theories, and others are in the area of history of thought, methodology and behavioural economics. The contributors range from Nobel Laureates to the promising new generation of innovative thinkers.

This volume is also a Festschrift in honour of Professor Kumaraswamy Vela Velupillai, the founder of Computable Economics, a growing field of research where important results stemming from classical recursion theory and constructive mathematics are applied to economic theory. The aim and hope is to provide new tools for economic modelling.

This book will be of particular appeal to postgraduate students and scholars in one or more of the following fields: computable economics, business cycles, macroeconomics, growth theories, methodology, behavioural economics, financial economics, experimental and agent based economics. It is also of importance to those interested in the general theme of algorithmic foundations for social sciences.

Stefano Zambelli is Professor of Political Economy in the Department of Economics at University of Trento, Italy.

Routledge frontiers of political economy

MJ sept 07

Computable, Constructive and Behavioural Economic Dynamics

Essays in honour of Kumaraswamy (Vela) Velupillai

Edited by Stefano Zambelli

Routledge
Taylor & Francis Group

LONDON AND NEW YORK

First published 2010
by Routledge
2 Park Square, Milton Park, Abingdon, Oxon OX14 4RN

Simultaneously published in the USA and Canada
by Routledge
711 Third Avenue, New York, NY 10017

Routledge is an imprint of the Taylor & Francis Group, an informa business

Typeset in Times by Wearset Ltd, Boldon, Tyne and Wear

British Library Cataloguing in Publication Data
A catalogue record for this book is available from the British Library

Library of Congress Cataloging in Publication Data
A catalog record for this book has been requested

ISBN13: 978-0-415-49263-8 (pbk)
ISBN13: 978-0-203-86014-4 (ebk)

Contents

Figures

Tables

Contributors

Abraham, Ralph, Mathematics Department, University of California, Santa Cruz, USA.

Boylan, Thomas A., Department of Economics, National University of Ireland, Galway, Ireland.

Bruun, Charlotte, Department of Economics, Aalborg University, Denmark.

Chaitin, Gregory, IBM – T.J. Watson Research Center, New York, USA.

Chen, Shu-Heng, National Chengchi University, Taipei, Taiwan.

Chiodi, Guglielmo, Università della Sapienza, Rome, Italy.

Clower, Robert W., University of South Carolina – Moore School of Business Economics, USA.

Corsino, Marco, Department of Informatics and Business Studies, Faculty of Economics, University of Trento, Italy.

Da Costa, N.C.A., Academia Brasileira de Filosofia, Rio de Janeiro, Brazil.

Day, Richard H., Department of Economics, University of Southern California (USC), California, USA.

De Antoni, Elisabetta, Department of Economics, University of Trento, Italy.

Doria, F.A., Academia Brasileira de Filosofia, Rio de Janeiro, Brasil.

Feldman, Todd, Economics Department, University of California, Santa Cruz, USA.

Foley, Duncan K., Department of Economics, New School, New York, USA.

Friedman, Daniel, Economics Department, University of California, Santa Cruz, USA.

Gabriele, Roberto, Department of Informatics and Business Studies, Faculty of Economics, University of Trento, Italy.

Harcourt, G.C., Jesus College, Cambridge University, Cambridge, UK.

Heyn-Johnsen, Carsten, Department of Economics, Aalborg University, Denmark.

Holm, Håkan J., Department of Economics, Lund, University, Sweden.

Huang, Ya-Chi, National Chengchi University, Taipei, Taiwan.

Kerr, Prue, Jesus College, Cambridge University, Cambridge, UK.

Lawson, Tony, Faculty of Economics, University of Cambridge, Cambridge, UK.

Lee, Cassey, Business School, University of Nottingham, Malaysia.

Leijonhufvud, Axel, Department of Economics, University of Trento, Italy, and University of California of Los Angeles (UCLA).

Luna, Francesco, International Monetary Fund, Washington, USA.

McCall, John J., University of California of Los Angeles (UCLA), University of Santa Barbara, California, USA.

McCauley, Joseph L., Physics Department, University of Houston, Texas, USA.

O'Gorman, Paschal F., Department of Philosophy, National University of Ireland, Galway, Ireland.

Prasad, Kislaya, Robert H. Smith School of Business, University of Maryland, USA.

Rissanen, Jorma, Technical Universities of Tampere and Helsinki Institute for Information Technology, IBM Research, San Jose, California, USA.

Rosser, J. Barkley, Jr., Department of Economics, James Madison University, Virginia, USA.

Samuelson, Paul A., Massachusetts Institute of Technology, Department of Economics, Cambridge, MA, USA.

Solow, Robert, Massachusetts Institute of Technology, Department of Economics, Cambridge, MA, USA.

Sordi, Serena, Department of Political Economy, University of Siena, Siena, Italy.

Thalberg, B., Department of Economics, Lund University, Sweden.

Velupillai, Viveka, Department of English, Justus Liebig Universität Gießen, Gemany.

Wang, Jen-Fu, National Chengchi University, Taipei, Taiwan.

Zambelli, Stefano, Department of Economics, University of Trento, Italy.

Zaninotto, Enrico, Department of Informatics and Business Studies, Faculty of Economics, University of Trento, Italy.

Foreword

In March 2007 I arrived at Tooreeny, near Galway, at Prof. Kumaraswamy Vela Velupillai home (hereafter just Vela). It was not the first time that I had visited Vela there. Before arriving at his home I thought about the many different places where I had visited him since I met him. I have had the pleasure of visiting him at Badia Fiesolana, Fiesole, where he and his family were living in a beautiful house just outside Caldine, viewing the beautiful landmark of Tuscany. I visited him at his house at Castello (just outside Dervio at Lago di Como), where the view over the lake was absolutely wonderful. I visited him at Svanshall, Sweden, where the view over the sea was just splendid. I visited him at Los Angeles (Santa Monica, Pacific Palisades and Westwood) where the surroundings were the quintessence of beauty and modernity American style.

As I was approaching Vela's residence I found myself wondering how many different homes he had had. On my arrival I asked Vela about it. To my surprise his reply was very precise: 61! To such a type of personal question he is normally evasive, but not this time!

Anyone who has visited Vela at any of his homes will know that no matter what, he is surrounded by books. Books that, as if it was some sort of magic, seem to follow him wherever he goes. Although some old books, donated to colleagues and friends, are replaced with new ones, no matter what: books are there around him.

Also the views you can enjoy from his homes are always very spectacular: and Tooreeny was no exception – it had a beautiful view over a very nice lake. During my stay Vela gave a party and during the party I went upstairs – where most of the books were and from where one could enjoy the view over the lake. To browse through his books is an experience in itself: there is always either an important old book or a very nice new one. You pick a book and it would have a story. Obviously a story of its own – for the reasons it came into being – but also a story associated with why, when and where Vela bought the book: you ask and he will tell about both ... and if you have time to spare and Vela has time to talk it will end up into being a lecture on this or that topic.

Vela always has a good reason why he got the book and a good story to be told about the book. Books are lively entities. Moreover, all of Vela's books are underlined with a ruler and a pencil and comments are to be found at the margin. And what he underlines and the comments are always interesting to read.

As I said I was, and I am, used to looking through Vela's bookshelves. Each move from the previous home to the next one allows him to rearrange the books, so that it is interesting to see where he locates a certain class of books with respect to another class and it is also interesting to see which 'new' bookshelves have appeared and where the 'classics' happen to be located.

With respect to what I had experienced before, in Tooreeny I saw something totally different: at a particular corner – as if it was hidden – there was a bookshelf with only his publications.

This was quite unusual. I have known Vela since 1982–1983 and since then Vela has always shared with me most of his intellectual thoughts and has always sent me copies of his work. Therefore I was aware of his publications, but to see all of them being so nicely arranged was a great thrill for me. I started browsing through the books with great interest.

One shelf was totally devoted to the books he edited or authored. Five were Festschrifts volumes, two were a collection of original articles and one was his *Computable Economics* book. On the shelves below and above there was also a long series of books where he was a contributor mixed with reprints of his articles. As I said, what really struck me was that this was the first time that his works were to be seen assembled all together. Yes, the bookshelf was located in a corner and not immediately visible, but yet it was there. I had not seen this in his previous homes. In his apartment in Trento, where he has now moved together with his family and with his books, I have not been able to see the same bookshelf. His publications are somewhat scattered 'in between' the work of others.

In his life he has always shown great appreciation to the work of others. This is clear from his own works and it is clear from the Festschrifts he has edited. It is at that point that I was sure that he too deserved a Festschrift. I had been thinking about it for sometime, but I had some trepidation in taking up the task. Many of those that have done it know what I mean. I was a little hesitant for two reasons. First there was the risk that in such a project not many will contribute, not because they did not want to but because almost all of those which I thought should contribute are very busy people and although they surely appreciate Vela's tremendous intellectual capacity and work may not have had time to devote to a contribution to a Festschrift. This was really my major concern: that there would have not been enough contributors. A second problem was that I was not able to figure out whether Vela would like it or not. It is always very difficult to know whether he appreciates to be at the centre of attention or not. His shyness and modesty is counterbalanced by his intellectual curiosities: a Festschrift of original articles would certainly have embarrassed him but it would have been counterbalanced by the curiosity of reading what people would write about.

Being in front of that bookshelf I put aside all my concerns and decided that a Festschrift had to be put together. The following day I asked Vela's wife, Maria Johansson, on whether she thought it was a good idea. She said that it was. A few days later I called Viveka Velupillai, his eldest daughter: she too thought it would be a great idea.

Having the approval of his wife and his eldest daughter I went back to my University and started with some trepidation to send mails around. The first mail I sent was to Routledge. I got from them an immediate response and support. All those that I have been in touch at Routledge have been very cooperative and understanding. In particular I wish to thank Terry Clague, Tom Sutton and Bethany Lewis for their constant support. I have to thank the anonymous referees for providing thoughtful and encouraging reports. I apologize for not being able to follow all of their suggestions.

All those who I contacted accepted right away and with great enthusiasm. Only very few – less than a handful – were not able to deliver simply because they were too busy with other things.

In a few months all those that had accepted had delivered a title and an abstract so that by his sixtieth birthday Vela received at Tooreeny as a surprise gift a little booklet with a Table of Contents and the abstracts. I am sure he placed it in the hidden bookshelf with his publications. The booklet was assembled and delivered as a surprise to Vela. This was possible thanks to the help of his wife Maria Johansson and of his daughter, Viveka Velupillai – who did most of the assembly and made sure that Vela did not suspect anything. This was the first present coming from all the contributors.

The second present from the contributors are the final versions published in this volume.

The booklet had as a front page a drawing of Vela that his wife made. The drawing is in this volume facing the title page: it is the homage of his wife to her husband. A beautiful homage from his daughter is here reproduced at the end of this volume as an independent chapter with the title: 'A homage to my father'. Viveka is in this case representing all of Vela's five daughters: Viveka, Sumithra, Aruna, Alva and Kalyani (ordered by age).

Viveka has been of incredible help. When I first asked her opinion on whether it was a good idea to organize a Festschrift for her father, she said that she would have liked to help in any possible way. She kept her promise and she has helped more than it was imaginable. She has a PhD in linguistics and has several important publications in her field: to have her as a volunteer (meaning not paid!) editorial assistant has been a real luxury. Almost every contributor has been in touch with her and has been able to appreciate her qualities. She has been great. It is obvious that any infelicities in the volume are to be blamed on me. To try to put the blame on her would be pathetic: she is too good to make mistakes. I do not know whether this is due to genetic or family-cultural influence, but she has a lot of her father ... and a lot of her own. Thank you.

Vela is now a citizen of a globalized world. He does not have a blog, does not have a face book, but uses the email. Does he! Almost each of his emails are the work of a scholar: they are first draft articles. He writes to all sorts of scholars on whichever topic he might be interested at the moment. Scholars around the world may not be aware of Vela's existence, but as soon as they get a mail from Vela, one thing is sure: they will never forget him. All his thoughts are deep and original, but are always conveyed in a very simple way and to the point. Those who know him know what I mean. Whichever is the topic the contacted scholar is an expert on, whether it is on the complexity of the game of Go, on the Phillips machine, on some obscure reference appeared in an obscure book and so on, whatever the reason, Vela would most likely have raised a great interest from the scholar. Moreover and as I said above Vela has been somewhat permanent in 61 different places (plus all the other places he has visited 'in between'). In each place he left a mark and he met people with which he keeps some form of contact. Therefore, I surely owe an apology to all those scholars who deserved to be invited to contribute, but who weren't. My excuse is that Vela has 'parallel' lives and not all of them are known to me and to keep track of everything is impossible. Sorry.

I have to thank also Nicole Bertotti, the secretary at the Interdepartmental Research Training in Economics and Management (CIFREM – Faculty of Economics – University of Trento) who during the first stage has helped in finding the addresses of the contributors.

My two daughters, Martina Lucia and Sofia, are also to be thanked for their support. Sometimes the deadlines do conflict with family plans, but they too love Vela and his family; when I told them it was something I was doing for Vela, their protests were milder. My wife Silvana is always supportive, but when it comes to matters related to Vela she is even more supportive. Silvana has known Vela almost as long as I have and has great memories of the time we spent together, in particular to the time together at UCLA.

Finally, I have to thank all the distinguished contributors, who have responded so warmly and with such original articles. As I mentioned above, all those that I contacted responded immediately and with great enthusiasm: this is alone the best present and recognition of his intellectual and human qualities that Vela could get.

Thank you all.

Stefano Zambelli
Department of Economics – University of Trento

Postscript

As the final manuscript was ready to be sent to the printers, I received the news that Paul Samuelson had passed away. To correspond with him has been one of the greatest professional and personal thrills of my life. I am sure that all the contributors to this volume agree that there are no words to express the emptiness that his departure leaves to the profession.

I take this opportunity to express solidarity and moral support to Janice Murray, his assistant, and to Robert Solow, who have walked during most of their lives side by side with him.

Any economist worth his or her salt knows how Paul Samuelson and Robert Solow have been, academically speaking, strongly linked. During my editorial work, I also came to understand how close Robert Solow and Paul Samuelson must have been in their private lives, when I realized that they were sharing the same fax number.

All the contributors to this volume express their warm condolence to all those, like Janice Murray and Robert Solow, who feel the absence of their dear friend and colleague, Paul Samuelson, in their daily life.

Introduction

Stefano Zambelli

The 30 different contributions forming this volume have been arranged into eight major parts. The 'Prelude', contains two contributions. There is my contribution 'Computable and constructive economics, undecidable dynamics and algorithmic rationality: an essay in honour of Professor Kumaraswamy (Vela) Velupillai' (Chapter 1) where I try to give a sketch of Velupillai's intellectual path. Here I focus on Velupillai's works on the Stockholm school, on phenomenological dynamics, on constructive and computable economics and algorithmic social sciences. Great emphasis is posed on the constructive and computability elements of his research which leads both to negative results (for example the uncomputability of Walrasian general equilibrium and of the first and second welfare theorems) and positive ones like the definition of the Keynes–Simon–Velupillai rationality. That is a concept of rational behaviour which does not imply Olympic capacities on the part of human agents. This provides new foundations for Simon's behavioural economics.

The second chapter, 'From an admirer and a friend' (Chapter 2), is a short letter from Robert Clower. This is a cameo expressing the appreciation of a great economist to another great one; Clower has made very important contributions to economics with respect to rational decision making and to the functioning of the economic systems as a whole. In a way his previous work links well with the work of Velupillai on phenomenological Keynesian dynamics and on the foundations of computable economics. Several of Velupillai's works are based on Clower's contributions. The letter is a homage from Clower to Velupillai. Velupillai was criticized for having published in his edited volume in honour of Richard Goodwin (Velupillai 1989) a short letter from Kenneth Galbraith. I also wish to be criticized for having done a similar thing. I thank Clower for having given the permission to publish his letter.

Part II, 'Dynamical systems, business cycles and macroeconomics' contains the contributions of three great macroeconomists: Paul Samuelson, Robert Solow and Axel Leijonhufvud, who each in their own way deals with issues related with phenomenological macroeconomic dynamics.

In 'The Richard Goodwin circle at Harvard (1938–1950)' (Chapter 3) Paul Samuelson pays a homage to Velupillai by providing recollections of his mentor at Harvard. This chapter gives a glimpse of what Harvard was in the 1940s and

1950s. Personal recollections involve scholars of the calibre of Schumpeter, Leontief, Haberler, Hansen. Samuelson's writings are always full of content and of elements for future reflections or elaborations. The reading of this contribution is a breath of fresh air. From the point of view of the birth and development of phenomenological macrodynamics Samuelson gives an important credit to Richard Goodwin's importance – in a way also supporting Velupillai's work on Goodwin's one-sided oscillator. He concludes his contribution in this volume with the following:

> Just as John Hicks gained much from talking to Harrod, Meade and whomever about Keynesian matters, in my recollection much of what ended up in Hick's 1950 *A Contribution to the Theory of the Trade Cycle* would not have been possible if he had not earlier talked over those issues with Dick Goodwin. That's the way the dynamics of scientific discovery works. Bees take elsewhere my honey; and much of what is 'mine' was brought to me by those same busy bees. Insiders know these things. But historians never can get things perfectly right.
>
> (Chapter 3: 54)

The contribution by Solow connects nicely with the above. In his contribution 'Not growth, not cycles, but something in-between' (Chapter 4) we find a certain dissatisfaction with the modern macro encapsulated in the Dynamic Stochastic General Equilibrium (DSGE) model which poses emphasis in the long-run trend of the economy and deviations from it given by the short run demand shocks. The connection between trend and cycles explained by a single process is what Solow does appropriately define as the Goodwin approach (Goodwin 1967), an approach which is followed in much of Velupillai's work on phenomenological dynamics (Velupillai 1982a, 1982b, 1999, 2006a, 2008a, 2008b). Solow has no doubt the authority of setting an agenda for further research in economic dynamics. Here he calls for further investigations with respect to the link between short run and long run and between optimizing agent models and phenomenological functional relationships. It is somewhat reassuring that this reveals Solow's ' "Keynesian" overtones' (Chapter 4, page 61), but it is also encouraging for those like Velupillai that are working on one aspect of the 'in between' approach. Namely, the non-equilibrium economic dynamics.

The chapter 'The nonlinear path of macroeconomic dynamics' (Chapter 5) by Axel Leijonhufvud also takes up the issue of the different approaches to business cycles: on one hand that embedded in the DSGE model and on the other the one embedded in the Goodwin–Velupillai phenomenological approach. What Leijonhufvud proposes, following Clower (1967) is a structure in which credit transactions are intertemporal trades in money. But if one takes this road one has also to recognize that 'the transversality condition imposed in intertemporal general equilibrium models has no empirical counterpart'. Moreover, new types of foundations for individual rational behaviour and for the working of the economic system in its whole are necessary. The conclusion of Leijonhufvud is the important recognition that 'While other macrotheorists have busied themselves with general equilibrium theory, Vela has spent the last 20 or so years laying the foundational groundwork for a theory able to tackle these issues' (Chapter 5, page 68). That is, the issues concerned with the proper foundations of rational behaviour and the foundations of the aggregate functioning of the whole economic system. Specifically, that is the work on Computable Economics and Algorithmic Social Sciences.

Another set of chapters have been grouped in Part III under the heading of 'Computable Economics'. One of the most important contributions of Velupillai is the understanding that if the economic agents and their collections forming the aggregate system are to be modelled formally as some sort of computing devices, then the results stemming from classical recursion theory have not to be ignored and have to be at the centre of the analysis … and this is what forms his Computable Economics approach to economic theory. In this part we find the contribution of four giants in computability (Gregory Chaitin, Jorma Rissanen, N.C.A. da Costa, F.A. Doria) and the work of Duncan K. Foley which has been inspired by the work of Rissanen.

'The information economy' (Chapter 6) is a contribution by Gregory Chaitin, one of the fathers of Algorithmic Information Theory. Chaitin is consistently developing the implications that a view of an economic system modelled as an information economy would become in the future. His conclusion is that:

> Clearly, we are not yet living in an information economy. Oil, uranium, gold and other scarce, precious limited natural resources still matter. But someday we may live in an information economy, or at least approach it asymptotically. In such an economy, everything is, in effect, software; hardware is comparatively unimportant. This is a possible world, though perhaps not yet our own world.
>
> (Chapter 6: 78)

And if this is the case – the real issue would be not what and how to produce, but what and how to distribute the product among those forming the system.

The issue of what an economic system can and cannot compute is somewhat indirectly addressed by N.C.A. da Costa and F.A. Doria in 'Hypotheses that imply the independence of P = NP from strong axiomatic systems' (Chapter 7). Da Costa and Doria are here following their research path where they try to assess the issue of whether P = NP or not. This is one of the millennium prize problems, the solution or assessment of which is going to be rewarded with $1 million dollars. I must admit that being the editor of this volume I have been tempted to ask to F.A. Doria to provide a 'friendly' version of their contribution. That is a version more adequate to a broad public of economists. Given the joyful spirit of this volume I have avoided to do so and those interested may surely contact Doria for further explanations. I might here simply comment by saying that Chaitin may have omitted, in his mentioning of scarce resources ('Oil, uranium, gold and other scarce, precious limited natural resources') the limited resource of time. Therefore his vision that hardware may in the future be comparatively unimportant with respect to software might depend on whether $P = NP$ or $P < NP$. In this last case time is important. While we are waiting for this issue to be settled we shall take da Costa and Doria's support of Chaitin seriously. 'The idea that one should start out of reasonable, even if unproved, hypotheses, more or less follows from Chaitin's suggestion that one should consider "empirically" verified hypotheses in mathematics.'

Chaitin is one of the fathers of Algorithmic Information Theory and Jorma Rissanen is one of the fathers of Stochastic Complexity. In his contribution 'Universal models' (Chapter 8) Rissanen explains the idea of universal models for statistics. Given a class of (stochastic) models a universal model for the class is any parameter free distribution, which behaves like any model in the class. The idea is new in statistics here borrowed from recursion theory.

The work of Duncan K. Foley 'Model description length priors in the urn problem' (Chapter 9) is an application of Rissanen's Minimum Description Length to the urn problem. In his own words:

> The choice of ways to describe significant aspects of the world, the classification, ordering and interpretation of data, and the establishment of plausible theoretical categories within which to analyze it are all ultimately aspects of prior specification which cannot be reduced to a single prescription. Rissanen makes this point extremely cogently, in arguing that the best statistics can do is to find the optimal description of the data within a class of models specified externally to the statistical analysis.
>
> (Chapter 9: 120)

Part IV, 'Constructivity, rationality and complexity in economic theory' includes the contributions of John J. McCall, J. Barkley Rosser, Richard H. Day, Håkan J. Holm and Kislaya Prasad.

John McCall is well known for his pioneer work on search theory. I am particularly pleased that he has chosen to contribute to this volume with a very substantial chapter centred on behavioural biology and its related disciplines such as cultural anthropology, neurobiology and the cognitive sciences. Although McCall considers this an 'introduction', 'The honeybee as teacher' (Chapter 10) is surely much more than an introduction. It encapsulates a vision on how economic theory ought to be done and it is an attempt to provide some foundations to evolutionary economics as biological mechanisms. 'Biological and economic decision making are similar in that search and exchange of information comprise their essence' (Chapter 10: 127). Clearly, McCall's choice to have this essay published as a homage to Velupillai dates back to a set of mimeos they have been writing together and which were never published. One of them had as a title 'Constructive Foundations for Economics'. In a way this long chapter by John McCall is a Biological Foundations for Economics.

J. Barkley Rosser is offering to us another important contribution. In 'Constructivist logic and emergent evolution in economic complexity' (Chapter 11) he discusses alternative complexity measures and discusses some of the work of

Velupillai as a constructivist critique of formal, classical mathematics (Velupillai 2005a, 2006b, 2009). Rosser concludes the chapter by suggesting the importance of the markomata idea of Mirowski that sees markets being simultaneously algorithmic systems that are evolving higher order structures. Unfortunately Mirowski's markomata, as I have explained elsewhere (Zambelli 2007), are not equivalent to Turing machines and hence are not able to generate higher order degrees of complexities (structures). This means that Mirowski's markomata are able to perform only algorithmic trivial computations, i.e. they are not complex at all and are incapable of producing new emerging structures. Either Rosser and Mirowski think that markets are simple or they must change the definition of markomata so as to allow for Turing machine equivalent computations.

In 'Remarks on numerical systems, algorithms and economic theory' (Chapter 12) Richard Day points to the fact that the domain of economics magnitudes is in the rational numbers and not real numbers. But most importantly, he fully supports Velupillai's call for a reconstruction of the economics discipline based directly on computation. Day makes a

ringing endorsement of Velupillai's algorithmic point of view. It presents economizing activity as *functioning through* time, that is, as a dynamic process. The economic aspects of life – as in all the biosphere of which it is a part – is always changing, ever evolving. The essence of algorithmic theory and dynamic theory generally is the symbolic and computational representation of this fundamental character of life as we know it. They deserve all the emphasis that Velupillai demands. Surely, the time will come when the self-appointed optimal control 'mainstream' will have surpassed its flood stage with its suffocating purge of any consideration of the out-of-equilibrium, algorithmic character of real world dynamics. Surely, it will in turn be overcome by a renewed surge of theoretical research into the nature of actual economizing behaviour and market exchange.

(Chapter 12: 201)

If Richard Day has posed the focus on the serious problem of the existence and effective computation of equilibrium in the articulated context of Walrasian General equilibrium which some of the work of Velupillai has emphasized, Håkan Holm, in his 'An experiment on equilibrium selection: The relative unimportance of context' (Chapter 13), presents an experiment in which a game where the existence of an equilibrium is computationally trivial, but in which the coordination problem is relevant. The results confirm the prediction present in classical game theory, but in spite of the simplicity of the game he finds that there are degrees in which payoff effects dominate strategy label effects. An interesting question which calls for further investigation is whether these degrees are consistent with classical assumptions on rational behaviour.

Kislaya Prasad in 'The complexity of social choice' (Chapter 14) acknowledges the result implicit in Arrow's famous impossibility theorem (1951) that it is impossible to devise ideal voting systems, but does also point out that 'different rules governing the political process matter, and there is scope for weighing in on the computational properties of alternatives' (Chapter 14: 212). He then proceeds with the study of computational and combinatorial complexities of social choice functions and of voting rules. Following the classical work of Garey and Johnson (1979) Prasad analyses the computational complexity of the different rules in terms of P versus NP-hard problems (discussed in depth in Chapter 7 of the present volume). He first reduces the choice function in terms of Turing machine computations and subsequently computes the computational complexity of the specific Turing machine. This procedure is very powerful, but does, as also acknowledged by Prasad, assume that the choice functions are always computable (i.e. the Turing machines always halt) and that $P < NP$. Implicitly Prasad is here assuming that the social choice functions belong to the set of computable functions. I am sure he has good reasons to assume so, but from him one would expect an explanation of why these social functions are all terminating, computable processes. In a way what he does is to bypass Velupillai's result that an effective theory of policy is impossible for a complex economy (see for example Velupillai 2007: 477). But obviously, computable processes can be NP-hard and here Prasad concludes that a number of calculations happen to be NP-hard, i.e. intractable. And this is important information, especially when choices of social choice functions have to be made.

The four contributions of Tony Lawson, Carsten Heyn-Johnson, Thomas A. Boylan, and Paschal F. O'Gorman, and of B. Thalberg are grouped in Part V under 'History of thought and methodology'.

Tony Lawson in his 'Varieties of internal critique' (Chapter 15) departs from the analysis of 'The unreasonable ineffectiveness of mathematics in economics' (Velupillai 2005b) – where it is pointed out that wrong economic theory conclusions and/or economic policy prescriptions are obtained through the use of the inadequate mathematics – to focus on the possible alternative effective paths to take. What Lawson does is to start from an internal critique with the aim of proposing a strategy for the development of a better model. He explains:

> For I have argued for a different social ontology, of openness, structure, process, internal relationality, emergence, meaning and value, a perspective against which the implicit ontology of the mainstream approach is seen to be highly impoverished, and which if correct, explains the generalised failings of modern economics. For, if the ontology I defend is correct, then methods that presuppose atomism and closure are questionable, and the reason for the continuing failure of a project that insists on them is evident.
>
> (Chapter 15: 225)

What he concludes is that his proposed methodological approach could proceed in parallel with Velupillai's work:

> Vela provides internal critiques of the types of mathematical methods that economists employ (not of specific models per se), by showing that they

cannot achieve what is expected of them (and indeed even thought to have been achieved by them). And Vela does this whilst keeping open, and enthusiastically discussing, the possibility of a mathematical approach eventually emerging that is free from the sort of problems he identifies in existing approaches.

(Chapter 15: 226)

This type of adherence and support of Vela's work is for many of us like fresh air.

In his 'Rational economic man: A centrepiece in social science?' (Chapter 16) Carsten Heyn-Johnsen takes us from Augustinus to Vela Velupillai through the works of Adam Smith, Jerremy Bentham, Willhelm Friedrich Hegel, Jean-Baptiste Say, John Stuart Mill, John Elliot Cairnes, Karl Marx, Lèon Walras, Wilfredo Pareto, Henry Sidgwick, George Moore and Francis Herbert Bradley, Francis Edgeworth, Maynard Keynes, John Hicks, Kenneth Arrow, Gèrard Debreu, Brennan and Buchanan. And reaches the conclusion, following some of Velupillai's results (2000: 32) that the rational economic agent cannot always effectively generate as preference ordering the relevant series of statements that are choices from sets containing two elements simply because there is 'no effective procedure to decide whether a preference order can be generated by methodically – i.e. systematically – evaluating alternatives' (Velupillai 2000: 39). After his very lucid and imaginative path through the history of thought Heyn-Johnsen concludes that Velupillai's result 'marks an unsurmountable intellectual obstacle for any conventional microeconomic foundation of economics' (Chapter 16: 253). And surely the concept of Rational Economic Man as optimizing mechanism reveals totally its emptiness. Should it be relegated to the history of economic thought? There is an alternative which pairs with the research made by Simon and Velupillai which is at the foundation of the new behavioural economics. As Herbert Simon wrote to Velupillai

There are many levels of complexity in problems, and corresponding boundaries between them. Turing computability is an outer boundary, and as you [Vela Velupillai] show, any theory that requires more power than that surely is irrelevant to any useful definition of human rationality.

(quoted in Chapter 1: 33)

And a new *homo economicus* is the one where 'there is ... an inherently unpredictable element in rational behaviour' (Velupillai 2000: 29) because one cannot 'prohibit thoughts to be thought and stories to be told' (Chapter 16).

Tony Lawson credits Velupillai's work to provide an important parallel contribution to his critical realism approach, Carsten Heyn-Johnsen considers the implications that some of Velupillai's results have for the 'death' of the rational economic man and the survival of *homo economicus* and Thomas Boylan and Paschal O'Gorman in their 'Resisting the sirens of realism in economic methodology: A Socratic odyssey' (Chapter 17) support that 'there is no given, *a priori*, single formal framework that is natural, in any sense, for the formalization of economics' (Velupillai 2000: 2). Having this as a conclusion they provide us with a taxonomy between realist and anti-realist economists and constructive and non-constructive mathematics. Naturally it seems that they have difficulties in locating the Velupillai's Computable Economics inside this taxonomy. One could say that this is actually consistent with Velupillai's innovative contributions which are in their very nature of true innovations difficult to characterize: in a way they are intrinsically undecidable. Therefore I welcome these difficulties positively 'precisely because there is no single framework that is natural for the formalization of economics'.

'Who, in Scandinavian economic theoretic literature, picked up major threads from Wicksell's writings?' (Chapter 18) by B. Thalberg is a clear celebration to Velupillai's contribution to Scandinavian economics (see also Chapter 1: 17–22) and is economic history at its best. Thalberg, who was Ragnar Frisch's student, was Professor at Lund, Wicksell's university, and has made several important contributions following the work of great Scandinavians. Clearly this contribution can be interpreted as a wish that 'elements of the [Stockholm] School' (Chapter 18: 287) could survive in Velupillai's non-mainstream economics.

G.C. Harcourt, Guglielmo Chiodi and Serena Sordi have been, respectively, Velupillai's teacher, fellow student and pupil. Their contributions, here grouped in Part VI under 'Capital, viability and growth', all have very strong Cambridge tones.

'*The Accumulation of Capital* over 50 years on' (Chapter 19) by G.C. Harcourt and Prue Kerr is, as the title indicates, an historical and critical analysis of Joan Robinson's important contribution. This chapter is an excursus into Joan Robinson's ideas in relation to the scholars and ideas of her time; in particular Harrod, Kaldor, Kalecki and Sraffa. It is probably not coincidental that at Girton College, the office that once was that of Joan Robinson was assigned to Velupillai.

Guglielmo Chiodi pays homage to Vela with a chapter which is one of Chiodi's major research areas. The concept of viability is fundamental also for the accumulation of capital and surely for the existence of the Robinson's golden age. Clearly Piero Sraffa had an impact on the research work of Velupillai. Here with the work of Chiodi it is confirmed the distinction between viability when the system is capable of producing a physical surplus and viability as a socially determined condition when considering the socially determined 'living wage'. The conclusion leads to the interesting suggestion that there may be alternative profiles of viabilities which accommodate to alternative survival wage bundles, which may include

> *disabled* people of the family, who by definition cannot be 'productive' in the economic sense [...] The point is that whoever the 'beneficiaries' are the model can accommodate their inclusion so as to have a set of alternative profiles of 'viability'. It is worth noting that each will be based on the circumstance that the commodities that feature as inputs to production com-

prise in part an appropriate or *decent* standard of subsistence, for if a society is to reproduce itself, then it must be such as to permit its members to appear in public without shame.

(Chapter 20: 328)

If with the work of Guglielmo Chiodi we have a concern with the proper definition of the social notion of viable system in relation with subsistence wage levels, in 'A disequilibrium growth cycle model with differential savings' (Chapter 21) by Serena Sordi we see a model that is based on the very strong tradition of the functional distribution of income concept. Her model builds and expands on the previous works of Kaldor, Goodwin, Velupillai and Pasinetti and it is shown the existence of at least one limit cycle and one Hopf bifurcation. This is the least one can expect from Vela's former student.

Part VII, 'Markets and their behaviours', groups the outstanding works of several scholars which with their own methods try to shed light to the functioning of the world we live in.

Joseph L. McCauley in his 'Evolution of FX markets and new financial economics' (Chapter 22) presents both a strong critique of current efficient market hypothesis and of neo-classical equilibrium (including rational expectation equilibria and Lucas policy prescriptions). An important point put forward in the chapter is that 'fat tails' maybe 'spurious stylized facts' (Chapter 22: 370–3). It is a beautiful example of the power of Econophysics as well as an essay through the history of financial economics.

Shu-Heng Chen, Ya-Chi Huang and Jen-Fu Wang in 'Elasticity puzzle: an inquiry into micro–macro relations' (Chapter 24) use an agent based model with the aim to shed light to the problem that in the representative agent models if the estimated intertemporal elasticity of substitution is very low the implied relative risk aversion can be very high. They develop an agent based model so as to introduce heterogeneity and to be able to run computer experiments. The construction is impressive and the results shed light on the puzzle by focusing on the problems that emerge when trying to estimate the coefficients in the aggregate macro when actually the data is micro generated.

Ralph Abraham, Todd Feldman and Daniel Friedman in 'Bubbles and crashes: a cyborg approach' (Chapter 24) developed an agent based model with both robot agents and human agents. Their scope is twofold – on one hand they want to test a couple of simulation platforms, on the other they want to compare the performance of their robot with respect to the performance of their human agents (and vice versa). The results are only partially conclusive and there is, by declaration of the authors, 'still more work to be done'. This is good news.

Francesco Luna, in his 'Is there gold in Taylor's rule? A note on the treasure hunt' (Chapter 25), addresses in a meaningful way the issue of the learnability of the Central Bank policy rules. The approach is that of a computable economist which takes seriously the issue of the effective procedures from the point of view of computability. The chapter, including the title, is filled with subtle and sometimes implicit references to previous work. The conclusion is that there are serious limits to the hopes of learning the policy rule for the agents and on the capacity of the monetary authority to learn the economy's behaviour. These limits are to be identified in the (formally and properly defined) complexity of the finite automata representing the functions: if learning has to take place the complexity has to be low. So much for the Taylor rules!

'The economics of Keynes in an almost stock-flow consistent agent-based setting' (Chapter 26) by Charlotte Bruun provides a noteworthy example of stock-flow consistency and in this sense represents one of the few agent based models where accounting consistency is required both at the agent level as well as at the aggregate level. This is an important feature of the model where there are concurrent micro foundations to macro and macro foundations to micro and where the distinction between real magnitudes and nominal magnitudes is somewhat and willingly blurred. The models seem also to generate cyclical behaviour and this is not at all irrelevant result.

'Minsky's 'financial instability hypothesis': the not-too-Keynesian optimism of a financial Cassandra' (Chapter 27) by Elisabetta De Antoni is a lucid contribution which attempts to systematize some aspects of Minsky's work. De Antoni is an expert of Minsky's work and it has to be acknowledged that she has claimed its relevance also when financial crises were not a popular issue as they are now. This has to be said also because in her chapter she is providing a graphical formalization, in a Kaldorian fashion, of Minsky's informal arguments. This is for her a new territory, but it is a proper homage which stems from and is inspired by some of Velupillai's own recent work (Velupillai 2008b). As it is often the case explorations into new territories are particularly fertile ... and this seems to be the case.

The chapter by Marco Corsino, Roberto Gabriele and Enrico Zaninotto, 'Organizational capabilities and industry dynamics: a computational model' (Chapter 28) closes the part devoted to the markets and their behaviours. Here the focus is on the problem of the firm size which has very strong Simon-like flavour and hence is surely a proper homage to the behavioural and hence the Simon side of Vela's work. The model is interesting for several reasons. One property which is particularly striking is the way in which firms are seen as being a set of business opportunities so that production is more like a process than a function. The organization of the firm is essential and these firms adapt to the structure of the market. The authors define this as being 'boundedly rational', but in light of Vela's own research (and that of Simon) one could also drop the 'bounded' and claim that 'to adapt to the structure of the market' is just highly rational: full stop. Extremely interesting is the set of 'emerging regularities' that with their model they are able to generate.

The chapters by Cassey Lee and Viveka Velupillai do represent a proper 'Finale'. In his 'The most difficult questions: a brief reflection inspired by K. Vela Velupillai's contributions in computable economics, evolution and complexity' (Chapter 29) Cassey Lee succinctly and forcefully summarizes the most difficult question to which Vela Velupillai aims at providing a tentative answer. I will here not summarize it and I invite the reader to go directly to the chapter. Viveka Velupillai encapsulates, in a few pages, the love of his daughter(s). I think it is a proper conclusion to this exceptional set of contributions. We all have our own experience and our own understanding of Vela. The articles collected in this volume deal with some aspects of Vela's research or are anyway related to it, but ideas come from a context and Viveka tells also about that. Thank you.

This is a Festschrift in honour of Kumaraswamy Vela Velupillai. The collection of authors and the themes here discussed are impressive, but they are not the end. 'Caminante no hay camino, se hace camino al andar. Al andar se hace camino, y al volver la vista atras se ve la senda que nunca se ha de volver a pisar' (Machado's *Cantares* cited in Velupillai 2005a: 863).

Thanks.

References

Arrow, K.J. (1951) *Social Choice and Individual Values*, New York: Wiley.

Clower, R. (1967) 'A reconsideration of the microfoundations of monetary theory', *Western Economic Journal*, December 1967, reprinted in D.A. Walker (ed.) (1984) *Money and Markets: Essays by Robert W. Clower*, Cambridge: Cambridge University Press.

Garey, M. and Johnson, D. (1979) *Computers and Intractability: A guide to the theory of NP-completeness*, New York: W.H. Freeman.

Goodwin, R. (1967) 'A growth cycle', in C.H. Feinstein (ed.), *Socialism, Capitalism and Economic Growth: Essays presented to Maurice Dobb*, Cambridge: Cambridge University Press, 54–8.

Hicks, J. (1991) *A Contribution to the Theory of the Trade Cycle*, Oxford: Oxford University Press.

Velupillai, Vela K. (1982a) 'When workers save – and invest: Some Kaldorian dynamics', *Zeitschrift für Nationalökonomie*, 42(3): 247–58.

Velupillai, Vela K. (1982b) 'Linear and nonlinear dynamics in economics: The contributions of Richard Goodwin', *Economic Notes*, 11(3): 73–91.

Velupillai, Vela K. (1989) 'The (nonlinear) life and (economic) times of Richard M. Goodwin', in Velupillai, Vela, K. (ed.), *Nonlinear and Multisectoral Macrodynamics: Essays in Honour of Richard Goodwin*, London: Macmillan, 7–27.

Velupillai, Vela K. (1999) 'Non-maximum disequilibrium rational behaviour', *Economic Systems Research*, 11(2): 113–26.

Velupillai, Vela K. (2000) *Computable Economics*, Oxford: Oxford University Press.

Velupillai, Vela K. (ed.) (2005a) *Computability, Complexity and Constructivity in Economic Analysis*. Oxford: Blackwell.

Velupillai, Vela K. (2005b) 'The unreasonable ineffectiveness of mathematics in economics', *Cambridge Journal of Economics*, 29: 849–72.

Velupillai, Vela K. (2006a) 'A dis-equilibrium macrodynamic model of fluctuations', *Journal of Macroeconomics*, 28: 752–67.

Velupillai, Vela K. (2006b) 'Algorithmic foundations of computable general equilibrium theory', *Applied Mathematics and Computation*, 179: 360–9.

Velupillai, Vela K. (2007) 'Variations on the theme of *conning* in mathematical economics', *Journal of Economic Surveys*, 21(3): 466–505.

Velupillai, Vela K. (2008a) 'Japanese contributions to nonlinear cycle theory in the 1950s', *Japanese Economic Review*, 59(1): 54–74.

Velupillai, Vela K. (2008b) 'A perspective on a Hicksian Non-Linear Theory of the trade cycle', in Roberto Scazzieri, Amartya Sen and Stefano Zamagni (eds), *Markets, Money and Capital: Hicksian economics for the 21st century*, Cambridge: Cambridge University Press, 328–45.

Velupillai, Vela K. (2009) 'A computable economist's perspective on computational complexity', in J.B. Rosser, Jr, (ed.), *Handbook of Complexity Research*, Cheltenham: Edward Elgar, 36–83.

Zambelli, S. (2007) 'Comments on Philip Mirowski's article: "Markets come to bits: Evolution, computation and markomata in economic science"', *Journal of Economic Behavior and Organization*, 63: 354–8.

Part I

Prelude

1 Computable and constructive economics, undecidable dynamics and algorithmic rationality

An essay in honour of Professor Kumaraswamy (Vela) Velupillai

Stefano Zambelli

Introduction

Kumaraswamy (Vela) Velupillai was born in Colombo, Sri Lanka, 25 September 1947, that is a little more than a month after (15 August 1947) Nehru had declared India to be an independent country and only a few months before Sri Lanka, then Ceylon, also became an independent country (4 February 1948).

Events, anecdotes and almost unbelievable stories about his youth in Sri Lanka are many and I will here not attempt at all to report them as they were told to me by Professor Velupillai (from now on Vela) himself or reported to me by some of his friends and/or family members. This type of story telling is something that Vela should write about in his own autobiography.

What I will try to do here is to attempt to follow some of Vela's thought processes and creative path. I will certainly not try to systematize his intellectual production. I will be presenting the work of this deep and innovative scholar in an unusual way. What I will do is to link Vela's actual life journey with his intellectual journey. What this will determine is a very ad hoc association between places and intellectual production. Some have described the intellectual work of Vela as kaleidoscopic – I too will give a 'seemingly' kaleidoscopic picture, but the theme of this chapter will be that the seemingly kaleidoscopic fragmented work is actually a coherent and aesthetically beautiful whole: a whole whose composition started the day Vela left Colombo for Kyoto ... and has practically never ended, as he never returned back Sri Lanka. 'Caminante no hay camino, se hace camino al andar. Al andar se hace camino, y al volver la vista atras se ve la senda que nunca se ha de volver a pisar' (Machado's *Cantares* from Velupillai 2005: 863).

The University of Kyoto: problem solving and phenomenological thermodynamics

On 5 May 1965 the young Vela arrived at Kyoto. From Vela's own writings we read:

> Close, now, to almost forty years ago, I was taught, by example and patience, by Professor Ryoichiro Kawai, the meaning of proof in a mathematical setting. It was during special lectures on Linear Algebra, during my undergraduate days at Kyoto University, in 1966. As an undergraduate in the Faculty of Engineering, but specialising in Precision Mechanics, I am not sure whether by accident or predilection, I ended up by choosing most of the applied mathematics options. *The mathematical training from that background was, mostly, about methods of solutions rather than proof of propositions in an axiomatic framework.* However, Professor Kawai, voluntarily, gave me some special lectures and tuition in the more 'rigorous' aspects of pure mathematics and some of the precepts I learned from him must have remained etched in my memory cells.
>
> (Velupillai 2003a: 1, emphasis in original)

And

> As a young student in the Faculty of Engineering at Kyoto University in the late 60s, I was introduced to two kinds of Thermodynamics: phenomenological thermodynamics and statistical thermodynamics. The former was *about broad aggregates – pressure, volume, temperature, etc., – and the relationships that held between them; the latter was about the micro underpinnings of the aggregates.*
> The 'laws' of the former (like the 'stylized facts' of macroeconomics) – Boyle's law, Charles' law, the Second Law of Thermodynamics, and so on – were derived by imposing dimensional and 'accounting' constraints on flows and stocks ... as Phenomenological Macroeconomics.
>
> (Velupillai 2003b: 85, emphasis in original)

And

> I wish to add a personal 'Japanese' connection at this point. I myself learned the mathematics of the van der Pol equation as an undergraduate in the Department of Mechanical Engineering at Kyoto University (the alma mater also of Shinichi Ichimura and Michio Morishima) during Professor Chihiro Hayashi's lectures on electric circuit theory. Chihiro Hayashi was one of the great pioneers of nonlinear dynamics in its experimental mode. The importance of his analogue approach to the study of nonlinear dynamics was brought to my attention by my friend, another pioneer of dynamical systems theory, Ralph Abraham, in the late 1980s. Ralph Abraham has been tireless

in his efforts to resurrect Yoshisuke Ueda's priorities in the re-discovery of chaotic phenomena in nonlinear dynamical systems. Ueda re-discovered, independently of Lorenz, the existence of exotic dynamics in Duffing's equation in November, 1961; however, unlike Lorenz's investigation using digital computers, Ueda, in true 'Hayashi-spirit', conducted the investigations that led to his discovery using analogue computers. *Although Ueda's work was well known to Japanese economists, his method did not penetrate economic methodology in that analogue investigations simply disappeared from economic modelling after the initial attempts in the early 1950s.*

(Velupillai 2008a: 55, emphasis added)

The University of Lund: the 'Scandinavian' School of Economics

After graduation at Kyoto I entered the University of Lund to continue postgraduate studies in economics and was fortunate to come under the gentle and wise influence of Professor Björn Thalberg. The kind of macrodynamics he was working on at that time, stabilisation policies in the Phillips–Goodwin tradition that had even been popularised in Roy Allen's textbooks of the time, *emphasised the kind of applied mathematics I had learned at Kyoto.*

(Velupillai 2003a: 1, emphasis added)

The first exposure to economics was through what Vela defines Phenomenological Macroeconomics and the mathematical training he had from Kyoto University 'was, mostly, about methods of solutions rather than proof of propositions in an axiomatic framework' (Velupillai 2003a: 1).

The introduction to 'proof of propositions in an axiomatic framework' had yet to come in the sense that the axiomatic approach to economics was totally foreign to him. What he had learned in Kyoto was that given a problem one had to find a solution.

Professor Thalberg had himself worked with aggregate systems of differential equations and had been under the guidance of Ragnar Frisch in Oslo and Richard Goodwin in Cambridge. As known, both Frisch and Goodwin had developed models of the trade cycles where the study of the emergence of cycles for the economic system, when seen in its whole, had to be made with a low dimension system of difference, differential or difference-differential equations. Much of Frisch's work was addressed towards the study of the numerical solution of linear economic dynamical system, while Goodwin's was on the qualitative solutions of nonlinear economic dynamical systems. Their approaches diverged on what would explain the persistence of cycles (Frisch would turn to erratic impulses, while Goodwin emphasized nonlinearities), but one could agree that they shared as a method the need of identifying solutions and show results, 'methods of solutions', rather than 'proofs of propositions in an axiomatic framework'.[1]

The reasons that first led the young mechanical engineer to land at Lund University was a fascination of the work of Gunnar Myrdal (*An American dilemma: The Negro problem and modern democracy* – see also Velupillai 1992a: 12), as well as a fascination of the way in which Olof Palme spoke unambiguously against the Vietnam war (and communist dictatorships).

Clearly, Lund had other things to offer. The introduction to economics must have made him aware of the debates of that time: 'monetarism' versus 'American Keynesianism', but most importantly he got what Lund had to present at its best: the tradition of the (Scandinavian) Swedish School of Economics. He became quickly knowledgeable about the first Swedish School (Knut Wicksell, Gustav Cassel, Eli Hecksher and David Davidson) as well as of the second (Gustaf Åkerman, Johan Åkerman, Bertil Ohlin, Erik Lindahl, Gunnar Myrdal, Erik Lundberg and, although from Norway, Ragnar Frisch and Tryge Haavelmo).[2]

Some of the themes that characterized the work of the Swedish economists were the particular emphasis put to the study and understanding of an economy in its whole. It is for this reason that there is a good point in claiming that the Swedish economists are antecedents of Keynes in defining modern macroeconomics, but whether it is totally justified is still an open question (see for example Clower 1991, Hicks 1991 and Samuelson 1991). Efforts were put on the impacts that centrally controlled policies would have to the functioning of the system. And this would be so when considering modern monetary policy and fiscal policy.

Whether the claims of priority are well justified or not, there is substance in the claim that the approach of the Swedes was more towards process (period) analysis than equilibrium (also recognized, for example, by Hicks 1991, who acknowledged the importance of Lindahl (1933) and the 'Concept of Income'). The study of the process (period analysis) would be essential especially when considering the implicit connection between stocks and flows and the understanding of the deep and profound role to be given to expectations (see the Myrdal–Lindhal *ex ante* and *ex post*) and to proper book-keeping. The last section of Ohlin's notes has the title 'Keynes' Equilibrium Theory versus a Process Theory of the Stockholm Type'.

As Ohlin put it:

> To analyse and explain what happens or what will happen in certain circumstances it is necessary to register the relevant events. One needs a system of book-keeping which is relative to time. Not only is the time sequence of events as a rule important, the same is often true of the time-lags. It is therefore practical to use periods of time as a basis for the book-keeping. At the end of each period one can survey the registrations which refer to that period. This answers the question what has happened during a passed period. It is an account ex-post. This, however, explains nothing, for it does not describe the causal or functional relations.
>
> (1937: 58)

Although Ohlin was not himself highly esteemed by many Swedes,[3] the above quote well summarizes important points of the Swedish School and the emphasis to be posed to the process and the almost total irrelevance of the concept of equilibrium, its existence and stability. And this is too a thread characterizing Vela's mature work.

Those that have had the pleasure of observing Vela 'doing' research have certainly noticed that he actually reads all the literature which is available on the specific topic he happens to be interested in. Apart from the sheer pleasure that he finds in the act of reading (almost anything!), what he specifically looks for in the literature of economics is 'plausible' historical and/or methodological connections that might help in explaining and understanding the present state of economic theory. As we will see below, many of his published contributions have this characteristic.

Even the two works that he published while still in Lund are an example of this. He had to read the original works of the authors that were and are shaping economic theory as we know it today. In the article 'Cobb–Douglas or the Wicksell production function: A comment' (Velupillai 1973a) Vela identifies the antecedent of the Cobb–Douglas in a work of Wicksell. The identification of an historical antecedent is important. Not only does he point to the fact that Wicksell had the Cobb–Douglas 27 years earlier (Wicksell 1900), but also revealed that Wicksell had the view that 'It is [...] clear that the theory of production cannot be separated from the theory of *distribution*' (Wicksell 1990, quoted in Velupillai 1973a: 113).

The young engineer that had arrived only two years before to Sweden was now not only reading Swedish, but was already a Swede in the theoretical approach: distribution, public finance and taxation, economic processes, accounting, expectations were now a part of his theoretical tool box.

The second publication he had while at Lund shows the great concern for history and methodology. In his piece 'A note on the origins of the correspondence principle' (Velupillai 1973b) Vela was able to link Quantum Physics with the contributions of Hicks (Value and Capital) and Samuelson (Foundations). But while he was pointing to the correlations of the two correspondence principles (those in economics and those in physics) and to the parallels between Hicks' and Samuelson's works, he was already looking ahead towards concepts and ideas to treasure and develop. As a concluding statement of his article he wrote:

> If there is one lesson that we can draw for the economic correspondence principle from the Bohr principle, then it is that both comparative statics and dynamics are necessary for the better analysis of economic phenomena – the two are complementary, and only a discussion based on a combination of the two can yield fruitful results.
>
> (Velupillai 1973b: 304)

And this is also what most members stemming from the Scandinavian tradition would certainly subscribe to: process analysis. Furthermore Hicks has openly recognized the impact that Lindahl might have had on his work: 'The Swedish influence on Value and Capital' (Hicks 1991b). It is in 'Value and Capital' that Hicks introduced period analysis in his famous Monday process.

Later, in the article, 'Some Swedish stepping stones to modern macro-economics' (Velupillai 1988), Vela made a convincing case in support of the importance of the Swedish School. It is certainly not coincidental that the title mimics the review made by Abba Lerner (1940): '"Some Swedish stepping stones to economic theory"', Review of Myrdal (1939), Monetary Equilibrium and Lindhal (1939), Studies in the theory of money and capital. In his review of the two translated works, Lerner claimed that Lindhal and Myrdal had really nothing substantial to contribute with respect to what had already been done by English–American authors (mostly Keynes and Hicks). In the choice of the title for this contribution and in the contribution itself Vela maintains that there are in fact important stepping stones to modern macroeconomics, and, moreover, that there is much to be learned from reading the Swedes (Scandinavians). However, although the Scandinavians might claim some priorities with respect to Keynes' work, this is not the main aspect that Vela is trying to highlight. It is not only the Keynesian Modern Macro, but also the Lucasian Modern Macro that should pay proper consideration on the work of the Swedes (when it comes to expectation formations, to mention only one example).

In the above mentioned piece (Velupillai 1988) Vela reminds (post-, neo-, new-) Keynesian macroeconomists of the importance of the contributions of these Swedes because:

> The accounting conventions necessary to coherently consider [the interactions between Public Finance, Taxation and Capital Theory] led them to be pioneers in Social Accounting Theory. The book-keeping that an accounting theory requires is, naturally, over some period of time and the sequence of such periods cannot be considered without imposing *accounting discipline*.
>
> (Velupillai 1988: 96, emphasis added)

But the accounting discipline and issues of 'just taxation' require the acceptance of the setting implicit in any Monetary Policy and a profound understanding of its means and objectives – a theme well understood and recognized in the early works of Lindhal, Myrdal and supplemented with the works of Hammarskjöld, Johansson and Lundberg.

The Lucasian themes and criticisms on Econometric Policy Evaluations and Optimal Policy Proposals were, so Velupillai (1988) argues, somewhat anticipated by the Swedes. He also convincingly pointed out in 'Political arithmetics of the Stockholm School' that

> The very same issues the New Classicals now discuss at the frontier of research in macroeconomic theory had been the subject of analytical and policy deliberations by the Swedes from Davidson to Lindhal, *but not on the sort of microeconomic theory that the Lucasians advocate.*
>
> (Velupillai 1991: 342, emphasis added)

The difference in the *sort of microeconomic theory* is stressed in many of Vela's writings. For example, about Myrdal's view Vela wrote:

> The postulate of rational behaviour has on the whole been very badly handled in economic theory. The marginal utility school has set about propping it up with an explanation involving a complete popular psychology in terms of Pleasure-Pain mechanics ... What concern is it of economic theory, and what does it matter, that there was, and still is, a liberal–metaphysical rationalization which calls behaviour 'rational' in a deeper sense, in order to lay the foundation of social apologetics? Just how far does that provide the sort of explanation we require for scientific purposes? Why not start immediately on the same empirical basis as practical 'business economics'?

> (Velupillai 1989a: 42)

How and what enters and keeps staying in our 'memory cells' is a mystery. In between Lund and Cambridge the young Vela was exposed to Sraffa's major work and this was something that would affect his memory cells. In the article written in the Festschrift in Honour of his teacher, Professor Thalberg, Vela writes:

> in late autumn 1972 ... I was in my office [Lund University] reading Piero Sraffa's Production of Commodities by Means of Commodities, I was still a young man and had the usual share of arrogance and confidence in my make-up. Björn Thalberg dropped by to talk to me ... His only remark was: 'A very difficult book – isn't it?'. My reply: 'No, not at all!'. Now, ... some years later, I am still struggling with that same book...

> (Velupillai 1992a: 18)

In the article published years later about Myrdal, 'Reflections on Gunnar Myrdal's contributions to economic theory' (Velupillai 1989a), Vela would make an extremely interesting and profound analysis between Myrdal's Monetary Equilibrium, Sraffa's Production of Commodities by Means of Commodities (and Hayek's 1932 review) and Keynes' Chapter 17 in the *General Theory*. Myrdal, Sraffa and Keynes were all at discomfort with Wicksell and most importantly with Hayek's interpretation of Wicksell as presented in Hayek's *Prices and Production* (1931). Here, one of the points developed by Myrdal and stressed by Vela was that 'Wicksell had at its disposal a theoretical apparatus – NOW CONSIDERED RATHER OBSOLETE – which made him define the natural rate as a physical or technical marginal productivity' (Velupillai 1989a: 12, quoting Myrdal 1939, emphasis in the original).

Clearly this apparatus, the aggregated Wicksell–Cobb–Douglas production function (as it seems appropriate to be named, see above and Velupillai 1973a), was also one of the implicit critiques to be found in Sraffa's debate with Hayek (Sraffa 1932) to be made explicit later on in Sraffa (1960).

But according to Vela the contributions of Myrdal were more than this:

> Myrdal, like Keynes, believed almost passionately in the power of reason in human affairs; but it was not the reason of the rational economic man of economics. It was the reason of the ethically tempered rational economic man of Adam Smith. Thus he would have felt quite at home amongst those who are trying to enrich the content of rationality by broadening to include ethical elements in the formalization of economic theory.
>
> (Velupillai 1989a: 15)

One element that characterized much of the work of members of the Stockholm School(s) was the emphasis posed on the accounting principles for the foundations of analytical economic theory. Myrdal put it quite clearly. He dismissed the postulate of neoclassical rational behaviour and proposed as an empirical basis that of practical 'business economics', that is accounting. And accounting is also in the *ex-ante ex-post* concepts and in public finance (just taxation) and monetary policy as well as in the monetary tautological quantity equation. They are all deeply rooted in the distinction between stocks and flows ... and this is following the Stockholm School of Economics.

Cambridge University and non-standard economics

Cambridge. Kaldor and Goodwin nonlinear aggregate dynamics and the (functional) distribution of income

> After obtaining my Master's degree in economics at Lund, in January 1973, I arrived at Cambridge in October of that year to work under Richard Goodwin for a Ph.D. The wise and enlightened way he supervised me emphasised the same applied mathematics tradition in which I had been trained at Kyoto and which Thalberg reinforced in Lund.
>
> (Velupillai 2003a: 1)

After having being exposed to Swedish air, the young graduate student came to breathe Cambridge air (where at the time of his arrival Joan Robinson, Luigi Pasinetti, Nicholas Kaldor, Geoff Harcourt, Richard Goodwin and Piero Sraffa, with Roy Harrod among many others, as well as John Hicks in Oxford, were at their pick).

Vela came to deal with the Functional Theory of Income of Nicholas Kaldor (and Pasinetti), the Non-Linear Dynamics of Richard Goodwin, the Value Theory (both unorthodox, Piero Sraffa and Geoff Harcourt, and orthodox – through Frank Hahn) and simply the Keynesian spirit encapsulated by Joan Robinson and Kahn (and clearly Oxford was not too far – as the influence of Hicks proves).

At Vela's arrival Nicholas Kaldor was assigned as his supervisor. And although he 'began seeing Richard Goodwin almost from the outset' the Kaldor–Pasinetti Cambridge functional theory of income was important in Cambridge and a nonlinear approach to the business cycles was specific to both Kaldor and Goodwin. Naturally, some marks in the theoretical applications of the functional theory of income are to be found a few years later in the contributions: 'When workers save – and invest: Some Kaldorian dynamics' (Velupillai 1982a), 'Linear and nonlinear dynamics in economics: The contributions of Richard Goodwin' (Velupillai 1982b), 'A neo-Cambridge model of income distribution and unemployment' (Velupillai 1983), 'A note on Lindahl's theory of distribution' (Velupillai and Chiodi 1983) and more recently 'A dis-equilibrium macrodynamic model of fluctuations' (Velupillai 2006a).

In the first two contributions Vela presents a model where Kaldor's idea that the workers and producers had two different propensities to save was combined with Pasinetti's remark that if workers save they must also be owners of a share of the aggregate capital. Although some properties of the model(s) would show local convergence and stability, here Vela was already pointing out that

> the theory of dynamical systems is a vast and complex field where concepts of solutions and stability do not have *absolute* validity and unambiguous interpretations. The strong statements and assumptions we have made to ensure existence, uniqueness, stability (global, asymptotic and structural) must therefore be interpreted with caution.
>
> (Velupillai and Chiodi 1983)

These contributions are certainly inside what Vela would define as *phenomenological macroeconomics*. Here the approach is of postulating behavioural equations for a small set of crucial variables and subsequently to derive conclusions with respect to the dynamic behaviour of these crucial variables. Currently, this approach, when seen in the light of the Lucasian fundamentalism demanding Walrasian microfoundations for macroeconomics, might seem obsolete and not in line with the modern mainstream standard approach. But as early as 1982, Vela explicitly formulated his methodological view on this topic:

> It will be evident that the analysis ... owe nothing to neoclassical methodology. Marginal productivities, marginal cost pricing, competitive markets, aggregate production functions, profit maximization, and other well-known concepts and methodology of neoclassical economics, though not inconsistent with an appropriately modified form of the model developed here, are *not necessary for any of the conclusions* ... recent research in so-called 'microeconomic foundations of macroeconomics' or the attempts to make compatible Walrasian microeconomics and Keynesian macroeconomics ultimately reduce to providing choice-theoretic framework such that the two fields can be reconciled.... However, the passage from the micro choice-theoretic framework to macro seems to be as ad hoc as the Keynesian macroeconomics that has been criticized ... It is our conjecture that there are *macroeconomic relations* that cannot (and indeed should not) be given microfoundations. The foundations for such relations should be sought not

in microeconomics as *conventionally* understood ... It is perhaps ironic that such a conjecture can even be extrapolated from the recent results of Sonnenschein (1972, 1973a, 1973b) and Debreu (1974).'

(Velupillai 1993b: 440)

The relationship between Richard Goodwin and Vela was a special one. Of the many students that Goodwin had, Vela was certainly one he was closest to. Those that have had the fortune of seeing them together, which I have had,

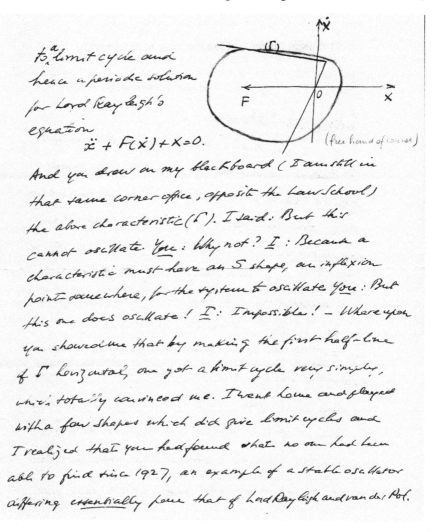

Figure 1.1 The Goodwin–Velupillai 'One sided oscillator' and the 'Goodwin characteristic' (source: letter from Le Corbellier to Goodwin 1960, reproduced in Velupillai 1989b: 21).

would know that for them research was a joyful play: a child's journey in a world of intellectual discoveries. Goodwin was for Vela first a mentor and later both a mentor and a friend.[4] Several of Vela's works focus and expand specifically on Professor Goodwin's intellectual work (for example Velupillai 1982b, 1989b, 1992b, 1998a, 1998b). I leave to the interested readers to consult the above sources where one would find the appreciation that Vela had for his mentor. In particular I would advise the readings of 'The (nonlinear) life and (economic) times of Richard M. Goodwin' (1989b), 'The vintage economist' (1998a) and 'Richard Goodwin: 1913–1996' (1998b).

One of the great achievements of Richard Goodwin was the claim and discovery that in order to maintain cycles only one 'nonlinearity' was sufficient. Richard Goodwin was in contact with Philip Le Corbellier who, as early as 1933 in the very first issue of *Econometrica*, wrote an article suggesting that endogenous cycles could be modelled by a nonlinear dynamical model and not a linear one, maintained with impulses (Le Corbellier 1933). It was well recognized by Le Corbellier that in order for a limit cycle to exist (in the case of a two dimensional dynamical system) an S shaped characteristic was necessary (as in the cases of Rayleigh and Van der Pol equations). In a correspondence they had, Corbellier[5] admitted that Goodwin had found an economic justification[6] for the existence of a characteristic for the second order nonlinear differential equation known as the Rayleigh equations (which, with a transformation, is also known as the Van der Pol equation) that would give rise to oscillations that were overlooked by mathematicians. This is a beautiful and one of few instances where a serious search has been conducted to an economic problem so as to allow for a new mathematical discovery. In correspondence from Le Corbellier to Goodwin we read:

> you came one day in my office in great elation ... and told me that you had found economic justification for a characteristic which gave rise to a limit cycle and hence a periodic solution for Lord Rayleigh's equation. I went home and played with a few shapes which did give limit cycles and I realized that *you had found what no one had been able to find since 1927*, an example of a stable oscillator differing essentially from that of Lord Rayleigh and van der Pol.Le Corbeiller.
>
> (Velupillai 1998a: 11, emphasis added by Velupillai)

Vela's merit is to have emphasized this contribution. What is important here is that a property of the beautiful Rayleigh differential equation was discovered because 'there was an economic justification' (Velupillai 1998a: 11). This should be of interest for the history of thought and it is to Vela's merit that this result was brought to the attention of the economists.[7]

Capital theory, Sraffian schemes and general equilibrium

Obviously, being in Cambridge in the 1970s one could not ignore, as it is done today, the Cambridge–Cambridge controversy and the implications it had for capital theory. Harcourt (1972) had just published *Some Cambridge Controversies in the Theory of Capital*. Having read Sraffa before and having been exposed to capital theory through the study of Wicksell, it was only natural that the young Vela approached the much discussed topic of reswitching techniques and Sraffian schemes his own way: that is by making a thorough investigation of the historically relevant sources and by asking, again and again, relevant methodological questions. These led to an important discovery of a relevant historical link that he made shortly after his arrival in Cambridge. He spotted a first historical instance of Reswitching in the Theory of Interest by Irving Fisher: 'Irving Fisher on "Switches of Techniques": A historical note' (Velupillai 1975). This demonstrates once again his scholarly qualities. Obviously, Vela could not read Wicksell without reading Fisher and once he was to read Sraffa he came to see that Fisher had an example of reswitching. Not all scholars would do that.

The reading of *Production of Commodities by Means of Commodities* is for Vela something that happens over and over. An important point Vela has made is that Sraffa's method is constructive in at least two different ways. First, Sraffa proceeds by ways of examples and, second, Sraffa's method is deeply constructive in the sense used inside constructive mathematics. Not only Sraffa's book contains 'no formal proposition which [Frank Hahn] considered to be wrong' (Velupillai 2007a: 7), but is also a highly mathematical book: Sraffa's method is constructive and not formalistic. In a way, in *Production of Commodities by Means of Commodities*, Sraffa is following his friend Wittgenstein in writing only about things for which meaningful propositions can be made. This is a huge difference between his formal approach and the one of standard mathematical economics where the focus is on existence proofs and the method is far from being constructive: if an object is 'said' to exist, but cannot be 'constructed' then the object cannot be part of a rigorous logical construction. In a way Sraffa's schemes and the set of propositions that are to be found in *Production of Commodities by Means of Commodities* are all rigorous logical propositions, but the same cannot be said, for example, about Debreu's Theory of Value, because there most of the results, being derived by using formalistic mathematics and not constructive mathematics, cannot be considered as forming a set on consistent and/or constructible logical propositions.

Given the current fashion the above statement will certainly encounter a certain degree of scepticism, but the point is clearly stated in several of Vela's works. In Velupillai (1989c) Vela convincingly showed that Sraffa did provide a constructive proof for the determination of the standard commodity, without using the Perron–Frobenious theorem. Many authors have criticized Sraffa for not using the available mathematical results and by so doing they have attempted to undermine the approach and the results. This is too unfortunate. In one of Vela's recent papers (Velupillai 2007a) the case is made clear. It is almost common sense, that if we imagine a mathematics useful for economics, we have to think of constitutive elements that we observe in the real world. A fundamental observation is that any accounting of the exchanges that define the observable economic activity can occur only by using a subset of the rational numbers (which is enumerable) while standard formal economics results are derived by measuring magnitudes as real numbers (which are not enumerable). This means that these magnitudes cannot and do not belong to the world of economic facts! Moreover, an ordering of the non-enumerable elements of the real line imply the use of the axiom of choice (and of the fix point theorem), but the axiom of choice is not constructive (because it cannot be used operationally to chose the elements that belong to the set, see below the section on *Computable Economics*). According to Vela, Sraffa made a formal proposition using the constructive method – for which, I would say in a Wittgenstein's meaning – it would be actually possible to talk about and hence he was able to exclude propositions that not being constructive would belong to the world of objects for which we should not theorize about. Whether Sraffa was totally aware of this is not important, but what is relevant is that Sraffa's own method, being constructive, allowed him to produce meaningful and rigorous propositions.

Imperial College and the estimation of Frisch's policy makers functions

The necessity of developing tools to be used for the practical solutions of problems has been a characterizing element of Vela's research. Although some of the articles and of the themes developed by Vela are highly theoretical, the approach is and has always been a constructive one. Constructive in the sense that an effective procedure, an algorithm, would have to be, at least in principle, provided by the researcher. This would always be the case for both his theoretical work as well as for his applied work. During his collaboration with the researchers located at Imperial College which initiated around 1976 Vela participated in a research programme: *Cooperation Between Politicians and Econometricians and the Search for Optimal Economic Policy*. Here the problem was that of developing methods that would allow the construction of the objective function of the policy maker (Velupillai *et al.* 1978, Velupillai and Rustem 1984, 1986 and 1987).

The approach is another example of Vela's search for practical means for the solution of a relevant theoretical and applied economic problem. Again a Scandinavian mark is found in the guiding lines set in some of Frisch's articles and also in his (Frisch 1981) Nobel Laureate lecture, 'From utopian theory to practical application: The case of econometrics'.

> It goes without saying that econometrics as thus conceived does not exhaust all the contents of economics. We still need – and shall always need – also broad philosophical discussions, intuitive suggestions of fruitful directions of research, and so on. But this is another story with which I will not be concerned here (7). Let me only say that what econometrics – aided by electronic computers – can do, is only to push forward by leaps and bounds the line of demarcation from where we have to rely on our intuition and sense of smell.
>
> (Frisch 1981: 6)

And of course here Frisch meant Econometrics as he envisaged it when he coined the term and not Playometrics as he meant that it had became (Frisch 1965 (1970): 163).

Vela's articles written in cooperation with Berc Rustem on the Frisch problem of the determination of the objective function of the policy makers are innovative because: (a) they provide a solution to Frisch's problem of the determination of the preferences of the politicians to be obtained through interviews; (b) they implement the updating of information using the Kalman Filter; (c) they provide important reflections on the link between the updating of information and numerical calculations; (d) they provide a general procedure to estimate an agent's expectations (of which a special case would also be that of the estimation of the agent's eventual rational expectations).

One element which is characteristic of Vela's approach to problems and which shows his intellectual drive is that of always taking into account the limits of what one can achieve with whatever analytical tool one may use to express reasoning – mathematical or literal, as the case might be. But at the same time he pushes the frontiers of what we can actually do as far as it is possible ... with the theoretical tools that one has at one's disposal.

The first article of this series is an example of this approach. On the one hand it is shown that in principle the studied iterative process would converge to the optimizing weighting matrix (Velupillai et al. 1978: 570–1), on the other it is shown also through numerical examples that such a conceptual process is not computationally feasible' (ibid.: 582). Is one to conclude that these methods are not to be used? Certainly not; they are important to push forward ... the line of demarcation from where we have to rely on our intuition and sense of smell.

Badia Fiesolana fix-price models and 'modern and new classical macroeconomics'

In 1981 Vela was appointed Professor at the European University in Florence: 'Badia Fiesolana'. As the story goes his mentor and now also friend Richard Goodwin was at Siena University and wished to have his pupil nearby. Vela would most likely not have gone to Florence if Goodwin had not insisted. This probably explains why the young Vela left his post at Peter House, Cambridge: his mentor was not there any longer and he felt he had to follow him. Anyway, this is probably only part of the whole explanation. At Badia Fiesolana Vela was in one way following and expanding on the elements that had influenced and characterized his previous research at Lund and Cambridge, but was also opening and trying to understand why the emergent new classical macroeconomics was taking over the main stream of the profession. While the Lucasians were already prominent in the profession some of the articles which were to mould much of the future research in macroeconomics had yet to be published or were published in those years (see Kydland and Prescott 1982; Lucas 1988; Romer 1986). Badia Fiesolana was a very lively place where most of the prominent scholars of that time – if and when invited – liked to go. Obviously the beautiful surroundings helped, but the European University was at that time also run in a way that required, as part of the PhD training, the organization of advanced level seminars.

It is at Badia Fiesolana that the young Professor reinforced the reputation he had already acquired in Cambridge. Those years were the years where on the other side of the Atlantic the Lucasians were winning their battle against the American Keynesians while on this side the fix-price theories of the French flavour were trying to reconcile the fully flexible full equilibrium models with the more Keynesian fix-price disequilibrium models. Vela was on this side of the Atlantic and was developing strong personal and academic relations with Sir John Hicks and with Axel Leijonhufvud who were in part advocating the importance of the fix-price approach especially in the attempt of reconciling the monetary and real elements of the economic magnitudes.

'Growth cycles in distributive shares, output and employment' (Velupillai and Fitoussi 1983) is a contribution that links the fix-price methodology and the Lucas–Sargent New Classical Macroeconomics through an extension of the original Goodwin's growth model to the case in which wage and price dynamics are endogenous. The model is a pioneer one because it shows that the 'theoretical technology (in colourful Lucasian terminology) of non-linear dynamics allows many more exotica than those allowed in planar-dynamics and saddle points characterizations' (ibid.: 49).[8] The saddle-path dynamics and the market clearing prominent in the New Classical Macroeconomic tradition here become a special case with respect to the wide dynamic behaviours that the model could and can generate.[9]

The search for new macroeconomic perspectives is clear in two important works also originated during this period: the review of Lucas' collected articles, 'Studies in business cycle theories' (Velupillai and Fitoussi 1987) and 'Macroeconomic perspectives' (Velupillai and Fitoussi 1990a). Both contributions contain critical remarks with respect to two neoclassical economists – Lucas and Patinkin – which would make use of two different theoretical tool boxes but that would be united in thinking that the full employment macroeconomic equilibrium would be a general case solution and not a particular one – as in the Keynesian approach.

These two critical essays contain elements that would become central in the future research in Vela's Computable Economics. As he put it in 'Macroeconomic perspectives':

> Patinkin conceptualized the central construct of his analytical framework – the excess demand function – by imagining the existence of a utility computer in a thought experiment. Lucas and the new-classicals made the signal processing agent the centerpiece of their equilibrium macroeconomics.
>
> (ibid.: 225)

Lucas would focus on the view that 'theoretical economists' and the econometricians should get:

better and better abstract, analogue economic models, not better verbal observations about the world [that should allow the econometrician to] write a FORTRAN program that will accept specific economic policy rules as 'input' and will generate as 'output' statistics describing the operating characteristics of time series we care about.

(Lucas 1982: 285; Velupillai and Fitoussi 1987: 126)

In commenting on this approach Vela would point out that 'This *Turing Machine Philosophy*, as we call it, it is matched for its audacity only by its naivité'. Here Vela is referring, as we would learn from his future work, to the fact that not everything is computable – as Turing results would imply – and hence to the fact that it is not said that for non-trivial problems when a question is posed to a computer as an 'input' it is not to be expected that the computer will deliver an 'output' (see the famous Turing Halting Problem). This would be part of Vela's future and innovative research programme (see among others, Velupillai 1989d, 1990b, 1997, 2000, 2002, 2003a, 2005, 2006b, 2007b, 2009).

The review article of Patinkin's work contains a full section with the title '"Utility Computers" and all that'. Here we find a clear and lucid attachment to the ad hockery of neoclassical economics and new classical macroeconomics that Patinkin and Lucas represent. Vela writes:

the point we wish to make in this section is the following: every metaphor that has been suggested, in formal economic theory, to model Rational Economic (Wo)Man (REM) has a representation that can be formalized in terms of a finite automaton. The implications of this assertion are many: – Patinkin's utility computer cannot be fed *any* arbitrary sequence (*sic!*) of prices to obtain, as output, 'a corresponding sequence of "solutions" in the form of specified optimum positions' to 'conceptually generate the individuals' excess demand function. The sequence of prices, or the domain over which prices are defined, must possess a certain mathematical structure, for example, recursive enumerability for the feasibility of *effective* computation of optima. – Similarly, Lucasian Signal processors cannot process any arbitrary signal. This is easily shown consequence of a variety of results from mathematics and computability theory. Above all it is not the case that any arbitrary signal can be deciphered for patterns – systematic elements – by demonstrable learning algorithms – and most certainly not by the standard formalism of new-classical macroeconomics.

(Velupillai and Fitoussi 1990: 226–7)

The above encapsulates a full research programme and it is what became Computable (Macro)economics. Almost two decades later Vela would give a full and detailed description of what was meant with the above in the article 'Rational expectation equilibria: A recursion theoretic tutorial' (Velupillai 2004: 169ff) which was to appear in the Festschrift he edited in honour of one of his co-authors.

How are the Patinkinian Utility Computer and the Lucasian Signal Processor learning to compute optimally? How can this question be addressed rigorously? The first problem is that:

> The topological definition of a function is not algorithmic. Therefore, the expressions formed by from the language of economic theory, in a topological formalization, are not necessarily implementable by a program, except by fluke or by illegitimate and vague approximations.

> (ibid.: 180)

What Vela does is to 'dichotomize' the proofs by first transforming the problem into a problem which has meaning from a recursive theoretical point of view and second to derive computable meaningful propositions from it. In essence both the Utility Computer and the Signal Processors have to be equipped with algorithmic structures so that both learning and decision making might have an effective and procedural content, otherwise any propositions about their decisions has no meaning: it is a pure act of faith.

The algorithmic structures are in terms of Turing equivalences. In 'Rational expectation equilibria: a recursion theoretic tutorial' (ibid.: 169ff.) Vela first demonstrates that a standard Recursive Expectation Equilibrium of a standard Overlapping Generations Model can be learned by a Turing Machine Rational Algorithmic agent, but warns the reader that this result 'does embody an unpleasant epistemological implication: there is no effective way for the learning agent to know when to stop applying the learning mechanism!' (ibid.: 182).

From UCLA on his way to Trento University: the birth and discrete growth of computable (macro) economics

Computable Economics is a neologism invented by Vela. Where and when he developed the idea is not clear to me and I suspect it is not clear to him as well. Certainly his whole research has always had as a basic ingredient the need of understanding what it means to say that a solution to a problem exists and that it has been found. When he first arrived at UCLA, January 1987, he had already been thinking about Computability Theory and Undecidability (see the discussion above on the review of Lucas' book *Studies in Business-Cycle Theory*, Velupillai and Fitoussi 1987: 126), but it is probably from this period that he started thinking more and more rigorously about the implications that results obtained inside classical recursion mathematics might have for economic theory.

The very term Computable Economics – which is a concept substantially very different from what is normally understood by economists as *Computational Economics* – was coined by Vela during his stay at the Department of Economics, UCLA. The idea of Computable Economics, which is explained and presented in his 'little book' (Velupillai 2000), was during the first phase that of admitting the results of *Classical Recursion Theory* (known also as *Computability*) into economic theory. It is only subsequently that the implications to economic theory of *Constructive Mathematics* were added to those derived from *Computability*. The computable approach to economic theory was crystallized around the end of the 1980s and the beginning of the 1990s during his stay at UCLA. Written proofs of this are to be found in some of the publications of those years (Velupillai 1989d, 1990b) and in the publications that were published with some delay but that were substantially written during the same period (Velupillai 1997, 1999, 2000). In fact, it is during 1990 that the *Centre for Computable Economics* (please note again 'computable' and *Not* 'computational') at UCLA took off and it was in 1992 that the *First Summer School in Computable Economics* was organized at Aalborg University (in collaboration with the *Centre for Computable Economics* at UCLA). And, again, if we find today, at the University of Trento, a *Computable and Experimental Economics Laboratory* (CEEL), is due to the very ideas associated with Vela's Computable Economics. The tools and implications of Computable Economics, if not just for its algorithmic content alone, should be part of the theoretical tool box of every modern economist.

Computable Economics (I) and/or the Keynes–Simon–Velupillai rationality[10]

Obviously theoretical abstractions may be useful even if they don't match reality, but up to which point is this reasonable? While in physics real magnitudes, that define the physics proper, are often approximated with rational ones, and continuous functions with discrete, the contrary seems to occur in economics, where the abstraction of continuous functions defined over the real domain is often assumed to be an approximation of the rational magnitudes – actually the integers – that constitute the empirical essence of the economic proper. In essence it seems that most economic theorists use real analysis because it should be 'easier'. Easier because one can in that way use the theorems 'proved' in real analysis and use also a particular type of topological space for the existence proofs of solutions.

What Vela did, in the approach which he was supporting and advocating, Computable Economics (I), was to investigate the results that one obtains when including 'a more consistent assumption of computability in the formulation of economic hypothesis' (Velupillai 2000: 29) so as to be aware from the very beginning that 'not everything is computable' (ibid.) and that 'there is in this sense an inherently unpredictable element in rational behaviour' (ibid.).[11]

The results of computability theory shed light on what one can actually compute and what one cannot. Famous results of computability are Gödel's *Incompleteness Theorems*[12] and Turing's *Halting Problem.*[13] Particularly relevant in this context is the concepts of Turing Machine computations and Turing machine equivalent computations.[14] Here a reliance to the *Church–Turing* thesis allows the claim that every computation is computable by an appropriately programmed Turing Machine. Hence, if economic agents and if markets can be seen as computing mechanisms they can in principle be simulated by the computation of a *Universal Turing Machine*.

Thus complexity can also be measured in terms of Turing Machine complexity (whether in terms of computational complexity and/or algorithmic complexity is not essential here) which sets an upper computable boundary to agents' rationality.

Herbert Simon, in private correspondence with Vela and commenting on the book *Computable Economics* (Velupillai 2000), coherently with his own work fully supports this view.

> There are many levels of complexity in problems, and corresponding boundaries between them. Turing computability is an outer boundary, and as you [Vela Velupillai] show, any theory that requires more power than that surely is irrelevant to any useful definition of human rationality.
>
> (Simon 2000 (2009))

Herbert Simon here forcefully asserts that 'any useful definition of human rationality' (ibid.) which implies a computational capacity which is above that capable by a Universal Turing Machine is 'irrelevant' (and one can safely add that it is also conceptually and practically impossible to construct). This being the case the rationality assumed for the economic agents as described in standard microeconomics make the Arrow–Hahn–Debreu type of models 'irrelevant'.

From a recursion theoretical point of view a salvation from the Simon–Velupillai attack on the Olympian rationality assumption typical of standard neoclassical models could occur if it was possible to show that agents can actually compute and precisely generate their own preferences (ordering) so as to be able to decide on the memberships of the elements for any arbitrary partition and composition of any subset of the universal set of alternatives. But one of the results derived by Vela is that 'there is no effective [universal] procedure to generate preference orderings' (Velupillai 2000: 38), which means that there is no effective way to know whether the choices made are consistent or not with the standard assumptions about rational choice. Most economists who are used to assume from the very beginning that an ordering of all possible alternatives is known (or knowable) to the economic agents, might find this to be irrelevant, but it is possible to ignore this problem only because it is 'assumed' away by economists themselves, not for any other reason. The assumption that a set of all possible alternatives and an ordering of them is given has, if not for very trivial and uninteresting cases, no operational content.

Computable Economics (II) and/or new mathematical foundations for economic theory

In Vela's writings we find instances in which the *Church–Turing* thesis and the *halting problem* are fully adopted in the analysis and others in which qualification are requested, and where the constructive mathematics approach and qualifications are adopted for the analysis. This represents an evolution with respect to the *Computable Economics* book (Velupillai 2000). Vela has explained in several places what the distinction between the *computable* and the *constructive* is. In Velupillai (2002: 308), Vela explains:

> Both computable and constructive refer to procedures that are describable in terms of clearly specified algorithms or rules where no appeal or resort is made to undecidable disjunctions. However, in constructive mathematics the *law of the excluded middle* is never invoked in infinitary domains, whereas no such restriction is observed in computable mathematics ... Every mathematical existence proposition in constructive analysis comes with a proof that can, in *principle*, be implemented step-wise, with a clearly specified and finite termination criterion at which the object of the proposition is, in fact, 'produced' as the result. Exactly the same description can be given for *computable existence* with the added proviso that the Church–Turing thesis is invoked in computable mathematics.... Hence, there may exist constructive functions that are uncomputable: and the converse is also possible; i.e. the existence of computable functions that are not constructive. It is, therefore, also possible to envisage cases where an uncomputable function can be effectivized using constructive mathematics: and conversely, nonconstructive functions could be effectivized using computable mathematics. In the latter case, it will usually be possible only because the law of the excluded middle is re-introduced at some point in a proof from which it was, originally, banished in view of constructive strictures. In the former case, it will normally be the case that the Church–Turing thesis is re-invoked at some point in a mathematical procedure where it was, originally, ignored. In both cases these paradoxical possibilities come about by finessing the domains of definitions of mathematical objects and procedures.

Among the purists in *classical recursion* theory and the purists in *constructive* mathematics there would be disagreement with this somewhat unorthodox view. But the point is clear: any reasoning in terms of economic theory is meaningful only if one can produce an effective algorithm for the solution of a problem.

The axiom of choice, the Bolzano–Weierstrass theorem, the law of the excluded middle, the Hahn–Banach theorem and the fixed-point theorems are all meaningless from a constructive mathematician point of view, but they should also be 'irrelevant' for economists simply because only somebody equipped with Olympian rationality could generate the bounded infinite subsequences necessary for the Bolzano–Weierstrass to hold, could identify the 'middle' element from an infinite number of alternatives for the law of the excluded middle, could pick a member from each of an infinite number of sets for the axiom of choice to be algorithmically relevant and so on and so forth.

As Vela has amply demonstrated, the algorithmic approach (from the computability or/and constructive point of view) allows the assertion of several different propositions, theorems or statements which are in sharp opposition with respect to the commonly accepted economic results.

The result concerning the undecidability of the optimality of choices as presented in Velupillai (2000) is, in my view, sufficient to reject the validity of the existence of the Walrasian general equilibrium.

But Vela, in exploring the non-constructive elements of proofs, demonstrates the irrelevance of the Walrasian general equilibrium also relying on constructive mathematics alone. Simply by exploring the validity of the Uzawa's *equivalence theorem* (which states that the Walrasian general equilibrium is equivalent to Brouwer's fixed-point theorem (see Velupillai 2002, 2006b; Tanaka 2008)), he is able to show the irrelevance (non-constructivity) of the proof of the existence of a Walrasian equilibrium price vector.

Vela summarizes for us and with great clarity that every celebrated theorem in mathematical economics, from Arrow's Impossibility Theorem, via the Nash and Arrow–Debreu equilibria, the two fundamental theorems of welfare economics, to macroeconomic recursive competitive equilibria, is plagued by the infelicities common to one or more of the above theorems (i.e. those proved non-constructively). Hence every one of them is rich in uncomputable, non-constructive, undecidable and unsolvable content (Velupillai 2007b).

Computable economics and bounded rationality

The current interpretation that most economists pose on Simon's *bounded rationality* (of which Simon himself might also be responsible) is that bounded rationality is anyway related (or just a special case) of the rationality of an *optimizing economic agent*. After all, in one of Simon's much quoted articles, 'From substantive to procedural rationality' (Simon 1976), the (bounded) *procedural rationality* is confronted with the optimizing *substantive rationality* of the ideal economic agents. It is Simon himself who, by accepting the idea of *optimizing economic agents* (*substantive rationality*), provides a benchmark to be used to measure irrational (i.e. non-optimizing) bounded behaviour (*procedural rationality*).

The usual argument in support or defence of *substantive rationality* is the *as if* one: the ideal optimizing agents are considered *as if* they knew the whole set of alternatives and *as if* they were able to effectively compute an ordering on this set; an ordering from which to pick the optimal alternative in accordance with a specified criterion function. Hence, Simon's bounded rationality is, in a way, subordinated to the *normative* substantive rationality: real agents may not be able to decide according to substantive rationality, but if one accepts the *as if* assumption it is almost straightforward to conclude that they actually should. If the above argument was correct it would not justify the diffuse broad neglect of Simon's work, but it would provide a partial explanation of it.

The approach followed by Vela in his *Computable Economics* does not allow any recuperation of the standard neoclassical substantive rationality approach.

Inside *Computable Economics* the concept of substantive rationality is meaningless or its validity is at most restricted to uninteresting trivial cases. Either the agent equipped with substantive rationality is also equipped with effective algorithms that allow him to find the optimal choice or he simply cannot find the optimal choice by construction. When considering the Church–Turing thesis this is almost tautological.

If we consider the Velupillai result that 'there is no effective [universal] procedure to generate preference orderings' (Velupillai 2000: 38), we see the difficulty that a supporter of the *as if* argument would have in defending the substantive rationality assumption. To repeat and emphasize, an implicit and indirect defence is by assuming that a complete set of alternatives is a priori given to the optimizing agent and that a choice function exists and is accessible to the agent. This is possible only if the ordering itself has been previously computed. But this means, given the Church–Turing thesis, that there is a (Universal) Turing Machine that can be programmed to generate this ordering (here each alternative will be an input of the tape and the Turing Machine the specific choice function). Vela has demonstrated that the problem of attributing the membership (ordering) to a member of a set (of alternatives) can be *undecidable*. (And this leads also to the uncomputability of Walrasian general equilibrium.) Therefore substantive rationality is almost always impossible.

In analogy with physics, it is known and accepted as an undeniable truth that the highest speed any particle might have is the speed of light. A physicist might surely imagine a universe *as if* the maximum speed was above the speed of light, but this will not make a particle go faster than the speed of light. This is impossible. In the same way, an economist might assume, as it is standard to do, that economic agents decide on the undecidable, *substantive rationality*, but this does not make agents able to actually do so. This is impossible and to assume the contrary means to negate the twentieth century development in logic (classical recursion theory). To do so is appealing to magic, but it is not scientific.

A slightly different, but substantially equivalent defence of substantive rationality is put forward by the sustainers of the *rational expectations hypothesis*: the economic agents are assumed to be smarter than the economists themselves (as if economists were not agents themselves!). The undecidability of the preferences generating process poses serious limitations on the logical possibility of knowing whether a particular choice is the optimal one or not. This means that it may be impossible to know whether and if *substantive rationality* is exercised by the agent. While the exercise of *procedure rationality* is tautologically true, that of the exercise of *substantive rationality* is almost always not verifiable. In this last case we are again back to magic and the rational expectation inference concerning the capacity of the agents without any substance.

In sum: optimizing choices (being not knowable) cannot be used as if they represented a type of benchmark – a type of measurement unit. To assume that an agent does solve the unsolvable is not logically defendable. Clearly, something which is proven or simply known to be unsolvable, cannot be assumed to be solvable (without at least questioning the method used to prove its unsolvability). To do so is absurd, non-scientific and hence *substantive rationality* cannot be defended.

Simon's approach leaves ample space to the concept of optimizing rationality and does therefore make it possible to claim by some that his views may be incorporated as a special case of standard choice theory. This is not at all conceivable for the case of Computable Economics where any decision is *procedural* (algorithmic) and hence the very limited and trivial cases in which a procedure is known so as to compute an optimal choice, *substantive rationality*, represent a subset of the broader set in which procedures allowing a choice to be made are available (Velupillai 2007b: 7). In essence Computable Economics' results, by negating the conceptual priority and relevance of substantive rationality, while providing formal computability contents to procedural rationality, represent a serious foundation to be used in support of behavioural economics.

Algorithmic social sciences at the University of Trento: non-equilibrium dynamics, impossibility of policy, conning in mathematical economics and busy beavers.

'Given the availability of a variety of mathematical structures that could have been harnessed for the formalisation of economic theory, why and how did economists choose the one formalism that was most conspicuously devoid of numerical content?' (Velupillai 2005: 858).

Between the position Vela had at the Department of Economics, UCLA and the one he holds now at the Department of Economics, University of Trento, he has had others at different universities. Surely all these places have had an influence on him as he had an influence on the places and on the people he met.[15] I have now the pleasure of being one of his colleagues at Trento – so I like to think that Trento is an important stop in his never ending intellectual journey.

At the University of Trento Vela has found an environment that allows him to focus on his stimulating work. The Working Paper series of the Department of Economics now hosts a substantial collection of his recent papers. These working papers have become published papers in journals or in collected volumes, but with respect to the published versions they are more complete: in a way they are like "director's cuts" – a well known concept in the film industry and that are so much appreciated by movie fans.

Inside the Computable Economics approach Vela has been able to give algorithmic contents to important results. In the following I list some of these results.

- 'there is no effective [universal] procedure to generate preference orderings' (Velupillai 2000: 38). The generation of preference orderings is undecidable or 'rational choice, understood as maximizing choice, is undecidable' (Velupillai 2008c: 8)
- The Walrasian excess demand '$X(p^*)$ is undecidable, i.e., cannot be determined algorithmically' (Velupillai 2006b: 363). Alternatively the existence of a 'Walrasian equilibrium price vector is undecidable' (Velupillai 2002: 318)

- 'Uzawa equivalence theorem is neither constructive nor computable' (Velupillai 2005: 862)
- 'The Recursive Competitive Equilibrium of New Classical Macroeconomics, Recursive Macroeconomic Theory, is uncomputable' (Velupillai 2008b: 10)
- 'Scarf's Computable General Equilibrium is neither computable nor constructive' (Velupillai 2006b)
- 'neither the first nor the second welfare theorems are computationally feasible in the precise senses of computability theory and constructive analysis' (Velupillai 2007b: 27–8)
- 'Nash equilibria of finite games are constructively indeterminate' (Velupillai 2008b: 21).

Simply put, Computable Economics is algorithmic economic theory in the sense of being constructive and recursive in accordance with constructive mathematics and computability theory.

The Computable Economics approach is innovative, it is new to most economic theorists, but it is also almost trivial, it demands that every concept must have an operationally relevant content so as to be understood and implemented by the virtual economic agents. The Computable Economics approach does not demand Olympic rationality to the decision takers and recognizes from the outset the limits to the capacity of the theorist, who is not allowed to use intangible non-constructive concepts to demonstrate the existence of uncomputable intangible objects.

Regardless of its obvious relevance it seems that Computable Economics is having a very little impact on the profession. This is quite discomforting. Vela does himself attempt to provide an explanation:

> My conviction, after all these years of struggling with an understanding of the non-algorithmic content of mathematical economics, is that the teleological element in mathematical economics is entirely attributable to the kind of mathematics that is used in its formalization.
>
> (Velupillai 2007b: 20)

Vela's Computable Economics is constructive, effectively algorithmic and not teleological. Hence, for effective, procedural and behavioural economics to be at the centre of economic theory one has to hope for the serious use of a different type of mathematics and approach to it (computability and constructive mathematics). One should try to take this approach seriously and value the results that would be derived.

In an email to me on the question about why the results listed above were not taken seriously by the profession, Vela gave an indirect answer but actually did provide an indication of a direction to take. Vela wrote:

> How does one derive these kinds of results? By recasting traditional economic concepts – both at the individual and institutional level – in altern-

ative mathematical and logical frameworks and asking the same questions. How many different such mathematical frameworks can be harnessed? At least four: classical real analysis, constructive analysis, computable analysis and non-standard analysis – but there are other alternatives, too. How many different mathematical logical systems can be used? Again, at least four: set theory, proof theory, recursion theory and model theory. Why, then has economic formalization and, hence, mathematical economics been appealing just to classical real analysis and set theory for its formalizations? There has never been an adequate answer given – indeed the question has never been posed by the internal practitioners of the subject and, when asked such a question, the reaction is, invariably, incomprehension.

This is why I am forced to embark on an interdisciplinary research program – harnessing the power of alternative mathematics, different mathematical logics, mathematical epistemologies […] and varieties of phenomenologies […], in the hope that such an unfashionable and unorthodox combination of foundations may generate an interest in the results that would convince economic theorists, game theorists and mathematical statisticians that behavioural social science has, above all, to become, first and foremost, an *Algorithmic Social Science* and live with unsolvable and undecidable ambiguities, tempered by humane attitudes to failures, weaknesses and ineffectivities.

Obviously Vela is looking ahead. In 1989–1990 Vela created the neologism Computable Economics where the Turing Machine type of computations and Gödel types of undecidability, together with the Church–Turing thesis, were to be considered at the foundation at economics theorizing and of decision theory. Now, twenty years later an extension from Computable Economics is made to Algorithmic Social Sciences; where an interdisciplinary road is taken. Meanwhile Computable Economics has been enriched by Vela, as we have seen above, with the Brouwer type of constructive mathematics.

In 1989 I received from Vela as a gift the book *From Cardinals to Chaos, Reflections on the Life and Legacy of Stanislaw Ulam* (Cooper 1989). At the end of the book there is an interview by Rota to Ulam. Vela has several times quoted that interview.

ROTA: What about l'avenir des mathématiques today?

ULAM: Mathematics will change. Instead of precise theorems, of which there are now millions, we will have, fifty years from now, general theories and vague guidelines, and the individual proofs will be worked out by graduate students or by computers.... In the next fifty years there will be, if not axioms, at least agreements among mathematicians about assumptions of new freedoms of constructions, of thoughts. Given an undecidable proposition, there will be a preference as to whether one should assume it to be true or false. Iterated this becomes: Some statements may be undecidably undecidable.

(ibid.: 312)

It is only recently that branches of mathematics seems to go in the direction predicted by Ulam. For some reasons theoreticians do not like to have to conclude that some propositions may be undecidably undecidable or uncomputably uncomputable. Certainly, economists seem not to like to have to admit that there exist problems that are undecidably undecidable. For most of orthodox economics the rational economic agent is equipped with Olympic rationality that renders the work on undecidability made by giants like Turing, Gödel, Rabin and Matiyasevich totally irrelevant. But economics should not be magic: theoretical as well as hard practical problems should not be assumed away.

Let us hope that the work of these giants, together with the work of the giant that this volume is celebrating, will become bread and butter of mathematical economics. And subsequently part of the core of economics. If economic theory aims at being relevant this is the path to take. Theoretical economists should only talk about things they can talk about, the rest is magic. And what they can talk about is only what they can compute in the deep sense given to the word in classical recursion theory.

The path taken from Colombo to Trento has been a complicated one. Along the way many have joined. Some of them are here as contributors. Others are not. But surely in the years to come there will be many following the same path. The sooner the better.

Notes

1 Frisch's celebrated work on the business cycles was precisely about the construction of macrodynamic system that would generate 'free-oscillations'. A great deal was devoted to the numerical calculation of the principal roots of the low dimension difference-differential equations. Later on Frisch made several studies on the numerical solution of difference equations. As for Goodwin, he was definitely concerned with the qualitative determination of solutions of low dimensional economic systems with nonlinearities. Even in one of his last works Chaotic Economic Dynamics, Goodwin (1990) was concerned mostly with the presentations of numerical examples than on the proofs themselves and certainly was not concerned at all with an axiomatic framework (see also Velupillai 1992b).

2 Lars Jonung (1991) has as an opening sentence of his preface to the volume The Stockholm School of Economics Revisited an acknowledgement that the idea of the collected book was due to Kumaraswamy Velupillai.

3 One reason is that many thought that Ohlin's interpretation of the Stockholm School had received far too much attention and was not complete. Also Vela seems to share this view.

4 All those who have had the fortune to know him, would agree that Goodwin was a very gentle man. The young Vela found in him somebody to look up to and somebody who would guide him through the difficulties of academic life. And all those that have known and know Vela, also know how he makes an effort to look after his students with a generosity which is extremely unusual in the academic profession. How much was Vela influenced by the kind behaviour of his mentor is not possible to assess. Nevertheless, Vela himself has in writing and with personal conversations expressed gratitude with respect to the teachings of his mentor. One thing Vela would tell to his pupils would be that Goodwin taught him to be hard and demanding with colleagues and senior people and to be soft and understanding with junior. I think that most who have had at least one of the two types of contacts with him would agree this to being the case.

5 The details of this story and the letter from Le Corbellier to Goodwin are to be found reproduced in Velupillai (1989b) and further developed in Velupillai (1998a and 1998b).

6 The economic justification was that either a limit in the maximum speed of accumulation of capital (investment) or its speed of natural destruction of capital (disinvestment) could be sufficient to explain the persistence of cycles. This was one of the major points raised in Goodwin's review of Hicks' *A Contribution to the Theory of the Trade Cycle* (see Goodwin 1950)

7 But obviously, no result or contribution of Vela is ever final. One of Goodwin's important contribution is the review article of Hicks' *A contribution to the theory of the trade cycle* (Hicks 1950; Goodwin 1950). Recently Vela has reinterpreted both Hicks' work and Goodwin's review in terms of a Van Der Pol equation *A perspective on a Hicksian non-linear theory of the trade cycle* (Velupillai 2008b) where the Hicks–Goodwin cycles are interpreted in terms of the Canard. And this is a whole new story.

8 This model was in fact a precursor of the KMG model of Carl Chiarella and Peter Flaschel.

9 Twenty years later when writing a very articulated and detailed book review of some work inspired by Keynes, Goodwin and Metzler done by Chiarella, Flaschel and Franke (Chiarella and Flaschel 2000; Chiarella *et al.*, 2000) Velupillai (2003b) did not refer at all to his previous work (Velupillai 1982a, 1982b, 1983, 1990b; Velupillai and Fitoussi 1983). One of the reasons, I conjecture due to modesty, is the fact that Vela's work was already taking into account – as early as 1983 – of the importance of the contributions of New Classical Macroeconomics and in particular to the point that the Keynesian approach was a general one and what proposed by neoclassical macroeconomists – in whichever variety – was a special case. This was positively presented in Velupillai and Fitoussi (1983) and also pointed out in the critique of Patinkin's work in *Macroeconomic Perspectives* (Velupillai and Fitoussi 1990).

10 For reasons of space I will here not elaborate on the Keynes part of the Keynes–Simon–Velupillai concept of rationality. The distinction between common (for economists) definitions of rational behaviour and Keynes understanding of it is known to most – for a reference see Keynes' *General Theory*, Chapter 12.

11 The reader will most likely recognize here Arrow's quotation made famous mostly thanks to Velupillai (2000: 29).

12 Very briefly, any effective theory able of expressing mathematics cannot be both consistent and complete.

13 A general algorithm to determine for any couple program-inputs whether the program will stop or will continue running forever does not exist.

14 The connection between Gödel's formally undecidable propositions and Turing formalism is well explained by Gödel himself in the note added to the reprint of the original 1931 article (Gödel 1931(1977): 616).

15 From when he left his post as Associate Director, Center for Computable Economics and Adjunct (Full) Professor (appointed for the period 1993–1998, but resigned in 1993), Department of Economics, UCLA Vela has held different posts: Consultant, International Economics and Socio-Economic Data Division, the World Bank, Washington DC 1991–1993; Visiting Professor at the Central European University, Prague 1993 (July–August). Senior Research Fellow, Statistics Norway, Oslo, Norway; Professor of Economics (tenured) Department of Economics, Queen's University of Belfast 1994–1995; John E. Cairnes Professor of Economics (tenured), Department of Economics, National University of Ireland, Galway, Republic of Ireland (2001–2008); since 1999, Standing Senior Visiting Professor at the Madras School of Economics, Madras, India; 2006–2008 Fellow, College Lecturer and Director of Studies in Economics Girton College, Cambridge 2006–2008.

References

The entries are listed following standard rules, but with one exception which concerns the entries associated with Velupillai. In this case the co-authors which would normally come, given the alphabetical order before Velupillai, have been placed after. This for the clarity of the exposition. The involved co-authors are: Guglielmo Chiodi, Berc Rustem and Jean-Paul Fitoussi.

Chiarella, C. and Flaschel, P. (2000) *The Dynamics of Keynesian Monetary Growth: Macro foundations*, Cambridge: Cambridge University Press.

Chiarella, C., Flaschel, P., Groh, G. and Semmler, W. (2000) *Disequilibrium, Growth and Labor Market Dynamics: Macro perspectives*, Berlin: Springer Verlag.

Clower, R. (1991) 'Ohlin and the general theory', in L. Jonung (ed.), *The Stockholm School of Economics Revisited*, Cambridge: Cambridge University Press, 245–62.

Cooper, N. (1989) *From Cardinal to Chaos: Reflections on the life and legacy of Stanislaw Ulam*, Cambridge: Cambridge University Press.

Frisch, R. (1965 (1970)) 'Econometrics in the world today', in W. Eltis, M. Scott and J. Wolfe (1970) *Induction, Growth and Trade: Essays in honour of Sir Roy Harrod*, Oxford: Clarendon Press, 152–66.

Frisch, R. (1981) 'From utopian theory to practical applications: The case of econometrics', *American Economic Review*, 71(6): 1–16.

Gödel, K. (1931 (1977)) 'On formally undecidable propositions of Principia Mathematica and related systems I', in J. van Heijenoort (ed.), *From Frege to Gödel*, Harvard, MA: Harvard University Press, 596–616.

Goodwin, R. (1950) 'A non-linear theory of the cycle', *Review of Economics and Statistics*, 32(4): 316–20.

Goodwin, R. (1990) *Chaotic Economic Dynamics*, Oxford: Oxford University Press.

Harcourt, G. (1972) *Some Cambridge Controversies in the Theory of Capital*, Cambridge: Cambridge University Press.

Hayek, F. (1931) *Prices and Production*, London: George Routledge and Sons.

Hicks, J. (1991a) *A Contribution to the Theory of the Trade Cycle*, Oxford: Oxford University Press.

Hicks, J. (1991b) 'The Swedish influence on value and capital', in L. Jonung (ed.), *The Stockholm School of Economics Revisited*, Cambridge: Cambridge University Press, 369–76.

Jonung, L. (1991) *The Stockholm School of Economics Revisited*, Cambridge: Cambridge University Press.

Kydland, F. and Prescott, E. (1982) 'Time to build and aggregate fluctuations', *Econometrica*, 50(6): 1345–70.

Le Corbellier, P. (1933) 'Les systemes autoentretenus et les oscillations de relaxion', *Econometrica*, 1: 328–38.

Lerner, A. (1940) ' "*Some Swedish stepping stones to economic theory*" ' Review of Myrdal (1939), Monetary Equilibrium and Lindhal (1939), Studies in the theory of money and capital', *Canadian Journal of Economics and Political Science*, 6(4): 574–91.

Lindahl, E. (1933) 'The concept of income', in G. Bage (ed.), *Economic Essays in Honour of Gustav Cassel*, London: Allen and Unwin, 399–407.

Lindhal, E. (1939 (1970)) 'Studies in the theory of money and capital', *Reprints of Economic Classics*, New York: Augustus M. Kelly.

Lucas, R. (1982) *Studies in Business-Cycle Theory*, Cambridge, MA: MIT Press.

Lucas, R. (1988) 'On the mechanics of economic development', *Journal of Monetary Economics*, 22: 3–42).

Myrdal, G. (1939) *Monetary Equilibrium*, London: Hodge.

Ohlin, B. (1937) 'Some notes on the Stockholm theory of savings and investment I', *Economic Journal*, 47(185): 53–69.

Romer, P. (1986) 'Increasing returns and long-run growth', *Journal of Political Economy*, 94(5): 1002–37.

Samuelson, P. (1991) 'Thoughts on the Stockholm School and on Scandinavian economics', in L. Jonung (ed.), *The Stockholm School of Economics Revisited*, Cambridge: Cambridge University Press, 391–407.

Simon, H. (1976) 'From substantive to procedural rationality', in S.J. Latsis (ed.) *Method and Appraisal in Economics*, Cambridge: Cambridge University Press, 424–43.

Simon, H. (2000 (2009)) Letter to Kumaraswamy Vela Velupillai: 25 May 2000, in *Complexity Theoretic Bounded Rationality and Satisficing* (mimeo, Department of Economics, University of Trento).

Sraffa, P. (1932) 'Dr. Hayek on money and capital', *Economic Journal*, 42(165): 42–53.

Sraffa, P. (1960) *Production of Commodities by Means of Commodities: Prelude to a Critique of Economic Theory*, Cambridge: Cambridge University Press.

Tanaka, Y. (2008) 'Undecidability of Uzawa equivalence theorem and LLPO (Lesser Limited Principle of Omniscience)', *Applied Mathematics and Computation*, 197: 598–603.

Velupillai, Vela K. (1973a) 'Cobb–Douglas or the Wicksell production function: A comment', *Economy and History*, 16: 111–13.

Velupillai, Vela K. (1973b) 'A note on the origins of the correspondence principle', *Swedish Journal of Economics*, 75: 302–4.

Velupillai, Vela K. (1975) 'Irving Fisher on "switches of techniques": A historical note', *Quarterly Journal of Economics*, 89(4): 679–80. Reprinted in M. Blaug (ed.) (1992) *An Elgar Reference Collection: Pioneers in Economics – Piero Sraffa (1898–1983)*, Aldershot: Edward Elgar.

Velupillai, Vela K., Rustem, B. and Westcott, J. (1978) 'Respecifying the weighting matrix of a quadratic objective function', *Automatica*, 14: 567–82.

Velupillai, Vela K. (1982a) 'When workers save – and invest: Some Kaldorian dynamics', *Zeitschrift für Nationalökonomie*, 42(3): 247–58.

Velupillai, Vela K. (1982b) 'Linear and nonlinear dynamics in economics: The contributions of Richard Goodwin', *Economic Notes*, 11(3): 73–91.

Velupillai, Vela K. (1983), 'A neo-Cambridge model of income distribution and unemployment', *Journal of Post Keynesian Economics*, 5(3), 454–73.

Velupillai, Vela K. and Chiodi, G. (1983) 'A note on Lindahl's theory of distribution', *Kyklos*, 36(1): 103–11.

Velupillai, Vela K. and Fitoussi, J-P. (1983) 'Growth cycles in distributive shares, output and employment', invited presentation at the *Conference on Macrodynamics*, OFCE, Paris, France, September 1983. Published in J-P. Fitoussi and P.A. Nuet (eds.) (1987), *MacroDynamique et Disequilibres*, Paris: Economica.

Velupillai, Vela K. and Rustem, B. (1984) 'Cooperation between politicians and econometricians and the search for optimal economic policy', *Journal of Policy Modeling*, 6: 341–50.

Velupillai, Vela K. and Rustem, B. (1986) 'On rationalizing expectations using rank-one updates of the Kalman Filter', *Journal of Economic Dynamics and Control*, 10: 119–24.

Velupillai, Vela K. and Rustem, B. (1987) 'Objective functions and the complexity of policy design', *Journal of Economic Dynamics and Control*, 11: 185–92.

Velupillai, Vela K. and Fitoussi, J-P. (1987) 'A review essay on: *Studies in Business-Cycle Theory* by R.E. Lucas, Jr.', *Journal of Money, Credit, and Banking*, 19(1): 122–30.

Velupillai, Vela. K. (1988), 'Some Swedish stepping stones to modern macroeconomics', *Eastern Economic Journal*, XIV, January–March: 87–98.

Velupillai, Vela K. (1989a) 'Reflections on Gunnar Myrdal's contributions to economic theory', mimeo, (a version in French published (1990) as 'Gunnar Myrdal – The universal social scientist (1898–1987)', in G. Dostaler, *Gunnar Myrdal et son Oeuvre*, Paris: Economica.)

Velupillai, Vela K. (1989b) 'The (nonlinear) life and (economic) times of Richard M. Goodwin', in Velupillai, Vela K. (ed.), *Nonlinear and Multisectoral Macrodynamics: Essays in Honour of Richard Goodwin*, London: Macmillan, 7–27.

Velupillai, Vela K. (1989c) 'The existence of the standard system: Sraffa's Constructive Proof', *Political Economy – Studies in the Surplus Approach*, 5(1): 3–12.

Velupillai, Vela K. (1989d) 'What have we learned in the path from Gödel and Turing to artificial intelligence', in A.E. Andersson, D. Batten and C. Karlsson (eds.), *Knowledge and Industrial Organization*, Berlin: Springer Verlag.

Velupillai, Vela K. and Fitoussi, J-P. (1990) 'Macroeconomic perspectives', invited presentation at the *Conference in Honour of Don Patinkin*, the Hebrew University of Jerusalem, September 1990. Published version in H. Barkai, S. Fischer and N. Liviatan (eds) (1993), *Monetary Theory and Thought: The Patinkin Festschrift*, London: Macmillan.

Velupillai, Vela K. and Rustem, B. (1990) 'Rationality, computability and complexity', *Journal of Economic Dynamics and Control*, 14: 419–32.

Velupillai, Vela K. (1991) 'Political arithmetics of the Stockholm School', in L. Jonung (ed.), *The Stockholm School of Economics Revisited*, Cambridge: Cambridge University Press, 333–45.

Velupillai, Vela K. (1992a) 'Björn Thalberg – Teacher, mentor and friend', in V.K. Velupillai (ed.), *Nonlinearities, Disequilibria and Simulation: Essays in Honour of Björn Thalberg*, London: Macmillan, 12–19.

Velupillai, Vela K. (1992b) 'Review of R.M. Goodwin's *Chaotic Economic Dynamics*', in the *Journal of Economic Behaviour and Organization*, 17(2): 306–10.

Velupillai, Vela K. (1997) 'Expository notes on computability and complexity', *Journal of Economic Dynamics and Control*, 21: 955–79.

Velupillai, Vela K. (1998a) 'The vintage economist', *Journal of Economic Behaviour and Organisation*, 37(1): 1–31.

Velupillai, Vela K. (1998b) 'Richard Goodwin: 1913–1996', *Economic Journal*, 108: 1436–49. (Awarded the Anbar Prize for Excellence in Writing).

Velupillai, Vela K. (1999) 'Non-maximum disequilibrium rational behaviour', *Economic Systems Research*, 11(2): 113–26.

Velupillai, Vela K. (2000) *Computable Economics*, Oxford: Oxford University Press.

Velupillai, Vela K. (2002) 'Efficiency and constructivity in economic theory', *Journal of Economic Behavior and Organization*, 49: 307–25.

Velupillai, Vela K. (2003a) 'Essays on computable economics, methodology and the philosophy of science', *Discussion Paper No. 8*, Department of Economics, University of Trento.

Velupillai, Vela K. (2003b), 'Book reviews: Chiarella, C. and Flaschel, P. The Dynamics of Keynesian Monetary Growth: Macro Foundations and Disequilibrium Growth and Labor Market Perspectives', *Journal of Economics*, 24: 83–96.

Velupillai, Vela K. (2004), 'Rational expectations equilibria: A recursion theoretical tutorial', in Velupillai K. (ed.), *Macroeconomic Theory and Economic Policy, Essays in honour of Jean-Paul Fitoussi*, London and New York: Routledge.

Velupillai, Vela K. (2005) 'The unreasonable ineffectiveness of mathematics in economics', *Cambridge Journal of Economics*, 29: 849–72.

Velupillai, Vela K. (2006a) 'A dis-equilibrium macrodynamic model of fluctuations', *Journal of Macroeconomics*, 28: 752–67.

Velupillai, Vela K. (2006b) 'Algorithmic foundations of computable general equilibrium theory', *Applied Mathematics and Computation*, 179: 360–9.

Velupillai, Vela K. (2007a) 'Sraffa's mathematical economics – A constructive interpretation', Discussion Paper, Department of Economics, University of Trento, WP.2.

Velupillai, Vela K. (2007b) 'Taming the incomputable, reconstructing the nonconstructive and deciding the undecidable in mathematical economics', Department of Economics, University of Trento, WP.22, forthcoming (2010) *Mathematics and Natural Computation*.

Velupillai, Vela K. (2008a) 'Japanese contributions to nonlinear cycle theory in the 1950s', *Japanese Economic Review*, 59(1): 54–74.

Velupillai, Vela K. (2008b) 'A Perspective on a Hicksian non-linear theory of the trade cycle', in Roberto Scazzieri, Amartya Sen and Stefano Zamagni (eds), *Markets, Money and Capital: Hicksian Economics for the 21st Century*, Cambridge: Cambridge University Press, 328–45.

Velupillai, Vela K. (2009) 'Undecidability and uncomputability in economic theory', Invited Lecture at the *Workshop on Physics and Computation 7th International Conference on Unconventional Computation*, Vienna, 25–28 August 2008 (printed (2008) in *Discussion Paper 6*, Department of Economics, University of Trento). In *Applied Mathematics and Computation*, 215(4): 1404–16.

Wicksell, K. (1900) 'Om gränsproduktiviteten såsom grundval för den nationalekonomiske fördelingen', *Ekonomisk Tidskrift*, 305–37.

2   From an admirer and a friend

Robert W. Clower

January 18, 2008

Dear Stefano:
I am much honored by your invitation to contribute to the forthcoming Festschrift for Vela, and consider it a privilege to express my deep respect for Vela as a scholar and my gratitude for his friendship over many decades. Because o. my current physical (though not medical) infirmities and the fact that I have no kept up with the profession since my retirement, I cannot do justice to Vela's considerable contributions. Indeed my admiration for Vela's work in recursive functions and computable economics is such that I feel anything short of a Nobe. Prize would be a virtual insult. Nothing I write can adequately convey my esteem for Vela's intellectual breadth, his discriminating focus and, not least, the grace and eloquence of his writing.

The world does not often produce such generous and fertile mind and I consider myself fortunate to be counted among his friends. I wish Vela a long future in which he may continue to enlighten his colleagues and fans.

Sincerely,
Robert W. Clower

Part II

Dynamical systems, business cycles and macroeconomics

3 The Richard Goodwin circle at Harvard (1938–1950)

Paul A. Samuelson

These will be selective affectionate remembrances of times long gone by. Any errors in memory may themselves be of interest. Surprisingly, the bare biographical facts about Dick cannot be found in the 1999 *Who's Who in Economics* (3rd edn), for the reason that its editors scandalously omitted to include Goodwin's name.

When I arrived at the Harvard Graduate School in 1935, already present were the two Sweezys (Alan and Paul); and also Abram Bergson, Alice Bourneuf, Wolfgang Stolper and Richard Musgrave. Memories still were fresh of earlier staff and students – Professors Lauchlin Currie and Allyn Young; students Emile Despres and Albert Hart, class of 1930; Moe Abramowitz and Walter Salant, class of 1934.

But never in the 1935–1937 period did I ever hear the name of Richard Goodwin (class of 1934).

I think it was early in 1938 that a lunchtime guest at Harvard's Society of Fellows mentioned that a bright friend of his, one Richard Murphy Goodwin, would be soon returning to Harvard economics after his three years at Oxford as a Rhodes Scholar.

New boy on the block

My 1938–1950 period of course followed an earlier 1930–1934 Harvard era, and was followed by the longer 1950–1996 third act. If copies of Dick's undergraduate articles for the *Harvard Advocate* still exist, they would be worth examining microscopically. How naive or sophisticated were his youthful Marxist views? He once described himself as both a lapsed Catholic and a lapsed Marxian. This resembles the sociologist Paul Lazarfeld who once claimed to be a 'Marxist on leave'. 'Who gave you leave?' Lazarfeld's friend Jacob Marschak enquired. In Goodwin's post-1938 Harvard Yard sojourn, I don't remember hearing that he had any connection with the senior Marxist *Science and Society* periodical.

That Goodwin from Indiana had ever been a Catholic would have surprised his Cambridge, Massachusetts friends. Such were not common in the Hoosier state of Indiana that he and I were born in. The middle name 'Murphy' should perhaps have lessened our surprise.

An important fact should be mentioned. When Dick and I were boys in Indiana, at the time he and I were in grade school, Indiana was a leading northern centre for the extremist Klu Klux Klan. When Dick was 12, the Indiana KKK numbered almost half a million members (a tenth of total US membership), and the Klan controlled virtually all elected officials from the governorship downward. With a private slogan, 'Join the Klan and lynch a [what shall I write?] "black"', there weren't all that many folk of colour around Greencastle, Indiana. So in the north, the KKK's anti-Catholicism had to trump its anti-Negroism. 'The only good Catholic is a dead Catholic', was a borrowed KKK locker-room phrase. Maybe it was non-Darwinian creative design that the Klan's northern head, in a drunken orgy, raped, mutilated and killed a woman – who lived long enough to provide the data that sent the Klan leader to prison for life, while the governor and other high officials' careers were terminated by criminal indictments. Richard and I, as two Hoosier natives, never happened to discuss these historic factoids.

An open question is this. How, within a year after the October 1929 stock market crash, did Dick get the money to attend Harvard? Unlike Jim Tobin, class of 1939, who was a first-time Conant Merit Scholar, Goodwin must have had to rely on private financing to attend the Harvard that was in his time still an eastern private school destination.

Settled in

After 1938 the attractive couple of Dick and his Dutch-born wife Jackie were popular ornaments to the Harvard social scene. Before the 1939 Second World War, America's Great Depression had not fully ended. Therefore, a backlog of untenured instructors and assistant professors marked time at Harvard until good jobs elsewhere could be attained.

Closest to Dick and Jackie were her sister Suzanne and Dick's Oxford buddy, Dick Schlatter (later Provost at Rutgers University). Unmarried Dan Bourstin completed a threesome of recent Rhodes Scholars. I must mention them specifically because later, when Joe McCarthy's witch hunting for subversive communists was burgeoning, the FBI publicly announced that Richard Goodwin, Richard Schlatter and Dan Bourstin had been part of a small cell of communist party members at Oxford.

This news seemed almost comical: three such unworldly academics, scarcely capable of catching a mosquito. Professor Wassily Leontief and his wife Estelle were stunned at the news; and even resentful that they had not been 'told'! My wife Marion and I were glad that we had been kept in the dark. In these matters dates can be important. 'When did you join the French resistance movement? And did you, two months before me, succumb to Vichy blandishments?'

In the US before post-1945 cold war days, it was no crime to be a 'card-carrying' member of the Communist Party. Apparently the members of the Oxford cell broke with the Communist Party when Stalin in 1939 formed a pact with the Nazi Adolf Hitler. A good time to jump ship. By hindsight, we know that each of these Rhodes troika later did achieve deserved scholarly and academic recognition.

No exact answer can be given to the following question: Was Goodwin deprived of a tenured Harvard professorship because of his radical associations?

Before Cambridge folk had been able to know about the Oxford cell connection, my guess is that the prognosis of Goodwin's future at Harvard was a gloomy one. Why should a good teacher and fruitful researcher not be a shoe-in for retention and promotion? Here are some reasons.

1   The Economics Department at Harvard in the 1930–1950 period, records show, resented excellence in scholarship. In Goodwin's 1930–1934 undergraduate time, outmoded luminaries such as Professors Gay, Bullock and Carver still ruled the roost. Statistics at Harvard both in Goodwin's time and mine were a feeble jest. How come top student Jim Tobin was permitted to go to Yale around 1950? He was brilliant from age five on in Champagne, Illinois. Why no Lloyd Metzler permanently at Harvard? To the department chairman Metzler's name may have sounded Jewish, but actually Lloyd was a Kansan-born Protestant. Why did Chairman Burbank discourage Franco Modigliani from accepting the Harvard offer to come there? Why no Solow permanently at Harvard? The list of like cases is a long and unsavoury one.

2   Dick was regarded as a 'dilettante' – an eccentric who preferred half-time pay to full-time. He liked to do serious painting. His later aristocratic love for once-expensive Edwardian automobiles belied his frugal, ascetic living style. It wasn't easy to find in Cambridge the Revere Street living quarters that lacked central heating, but Dick and Jackie managed to do so. They bought whisky by the pints, not litres. When we students persuaded Schumpeter not to let his disgust for Harvard colleagues make him accept a Yale chair, we celebrated by holding in his honour a dinner at an expensive Boston restaurant. Though Dick had been a leader in the full-court press to keep Schumpeter at Harvard, he protested at the cash outlay. Probably the pro-rated restaurant bill equalled his monthly living-expenses budget.

Witch hunt days

Somewhere I have published that during the 1949 American Economics Association meetings, I was the last economist to talk to Schumpeter a few days before his death. What we talked about in the hotel bar was how to get a good job for Dick Goodwin.

Said Schumpeter, 'I told Dick I would try to gain for him a permanent non-professorial lectureship at Harvard even though such deals are being phased out. Goodwin replied, "I'm not willing to be a second-class member of any club." I understood that.'

My next suggestion was, 'What about a good big-ten university like Michigan or Wisconsin?' Schumpeter said that Dick had no interest in them. Even Amherst or Williams were not to his taste.

So, the only root to our equation had to be a British elite university. This carried the extra advantage that going abroad would free Goodwin from having to testify before the bullying McCarthy committees that would require naming of names of one's associates (which the Committee of course already knew). Also part of that ordeal was arm-twisting pressure to express remorse and regret over earlier quite legal decisions. Hindsight confirms that the Oxford three all achieved highest academic and scholarly achievements.

If Schumpeter believed that only he and Haberler would vote tenure for Goodwin, I believe he miscalculated. Surely Hansen and Leontief valued Goodwin's scholarly merits.

On the road to the wake

I ought not to ramble on and on. So let me conclude with an account connected with Schumpeter's Connecticut funeral only ten days into 1950. Schumpeter died, so to speak, with his boots on. He expired in his sleep after a day spent on composing an important University of Chicago lecture, and working on his almost finished *History of Economic Analysis*.[1]

On a snowy New England January day, in the back seat of Gottfried Haberler's car, I was sandwiched between instructor Alfred Conrad on the left and Dick on my right. Professor Haberler drove, while his wife Friedl sat in the front passenger seat. Naturally we back three talked during the long drive. Most of it was about Schumpeter. But some concerned the arch enemy, Harold Hitching Burbank. Burbank was a rogue scholar with zero scholarly credentials. From 1913 to 1930 he had wormed his way to the long-term chairmanship of the Harvard economics department. Burbank would have preferred an affable Goodwin to an able Abram Bergson, but Dick was not the type to suck up to his bullyings.

For the record I will reconstruct some of our random car conversations.

GOODWIN: Burbie urged me to accept every job offer I ever got except, strangely, one from Amherst. Go figure.

SAMUELSON: I can explain that. It had nothing to do with you. As a 1913 Dartmouth College ruffian, he had a life long distaste for Amherst.

CONRAD: Say what you will, in the cold Cambridge milieu, it was Burbank who knew that I once was tubercular. Often he would ask about my health. Once he invited me in to talk about a thesis topic. 'Alf', he said, 'you are a warm human being. You should not pick an arid subject in pure theory.' It was not easy to have to tell him then that I had just decided on a topic involving Leontief's input/output matrix algebra.

GOODWIN: You say Burbank was in a warm human relationship with some students. One day he did call me in to say, 'Dick, I'd like to tie you to a wagon much the way my father did with me, and whip you into sense.' That's warmth for you.[2]

My next vignette is a bit of a digression, but illuminates what gets lost below the radar screen of history writers. Alf Conrad was co-author with Harvard's John Meyer of the seminal paper (1958) that launched the *cliometrics* vogue among economic historians. (The seed that they sowed, denying that ante-bellum slavery was doomed to die of its own weight as a bankruptcy operation, was harvested more intensely by Robert Fogel later.) At the time of Schumpeter's death, Conrad was his paid assistant.

CONRAD: Recently I asked Professor Schumpeter what he thought of the economist Nicky Kaldor. His reply, which I will quote, mystified me.

SCHUMPETER: Oh, these Asiatic Magyars. They are only early bloomers as scholars, thereby usurping chairs away from deeper thinkers.

CONRAD: Magyars. Are you referring to Professor Kaldor's Hungarian birth?

SCHUMPETER: No, my dear Alf. To spare your sensibilities, that was my way of identifying Kaldor's Mosaic heritage.[3]

One anecdote begets another. One of Schumpeter's best subsequent biographers, the Swedish econ-sociologist Richard Swedberg, at one point writes (in my paraphrase): 'And now we must address the question, was Schumpeter anti-Semitic? Stolper and Galbraith say No. X and Samuelson say Yes.' Surprised by the last part of the previous sentence, I read its footnote, which read: 'From personal conversation with Samuelson' (at earlier specified date).

This persuaded me to write to my admired acquaintance Swedberg that I wished he had quoted exactly what I said to him, which was, 'One of the many forms of anti-Semitism is to say that Jews do not lack competence, but are only "early bloomers". Schumpeter's view was shared by America's great mathematician George Birkhoff at Harvard, who believed in just that.' Conrad's 1950 account was precisely that which I had reported to Swedberg. The nuances of Schumpeter's 'politically incorrect' (or correct) views are so complex that I have avoided reporting on them. I will only venture here the following vague summary. After reading Melvin Reder (2000) on anti-Semitism among eminent economists, I judged that Keynes was worse than Schumpeter or Hayek; and that Hayek, incompletely successful, at least tried hardest to overcome what he could not completely overcome. Long and late he believed his Indian students at the LSE were offspring of 'money lenders'.

Personal piffle, like all of the above, is admissible in a family portrait. But even more important, the following information may be new. As the five of us wended our 100+ snowy miles between eastern Massachusetts and western Connecticut, Dick Goodwin engaged in extensive conversations with Friedl Haberler about their respective painful and frequent migraine headaches. Never had any in our circle even known that Goodwin had a migraine problem at all. In my mind this puts a new light on his role as a 'dilettante painter'. Half-time leisure and recreation may at some point in one's life in fact be the optimal paradigm for maximizing one's inherited biblical pound.[4]

Limit-cycle stable periodic limit cycles

My frenetic pen has left me epsilon time to discuss the Goodwin–LeCorbeiller greatest claim to theoretical fame. Just as John Hicks gained much from talking to Harrod, Meade and whomever about Keynesian matters, in my recollection much of what ended up in Hick's 1950 *A Contribution to the Theory of the Trade Cycle* would not have been possible if he had not earlier talked over those issues with Dick Goodwin. That's the way the dynamics of scientific discovery works. Bees take elsewhere my honey; and much of what is 'mine' was brought to me by those same busy bees. Insiders know these things. But historians never can get things perfectly right.

Notes

1 Goodwin was one of the few who helped widow Elizabeth Boody (Firuski) Schumpeter edit uncompleted fragments of the great history-of-thought book.
2 A story has been told that Goodman faced up to command Burbank to destroy 'the little black book' containing the names of minority students he was opposed to. One must wonder whether memory got somehow garbled. Burbank needed no written list to identify non-favourites. Breakfast, lunch and supper he fretted over them.
3 Alfred Conrad, I believe, may have been born Alfred Cohen. I ought to add that in the 37 years between 1949 and his 1986 death at age 78, Kaldor was as prolific as he had been in his post-1932 youth – with about the same fraction of interesting speculations and a few doubtful ones.
4 Often later in life, migraine sufferers do enjoy some relief; maybe one of the few benefits from getting old. Certainly Goodwin did find in Siena, Italy, a new burst of scholarly productivity.

References

Blaug, M. (ed.) (1999) *Who's Who in Economics*, 3rd edn, Cheltenham: Edward Elgar Publishing Limited.
Conrad, A. and Meyer, J. (1958) 'The economics of slavery in the ante-bellum south', *Journal of Political Economy*, 66(April): 95–130.
Hicks, J. (1950) *A Contribution to the Theory of the Trade Cycle*, Oxford: Clarendon Press.
Reder, M. (2000) 'The anti-semitism of some eminent economists', *History of Political Economy*, 32(winter): 833–56.
Schumpeter, J. (1954) *History of Economic Analysis*, New York: Oxford University Press.

4 Not growth, not cycles, but something in between

Robert Solow

Most economists these days accept some version of the neoclassical growth model as an aggregative first-order representation of undisturbed trend growth. The basic model is supply-side oriented. It is a story about the growth of potential output in an economy that always stays close to producing at its potential.

We know (but see below) that real market economies experience frequent deviations from this potential growth path. The deviations are mostly small and transitory. But occasionally there are large and persistent gaps between actual and potential output. The worldwide depression of the 1930s is the most celebrated example, Japan in the 1990s another. The past couple of decades in France and Germany may be another much milder case, though the majority view holds otherwise. And some recessions are bigger than others.

In principle, deviations from potential can and do go in either direction, but one's casual impression is that recession is more frequent than overheating. If that is actually so, it is an invitation to a line of research that was once followed but has become unfashionable. Remember 'pushing on a string'. (It is important here not to rely on definitions of potential output that impose some kind of average symmetry.)

Typically a differently oriented macroeconomic model is invoked to cope with these departures from the potential growth path (but see below), to understand their causes, and to think about possible policy responses. There are many candidate models for this role, though there is a broad similarity among them. This is an activity that has to proceed in real time, in order to produce quarterly forecasts and analyse the likely effects of currently proposed policies. So the producers of this kind of analysis are usually consulting firms, central banks, ministries of finance and the like. The commonest presumption is that fluctuations in aggregate demand are responsible for fluctuations in actual output on either side of the growth path; so the models are usually aimed at the main components of the demand for goods and services. I do not intend to focus on the choice among such models, although many important issues about macroeconomics arise in that context.

This dichotomy between supply-oriented growth models and demand-oriented business-cycle models creates an analytical problem: how to knit the short run and the long run together. It is not as if there is a time interval called the short run and another called the long run, with some kind of moment of transition between them; instead there are slow and fast processes going on all the time, and they influence one another. The analogy with Marshall's terminology is close.

One sort of influence is generally agreed, working through investment and the stock of capital. Investment is one component of aggregate demand, and the stock of capital is one determinant of potential output. So the growth path bears the mark of past recessions and booms, and each recession or boom is conditioned by a stock of capital determined by past growth. The other main determinant of (per capita) potential output is the level of total factor productivity. But there the interactions between short-run events and long-run developments are at best still poorly understood.

There is no broad agreement about the best way to deal with the trend-and-cycle problem. By the way, my use of this language does not imply any commitment to the notion that aggregate motions around the growth path are periodic, or anything like that; 'trend-and-short-run-fluctuations' would be more accurate but too awkward. The vogue for true periodic-motion categories has given way to the Wicksell–Frisch–Goodwin impulse-propagation stories, with more emphasis on the impulses. All I intend is a brief sketch (or caricature) of three current approaches to this task. It will be fairly obvious where my sympathies lie, but I do not want to make a case; the attitude I will try to achieve might be called *faute de mieux* pragmatism. The order in which I take up the various approaches is not chronological, maybe the reverse, but seems to serve the exposition best.

I will start with what is sometimes described as 'modern macro'. (It is the 'below' that I referred to above.) I do not know if it is actually a majority view among economists today, but it is certainly favoured by elite journals and leading-edge researchers. I am told that many central banks maintain 'dynamic stochastic general equilibrium' (DSGE) models – the verbal hallmark of modern macro – even though they do not find them very useful for the business at hand. The origin of these models is the famous 1982 paper by Kydland and Prescott, but there is by now a perfectly enormous literature.

The standard 'micro-founded macro model' consists of a single 'representative' agent who maximizes a discounted time-additive utility (of consumption) function over an infinite horizon under perfect foresight or rational expectations. Initially the only constraints considered were budgetary and technological, but later research has enriched the model with various rigidities and lags. Also at the beginning, the technological, organizational and informational assumptions were chosen so that the solution to the optimization problem could be naturally decentralized to competitive markets. In effect the industrial side of the economy just carried out the plan or dynamic programme of the representative consumer–worker–owner. Here too later research has added some non-competitive features, and this has surely given the model more realism. What cannot be tacked on, however, is a serious scope for conflicting interests among the participants in the model economy. It is certainly possible, I should think likely, that this limitation forces the output of the model to have more coherence than can be justified either by theory or by comparison with actual economic performance. It is a bit like the macroeconomist's version of 'intelligent design'. There is some incidental irony in the fact that these DSGE models tend to be favoured by rather conservative right-of-centre economists who in other contexts react negatively to the notion of anyone managing or guiding the economy. The DSGE model does just that, only the manager or guide is called the representative agent. My point is precisely that a capitalist economy does not have such a guide, public or private.

The essential point for present purposes is that modern macro provides a single model for *all* runs. There is no real distinction between trend and cycle. If the model runs from some initial conditions, with no exogenous disturbances, it will trace out a growth path. Then, if preferences or technology or indeed any other features of the model are subject to unforeseeable random or arbitrary disturbances, the model will adapt to them (constrained-optimally, of course, in view of the representative agent's intertemporal utility) and some other trajectory will emerge from the same initial conditions. The differences between the two paths are the fluctuations induced by the disturbances interacting with the model. Some of those differences will be short lived; some may persist for a while, even if the corresponding disturbance was only a transitory blip. The 'events' of common parlance are merely optimal adaptations to these exogenous shocks.

This is in some ways a satisfying way to deal with the trend-cycle problem. There is no awkward shifting between supply-side and demand-side considerations. It is seamless. The question is whether this picture of macroeconomic behaviour is satisfactory in other ways. It is sometimes, though not very often, criticized for short-changing the aggregate-demand-side complications and pathologies that had been the focus of earlier brands of macro theory. Some of those have traditionally been related to inconsistent beliefs and expectations held by participants in the economy. These would seem to be inherently excluded by a model based on representative-agent optimization. This approach is usually defended, not in particular, but by the general claim that it is the only 'theory-based' approach to macroeconomics that is available. I think that this claim does not stand up to careful inspection, but that is not the argument I want to pursue now.

There is an alternative branch of the growth-and-cycles literature that differs from 'modern macro' in just about every respect but one. The natural example is the work of Richard Goodwin (1967). It is natural both because of its intrinsic interest and because Goodwin was Vela Velupillai's much admired teacher, mentor and friend (and mine as well). There are other protagonists of this approach, among whom one would surely have to count Joseph Schumpeter, but I will refer to it as the Goodwin approach when I need a shorthand label.

The Goodwin approach also generates trend and fluctuations out of a single process. Trend and cycle can be separated *ex post* by statistical decomposition, but they arise out of a common economic mechanism. In other respects this mechanism is very different from the one that underlies modern macro. There is certainly no background optimization going on. Quite the contrary, in Goodwin's case, the heart of the causal process is the push and pull over the distribution of total income between workers and employers. In my reading, the Goodwin growth cycle is a peculiar hybrid. Its basic infrastructure is a Domar model, but with an exogenous, exponentially growing labour productivity. In the simplest version, all profits are saved and invested, and all wages are consumed. The constancy of the capital–output ratio is a tacit assumption that capital is always fully utilized, though labour may be unemployed. The characteristic property – or peculiarity – of the Domar model is that there is a well-known balance condition – savings ratio times capital–output ratio equals growth rate of effective labour force – that must be satisfied if employment is to keep pace with the labour force. If the required equality happens to be replaced by inequality in one direction or the other, the result is perpetually growing labour shortage or perpetually growing unemployment.

Goodwin's innovation is a real-wage Phillips curve, with sharply rising real wages as the unemployment rate becomes small. Now suppose the Domar condition is not satisfied, and employment is outrunning the growth of the labour force. Eventually real wages will explode, profits will fall and, since profits are saved and invested by assumption, the savings-investment rate will fall, and the Domar condition will move towards balance. Indeed it will overshoot, the inequality will turn the other way and unemployment will rise. But then the real wage will decelerate or fall; in either case wages will fall short of productivity growth, profits will rise and investment with it. So at the very least the growth rate of the Goodwin economy will oscillate around its long-run value (which is the growth rate of the effective labour force). There may be intervals in which the level of output falls.

This is indeed, as advertised, a seamless model of growth with cyclical interruptions. It does not much look like the short-run fluctuations of modern capitalist economies, however. Characteristically the profit share rises in booms and falls in slumps, unlike the machinery that drives this model; nor do recoveries from recessions await a collapse of real wages. But there are clearly some realistic traits, maybe more akin to slower motions of aggregate output. How the Goodwin story would look if it were grafted to a more complex model of underlying growth is not clear. Goodwin speaks of serious complications.

This characteristic, that a single model generates both the trend and the fluctuations around it, is certainly more intellectually satisfying than any patchwork procedure. It is the one respect in which these two approaches resemble one another. The big difference is that the cycles of Goodwin and the fluctuations of Kydland–Prescott and successors belong to entirely different species. The first are fairly repetitive (although of course irregular disturbances could be tacked on) and presumably have a longish period. As I have mentioned, many of the Goodwin-style models tell a story centred on endogenous distributional shifts between wages and profits. (There is an element of distributional shift in the Schumpeter mechanism too, via entrepreneurial profits, but the story is entirely different.) In contrast, the fluctuations of modern macro are a response to irregular exogenous shocks: they must be irregular because they are unforeseeable, and they are therefore short lived, and in an obvious sense non-structural.

This way of distinguishing between the two model approaches is, so to speak, entirely internal, stemming from differences in goals and modelling strategies. From the standpoint of an outside observer the difference is that modern macro purports to be dealing with the everyday alternation between recession and expansion, while the Goodwin model is not about that at all, but about a qualitatively different sort of dynamic motion. To take a single simple example, Goodwin models have no place for inventory fluctuations, although changes in inventory investment were an important component of the business cycle at the time Goodwin was writing. Both species of fluctuation have appropriate niches in economics. My concern in this note is primarily with the shorter, more casual fluctuations; ultimately they ought to find a place in Goodwin-type models aimed at lower-frequency motions.

There is an older, though still living, tradition that has a harder time bridging the gap between short-run macroeconomics and long-run growth theory. In practice, the growth part of the story is handled through some version of the neoclassical growth model, and the short-run deviations through some more or less 'Keynesian' apparatus. Neither specification is necessary; any consistent growth model along with any consistent way of dealing with aggregate demand. The significant distinguishing characteristic of this tradition is that it focuses more explicitly on the relation between demand and supply (at any level of aggregation). For instance the rather different 'New Keynesian' approach would do quite well, though, in the interest of simplicity, I will not go down that path. I will be as generic as I can.

So imagine an economy following some growth path that describes the evolution of its potential output. (It might be convenient to suppose that it would approach a steady, though not stationary, state if it were undisturbed, but I will not make use of this property). The main restriction I want to impose is that the underlying machinery is not the Ramsey model; this economy is not anthropomorphically trying to optimize an intertemporal utility. The central property of a growth model is that $Y^P = F(K, A(t)L(t))$, where of course Y^P is potential output, $K(t)$ is the current stock of capital and $L(t)$ is the level of employment that defines potential, with whatever allowance for inflation-proofness dynamic frictions, etc., seems desirable. In the usual way, appending some mechanism for fixing saving and investment allows the model to calculate a trajectory for future potential output corresponding to any given path for $L(t)$ and $A(t)$.

Now suppose there is a sudden reduction (or increase) in aggregate demand, say in consumption (an unexpected increase in the saving rate). An alternative possibility is that saving is unchanged, but the willingness to invest exceeds it or falls short of it, the sort of maladjustment not contemplated in growth models. This failure takes place at t_0. In principle there is a new growth trajectory for Y^P and K emanating from the initial conditions $K(t_0)$, $L(t_0)$, with capital and labour both fully utilized as before. This is simplest to see if the disturbance is simply a sustained rise in the saving rate. But perhaps wage and price rigidities or some other obstacles to the immediate restoration of long-run equilibrium make this impossible.

We are now in the domain of short-run demand-oriented macroeconomics. I do not want to promote any particular theory of aggregate demand. There was a time when the textbook solution was a version of the ISLM model. Outside DSGE circles, it is still fairly acceptable, except that the LM curve (with an exogenous money supply) is commonly superseded by the direct determination of the short-term nominal rate of interest by the central bank, perhaps operating according to a so-called 'Taylor rule'. For my purposes anything will do that provides a dynamic path for y^D (and the price level too) until it settles back at the appropriate y^P, assuming it does so.

Imagine two identical island economies that had been moving along identical growth paths. The disturbance at t_0 affects only one of them; the other continues along its merry way, well represented by the standard growth model. The other island has at least a spell during which $y = y^D < y^P$, and it evolves at least for a while according to a different model. Real instability is a possibility; but suppose that is not the case. The question then is: does this island return to a growth path with new initial conditions? How and when? How is that path related to what has been happening in the sister island? This is exactly what I mean by the problem of bridging between short-run and long-run dynamics. It is pretty obvious that the main connective tissue will be the evolution of $K(t)$ off the growth path, which is not exactly the easiest part of macroeconomics. Notice how the DSGE model avoids this problem: once the unforeseen disturbance at t_0 has taken place, the economy just optimally selects it own future among all the futures that are now possible; on most sets of assumptions it converges along a saddle-path to a steady state much like the one its sister island never left, though perhaps lagging a little behind. If only, one is tempted to say; but of course something similar could happen in an economy without a guardian angel. A Goodwin model, on the other hand, has no vocabulary for dealing with deviations of aggregate income from potential. It is telling a different kind of story.

I would like to explicate a bit further, without actually proposing a medium-run model. It seems to me that the key feature of a successful model will have to be a theory of the evolution of investment, capital stock and level of technology under conditions that are neither like those of short-run macroeconomics, where K is treated as constant, nor like growth theory, where anticipated and actual full utilization is the rule.

As long as $y = y^D < y^P$, the underlying technology says that $y = F([1 - v]K, [1 - u]AL)$. Here u is the unemployment rate over and above the rate that passes for full employment, and v is, so to speak, the unemployment rate of capital, the proportion of capital left idle. This formulation brings to the surface an issue not often discussed: the relation between v and u. Given y on the demand side, the production function itself determines v once u is determined, or vice versa. But that is too simple: the amount of investment, and thus y^D itself, could depend on how v and u behave in practice. There are standard user-cost arguments that are relevant; if we ignore user costs and allow easy substitution, we are led to the usual practice of treating v as zero. Realistically speaking, there are user costs (about which little is known) and aggregate substitutability is not uniformly easy; it would be a reasonable first step just to impose some empirically plausible relation $v = g(u)$. Then the production function connects u and y.

I have dwelt on this point not because it is important for itself, but rather to indicate some of the complexity of the truly important medium-run problem: the valuation of capital and the determination of investment when the economy is off the growth path, and how y will later wind its way around y^p is uncertain. The Brainard–Tobin q-theory is an obvious candidate; but it transfers the problem to the way the stock market values tangible and intangible capital.

However that basic analytical problem is resolved, if the short-run model's dynamics are stable, then the economy will converge to something in the absence of further disturbances. A good formulation will imply that it converges to a trajectory of the accepted growth model. The recent reduction in macroeconomic volatility – what is sometimes called the Great Moderation in the US – seems to point in that direction. How would one proceed in the opposite case, if there were too many very large disturbances? In that case the growth model itself would have little descriptive validity; some other model of evolution would be needed.

I realize that this brief exposition has 'Keynesian' overtones. That merely reveals my own preferences. Actually, my argument depends only on the acknowledgement that market economies experience non-trivial intervals when aggregate output is effectively determined by aggregate demand. Whether this fact can be traced to market imperfections or to something more basic is not my concern. Any coherent model of aggregate demand will do. What will not do is to ignore the problem of bridging between an adequate model of a recession or inflation and a lower-frequency model of undisturbed trend or even cyclical (Goodwin-like) growth.

References

Goodwin, R. (1967) 'A growth cycle', in C.H. Feinstein (ed.), *Socialism, Capitalism and Economic Growth: Essays presented to Maurice Dobb*, Cambridge: Cambridge University Press.

Kydland, F.E. and Prescott, E.C. (1982) 'Time to build and aggregate fluctuations', *Econometrica*, 50(6): 1345–70.

5 The nonlinear path of macroeconomic dynamics

Axel Leijonhufvud

Introduction

Having completed a degree in Mathematics and Engineering at the University of Kyoto, Vela began his studies in Economics at the University of Lund in Sweden.[1] Björn Thalberg became his first mentor in Economics. Vela became extremely well versed in the Swedish macroliterature from Wicksell through Lindahl, Myrdal, Ohlin and Lundberg. From Thalberg he also learned the dynamic multiplier–accelerator models of that day. Moving on to Cambridge, he first studied with Nicholas Kaldor and then Richard Goodwin became his friend and mentor. With this economics training added to the excellent mathematical skills and an engineer's understanding of general systems that he had brought with him from Japan, no one could have been better prepared than Velupillai to contribute to the development of a genuine macroeconomic dynamics. In his mastery of the economics and the mathematics of business cycle models, as well as of the historical development of both, he is without equal.[2]

But in the intervening decades macroeconomics took a very different and less than straightforward course. It has changed direction about as many times as a hunted hare. The question is: Will the hare obey Dennis Robertson's *dictum* and eventually come around pretty much to the same place?

Tracking the hare

The economics of the multiplier–accelerator models that became the first training ground for economists to learn about nonlinear (or piece-wise linear) dynamics was of course simplistic. The constancy of the capital–output ratio which gave the accelerator its 'kick', for example, was a pretty crude assumption and the adaptive behaviour that it generated certainly fell short of the 'rationality' on which later generations of economists would insist.

But the property that became the eventual downfall of these models was another one, namely, that their cycles consisted of a sequence of 'Keynesian' short runs. First, stagflation in the 1970s became an embarrassment for the Keynesian model. Then, there followed the debacle over the unstable Phillips curve. Friedmanian monetarism seemed to handle both problems with ease. Textbook

Keynesianism went into abrupt decline – and took the earlier business cycle theories with it into limbo.

With the Lucasian rational expectations twist to the story, however, monetarism became too clever for its own good. The hypothesis that 'unanticipated money' drove employment fluctuations had an unanticipated good run for the money but eventually proved untenable. Since by that time aesthetic criteria of what constituted 'good economics' in modelling had come to dominate theory choices, the leading fashion in macroeconomics made a quick about-turn, abandoning the belief that the money stock meant everything in generating cycles in favour of the belief that it meant basically nothing of 'real' consequence. With the fleeting misperception disequilibria of Lucasian theory relegated to a footnote, thoroughly general (stochastic) intertemporal equilibrium, complete with efficient financial markets, became the ruling macroeconomic paradigm – and remains so today.

There have been endless criticisms of the unrealistic assumptions of the models belonging to this family – rational expectations, continuous market clearing, representative agent – all to little effect. We might try, instead, to start from the other end, confronting dynamic stochastic general equilibrium (DSGE) theory with the reality around us. When the theory seems more of a hinder than a help in understanding events, we may then ask what assumption or assumptions may need to be changed and what consequences this would have for the theoretical structure as a whole.

Theory in the light of events

In retrospect we can see that the failures of Monetarist theory were more far-reaching than the reasons that prompted its demise and that they implicate other versions of DSGE theory as well.

In rational expectations monetarism, the real interest rate was determined by real factors and could not be manipulated by the central bank. Any attempt to do so would quickly destabilize the price level in Wicksellian fashion. The Federal Reserve System under Greenspan put this proposition to the test in the years following the dot.com crash, pursuing an extreme low interest policy. The result was more Austrian than Monetarist: virtually no CPI inflation, but drastic asset price inflation and very serious deterioration of credit standards (Leijonhufvud 2007).

So the theory failed and needs to be fixed. What might this involve? Repair might start from the recognition that the 'real' interest rate does not exist in 'reality' but is a constructed variable. What does exist is the money rate of interest from which one may construct a distribution of perceived 'real' interest rates given some distribution over agents of inflation expectations. Central banks have considerable influence over money rates of interest. Intertemporal non-monetary general equilibrium (or finance) models deal in variables which have no real world counterparts.

What is needed is a structure in which credit transactions are intertemporal trades *in money*. This is a task similar to that posed by Clower (1967) 40 years ago, namely, of providing a model in which money is used in almost all spot transactions. But constructing a general equilibrium model where the role of money goes beyond just determining the nominal scale of already determined 'real' variables is a problem that has by now remained unresolved for decades.

Similarly, Ricardian equivalence was a property of rational expectations Monetarism. The Bush administration swung the federal budget into large deficit. The increase in the deficit was not compensated by increased private saving. Instead, American households decreased their saving to basically nothing.

So, again, the theory failed and needs to be fixed. What might this involve? The violation of Ricardian equivalence suggests that the transversality condition imposed in intertemporal general equilibrium models has no empirical counterpart. Without such a condition consistency of all decisions is no longer guaranteed in intertemporal models. But bubbles and crashes are admitted. To retain as much of a family resemblance to recent general equilibrium theories as possible would require turning back to two of Vela's favourite economists, Erik Lindahl and John Hicks, and making their temporary equilibrium models the starting point for further work.

Modern financial theory constitutes a crucial component of dynamic stochastic general equilibrium theories. It has been subject to weighty criticism for a long time (Mandelbrot and Hudson 2004) much of it stressing that the core assumption that future returns are normally distributed has been proven false innumerable times (Taleb 2007). For macroeconomics, the repeated occurrence of financial crashes or crises has become the more pressing concern since they hardly seem consistent with intertemporal equilibrium theory. A list covering only the last 20 years would include the October 1987 stock-market crash on Wall Street and the Norway banking crisis in the same year, followed by Japan (1990), Sweden and Finland (1991), the East Asian crises (1997), Russia (1998) and Brasil (1999), the US dot.com crash (2000), Argentina (2001) and now the ongoing credit crisis triggered by the 'subprime meltdown' in the United States (2007–?).

In intertemporal equilibrium models all agents are endowed with rational expectations. It is convenient to suppose that this means that all have the same expectation and thence tempting to assume that the collective of agents behaves as one. So modelling the behaviour of the entire economy as the behaviour of a single representative agent became a widespread practice. The usual objection to ignoring the heterogeneity of agents has been that it fails to take into account well-documented systematic differences in behaviour between age groups, income classes, etc. Disregarding the fact that different people react differently to events is bad enough. But what is probably far worse is that these models are blind to the consequences of too many people doing the same thing at the same time. The fallacy of composition comes as a built-in feature of representative agent models. The representative lemming is not a rational expectations intertemporal optimizing creature. But he is responsible for the 'fat tail' problem that macroeconomists have the most reason to care about.

These intertemporal equilibrium models do if anything worse at the other extreme of monetary instability. The work that Daniel Heymann and I did on high inflations[3] years ago resulted in a number of stylized facts which, from the standpoint of DSGE theory, are to be regarded as anomalies. The major anomalies were five. First, the domestic money remains in use even at rates of 'inflation tax' amounting to thousands of percentage points per year. Second, the legal unit of account plays a far more important role than recognized by standard theory. When the value of money becomes sufficiently unstable monetary accounting becomes meaningless. But monetary accounting is vital to the monitoring of innumerable principal agent relationships in a modern economy. So unstable money disrupts economic organization in innumerable ways. Third, almost all intertemporal markets simply disappear. Only a few quite thin markets in ultrashort maturities survive. Fourth, spot markets instead fragment as spatial arbitrage fails even between close locations. Fifth, relative prices become extremely volatile. None of these characteristic high inflation phenomena are predicted by monetary general equilibrium models. In fact they constitute strong evidence against them.

Axiomatic macroeconomics?

Real Business Cycle Theory came to rule the macroeconomic roost about 20 years ago – just in time for the start of the long series of financial crashes and crises to the understanding of which that theory contributes precisely nothing. Dynamic stochastic general equilibrium theory must, I believe, be judged a failure. But it is important to realize that the failure with which we have to deal is not just that of some particular properties of this class of models, such as the lack of a general non-*tâtonnement* stability theorem, or the fundamental aggregation problem uncovered by Sonnenschein, Mantel and Debreu – or even the failure of incorporating money in a non-trivial manner. The enterprise that has fundamentally failed is that of basing macroeconomics on an axiomatic foundation.[4] This is not only because in a complex system the whole is not just the sum of its parts (so that representative agent constructions mislead). It is also because several of our 'axioms' are themselves far from 'self-evident' and, indeed, rather doubtful as a steadily growing body of evidence in experimental and behavioural economics and econophysics is demonstrating.

How did we come to invest so heavily in this bankrupt enterprise? It is of course a complex story. But one important strand of it starts with the ambition of Robert Lucas to consolidate the victory over Keynesianism by putting Friedman's monetarism on 'solid microfoundations'. This involved most particularly replacing the uncertain future with the known Gaussian future that the rational choice agent requires. But something more fundamental than changing a couple of assumptions was going on underneath all the excitement and controversy surrounding the rise of the New Classical Economics. Friedman's monetarism had been *inductively* based. His work was in the old tradition of the NBER as shaped by Wesley Mitchell and Arthur Burns. Theory to Friedman was a matter of seeing some coherent order in the patterns found in long years of work with the primary data.[5] This ontological anchoring (Lawson 1997) was lost in the turn to axiom-based theorizing.

It is interesting to reflect that one of the most outspoken of all critics of Friedmanian Monetarism, Vela's one-time teacher, Nicholas Kaldor, nonetheless had the same basic approach to economic theorizing. To Kaldor, the 'stylized facts' dictated what a theory should explain. The ambition to deduce how the world behaves from a small set of axioms was alien to the entire generation to which Friedman and Kaldor belonged. They were the better for it.[6]

The macroeconomics of 'inflexibilities'

For many years now the main alternative to Real Business Cycle Theory has been a somewhat loose cluster of models given the label of New Keynesian theory. New Keynesians adhere on the whole to the same DSGE modelling technology as RBC macroeconomists but differ in the extent to which they emphasize inflexibilities of prices or other contract terms as sources of short-term adjustment problems in the economy. The 'New Keynesian' label refers back to the 'rigid wages' brand of Keynesian theory of 40 or 50 years ago. Except for this stress on inflexibilities this brand of contemporary macro theory has basically nothing Keynesian about it.

The obvious objection to this kind of return to an earlier way of thinking about macro problems is that the major problems which have had to be confronted in the last 20 or so years have originated in the financial markets – and prices in those markets are anything but 'inflexible'. But there is also a general theoretical problem that has been festering for decades with very little in the way of attempts to tackle it. Economists talk freely about 'inflexible' or 'rigid' prices all the time, despite the fact that we do not have a shred of theory that could provide criteria for judging whether a particular price is more or less flexible than appropriate to the proper functioning of the larger system. More than 70 years ago, Keynes already knew that a high degree of downward price flexibility in a recession could entirely wreck the financial system and make the situation infinitely worse. But the point of his argument has never come fully to inform the way economists think about price flexibility.

What matters for the dynamic behaviour of a system is *relative* speeds of adjustment. A pertinent example of this point is given in Bookstaber's (2007) account of how the October 1987 market crash was triggered. The stock market had gone through three consecutive days of big declines in the week ending Friday 16 October. The managers of portfolio insurance programmes started out to reset their dynamic hedges first thing on Monday morning, 19 October. This required selling S&P futures. A massive amount of sell orders flowed into the Chicago futures market and the price of futures fell rapidly. Induced by the widening gap between the current futures price and the Friday stock closing prices, cash–futures arbitrageurs stepped in to buy futures with the intention of shorting the stocks underlying the S&P index. However, at this point the New York Stock Exchange had not yet opened. When, half an hour later, NYSE did open it was hit by a surge of sell orders. The wave hit a wall. The volume was too large for the specialists to add to inventory so they tried to find buyers by dropping prices.

But the equity investors initially were not ready to re-evaluate their positions that quickly and later on were frightened off by the very speed with which prices were falling. Thus, concludes Bookstaber (2007: 22), there was 'a dislocation between the hair-trigger execution of the futures and the ponderous decision making on the cash–equity side, compounded by the insufficient capital of the specialist to bridge the gap'. Rephrasing the point, the specialists did not have the *buffer stock capacity* to keep the process orderly – to keep it within its 'corridor'. The deviation-amplifying process gathered ever more momentum so that 'in the last 75 minutes of the trading day, the Dow dropped … three times as much … as it had in any other full trading day in history' (ibid.: 25).

The story is worth retelling at some length because, obviously, this disaster was not fashioned by 'inflexibility' of prices. It makes two points. First, 'the time frame for being able to do transactions in the futures market was substantially different from the time frame in the equity market' (ibid.: 21). Second, price formation in one market will be dependent on that in one or more other markets.

In a somewhat different context, these points were made long before in a splendid but little known paper by Art DeVany (1996) in a volume edited by Vela and Daniel Vaz. DeVany is one of the rare economists who realizes that higher price adjustment velocities are not always beneficial. Markets operate on different frequencies:

> Consider the simple case of bread. The wheat market clears annually. The inventory is drawn down monthly. It can be hedged with three-month futures contracts. Bakers rent their shops on five-year contracts. Rental contracts are adjusted yearly, contingent on the price level. Bakers own their equipment in perpetuity, but borrow on three-year notes to buy it. The commercial note market clears hourly. Equipment orders take six months to produce. The used equipment market is thin; its transactions are episodic and few. Bakery employees are hired weekly. Bread is baked and consumed daily.
>
> (DeVany 1996: 325)

The synchronization of all these activities operating on different time frames, DeVany makes clear, is a genuine problem that general equilibrium falsifies by the 'artefact of the common dating of all commodities' (ibid.: 324). All markets are supposed to operate simultaneously on all dates. But the appropriate time frames differ. Moreover, this will condition how the network of markets is structured and how information flows through it. They will automatically form a hierarchical order in which 'commodities that trade in low frequency markets [will] condition on the high frequency markets' (ibid.: 329). DeVany's paper in effect outlines an entire programme of research that needs to be done in order to provide meaningful microfoundations for adaptive dynamic macroeconomics.

The last two of the five anomalies about high inflations mentioned earlier were that spot markets fragment and that relative prices (among the fragments) become exceedingly volatile. The interpretation of this relative price volatility commonly seen in the literature has been that it would be due to 'menu costs' keeping some markets from adjusting as frequently as others. Heymann and I came to the very opposite conclusion, namely, that most of the excess volatility was due to the movements of the most frequently adjusted prices. High inflation forces markets away from the natural relative frequency equilibrium described by DeVany – and the result is chaos.

After DSGE what next?

Tremendous ingenuity has been applied over several decades to the task of adapting general equilibrium theory to the needs of macroeconomic theory. This effort, I believe, must by now be judged a failure.[7]

What next then? Will Robertson's hare return pretty much to the same place where Vela started in economics? In some respects, we are likely to see a family resemblance to the business cycle models of that time. Macroeconomists are likely to build models with heterogeneous adaptive not-to-rational agents rather than the optimizing superhumans of DSGE models. And that means a return to the study of nonlinear dynamic processes.

But the low-dimensional models of yore will not be of much interest any longer and will of course not be of any help in trying better to understand systems of multiple markets operating on different time scales. The investigation of higher dimensional dynamical systems will take us beyond what can be done with purely analytical methods. Moreover, the old Keynesian business cycle models were hardly more suited to the analysis of the economy's self-organizing, self-regulating properties – *and* their limits – than is modern general equilibrium theory. And these are the issues that should belatedly come on to the agenda.[8]

While other macro theorists have busied themselves with general equilibrium theory, Vela has spent the last 20 or so years laying the foundational groundwork for a theory able to tackle these issues. Dennis Robertson advised that if one stood still the hare of high brow opinion would come around to the same place. Vela has not stood still.[9] It is devoutly to be hoped that the hare comes around to the fields that he has been cultivating. Our subject would be better for it.

Notes

1 I first met Vela in Lund in 1971. Having been told that a Mr Velupillai had made an appointment to see me, I formed the hypothesis that the name must be Finnish. As forecasts of economists go, this was not too far off (at least geographically). Vela, of course, is Swedish.

2 His command of these fields is on display in his recent contribution to the Hicks memorial volume (Velupillai 2008).

3 Heymann and Leijonhufvud (1995). The major anomalies are briefly summarized in Leijonhufvud (1997).

4 Some 20 years ago a leading macro theorist (to me a new acquaintance) told me that he foresaw great progress in the near future 'now that we have put macroeconomics on an axiomatic foundation'. I recall the incidence so vividly because the statement stunned

me and made me realize how drastically the entire conception of the field had changed from one generation to the next.
5 Cf. the fine book by Hammond (1996).
6 Vela has had a long-standing interest in the role of induction in science. Cf., for example, his critique of Popper in 'Trans-Popperian suggestions on falsification and induction' (Velupillai 2003, Chapter 6).
7 An opinion, of course, that does not command widespread acceptance – not yet, at any rate.
8 There is also the question, which I remember discussing with Vela 30 or more years ago, whether one should aim for a purely endogenous theory of fluctuations. On this issue, I remain an impulse-propagation advocate on the grounds that endogenizing all impulses involves enlarging models by adding equations that are no more than speculations about possible relationships on which we have no reliable knowledge.
9 He is known, rather, for never staying in the same place very long!

References

Bookstaber, R. (2007) *A Demon of Our Own Design: Markets, Hedge Funds, and the Perils of Financial Innovation*, Hoboken, NJ: John Wiley & Sons.

Clower, R.W. (1967) 'A reconsideration of the microfoundations of monetary theory', *Western Economic Journal*, December 1967, reprinted in D.A. Walker (ed.) (1984) *Money and Markets: Essays by Robert W. Clower*, Cambridge: Cambridge University Press.

DeVany, A. (1996) 'Synchronising markets, mutual information and the price level: Co-ordination in a non-general equilibrium world' in D. Vaz and K. Velupillai (eds), *Inflation, Institutions and Information*, London: Macmillan.

Hammond, J.D. (1996) *Theory and Measurement: Causality issues in Milton Friedman's monetary economics*. Cambridge and New York: Cambridge University Press.

Heymann, D. and Leijonhufvud, A. (1995) *High Inflation*, Oxford: Oxford University Press.

Lawson, T. (1997) *Economics and Reality*, London: Routledge.

Leijonhufvud, A. (1997) 'Macroeconomics and complexity: Inflation theory', in B. Arthus, S. Durlauf and D. Lane (eds), *The Economy as an Evolving Complex System II*, New York: Addison-Wesley.

—— (2007) 'The perils of inflation targeting', VoxEU.org. Online, available at: www.voxeu.org/index.php?q=node/322 (accessed 26 October 2007).

Mandelbrot, B. and Hudson, R.L. (2004) *The (mis)Behavior of Markets: A Fractal view of risk, ruin and reward*, New York: Basic Books.

Taleb, N.N. (2007) *The Black Swan: The impact of the highly improbable*, New York: Random House.

Velupillai, K.V. (2003) 'Essays on computable economics, methodology and the philosophy of science', Discussion Paper No. 8, University of Trento, Department of Economics.

—— (2008) 'A perspective on a Hicksian "non-linear" theory of the trade cycle', in R. Scazzieri, A. Sen and S. Zamagni (eds), *Markets, Money and Capital: Hicksian economics for the 21st century*, Cambridge: Cambridge University Press.

Part III
Computable economics

6 The information economy

Gregory Chaitin

Introduction

I am not an economist; I work on algorithmic information theory (AIT). This chapter, in which I present a vision of a possible future information economy, should not be taken too seriously. I am merely playing with ideas and trying to provide some light entertainment of a kind suitable for this Festschrift volume, given Vela's deep appreciation of the relevance of foundational issues in mathematics for economic theory.

In algorithmic information theory, you measure the complexity of something by counting the number of bits in the smallest program for calculating it:

program $\rightarrow$ *Universal Computer* $\rightarrow$ output.

If the output of a program could be a physical or a biological system, then this complexity measure would give us a way to measure of the difficulty of explaining how to construct or grow something, in other words, measure either traditional smokestack or newer green technological complexity:

software $\rightarrow$ *Universal Constructor* $\rightarrow$ physical system
DNA $\rightarrow$ *Development* $\rightarrow$ biological system

And it is possible to conceive of a future scenario in which technology is not natural-resource limited, because energy and raw materials are freely available, but is only know-how limited.

In this chapter, I will outline four different versions of this dream, in order to explain why I take it seriously:

1 magic, in which knowing someone's secret name gives you power over them;
2 astrophysicist Fred Hoyle's vision of a future society in his science-fiction novel *Ossian's Ride*;
3 mathematician John von Neumann's cellular automata world with its self-reproducing automata and a universal constructor;

4   physicist Freeman Dyson's vision of a future green technology in which you can, for example, grow houses from seeds.

As these four examples show, if an idea is important, it's reinvented, it keeps being rediscovered. In fact, I think this is an idea whose time has come.

Secret/true names and the esoteric tradition

> In the beginning was the Word, and the Word was with God, and the Word was God.
>
> (John 1:1)

Information – knowing someone's secret/true name – is very important in the esoteric tradition (Coudert 1995):

* Recall the German fairy tale in which the punch line is 'Rumpelstiltskin is my name!' (the Brothers Grimm).
* You have power over someone if you know their secret name.
* You can summon a demon if you know its secret name.
* In the Garden of Eden, Adam acquired power over the animals by naming them.
* God's name is never mentioned by Orthodox Jews.
* The golem in Prague was animated by a piece of paper with God's secret name on it.
* Presumably God can summon a person or thing into existence by calling its true name.
* Leibniz was interested in the original sacred Adamic language of creation, the perfect language in which the essence/true nature of each substance or being is directly expressed, as a way of obtaining ultimate knowledge. His project for a *characteristica universalis* evolved from this, and the calculus evolved from that. Christian Huygens, who had taught Leibniz mathematics in Paris, hated the calculus (Hofmann 1974: 299), because it eliminated mathematical creativity and arrived at answers mechanically and inelegantly.

Fred Hoyle's *Ossian's Ride*

The main features in the future economy that Hoyle imagines are:

* cheap and unlimited hydrogen to helium fusion power;
* therefore raw materials readily available from sea water, soil and air (for example, using extremely large-scale and energy intensive mass spectrometer-like devices (Gordon Lasher, private communication));
* and with essentially free energy and raw materials, all that counts is techno-logical know-how, which is just information.

Perhaps it's best to let Hoyle explain this in his own words:

> [T]he older established industries of Europe and America ... grew up around specialized mineral deposits – coal, oil, metallic ores. Without these deposits the older style of industrialization was completely impossible. On the political and economic fronts, the world became divided into 'haves' and 'have-nots', depending whereabouts on the earth's surface these specialized deposits happened to be situated...
>
> In the second phase of industrialism ... no specialized deposits are needed at all. The key to this second phase lies in the possession of an effectively unlimited source of energy. Everything here depends on the thermonuclear reactor ... With a thermonuclear reactor, a single ton of ordinary water can be made to yield as much energy as several hundred tons of coal – and there is no shortage of water in the sea. Indeed, the use of coal and oil as a prime mover in industry becomes utterly inefficient and archaic.
>
> With unlimited energy the need for high-grade metallic ores disappears. Low-grade ones can be smelted – and there is an ample supply of such ores to be found everywhere. Carbon can be taken from inorganic compounds, nitrogen from the air, a whole vast range of chemical from sea water.
>
> So I arrived at the rich concept of this second phase of industrialization, a phase in which nothing is needed but the commonest materials – water, air and fairly common rocks. This was a phase that can be practiced by anybody, by any nation, provided one condition is met: provided one knows exactly what to do. This second phase was clearly enormously more effective and powerful than the first.
>
> Of course this concept wasn't original. It must have been at least thirty years old. It was the second concept that I was more interested in. The concept of information as an entity in itself, the concept of information as a violently explosive social force.
>
> (Hoyle 1959: 157–8)

In Hoyle's fantasy, this crucial information – including the design of thermonuclear reactors – that suddenly propels the world into a second phase of industrialization comes from another world. It is a legacy bequeathed to humanity by a non-human civilization desperately trying to preserve anything it can when being destroyed by the brightening of its star.

John von Neumann's cellular automata world

This cellular automata world first appeared in lectures and private working notes by von Neumann. These ideas were advertised in an article in *Scientific American* in 1955 that was written by John Kemeny (1955). Left unfinished because of von Neumann's death in 1957, his notes were edited by Arthur Burks and finally published in 1966 (Neumann 1966). Burks then presented an overview (1970) with the key points:

- World is a discrete crystalline medium.
- Two-dimensional world, graph paper, divided into square cells.
- Each square has 29 states.
- Time is quantized as well as space.
- State of each square the same universal function of its previous state and the previous state of its four immediate neighbours (square itself plus up, down, left, right immediate neighbours).
- *Universal constructor* can assemble any quiescent array of states.
- Then you have to start the device running.
- The universal constructor is part of von Neumann's self-reproducing automata.

The crucial point is that in von Neumann's toy world, physical systems are merely discrete information, that is all there is. And there is no difference between computing a string of bits (as in AIT) and 'computing' (constructing) an arbitrary physical system.

I should also mention that starting from scratch, Edgar Codd (1968) came up with a simpler version of von Neumann's cellular automata world. In Codd's model cells have eight states instead of 29.

Freeman Dyson's green technology

Instead of Hoyle's vision of a second stage of traditional smokestack heavy industry, Dyson (1999, 2007) optimistically envisions a green-technology small-is-beautiful do-it-yourself grass-roots future.

The emerging technology that may someday lead to Dyson's utopia is becoming known as 'synthetic biology' and deals with deliberately engineered organisms. This is also referred to as 'artificial life', the development of 'designer genomes'. To produce something, you just create the DNA for it. Here are some key points in Dyson's vision:

- Solar electrical power obtained from modified trees. (Not from thermonuclear reactors!)
- Other useful devices/machines grown from seeds.
- Even houses grown from seeds?!
- School children able to design and grow new plants as well as animals.
- Mop up excessive carbon dioxide or produce fuels from sugar (actual Craig Venter (2007) projects).

On a much darker note, to show how important information is, there presumably exists a sequence of a few-thousand DNA bases (A, C, G, T) for the genome of a virus that would destroy the human race, indeed, most life on this planet. With current or soon-to-be-available molecular biology technology, genetic engineering tools, anyone who knew this sequence could easily synthesize the corresponding pathogen. Dyson's utopia can easily turn into a nightmare.

AIT as an economic metatheory

So one can imagine scenarios in which natural resources are irrelevant and all that counts is technological know-how, that is, information. We have just seen four such scenarios. In such a world, I believe, AIT becomes, not an economic theory, but perhaps an economic meta theory, since it is a theory of information, a theory about the properties of technological know-how, as I will now explain.

The main concept in AIT is the amount of information $H(X)$ required to compute (or construct) something, X. This is measured in bits of software, the number of bits in the smallest program that calculates X. Briefly, one refers to $H(X)$ as the *complexity* of X. For an introduction to AIT, please see Chaitin (2006, 2007).

In economic terms, $H(X)$ is a measure of the amount of technological know-how needed to produce X. If X is a hammer, $H(X)$ will be small. If X is a sophisticated military aircraft, $H(X)$ will be quite large.

Two other concepts in AIT are the *joint complexity* $H(X, Y)$ of producing X and Y together, and the *relative complexity* $H(X|Y)$ of producing X if we are given Y for free.

Consider now two objects, X and Y. In AIT,

$$H(X) + H(Y) - H(X, Y)$$

is referred to as the *mutual information* in X and Y. This is the extent to which it is cheaper to produce X and Y together than to produce X and Y separately, in other words, the extent to which the technological know-how needed to produce X and Y can be shared, or overlaps. And there is a basic theorem in AIT that states that this is also

$$H(X) - H(X|Y),$$

which is the extent to which being given the know-how for Y helps us to construct X, and it's also

$$H(Y) - H(Y|X),$$

which is the extent to which being given the know-how for X helps us to construct Y. This is not earth-shaking, but it's nice to know. (For a proof of this theorem about mutual information, please see Chaitin 2001: 95–6.)

One of the reasons that we get these pleasing properties is that AIT is like classical thermodynamics in that time is ignored. In thermodynamics, heat engines operate very slowly, for example, reversibly. In AIT, the time or effort required to construct something is ignored, only the information required is measured. This enables both thermodynamics and AIT to have clean, simple results. They are toy models, as they must be if we wish to prove nice theorems.

Conclusion

Clearly, we are not yet living in an information economy. Oil, uranium, gold and other scarce, precious limited natural resources still matter. But someday we may live in an information economy, or at least approach it asymptotically. In such an economy, everything is, in effect, software; hardware is comparatively unimportant. This is a possible world, though perhaps not yet our own world.

References

Burks, A. (ed.) (1970) *Essays on Cellular Automata*, Urbana, IL: University of Illinois Press.

Chaitin, G. (2001) *Exploring Randomness*, London: Springer Verlag.

—— (2006) *Meta Maths*, London: Atlantic Books.

—— (2007) *Thinking about Gödel and Turing*, Singapore: World Scientific.

Codd, E. (1968) *Cellular Automata*, New York: Academic Press.

Coudert, A. (1995) *Leibniz and the Kabbalah*, Dordrecht: Kluwer.

Dyson, F. (1999) *The Sun, the Genome, and the Internet*, New York: Oxford University Press.

—— (2007) *A Many-Colored Glass*, Charlottesville, VA: University of Virginia Press.

Hofmann, J. (1974) *Leibniz in Paris 1672–1676*, Cambridge: Cambridge University Press.

Hoyle, F. (1959) *Ossian's Ride*, New York: Harper & Brothers.

Kemeny, J. (1955) 'Man viewed as a machine', *Scientific American*, April, 58–67.

Neumann, J. von (1966) *Theory of Self-Reproducing Automata*, Urbana, IL: University of Illinois Press. (Edited and completed by Arthur W. Burks.)

Venter, C. (2007) *A Life Decoded*, New York: Viking.

7 Hypotheses that imply the independence of $P = NP$ from strong axiomatic systems

N.C.A. da Costa and F.A. Doria

Prologue

In a nutshell: the P vs NP question deals with a class of problems whose solutions are easy to test but hard to find. The best known example is the travelling salesman problem: given n cities and k gallons of gas, which is the route, if any, that goes through all n cities and uses at most k gallons of gas? There are many known algorithms that get the solution – alas! – all known algorithms operate in exponential time on the length of the input. However given a possible solution which was whispered to us by some well-meaning guardian angel, it is easy (that is, it is time-polynomial on the length of the input) to test for it – to make sure that the guardian angel wasn't some mischievous little devil in disguise...

So, if solutions are easy to test, we may ask, are they also easy to find?

Is there a fast, time-polynomial, algorithm that finds a solution for the travelling salesman problem?

This is the $P = NP$ problem. Its negation will be noted $P < NP$: it means, there is no such a fast algorithm.[1]

The P vs NP question has been around for nearly 40 years, and so far nobody has advanced a single clue about its solution. Moreover one wonders why such a practical, down to earth problem, has so far resisted all attacks. Why is P vs NP such a difficult problem?

In this chapter we suggest an answer: we do not in fact need new concepts or techniques to deal with the P vs NP question. However we must get ready for the unexpected in the answer of the problem. We present here a proof of the independence of the formal sentences $[P < NP]$ and $[P = NP]$ from strong axiomatic systems that include arithmetic, given two hypotheses. In our viewpoint these hypotheses are quite intuitive, and we sketch naive, informal arguments for them at the appendix.

Main themes

We will deal here with *poly machines*, or *poly Turing machines*. These are Turing machines that input a word over a binary alphabet and output a similar word, and whose operation time is polynomial on the length of the input.

The formal sentence $[P < NP]$ is a Π_2 arithmetic sentence (it will be explicitly written out later on), that is, it has the form $\forall x \exists y P(x, y)$, with P primitive recursive. It is known that $\forall x \exists y P(x, y)$ is provable in some reasonable axiomatic system S – see below for a more precise characterization of S – if and only if function $f(x) = \min_y P(x, y)$ is proved by S to be total. We use that idea here.

As we will soon see, f is the so-called BGS counterexample function.

Functions f and f

In our opinion, the key to the solution of the problem is the fact that the so-called full counterexample function f to $P = NP$ grows in its peaks at least as fast as the Busy Beaver function.

Remark 1. The full counterexample function f to the $P = NP$ hypothesis is given by the following construction. Consider a primitive recursive Gödel numbering of all Turing machines which is on to ω. Then the full counterexample function f is given by:

i   If m codes a poly machine, then $f(m) =$ the first integer x (in binary form) input to poly machine $\{m\}$ that fails to output a satisfying line for x seen as an instance of SAT.

ii   If m codes no poly machine, then $f(m) = 0$.

SAT is the set of satisfiable Boolean expressions in conjunctive normal form, which is our model problem in the NP-class (Machtey and Young 1979).

However f turns out to be noncomputable and in order to apply the result just mentioned about Π_2 sentences we must obtain a recursive function which has the same information contained in the full counterexample function and which is relevant to the matter. We do so by the restriction of the full counterexample function f to the so-called BGS set of Turing machines and get function f, the BGS counterexample function. (For its definition, as well as the definition of the exotic counterexample function see Remark 23.)

The BGS set is a well-known recursive set of poly machines (Baker *et al.* 1975) with the following properties:

•   Every Turing machine in the BGS set is a poly machine.
•   Given any poly machine M, there is a poly machine M′ in the BGS set so that for every input x, $M(x) = M'(x)$.

So, the BGS set adequately mirrors the set of all poly machines. Moreover, it is a recursive set.

However there are problems when we go from the full counterexample function f to the BGS function f. When we restrict the counterexample function to the BGS machines, we get a function whose behaviour is difficult to check when it comes to its growth properties. More precisely: we must find in our theory some procedure that 'develops', as in a photograph, the fast-growing properties of the recursive counterexample function.

Such is the exotic formulation trick introduced by the authors (da Costa and Doria 2003, 2006; da Costa *et al.* 2007), together with the two hypotheses we will introduce here and which we believe are quite intuitive.

Given our two hypotheses, we conclude that:

* The full, noncomputable, counterexample function to [*P* = *NP*] can be restricted to a computable function within an axiomatic theory *S* as briefly described below. However the ability of *S* to 'see' the fast-growing properties of such a computable function is restricted; therefore we require our hypotheses to allow for *S* to notice those properties.
* If we add the two hypotheses spelled out below, both the [*P* = *NP*] and [*P* < *NP*] (or [*P* ≠ *NP*]) formal sentences become independent of Peano Arithmetic (PA) and of a whole family of strong theories that include arithmetic and have models with a standard arithmetic part.

   Moreover, a nonrecursive extension of Peano Arithmetic (with the same language as PA) proves [*P* < *NP*], since if it is independent it holds of the standard model for arithmetic. (We ignore here the trivial situations such as theory PA + [*P* < *NP*] which immediately proves [*P* < *NP*].)
* As side results we deal with some properties of theory *S* + [*P* < *NP*], which we consider in the last part of the chapter.

Incompleteness as a widespread phenomenon in axiomatic theories

We will later characterize our theory *S*; most axiom systems used in mathematics such as Peano Arithmetic or Zermelo–Fraenkel Set Theory with the Axiom of Choice (ZFC) satisfy the conditions we ask for *S*.

Why should we expect that [*P* = *NP*] and [*P* < *NP*] are independent of strong axiomatic systems? Because among other things undecidability and incompleteness are widespread phenomena. Hartmanis and Hopcroft showed in 1976 that several interesting questions in computer science are independent of systems like *S*. (For more examples see Carnielli and Doria 2008.)

We can also quote other examples in that direction:

Proposition 2. There is a set $\mathcal{P}$ of Turing machines so that ZFC can neither prove nor disprove the (adequately formalized sentence) '$\mathcal{P}$ is a set of poly Turing machines.'

A similar result, with analogous proof (Carnielli and Doria 2008, da Costa and Doria 2004):

Proposition 3. There is a set $\mathcal{A}$ of Turing machines so that ZFC can neither prove nor disprove the sentence (again properly formalized) '$\mathcal{P}$ is a set of finite automata.'

A curious fact is:

Proposition 4. There is a real number s whose decimal expansion is proved by ZFC to be generated by an algorithmic procedure and yet such that ZFC cannot compute a single digit of it.

(For the proof see the Appendix.) Another result, related to a result by Solovay (in Calude 2007):

Proposition 5. There is a real number Ω' related to Chaitin's Ω so that ZFC cannot compute a single digit of it.

(See the Appendix.) So among other things, if undecidability and incompleteness are a widespread phenomenon and affects even naively looking sentences, then one must seriously consider that possibility when dealing with the P vs NP problem.

The two main hypotheses: a preliminary discussion

We refer here to Remark 11 for the formal sentences $[P = NP]$ and $[P < NP]$. We will deal with a class of axiomatic systems S that satisfy:

- S has a recursively enumerable set of theorems.
- S includes Peano Arithmetic.
- S has a model with standard arithmetic. That is, theory S is *arithmetically sound*.

We will require:

Hypothesis 6. If $S \vdash [P < NP]$ then theory S has the same provably total recursive functions as theory $S + [P < NP] \leftrightarrow [P < NP]^F$.

If we add that hypothesis to our results on the exotic formulation, we see that $S \vdash [P < NP]$. Given that:

Hypothesis 7. If $S \vdash [P < NP]$ and $S = [P < NP]$, then S proves that the set of BGS poly machines that solve any problem in the NP class is recursively enumerable.

$[P < NP]^F$ is our exotic formulation (da Costa and Doria 2003, 2006; da Costa *et al.* 2007); see below. We present extensive plausibility arguments in favour of these hypotheses in the Appendix.

Remark 8. Both hypotheses are quite reasonable, as we now argue. We will prove below that the counterexample function to $[P = NP]$ grows at least as fast as the Busy Beaver function, since its peaks dominate any total recursive function. If S proves $[P < NP]$, the counterexample function is total; as there is a recursive function with the required information, namely being total, we show that it, sort of, has also coded in itself the fast-growing properties of the full noncomputable, counterexample function. So, as S proves $[P < NP]$, it is reasonable to suppose that both S and $S + [P < NP] \leftrightarrow [P < NP]^F$ have the same provably total recursive functions, as the extra condition only adds, if anything, data about F.

From the first hypothesis:

- Suppose that S proves $[P < NP]$.
- It will then hold of the standard model for arithmetic.
- Then consistent theory $S + [P < NP] \leftrightarrow [P < NP]^F \vdash [P < NP]$.
- But da Costa and Doria (2003, 2006; da Costa *et al.* 2007) $S \vdash [P < NP]^F$.
- From Hypothesis 6, $S + [P < NP] \leftrightarrow [P < NP]^F \vdash [P < NP]^F$.
- Then $S + [P < NP] \leftrightarrow [P < NP]^{FF} \vdash [P < NP]$.
- A contradiction. Thus $S \nvdash [P < NP]$.

Remark 9. The second hypothesis is also quite reasonable. Suppose that $S \vdash [P = NP]$. Then there are infinitely many time-polynomial (poly) algorithms that fully settle all problems in some NP-complete class, say, the satisfiability problem SAT (da Costa and Doria 2003, 2006; da Costa *et al.* 2007). Think of S as a Turing machine that lists all theorems of S. We know that the recursive set of poly machines (the BGS set, cf. Baker *et al.* 1975) is such that the set of machines that *do not* solve the whole of SAT form a recursively enumerable set. Then the poly machines that S proves that settle all of SAT is recursively enumerable, and a simple concluding argument shows that such a listing has to be exhaustive. See also the Appendix for a more detailed discussion and a naive argument for Hypothesis 7.

The second hypothesis implies that $S \nvdash [P = NP]$, or equivalently that $S + [P < NP]$ is consistent if so is S. However the argument is a bit more involved, so, we skip it and we present it in full detail below in the part of the chapter that deals with Hypothesis 7.

Hypothesis 6 implies that $S \vdash [P < NP]$: full discussion

We base our presentation here on da Costa and Doria (2003, 2006; da Costa *et al.* 2007). Folklore has long asserted that the counterexample function to $P = NP$ would be of extremely fast growth in its peaks (for definitions see Remarks 1 and 23). This fact suggested the Paris–Harrington like approach to the P vs NP question that we have followed.

This idea led to what the authors have called the exotic formalization for $P < NP$: a Π_2 sentence $[P < NP]^F$ that naively translates as $P < NP$, is in fact equivalent to $[P < NP]$ in the standard model for arithmetic (Doria 2007), but cannot have that equivalence established within theories such as S, for adequate fast-growing functions F (da Costa and Doria 2003, 2005, 2006; da Costa *et al.* 2007), for that equivalence is actually independent of such theories.

We present here our previous results for the sake of completeness and give both naive proofs for them, and then rigorous proofs. Our axiomatic framework

S is taken to be at least ZFC, in order to ensure enough 'elbow room' for our arguments, but they apply to any *S* as described.

More on the exotic formalization

The exotic formalization for $P < NP$ is naively the same as the standard formalization, but cannot (in general) be proved equivalent to the latter within even strong systems such as ZFC. Let $t_m(x)$ be the (primitive recursive function that gives the) operation time of Turing machine $\{m\}$ of Gödel number m over an input x of length $|x|$.

Remark 10. Recall:

- The standard formalization for $[P = NP]$ is:

$$[P = NP] \leftrightarrow \exists m \in \omega, a \forall x \in \omega[(t_m(x) \leq |x|^a + a) \wedge R(x, m)].$$

- $[P < NP] \leftrightarrow _{Def} \neg[P = NP].$
- R is a poly predicate, that is to say, $\langle x, m \rangle$ satisfies R if and only if there is a poly machine $M_R(x, y) = 1$. Otherwise $M_R(x, y) = 0$.

Suppose that $\{e_f\} = f$ is total recursive and strictly increasing. The naive version for the exotic formalization is:

$$[P = NP]^f \leftrightarrow \exists m \in \omega, a \forall x \in \omega[(t_m(x) \leq |x|^{f(a)} + f(a)) \wedge R(x, m)].$$

Now, for the next definitions and results let f be in general a (possibly partial) recursive function which is strictly increasing over its domain, and let e_f be the Gödel number of an algorithm that computes f. Let $p(\langle e_f, b, c \rangle, x_1, x_2, \ldots, x_k)$ be (Davis 1982) a universal Diophantine polynomial with parameters e_f, b, c; that polynomial has integer roots if and only if $\{e_f\}(b) = c$. We may if needed suppose that polynomial to be ≥ 0. We omit the '$\in \omega$' in the quantifiers, since they all refer to natural numbers.

Definition 11. $\begin{array}{c} M_{f(x,y)} \leftrightarrow Def \\ \exists x_1, \ldots, x_k[p(\langle e_f, x, y \rangle, x_1, \ldots, x_k) = 0]. \end{array}$

Actually $M_f(x, y)$ stands for $M_{e_f}(x, y)$, or better, $M(e_f, x, y)$, as dependence is on the Gödel number e_f.

Definition 12. $\neg Q(m, a, x) \leftrightarrow _{Def}[(t_m(x) \leq |x|^a + a) \rightarrow \neg R(x, m)].$

Proposition 13. $[P < NP] \leftrightarrow \forall m, a \exists x \neg Q(m, a, x).$

Definition 14. $\neg Q_f(m, a, x) \leftrightarrow _{Def} \exists a'[M_f(a, a') \wedge \neg Q(m, a', x)].$
We will sometimes write $\neg Q(m, f(a), x)$ for $\neg Q_f(m, a, x)$, whenever f is total.

Definition 15. (Exotic formalization) $[P < NP]^t \leftrightarrow_{Def} \forall m, a \exists x \neg Q_t(m, a, x)$.
Notice that this is also a Π_2 arithmetic sentence.

Definition 16. $[P = NP]^t \leftrightarrow_{Def} \neg [P < NP]^t$.

We now use a well-known recursive function that is diagonalized over all
S-provably total recursive functions. We note it $\mathbf{F}$, or sometimes $\mathbf{F}_S$, see da Costa
and Doria (2003, 2006) and Kaye (1991: 51–2) on it.

Remark 17. For each n, $\mathbf{F}(n) = \max_{k \leq n}(\{e\}(k)) + 1$, that is the sup of those $\{e\}(k)$
such that:

1    $k \leq n$.
2    $\lceil \mathrm{Pr}_S(\lceil \forall x \exists z T(e, x, z) \rceil) \rceil \leq n$.

$\mathrm{Pr}_S(\lceil \xi \rceil)$ means, there is a proof of ξ in S, where $\lceil \xi \rceil$ means: the Gödel number
of ξ. So $\lceil \mathrm{Pr}_S(\lceil \xi \rceil) \rceil$ means: 'the Gödel number of sentence "there is a proof of ξ in
S"'. Condition 2 above translates as: there is a proof of $[\{e\}$ is total] in S whose
Gödel number is $\leq n$.

Proposition 18. We can explicitly compute a Gödel number e_F so that $\{e_F\} = \mathbf{F}$.

Proposition 19. If S is consistent then $\forall m \exists n[\{e_F\}(m) = n]$ is independent of the
axioms of S.

The idea of such fast-growing functions goes back to Kleene (1936, 1967)
and was first thoroughly explored by Kreisel (1951, 1952). Also, keep in mind
that $[P < NP]^t \leftrightarrow \forall m, a \exists x \neg Q_t(m, a, x)$.

Lemma 20. If $I \subseteq \omega$ is infinite and $0 \in I$, then: $S \vdash \{[\forall m \forall a \in I \exists x \neg Q(m, a, x)] \rightarrow [\forall m \forall a \in \omega \exists x \neg (m, a, x)]\}$

The meaning of this result is: as long as we have an infinite succession of
ever larger bounds that make the Turing machines polynomial, our definitions
and equivalences hold. The size of the intermediate gaps between each pair of
bounds doesn't matter.

Proposition 21. $S \vdash [P < NP]^F \leftrightarrow \{[\mathbf{F}$ is total $] \wedge [P < NP]\}$.

Sketch of proof: We first present a naive, short, argument. It is easy to see that:
$S + [P < NP] + [\mathbf{F}$ is total$] \vdash [P < NP]^F$.

For the converse, the fact that the exotic counterexample function f_F (see
below after Lemma 22) is total implies that $[P < NP]$ and $[\mathbf{F}$ is total$]$ hold at the
same time (we will require Lemma 20 here).

Proof: We will require here the formal definitions for $[P < NP]$, $[P < NP]^F$ and
so on.
[$\Leftarrow$]. Suppose that $[P < NP] \wedge [\mathbf{F}$ is total$]$ holds.

1    $\forall a \exists a' M_F(a, a')$.
2    $\forall m \forall b \exists x \neg Q(m, b, x)$.
3   By restriction to Im(F) in (2), $\forall m \forall b \in \text{Im}(F) \exists x \neg Q(m, b, x)$.
4   For $b = F(a)$ due to step (1) above: $\forall m \forall b \in \exists Dom(F) \exists x \neg Q(m, F(a), x)$.
5   Then, $\forall m \forall b \exists x \neg Q_F(m, a, x)$.
6   That is, $[P < NP]^F$.

[$\Rightarrow$]. Now suppose that $[P < NP]^F$ holds:

1   That is, $\forall m \forall b \exists x \neg Q_F(m, a, x)$.
2   We get that $\forall a \exists a' M_F(a, a')$. (See below, Lemma 22.)
3   Then for $b = F(a)$, into (1), we get: $\forall m \forall b \in \text{Im}(F) \exists x \neg Q(m, b, x)$.
4   This is equivalent to $[P < NP]$. (See Lemma 20.)
5   From (2) and (4) we finally get: $[P < NP] \wedge [\text{F is total}]$.

We quote an important result that is actually a scholium of the preceding result:

Lemma 22. $S \vdash [P < NP]^F \rightarrow [\text{F is total}]$.

Proof of the lemma:

1    $\neg Q_F(m, a, x) \leftrightarrow_{\text{Def}} \exists b[M_F(a, b) \wedge \neg Q(m, b, x)]$. (definition of $\neg Q_F$.)
2   Assume $\neg Q_F(m, a, x)$. From step (1):

    a $\exists b[M_F(a, b) \wedge \neg Q(m, b, x)]$. (Assumed.)
    b $[(\exists b[M_F(a, b)]) \wedge (\exists b \neg Q(m, b, x))]$. (From step (2a), and *modus ponens*.)

3    $\neg Q_F(m, a, x) \rightarrow [(\exists b M_F(a, b)) \wedge (\exists b \neg Q(m, b, x))]$. (The assumption in step (2a) implies step (2b).)
4   Recall that the following is a propositional theorem: $[A \rightarrow (B \wedge C)] \rightarrow [A \rightarrow B]$.
5    $[\neg Q_F(m, a, x)] \rightarrow [\exists b(M_F(a, b)]$ (From step (4) applied to step (3) plus *modus ponens*.)
6   Generalization rule applied to the unquantified variable x: $\forall x \{[\neg Q_F(m, a, x)] \rightarrow [\exists b(M_F(a, b)]\}$.
7   Internalization of $\forall x$, and *modus ponens*: $\{[\exists x \neg Q_F(m, a, x)] \rightarrow [\exists b(M_F(a, b)]\}$
8   Generalization Rule applied to the unquantified variables m, a: $\forall m, a\{\exists x[\neg Q_F(m, a, x)] \rightarrow [\exists b(M_F(a, b)]\}$.
9    $[\forall m, a \exists x[\neg Q_F(m, a, x)]] \rightarrow [\forall a \exists b M_F(a, b)]$. (Operations, *modus ponens* and elimination of empty quantifier.)
10   That is, $[P < NP]^F \rightarrow [\text{F is total}]$.

Remark 23. The following argument clarifies the meaning of the lemma and gives a naive proof for it: let:

$$f_F(\langle m, a \rangle) = \min_x [\neg Q(m, F(a), x)],$$

where we can look at F as a (partial) recursive function. (The brackets $\langle \ldots, \ldots \rangle$ note the usual 1–1 pairing function.) Now if f_F is total, then $F(a)$ has to be defined for all values of the argument a, that is, F must be total. The function f_F is the so-called *exotic counterexample* function to $[P = NP]^F$. We can similarly define a *standard counterexample function*:

$$f(\langle m, a \rangle) = \min_{x} [\neg Q(m, a, x)].$$

As $S \vdash [\text{F } is \; total] \leftrightarrow [S \text{ is } \Sigma_1\text{-sound}]$ (see Carnielli and Doria 2008 on that equivalence), and also as $S \vdash [S \text{ is } \Sigma_1\text{-sound}] \rightarrow \text{Consis } (S)$, $S \vdash [\text{F } is \; total] \rightarrow$ Consis (S). Then:

Lemma 24. $S \vdash [P < NP]^F \rightarrow$ Consis (S).

Proposition 25. If S is consistent, then S doesn't prove $[P < NP]^F$.

Proof: $S \vdash [[P < NP]^F \rightarrow (\text{F is total})]]$. (Lemma 22.) So, S cannot prove $[P < NP]^F$.

Corollary 26. $[P = NP]^F$ is consistent with S.
  If **N** is a model for S and makes it arithmetically sound, that is, **N** has a standard arithmetic part for the arithmetic in S:

Proposition 27. $\mathbf{N} \models S + [P < NP] \leftrightarrow [P < NP]^F$.

Proof: F is total in the standard model for arithmetic.

Proposition 28. $[P < NP] \leftrightarrow [P < NP]^F$ is independent of S.

Proof: Suffices to show that S doesn't prove that equivalence due to Proposition 21, since otherwise it would prove [F is total].
  Now since the sentence $\neg$ [F is total] holds in some model for our theory S, the fact that we have in that model $\exists x(F(0) = x)$, $\exists x(F(1) = x)$, $\exists x(F(2) = x), \ldots$, together with $\neg$ [F is total] shows that: if $\neg$ [F is total] holds, then $S + \neg$ [F is total] is ω-inconsistent. More precisely: if some theory S' proves $\neg$ [F is total], then it is ω-inconsistent. So, if some theory S' is ω-*consistent*, then [F is total] is consistent with it. Thus a preliminary result:

Proposition 29. If $S + [P = NP]^F$ is ω-consistent, then $S + [P = NP]$ is consistent.

First consistency result

But we may go beyond that. Let us now repeat what has been stated in the introduction:

- Suppose that S proves $[P < NP]$.
- Suppose that Hypothesis 6 holds.

- Then $S + [P < NP] \leftrightarrow [P < NP]^F \vdash [P < NP]$.
- But $S \vdash [P < NP]^{FF}$.
- From Hypothesis 6, $S + [P < NP] \leftrightarrow [P < NP]^F \vdash [P < NP]^F$.
- Then $S + [P < NP] \leftrightarrow [P < NP]^F \vdash [P < NP]$.
- A contradiction. Thus $S \vdash [P < NP]^F$.

Or,

Proposition 30. Hypothesis 6 implies that $S \vdash [P < NP]$.

The counterexample function is fast growing

The next construction was originally developed in 1995 as a preliminary, alternative way to obtain our result on exotic formulations by the direct construction
of a segment of the counterexample function to the exotic $[P = NP]^F$ that is
shown to grow faster than any S-provably total function, where S is the theory
that serves as our axiomatic background. We use fast-growing functions to com-
press the Gödel numbers of machines in the BGS set.

More precisely: the idea in the next proof goes as follows:

- Use the *s-m-n* theorem to obtain Gödel numbers for an infinite family of
  'quasi-trivial machines' (see below). The table for those Turing machines
  involves very large numbers, and the goal is to get a compact code for that
  value in each quasi-trivial machine so that their Gödel numbers are in a
  sequence $g(0), g(1), g(2), \ldots$, where g is primitive recursive.
- Then add the required clocks as in the BGS sequence of poly machines, and
  get the Gödel numbers for the pairs machine + clock. We can embed the
  sequence we obtain into the sequence of all Turing machines.
- Notice that the subsets of poly machines we are dealing with are (intuitive)
  recursive subsets of the set of all Turing machines. Moreover, if we formalize everything in some theory S, then the formalized version of the sentence
  'the set of Gödel numbers for these quasi-trivial Turing machines is a recursive subset of the set of Gödel numbers for Turing machines' holds of the
  standard model for arithmetic in S, and vice versa.

      However S may not be able to prove or disprove that assertion, that is to
  say, it will be formally independent of S.
- We can thus define the counterexample functions over the desired set(s) of
  poly machines, and compare them to fast-growing total recursive functions
  over similar restrictions.

Definition 31. For f, g: $\omega \to \omega$,

   f *dominates* g $\leftrightarrow_{Def} \exists y \forall x (x > y \to f(x) \geq g(x))$.

We write $f \varphi g$ for f dominates g.

Quasi-trivial machines

Recall that the operation time of a Turing machine is: if M stops over an input x, then the operation time over x,

$$t_M = |x| + \text{number of cycles of the machine until it stops.}$$

Example 32:
- *First trivial machine.* Note it O. O inputs x and stops.
  $t_O = |x| +$ moves to halting state + stops.
  So, operation time of O has a linear bound.
- *Second trivial machine.* Call it O′. It inputs x, always outputs 0 (zero) and stops.
  Again operation time of O′ has a linear bound.
- *Quasi-trivial machines.* A quasi-trivial machine Q operates as follows: for $x \leq x_0$, x_0 a constant value, Q = R, R an arbitrary total machine. For $x > x_0$, Q = O or O′.
  This machine has also a linear bound.

Remark 33. Let H be any fast-growing, superexponential total machine. Let H′ be another such machine. Form the following family of quasi-trivial Turing machines with subroutines H and H′:

1   If $x = H(n)$, $Q^{H,H',n}(x) = H'(x)$;
2   If $x > H'(n)$, $Q^{H,H',n}(x) = 0$.

Proposition 34. There is a family of Turing machines $R_{g(n,|H|,H')}(x) = Q^{H,H',n}(x)$, where g is primitive recursive, and $|H|$, H′ denote the Gödel number of H and H′.

Proof: By the composition theorem and the *s-m-n* theorem.

We first give a result for the counterexample function when defined over all Turing machines (with the extra condition that the counterexample function = 0 if M_m isn't a poly machine). Suppose that H′ = T, where T is the Turing machine that exponentially settles all of SAT. We have:

Proposition 35. If $N(n) = g(n)$ is the Gödel number of a quasi-trivial machine as in Remark 33, then $f(N(n)) = k(n) + 1 = H(n) + 1$.

Proof: Use the machines in Proposition 34 adequately modified.

Proof of non-domination

Our goal here is to prove the following result:

Proposition 36. For no total recursive function h *does* h φ f.

Proof: Suppose that there is a total recursive function h such that h φ f.

Remark 37. Given such a function h, obtain another total recursive function h′ which satisfies:

1   h′ is strictly increasing.
2   For $n > n_0$, h′$(n) >$ h$(g(n))$.

Lemma 38. Given a total recursive h, there is a total recursive h′ that satisfies the conditions in Remark 37.

Proof: Given h, obtain out of that total recursive function by the usual construc-tions a strictly increasing total recursive h*. Then if, for example, F_ω is Acker-mann's function, h′ = h* o F_ω will do. (The idea is that F_ω dominates all primitive recursive functions, and therefore h* composed with it dominates $g(n)$.)

We have that the Gödel numbers of the quasi-trivial machines Q are given by $g(n)$. Choose adequate quasi-trivial machines, so that $f(g(n)) =$ h′$(n) + 1$, from Proposition 35. From Remark 37 and Lemma 38 we conclude our argument. If we make explicit the computations, for $g(n)$ (as the argument holds for any strictly increasing primitive recursive g):

$$f(g(n)) = \text{h}′(n) + 1 = \text{h}^*(F_\omega(n)) + 1,$$

and

$$\text{h}^*(F_\omega(n)) > \text{hh}^*(g(n)).$$

For $N = g(n)$,

$$f(N) > \text{h}^*(N) \geq \text{h}(N), \text{ all } N.$$

Therefore no such h can dominate f.

Corollary 39. No total recursive function dominates f.

Exotic BGS^F machines

Now let F be as in Remark 17. We consider exotic BGS^F machines, that is, poly machines coded by the pairs $\langle m, a \rangle$, which code Turing machines M_m with bounds $|x|^{F(a)} + F(a)$. Since the bounding clock is also a Turing machine, now coupled to M_m, there is a primitive recursive map c so that:

$$\langle M_m, |x|^{F(a)} + F(a) \rangle \rightarrow M_{c(m,a,|F|)},$$

where $M_{c(m,a,|F|)}$ is a poly machine within the sequence of all Turing machines.

For BGS$_F$ (the exotic BGS machines) restricted to the quasi-trivial ones we have the following pairs:

$$\langle k(a,|F_S|), g(n,|H|,|H'|)\rangle,$$

where k, g are primitive recursive. We then argue as above, for f.

We similarly proceed as above, and follows:

Proposition 40. Given the counterexample function f_F defined over the BGS^F machines, for consistent ZFC, no ZFC-provable total recursive h does h φ f.

Proof: As in Proposition 36.

Hypothesis 7 implies that $S \vdash [P = NP]$

Suppose that:

- $S \vdash [P = NP]$.
- Hypothesis 7 holds.

Let K be the set of Gödel numbers of all poly machines that settle the whole of SAT. For our purposes here, we consider K a subset of the BGS set. Recall that from our hypothesis we get that S proves 'K is recursively enumerable' in BGS. The immediate consequence for the BGS set is that K is proved recursive by theory S. Then if f is the BGS recursive counterexample function:

Proposition 41. If $S \vdash [P = NP]$, then the following function f*:

1 If n is in K, then f*(n) = 0.
2 If n isn't in K, then f*(n) = f(n).

is provably total and recursive in S.

Remark 42. We can give an expression for that function with the help of the ι-symbol added to the language S and with the help of a recursive function K so that $K(x) = 1$ if and only if x is in K, and 0 otherwise:

$$f*(n) = \iota_x \{[(x = 0) \wedge (K(n) = 1)] \vee [(x = f(n)) \wedge (K(n) = 0)]\}.$$

Again f is the BGS counterexample function to $[P = NP]$.

Now, for the function f*, put $h* = f*|_{\omega-K}$, where $|_A$ denotes restriction to A:

Proposition 43. If $[P = NP]$ holds, since f* is recursive and proved total by S, then so is h* (over $\omega - K$).

From the exotic function that corresponds to f*, namely $f*_F$. We have:

Proposition 44. $S \vdash [(f^*)_F \text{ is total}] \rightarrow [F \text{ is total}]$.

Proof: To prove the result consider the restriction $(f^*)_F|_{\omega - K}$.

Remark 45. To conclude one has to establish the equivalence: $[(f^*)_F \text{ is total}] \leftrightarrow [(f^*) \text{ is total}]$.

That equivalence is $[P = NP] \leftrightarrow [P = NP]^F$. As we have supposed that $S \vdash [P = NP]$,

$$S + [P = NP] + [P = NP] \leftrightarrow [P = NP]^F$$

is consistent and holds of a model for S with standard arithmetic part. So, the results in the previous part of the chapter apply here.

Follows:

Proposition 46. $S \vdash [P = NP] \rightarrow [f^* \text{ is total}]$.

Proof: From the hypotheses, we have that $S + [P = NP] \vdash [f^* \text{ is total}]$.

Proposition 47. If Hypothesis 7 holds, then $S \vdash [P = NP]$.

Proof: Suppose that $S \vdash [P = NP]$. Then $S \vdash [P = NP] \rightarrow [f^* \text{ is total}]$. From the preceding equivalences, $S \vdash [P = NP] \rightarrow [F \text{ is total}]$. Then $S \vdash [F \text{ is total}]$. A contradiction, as S cannot prove that F is total.

A strong theory that proves [P < NP]

Remark 48. We show in the Appendix that if $[P = NP]$ holds true of the standard integers, then there is a theory very close to PA which proves $[P = NP]$. Such a theory has the language of PA, includes the axioms of PA and shares with PA the same provably total recursive functions.

Call that theory PA'. Therefore, if there is no theory like PA' that proves $[P = NP]$, then either it proves $[P < NP]$ or both $[P < NP]$ and $[P = NP]$ are independent of PA'.

In that case, $[P < NP]$ holds true of the standard integers. Moreover, if independence holds, e.g. with respect to ZFC or even stronger theories, then $[P < NP]$ must hold true of the standard integers.

We have:

Proposition 49. Given Hypotheses 6 and 7, PA + Shoenfield's ω-rule $\vdash [P < NP]$.

Remark 50. This is just a kind of metaphor, to give an idea of what seems to be going on here. Let us be given a nonstandard polynomial:

$$p_N(x) = 1 + x + \frac{x^2}{2!} + \frac{x^3}{3!} + \ldots + \frac{x^{N-1}}{(N-1)!} + \frac{x^N}{N!},$$

where N is a nonstandard (infinite) integer. So, if p_N bounds the operation time of some Turing machine, it is a polynomial when seen within a nonstandard model, but its restriction to the standard part looks exponential.

For Shoenfield's ω-rule see (Franzen 2004) and the next part of the chapter.

Informal arguments about independence

The following argument circulates in a folklore-like way; we do not know where it originated, and to our knowledge it has never appeared in print – nor has been discussed in depth.

Let S be a theory that includes arithmetic, has a recursively enumerable set of theorems, is based on a first-order classical language, and has a model with standard arithmetic. Get some formal version for the $P = NP$ hypothesis as an arithmetic sentence, and note that formal version $[P = NP]$. Again $[P < NP] = \neg\, [P = NP]$:

- Suppose that you've proved independence of $[P < NP]$ and $[P = NP]$ with respect to S.
- Then $S + [P < NP]$ is consistent.
- Better: $S + [P < NP]$ satisfies the conditions above. Thus we can take it as our new starting theory and may argue for it.
- We conclude that $S + [P < NP] + [P = NP]$ is consistent. A contradiction.
- Thus independence proved in this way actually proves that $S \vdash [P = NP]$.

(The argument concludes: as almost nobody believes that $P = NP$ holds true, then any independence proof must contain a flaw somewhere, since (if we follow the preceding argument) it leads to the proof of $P = NP$.)

This is the best-known paradoxical argument. We'll present some similar arguments in due course. Now: can we get around them?

Difficulties avoided

Suppose that independence holds. Consider our arguments involving standard and exotic definitions as in the preceding part of the chapter. One would then get, for the paradoxical reasoning sketched at the introduction:

- $S + [P < NP]$ is consistent and arithmetically sound.
- Then argue as we do and get that $S + [P < NP] + [P = NP]^F$ is consistent.
- However if independence holds, that theory isn't arithmetically sound; moreover we cannot add to it as a new axiom $[P < NP] \leftrightarrow [P = NP]^F$ to derive $[P = NP]$, for we would therefore get a contradiction.

The point is, we cannot have $[P < NP] \leftrightarrow [P = NP]^F$ in that theory, or it is trivialized.

Remark 51. Let's elaborate on that. If ZFC + $[P < NP]$ is consistent, then so is ZFC + $[P < NP] + [P = NP]^F$. However this latter theory isn't arithmetically sound, for it only has nonstandard models – and moreover models where [F has a finite domain] holds, so that the equivalence $[P = NP] \leftrightarrow [P = NP]^F$ will never hold.

An alternative viewpoint:

- We cannot start from a consistent $S + [P < NP] \leftrightarrow [P < NP]^F + [P < NP]$.
- For $S \vdash [P < NP]^F \to$ [F is total].
- Thus $S + [P < NP] \leftrightarrow [P < NP]^F + [P < NP] \vdash$ [F is total], and we cannot argue (as in the preceding parts of the chapter) to show that $[P < NP]^F$ is consistent, for in order to do so we require that [F is total] be unprovable in our theory.

More about theory $S + [P < NP]$

This is a rather weird theory. If $[P < NP]$ is independent of S, $S + [P < NP]$ has a model with standard arithmetic and thus we can consistently add to it a finite set of conditions $[P < NP] \leftrightarrow [P < NP]^{Fi}$, i ranging over a finite set. Then theory:

$$S + [P < NP] + \sum_i [P < NP] \leftrightarrow [P < NP]^{Fi}$$

has the same provably total recursive functions as $S + [P < NP]$ (we use here Kreisel's Lemma (Ben-David and Halevi 1991) and Hypothesis 6; see Appendix). However if we add an *infinite* set of conditions $[P < NP] \leftrightarrow [P < NP]^{Fi}$ so that given each intuitively total recursive g there is some F_i in the added set so that F_i dominates g, then the resulting theory becomes a nonrecursive theory, for it proves all arithmetical truths.

Another fact: suppose that h is any strictly increasing total recursive function. Form theory $S' = S + [P < NP]$. Then theory $S' + F_{S'} \varphi$ h is consistent. That is to say, F_S cannot be precisely placed among all total recursive functions! This isn't surprising, as the set of all total recursive functions is plagued with undecidabilities of all sorts.

Conclusion

We rest our case. While our arguments for Hypotheses 6 and 7 are certainly incomplete (but see Appendix), we believe that they do hold water and can be extended to a fully fledged rigorous proof. We will then conclude that $[P = NP]$ and its negation are independent of ZFC, and that $[P < NP]$ holds of the standard model for arithmetic – that is to say, is true in the real world, and is what happens in our everyday life.

The idea that one should start out of reasonable, even if unproved, hypotheses, more or less follows from Chaitin's suggestion that one should consider 'empirically' verified hypotheses in mathematics.

We notice that informal, incomplete arguments have a long tradition in mathematics, and that they have never detained anyone from stating interesting results, even on technically shaky grounds. Two well-known examples are the original proof of Shannon's coding theorem for noisy channels, and the Seiberg–Witten theory in the domain of four-manifolds. So our approach here has well-known, accepted precedents.

And if our arguments can be extended to a full, strict proof, then we conclude that the *P* vs *NP* question isn't difficult because of the need of novel techniques to attack it; it is difficult because it reveals a very weird and unexpected phenomenon – a question which is highly insensitive to non-arithmetic axioms in set theory and beyond – but which can be settled in a rather reasonable, albeit non-recursive, theory, namely PA + Shoenfield's ω-rule.

Acknowledgements

The authors wish to thank Professor S. Zambelli for his kind invitation to contribute to this Festschrift.

The ongoing research programme that led to this text has been sponsored by the Advanced Studies Group, Production Engineering Program, COPPE-UFRJ, Rio, Brazil.

The authors also wish to thank the Institute for Advanced Studies at the University of São Paulo for support of this research project; we wish to acknowledge support from the Brazilian Academy of Philosophy and its chairman Professor J.R. Moderno. Portions of this work were done during the COBERA March 2005 Workshop at Galway, Ireland; Doria wishes to thank Professor Vela Velupillai for the stimulating and fruitful environment he so kindly sponsored at that meeting. Finally Doria wishes to thank Professors R. Bartholo, C.A. Cosenza and S. Fuchs for their invitation to join the Fuzzy Sets Lab at COPPE-UFRJ and the Philosophy of Science Programme at the same institution.

The authors acknowledge partial support from CNPq, Philosophy Section.

We wish to stress that many ideas discussed here owe deeply to our exchanges with M. Guillaume (2003, as well as email correspondence with the authors during the years 2000–2003), whom we heartily thank.

Appendix

Plausibility arguments for the hypotheses

We present here plausibility arguments to support Hypothesis 6 and Hypothesis 7. We stress that the discussions below around Hypotheses 6 and 7 are to be strictly understood as waving-hands arguments.

A plausibility argument for Hypothesis 6

Suppose that predicate $K(m, a, x)$ means 'poly Turing machine of Gödel number m bounded by polynomial $|x|^a + a$ on the length of input $|x|$ outputs a satisfying line of truth-values for input x'. We take our poly machines in the BGS family (Baker *et al.* 1975).

Now:

- Suppose that theory:

$$S^* = S + \forall m, a, a'[\exists x \neg K(m, a, x) \leftrightarrow \exists x' \neg K(m, F(a'), x')]$$

  is consistent and holds of $\mathbf{N} \models S$, a model with standard arithmetic part. (The naive interpretation of sentence:

$$\forall m, a, a'[\exists x \neg K(m, a, x) \leftrightarrow \exists x' \neg K(m, F(a'), x')]$$

  in the standard model for arithmetic is quite straightforward; roughly it means that a poly machine coded by m with bound $|x|^a + a$ fails to output a satisfying line for input x if and only if the same machine with bound $|x|^{F(a')} + F(a')$ again fails to output a satisfying line given x as input.)
  We believe that a rigorous proof can be found for this statement.
- Then a few computations show that $S^* \vdash [P < NP] \leftrightarrow [P < NP]^F$.
- Now: we have supposed that $S \vdash [P < NP]$.
- Then the first x where BGS machine m fails to output a satisfying line of truth-values is bounded by a total provably recursive function g (as we prove the Π_2 sentence $[P < NP]$ in S, which means that the counterexample function f is provably total recursive in S).
- Therefore, we get that S^* proves:

$$\forall m, a, a'[\exists x < g(m, a, a') \neg K(m, a, x) \leftrightarrow \exists x' < g(m, a, a') \neg K(m, F(a'), x')]$$

  for some provably total recursive g. This is a Π_1 sentence.
- Recall Kreisel's Lemma (Ben-David and Halevi 1991): if S has a recursively enumerable set of theorems, contains arithmetic and has a model with standard arithmetic, then S and S + {all the true Π_1 arithmetic sentences} have the same provably total recursive functions.
- Now, we apply Kreisel's Lemma to that Π_1 sentence in S^*. We then conclude that S and S^* have the same provably total recursive functions, as these theories only differ by a true Π_1 sentence.
- Now: we know that (da Costa and Doria 2003, 2006) $S \vdash [P < NP]^F \rightarrow [F$ is total].
- Since S^* proves the equivalence $[P < NP] \leftrightarrow [P < NP]^F$, $S^* \vdash [F$ is total], from the hypothesis that $S \vdash [P < NP]$ we get that $S^* \vdash [F$ is total].
  A contradiction, since S^* cannot prove [F is total].
- Thus $S \vdash [P = NP]$.

A plausibility argument for Hypothesis 7

Definition A.1. Any poly algorithm that settles all of SAT is a *good algorithm.*
 Our goal here is to argue that:

Lemma A.2. S proves the (formal version of the) sentence: [The set of Gödel numbers of BGS good algorithms is recursively enumerable].
 We note that set $K \subset \omega$. Of course, if $K = \varnothing$, then the lemma holds. We now consider the nontrivial case, that is, we suppose that $S \vdash [P = NP]$ (see below Hypothesis A.5).

WE NEED AN ALTERNATIVE FORMULATION FOR $[P = NP]$:

Lemma A.3. $[P = NP] \leftrightarrow \exists e, a \forall x \exists z \leq (|x|^a + a)[T(e, x, z) \wedge R(x, U(T(e, x, z)))].$
 Define:

Remark A.4. For our purposes, we specifically consider in this section Π_1 sentences of the form:

1   $\forall x P$, P primitive recursive.
2   $\forall x \exists y \leq g(x)$ P, where g, P are primitive recursive.

 Then:

$$\forall x \exists z \leq (|x|^a + a)[T(e, x, z) \wedge R(x, U(T(e, x, z)))]$$

is a Π_1 sentence, if a $\in \omega$ is seen as a constant.

Remark A.5. We suppose that $S \vdash [P = NP]$.

Corollary A.6. $N \models [P = NP]$.
 Moreover, for integers e, a:

Corollary A.7. $N \models \forall x \exists z \leq (|x|^a + a)[T(e, x, z) \wedge R(x, U(T(e, x, z)))].$
 Now let PA_1 be the (nonrecursive) theory that consists of PA plus all true Π_1 sentences. Then clearly:

Lemma A.8. If there are constants e, a so that $\forall x \exists z \leq (|x|^a + a)[T(e, x, z) \wedge R(x, U(T(e, x, z)))]$ holds true of the standard model for arithmetic, then:
$PA_1 \vdash [\forall x \exists z \leq (|x|^a + a)[T(e, x, z) \wedge R(x, U(T(e, x, z)))]].$

Corollary A.9. If there are constants e, a so that: $\forall x \exists z \leq (|x|^a + a)[T(e, x, z) \wedge R(x, U(T(e, x, z)))]$ holds true of the standard model for arithmetic, then:
$PA_1 \vdash [P = NP].$

For we have:

$$[\forall x \exists z \leq (|x|^a + a)[T(e, x, z) \wedge R(x, U(T(e, x, z)))]] \rightarrow$$
$$[\exists e, a \forall x \exists z \leq (|x|^a + a)[T(e, x, z) \wedge R(x, U(T(e, x, z)))]].$$

Then by detachment we get $[P = NP]$ (Ben-David and Halevi 1991).

FROM THE ARITHMETIC SOUNDNESS OF S, FOR A MODEL FOR S WITH STANDARD ARITHMETIC **N**:

Corollary A.10. If Remark A.5 holds, then **N** $\models [P = NP]$.
   We give a waving-hands argument for the assertion:

- Suppose $S \vdash [P = NP]$.
- Then **N** $\models [P = NP]$.
- Therefore it is true that there is at least a (standard) pair $e, a \in \omega$ so that $\{e\}$ with bound $|x|^a + a$ settles all of SAT.
- Let PA_1 be Peano Arithmetic plus all true Π_1 arithmetic sentences.
- Since $PA_1 \vdash [P = NP]$, then either PA proves it or, at worst,

$$PA' = PA + \forall x \exists z \leq (|x|^a + a)[T(e, x, z) \wedge R(x, U(T(e, x, z)))]$$

trivially proves it. Both are arithmetically sound theories with a recursively enumerable set of theorems.

   Both PA and PA$'$ have the same provably total recursive functions, and therefore have (in that sense) the same provability strength. This stems from Kreisel's Lemma (Ben-David and Halevi 1991; da Costa *et al.* 2007).
   We now consider BGS poly Turing machines, coded by pairs $\langle e, a \rangle$ (see below). Then if:

- $K(e, a) \leftrightarrow_{Def} [\forall x \exists z \leq (|x|^a + a)[T(e, x, z) \wedge R(x, U(T(e, x, z)))]]$, for infinitely many numerals e, a, the sentences $K(e, a)$ will be theorems of PA$'$.
- Moreover, for numerals e, a, the set of all PA$'$-provable $K(e, a)$ is a recursively enumerable set coded by the pair $\langle e, a \rangle$. This pair is the BGS code for poly machines.
      (A BGS pair (Baker *et al.* 1975) can be interpreted as a Turing machine $\{e\}$ coupled to a clock that stops its operation on binary input x before $|x|^a + a$ cycles. Every BGS pair then codes a poly machine, and every poly machine can be represented as a BGS pair. Finally, if e runs over all of ω, then the BGS pairs run over $\omega \times \omega \times \omega$.)
- Now suppose that there is $\langle e, a \rangle$ that settles SAT, that is to say, there is some Turing machine $\{e\}$ with polynomial bound $|x|^a + a$ so that **N** $\models K(e, a)$, but such that $K(e, a)$ doesn't come up among the theorems of PA$'$.

- Note that machine P'_m Then there is a machine M so that, for a machine that comes up in the theorem's enumeration, PP_m, we have: $P'_m = M \text{ o } P'_m$. (Of course M must be total and polynomial.)
- We then agree that P'_m is in the enumeration of theorems:

  - $K(e, a)$ is a theorem, that is, P_m settles all of SAT.
  - Then there is a poly Turing machine M so that $P'_m = M \text{ o } P'_m$.
  - Therefore P'_m settles all of SAT, that is, for $m' = \langle e', a' \rangle$, $K(e', a')$ is a theorem.

Proposition A.11. Given Hypothesis A.5, the nonempty set K of all BGS-coded $\langle e, a \rangle$ poly Turing machines so that K(e, a) holds true of the standard model for arithmetic is recursive.

For it is recursively enumerable, and its complement (the set of counterexamples over BGS) is also recursively enumerable, as it is the image of a partial recursive function.

Proposition A.12. We can effectively compute the Gödel number of an algorithm that recursively enumerates the K(e, a).

Begin a listing of all integers, 0, 1, 2, ... Input $k \in \omega$:

- We fit check whether it is the Gödel number of a proof in PA'. If not, go to $k + 1$. If it is, go to the next step.
- Check whether the last code in the proof is a code for $K(e, a)$, for some pair e, a.
- If not, go to $k + 1$. If so, output e, a and go to $k + 1$.

Let e_K be that Gödel number.

Corollary A.13. Given Hypothesis A.5, for the nonempty set K, we have that $S \vdash [K \in \omega$ is recursive].

By the representation theorem, given Hypothesis A.5, as we can compute a Gödel number for the algorithmic procedure that recursively enumerates K, we can represent it in PA, and therefore also in S; by definition it is (PA)-provably recursively enumerable, and as the complement of a recursively enumerable set it is recursive in PA and therefore in S.

More precisely:

- If $\{e_K\}$ is the algorithm that enumerates K as described above, then we can explicitly construct a Diophantine polynomial $p_K(y, x_1, \ldots, x_k)$ so that it holds of a model **N** with standard arithmetic that:

$$[\{e_K\}(a) = b] \leftrightarrow \exists x_1, \ldots, x_k p_K(\langle a, b \rangle, x_1, \ldots, x_k) = 0.$$

- We then have that $\{e_K\}(a) = b$ if and only if:

$$S \vdash \exists x_1, \ldots, x_k p_K(\langle a, b \rangle, x_1, \ldots, x_k) = 0.$$

- Then (with perhaps some abuse of language): S proves:

$$[\{y \in \omega: \exists x_1, \ldots, x_k p_K(\langle a, b \rangle, x_1, \ldots, x_k) = 0\} \text{ is recursively enumerable}].$$

- As its complement is also a recursively enumerable set – it is the set of values of the counterexample function to $[P = NP]$ – we have that S proves that K is recursive.

Unbounded theories

Recall that S is *arithmetically sound* if it has a model with a standard arithmetic part. From the arithmetic soundness of S, for a model for it with standard arithmetic (which will always be noted) $\mathbf{N}$:

Definition A.14. Let theory S be such that $\mathbf{N} \models S$, and such that we can construct a function F_S for it as in Remark 17. Then S is *unbounded* if for any f so that $\mathbf{N} \models$ [f is strictly increasing total recursive], then $S + [F_S$ dominates f] is consistent and holds of $\mathbf{N}$.

The idea is that we can take the bounding fast-growing function F_S as fast-growing as possible.

Remark A.15. From here on we will consider a theory S that:

- S includes Peano Arithmetic.
- S is arithmetically sound, and model $\mathbf{N}$ makes it so.
- S has a recursively enumerable set of theorems.
- S is based on a first-order classical language.
- S isn't unbounded.

We notice that both PA and ZFC satisfy the above requirements.

Remark A.16. If Hypotheses 6 and 7 hold, then $S + [P < NP]$ is unbounded. We see this as a kind of consequence of the huge fast-growing behaviour of the counterexample function when seen within that theory.

More comments about undecidability and incompleteness in strong theories

See the Introduction for more comments on these results. Chaitin's pioneering results had already convinced us that undecidability and incompleteness are everywhere. The next propositions just add to that.

Proposition A.17. There is a real number s whose decimal expansion is proved by ZFC to be generated by an algorithmic procedure and yet such that ZFC cannot compute a single digit of it.

Proof: Let r and r' be real numbers which are algorithmically generated. Impose also that, for all i, the i-th digits $r_i \neq r_i'$. Then for β as in da Costa and Doria (2004), $s = \beta r + (1 - \beta)r'$.

A second result:

Proposition A.18. There is a real number O. so that ZFC cannot compute a single digit of it.

Sketch of proof: List (this isn't a recursive enumeration!) all instances of the halting problem for some partial recursive algorithm that cannot be proved to diverge within ZFC. Those instances appear as .1 sentences. Order them by their respective Gödel numbers. This is a noncomputable function, which can be coded as a real number in several ways.

ZFC cannot prove by construction a single digit of that number.

Another construction:

Proposition A.19. There are infinitely many real numbers in ZFC so that none of its decimal places are computable.

Proof: Recall that no well-orderings of the real numbers are expressible in ZFC, but there are infinitely many such orderings.

Let Γ be one such ordering, and let r be the first real number in Γ so that none of its decimal places are definable – there is one such r, as the set of numbers which have definable decimal places is denumerable.

Remark A.20. Still another simple but interesting result about the decidability of Π_1 sentences and hierarchies of theories goes as follows. Π_1 arithmetic sentences code several interesting facts, e.g. Riemann's Hypothesis. If we are able to ascertain by some analogue procedure (da Costa and Doria 2004) that Riemann's Hypothesis is true of the standard model for arithmetic, then given the Fefermann hierarchy (Franzen 2004) of theories $S_0 = S$, $S_1 = S + \text{Con } S$, $S_2 = S + \text{Con}(S + \text{Con } S), \ldots$, there will be a S_j so that $S_j \vdash$ Riemann's Hypothesis.

Another interesting series of results about undecidability and incompleteness in the theory of partial differential equations was recently presented by E. Reyes (2007).

Note

1 We will use $[P = NP]$ or $[P < NP]$ for loose, intuitive formulations of the hypotheses, and $[P = NP]$ and $[P < NP]$ for their formulation as Σ_2 and Π_2 arithmetic sentences, respectively.

References

Baker, T., Gill, J. and Solovay, R. (1975) 'Relativizations of the $P = ?NP$ question', *SIAM Journal*, 4: 431–42.

Ben-David, S. and Halevi, S. (1991) 'On the independence of P vs. NP', *Technical Report* #699, Technion.

Calude, C. (2007) 'Preface' to *Randomness and Complexity, from Leibniz to Chaitin*, Singapore: World Scientific.

Carnielli, W. and Doria, F.A. (2008) 'Are the foundations of computer science logic-dependent?' in C. Dégremont, L. Keiff and H. Rückert (eds), *Dialogues, Logics and Other Strange Things: Festschrift in Honor of Shahid Rahman*, College Publications.

da Costa, N.C.A. and Doria, F.A. (2003) 'Consequences of an exotic formulation for $P = NP'$, *Applied Mathematics and Computation*, 145: 655–65.

—— (2004) 'On set theory as a foundation for computer science', *Bulletin of the Section of Logic* (University of Lodz), 33: 33–40.

—— (2005) 'Computing the future', in K. Velupillai (ed.), *Computability, Complexity and Constructivity in Economic Analysis*, Oxford: Blackwell.

—— (2006) 'Addendum', *Applied Mathematics and Computation*, 172: 1364–7.

da Costa, N.C.A., Doria, F.A. and Bir, E. (2007) 'On the metamathematics of the P vs. NP question', *Applied Mathematics and Computation*, 189: 1223–40.

Davis, M. (1982) 'Hilbert's Tenth Problem is unsolvable', in M. Davis (ed.), *Computability and Unsolvability*, New York: Dover.

Doria, F.A. (2007) 'Informal vs. formal mathematics', *Synthèse*, 154: 401–15.

Franzen, T. (2004) 'Transfinite progressions: a second look at completeness', *Bulletin of Symbolic Logic*, 10: 367–89.

Guillaume, M. (2003) 'What counts in an exotic formulation', unpublished ms.

Kaye, R. (1991) *Models of Peano Arithmetic*, Oxford: Clarendon Press.

Kleene, S.C. (1936) 'General recursive functions of natural numbers', *Mathematische Annalen*, 112: 727.

—— (1967) *Mathematical Logic*, New York: Wiley.

Kreisel, G. (1951) 'On the interpretation of non-finitist proofs I', *J. Symbol. Logic*, 16: 241.

—— (1952) 'On the interpretation of non-finitist proofs II', *Journal of Symbolic Logic*, II, 17: 43.

Machtey, M. and Young, P. (1979) *An Introduction to the General Theory of Algorithms*, Amsterdam: North-Holland.

Reyes, E. (2007) 'Undecidability and incompleteness in the theory of partial differential equations', preprint ms.

8 Universal models

Jorma Rissanen

Introduction

It is a great pleasure for me to write this contribution to honour Vela's 60th birthday. Although our fields are somewhat different we both share the same interest in applying the ideas of the algorithmic theory of complexity to real world problems, he to economics and I to statistical inference. This has been a daunting task for both of us, for most people who are interested in finding solutions to their every day problems do not care whether the solutions are rational or not. By contrast, Vela, who is a true scholar, and I to a much lesser degree, would like the techniques we use to make sense and to be founded on fundamental principles.

In this chapter I would like to explain the ideas of universal models for statistics. The basic idea is taken from recursive function theory, where a universal computer can imitate the actions of any special computer or program and execute them. Hence, given a class of models, each a parametric distribution, a universal model for the class is any parameter free distribution, which behaves like any model in the class on data generated by the model in the sense of assigning almost as large a probability or density to the data as the model. Unlike in recursive function theory the imitation is not exact except in the per symbol limit as the sample grows. We define this more precisely later.

Universal models are new in statistics, although some of their uses are handled by the familiar concepts like consistency, estimator and criterion, all of which may in fact be replaced and generalized by universal models. In information theory the related constructs of universal data compression systems are ubiquitous and, one may say, most practical data compression systems are of that kind.

Universal model

Consider a parametric class of models $M_k = \{f(y^n|x^n; \theta): \theta \in \Omega \subset R^k\}$, where $y^n = y_1,\ldots, y_n$ and $x^n = x_1,\ldots, x_n$ denote any kind of data, and θ denotes parameters.

A density function $f(y^n|x^n)$ for a class of parametric models M_k is called universal, if

$$\frac{1}{n} \log \frac{f(y^n|x^n; \theta)}{f(y^n|x^n)} \to 0$$

for all parameters $\theta = \theta_1, \ldots, \theta_k \in \Omega$, and *optimal universal* if the convergence is the fastest possible for almost all θ; the convergence is either in the mean, taken with respect to $f(y^n|x^n; \theta)$, or almost surely or both. The qualification 'almost all θ' may be slightly modified; see Rissanen (1984, 1986). The fastest asymptotic rate is $(k/2n) \log n$. We may also extend the definition to the model class $M = Y_k M_k$.

Non-asymptotically a question arises in comparison of two universal models f_1 and f_2. Since both are density functions it is clear that there must be data z^n where $f_1(z^n|x^n) < f_2(z^n|x^n)$ and another set u^n where $f_2(u^n|x^n) < f_1(u^n|x^n)$. Hence, one may wonder how to prefer one over the other. We prefer the one which assigns a greater probability or density to data which we consider relevant. We discuss this further below. Further significant possibilities arise when we ask for the fastest convergence rate in the mean, the mean taken with respect to the worst case model outside the family M_k.

Clearly, being able to imitate any model in the class implies in effect consistency, which, however, is not necessarily of the kind where the parameter estimates converge to the one defining the model that generates the data. In some universal models exactly this takes place. The negative logarithm of a universal model for the class M_k automatically provides a criterion for the number of parameters without any prior on the number of parameters as in the case of a Bayesian posterior.

Universal models for M_k

We drop the regression data x^n from the density function to simplify the notations, and consider first the model class M_k.

Normalized ML model

Let $\hat{\theta}(y^n)$ be the Maximum Likelihood (ML) estimate. The Normalized ML or *NML* model (Baron *et al.* 1998; Rissanen 1996; Shtarkov 1987),

$$\hat{f}(y^n; k) = \frac{f(y^n; \hat{\theta}(y^n))}{C_{n,k}}$$

$$C_{n,k} = \int_{y^n : \hat{\theta}(y^n) \in \Omega} f(y^n; \hat{\theta}(y^n)) dy^n,$$

defines a universal model, where Ω is such that the integral is finite. It is the unique solution to Shtarkov's minmax problem

$$\min_q \max_{y^n} \log \frac{f(y^n; \hat{\theta}(y^n))}{q(y^n)}.$$

It is also the unique solution to the related maxmin problem (Rissanen 2007),

$$\max_g \min_q E_g \log \frac{f(Y^n; \hat{\theta}(Y^n))}{q(Y^n)},$$

where g ranges over any set that includes $\hat{f}(y^n; k)$, as well as the associated minmax problem – although the maximizing distribution is then nonunique.

We have defined (Rissanen 1996)

$$\log 1/\hat{f}(y^n; k) = \log 1/f(y^n; \hat{\theta}(y^n)) + \log C_{n,k}.$$

as the *stochastic complexity* of the data y^n. This also provides a powerful criterion for finding the number of parameters $\hat{k}(y^n)$ by minimization. A difficulty is to calculate the normalizing coefficient. For discrete data the integral becomes a sum, for which efficient algorithms are needed for large n. In a number of special cases such algorithms have been developed.

One can show (Rissanen 1996) that if the model class satisfies the central limit theorem and other smoothness conditions the stochastic complexity is given by the decomposition

$$\log \frac{f(y^n; \hat{\theta}(y^n))}{\hat{f}(y^n; k)} = \frac{k}{2} \log \frac{n}{2\pi} + \log\int_\Omega |J(\theta)|^{\frac{1}{2}}d\theta + o(1), \tag{1}$$

where $J(\theta)$ is the Fisher information matrix

$$J(\theta) = \lim n^{-1} E \left[\frac{\partial^2 \log 1/f(y^n; \theta)}{\partial \theta_i \partial \theta_j} \right].$$

Taking the mean we see in light of theorems in Rissanen (1984 and 1986) that $\hat{f}(y^n; k)$ is optimal universal.

Mixture model

The second example is the mixture model, which requires a prior $w(\theta)$

$$f_w(y^n; k) = \int_\Omega f(y^n; \theta)w(\theta)d\theta.$$

Such a mixture model $\hat{q} = f_w(y^n; k)$ satisfies the problem

$$\min_q \int w(\theta)D(f(Y^n; \theta) \| q(Y^n))d\theta$$

where $D(f(Y^n; \theta) \parallel q(Y^n))$ is the Kullback–Leibler distance between the two density functions shown. There is a special prior w^* maximizing the minimized result

$$\max_w \int w(\theta) D(f(Y^n; \theta) \parallel f_w(y^n; k)) d\theta = K_{n,k},$$

which is the capacity of the channel $\Theta \rightarrow Y^n$. For this prior the mixture lies at the centre of a hyperball with the model class M_k as the surface and the radius given by the constant distance $D(f(Y^n; \theta) \parallel f_{w^*}(Y^n; k))$. Needless to say such a prior is not easy to calculate.

However, asymptotically one can show (Clarke and Barron 1990) that with Jeffreys' prior

$$w(\theta) = \frac{|J(\theta)|^{\frac{1}{2}}}{\int_\Omega |J(\eta)|^{\frac{1}{2}} d\eta},$$

we get

$$E_\theta \log \frac{f(Y^n; \theta(Y^n))}{f_w(Y^n)} = \frac{k}{2} \log \frac{n}{2\pi} + \log \int_\Omega |J(\eta)|^{\frac{1}{2}} d\eta + o(1).$$

Since the right hand side does not depend on θ the channel capacity achieving prior coincides in the limit with Jeffreys' prior. Also we see that with Jeffreys prior the mixture universal model is optimal.

The negative logarithm of the mixture universal model also provides a criterion for the selection of the number of parameters, but non-asymptotically the prior must be taken so that the mixture can be computed. Hence, the result will depend on the prior. The criterion of the asymptotic version behaves more or less like BIC, or equivalently, the crude version of the MDL criterion, and for most cases it is not a very good criterion.

Sequentially normalized universal model

There is yet another way to obtain a universal model by normalization. Let $\hat\theta_t = \hat\theta(y^t)$ denote the maximum likelihood estimate with maximum number of components, not exceeding a selected k, which can be uniquely solved from the data y^t. Consider the sequentially maximized likelihood

$$f(y^n; \hat\theta^n) = \prod_{t=0}^{n-1} f(y_{t+1}|y^t; \hat\theta_{t+1}), \tag{2,}$$

where $\hat\theta^n = (\hat\theta_1, \hat\theta_2, \ldots, \hat\theta_{m+1}, \hat\theta_n)$, repetitions allowed. We take $f(y_1|x_0, \hat\theta^1) = f(y_1)$ a suitable density function with $\hat\theta_1$ empty. Also, for $t < m$ we may have $\hat\theta_{t-1}^t = \hat\theta_t^{t+1}$. One can show that $f(y^n; \hat\theta^n) \geq f(y^n; \hat\theta_n)$ so that it is bigger than the ordinary maximized likelihood!

We wish to normalize the conditionals equation (2) to generate recursively a density function $\hat{f}(y^t) = \hat{f}(y^{t-1})\hat{f}(y_t|y^{t-1})$:

$$\hat{f}(y_t|y^{t-1}) = \frac{f(y_t|y^{t-1}; \hat{\theta}(y^t))}{K(y^{t-1})}$$

$$K(y^{t-1}) = \int f(y_t|y^{t-1}; \hat{\theta}(y^t))dy_t$$

where the ranges of the integrals may have to be restricted to be finite. This gives the universal *SNML* model as a random process

$$\hat{f}s(y^n; k) = \prod_{t=1}^{n} \hat{f}(y_t|y^{t-1}).$$

For a family of models that define random processes one can show that $K(y^{t-1}) = K_{t-1}$.

We mention to this end that if the estimate $\hat{\theta}(y^{t+1})$ in equation (2) is replaced by $\hat{\theta}(y^t)$ we get Dawid's (1984) prequential model. Such a model is also universal. It would be worse than the *SNML* model except for data where y_{t+1} adds little new information; for instance, where it is easy to predict. Pushing the point to an extreme, the model where the ML estimate is formed from the first part of the past data is also universal, but worse than the SNML *model* except for data of little interest.

Universal model for $M = Y_K M_K$

We conclude this paper with a model for the family *M* which is optimal universal. Let $w^*(n) = C/[n(\log n)(\log \log n)\ldots]$ be a universal prior for the positive integers (Rissanen 1983) where $C^{-1} \cong 2.85$ and the product ends with the last positive factor. The logarithms are binary. Put

$$\hat{f}(y^n) = \sum_{k\geq 1} \hat{f}(y^n; k)w^*(k).$$

Since $\hat{f}(y^n) \geq \hat{f}(y^n; k)w^*(k)$ we have for $\theta \in \Omega \subset R^k$

$$D(f(Y^n; \theta) \| \hat{f}(Y^n)) \leq D(f(Y^n; \theta) \| \hat{f}(Y^n; k)) + \log 1/w^*(k).$$

By equation (1) $\hat{f}(y^n)$ is optimal universal.

In light of Rissanen (1984) $D(f(Y^n; \theta) \| \hat{f}(Y^n)) \geq D(f(Y^n; \theta) \| \hat{f}(Y^n; K))$, and the right hand side divided by $\log n$ converges to $k/2$, except for θ in a set whose volume goes to zero as n grows to infinity.

References

Barron, A.R., Rissanen, J. and Yu, B. (1998) 'The MDL principle in modeling and coding', special issue of *IEEE Transactions on Information Theory* to commemorate 50 years of information theory, IT-44 (October 6 1998): 2743–60.

Clarke, B.C. and Barron, A.R. (1990) 'Information-theoretic asymptotics of Bayes methods', *IEEE Trans. Information Theory*, IT-36: 453–71.

Dawid, A.P. (1984) 'Present position and potential developments: Some personal views, statistical theory, the prequential approach', *Journal of the Royal Statistics Society A*, 147(2): 278–92.

Rissanen, J. (1983) 'A universal prior for integers and estimation by minimum description length', *Annals of Statistics*, 11(2): 416–31.

—— (1984) 'Universal coding, information, prediction, and estimation', *IEEE Trans. Information Theory*, IT-30(4): 629–36.

—— (1986) 'Stochastic complexity and modeling', *Annals of Statistics*, 14: 1080–1100.

—— (1996) 'Fisher information and stochastic complexity', *IEEE Trans. Information Theory*, IT-42(1): 40–7.

—— (2007) *Information and Complexity in Statistical Modeling*, London: Springer Verlag.

Shtarkov, Y. (1987) 'Universal sequential coding of single messages', *Problems of Information Transmission*, 23(3): 175–86.

9 Model description length priors in the urn problem

Duncan K. Foley

The urn problem

An old and very fruitful problem is statistics is the *urn problem*. The statistician is given a sample of n balls of r colors, drawn without replacement from an urn. The problem is to infer the composition of the urn given this information. This problem is well-suited to Bayesian methods.

Bayesian statistics

Bayesian statistics follows directly from the definitions of joint and conditional probability. Given a finite set of descriptions of exclusive elementary events, X, and a system of probabilities or *probability distribution*, that is, an assignment of non-negative numbers $P[x]$ to each element $x \in X$, with the property that $\Sigma_{x \in X} P[x] = 1$, for each subset $H \in X$, the probability of the event described by H is $P[H] \equiv \Sigma_{x \in H} P[x]$. For any two events H, D, the *joint probability* $P[H \wedge D] \equiv \Sigma_{x \in H \wedge D} P[x]$ is the probability of the elementary events contained in both H and D. If $P[D] > 0$, the *conditional probability* $P[H|D] \equiv P[H \wedge D]/P[D]$. From these definitions it follows that when $P[H \wedge D] > 0$, $P[H|D]P[D] = P[H \wedge D] = P\{D|H]P[H]$. Bayes' Theorem is the restatement of this relationship in the form:

$$P[H|D] \equiv P[H]\frac{P[D|H]}{P[D]}$$

In the terminology of Bayesian statistical inference, H is the *hypothesis*, D is the *data*, $P[H]$ is the *prior probability* of the hypothesis, $P[D|H]$ is the *likelihood* of the data given the hypothesis, and $P[H|D]$ is the *posterior probability* of the hypothesis given the data. $P[D]$ can be regarded as a normalizing factor since $P[D] = \Sigma_{H'} P[D|H']P[H']$, and is called the *evidence*. The likelihood, $P[D|H]$ is a normalized conditional probability when it is viewed as a function of the data for a given hypothesis, but is not normalized when it is viewed as a function of the hypothesis for given data. The normalized posterior probability is the normalized product of the likelihood (as a function of the hypothesis) and the prior.

In statistical applications the data is a set of observations and the hypothesis is a model depending on parameters which generates a probability distribution over possible sets of observations. The prior probability expresses the observer's relative degrees of belief over a set of possible models, given whatever information is available before the current set of observations. The use of Bayes' Theorem to update these prior beliefs taking account of the observed data guarantees the logical consistency of the statistical conclusions. As Jaynes (Jaynes and Bretthorst 2003) shows, any foundation for the theory of statistical inference which is not equivalent to the Bayesian framework worked out by Laplace (1814) is vulnerable to inconsistencies and paradoxes.

Other statistical methods may coincide with the Bayesian approach in specific situations, or for specific priors, but the Bayesian framework has two decisive advantages. First, the Bayesian framework requires the explicit specification of a consistent system of beliefs in the form of the prior probability over the hypothesis space. Thus controversies over the interpretation of data takes the coherent and fruitful form of a debate over the appropriate prior. Second, the Bayesian approach expresses the conclusions of a statistical analysis in the form of a posterior probability distribution over all possible hypotheses, thereby avoiding the fallacy of "rejecting" hypotheses that have low posterior probability but could logically have produced the observed data. Every hypothesis in the set of models assigned a positive prior probability that is logically consistent with the observed data will have a positive (though perhaps very small) posterior probability. The posterior probability depends on the class of models being considered, the prior probability the observer assigns to each model in the class, which can encode preferences for model features like "simplicity" and "smoothness", and on the observed data. Thus the posterior probability can reflect both the "fit" of a model to the data and other important characteristics of models, such as parsimony and continuity.

The urn model

As a concrete example of how this works out, let us take the urn problem.

The data takes the form of a *sample*, which is an ordered list of colors of balls. The sample is summarized in a histogram $n = \{n_1, \ldots, n_r\}$, where n_s is the number of balls of color s. The sample size is

$$N[n] = \Sigma_{s=1}^{r} n_s.$$

(We can also describe the sample data by reporting its size N, and the frequencies with which each category has been observed,

$$p = \left\{ \frac{n_1}{N}, \ldots, \frac{n_r}{N} \right\}.)$$

The case $r = 2$, where there are only two observed colors in the sample, plays a central role in the history of statistics as the *Bernoulli model*. Bruno DeFinetti's *exchangeable* priors (1975) assign the same prior probability to samples that are permutations of each other. It is immediate that exchangeable priors in this setting assign the same probability to samples with the same histogram. A little more thought establishes that only priors that can be written as functions of the histogram of a sample are exchangeable. In what follows we will assume that the prior is exchangeable, and describe the sample as a histogram.

Given a sample $n = \{n_1, \ldots, n_r\}$, we can regard it as coming from an urn, the composition of which is described by the histogram $m = \{m_1, \ldots, m_k\}$. (We can also describe the urn by giving its size, M, and the frequencies of each color of ball,

$$q = \left\{\frac{m_1}{M}, \ldots, \frac{m_k}{M}\right\}.)$$

Let the set of all possible urns be $\mathcal{M} = \{\{m_1, \ldots, m_k\} \mid k \in \{1, 2, \ldots\}, m_s \in \{0, 1, 2, \ldots\}\}$. If $k \geq r$, $m - n = \{m_1 - n_1, \ldots, m_k - n_k\}$ is the *unobserved* part of the urn (padding out with 0s where $k > r$). Note that r is not necessarily equal to k, because there may be balls in the urn with colors that were not selected in the sample. For a prior distribution $P[.]:\mathcal{M} \to (0, 1)$, the posterior probability that the sample n came from an urn with histogram m is $P[m|n] \propto P[m]P[n|m]$. In Bayesian language the hypothesis is the composition of the urn, m, and the data is the observed sample, n.

The number of actual ordered urns that have the histogram m is Multinomial@@m (using *Mathematica* notation), or alternatively Multinomial $[m_1, \ldots, m_k]$. (The multinomial coefficient is defined as

$$\text{Multinomial } [m_1, \ldots, m_k] = \text{Multinomial@@}m = \frac{(m_1 + \ldots + m_k)!}{m_1! \ldots m_k!}.)$$

Of these, the number that have the histogram n for a fixed position, say the first N observations, is Multinomial@@nMultinomial@@$(m - n)$. Thus the likelihood of the sample n given the urn m (in the case where $m \geq n$, so that the sample could have come from the urn) is proportional to the joint hypergeometric probability:

$$P[n|m] \propto \frac{\text{Multinomial@@}n\text{Multinomial@@}(m - n)}{\text{Multinomial@@}m}$$

The sum of the hypergeometric probability over n holding $m - n$ constant is

$$\frac{\text{Binomial}[M + k - 1, k - 1]}{\text{Binomial}[M - N + k - 1, k - 1]}$$

and symmetrically over $m - n$ holding n constant,

$$\frac{\text{Binomial}[M + k - 1, k - 1]}{\text{Binomial}[M + k - 1, k - 1]}.$$

For a given sample n, knowledge of the unobserved part of the urn $m - n$ is equivalent to knowledge of the urn itself, m. What we are interested in, however, is actually the unobserved part of the urn, so that we need to normalize the likelihood by summing over all possible samples n of size N, holding constant $m - n$. This results in the likelihood (with the convention that the multinomial coefficient is zero when any argument is negative):

$$P[n|m] = \frac{\text{Binomial}[M - N + k - 1, k - 1]}{\text{Binomial}[M + k - 1, k - 1]}$$

$$\frac{\text{Multinomial}@@n\text{Multinomial}@@(m-n)}{\text{Multinomial}@@m}$$

For a prior $P[m - n|M, k]$ the posterior probability of an urn with composition m conditional on the sample, n, the size of the urn, M, and the number of colors, k, is proportional to the product of the prior and this likelihood:

$$P[m - n|n, M, k] \propto P[m - n|M, k] \frac{\text{Binomial}[M - N + k - 1, k - 1]}{\text{Binomial}[M + k - 1, k - 1]}$$

$$\frac{\text{Multinomial}@@n\text{Multinomial}@@(m-n)}{\text{Multinomial}@@m}$$

For example, if the prior (as is typically the case in standard statistical inference) is uniform over all urn compositions, the normalized conditional posterior will be:

$$P[m - n|n, M, k] = \frac{\text{Binomial}[N + k - 1, k - 1]}{\text{Binomial}[M + k - 1, k - 1]}$$

$$\frac{\text{Multinomial}@@n\text{Multinomial}@@(m-n)}{\text{Multinomial}@@m}$$

This posterior is the familiar binomial distribution of the composition of the urn as Figure 9.1 shows.

Probability theory and information theory

Claude Shannon and WarrenWeaver's work (Shannon and Weaver 1949) shows the close links between the theory of probability and the theory of information (or communication). Shannon and Weaver consider the problem of encoding a finite set of possible messages $\mathcal{M}$ with cardinality $|\mathcal{M}|$ in binary strings. One way to accomplish this encoding is to number the messages in some order and use the binary expression of the message number as its code. This procedure requires $\text{Log}_2[|\mathcal{M}|]$ bits for each code word. Shannon and Weaver observe, however, that if some messages will be transmitted more frequently than others, it is possible

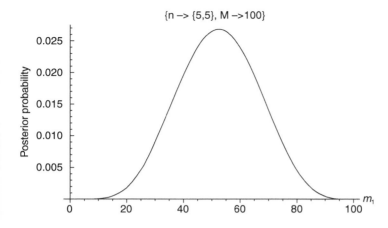

Figure 9.1 Binomial distribution of the composition of the urn.

to economize on this coding and achieve a shorter average bit length for the codes. In fact if we have a prior probability distribution $P[m]$ defined over all $m \in \mathcal{M}$, we can rank the messages by their prior probabilities and assign shorter code words to the higher probability messages. A basic theorem of information theory asserts that (ignoring issues of rounding) it is possible to find a coding scheme in which the code length of a message with probability

$$P[m] \text{ is } \mathrm{Log}_2\left[\frac{1}{P[m]}\right] = -\mathrm{Log}_2[P[m]].$$

With this coding scheme the expectation of the code length of a message given the prior probability distribution is:

$$H[\{P[m_1],\ldots,P[m_{|\mathcal{M}|}]\}] \equiv -(P[m_1]\mathrm{Log}_2[P[m_1]] + \ldots + P[m_{|\mathcal{M}|}]\mathrm{Log}_2[P[m_{|\mathcal{M}|}]])$$

Shannon and Weaver called this expected code length the *informational entropy* of the probability distribution $P = \{P_1,\ldots,P_{|\mathcal{M}|}\}$. It reaches its maximum value $\mathrm{Log}_2[|\mathcal{M}|]$ when the prior probabilities are uniform:

$$P[m_1] = \ldots = P[m_{|\mathcal{M}|}] = \frac{1}{|\mathcal{M}|}.$$

An immediate consequence of this definition is that we can measure the contribution of data to reducing the uncertainty of the observer in a Bayesian system by the difference between the informational entropy of the prior and the posterior probability distributions.

The model description length principle

In statistical practice we frequently encounter the following situation. The relevant hypotheses are organized into classes, $\{\mathcal{H}_1, \ldots \mathcal{H}_r\}$. Each hypothesis H_i is a member of one class. These classes are often referred to as statistical *models*. One common way for models to be defined is in terms of the number of parameters the hypotheses in the class require. For example, linear models of two dimensional data require two parameters (a slope and an intercept), while quadratic models require three parameters and so on. Given a statistical model (a class of hypotheses) equipped with a prior probability distribution over the model and some data that could be generated by hypotheses in the model, we can turn the crank of Bayes' Theorem to find a posterior probability distribution over the model. Everyday statistical practice, however, gives little guidance as to the choice of a model. This has proved disastrous in many contexts. In particular, once the attention of a scholarly audience has been focused on how well a given model can fit particular data, there is a strong pressure to move to more and more complex models, with more parametric degrees of freedom, in a search for a better fit. (Since models often nest in terms of parametric degrees of freedom, adding more parameters generally will not degrade the fit.) This curse of *overfitting* haunts many empirical scholarly discourses, including prominently my own field of economics. There is some protection against overfitting in the tendency of limited data to produce flatter and flatter posterior distributions over more complex (and hence larger) model classes. This leads to the quaint practice of assigning target levels of statistical significance which empirical studies must meet to be published in the journals of particular disciplines. These levels of statistical significance seem to arise from a consensus of the wise and experienced (and sometimes dead) practitioners of the discipline, whose judgment seems to be the only guide to this puzzle for researchers. The problem is that the choice of a particular hypothesis or model class of hypotheses along these lines is capricious and without logical foundation. Sometimes it works pretty well, and sometimes it goes completely haywire. In recent years the problem of model choice has been the frontier of statistical methodology.

Jorma Rissanen (Wallace and Boulton (1968) develop a theory based on similar insights) has pointed to a far-reaching ramification of Shannon's information theory for statistical method. Rissanen (2005a, 2005b) notes that we can measure the complexity of a hypothesis by the code length necessary to transmit it as a message. An old scientific-philosophical tradition associated with William of Occam (whose "razor" shaved away unnecessary hypotheses) recommends putting more belief in simpler and more parsimonious scientific hypotheses. This is clearly a principle which is prior to the analysis of data, and suggests that the complexity of a model has to be evaluated against the ability of that model to explain, that is, in statistical terms, fit the data. Rissanen's breakthrough, like many scientific turning points, is his proposal to *quantify* the complexity of statistical hypotheses in terms of the code length necessary to transmit them.

It turns out that cashing this insight out into actual statistical procedures requires considerable insight in each concrete case. Rissanen himself has constructed a system of "normalized maximum likelihood" estimation to exploit the tradeoff between fit and complexity. The current chapter owes its whole conceptual framework and much of its technical detail to Rissanen's method. Where I part from Rissanen is in incorporating the model description length principle consistently within the Bayesian framework of statistical inference. (See MacKay (2003) for further elaboration of this program for a wide variety of models.)

(One of the delights of my friendship with Vela Velupillai was his introducing me to Jorma Rissanen and his ideas at a workshop at the National University of Ireland, Galway, in March, 2005.)

Minimum description length and the maximum model description length posterior

The model description length principle can provide a prior for general Bayesian analysis.

Assume that we have a finite set of hypotheses $\mathcal{H} = \{H_1, \ldots, H_R\}$ chosen on prior grounds to be relevant to the explanation of given data $D \in \mathcal{D}$, where $\mathcal{D}$ is the set of all possible values of the data. For each hypothesis H_i we have a likelihood function, $P[.|H_i]: \mathcal{D} \to [0, 1]$ with $\Sigma_{D \in \mathcal{D}} P[D|H_i] = 1$, defined for a given hypothesis as a function of the possible values of the data. In the Bayesian framework, we will assign a prior distribution $P[.]: \mathcal{H} \to [0, 1]$, and calculate the posterior probability of each hypothesis H_i as $P[H_i|D] \propto P[H_i]P[D|H_i]$. As we have seen, the posterior can be normalized by dividing by $P[D] = \Sigma_{H' \in \mathcal{H}} P[H'] P[D|H']$.

Suppose we have calculated the minimum description length of each hypothesis $\varphi[H_i]$, the number of bits required to describe the hypothesis within the class $\mathcal{H}$. Then we can take the prior probability of the hypothesis $P[H_i]$ to be proportional to $2^{-\varphi[H_i]}$. With this prior, the posterior probability of any hypothesis is $P[H_i|D] \propto 2^{-\varphi[H_i]}P[D|H_i]$. If we take the logarithm of the posterior, we see that:

$$\text{Log}_2[P[H_i|D]] = -\varphi[H_i] + \text{Log}_2\left[\frac{P[D|H_i]}{P[D]}\right]$$

The log-posterior probability of a hypothesis can thus be expressed in bits as its fit, $\text{Log}_2[P[D|H_i]/P[D]]$, which measures the reduction in entropy (increase in information) the hypothesis provides, less the "complexity" of the hypothesis, $\varphi[H_i]$. As is generally the case for Bayesian statistical analysis, no hypothesis which is logically consistent with the data is "rejected", though poorly fitting or very complex hypotheses may have a very small posterior probability.

The model description length prior for the urn problem

In the urn problem, for any given size of urn, M, the likelihood function reaches its maximum when the composition of the urn is the same as the composition of the sample. The likelihood increases with the size of the urn, as Figure 9.2 illustrates.

The Model Description Length (MDL) principle assigns a prior probability to any hypothesis H proportional to $2^{-\varphi[H]}$, where $\varphi[H]$ is the minimum coding length for the hypothesis. In the case of the urn model, $m = \{m_1,\ldots, m_k\}$, the description of the hypothesis requires the transmission of the total urn size, M, and $k - 1$ integers between 0 and M reporting the number of balls in the urn of each color but the last. (From this information one can infer the number of balls of the last color.) A well-known result from information theory (see Grunwald, 2004) tells us that the minimum coding length of an arbitrary integer $M = 1$, $2,\ldots, \infty$ is $2\mathrm{Log}[M] + 1$. The minimum coding length of an integer less than or equal to a given M is $\mathrm{Log}[M]$. Thus we need $(k + 1)\mathrm{Log}[M] + 1$ bits to transmit the urn histogram, m. Thus the MDL prior for the urn model assigns a prior probability of $P[M, k] = M^{-(k+1)}$ to an urn of size M with balls of k different colors. (This distribution is normalized.)

Thus the MDL prior makes the posterior distribution in the urn model proportional to:

$$P[m|n] \propto M^{-(k+1)}\frac{\mathrm{Binomial}[M - N + k - 1, k - 1]}{\mathrm{Binomial}[M + k - 1, k - 1]}$$

$$\frac{\mathrm{Multinomial}@@n\,\mathrm{Multinomial}@@(m- n)}{\mathrm{Multinomial}@@m}$$

$$n \to \{50,50\},\ q \to \{\tfrac{1}{2},\tfrac{1}{2}\}$$

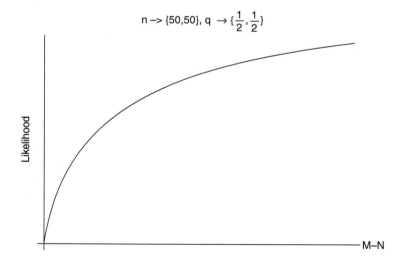

Figure 9.2 Likelihood function.

The MDL prior penalizes large urns, despite the fact that they fit the sample better, as Figure 9.3 shows.

If we marginalize the conditional uniform posterior in the urn problem over all possibilities for the composition of the unobserved part of the urn we find the likelihood that the sample came from an urn of size M with k colors:

$$P[n|M, k] = \frac{\text{Binomial}[M - N + k - 1, k - 1]}{\text{Binomial}[N + k - 1, k - 1]}$$

This likelihood rises (linearly) with the size of the urn M, as Figure 9.4 illustrates.

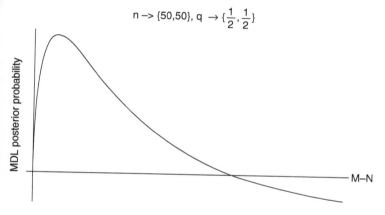

Figure 9.3 Model description length posterior probability.

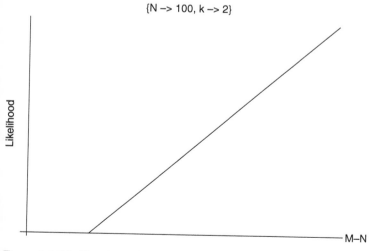

Figure 9.4 Likelihood as a function of urn size, M.

Combining this likelihood with the MDL prior, ignoring constant factors, the posterior probability for number of colors and the size of the urn is:

$$P[M, k|N] = \frac{\text{Binomial}[M - N + k - 1, k - 1]}{\text{Binomial}[N + k - 1, k - 1]}$$

While the fit of any hypothesis M, as represented by the likelihood function rises with M, the prior probability, representing the inverse of the description length, falls with M. This creates a tradeoff, as illustrated in Figure 9.5, which plots the posterior distribution of M, conditional on $k = 2$.

It might at first seem odd to calculate a posterior probability distribution over the urn size M, particularly because the traditional exposition of the urn model takes **M** as given and then allows it to grow without limit in order to derive the asymptotic posterior distribution of the hypothesis frequencies, $q = \{q_1, \ldots, q_k\}$. In many parametric expositions of this model, these limiting frequencies are regarded as parameters, $\theta = \{\theta_1, \ldots, \theta_k\}$ representing the propensity of the balls to be of each color.

But, in line with Rissanen's basic insight, the posterior probability distribution over M is actually reporting a critical dimension of the statistical analysis, the precision of the inferred statistics. When $M = 100$, for example, the effective precision with which q_s is known is two significant digits, and when $M = 10,000$ four significant digits. A sample with a small N does not give much data for a hypothesis q expressed to many significant digits. The value of M with maximum posterior probability gives a good working notion of the precision the data supports.

The maximum posterior sized urn is not very large. For $k = 2$, for example, the posterior distribution over the size of the original urn reaches its maximum at $\frac{3}{2}(N - 1)$.

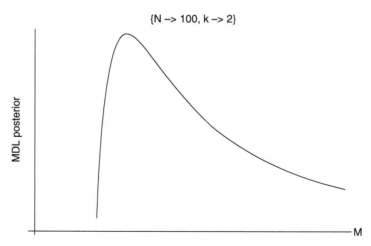

{N –> 100, k –> 2}

MDL posterior

M

Figure 9.5 Posterior distribution of M, conditional on $k = 2$.

Model description length and maximum entropy

The Model Description Length principle provides an elegant and persuasive solution to a long-standing nagging problem in Bayesian statistics. Laplace understood that the function of the prior in probability analysis is to make explicit the informational state of an observer of a system. This way of looking at the problem follows logically from the view that probabilities are measures of degrees of belief of an observer in alternative hypotheses. Later in the nineteenth century this understanding got garbled in the hands of mathematicians such as John Venn (1866) and George Boole (1854), who for reasons of their own regarded the prior as introducing a "subjective" element into probabilistic reasoning. What Jaynes calls the "mind projection fallacy", the tendency to project limited information of an observer as inherent indeterminacy of an observed phenomenon in the real world, took over, leading to the suppression of the prior in statistical practice, various ad hoc attempts to supply its functions, such as "significance tests" and "confidence intervals", and the general disaster of twentieth century statistical pedagogy.

Jaynes (following the work of Jeffreys (1939) and in sometimes uncomfortable collaboration with Savage (1954) and de Finetti (1975)) returned sanity to this dialog by reiterating Laplace's point that the prior is a description of the information state of an observer, not an expression of the observer's private idiosyncratic opinions about life. Jaynes expended considerable effort in seeking general and "objective" principles for the selection of priors in particular situations. He is best known for his advocacy of choosing priors that have maximum entropy as a way of introducing the minimum of information into the analysis through the prior. Jaynes also worked with other important ideas, such as using scale invariances built into specific situations to suggest priors. (See, however, Frank Lad (1996) for a principled defense of priors as an expression of subjective belief.)

Nonetheless, the mathematical arbitrariness of the prior has been a consistent drag on Bayesian probability theory. Pretty much everyone accepts one or another version of the likelihood principle as a measure of goodness of fit of models, but for many reasonable people the explicit introduction of a prior seems to be pulling a rabbit out of a hat. Since you can't have a posterior distribution to answer all the questions we want to ask of data without some prior, the lack of a compelling theory of prior specification presents a real problem for statistical method and pedagogy. One purely formal approach to this problem when models are specified in terms of parameters is the use of "conjugate" priors, which have the appealing mathematical property that their product with a particular likelihood function yields a tractable integral as the posterior. In two ways, however, the conjugate prior approach makes things worse. First, it isn't rooted in the empirics of statistical problems. How can a purely mathematical principle make any contribution to our understanding of a real phenomenon? Second, the mathematical sophistication required to grasp the conjugate prior idea is considerably higher than one can expect from students in

introductory courses in probability and statistics, which discourages the peda-
gogical use of the Bayesian framework, despite its simplicity and logical
transparency.

We must, however, remember that there can be no universal rule for forming
priors in all situations. Such a rule would amount to an algorithm for doing science. The choice of ways to describe significant aspects of the world, the classification, ordering and interpretation of data and the establishment of plausible
theoretical categories within which to analyze it are all ultimately aspects of
prior specification which cannot be reduced to a single prescription. Rissanen
makes this point extremely cogently, in arguing that the best statistics can do is
to find the optimal description of the data within a class of models specified
externally to the statistical analysis.

The Model Description Length principle goes a long way toward answering
these questions within the framework of Bayesian statistics. It incorporates an
ancient and powerful scientific principle, to prefer simpler explanations over
more complex ones and to dispense with unnecessary complication in hypotheses. These ideas have very different implications in different scientific contexts,
but they re-emerge over and over again in one form or another. The Model
Description Length approach has the very powerful consequence of allowing us
to measure the complexity of hypotheses quantitatively. (In practice it is not
always obvious how to do this. Caveat emptor!) This in turn allows statistical
analysis to trade off the complexity of an hypothesis against its ability to explain
observed data in an unambiguous manner. The incorporation of the Model
Description Length principle into the Bayesian prior insures that the resulting
analysis will be free of inconsistencies and hidden paradoxes.

From a Bayesian point of view the Model Description Length principle
replaces Laplace's and Jaynes' Maximum Entropy principle as a guide to the
specification of priors. In doing this MDL respects the Maximum Entropy principle's insistence that the prior should reflect the informational state of an unin-
formed observer confronting data. But MDL goes beyond the Maximum Entropy
principle to endow the observer with a philosophy of science and explanation
which is prior to the actual collection and analysis of data. The MDL prior is
hostile to complicated hypotheses on principle, and allows the posterior to con-
template them only grudgingly when the data require it.

References

Boole, George (1854) *An Investigation of the Laws of Thought*, London: Macmillan.
    Reprinted by Dover Publications, Inc., New York (1958).
de Finetti, B. (1975) *Theory of Probability Volume 2*, New York: Wiley.
Grunwald, P. (2004) "A tutorial introduction to the Minimum Description Length prin-
    ciple", in P. Grunwald, I.J. Myung, and M.A. Pitt (eds), *Advances in Minimum
    Description Length: Theory and Applications*, Cambridge: MIT Press. (Online, avail-
    able at: www.mdl-research.org/ accessed October 21, 2009).
Jaynes, E.T. and Bretthorst, L.G. (2003) *Probability Theory: The Logic of Science*, Cam-
    bridge: Cambridge University Press.

Jeffreys, Harold (1939) *Theory of Probability*, Oxford: Clarendon Press. Later editions, 1948, 1961, 1967, 1988.

Lad, F. (1996) *Operational subjective Statistical Methods: A mathematical, philosophical and historical introduction*, New York: Wiley.

Laplace, P.S. (1814, 1819) *Essai Philosophique sur les Probabilités*, Paris: Courcier Imprimeur. Reprinted in *Oeuvres Complétes de Laplace*, Vol. 7, Paris: Gauthier-Villars, 1886.

MacKay, D.J.C. (2003) *Information Theory, Inference, and Learning Algorithms*, Cambridge: Cambridge University Press.

Rissanen, J. (2005a) "Complexity and information in modeling", in K. Velupillai (ed.), *Computability, Complexity and Constructivity in Economic Analysis*, Oxford: Blackwell.

Rissanen, J. (2005b) *Lectures in Statistical Modeling Theory*. Online, available at: www.mdl-research.org/reading.html (accessed November 24, 2008).

Savage, L.J. (1954) *Foundations of Statistics*, New York: Wiley.

Shannon, C. and Weaver, W. (1949) *Mathematical Theory of Communication*, Urbana, IL: University of Illinois Press.

Venn, John (1866) *The Logic of Chance*, London: MacMillan & Co. Later editions 1876, 1888.

Wallace, C. and Boulton, D. (1968) "An information measure for classification", *Computer Journal*, 11(2): 185–94.

Part IV

Constructivity, rationality and complexity in economic theory

10   The honeybee as teacher

John J. McCall

Introduction

This chapter is an introduction to several outstanding theoretical and empirical studies in behavioural biology and its closely related disciplines: cultural anthropology, neurobiology and the cognitive sciences. The three major components of behavioural biology are foraging, mate selection and the choice of a settlement or nest. From our perspective search theory is a unifying ingredient of this research with game theory also assuming a conspicuous role. We believe there is a fundamental connection between biology and economics where search is merely a single manifestation. Another way of recognizing this linkage is to show the close connections among Adam Smith, David Hume, Charles Darwin and other prominent biologists and economists. We are always aware of egregious mistakes attached to the supposition that economics is a universal life-saver for any of the problems endogenous to another discipline.[1] Context must never be overlooked either within or, especially, across disciplines. Given this basic restriction, we agree wholeheartedly with Frank (1998):

> The theory of natural selection has always had a close affinity with economic principles.[2] Darwin's masterwork is about scarcity of resource, struggle for existence, efficiency of form, and measure of value. If offspring tend to be like their parents, then natural selection produces a degree of economic efficiency measured by reproductive success. The reason is simple: the relatively inefficient have failed to reproduce and have disappeared.

Exchange, division of labour, the 'invisible hand' and decision making under uncertainty are hallmarks of Smithian economics. Frank considers three exchange rates connected with natural selection:

1   Fisher's (1958a, b) formulation of reproductive value by analogy with the discounted value of money.[3]
2   The second factor is marginal value. Frank maintains that this gives the proper scale for comparing costs and benefits.
3   The third exchange is also a scaling factor: the coefficient of relatedness from kin selection theory (Hamilton 1964a, b). This appears to be peculiar

to evolutionary theory, but Frank shows that kin selection is tightly connected with the notion of correlated equilibrium in game theory and economics. He also presents the nexus with the basic ideas of statistical information and prediction. Thus, he shows that not only are Smith and Darwin joined by exchange, but so too are Bayes, Fisher, and Hamilton, i.e. there exists a 'logical unity of social evolution, statistical analysis of cause, aspects of Bayesian rationality, and economic measures of value'.

In this chapter, we concentrate on the similarities among Smith, Darwin and Hamilton. The close nexus with Bayesian methods are introduced, but are not explored in detail.[4]

The biological marketplace

The exchanges described by Frank (1998) are also spelled out in great detail by Noe *et al.* (2001). In the Preface, Noe observes:

> The constraints of life force every organism to behave economically. The study of economic behaviour is not limited to 'economics'. Scientific disciplines that concentrate on other aspects of human behaviour, such as psychology, sociology, and anthropology have to pay close attention to the economic decisions that drive human behaviour. The same is true for biological disciplines.... In order to determine in how far a behavioural strategy is 'economical', it has to be compared to some ideal norm: the strategy that would yield maximum payoff.... Evolutionary biologists have realized ... that even the dimmest of organisms, such as fungi and flatworms, often use 'super-rational strategies', because a process of selection running over a vast number of generations can shape the behaviour of every species to near perfection.... There lies the common ground between biology and economics: while Adam Smith's human producers and consumers are driven by the 'invisible hand' of self-interest, Charles Darwin's living organisms are driven by the selection for maximizing individual fitness....
>
> The idea to apply the principles deduced by economists for human markets to cooperative and mutualistic interactions in biology is relatively recent, but the idea of a 'mating market' has been around ever since Darwin identified sexual selection as a powerful motor of evolution.

In Chapter 5 of Noe *et al.*: '*Biological markets*: partner choice as the driving force behind the evolution of mutualisms', he defines 'systems such as the peacock's mating system, in which the members of one class of organisms benefit from being chosen by members of another class, have properties similar to human markets on which goods or services are exchanged'.

The properties of these biological markets are:

- Commodities are exchanged between individuals that differ in the degree of control over these commodities.

- Trading partners are chosen from a number of potential partners....
- There is competition among the members of the chosen class to be the most attractive partner.
- Supply and demand determine the bartering value of commodities exchanged.
- Commodities on offer can be advertised.

Two classes of biological interactions possessing these biological market properties are identified. They are mating systems and mutualistic interactions between members of diverse species. The beehive which we study in the fourth section of this chapter entails both classes of interactions. Cooperation is manifest in the hive and is a consequence of Hamilton's kin selection. In a sense then the honeybee hive is a perfect example of a biological marketplace.[5] However, its perfection means we must look elsewhere for cheating and freeriding.

Noe observes that inclusion of supply and demand renders the market approach quite different from other cooperative theories used in biology. A simple game theoretical market model predicts only the direction that the exchange rate will shift as the supply–demand conditions change. Noe is hopeful that the exact value of the exchange ratio will be predicted by more sophisticated models.

Interdisciplinary research is strongly supported by Noe. In the conclusion he describes three interrelated disciplines that stress the theory of markets: Economics, Anthropology and Biology. In Biology he notes that empirical and theoretical research has been accomplished on mating markets, in the context of sexual selection, whereas research on intra-specific cooperation has emphasized game theory.

Biological and economic decision making are similar in that the search and exchange of information comprise their essence. Search lies at the foundations of foraging, mate selection and nest(house) hunting problems – the three basic problems in behavioural biology. An organism's life is a learning process and it is exactly this learning which constructs and shapes the unique individual self. Adjustments to the environment are central to learning. Environmental fluctuations affect all organisms, where the precise impact on individual behaviour depends on its life history and the unique cognitive(neural) structure assembled in response to this history.

In economic terms, the environment confronting each individual in a particular society is characterized by the marketplace. Exchange is the decisive activity of each individual as he responds to changes. The repeated exchanges by each of society's members yields a spontaneous order. It is precisely this unplanned order which enables each member to exploit all the pertinent information dispersed throughout society. The prices in a pure economy carry this information, enabling each and every exchange among individuals to be based on all the relevant information *available* throughout the society. It is exchange which gives rise to the division of labour, the mechanism which enhances both individual productivity and society's welfare.

The recognition that a man's effort will benefit more people, and on the whole satisfy greater needs, when he lets himself be guided by the abstract signals of prices rather than by perceived needs, and that by this method we can best overcome our constitutional ignorance of most of the particular facts, and can make the fullest use of the knowledge of concrete circumstances widely dispersed among millions of individuals, is the great achievement of Adam Smith.

(Hayek 1978: 269)

The crucial point yoking these familiar Smithian principles is that every economic response is a reply to *unforeseen changes*. Uncertainty lives in both the social–economic 'order' and is the source of the idiosyncratic cognitive architecture of each of society's members. One might say that at the level of society there is an unfolding 'objective' order, whereas each individual is busy constructing his own 'subjective' self.

In our discussion of Biological Behavioural systems we rely heavily on the intensive research of the behaviour of honeybees by Seeley (1985, 1995) and his colleagues. The bee attracted the interest of Bernard Mandeville and led to the development of both evolution and spontaneous order together with division of labour and the central position of exchange. His original poem, composed in 1705, had as its major thesis the paradoxical assertion that private vices combine to create public virtue. We will discuss Mandeville in our section on the honeybee.

The second section of this chapter is a detailed presentation of the foraging problem and its link with search theory. We present a heuristic account of the Gittins index following the introduction. We then outline an exchangeable approach to foraging, extending the Bayesian formulation by Krebs and Davies (1987). This is followed by a fairly detailed discussion of adaptive sequential search. The problems of patch use and prey choice are then studied. An important new approach to foraging via game theory is outlined in the seventh subsection on social foraging theory. We then analyse the foraging and nesting behaviour of bumblebees. The section concludes with a brief discussion of the cognitive architecture of bumblebees.

The third subsection is a rather complete discussion of mate choice. Both one-sided and two-sided models are investigated. We also discuss the handicap (or signalling) model and note its renewal by Grafen (1990a). Two-sided mating models can now be designed with search on one side and signalling on the other.

A study of the honeybee is the subject of the fourth subsection. As we will see almost all of the economic analysis that is covered in a complete course in *microeconomics* and that is presented in a course in the *economics of information* have applications and extensions in the marvellous research by Seeley and his colleagues. The topics range from division of labour as it is sequentially practised by the clever honeybees to the notion of a superorganism which addresses current controversies over the level of selection.

The final section of the chapter is the most challenging as it summarizes some of the important and recent research in neuroscience and its economic implications. We rely heavily on the research by Edelman (1987, 1989, 1992, 2004, 2006), LaCerra and Bingham (2002), Quartz and Snejowski (1997, 2000). Their articles combine basic market economics with complex neuronal structures. We summarize their work emphasizing the important interchange among economics and neuroscience. Our final subsection suggests that Bayesian analysis may be useful in analysing neuroscientific structures. This is compatible with recent recommendations by, among others, Shepherd (1988) and Tennenbaum and Griffiths (2001), and can be translated into an exchangeability approach similar to that flourishing in population genetics and econometrics.

Foraging theory and applications

Introduction

The application of economics to biology *and* the application of biology to economics have venerable histories. It is well known that Adam Smith, David Hume and Thomas Malthus have had and continue to have a profound influence on biology and that Charles Darwin and his followers have had a similar impact on economics.[6]

Over the last 30 years, economists, specializing in microeconomics and the economics of information, and behavioural biologists specializing in the foraging and mating behaviour of animals and insects have realized that these seemingly diverse disciplines are, in fact, two important applications of the same evolutionary and economic principles.[7] These two disciplines have both made substantial progress over this period of interdisciplinary study, with search, adaptive search, equilibrium search, evolutionary stable systems, the evolution of cooperative behaviour and signalling comprising a few of the important advances.

This chapter concentrates on foraging theory and its decisive link with search theory. We present three topics that have received little or no attention in the biological literature: the Gittins index, Bayes adaptive search and the significance of exchangeability and the Polya urn.

A significant exception is the discussion of Bayes theory and adaptive foraging models in Chapter 4 of the comprehensive and seminal study by Stephens and Krebs (1986). They remark, perspicaciously, that 'we consider information, viewing learning from the perspective of gaining and using information economically. *This approach differs greatly from the way psychologists usually analyze learning*' (italics added). Stephens and Krebs are on the verge of studying optimal stopping rules which would have led them to optimal adaptive search in the sense of Bayes (they reference DeGroot (1970)), but somehow they don't make it over the threshold. Nevertheless, their treatment of foraging is a landmark in revealing both the huge benefits of biological cooperation with economics and the obstacles imposed by psychologists in their 'theory of learning', on applications of Bayesian methods to the many disciplines touched by psychology, especially neuroscience. An important demurral is Shepherd's research as interpreted by Tennenbaum and Griffiths (2001). They show that the 'similarity' studied by Tversky (1977) is 'equivalent' to Shepherd's Bayesian approach. We elaborate on this in the last section of the chapter.

In our first application we make the simplest assumption, namely, that foraging takes place in a patchy habitat. By this is meant a foraging area (habitat) that is composed of n independent feeding patches. The problems for the animal are to decide which habitat to select, which patch to feed in and when to switch from patch i to patch j. These decisions are made when the food content of the habitat and its patches is known imperfectly. As the animal feeds in a patch it gains more information about its food content. The decision to stay or leave a particular patch is similar to the stay/leave decision made by an employee who is learning more about his job as time progresses. The search for food is analogous to the search for a high wage or a low price. It is the similarity between these decision processes that led us to believe that the search methodology could be fruitfully applied to the foraging behaviour of animals.[8]

There is the question of whether searchers actually pursue optimal search policies. The complexity of these policies has caused some to doubt their applicability. One might also question the optimality assumption for animals. For example it might seem absurd to some to assume that animals could solve these complicated optimal programmes. Our position on this point for both animals and humans has been lucidly stated by Royama (1970):

> It may reasonably be concluded that great tits have developed as efficient a method of hunting as their psychological capacity and their environmental conditions permit. Hence, our task is to postulate what the most efficient way of hunting should be and to compare it with what the great tits actually do.

Foraging as a multi-armed bandit process: a heuristic discussion

A bird flies over a meadow or habitat composed of n patches. It wishes to land on and forage in that patch i with the largest rate of food intake or capture rate θ_i. Following Royama (1970) and Smith and Dawkins (1971) our basic postulate is that the bird tries to maximize its hunting efficiency by sampling the food in different patches and spending the most time in those patches with high capture rates. The task then is to identify high capture rate patches. We assume that the bird makes tentative identification during its overflight. On the basis of information acquired during overflight it assigns numbers ξ_i, $i = 1, 2, 3, \ldots, n$ to each of the n patches. It then commences feeding on the patch with the largest ξ_i, say

$$\xi_1 = \max_i \xi_i.$$

As it searches the chosen patch it acquires more information about the parameter θ_1. (Another complication is that θ_1 is a function of t and declines as the bird feeds in the selected patch. Thus he may decide eventually to leave patch 1 even though the prior estimate of θ_1 is equal to the posterior value at $t = 0$. We study this complication later.) If on the basis of information required from s searches the posterior value of ξ_i say $\xi_i(s)$ drops below the critical number ξ_2 for what was initially the second best patch, then the bird switches to this second patch. The critical number, ξ_2 measures the opportunity cost of searching patch 1. When $\xi_2 > \xi_1(s)$, it pays to switch from patch 1 to what is now the highest expected yield patch. It continues the same process on patch 2 accumulating information and revising ξ_2. After feeding on patch 2 for m searches ξ_2 has been revised to the posterior value $\xi_2(m)$. If this value is less than ξ_3 and ξ_3 is greater than $\xi_1(s)$, the bird switches to patch 3. If $\xi_2(m)$ is less than $\xi_2(s)$ and ξ_3 is also less than $\xi_1(s)$, the bird returns to patch 1. The bird continues in this fashion until feeding is completed. This multi-armed bandit policy tells the bird how to choose a patch, when to leave a patch and finally which patch to occupy next. Several simplifying assumptions have been made. First, we assume that the birds do not have to evade predators during their feeding. Second, the characteristics of the $n - 1$ patches are unaltered during feeding on the nth patch.

It may be that it is sometimes impossible for the foraging animal to predict the attractiveness of patches not already visited. In this circumstance the prior over the food content of these patches is flat: they are all tied for first(last) place in the predator's ranking. The optimal policy is to pick a patch at random and switch when the posterior estimate of the food content falls below the average of the other patches. When this occurs the predator switches to another patch chosen at random. This proceeds until feeding is completed. The implications of this procedure are consistent with the laboratory findings of Dawkins and Smith. There were three low yield patches and one high yield patch.

The birds were provided with different densities of mealworms in each area so that the highest density area contained 16, the next highest 8, then 4 and finally one mealworm per 256 pots. The location of each density was kept constant between trials. The highest density was sited in the location that the bird had visited least during training and the lowest density in the most visited location. The actual location of the mealworms within the 256 pots in a feeding area was determined by random number tables with the restriction that no pot contained more than one mealworm.

The birds sampled the low yield patches about the same length of time before switching eventually to the high yield patch. The search time spent at the three low yield patches was approximately the same. This suggests that the prior was considerably higher than these yields so that the relative differences among them was slight, i.e. the sample sizes required to reject these patches were approximately equal.

The multi-armed bandit methodology

Posing the foraging problem in this way means that we can use the multi-armed bandit (MAB) methodology to resolve it. Recall that in the MAB the gambler is confronted with N slot machines (one-armed bandits) that may be played repeatedly in any order. The ith machine is characterized by a success probability θ_i which is unknown to the gambler. The Bernoulli sequence of successes and failures on the ith machine provides information used to obtain a Bayesian estimate of θ_i. The object is to choose the sequence of plays to maximize the total discounted expected reward.

During the past few years Gittins and his colleagues have solved this MAB problem. Simply stated the optimal policy has the following form: a policy is optimal if and only if at each decision point the selected bandit process is the one with the largest Gittins index, ξ, where this index is the MAB generalization of the reservation wage.

More concretely, suppose there are N projects indexed by $n = 1, 2, \ldots, N$. At any decision point exactly one project must be selected for further development. Suppose project n is in state i. If n is chosen a reward R_i^n is collected and project n moves from state i to state j with probability p_{ij}^n. The states of all other projects remain unchanged. The discount factor is β_i^n.

The solution to this problem is obtained by assigning each project a Gittins index and then choosing each period that project with the largest index. Intuitively, the Gittins index is the value of a fallback position which would make a decision maker indifferent between continuing with project n in state i and rejecting the project for the fallback position. For any fallback position ξ^0 the maximum expected discounted return $V_i^n(\xi)$ obtainable given the choice of either continuing with project n (in state i) or stopping and getting ξ satisfies

$$V_i^n(\xi) = \max\{\xi;\ R_i^n + \beta_i^n \Sigma P_{ij} V_j^n(\xi)\}.$$

Thus the Gittins index ξ_i^n is given by

$$\xi_i^n = V_i^n(\xi_i^n) = R_i^n + b_i \Sigma P_{ij}^n V_j(\xi_i^n).$$

The early optimization foraging theory is based on a simple but powerful result from microeconomic theory. Following Krebs *et al.* (1974) assume there are two types of patches, A and B, with P_A and P_B being the proportion of each in a habitat. The average travel time between patches is t. The amount of food taken from a patch $f(T)$ is an increasing concave function of T, the time spent in the patch. Let $T_A(T_B)$ be the time spent in an A-type(B-type) patch. The average time to use one patch T is the travel time t plus the time spent in the patch,

$$T = t + P_A T_A + P_B T_B.$$

The average food taken from one patch is

$$E = P_A f(T_A) + P_B f(T_B).$$

Krebs *et al.* chose T_A and T_B to maximize E/T. The first order condition is given by

$$\frac{\partial f(T_i)}{\partial T_i} = \frac{E}{T}, \; i = A, B.$$

The predator should leave the patch when the average rate of food intake in the habitat equals the marginal rate in the patch.

The Krebs *et al.* model allows for a declining capture rate, but does not permit learning as the animal searches a particular patch. Their model does permit switching, but does not predict which patch will be visited next. The main prediction of this model is the quitting time for a particular patch. It does not predict how this patch was chosen initially nor does it predict which patch will be visited next or when the habitat will be quit. All of these decisions are incorporated in the MAB approach to foraging.

An exchangeable approach to foraging

This section combines the Bayesian foraging model in Stephens and Krebs (1986) with the famous thumbtack model exposited in Lindley and Phillips (1976), Krebs (1989) and Schervish (1995).

Suppose a forager enters a patch and after one period hears a rustle in the underbrush. His prior distribution regarding the presence of prey in the patch is P(prey) = P(no prey) = 1/2. Using Bayes theorem the posterior distributions given rustling are:

$$P(prey|rustling) = \frac{P(rustling/prey)P(prey)}{P(rustling)}$$

and

$$P(no\ prey|rustling) = \frac{P(rustling/noprey)P(noprey)}{P(rustling)}$$

As new information accumulates these conditions are repeated with the posterior probabilities as the new prior probabilities.

We now consider the thumbtack version of this problem. An old-fashioned metal thumbtack is tossed on to a soft surface. When it stops, note whether the point is up or down. Successive tosses are treated symmetrically. Suppose we assume that this symmetry obtains for any number of tosses. Furthermore let an up on the ith toss correspond to a rustle in the brush which we represent by

$X_i = 1$. If there is no rustle in the ith period, $X_i = 0$. The standard procedure is to model the outcomes of the tosses as IID random variables with $X_i = 1$ indicating the toss is point up denoting a rustle, and $X_i = 0$ indicating point down and no rustle. The classical approach invents a parameter θ assumed fixed and not yet known to the experimenter. Succinctly put, the classical statistician says that the X_i are IID with $P(X_i = 1) = \theta$.

In the Bayesian setting, a probability μ is constructed for the unknown θ. The probability of a particular sequence of rustles and stillnesses is given by

$$P(X_i = x_1,\ldots, X_n = X_n) = \int\theta\sum_{i=1}^{n} x_i(1 - \theta)n - \sum_{i=1}^{n} sx_i d\mu(\theta). \tag{10.1}$$

Schervish (1995) shows how to replace the assumptions of IID and 'fixed but unknown parameter θ' with the symmetry that is natural to such a problem and is called *exchangeability*. The information garnered from one toss is the same as that derived from any other toss. This holds for information from two tosses – it is treated the same as any other two tosses regardless of their location in the sequence. Symmetry holds for 3,4,.... This process recognizes the symmetry among the tosses. Observe that the IID assumption implies this symmetry *and* more. Note that in equation (10.1), every permutation of the outcomes $x_1,\ldots, x_n$ yields the same value of the RHS of (10.1). If nothing more is assumed over and above permutation symmetry for a possibly infinite sequence of thumbtack tosses, then we can prove[10] that there is a μ such that (10.1) obtains. Implicitly, the quantity θ is now a random variable Θ rather than a fixed value. The distribution of Θ is frequently referred to as the *deFinetti measure*. Note $X_1, X_2,\ldots$ are not necessarily mutually independent; they are conditionally independent given Θ.

Let us look more closely at equation (10.1). Roughly speaking, equation (10.1) is a version of deFinetti's representation theorem – it is a mixture of Bernoulli random variables with μ the deFinetti mixing measure. That is

$$\mu(\theta)\infty\theta^{a-1}(1 - \theta)^{b-1}.$$

We wish to predict whether there will be a rustle in, say, the thirteenth time interval spent on the patch in question. There have been nine rustles (Us) and three silences (Ds). Then

$$P(X_{13} = U|9, 3) = \frac{P(10, 3)}{P(9, 3)} \tag{10.2}$$

and both numerator and denominator on the RHS of (10.2) can be calculated using (10.3). This gives:

$$P(U_{13}|9, 3) = \int_{1}^{0} \theta\{\theta^4(1 - \theta)^3 d\theta/p(9, 3)\} \tag{10.3}$$

The term in the braces of (10.5) is $p(\theta|9, 3)$, the posterior distribution when $p(\theta)$ is the prior distribution. Thus,

$$p(U13|9, 3) = \int_1^0 \theta p(\theta|9, 3)d\theta.$$

Let us assume that $p(\theta) \equiv \mu(\theta)$ is given by a beta distribution with parameters a, b > 0. That is,

$$p(\theta) \propto \theta^{a-1}(1 - \theta)^{b-1}, \text{ for some a, b} > 0.$$

Note that the binomial and beta are natural conjugates, that is,

$$p(\theta|r, s) \propto \theta^r(1 - \theta)^s p(\theta) \propto \theta^{r+a-1}(1 - \theta)^{s+b-1}.$$

The probability of a rustle on trial $n - 1$ in the patch is

$$P(U_{n+1}|r, s) = \frac{a + r}{a + b + n}.$$

It is important to note that the beta-binomial distribution is a Polya distribution. A Polya sequence is generated by an urn process and is exchangeable. It is extremely useful in the flourishing literature on Bayes nonparametric inference.

Foraging: patch use and prey choice

In their excellent survey paper, McNamara et al. (2001) apply renewal theoretic methods to both patch use and prey choice. They describe 'rate maximization strategies' when food occurs periodically and the animal renews itself at the end of each period. In the application to patch use, a cycle commences when the animal leaves one 'depleted' patch and looks for another richer patch. When search yields a new patch, the animal initiates consumption at a decreasing rate caused by the depletion of food on the patch being exploited. Thus, the animal eventually leaves the patch and a new cycle begins.[11] McNamara et al. (2001) let G be the net energy achieved during a cycle and T is the cycle length. They assume that both G and T are random variables determined by the animals 'behavioural strategy'. The mean net rate of the animal's energy accumulation is given by

$$\gamma = \frac{E(G)}{E(T)}$$

The maximum value of γ over all foraging strategies is

$$\gamma^* = \max \gamma.$$

A strategy is called optimal if and only if it maximizes $E(G - \gamma^*T)$. McNamara (1982) showed that this is equivalent to maximizing

$$H = E(\text{Gain from remainder of cycle} - \gamma^* \times \text{Time left on cycle}) \qquad (10.4)$$

at every stage of the cycle. This shows that γ^* is similar to a rate of exchange between time spent on the current cycle and energy given up in future cycles. McNamara *et al.* (2001) conclude with a perspicacious insight: 'We can thus think of γ^* as the opportunity cost per unit time. *This brings out the trade-off between time and energy that is at the heart of rate maximization.*' (ibid., italics added).

Two 'classic' renewal cycle paradigms are 'patch use' and 'prey choice'.[12]

Patch use. An animal searches for food in discrete patches. Let $G_i(t)$ be the total expected energy consumed by foraging a type i patch for time t. G_i is increasing ($G_i' > 0$) and concave ($G_i'' > 0$). When the forager quits a patch at t, the renewal time, it spends an expected time τ finding a new patch. Maximizing (10.4) implies that the optimal time t_i^* on type i patch maximizes

$$G_i(t) - \gamma^*t$$

and therefore is the solution to

$$G_i'(t_i^*) = \gamma^*.$$

This is Charnov's (1976) marginal value theorem.

Prey choice. McNamara *et al.* (2001) consider an animal foraging in a milieu containing several different prey, where prey i yields energy e_i when consumed and this activity takes time h_i to handle and consume. Types arrive according to independent Poisson processes, with λ_i the rate of arrival of type i prey. Handling time completely occupies the forager and no prey arrive during this period. The question is: Which prey that arrive should be consumed by the forager? If a prey of type i arrives, the optimal decision maximizes (10.4), which implies

$$H_{(\text{accept})} = e_i - \gamma^*h_i \text{ and } H_{(\text{reject})} = 0.$$

Thus prey i is accepted if and only if

$$e_i/h_i > \gamma^*.$$

The calculation of γ^* is based on an iterative method devised by McNamara (1985). In particular γ^* can be computed by constructing a sequence $\gamma_1, \gamma_2, \ldots$ as follows. Consider any strategy and let γ_1 be its expected rate ($\gamma_1 > 0$). Then at step n, let $\gamma_n = f(\gamma_n - 1)$ for $n \geq 2$, where $f(\gamma) = E(G)/E(T)$ under a strategy maximizing $E[G - \gamma T]$ for each $\gamma > 0$. See McNamara *et al.* (2001) for a complete discussion which includes their Figure 2.

Risk-sensitive foraging[13]

Consider an animal with reserves x at time t. The animal has two consumption opportunities, u_1 and u_2. Option u_1 gives a net change in reserves by $t + 1$ of γ, so the level of reserves at $t + 1$ is simply $X' = x + \gamma$. Associated with u_2 is a net change in reserves from t to $t + 1$ is $X' = x + Y$, where Y is a random variable with mean γ. Let $V(x', t + 1)$ be the reproductive value of occupying state x' at $t + 1$. Then the reproductive value of choosing u_1 at t is

$$H(x, t; u_1) = V(x + \gamma, t + 1)$$

and the similar measure for u_2 is

$$H(x, t; u_2) = E[V(x + Y; t + 1)].$$

Hence an animal choosing u_2 (is risk-prone) if and only if

$$V(x + \gamma, t+1) < E[V(x + Y, t + 1)].$$

If V is linear what produces deviations from linearity?

Let $[O, T]$ be a time interval in which there is no reproduction. Assume that energy gained in any time interval is independent of x, its energy reserves. Let $R(x)$ be the terminal reward and suppose $R(x) = k_0 + k_1 x$.

If an animal with reserves x at t augments reserves by a random variable Y between t and T, then its reproductive value is

$$V(x, t) = E[R(x + Y)] = k_0 + k_1[x + E(Y)].$$

Houston and McNamara (1999) note that V is independent of $\mathrm{Var}(Y)$ and is a linear function of x. This implies that the animal should rate-maximize.

In some situations, the terminal reward is nonlinear. Also, the amount of energy acquired in an interval does not depend on x.

Social foraging theory[14]

In social foraging, decisions are based on the frequency-dependence of their pay-offs. A primary decision in social foraging is determining group membership. The payoff obtained from joining a hunting party depends on its size, that is, the number of individuals who have made a similar decision. Social foraging decisions sometimes consider patch use when foraging parties simultaneously search a patch. The returns to an individual from time spent on a patch depends on the number of foragers that have stayed or left the patch. A familiar social foraging decision is whether to participate in the discoveries made by other group members. This decision is the essence of the producer–scrounger (PS) game. This game has been modelled by Vickery *et al.* (1991) and we base our description on that by Giraldeau and Livoreil (1998).[15]

A rate maximizing PS foraging game

A group of G foragers is decomposed into $G_S = (1 - q)G$ individuals playing S who always detect all food clumps discovered by $G_P = qG$, the number of individuals playing P. This game assumes that qG foragers search for patches independently, the time before a patch is found is large compared to the time of exploitation, and patches are never exploited together. Each food patch contains F items which are consumed by a single searcher; they cannot be shared. A P player is sure of receiving a $(0 \leq a \leq F)$ items for its own consumption. Vickery *et al.* (1991) call a the finder's advantage. Giraldeau and Livoreil treat a as a parameter of the game and not a decision variable.

When a P player discovers a clump, the g scroungers arrive together. The remaining food $(A = F - a)$ is shared equally among the $n = G_S + 1$ individuals in the patch. The producer average consumption (IP) after T time units of foraging is

$$I_P = \lambda T(a + A/n),\tag{10.5}$$

where λ is the rate at which patches are discovered. The corresponding consumption of scroungers is

$$I_S = \lambda q G T(A/n).\tag{10.6}$$

Solving (10.5) and (10.6) for the equilibrium q^* yields

$$q^* = a/F + \frac{1}{G}.$$

Note that $\lambda G q T$, the rate of encounter by the G_P producers does not influence q^*. The reason is that the G_S individuals have no impact on the encounter rate of individuals playing P. Thus $1 - q^*$ is independent of rate at which joining opportunities become available. Therefore the fraction using P and thus the fraction using S are determined only by G and a/F.

A number of predictions regarding the extent to which the use of S would be a frequent occurrence in foraging groups flow from the foraging model.

The rate maximizing P_S games of Vickery *et al.* (1991) predicts the observed proposition P, for a given finder's share, to be an inverse function of group size. Given group size, P should increase as a function of finders share. In an experiment, Giraldeau and Livoreil (1998), found that the proposition playing P moved towards the rate-maximizing P_S game's predictions.[16]

The foraging and nesting behaviour of bumblebees

Background

Bumblebees are social insects in that parent and offspring live together in a common hive and display cooperative behaviour towards one another. Yet in spite of being labelled social insects, the worker bees in their foraging activities behave individualistically. These female foragers do not cooperate with one another in their hunting. Each behaves as if she were maximizing her own utility function. The arguments of this function are the amounts of nectar and pollen that are brought to the hive. These are used to produce more bees. Early in the life cycle of the hive worker bees are the main output, while towards the end of the cycle the hive produces queens and drones. Given the environment in which bumblebees reside, the individualistic conduct is superior to the cooperative behaviour of honeybees.

> While a honeybee colony relies on cooperation and communication for success in foraging, a bumblebee colony relies on individual initiative. Each is suited to a specific life history strategy in a particular environment. A honeybee colony resembles a big corporation that goes after the big markets. It can wait out long lean periods and rapidly exploit windfalls because of its elaborate organization and huge communal storage capacities. In contrast, a bumblebee colony has a more individualistic cottage industry approach. It thrives by living hand-to-mouth, exploiting small, scattered energy sources that in most cases can be taken up by single workers operating individually. Windfalls, such as large banana inflorescences loaded with nectar, are rare for bumblebees but not for honeybees, which originated in tropical areas. Bumblebees do not need an elaborate communication system. In fact, it could be disadvantageous, for it could re-route bees who might be in the hive, and waiting to follow dances, the bumblebees keep track of changing resources through their minor specialties, and they explore for new food resources when their majors no longer satisfy.
>
> (Heinrich 1979)

Bumblebees do not accumulate inventories of nectar[17] and pollen.[18] Instead they convert most pollen and nectar directly into larvae. They can pursue this strategy because the amount of nectar and pollen collected each day is relatively constant. This follows from the bumblebee's ability to forage in almost all kinds of weather.[19] Also in contrast to honeybees, bumblebees need not accumulate inventories to carry them through the winter.

The bumblebee hive begins in the spring with a single queen. She chooses a site for the hive and lays eggs that grow into workers. These workers relieve the queen of her foraging and hive-caring duties. In the first part of the hive's cycle, mostly worker bees are produced.

Towards the end of the cycle all larvae develop into queens and males. The cycle ends when the workers die and the queens are inseminated. The queens then search for a place to hibernate until next spring. In temperate regions the cycle begins in the spring and ends in the late summer or autumn.

Foraging

Heinrich in a series of papers and a book has emphasized the importance of economics in understanding the foraging behaviour of bumblebees.[20] Here we extend some of his findings by explicitly including uncertainty and information in the economic model of foraging behaviour.

Our basic point is that the attachment between a bee and a species of flower is akin to the relationship between employer and employee.[21] Just as the employer must advertise using want ads, etc., for workers, so too the flowers advertise for bees using their colour and fragrance. The bees pollinate the flowers and in return are paid a wage in pollen and nectar. The relationship is maintained as long as the bee lives, the flower blooms and the bee receives a wage that is higher than the alternatives.

A crucial observation about bumblebees is that their foraging is individualistic. There is no cooperation as, for example, occurs among the honeybees with their celebrated communication dance.[22]

A young and inexperienced bumblebee leaves its hive in quest of pollen and nectar. It soon discovers that extracting nectar from particular flowers requires a certain amount of skill. It tries out flowers much like a young worker tries out jobs. At some point it decides to acquire the specific capital enabling it to harvest, say, jewelweed. From that day on it only harvests jewelweed. The attachment that occurs here is very much like the employment relationship. The cement for this relationship is the specific bee capital investment, the promise by the flower to pay in nectar and pollen (whenever available), and the promise of the bee to pollinate.

Young and inexperienced bees wander around a lot testing various flowers, many with little nectar, while others are difficult to harvest. These bees also do not take the fastest route back to the hive. Thus they are unemployed a good portion of the time. This corresponds to the youth unemployment observed in capitalist countries. During this period the bees learn about different jobs and also about alternative routes to and from the hive. Each flower (job) has a wage rate that is transmitted by its colour and fragrance. If this wage rate exceeds the young bee's reservation wage, he visits the flower. If upon visiting he finds little nectar, he quits that flower. When he visits a flower that yields much nectar he learns how to harvest it efficiently and takes a permanent job.

A version of the belated information search model can be used to analyse this foraging behaviour. The bee first determines what nectar[23] is associated with the colour-scent combination. If this 'wage' is sufficiently large, namely, in excess of a critical number ξ, then the bee continues testing this flower learning the cost of the training required to extract 'w'. If this cost is sufficiently low, the bee makes the investment and harvests this species of flower.

Nesting behaviour

Suppose a queen bumblebee has just emerged from hibernation and is searching for a nest. The belated information model is relevant here. In fact, there may be two pieces of belated information. The bee discovers a site that looks acceptable, that is, its immediately observed characteristics are greater than a critical number x'_a. The bee checks it out and discovers the nest occupied by another bee. It checks x'_a, the critical number for occupied sites and the nest is still acceptable. Thus, it fights. If it wins, it stays and if it loses, it looks elsewhere. Suppose it wins. Now it gives the site a thorough look. If it remains acceptable, it stays; if a defect is revealed, it leaves and looks elsewhere. This can be formalized by slightly extending the belated model.

The cognitive architecture of bumblebees

The cognitive architecture of bumblebees was studied ingeniously by Real (1991a). Experiments with enclosed colonies of bumblebees, constrained to forage on artificial flowers imply that the cognitive architecture of bumblebees is efficiently constructed to consume in an efficient manner the floral resources from spatially designed environments, where there are recognized limits on memory and neuronal information processing.

Real (1991a) chose bumblebees for his experimental organism because they possess properties that facilitate investigations of how the decision-making process evolves. The worker bee tends to specialize almost completely in a single task or job, namely, finding and harvesting nectar and pollen for the colony. Being sterile they do not search for mates. They are designed to be almost invulnerable to predators and they do not exchange information with other bees about resource location. Heinrich conjectures that these information exchanges would lead to less productive search. The colony's reproductive success relies on the foraging ability of the worker bee which thereby affects future genetic composition. Real (1991a) concludes that 'the bumblebee is an autonomous agent engaged solely in one important activity of obvious evolutionary significance'.

Real's experiments show that bees are risk averse in fair gambles. By increasing the mean return of the more variable flowers, he induced the bees to switch to the more risky patch. A plot of mean-variance combinations generating indifferent foraging (50 per cent constant and 50 per cent variable) displayed a significant positive linear relation. Thus, increased variability in floral reward can be offset by increasing the mean reward. This type of trade-off between mean and variance is compatible with the Markowitz portfolio analysis. Real also relates bumblebee behaviour to biomechanical principles.

He measures subjectivity bias in bumblebees. A clever experiment showed that bees over-represent events that are common, whereas rare events are under-represented. This is exactly opposite of the results obtained for human subjects when they assess probabilities. Real attributes these results to short-term computational rules and/or truncated sampling. Such short-term rules may be adaptive when organisms are subject to memory or conceptual constraints and other cognitive limitations. Then, misperception is adaptive. Tversky and Kahneman (1974) believe these perceptual biases may be caused by the use of heuristic 'rules of thumb' for complex decision processes. Real observes: 'what is adaptive heuristic for one species in a specific environment may not be adaptive for another species in a different environment' (1991a).

Sexual selection and a sequential search for mates by female sticklebacks

Despite the absence, by and large, of man, the book [*Mate Choice*, edited by P. Bateson (1983)] certainly cannot be read without thought of him (and her). Or indeed without noticing the busy trade in terms and ideas between, on the one hand, the exciting, agonizing world we all know so well from the inside and, on the other, the parody world of animals that we can observe a little more objectively – a world of nest and plume and song and tiny combat. How seriously one takes the correspondence to human behaviour depends greatly on temperament, but it can be said that the more animals are studied the more human their problems and reactions seem.

(Hamilton 1983)

Sexual selection: Darwin's theory

In his first paragraph of the monograph *Sexual Selection*, Andersson (1994) states the major problems that provided the impetus for Darwin's theory of sexual selection (Darwin 1859, 1871). They are: Why are males and females so different in appearance? What are the selective pressures behind sex differences in size, shape, coloration and behaviour? And, most puzzling, how do extravagant male traits evolve, such as bright colours, huge feather plumes or fins, and other conspicuous male attributes that can hardly improve survival?

Darwin (1871) maintained that sexual selection was the consequence of the differences in reproductive success flowing from the competition for mates. Sexual reproduction is essential to sexual selection, where the former entails the combination of genetic material from two parents. Different sexes are not required, but the usual outcomes of sexual selection in plants and animals depend on the existence of two different sexes with their definitive gametes: large eggs produced by females and small, mobile sperm by males. Andersson notes that this anisogamy – two gametes of different size – is crucial to the evolution of sex differences in both behaviour and morphology. He also observes that explanations for anisogamy are easier to come by than explanations of sex. Apparently, sexual reproduction occurred before anisogamy. Anisogamy then followed from two distinct selective pressures. The first was for larger zygotes, improving their survival, while the second was for more gametes. These opposing forces were reconciled by the evolution of two different sexes: males producing many small gametes, while females produced only a few large gametes

A definitive relationship between zygote size and survival, anisogamy is specified by the evolutionary, stable strategy.[24]

This simple difference between size and number of gametes gave rise to sexual conflict within and between the sexes. Males with their abundance of sperm seek to mate with as many females as possible. Females, the other side of the coin, with larger and fewer eggs will seek to protect each of these investments by assiduous choice of a male partner. Andersson (1994) concludes that: 'the nature and consequences of competition over mates is the subject matter of the theory of sexual selection'.

Conspicuous male traits posed a major problem for Darwin's theory of evolution by natural selection. These traits seem to reduce survival and should not be favoured by natural selection. Darwin resolved this tension by distinguishing between sexual and other natural selection. Andersson (1994) summarizes the resolution:

Male ornaments, according to Darwin, evolve through sexual selection by female choice of mate, and male weapons evolve through sexual selection by contests over females.... Note that mate choice by one sex can suffice for there to be competition over mates in the other sex, even if there are no aggressive interactions.... Darwin's distinction between sexual and other natural selection is often useful; the evolutionary effects of competition over mates often differ in remarkable ways from those of other natural selection.[25]

Andersson defines competition as follows:

Competition occurs whenever the use of a resource (in this case, mates) by one individual makes the resource harder to come by for others. This is so whether or not the rivals meet in actual contests.... Mate choice by one sex therefore usually implies (indirect) competition over mates in the other sex, even if rivals never meet each other.

In short, mate choice is a mechanism of mating competition, which includes contests, scrambles and sperm competition.[26]

Andersson regards R.A. Fisher as Darwin's main disciple in constructing a sexual selection theory. If females mate with the 'most effective signaller', then they should have sons who are also effective signallers and this could lead to Fisher's runaway process.

Andersson makes a pregnant appraisal of sequential search as a tactic for mate choice. The most favourable tactic depends on the variation among males and *the cost of search for females*.[27]

Fisher's runaway process

Fisher (1930) put forward the following notion: 'A sexual preference of a particular kind may confer a selective advantage, and therefore become established in the species'. Andersson describes this as a two-step process. Suppose males with above-average tail length have a 'slight survival advantage'. Those females with preferences for long tails will mate accordingly and have sons with high survival. Thus alleles coding for longer tails in males will spread together with alleles associated with female preferences for long-tailed males. As this process continues a new effect is manifest:

> males with long tails are favoured not only by better survival, but also by higher mating success as the preference for long tails spreads among females. The higher mating success of long-tailed males helps carry the associated alleles for the long tail and the female preferences to yet higher frequency, and a feedback 'runaway process' develops at accelerating pace.

The process reaches an equilibrium when the high mortality of long tails balances the mating advantage. Andersson concludes: 'Fisher (1930) provided the capstone for Darwin's theory of sexual selection and made it a coherent if untested explanation for the evolution of secondary sex ornaments by mate choice.'

The handicap principle was developed by Zahavi (1975, 1977) and according to Andersson has its source in George Williams' explanation of Fisher's indicator mechanism:

> It is to the female's advantage to be able to pick the most fit male available for fathering her brood. Unusually fit fathers tend to have unusually fit offspring. One of the functions of courtship would be the advertisement, by a male, of how fit he is. A male whose general health and nutrition enables him to indulge in full development of secondary sexual characters, especially courtship behaviour, is likely to be reasonably fit genetically.... In submitting only to a male with such signs of fitness a female would probably be aiding the survival of her own genes.
>
> (Williams 1966: 184)

Thus was born the handicap principle, whose validity was doubted by Williams himself.

Hamilton–Zuk and mate choice in sticklebacks

The two papers by Grafen (1990a, b) contain rigorous proofs of the validity of the Zahavi handicap principle. Grafen sees little overlap between signalling in biology and signalling in economics. The Hamilton–Zuk hypothesis is a version of the handicap principle, which has received much attention. It is based on host–parasite cycles and maintains that genetic cycles of fluctuating resistance in hosts, and virulence in parasites, achieves heritability of resistance in hosts. The level of resistance appears in secondary sex traits like bright colours that can be used as a signal in mate choice. If these co-evolutionary cycles are rare, parasites and pathogens may still validate the Hamilton–Zuk hypothesis, that is, females select healthy fathers when they choose ornamented males.

To test whether female sticklebacks prefer brighter males, Milinski and Bakker (1990) arranged tanks starting with the lowest colour ranked male 1 and ending with the brightest ranked male 24. Females showed a significant preference for brighter males and therefore preferred the healthier males. These results support the Hamilton–Zuk hypothesis. Milinski and Bakker used the simple sequential search model. They compared it with Stigler's fixed-sample size model and found that when the appropriate costs were included, sequential search was preferred. When costs of search are increased, female sticklebacks become less selective, as predicted. Milinski (2001) notes that both theories of sexual selection and economic choice are used to develop optimal strategies. Their experiments support the Hamilton–Zuk hypothesis as well as the theory of sequential search.[28]

In an excellent two-part survey, Real (1990a, 1991b) applies one-sided and two-sided (equilibrium) sequential search models to the choice of a mate by an animal or insect. He begins with the observation that sexual selection has been an important research topic in evolutionary biology since Darwin emphasized that mate choice is advantageous to those individuals who have been preferred by natural selection. Clearly, when specific individuals are more attractive as potential mates, the characteristics associated with this preference become more prominent in the overall population. Real cites Wittenberger to support his contention that the decisive problem of processing information in mate choice remains an important topic of empirical and theoretical study.

> Mate choice may not be as simple a process as many authors seem to imply. It may entail a series of tactical choices during both information-gathering and decision-making phases. Choosing individuals must acquire information about one or more prospective mates before they make any choices, and they can employ any of several tactics to that end.... The information-gathering and decision-making processes involved in mate choice have not been addressed from this perspective.
>
> (Wittenberger 1983: 436)

Hamilton (1983) in his review of the Bateson volume, is more specific:

> What have theorists been doing while the new surge of data rolls in? Three interlinked themes, well-represented in the book, may be mentioned briefly. First, is there any *real* female choice? Second, granted choice, does R.A. Fisher's 'runaway' process of sexual selection really run; and does it underlie the exaggerated and the ornate in animal display to the extent that he supposed? Third, whether or not there exist genes subject to largely *arbitrary* preferences,... are females looking also for *utilitarian* 'good genes' for their offspring – genes concerned with non-sexual challenges in the battle for life?...

In 1975, Zahavi also suggested a persistent utilitarian function for sexual selection and tied it in with a seemingly perverse notion that selectors are looking for physical handicaps that prove the potential mate's vigour. This idea gets short shrift in the book.... Although it was carelessly presented, *I believe that Zahavi's general notion is sustainable.... While not denying the potential for arbitrariness and exaggeration latent in gene-inspired choosing, utilitarian 'good genes' as the original or ultimate objective of choice surely must exist.*

(italics added)

Finally, Hamilton (ibid.) observes, 'What I did *not* still find ... was reference to the considerable statistical literature on stopping rules in sequential searches ... not even in Parker's original and useful chapter on mating decisions.'

The survey by Real is a belated response to this last comment by Hamilton. Real (1990a) addresses three problems associated with male mate choice: Given a distribution of mate qualities and a sequence of encounters with potential mates, how should the unmated select mates and build preferences? Second, can rules be discovered which determine mate selection? And third, how do the quality distribution (and changes therein) and search cost affect mate selection? These problems are translated in four queries. How to find the best mate? How long should one search for the best? Is there a threshold value of mate quality? What are the consequences of increased uncertainty and increased cost?

Previous models of search in behavioural ecology include the important papers by Janetos and Cole (1981) and Parker (1978). However, neither of them posed the optimal stopping problem described by Hamilton and derived by Real in an ecological setting.

Real considers the Stigler fixed-sample size model. Recall that the expected value of W_n^* maximum mate quality when n is the fixed sample size

$$E[W_n^*] = n\int_\infty^0 wf(w)F(w)^{n-1}dw.$$

The optimal number of mates n^* is the largest n such at

$$\Delta(n) \geq c,$$

where c are the sampling costs.[29]

Real compares the Stigler result with that of sequential search. He assumes that active (searching) individuals discover passive (searching) mates one at a time and accept the current prospect if and only if $W \geq w^*$,[30] where w^* is the solution to:

$$c = H(w^*) = \int_\infty^{w^*} (w - w^*)dF(w).$$

Real gives a biological interpretation to this equation. The threshold value of W, w^*, is selected so that the cost of searching (c) equals the expected fitness gain from observing one more passive (non-searching) mate.

Real discovers that the sequential rule dominates Stigler's best-of-n rule for every $c > 0$. This is exactly opposite to the result of Janetos (1980), who assumes $c = 0$. Real notes that the preference for best-of-n over sequential search is an artefact of costless search.

Real notes that four conditions when altered, lead to a decrease in threshold mate quality. These are: finite time horizon, increasing search costs with time, systematic search and adaptive search. Adaptive search for sequential models was developed by Rothschild (1974), which is not cited by Real.

In making a transition to the situation in which both mates are active searchers, several comments are in order:

i   Hammerstein and Parker (1987) explicitly consider the interaction between searching males and females as an evolutionary game and have designed evolutionary stable strategies (ESS) for both sexes.

ii McNamara *et al.* (2001) note that the assumption of a non-searching male, which gives rise to the sequential search threshold policy, is not realistic. Assuming interactions among potential mates (males and females) requires a game theoretic approach.[31] If there also is a time cost of searching, the best threshold for one sex depends on the threshold chosen by the other. Thus, even if mates are not removed from the population, game theory is required. McNamara and Collins (1990) devise the general solution for the ESS. This solution entails assortative mating by class and has had an important influence on economics, where Burdett and Coles (1998, 1999), Smith (1983), Bloch and Ryder (2000), among others cite this valuable article.[32]

Real (1991b) assumes that males require a minimum fitness Y in females. Then, the expected discounted fitness to males is

$$\Gamma(y) = \int_y^x (x - w)dM(x) + \beta\Gamma(y^*)M(y),$$

where $M(y)$ is the probability that a discovered female is below the minimum acceptable fitness, and $\beta = (1 + r)^{-1}$. The optimal value of Y is the solution to

$$\Gamma(y^*) = \frac{(y^* - w)}{\beta}$$

Substitute (b) in (a) to yield

$$\Gamma(y^*) = \int_{y^*}^x (x - w)dM(x) + (y^* - w)M(y).$$

It follows from (*b*) and (*c*) that increases in male's adjusted fitness produce an increase in the minimum acceptable female fitness Y^*. Males with large fitness wait till a large fitness female is found, i.e. they display assortative mating by fitness.

Real (1991b) has an interesting application of Burdett and Judd (1983). Let *qk* be the probability of a female discovering *k* males during one search,

$$k = 1, 2, \ldots; \sum_{k=1}^{\infty} qK = 1.$$

Females have identical search costs *c*. The sequential search rule where the number of males observed during a single search is random, is:

$$c = \int_{W_c}^{x} (w - W_c)j(w)dw \tag{10.7}$$

where *j*(*w*) is the *p.d.f* for highest observed male fitness during a single search period. *F* is the *c.d.f* of male fitness, as

$$j(w) = \sum_{k=1}^{x} q_k[kf(w)F(w)^{k-1}], \text{ for any } w. \tag{10.8}$$

Substituting (10.7) into (10.8) gives the general search rule for 'noisy' search in terms of male fitness *f*(*w*):

$$c = \int_{W_c}^{x} \sum_{k=1}^{x} q_k k(w - W_c)f(w)F(w)^{k-1}dw$$

This equation can be used to calculate W_c for females.

The expected fitness to males given optimal behaviour is likewise restated to include this feature of female behaviour. Both of these 'corrected' search rules determine the male fitness equilibrium distribution. Assuming females have identical optimal preferences, Real includes their 'noisy' search in the males' expected net fitness function[33] giving

$$\pi(w) = \begin{cases} (x - w)\sum_{k=1}^{x} q_k \ kf(w)F(w)^{k-1}, & w \geq W_c \\ 0 & w < W_c \end{cases}$$

Applying (α) and (β) together yields an important implication: Given q_k and $c > 0$ are fixed, (i) for $q_1 = 1$, there is a unique equilibrium distribution for male fitness, where $w = W_c$; (ii) for $q_1 = 0$, there is a unique equilibrium for male fitness, with $w = x$; and (iii) for $0 < q_1 < 1$, there is a unique equilibrium distribution for male fitness and it is nondegenerate.

Real concludes his application of the Burdett–Judd results by observing that stable variation in male fitness occurs because there is uncertainty whether females searching for males will discover either one or more than one during each search. If females are certain to discover only one male at each search or more than one, then fixed point solutions occur. Real concludes: 'The major value of their approach is that it shows that equilibrium variation in male fitness can be obtained when all females have identical preferences.'

Bayesian search

With several recent exceptions,[34] most of the search models used to study mate choice have been non-adaptive. Clearly, learning while searching could be quite important in describing the actual behaviour of organisms. In the foraging section, several Bayesian models were described together with their important link with exchangeability and deFinetti's theorem.

Adaptive modelling also may be decisive in not only understanding mate choice, but also in obtaining a firmer grasp of honest advertising and the handicap principle. It is interesting that the signalling models and search models finally join hands in comprehending an extremely elusive phenomenon: the handicap principal.[35]

Lessons from the honeybee hive

Introduction

We have much to learn from the honeybee. The combined wisdom of Adam Smith, Charles Darwin, Norbert Wiener, F. Hayek and H. Simon is necessary to comprehend the decision making, organizational structure and vital information flows inherent in the smooth functioning of the honeybee society. There are striking lessons in the evolution of biological organizations that flow from the everyday behaviour of honeybees. Division of labour is a central feature. Seeley distinguishes four different kinds of labour specialization: forager, cleaner, nurse and food storer. Each honeybee engages in all four of these specialties at different periods in its life. These temporary modes of specialization are distinguished from the permanent specializations associated with other social organizations. Seeley surmises that permanent attachment to specialties by the members of a society or organization requires a relatively stable environment. A military organization has this kind of stability. Clearly a fluctuating milieu may render obsolete those rigid specialties that are unable to adjust to changes in demand for its services. The smaller the organization, the more vulnerable it is to this type of dynamic.

Adam Smith's famous pin factory is the foundation for the belief that division of labour in living systems is preferred by Darwinian selection. This preference is based on enhanced efficiency of special skills associated with special knowledge and/or special 'equipment' including morphology. The former is an investment in human capital by the individual whereas the latter is the 'long run' response of natural selection. Seeley emphasizes that *efficiency* is not the whole story. One must also recognize that the task performed has high *importance*: in the honeybee colony there are mechanisms that allocate individual bees to those tasks that have become significant.[36] Tofts and Frank (1992) recommend that labour in the hive be allocated according to the principle of 'foraging for work' which is based on three assumptions: (i) each worker actively searches for work and will switch to an adjacent job when the demand for its currently used specialty falls, (ii) tasks are concentrically arranged in the hive and (iii) the workers are born in the centre of the hive where their first job is located. These assumptions imply 'age polyethism', that is, central place of birth increases labour supply at the centre which shifts older workers to adjacent jobs, thereby augmenting labour supply at this job, etc. The effects percolate in this manner until they reach the last job zone where the oldest are employed and where they die.[37]

Seeley questions the first assumption of this model for honeybee behaviour. But even if it is correct, future studies should reveal that natural selection has constructed more elaborate mechanisms similar to those advocated by Tofts (1993). Seeley concludes that: 'many intriguing mysteries remain regarding the mechanisms by which honey bee colonies and other functionally organized groups achieve an effective division of labour. *Their elucidation is one of the fundamental problems of biology*' (italics added).

Another important aspect of the honeybee colony is a paucity of structural links among bees inside the hive. This has many interesting consequences. First, there is no nervous system connecting the bees in the hive. There are no synapses and indeed no neurons, although the bees themselves do have neurons and are sometimes regarded as analogous to neurons. Nevertheless, there is rapid communication among honeybees via chemical signals that connect them. These include the alarm pheromones coordinating defence responses and also the signals via the food that workers exchange. The food contains trophallaxis which notifies the honeybees about fluctuations in the protein content of their diet. This information seems to regulate pollen production.

This organizational feature is summarized by noting the profound differences in internal design between organizations with and without mobile subunits. In an important sense the honeybee is evolving into a system where each bee no longer resembles its solitary ancestor, but has merged into a connected component of the hive.

Information flows in the honeybee colony

In the honeybee colony information transfer among members is accomplished through a myriad of mechanisms that are diverse and subtle. Each bee has been made by natural selection so that it is responsive to essentially all useful information. Several of the extraordinarily diverse, incredible and opportunistic information transfer mechanisms include: recruitment dances of nest mates, the temperature of the nest interior, their hunger for protein (pollen), the hexagonal shape of the beeswax cell, the difficulty of unloading forage (the queuing effect), the scent of the queen and a host of others.

It is important to distinguish between signals and cues. Signals (which are actions or structures) were designed by natural selection to convey information. Cues also carry information, but were not made by natural selection for this purpose. An important lesson in the analysis of honeybee foraging is recognizing that cues are the major vehicle for the transfer of information. Three signals accompany honeybee foraging: the waggle dance, the tremble dance and the shaking signal. There are, however, numerous cues.

Natural selection favours cues over signals because they are ready and waiting, whereas a signal must evolve. Also, the process of group coordination depends on information flowing from the group to the individual. This flow is usually by cues. That is, group-level indicators which are used by individuals to guide their decision making are likely to be by-products of the joint action of the colony's members (cues) and not group-level structures that evolved for conveying information (signals).

Much of the information flow among bees is indirect. It occurs via some aspect of the shared environment. Almost all of this indirect flow is done by cues rather than signals. Seeley conjectures that the opportunism of natural selection suggests that the researcher must be alert to subtle forms of communication in colonies and that 'this lesson probably applies to the communication networks inside living systems at all levels of biological organization'.

With respect to the high economy of communication, Seeley suggests that the intensity of communication within colonies is less than that within organisms and cells. The reason is opportunity costs, that is, time spent in communication could have been spent foraging. Thus there is a trade-off between the two activities which restricts communication to an efficient level. This type of trade-off is present in the multiprocessor computer where computation time is restricted by communication. It would appear that there is a similar computation–communication trade-off in living systems.

The role of negative feedback

Negative feedback, which was first noted by Adam Smith and, of course, fine-tuned by Norbert Wiener, is extremely important in the honeybee's foraging because there can be rapid and extreme fluctuations in external supply and/or internal demand for the three forage commodities: nectar, pollen and water. Negative feedback conveys information to the colony's foragers that is used to eliminate mismatches between demand and supply. This feedback information is, of course, a proxy for the prices that are used to modify demand and supply in a competitive economy. In and of itself, the information used in lieu of prices is seemingly inconsequential like the search time during unloading used by water collectors. Why have bees evolved feedback loops based on control variables that are intrinsically unimportant? Seeley's answer is: 'Almost certainly because these variables are far more easily sensed than the underlying variables of supply and demand, yet they provide all the information that is needed to correct a mismatch between supply and demand.'

Coordination without central planning

A remarkable aspect of the honeybee colony is the extent to which it approximates Adam Smith's laissez-faire economy. The actions of the entire bee colony are coordinated by the prices implicit in the signals and cues. Neither the queen bee nor any distinguished group of bees has any effect on the coordination of the bee's decisions. Each bee acquires all the information it needs for efficient foraging from the dance hall and other subtle and ingenious sources of 'price' information. It is a decentralized economy par excellence, similar, but in many ways superior, to the human competitive market economics. The interaction of various forms of division of labour, of exchange in the pollen and nectar marketplace and of the dissemination of information primarily in the dance hall produces a spontaneous order. Two advantages of this order of the market, or catallaxy, are prominent. The knowledge and information used belongs to all of the actors in this society. The goals of this order are those of the individual honeybees.[38]

Natural selection combines with a competitive market to make a society that can cope with environmental uncertainties to yield a stable order which maximizes the welfare of each individual bee, where the bee's welfare is given by its kinship dominated utility function which equates its welfare to that of the colony.

An employed forager's advertisements conveyed in the dance hall may not be honest in which case the audience of unemployed foragers is misled. Any dishonest dancing should be eliminated by natural selection. If a mutation occurred causing dancers to fabricate by lying about the desirability of its discovered flower patch, the economic well-being of the colony would decline, as would its reproductive success. In this way dissembling would be eliminated.

Dance floor signals are honest!

> This 'open market' policy toward sources of information means that a colony can flexibly respond to changing conditions outside the hive, allocating foraging effort toward new opportunities whenever they arise. This openness and flexibility is illustrated by the fact that even though every food source is advertised at first by just one forager ... if a source offers a plentiful supply of high desirable forage, eventually it will become massively advertised in the hive and then it will become a major focus of the colony's foraging.
>
> (Seeley 1995)

Seeley answers his basic question: Why is there no central planning within a honeybee colony? Smith and Hayek have answered this question in economic terms. Seeley augments their response by implicating Darwin's natural selection – natural selection has devised elegant mechanisms whereby the members of a honeybee colony can solve the daunting forager allocation problem without assembling in one mind all the relevant information that is in fact dispersed among all the bees in her hive.

The wisdom of the hive

The analysis of the beehive as presented in Seeley (1995) contains almost the entire repertoire of Economics 101 and the Economics of Information. There is search for food, nectar, pollen and water; specialization and division of labour among the bees, dances which advertise the location of food supplies and attractive nests (the house hunting problem), coordination of nectar collection and nectar processing, the regulation and construction of symmetric honeycombs. All of these activities are in accord with economic design, *and* there are only honest signals. Unemployed foragers use honest signals transmitted by dancing foragers to locate a food source, thereby limiting bouts of unemployment, while prices do not explicitly appear there are almost perfect substitutes for them. For nectar and water, the analogue of price is the time expended searching in the hive for bees able to take the load of nectar or water. A short (long) search is like a high (low) price and production is correspondingly increased (decreased). For pollen, the price is represented by the hunger for protein felt by each forager. The greater the hunger the higher the price of pollen and the more likely foragers will switch from water and nectar to pollen. Seeley observes: 'The essential thing is that each of these three indicators reliably rises and falls in accordance with changes in the supply–demand ratio of its corresponding material, hence each one provides the same information as does price.'

There is also an absence of central planning in the hive. Why is this? The amount of information required to control the bee colony's food allocations is too large and ever-changing to be comprehended by a central planning authority. *A miracle of the hive is that the bees have been equipped* by natural selection with elegant processes such that they themselves solve the complex forager allocation problem. Seeley's perceptive answer to the absence of a central foraging plan is: 'This question is best answered, I believe, by noting the essence of the problem a colony must solve in allocating its foragers among food sources: *adaptation to countless changes in the particular circumstances of time and place*' (ibid., italics added). The elementary information and communication systems possessed by the honeybees can only resolve the foraging allocation problem by mimicking the price system of a competitive society. It is astounding that the response of each foraging bee to the cues and honest signals represented by dances, hunger pangs, etc. provides a decentralized information system comparable to the price system of a Smithian economy.

It should be emphasized that the hive is an extraordinary adaptive, cooperative system made possible by Hamilton's kinship theory and natural selection. Adverse selection and moral hazard are absent from the hive. All signals are honest.[39]

In the conclusion of his book, Seeley (1995) emphasizes that

> probably few biologists recognize that evolution has ... endowed certain animal societies with impressive abilities and has fashioned elaborate mechanisms of communication and control inside these societies to produce their

remarkable group-level skills ... it is only rather recently that we have ha
both the *conceptual framework* (Hull and Dawkins on replicators and inter
actors) and the empirical findings (such as those in this book) to demon
strate the reality of extremely rich functional organization at the group leve

A nice summary of this important book is contained in the following conclud
ing paragraph:

> In 1978, no one knew that a colony can *thoroughly monitor a vast regio*
> *around the hive for food sources*, nimbly *redistribute its foragers within a*
> *afternoon*, fine-tune its nectar processing *to match* its nectar collecting
> effect cross inhibition between different forager groups *to boost its respons*
> *differential between food sources*, precisely regulate its pollen intake in rela
> tion to its ratio of *internal supply and demand*, and limit the *expensive proc*
> *ess of comb building* to times of critical need for additional storage space
> Moreover, we lacked precise knowledge regarding many of the bee-leve
> actions underlying such colony-level abilities, including the performance o
> *tremble dances to reallocate labour, the transfer of proteinaceous food fror*
> *nurses to foragers to regulate pollen collection, the use of search time t*
> *assess supply/demand relations, and the use of friendly competition on th*
> *dance floor to allocate foragers among flower patches.* Today, in contras
> we easily see a honeybee colony as a sophisticated, group-level vehicle o
> gene survival, and we know that natural selection has equipped it with
> wealth of ingenious mechanisms for successful group functioning. It seem
> likely that future studies of social physiology, in honeybees and other socia
> animals, will further substantiate the view that *animal societies, like cell*
> *and organisms, can possess a high level of functional organization.*
>
> (ibid., italics added

It is interesting that Seeley's discoveries are compatible with the theories o
Hayek and Simon. The exchanges that take place almost continuously amon
bees and their environment in providing essential information for the well-bein
of the individual bee and the hive corresponds to Hayek's repeated emphasis o
the game of catallaxy (from the Greek word for bartering or exchanging
throughout his writings. Hayek notes that in addition to meaning exchanging thi
word, catallaxy, also meant to convert an enemy into a friend. It is catallax
which explains how markets operate. Hayek also observes that the market proc
ess is similar to a game of skill in a stochastic environment. Simon, on the othe
hand, is cited in Seeley's second paragraph where he presents Simon's watch
maker example which describes how complex assemblies emerge fron
sequences of stable sub-assemblies. Seeley maintains that: this Simon-like prin
ciple of constructing complexity through 'stratified stability' is almost surel
applicable to the evolution of life. Seeley points to the contributions of Hu
(1980, 1988) and Dawkins (1982).

Hamiltonian altruism and the wisdom of the hive

We now turn to the altruism of honeybees and its study by T.D. Seeley[40] which rely on the seminal studies of altruism by W. Hamilton.[41]

It is interesting to reflect on Hamilton's pioneering studies. We have just seen his work with Zuk on Fisher's indicator theory. It should also be noted that in his review of *Mate Choice* edited by Bateson (1983), he called for the use of optimal sequential search models in the study of mate selection. His 1964 articles linked altruism with genetic relatedness and made the work of Seeley and many others much more incisive. He then combined with Axelrod to show how repeated games give rise to an artificial (as opposed to genetic) relatedness and once again stimulated a huge research effort in repeated games. Thus, he moved from Darwin's theory of sexual selection to Fisher's indicator theory, to genetic justification for altruism, to a game theoretic extension of altruism to individuals who see each other repeatedly, but are not related genetically.

Relatedness and cooperative behaviour among honeybees

Honeybees are eusocial insects. Dugatkin remarks that there is some debate over the current definition of 'eusocial'. Let us use the definition by Holldobler and Wilson (1990) cited in Dugatkin (1997: 638). Those species are eusocial when they display

> cooperation in caring for the young; reproductive division of labour, with more or less sterile individuals working on behalf of individuals engaged in reproduction; and overlap of at least two generations of life stages capable of contributing to colony labour.

Hamilton's inclusive fitness theory (1963, 1964a, b) is 'the most famous theory explaining the evolution of eusociality in insects' (Dugatkin 1997).

This theory is summarized by Hamilton (cited in Dugatkin 1997):

> The social behaviour of a species evolves in such a way that in each distinct behaviour-evoking situation the individual will see to value his neighbour's fitness against his own according to the coefficients of relatedness appropriate to that situation.

Hamilton constructed formal genetic models which predict that individuals will be cooperative when interacting with relatives, the reason being that relatives are likely to share genes. Thus, helping a relative promotes the common genes. Maynard Smith (1995) observes that

> The mathematical treatment is difficult but it is easy to see that the more closely are the members of a (colony) related, the greater the risk an individual will run to confer a given advantage to the other members of the (colony). If the (colony) is merely a random sample of the whole population, selection will not favour the running of any risk at all.

Maynard Smith suggested the term kin selection for the Hamiltonian altruistic process. Haldane understood this process as is clear from his remark that he would surrender his life for two brothers *or* eight cousins. Fisher also was aware of Hamilton's altruism, but, of course, didn't work out the mathematics.

Maynard Smith relates the following story told by Hamilton.

> Social life has been evolved on at least four separate occasions by insects – by ants, bees, wasps, and termites. The first three of these four groups belong to the same insect order, the hymenoptera. What features of the hymenoptera have predisposed them to evolve societies? Hamilton suggests that the feature in question is their 'haploid-diploid' genetic mechanism. Among the hymenoptera, solitary or social, males develop from unfertilized eggs, and so are haploid (i.e., have only a single set of chromosomes); females develop from fertilized eggs and are diploid.... A female of a haploid-diploid species has ¾ of her genes in common with her sisters but only ½ of her genes in common with her daughters, whereas in a normal diploid species she has ½ of her genes in common with both her sisters and her daughters. Thus a female hymenoptera does more to preserve her own genes if she stays at home and looks after her sisters than if she goes out and starts a family on her own.

The simple explanation to what was regarded as a deep mystery deserves some more elaboration. Let us consider the social structure of a honeybee colony as presented in Seeley (1985).

A honeybee colony is a matriarchal family, with one long-lived female, the queen bee, who is the mother of the approximately 30,000 bees comprising a typical colony. Most of the queen's children (~95 per cent) are worker bees. These daughters never lay eggs while their mother is alive. They 'stay at home' and help their mother in her enormous reproductive task. Approximately 5 per cent of the queen's children do develop into queens and drones. A simple condition allows the queen to control the sex of her children. Males develop from unfertilized eggs and are haploid; females develop from fertilized eggs and are diploid. The diet during the first three days of life determines whether a fertilized egg becomes a worker or a queen. The essential difference is seemingly the concentration of hexose sugar in the diet during these crucial three days.

Not all bees in the colony share the same father. The average number of males inseminating the queen ranges between seven and 17. The value of multiple insemination to the queen is the increased viability of the colony. The key observation is that the females (workers and queens) are not all full sisters. They comprise 'several patrileal groups with females in the same group related as full sisters ($r = 0.75$) and females in different groups related as half sisters ($r = 0.25$)'. See Figure 3.1 in Seeley (1985).

We now present Hamiltonian kin selection in terms of benefit–cost ratios. Altruism is beneficial for an individual if $B/C > r_{A_Y}/r_{B_Y}$, where B and C are the benefits to the beneficiary and the cost to the altruist, and r_{A_Y} and r_{B_Y} are the probabilities of Ego having a gene in common with the young of the altruist (A) or with the young of the beneficiary (B). Seeley notes that Ego can be A or B or a relative of A or B. In honeybees, the queen is the beneficiary of the altruism of her worker-daughters.

Thus from the queen's perspective, and $r_{A_Y} = 0.25$ and $r_{B_Y} = 0.50$ so the threshold benefit: cost ratio is 0.50. Altruism by a queen's daughters is advantageous to the queen so long as her daughters are at least 50 per cent as efficient helping their mother produce offspring (reproductives) as they are in producing their own offspring.

Seeley (1985) shows that this threshold is almost surely exceeded. The threshold B/C ratio for worker altruism from the workers perspective has a numerator equal to 0.5 (Ego is the altruist). The denominator r_{B_Y} is more complicated, depending on how many males inseminated the queen, the distribution of paternities among these males, and the sex ratio of the reproductive offspring. Given that there is no inbreeding, the average relatedness of a worker to a female offspring of her mother is (r_{WF})

$$r_{WF} = \frac{1}{2}\left(\frac{1}{2} + \sum_{i=1}^{n} \hat{f}_i^2\right),$$

assuming the queen mates with n males with f_i the proportion of her progeny due to the ith male. If males contribute equally r_{WF} achieves its lowest value,

$$r_{WF} = \frac{1}{2}\left(\frac{1}{2} + \frac{1}{n}\right).$$

The relatedness of a worker to her mother's male offspring (males arise from unfertilized eggs) is always 0.25.

The last parameter for calculating r_{B_Y} is the ratio of investment between female (queens) and male offspring. Seeley observes that the workers have probably been selected to favour investing the fraction $(n + 2)/(2n + 2)$ of reproductive effort in females and $n/(2n + 2)$ of this effort in males, where n is the number of inseminators. Thus, we obtain

$$r_{B_Y} = \frac{1}{2}\left(\frac{1}{2} + \frac{1}{n}\right)\left(\frac{n+2}{2n+2}\right) + \frac{1}{4}\left(\frac{n}{2n+2}\right) = \frac{n^2 + 2n + 2}{4(n+1)(n)}.$$

Various values of r_{B_Y} is plotted as a function of n. For $n = 10$, $r_{B_Y} \geq 0.28$. Hence, the threshold benefit–cost ratio for worker altruism with the queen as beneficiary is at most

$$\frac{0.50}{0.28} = 1.8,$$

that is, altruism by a worker honeybee to be favoured by natural selection requires that a worker be about twice as efficient in rearing the queen's children as the worker's own.

Honeybee colonies as superorganisms

The notion of the honeybee colony as a single large organism goes back at least to Mandeville and no doubt was entertained by the Greek philosophers. This idea is expressed formally by Darwin in *On the Origin of Species* (1859). Seeley (1989: 546–8) has a modern interpretation:

> it is perhaps not surprising that even in most advanced insect societies such as colonies of ... honeybees, the differentiation and integration of a society's members have not reached the point at which each member's original nature has been erased. A colony of honeybees ... functions as an integrated whole and its members cannot survive on their own, yet individual honeybees are still physically independent and closely resemble in physiology and morphology the solitary bees from which they evolved. In a colony of honeybees two levels of biological organization – organism and superorganism – co-exist with equal prominence. The dual nature of such societies provides us with a special window on the evolution of biological organizations, through which we can see how natural selection has taken thousands of organisms that were built for solitary life, and merged them into a superorganism.... It seems correct to classify a group of organisms as a superorganism when the organisms form a cooperative unit to propagate their genes just as we classify a group of cells as an organism when the cells form a cooperative unit to propagate their genes.

Dugatkin (1997) studies the honeybee colony as a superorganism from three perspectives: foraging, anti-predator behaviour and thermo-regulation. If these behaviours display superorganism properties, selection among colonies – group selection – may be a powerful force in the evolution of cooperation in honeybee colonies. We concentrate on Dugatkin's evaluation of foraging behaviour.

Seeley and his colleagues have studied intensively how a honeybee colony functions as a superorganism from a foraging perspective.

Clearly, the 'waggle dance' transmits information among bees searching for food. This particular group behaviour is an extraordinary information transmission mechanism in that it entails a coded dance language which can be performed by those worker bees who have completed successful searches and now wish to inform their mates regarding the quality and location of this fuel source. Their mates, of course, must be able to translate the dance into quality and location information and compare it with information that is being simultaneously delivered by several dancing bees. An analogy with the neuronal behaviour of searchers who have just encountered a food source may be enlightening. Perception by a neuronal group search for a food source, the discovery of the source by perceptive neurons, the comparison of this food source with other possible sources with higher quality and less risk is made by neuronal dances between the memory and perception. A decision flows from an evaluation of these dances.

To push this a little further, it seems reasonable to suppose that a seasoned hunter will have constructed neuronal paths or networks such that the current information discovered by perception is immediately direct to the appropriate network which leads to the most favourable decision. If the search information is not comparable to an existing perceptual network, then a new network can be constructed and compared with those pertinent networks in the memory.

If there are several hunters searching for food, they may all defer to the group leader whose past performance is the reason for his leadership position. His perception, memory and decision-making success rate have been superior in the past. If each is equally adept, then a peaceful decision is made via a conversation, which is analogous to the actions of several dancing honeybees.

In the evolution of life, learning how each transition to a higher level of biological organization is a difficult enterprise. This is especially true of the early transitions of prokaryotic cells (3.5 billion years ago) and eukaryotic cells (1.3 billion years ago). This learning for superorganisms like the honeybee colony is less difficult. They appeared 100 million years ago and continue to be in transition. A honeybee colony is composed of an integrated group of bees whose members cannot survive in isolation. Nevertheless, individual honeybees are independent and bear a striking similarity to their ancestors, the solitary bees. In a honeybee colony both the organism and superorganism survive together. Their dual nature gives biologists a window on the evolution of biological organizations. Through this window biologists can observe how natural selection takes thousands of individual honeybees, that were initially designed for solitary life, and converts them via a host of ingenious transformations like dancing, nursing and building into an informationally coherent superorganism. This coherence or coordination is achieved without centralized decision making.

Each honeybee circulates in the hive and collects information about the colony's demands, and adjusts its supply accordingly. Lindauer (1952) followed individual workers within a glass-enclosed hive and noted the behaviour of a seven-day-old bee over a typical 30-minute period: 'patrolling, shaping comb, patrolling, feeding young brood, cleaning cells, patrolling, shaping comb, eating pollen, resting, patrolling, shaping comb. The task performed at any given moment presumably depends upon the specific labour need sensed by the bee'.

Swift response to local demands is a singular benefit of decentralized control. But Seeley conjectures that a better explanation of decentralization is: 'it is the best the bees can do given the limited communication processes that have developed through evolution'.

What is clear is that decentralized control is feasible because natural selection has constructed the honeybee so that it is extraordinarily adept both at sensing any stimulus that contains useful information and at generating signals that contain useful information.

Seeley observes that:

> within colonies there are various tappings, tuggings, shakings, buzzings strokings, wagglings, crossing of antennae, and puffings and streakings of chemicals, all of which seem to be communication signals. The result is that within a honeybee colony there exists an astonishingly intricate web of information pathways, the full magnitude of which is still only dimly perceived.

While they are more conspicuous and clearly represent little miracles, Seeley predicts that the subtle communication mechanisms of cues and the shared environment will reveal themselves to have greater informational import than the more spectacular signals like dancing.

Queuing as a source of information in the bee hive

Lindauer (1948) showed that when the rate at which honeybees collect nectar is high, foragers specialize in high energy sources. Seeley and Towne (1989) uncovered unambiguous evidence that foragers recruited more bees to search for food when the colony's food supplies were low. This increased recruitment was achieved via the foragers' dance patterns upon arrival at the hive. Seeley and Towne (1989) also presented an ingenious explanation of *how* the colony responds to changes in food supply. Using a variety of clever experiments they showed that foragers assess colony-level food supplies by the waiting time incurred to transfer their harvests to 'food storer' bees. This queuing explanation is especially interesting in that there is a close connection between the Gittins index and queuing. Dugatkin (1997) cites Seeley and Towne:[42]

> This hypothesis also neatly explains how nectar foragers might sense a change in their colony's nutritional status due to a change in the colony's rate of nectar intake, since it is known that as a colony's intake rate increases, the food storers become busier and busier and the nectar foragers experience increasing difficulty of unloading.

The honeybee's neural architecture

In their recent book and article, LaCerra and Bingham (2002, 1998) present a cogent and market-driven explanation of the neural architecture of honeybees. They note that the essence of behavioural intelligence systems is the ability to predict the future. The environment in which honeybees operate is a biological marketplace whose major concern is pollination. The bees are one of several classes of trader which, in addition to bees, include butterflies and other insects, flowers, hummingbirds and so on. These traders exchange commodities in this fluctuating marketplace. The two main commodities are pollen and nectar. The birds and bees provide a service to the flowers in carrying their genetic information contained in the pollen to other locations. They receive nectar from the flowers for providing this service. Both the nectar and the pollen are consumed by the bees.

LaCerra and Bingham observe that 'bees learn to associate the location, shape, symmetry, colour, and scent of flowers with the experience of getting ... the nectar (the rewards)'.

> This critical information is stored as representational forms which are then used in their next trip from the hive. In coping with uncertainty, the bees learn rapidly as the foraging landscape changes. The bee has evolved an integrated neuronal system that guides foraging behaviour. One part of this system is instinctual, reflecting the regularities of the foraging problem.... It (also) has a rudimentary cortex – a swatch of functionally plastic neural tissue – that can encode critical information ... about ... novel features of the environment.

There are several aspects of the bee's cognitive architecture that are emphasized. Each bee is confronted with a unique sequence of events as it adapts its marketing (exchange) behaviour using a cost–benefit calculus. The behaviour of the bee is not according to a fixed plan represented in an inherited neural endowment. Instead, the bee is a unique subjective entity whose mental representations reflect its very own idiosyncratic experience. Thus adaptive, market behaviour constructs a self associated with each bee. These same Darwinian, Smithian impulses are also at work in each human being. Consequently, every human extracts information from its fluctuating, uncertain market environment and makes a self that is a subjective entity also abiding by a cost–benefit calculus.

As we will see in the next section of the chapter, there are two competing models describing these phenomena. The first assumes that in early life a lavish array of neuronal networks are generated. From this extravagant number of mazes early experience selects those that correspond to the needs of the organism. Those networks not used wither away. Such a process, albeit *much* more sophisticated is associated with Edelman, Changeux and others. The other theory advanced by LaCerra and Bingham is characterized as follows:

> The temporally dynamic, individually specific cost–benefit analysis that any given social behavioural decision entails renders each information-processing problem an essentially novel and ephemeral construction, not an evolutionary static social adaptive problem that might be captured by selection processes. The critical issue for evolutionary behavioural scientists,[43] then, concerns the nature of the neural information-processing substrate capable of solving social survival and reproductive problems given the extent of fluctuation in the biological market environment and one's immediate position within it. The neuroscientific literature suggests that the plastic properties of the neocortex provided the requisite substrate: a matrix for the construction of representational networks.

These representational networks 'inform and are informed by, subcortical structures that select and sequence behaviours, facilitating, on line, the adaptive guidance of the behaviour of an individual, in a specific environmental situation and in a specific internal state'.[44]

The symmetry of the honeybees' honeycomb

The classic, Weyl (1952) discusses the honeycomb about which much has been written. By this time we are all convinced that honeybees are exceptional economists. In the pursuit of economy, the honeybees also became superb mathematicians. Weyl (1952) cites the *Arabian Nights*, where the bee proclaims: 'My house is constructed according to the laws of a most severe architecture; and Euclid himself could learn from studying the geometry of my cells.' The boast is, no doubt, true. Maraldi in 1712 measured the honeycomb precisely and discovered that the three bottom rhombs of a cell have an angle α of opportunity 110°, which equalled β, the angle they formed with the prism way. He inquired what α had to be in order to coincide with β.

Maraldi's answer was: $\alpha = \beta = 109°\ 28'$ and he concluded that the bees had solved this geometric problem. When economics was introduced via the mathematical theory of minima, the notion that α was calculated to make the most economical use of wax was entertained. Every other angle required more wax to construct cells of the same volume. This conjecture was confirmed by Koenig. Weyl humorously remarks that Koenig concluded that the bees' calculation was so accurate that it exceeded the methods of Newton and Leibnitz. The French Academy entered the ensuing debate and divined that the bees were as geometrically intelligent as Newton and Leibnitz but did not conclude that their use of such mathematics showed obedience to divine command and guidance. Darwin's appraisal is cited by Weyl (1952): the bee's architecture is

> the most wonderful of known instincts.... Beyond this stage of perfection in architecture natural selection (which has replaced divine guidance! Weyl) could not lead; for the comb of the hive-bee, as far as we can see, is absolutely perfect in economizing labour and wax.

This topic receives much attention in Thompson (1945). Thompson (1945: 537) cites Glaisher: 'the economy of wax has played a very subordinate part in the determination of the form of the cell.' Thompson (1945: 537) concludes:

> That the beautiful regularity of the bee's architecture is due to some automatic play of the physical forces, and that it was fantastic to assume that the bee intentionally seeks for a method of economizing wax, is certain; but the precise manner of this automatic action is not so clear.

In a more recent study, Toth (1964) states isoparametric problems for honeycombs. His careful analysis concludes with the following remarks:

Recapitulating our result, we can say: *Instead of choosing the bottom of a cell by three rhombi, as the bees do, it is always more efficient to use two hexagons and two rhombi.*

We must admit that this has no practical consequence.... So we would fail in shaking someone's conviction that the bees have a deep geometrical intuition.

The bee's navigational process is also astonishing. Over 50 years ago Karl von Frisch showed that bees can navigate using polarized light patterns in the sky. The mechanism used was unknown until Rossel and Wehner (1986) proposed a simple solution to this classic problem.

Their conclusion in brief is that although the bee has crude hardware, it 'has developed the single map most likely to be correct at any time' (ibid.).

Fable of the bees

F.B. Kaye's superb Introduction to Bernard Mandeville's (1924) *Fable of the Bees (or Private Vices, Publick Benefits)* begins: 'Heredity had its full share in Mandeville's genius'. Mandeville was born in Rotterdam in 1670. In London he was a medical specialist in the diseases of the nerves and the stomach. Today, we would call him a psychiatrist. His *Fable of the Bees* contained several extraordinary contributions to economics and biology. It is ironic that those modern specialists in the honeybee are discovering that the organization of the hive is founded on division of labour, a spontaneous order (an 'invisible hand') and of course, a range of evolutionary principles encompassing many of Darwin's basic insights. The irony is that Mandeville's basic discoveries were precisely these two economic principles, usually attributed to Adam Smith, and his remarkable evolutionary insights. These discoveries were, of course, transmitted as the behaviour of bees. As the subtitle of his masterpiece indicates 'Private vices, Publick Benefits' this remarkable book was an almost lethal thrust into the moral structure of seventeenth century society. His outrageous portrait of the beehive and its clear implications for the social order caused a public scandal. Hayek (1978: 142) notes that

> in 1728 at the age of 58, he added a second volume to it [and] the bearing of his thought became quite clear. By that time, however, he had become a bogey man, a name with which to frighten the godly and respectable ... whom everybody knew to be a moral monster.... Yet almost everybody read him and few escaped infection ... by making his starting-point the particular moral contrast between the selfishness of the motives and the benefits which the resulting actions conferred on others, Mandeville saddled himself with an incubus which neither he nor his successors to the present day could ever quite free themselves.

The evolution of institutions was central to his Fable and his central thesis was 'that we often ascribe to the excellency of man's genius ... what is in reality owing to the length of time, and the experience of many generations, all of them very little differing from one another ... in sagacity' (ibid.).

Consider the 'waggle-dance' of the honeybee as such an institution or the institutions of insurance and stock exchanges as outcomes based on the 'experience of many generations'.

While Mandeville's glimpse of human society contained several profound insights, his description of the beehive is almost completely defective. How could a man with the original economic insights of Mandeville produce such a wild caricature of the beehive? First, he really didn't study beehives and his objective was not to achieve true knowledge of their behaviour. Second, the hive was simply a platform from which he launched his parody of social morality. Depending on the reader, it was scandalous, hilarious or insightful.

Mandeville's major belief is that public benefits are derived from private vices rather than from private virtues. Rosenberg (1989) notes that Mandeville's paradox, widely considered as scandalous, was based on 'a highly ascetic and self-denying definition of virtue'. Any behaviour that had the slightest tinge of pride, vanity, avarice or lust, was regarded as vice. Thus, while the apparent behaviour of the honeybee is exemplary: cooperative, altruistic, honest and sharing, the hint that all of this is the working of a 'selfish gene' would, according to Mandeville's logic, sully the entire hive's conduct.[45] Hence, it was almost effortless for Mandeville to show that a successful social order could only be constructed according to a blueprint laden with private vices. Rosenberg (1989) together with Kaye (1924) regard as more enduring Mandeville's vision of socially beneficial outcomes flowing from the combined self-interested actions of all members of society:

> As it is Folly to set up trades that are not wanted, so what is next to it is to increase in any one Trade the Numbers beyond what are required. As things are managed with us, it would be preposterous to have as many Brewers as there are Bakers, or as many Woolen-drapers as there are Shoemakers. This Proposition as to Numbers in every Trade finds itself, and is never better kept than when nobody meddles or interferes with it.
> (Mandeville 1732, Vol. I: 299–300; cited in Rosenberg 1989)

Here we see a less provocative statement of Mandeville's philosophy which is agreeable with Adam Smith's 'laissez-faire' view of an economy that is self-organizing and relies on markets to allocate its produce.

This perception of the 'invisible hand' is closely tied to Mandeville's original formulation of the division of labour. Exchange is the crucial initiator of both Smith's and Mandeville's vision of the entire laissez-faire economic process.

Furthermore, Mandeville espoused the evolution by survival of the fittest of useful institutions and rules which regulated individual actions so as to produce results which were unintended and socially useful. Hayek comments on this evolutionary version of Mandeville's contribution as enlightening:

It was in the elaboration of this wider thesis that Mandeville for the first time developed all the classical paradigmata of the spontaneous growth of orderly social structures: of law and morals, of language, the market, and of money, and also of the growth of technological knowledge.

Perhaps the most important unintended consequence of the *Fable of the Bees* was the patient and lucid portrait of the division of labour, exchange, the invisible hand, etc. in Adam Smith's *Wealth of Nations* and of even greater import the development of sympathy. According to Griswold (1999),

> Sympathy not only allows us to escape the pain of selfishness … but also, in so doing, responds to the disinterested pleasure that arises from the apprehension of concord.… This pleasure is what one might call aesthetic, because it consists in the apprehension of harmony, symmetry, and peace between self and other.… The beauty of sympathy is its promise of wholeness and transcendence for self.… The longing for symmetry is the other face of our fear of measurelessness. The one is a longing to be part of a whole, the other a fear of being part of nothing. This interdependence of opposites is a fine example of what Smith calls 'the economy of nature' and it underlies … the exchanges Smith seeks to describe in his political economy.

The remarkable symmetry of the beehive reminds us that the tension between the selfish gene and sympathy is a ubiquitous component of the economy of nature.

Hexagons and honeycombs

The design of the honeybees' honeycomb has intrigued mathematicians for centuries. By 2000 they concluded that the actual design was not optimal. But the optimal design had not been discovered. In Kepler's *Six-Cornered Snowflake* the structure of the bee's honeycomb was carefully described. The honeycomb is a six-sided prism closed at one end by three rhombi. By closing the other end with three more rhombi, the honeycomb cell becomes the rhombic dodecahedron. In the nineteenth century, mathematicians conducted numerous studies and concluded that the actual honeycomb had the best structure. C. Maclaurin (1743) concluded: 'The cells, by being hexagonal, are the most capacious, in proportion to their surface, of any regular figures that leave no interstices between them, and at the same time admit the most perfect bases.'

In an important study L. Fejes Toth (1964), discovered that bees' honeycomb cell is not optimally designed. He concluded that:

> Recapitulating our result, we can say, Instead of choosing the bottom of a cell by three rhombi, as bees do, it is always more efficient to use two hexagons and two rhombi. We must admit that this has no practical consequence.… So we would fail in shaking someone's conviction that the bees have a deep geometrical intuition.

Let us also note that the bee's navigational prowess is also remarkable. Over 50 years ago Karl von Frisch showed that bees can navigate using polarized light patterns in the sky. The mechanism used was unknown until Rossel and Wehner (1986) proposed a simple solution to this classic problem. Their conclusion in brief was that although the bee has crude hardware, it has developed the single map most likely to be correct at any time.

Hales (2000) also observes that around 36 BC the Roman Marcus Terentius Varro composed a book on agriculture. In this early contribution, Varro presents the hexagonal form of the honeycomb. Two candidates were considered at this time as explanations of the hexagonal design. 'One theory held that the hexagons better accommodated the bees six feet. The other theory, supported by the mathematicians of the day, was that the structure was explained by the isoperimetric property of the hexagon honeycomb.' Varro wrote, 'Does the chamber in the comb have six angles.... The geometricians prove that the hexagon inscribed in a circular figure encloses the greatest amount of space.'

The proof has been lost but Hales notes that the

> Pythagoreans knew that only three regular polygons tile the plane: the triangle, the square, and the hexagon. Popper states that if the same quantity of material is used for the construction of these figures, it is the hexagon that will be able to hold more honey. Popper's reason for restricting his attention to the three regular polygons that the tile are not mathematical (bees avoid dissimilar figures). He also excludes gaps between the cells of the honeycomb without mathematical argument. If the cells are not contiguous, 'foreign matter' could enter the interstices between them and so defile the purity of their produce.

In 1999 Hales discovered the first general proof (Hales 2001):

Theorem (Honeycomb Conjecture): Any partition on the plane into regions of equal area has perimeter at least that of the regular hexagonal honeycomb tiling.

Hales notes that the main ingredient of the proof is a new isoperimetric inequality which has the regular hexagon as a unique minimum. Note that Figure 8 in Hales (2000: 447) presents a cell discovered (in 1964 by Toth) that is more efficient than the bee's honeycomb.[46]

Monopoly-power, externalities and the efficient beekeeper, or Ouch: has Coase been stung by bees?

The invisible hand works when externalities are present. Maskin (1994: 333) calls on Meade's (1952) example to show the issues generated by externalities. When the bees of this beekeeper pollinate the apple growers' apple blossom there is a positive externality accruing to the apple grower which means that the beekeeper keeps too few bees than are required for market efficiency. Coase's solution to this seeming dilemma is to have the beekeeper and the tree grower negotiate a fee paid by the apple grower to the beekeeper inducing the latter to keep the efficient number of bees. In these Coasian circumstances these negotiations produce an efficient solution without government intervention.

There remains the possible circumstance that the apple grower may not know the beekeeper production function and therefore is ignorant of the fee level that produces efficiency. Maskin shows that if the apple grower offers a fee, f, equal to the marginal benefit b, efficiency obtains if and only if the acceptable f exceeds c; the marginal cost of the beekeeper. For efficiency, $b - f$, the apple grower's net benefit, f is equal to zero. A rational beekeeper may offer an f such that f is strictly less than b. This implies that if $b > c > f$, then the additional bees will not be kept and efficiency is not obtained. There is symmetry in that if the beekeeper is uncertain about b, she may set f above b, which prevents an argument even though $b > c$, which means the outcome will not be efficient. Farrell (1987) argues that this inefficiency of negotiated agreements under incomplete information is a counterexample of Coase's theorem. Hence, there is a role for policy intervention, since the government can restore efficiency *ex ante* by imposing a scheme like that of d'Aspremont and Gerard-Varat (1979). This may leave one of the two parties worse off than were there no agreement at all.

Maskin concludes:

> Because it is not evident that situations entailing externalities are significantly more prone to the exercise of monopoly power than those involving purely private goods, a fairer test of whether externalities pose a particular problem for the invisible hand is one in which monopoly power (not but incomplete information) is kept out of the picture.

Maskin (ibid.) considers two more cases: 'Many bees and trees, Surplus-Maximizing Contracts, and the Nonexcludable case.'

The neural basis of cognitive development: a constructivist manifesto[47]

Introduction

In this section of the chapter we begin by presenting a simple example relating foraging behaviour with its neural foundations. The relationship has an economic interpretation which is described. We then turn to the recent papers by Quartz and Sejnowski (1997, 2001) where they describe 'neural constructivism' and distinguish it from the 'neural Darwinism' of Edelman, Changeux, Jerne, among others. The essence of 'neural constructivism' is that the representational features of the cortex are built upon the dynamic interaction between neural growth mechanisms and the neural activity generated by the environment. The next subsection elaborates on this statement. Then, we give a brief description of

Edelman's approach and note several of its attractive features. The section concludes by suggesting that a Bayesian approach to both neural constructivism and Edelman's model may bring them closer together. It appears that the Bayesian methodology makes perfect sense of the reinforced learning *à la* Hayek and Hebb. This Skinner survivor can be formulated as a simple Polya urn, which is an exchangeable entity.

The economics of neuroscience: a foraging example[48]

A hungry crayfish has been foraging for some time without success. Finally, it discovers a rich food patch and commences eating. At this point a small predator approaches the crayfish. The neuronal response of the crayfish would under normal circumstances have surpassed its *escape* threshold and rapid motion would ensue. However, the threshold has been raised by eating. The predator leaves, but is shortly replaced by the distant sound of a dangerous predator. This threat creates sufficient neuronal activity to exceed the escape threshold. The crayfish immediately stops eating, flips its tail and swims to the nearest sanctuary.

The economics of this behaviour is clear. The threshold corresponds to a reservation level. The neurotransmitter is a price which conveys environmental information. Each activity of the crayfish has an opportunity cost, determining the size of the reservation level. This level is high during eating and only high prices (threats or rewards) induce termination (and flight or attack).

This behaviour was reported in the illuminating review article by Bicker and Menzel (1989). In this elegant experiment, the *signals* (prices) were a combination of transmitters, modulators and hormones.[49] The action of transmitters in promoting information transfer along the synaptic connections among neurons is well known. These informational transfers are coordinated by modulators at the cell level and also by hormones. The action of the transmitters is rapid and proximate, the modulators operate on a longer time scale at greater distances and the hormones act like modulators, but on an even longer time scale and at greater distances. Hence, the tail flip that initiated the escape of the crayfish was the consequence of the coordinated activity of an information and control system operated by a plethora of spatio-temporal prices. This behaviour corresponds to a decentralized economy's dependence on the coordinated response of numerous agents to information conveyed by prices and interest rates in a stable environment.

The experiments reported by Bicker and Menzel were among the first to observe organisms perform routines in response to the coordinated information transfer among circuits at the cellular level. The experiments are wide-ranging including: the control of hormonal release *over the life cycle* to synchronize the timing of courtship and reproductive behaviour of crickets as well as the division of labour among honeybees.

Learning behaviour is also studied, 'as neuromodulators confer flexibility on neuronal circuits and trigger intracellular biochemical events that outlast the signal, they have been implicated in learning, memory, and the performance of learned tasks in vertebrates and mollusk' (Marder 1987: 288).

Marder's summary of this research concludes that it has 'exciting' ramifications for computational neuroscience. Using synaptic rules for linking neuron-like components, complex tasks have been performed by network models:

> The challenge is to elucidate how small neuronal networks work: how large networks of simple neuronal-like elements work; and how the complexity of neurons (conferred by their shape and ionic currents) and the richness of their connectivity define and constrain the possible functions of a neuronal network. So we need eventually to determine which properties of biological networks are not shared by networks of simple neuronal-like elements. Insights that have been gained from computer-modelled neuronal-like networks and studies of modulation in neuronal networks such as the stomato-gastric ganglion should help to understand how large biological networks generate behaviours and process information.
>
> (ibid.)

It appears that those chemicals transmitting information among the complex assemblies comprising the brain are the unifying force in neuroscience in the same way that the price mechanism unifies economics. Indeed, our basic hypothesis stipulates similarity between the two processes.

Edelman's neuronal, nativist theory is quite attractive.[50] He emphasizes that the perception of objects is not a passive activity. The world presents itself as a relatively homogeneous substance. Perception searches this seemingly incomprehensible hurly-burly of signals and noise. The search process associated with perception is able to select those objects that are important for its survival. It constructs cognitive representations of these objects. Every perception is a creative act. One of the major creative acts is to classify objects and place them in categories containing similar objects. This classification was stressed by Hayek.[51]

There are other admirable aspects to Edelman's theory. In Edelman (1992) a trenchant critique of cognitive science is presented. Edelman maintains that 'an extraordinary misperception of the nature of thought, reasoning, meaning, and of their relationship to perception has developed that threatens to undermine the whole enterprise (namely, cognitive science)'. Briefly put, the misconception is founded on a misplaced objectivism:

> Objects in the world come in fixed categories, things have essential descriptions, ... concepts and language rely on rules that acquire meaning by formal assignment to fixed world categories, and the mind operates through ... mental representations.... The brain in this view is a kind of computer.
>
> (ibid.)

This view is prevalent in psychology, linguistics, computer science and artificial intelligence. It clearly accounts for the anti-Bayesian attitude that pervades these disciplines. Although Edelman does not endorse the Bayesian position, his realism, and defence of metaphor and metonymy, and his Wittgenstein-view of categories are compatible with the subjectivist vision underlying Bayes. A key remark is: 'when symbols fail to match the world direction, human beings use metaphor and metonymy to make connections.... Minds *create* aspects of reality through cultural and linguistic interaction. Like biology itself, this interaction depends on historical events.'

His concluding sentences are:

> We must incorporate biology into our theories of knowledge and language. To accomplish this we must develop what I have called a biologically based epistemology on account of how we know and how we are aware in light of the facts of evolution and developmental biology ... a biologically based epistemology will enrich our lives.

Once again Bayes and Darwin are not only compatible, but are two sides of the same coin. This is being demonstrated in population genetics where Bayesian methods, especially exchangeability, is an intimate component.

As noted by Sachs, our sense organs sample the environment and create maps in the brain. Thus, the key to Edelman's theory is a neurological survival of the fittest: perceptions which prove to be important to survival have their neuronal mappings strengthened, whereas those mappings with little or no survival value are weakened until they disappear.

In Quartz and Sejnowski's constructivist theory no such selection takes place. Two themes distinguish their theory. First, development is a progressive increase in the structures underlying representational complexity and second, the increase depends on interaction with a structured environment to guide development. These are the bases of neuronal constructivism. The key difference between their theory and Edelman's is that the constructive or making process continues over the life of the mammal. It also belongs to the tradition beginning with Hayek and Hebb in that it rejects a dichotomy separating cognitive and neural and explores how learning guides the developing brain.[52] The selectionist theorists represented by Edelman apply selectionist thinking to brain development. Early in a mammal's life there is a surge in the production of representational maps. This surfeit is diminished by the selection argument noted above. More precisely, in the first stage of development there is an intrinsic construction of 'prerepresentations' by both genetic and epigenetic means. In the second stage, these prerepresentations go through a Darwinian sieve and those whose contribution to survival are below some critical number are eliminated. Those above this number are strengthened, the strongest being the most essential for survival. Quartz and Sejnowski call any developmental theory that specifies an initial exuberant growth followed by selective elimination, 'selectionism'. Development occurs as representational complexity diminishes. Changeux and Dehaene (1989: 82) summarize selectionism as 'activity does not create novel connections, but, rather contributes to the elimination of pre-existing ones'.[53] In contrast, neural construction regards development as an increase in representational complexity. Quartz and Sejnowski ask how they can measure representational complexity. Three measures are: synaptic numbers, axonal arborization and dendritic arborization.

Based on a detailed examination of empirical studies Quartz and Sejnowski conclude:

> Whereas many researchers believe that the major events in brain development end by 2 years of age, the evidence we have received illustrates these continue well past the first decade of life. Rather than being strictly reductive, neural constructivism points to the interaction between cognitive and neural processes in development, suggesting that cognitive and neural levels of description will need to be integrated into a single explanatory framework to explain this prolonged growth. Neural constructivism thus provides a meeting ground for cognitive scientists and neuroscientists. Although we are only beginning to understand how the world and brain interact to build the mind, the story that is unfolding already makes nativist theories appear implausible. What lies ahead promises to be an exciting – and far richer – account in which the mind is constructed from a prolonged interaction with a structured world.

LeDoux (2002) presents a balanced appraisal of these two approaches. The Neural Darwinism of Edelman is portrayed as a competitive struggle by the synapses 'to stay alive', which is similar to the Darwinism competition among animals. He cites Edelman regarding the negligible effects of 'external influences'. 'The pattern of neural circuitry ... is neither established nor rearranged instinctively in response to external influences' (ibid.). Instead, these environmental forces select synapses, of which there is an exuberance, by 'initiating and reinforcing certain patterns of neural activity that involve them' (ibid.). LeDoux also notes that 'selectionists assume that genetic and nongenetic factors interact at each step of brain development. Selection operates on pre-existing connections set up by the genes ... working in concert with nongenetic factors' (ibid.). But randomness also enters and opportunistic synapses are formed independently of any overall genetic plan. This randomness gives rise to a unique set of pre-existing connections. It is from this *unique* (due to randomness) set that selection is made giving rise to a novel person.

A Bayesian perspective

Psychologists have been reluctant to use Bayes' methods in their empirical work. There are several reasons for this reluctance. First, in their empirical work psychologists almost always use the Fisher–Neyman–Pearson brand of statistics which is the only type they have learned. That is, Bayesian statistics are usually not taught to psychology undergraduates. We surmise that most psychologists consider Bayes to be a subjective as opposed to objective approach to psychology questions. Thus, in their quest for an objective science they have disregarded

Bayes and its subjective 'prior distributions'. This attitude has been fortified by the experimental studies of Tversky and his colleagues, who find that few in their experimental studies behave according to Bayesian principles. This anti-Bayesian attitude has also infiltrated biological research which is closely related to psychology. Unfortunately, the recent collaboration of biologists with economists has not opened the door to Bayes. Economists also pursue objectivity in their quest for a scientific discipline. Thus, Bayesian methods have also tended to be given short shrift by econometricians.[54] With all of this negative news facing the Bayesian statistician, it is exhilarating to learn that Bayesian methods are the vehicle used in the probabilistic and statistical analyses of population geneticists. Another bright spot is the recent paper by Tennenbaum and Griffiths which elaborates on the Bayesian methods used by Shepherd, and shows that Tversky's early work on similarity has a Bayesian nexus. The text by Bradbury and Vehrencamp (1998) on animal communication also exposes a fully fledged Bayesian approach. Their descriptions contain the following sentence:

> We have seen that receipt of a signal is followed by a receiver's updating of the probabilities that a condition is true. *This is the whole point of communication*! How can a receiver combine its prior estimates with the information in the signal to produce a new estimate?... *No method, however, can produce a more accurate estimate than Bayesian updating.*
>
> (ibid., italics added)

They go on to give a detailed description of Bayes, which 'sets a benchmark against which to compare any alternative method' (ibid.).

Finally, in a recent study, Gigerenzer and Hoffrage (1995) show that

> Bayesian algorithms are computationally simpler in frequency formats... Frequency formats correspond to the sequential way information is acquired in natural sampling. In an extensive study, the authors found that when information was presented in frequency formats, statistically naive participants derived up to 50% of all inferences by Bayesian algorithms

Our view of learning is similar to that expressed by J.E.R. Staddon in 1988:

> The 'general laws of learning' refer to universal factors congenial to a Humean View of Causality: contiguity and relative frequency of association. All species rely to some extent on these general factors, using them as part of a Bayesian inference process to predict valued events. But more recent work shows that factors do not have for animals the exclusive role attributed to them by the philosophers. An animal's phylogeny can tell it that taste, for example, is more likely to be a valid predictor of sickness than a sound or a coloured light.... Animals operate as 'inference engines' with biases set by their phylogeny – which necessarily shares features in common with other species (and philosophers), as well as features peculiar to each

species' niche and phylogeny. Nevertheless, the process in all cases is the same: to use all available predictors in Bayesian fashion to gain access to value events or avoid noxious ones.

Random walks with reinforcement: a Bayesian encore[55]

In an unpublished paper, Coppersmith and Diaconis (1986) designed a random walk with reinforcement model specifically for neural networks. There are several discussions of the model (for example Diaconis (1988) and Pemantle (1989)) but as far as we know the model has not been used by mainstream neuroscientists. Diaconis presents the following example of city exploration by a new arrival. In the beginning all paths are equally unfamiliar and the newcomer chooses at random among them. However, as time passes, paths that have been taken more frequently up to the present, are more likely to be travelled in the future. This learning process is modelled formally as a reinforced random walk. A random walk is taken on the vertices of an undirected graph starting at a specific vertex. At the start of the process all edges are assigned a weight of unity. However, whenever an edge is walked across, that edge's weight is increased by Δ.

In selecting the next move from a given vertex, an edge leading out of the vertex is chosen, with the probabilities for the various edges proportional to their weights. For example, if after one step the random walk reaches a vertex with k neighbours, it returns to the starting vertex on the next move with probability $(1 + \Delta)/(k + \Delta)$. Pemantle (1989) shows how the Polya urn is the critical ingredient of the reinforced random walk. This urn is used to construct a random walk in a random environment (RWRE) that is equivalent to the original reinforced random walk. Pemantle also observes several other interesting results. The key construct is the Polya urn,[56] which produces an exchangeable sequence and is crucial to the genesis of a reinforced random walk. It is precisely this walk which applies to the neural nets first formulated by Hebb. This simple model and more complicated versions seem appropriate for studying the evolution of synaptic strengths in a Hebb-like brain.

As we saw, Edelman stresses the importance of classification (categorization) in his evolutionary model of the brain. Classification was also emphasized by Hayek (1945) in his seminal neural research. The point here is that there is a similarity among members of a particular classification which can be approximated by partial-exchangeability.[57]

It should also be noted that some of the learning problems encountered by Quartz and Sejnowski may be resolved by using an exchangeable framework. In particular, the Polya urn model is non-stationary (non-homogeneous) and this does not limit its prowess. Also the Kalman filter has an equivalent Bayesian version and a Bayesian non-parametric approach may be superior to the non-Bayesian method. Finally, most agree that Darwinian evolution produces hierarchical entities as first observed by Simon. These hierarchical structures are sometimes easily analysed using exchangeable methods. See Wedlin (2001) and the seminal paper by Lindley and Smith (1972). We conjecture that many of the disagreements between Quartz and Sejnowski (1997, 2000) and Edelman, and others,[58] may be resolved when a Bayesian analysis is adopted.[59]

'The 500th anniversary of the sharing problem (the oldest problem in the theory of probability', by Milton Sobel and Krzysztof Frankowski

These authors present a unified treatment for the general case with k players and equal or unequal cell probabilities. In order to achieve this unification, the authors developed the necessary Dirichlet integrals. They also extended the problem by assuming that the contest may be continued at some future time, conditional on the past results. As initial conditions they solve a host of problems including:

i   for the expected waiting time to complete the tournament and also higher moments;
ii   for the probability of each possible vector-ranking of the players at the tournament's termination;
iii   for four different disciplines for completion of the tournament;
iv   permitting a quota-free cell;
v   allowing ties.

The authors describe the problem as follows:

> A tournament with k players consists of games with all k players participating in each game. Each game has a single winner and the games are continued sequentially until a player wins n games. At a point when the ith player has won $w_i < n$ games ($i = 1, 2, \ldots, k$), or requires $n - w_i = r_i > 0$ games to win the tournament, the contest is abruptly stopped. How should the prize money be shared if we desire to distribute it in proportion to each player's conditional probability of winning the tournament, if the contest were resumed? The probability $p_i > 0$ that the ith player wins in a single game ($i = 1, \ldots, k$) is given and the games are independent of one another.

The article strikes me as having many applications in economics. For example, this sharing problem is analogous to the Banach match box problem and also to versions of the birthday problem.

Notes

1 See Dawkins (1986) for a lucid discussion of this error.
2 This is clear from the flourishing activity of the 'new' discipline: Evolutionary Economics.
3 This exchange rate is meaningful in that the value of tomorrow's offspring is discounted by the population growth rate, thus measuring the population's future.

4 The flourishing area of Bayesian applications in economics and especially population genetics, where almost every Bayesian article also mentions exchangeability, is only introduced here. A more complete discussion is McCall and McCall (2005).

5 In Box 5.2, Noe *et al.* (2001) present a pollination biological market. The two actors in this market when it is applied to the honeybee hive are flowers and honeybees, the pollinators. In Noe's example, there is cheating and game theory applications.

6 The influence of the early economists is treated comprehensively in Depew and Weber (1995). The first modern economist to perceive the extensive linkage between biology and microeconomics was Jack Hirshleifer. Evolutionary economics was initiated by Armen Alchian, and Herb Simon, with the classic study by Nelson and Winter (1982).

7 Chapter 1 of the definitive foraging study by Stephens and Krebs (1986) is titled: 'Foraging economics: the logic of formal modeling' and Chapter 5 is called: 'The economics of choice: tradeoffs and herbivory'.

8 This was spelled out in Lippman and McCall (1984).

9 If acceptance of a fallback position is ruled out by the problem's structure, set $\xi = 0$.

10 Theorem 1.49 in Schervish (1995).

11 This renewal procedure is similar to that used in optimal replacement policies. For example, see Jorgenson *et al.* (1967).

12 For a complete discussion see Stephens and Krebs (1986) and Houston and McNamara (1999).

13 This is based on Chapter 6 of Stephens and Krebs (1986). Also see the discussion in Chapter 5 of Houston and McNamara (1999).

14 This subsection is based on Giraldeau and Livoreil (1998). An excellent and comprehensive presentation of social foraging is contained in Giraldeau and Caraco (2000). Each of their models considers groups of interacting foragers. Each model asks one of the two central questions in social foraging theory: (i) How can the size of a foraging group be predicted given a certain set of ecological conditions? and (ii) How can the use of specific resources be predicted for individuals and groups of individuals, given a foraging group containing G members? The key to these questions and to the essence of social foraging theory is 'economic interdependence', that is, the return from a particular foraging policy depends simultaneously on the behaviour of all competitors. These interdependent returns imply that game theory must replace the conventional optimality models of foraging theory. Then predictions will be founded on evolutionary stable strategies. The conventional optimality theory is presented in Stephens and Krebs (1986) and illustrated in the previous section of the chapter. Thus, Stephens and Krebs mark the demarcation between one-sided and game theoretic foraging theory as well as the separation between conventional Bayes decision theory and adaptive optimal stopping rules.

15 An excellent discussion of PS games is presented in Chapter 6 of Giraldeau and Caraco (2000).

16 See Giraldeau and Livoreil (1998) for a complete description of the sequential experiment.

17 Nectar is the energy source that runs the entire system.

18 Pollen contains the protein needed to produce new bees.

19 The longevity of foragers varies with the environment. In the best of circumstances they live for two months with average longevity being three weeks.

20 See Heinrich (1979) and references therein.

21 See Lippman and McCall (1976).

22 See Seeley (1995).

23 We could just as well state this in terms of pollen or some combination of pollen and nectar.

24 See Maynard Smith (1982).

25 See Endler (1986) for elaboration.

26 See Table 1.1.1 in Anderson (1994).

27 See discussion below of Milinski's sequential search model for sticklebacks. Also see Real (1990a, 1991b) for discussions of sequential search in economics and its relevance for behavioural biology.

28 Milinski has been working with three-spined sticklebacks since 1977. He gives eight reasons for specializing in this small fish including their accessibility, their well-known behaviour based on Tinbergen's classic experiments, they are easily bred, etc. Milinski has addressed many important hypotheses with his sticklebacks. This is the type of division of labour that H. Simon recommended for economists!

29 For a full discussion, see McCall and McCall (2007).

30 See McCall and McCall (2007) for details.

31 Chade (2001) solves the two-sided search problem using optimal stopping rules.

32 These models are treated in Real (1991b). McNamara and Collins partition male and female quality into discrete classes: M_1, M_2,... and F_1, F_2,... respectively. In ESS males in M_i must mate with females in F_i, $i = 1, 2,...$

33 Expected net fitness to males of quality w is denoted by $\pi(w) = (x - w)G(w) + \beta\pi(w^*)$ $[1 - G(w)]$, where $\pi(w^*)$ is the maximum net quality to males from future meetings with females.

34 These include Dombrovsky and Perrin (1994), Krakauer and Rodriguez-Girones (1995), Luttbeg (1996).

35 For an excellent study of mate choice, coalition formation and honest signalling, see Gintis et al. (2001).

36 Seeley cites Simon (1976a), which also contains many pertinent insights. See also Simon 1976b, c and d.

37 This model has been validated by computer simulation (Tofts 1993).

38 See Hayek (1978: 183).

39 For the distinction between cues and signals and a critical assessment of signalling in biology via the 'handicap principle' of Zahavi, see Johnstone (1998).

40 See Seeley (1985, 1995), Seeley and Tautz (2001).

41 See Hamilton (1964a, b, 1971, 1982), Hamilton and Axelrod (1981) and Hamilton and Zuk (1982).

42 The hypothesis tested by them were: (i) whether a colony's nutritional status depended on storage space as well as the nectar intake, (ii) how foragers were informed about changes in the colony's food reserves and (iii) how queuing theory explained (ii). These hypotheses were also discussed by Lindauer (1948).

43 LaCerra and Bingham use evolutionary psychology as a contrasting and 'incorrect' model. The neuroscience model corresponding to evolutionary psychology is composed of a host of mental modules constructed by natural selection in such a way that each module was domain specific. That is, each model can resolve a particular subset of similar problems confronting the organism. This seems to be an unwieldy system theoretically and empirically does not accord with experimental observations (see Quartz and Sejnowski 1997). For a thorough description of the EP model see Barkow et al. (1992).

44 See Montague et al. (1995). They use a predictive form of Hebbian learning to describe the representational networks that control the foraging of the honeybee. They construct a simulation model of a honeybee searching for nectar in a new environment containing yellow and blue flowers. The model simulates the adaptive, foraging behaviour of a honeybee and explains experimental results of several studies of bees' learning. The mean returns of these two kinds of flowers are equal, but variances differ.

45 Some may regard the 'selfish gene' as a modern version of Mandeville's Fable. Mandeville himself, with a twinkle would consider Dawkin's contribution as the final episode of his Fable – the resurrection of the moribund, virtuous hive, expiring in the hollow of a tree, by the injection of the selfish gene. Recall the consequences of the 'Knaves turn'd Honest':

The building Trade is quite destroy'd/Artificers are not employ'd; /.../ As Pride and Luxury decrease,/So by degrees they leave the Seas. /.../ So few in the vast Hive remain,/The hundredth Part they can't maintain /.../ Hard'ned with Toils and Exercise,/They counted Ease itself a Vice;/Which so improv'd their Temperance;/ That, to avoid Extravagance,/They flew into a hallow tree,/Blest with Content and Honesty.

(Mandeville 1924, Vol. 1)

46 Honeycombs are subject to raids by bears, humans, etc. Thus, the time consumed in construction is an important variable. Perhaps the actual honeycomb can be built faster than the optimal.

47 This is the title, without the question mark, of the important article by Quartz and Sejnowski (1997).

48 This is drawn from McCall (1989). A modern version of this example is presented in Montague *et al.* (1995). The summary states that:

Recent work has identified a neuron with widespread projections to odour process-ing regions of the honeybee brain whose activity represents the reward value of gustatory stimuli. We have constructed a model of bee foraging in uncertain en-vironments based on this type of neuron and a predictive form of Hebbian synaptic plasticity. The model uses visual input from a stimulated three-dimensional world and accounts for a wide range of experiments on bee learning during foraging, including risk aversion.

Also see the excellent study by Hammer and Menzel (1995), which cites the article by Bicker and Menzel (1989).

49 Neuromodulators and neurohormones are controlled by the action of neuro-transmitters.

50 An excellent survey of Edelman's theory is by Oliver Sachs (1995).

51 *The Sensory Order* (1952).

52 It is interesting to note that the classification process introduced by Hayek into *neuro-nal constructivism* is the decisive beginning of Bayesian induction or learning. Classi-fication gives rise to partial exchangeability (see below).

53 This is quite different from Sachs' description of Edelman's theory, where creativity is of the essence.

54 This has been changing over the past few years, where Markov chain Monte Carlo methods have been used in Bayesian studies of economic data. The leaders in Baye-sian econometrics include Geweke, Poirier and others.

55 The olfactory conditioning paradigm described in Hammer and Menzel (1995) is a key to understanding the associative learning (reinforcement is described by the beha-viour of the VUMmx (neuron in the honeybee)) in honeybees. The Polya urn rein-forcement model is the natural mathematical generalization of this reinforcement learning process and may be the source of practical implications. For example, it sug-gests that non-parametric Bayes procedures are appropriate for 'testing' the properties of the learning process.

56 Recall that a Polya urn initially contains a black ball and a white ball. A ball is selected at random. If it is white(black) it is replaced in the urn with another white(black) ball. Polya used this model to study contagion. For a full discussion see McCall and McCall (2005).

57 See Wedlin (1982, 2001).

58 The Realistic view described in the Epilogue to Edelman (1992) has considerable overlap with the philosophical positions of deFinetti and Polya.

59 Two recent generalizations of the reinforced random walk which could play an important role in this resolution are Muliere *et al.* (2000, 2003).

References

Andersson, M. (1994) *Sexual Selection*, Princeton, NJ: Princeton University Press.

d'Aspremont, C. and Gerard-Varet, L.-A. (1979) 'Incentives and incomplete information', *Journal of Public Economics*, 11(1): 25–45.

Barkow, J.H., Cosmides, L. and Tooby, J. (eds) (1992) *The Adapted Mind: Evolutionary psychology and the generation of culture*, New York: Oxford University Press.

Bateson, P. (1983) *Mate Choice*, Cambridge: Cambridge University Press.

Bicker, G. and Menzel, R. (1989) 'Chemical codes for the control of behavior in arthropods', *Nature*, 337(6202): 33–9.

Bloch, F. and Ryder, H. (2000) 'Two-sided search, marriages, and matchmakers', *International Economic Review*, 41: 93–116.

Bradbury, J.W. and Vehrencamp, S.L. (1998) *Principles of Animal Communications*, Sunderland, MA: Sinauer Associates.

Burdett, K. and Coles, M.G. (1998) 'Separation cycles', *Journal of Economic Dynamics and Control*, 22(7): 1069–90.

—— (1999) 'Long-term partnership formation: Marriage and employment', *Economic Journal*, 109(456): F307–34.

Burdett, K. and Judd, K. (1983) 'Equilibrium price dispersion', *Econometrica*, 51(4) 955–70.

Chade, H. (2001) 'Two-sided search and perfect segregation with fixed search costs', *Mathematical Social Sciences*, 43: 31–51.

Changeux, J.P. and Dehaene, S. (1989) 'A simple model of prefrontal cortex in delayed response tasks', *Journal of Cognitive Neuroscience*, 1(3): 244–61.

Charnov, E.L. (1976) 'Optimal foraging: The marginal value theorem', *Theoretical Population Biology* 9: 129–36.

Coppersmith, D. and Diaconis, P. (1986) 'Random walk with reinforcement', unpublished ms, Stanford University, Palo Alto, CA.

Darwin, C. (1859) *On the Origin of Species by Means of Natural Selection, or the Preservation of Favoured Races in the Struggle for Life*, London: John Murray.

—— (1871) *The Descent of Man, and Selection in Relation to Sex*, London: John Murray.

Dawkins, R. (1982) *The Extended Phenotype: The gene as the unit of selection*, Oxford W.H. Freeman.

—— (1986) *The Blind Watchmaker*, New York: Norton.

DeGroot, M. (1970) *Optimal Statistical Decisions*, New York: McGraw-Hill.

Depew, D.J. and Weber, B.H. (1995) *Darwinism Evolving: Systems and the genealogy of natural selection*, Cambridge, MA: MIT Press.

Diaconis, P. (1988) *Group Representations in Probability and Statistics*, Hayward, CA Institute of Mathematical Statistics.

Dombrovsky, Y. and Perrin, N. (1994) 'On adaptive search and optimal stopping in sequential mate choice', *American Naturalist*, 144: 355–61.

Dugatkin, L.A. (1997) *Cooperation Among Animals*, Oxford: Oxford University Press.

Edelman, G.M. (1987) *Neural Darwinism: The theory of neuronal group selection*, New York: Basic Books.

—— (1989) *The Remembered Present: A biological theory of consciousness*, New York Basic Books.

—— (1992) *Bright Air, Brilliant Fire*, New York: Basic Books.

—— (2004) *Wider than the Sky: The phenomenal gift of consciousness*, New Haven, CT Yale University Press.

—— (2006) *Second Nature: Brain science and human knowledge*, New Haven, CT: Yale University Press.

Endler, J.A. (1986) *Natural Selection in the Wild*, Princeton, NJ: Princeton University Press.

Farrell, J. (1987) 'Information and the Coase Theorem,' *Journal of Economic Perspectives, American Economic Association*, 1(2): 113–29.

Fisher, R.A (1930) *The Genetical Theory of Natural Selection*, Oxford: Clarendon Press.

—— (1958a) 'The nature of probability', *Centennial Review*, 2: 261–74.

—— (1958b) 'Mathematical probability in the natural sciences', *Metrika*, 2: 1–10.

Frank, S.A. (1998) *Foundations of Social Evolution*, Princeton, NJ: Princeton University Press.

Gigerenzer, G. and Hoffrage, V. (1995) 'How to improve Bayesian reasoning without instruction', *Psychological Review*, 102: 682–704.

Gintis, H., Smith, E.A. and Bowles, S. (2001) 'Costly signaling and cooperation', *Journal of Theoretical Biology*, 213: 103–19.

Giraldeau, L.-A. and Caraco, T. (2000) *Social Foraging Theory*, Princeton, NJ: Princeton University Press.

Giraldeau, L.-A. and Livoreil, B. (1998) 'Game theory and social foraging', in L.A. Dugatkin and H.K. Reeve (eds), *Game Theory and Animal Behavior*, New York: Oxford University Press.

Grafen, A. (1990a) 'Sexual selection unhandicapped by the Fisher process', *Journal of Theoretical Biology*, 144: 473–516.

—— (1990b) 'Biological signals as handicaps', *Journal of Theoretical Biology*, 144: 517–46.

Griswold, C.L. Jr (1999) *Adam Smith and the Virtues of Enlightenment*, Cambridge: Cambridge University Press.

Hales, T. (2000) 'Cannonballs and honeycombs', *Notices of AMS*, 47(4): 440–9.

Halldobler, B. and Wilson, E.O. (1990) *The Ants*, Berlin: Springer Verlag.

Hamilton, W.D. (1963) 'The evolution of altruistic behavior', *American Naturalist*, 97: 354–6.

—— (1964a) 'The genetical evolution of social behaviour I', *Journal of Theoretical Biology*, 7: 1–16.

—— (1964b) 'The genetical evolution of social behaviour II', *Journal of Theoretical Biology*, 7: 17–52.

—— (1971) 'Geometry for the selfish herd', *Journal of Theoretical Biology*, 31: 295–311.

—— (1982) 'Pathogens as causes of genetic diversity in their host populations', in R.D. Anderson and R.M. May (eds), *Population Biology of Infectious Diseases*, Berlin: Springer Verlag.

—— (1983) 'Methods in March-hare madness: Review of *Mate Choice*', *Nature*, 304: 563–4.

Hamilton, W.D and Axelrod, R. (1981) 'The evolution of co-operation', *Science*, 211: 1390–6.

Hamilton, W.D. and Zuk, M. (1982) 'Heritable true fitness and bright birds: A role for parasites', *Science*, 218: 384–7.

Hammer, M. and Menzel, R. (1995) 'Learning and memory in the honeybee', *Journal of Neuroscience*, 15: 1617–30.

Hammerstein, P. and Parker, G.A. (1987) 'Sexual selection: Games between the sexes', in J.W. Bradbury and M.B. Andersson (eds), *Sexual Selection: Testing the alternatives*, New York: Wiley.

Hayek, F.A. (1945) 'The use of knowledge in society', *American Economic Review*, 35: 519–30.

—— (1952) *The Sensory Order*, Chicago, IL: University of Chicago Press.

—— (1978) 'Dr. Bernard Mandeville', *New Studies*, Chicago, IL: University of Chicago Press.

Heinrich, B. (1979–2004) *Bumblebee Economics*, Cambridge, MA: Harvard University Press.

Houston, R.I. and McNamara, J.M. (1999) *Models of Adaptive Behavior*, Cambridge: Cambridge University Press.

Hull, D.L. (1988) *Science as a Process*, Chicago, IL: University of Chicago Press.

Hull, D.L. (1980) 'Individuality and selection', *Annual Review of Ecology and Systematics*, 11: 31–32.

Janetos, A.C. and Cole, B.J. (1981) 'Imperfectly optimal animals', *Behavioural Ecology and Sociobiology*, 9: 203–9.

Johnstone, R.A. (1998) 'Game theory and communication', in L.A. Dugatkin and H.K. Reeves (eds), *Game Theory and Animal Behavior*, Oxford: Oxford University Press.

Jorgenson, D.W., McCall, J.J. and Radner, R. (1967) *Optimal Replacement Policy*, Amsterdam: North-Holland.

Kaye, F.B. (1924) 'Introduction', in B. Mandeville (ed.), *The Fable of the Bees: Or, Private Vices, Publick Benefits, with a Commentary Critical, Historical, and Explanatory by Benjamin Frederick Haye*, 2 vols, Oxford: Oxford University Press.

Krakauer, D. and Rodriguez-Girones, M.A. (1995) 'Searching and learning in a random environment', *Journal of Theoretical Biology*, 177(4): 417–29.

Krebs, J.R. (1989) *Introduction to Behavioral Ecology*, 2nd edn, Oxford: Blackwell Science.

Krebs, J.R. and Davies, N.B. (1987) *An Introduction to Behavioral Ecology*, Oxford: Blackwell Scientific Publications.

Krebs, J.R., Ruan, J.C. and Charnov, E.L. (1974) 'Hunting by expectation or optimal foraging: A study of patch use by chickadees', *Animal Behavior*, 22: 953–64.

LaCerra, P. and Bingham, R. (1998) 'The adaptive nature of the human neurocognitive architecture: An alternative model', *Proceedings of NAS*, 95: 11,290–4.

—— (2002) *The Origin of Minds*, New York: Harmony Books.

LeDoux, J. (2002) *Synaptic Self*, New York: Penguin Group.

Lindauer, M. (1948) 'Über die Einwirkung von Duft- und Geschmackstoffen sowie anderer faktoren auf die Tänze der Bienen', *Z. vergl. Physiol.*, 31: 348–412.

—— (1952) 'Ein Beitrag zur Frage der Arbeitsteilung im Bienenstaat', *Z. vergl. Physiol.*, 36: 299–345.

Lindley, D.V. and Phillips, L.D. (1976) 'Inference for a Bernoulli process (a Bayesian view)', *American Statistician*, 30: 112–19.

Lindley, D.V. and Smith, A.F.M. (1972) 'Bayes estimates for the linear model (with discussion)', *Journal of the Royal Statistical Society: Series B*, 34: 1–42.

Lippman, S.A. and McCall, J.J. (1976) 'Job search in a dynamic economy', *Journal of Economic Theory*, 12: 365–90.

—— (1984) 'Ecological decisionmaking and optimal stopping rules', unpublished ms, UCLA, LA.

Luttbeg, B. (1996) 'A comparative Bayes tactic formate assessment and choice', *Behavioral Ecology*, 7: 451–60.

McCall, B.P. and McCall, J.J. (2005) 'Estimation methods for duration models', *Working Paper*, 0205, Industrial Relations Center, University of Minnesota.

—— (2007) *Economics of Search*, vol. I, London: Taylor & Francis.

McCall, J.J. (1989) 'The Smithian self and the Bayesian brain', *Department of Economics Working Paper*, 596, UCLA.

McLaurin, C. (1743) 'Of the bases of the cells wherein the bees their honey', *Philosophical Transactions of the Royal Society of London*, 42: 561–71.

McNamara, J.M. (1982) 'Optimal patch use in a stochastic environment', *Theoretical Population Biology*, 21: 269–88.

McNamara, J.M. (1985) 'An optimal sequential policy for controlling a Markov renewal process', *Journal of Applied Probability*, 22: 87–94.

McNamara, J.M. and Collins, E.J. (1990) 'The job search problem as an employer-candidate game', *Journal of Applied Probability*, 28: 815–27.

McNamara, J.M., Houston, A.I. and Collins, E.J. (2001) 'Optimality models in behavioral biology', *SIAM Review*, 43: 413–66.

Mandeville, B. (1924 [1732]) *The Fable of the Bees: Or, Private Vices, Publick Benefits, with a Commentary Critical, Historical, and Explanatory by Frederick Benjamin Kaye*, 2 vols, Oxford: Oxford University Press.

Marder, E. (1987) 'Neurotransmitters and neuromodulators', in A.I. Selverston and M. Moulins (eds), *The Crustacean Stomatogastric Nervous System: A Model for the Study of Central Nervous Systems*, New York: Springer.

Maskin, E.S. (1994) 'The invisible hand and externalities', *American Economic Review*, 84(2): 333–7, Papers and Proceedings of the 106th Annual Meeting of the American Economic Association, May.

Maynard Smith, J. (1982) *Evolution and the Theory of Games*, Cambridge: Cambridge University Press.

Maynard Smith, J. (1995) 'Genes, memes and minds', *New York Review of Books*, (30 November): 46–8.

Maynard Smith, J. and Szathmary, E. (1995) *The Major Transitions in Evolution*, Oxford: Oxford University Press.

Meade, J.E. (1952) *A Geometry of International Trade*, London: Allen & Unwin.

Milinski, M. (2001) 'The economics of sequential mate choice in sticklebacks', in L.A. Dugatkin (ed.), *Model Systems in Behavioral Ecology*, Princeton, NJ: Princeton University Press.

Milinski, M. and Bakker, T.C.M. (1990) 'Female sticklebacks use male coloration in mate choice and hence avoid parasitized males', *Nature*, 344: 330–3.

Montague, P.R., Dayan, P., Person, C., Sejnowski, T.J. (1995) 'Bee foraging in uncertain environments using predictive Hebbian learning', *Nature*, 377: 725–8.

Muliere, P., Secchi, P. and Walker, S.G. (2000) 'Urn schemes and reinforced random walks', *Stochastic Processes and Their Applications*, 82: 59–78.

—— (2003) 'Reinforced random processes in continuous time', *Stochastic Proc. and Their Applications*, 104: 117–30.

Nelson, R.R. and Winter, S.G. (1982) *An Evolutionary Theory of Economic Changes*, Cambridge, MA: Harvard University Press.

Noe, R., van Hooff, J. and Hammerstein, P. (2001) *Economics in Nature*, Cambridge: Cambridge University Press.

Parker, G.A. (1978) 'Searching for mates', in J.R. Krebs and N.B. Davies (eds), *Behavioural Ecology*, London; Blackwell Science.

Pemantle, R. (1989) 'A time-dependent version of Polya's urn', *Journal of Theoretical Probability*, 3: 627–37.

Quartz, S.R. and Sejnowski, T.J. (1997) 'The neural basis of cognitive development: A constructivist manifesto?', *Behavioral and Brain Sciences*, 20: 537–96.

—— (2000) 'Continuing commentary', *Behavioral and Brain Sciences*, 23: 781–92.

Real, L.A. (1990a) 'Search theory and mate choice. I: Models of single-sex discrimination', *American Naturalist*, 136: 376–405.

—— (1990b) 'Predator switching and the interpretation of animal choice behavior: The case for constrained optimization', in R.N. Hughes (ed.), *Behavioral Mechanisms of Food Selection*, NATO ASI Series Vol. G20, Berlin: Springer Verlag.

—— (1991a) 'Animal choice behavior and the evolution of cognitive architecture', *Science*, 253: 980–6.

—— (1991b) 'Search theory and mate choice. II: Mutual interaction, assortative mating, and equilibrium variation in male and female fitness', *American Naturalist*, 138: 901–17.

Rosenberg, N. (1989) 'Bernard Mandeville', in J. Eatwell, M. Milgate and P. Newman (eds), *The Invisible Hand*, New York: W.W. Norton.

Rossel, S. and Wehner, R. (1986) 'Polarization vision in bees', *Nature*, 323: 128–31.

Rothschild, M. (1974) 'Searching for the lowest price when the distribution of prices is unknown', *Journal of Political Economy*, 82: 689–711.

Royama, T. (1970) 'Factors governing the hunting behavior and selection of food by the great tit', *Journal of Animal Ecology*, 39: 619–68.

Sachs, O. (1995) 'A new vision of the mind', in J. Cornwall (ed.), *Nature's Imagination*, Oxford: Oxford University Press.

Schervish, M.J. (1995) *Theory of Statistics*, Berlin: Springer.

Seeley, T.D. (1985) *Honeybee Ecology*, Princeton, NJ: Princeton University Press.

—— (1989) 'Social foraging in honey bees: how nectar foragers assess their colony's nutritional status', *Behavioral Ecology and Sociobiology*, 24: 181–99.

—— (1995) *The Wisdom of the Hive*, Cambridge, MA: Harvard University Press.

Seeley, T.D. and Tautz, J. (2001) 'Worker piping in honey bee swarms and its role in preparing for liftoff', *Journal of Comparative Physiology*, 187(8): 667–76.

Seeley, T.D. and Towne, W.F. (1992) 'Tactics of dance choice in honey bees: do foragers compare dances?' *Behavioral Ecology and Sociobiology*, 30: 59–69.

Shepherd, G.M. (1988) *Neurobiology*, Oxford: Oxford University Press.

Simon, H.A. (1969) *The Sciences of the Artificial*, 2nd edn, Cambridge, MA: MIT Press.

Simon, H.A. (1976a) *Administrative Behavior* (3rd edn), New York: The Free Press.

—— (1976b) 'The design of large computing systems as an organizational problem', in P. Verburg, C.A. Malotaux, K.T.A. Halbertsma and J.L. Boers (eds), *Organisatiewetenschap en Praktijk*, Leiden: H.E. Stenfert Kroese B.V.

—— (1976c) 'The information-storage system called "human memory"', in M.R. Rosenzweig and E.L. Bennett (eds), *Neural Mechanisms of Learning and Memory*, Cambridge, MA: MIT Press.

—— (1976d) 'Information processing', in A. Ralston and C.L. Meek (eds), *Encyclopedia of Computer Science*, New York: Petrocelli/Charter.

Smith, E.A. (1983) 'Anthropological applications for foraging theory: A critical review', *Current Anthropology*, 24: 625–51.

Smith, J.N.M. and Dawkins, R. (1971) 'The hunting behavior of individual great tits in relation to spatial variations in their food density', *Animal Behavior*, 19: 695–706.

Sobal, M. and Frankowski, K. (1994) 'The 500th anniversary of the sharing problem. (The oldest problem in the theory of probability)', *American Mathematical Monthly*, 101: 833–47.

Staddon, J.E.R. (1988) 'Learning as inference', in R.C. Bolles and M.D. Beecher (eds), *Evolution and Learning*, Philadelphia: Lawrence Erlbaum.

Stephens, D.W. and Krebs, J.R. (1986) *Foraging Theory*, Princeton, NJ: Princeton University Press.

Tennenbaum, J.B. and Griffiths, T.L. (2001) 'Generalization, similarity, and Bayesian inference', *Behavioral and Brain Sciences*, 24: 629–40.

Thompson, D.A.W. (1945) *On Growth and Form*, Cambridge: Cambridge University Press.

Tofts, C. (1993) 'Algorithms for task allocation in ants. (A study of polyethism theory.)', *Bulletin of Mathematical Biology*, 55: 891–918.

Tofts, C. and Frank, N.R. (1992) 'Doing the right thing: ants, honeybees and naked mole-rates', *Trends in Ecology and Evolution*, 7: 346–9.

Toth, L. Fejes (1964) 'What the bees know and what they do not know', *Bulletin of the American Mathematical Society*, 70: 468–81.

Tversky, A. (1977) 'Features of similarity', *Psychological Review*, 84: 327–52.

Tversky, A. and Kahneman, D. (1974) 'Judgement under uncertainty: Heuristics and biases', *Science*, 185: 1124–30.

Vickery, W.L., Giraldeau, L.-A., Templeton, J.J., Kramer, D. L. and Chapman, C.A. (1991) 'Producers, scroungers and group foraging', *American Naturalist*, 137: 847–63.

Wedlin, A. (1982) 'Partial exchangeability and inference in the risk process', in G. Koch and F. Spizzichino (eds), *Exchangeability in Probability and Statistics*, Amsterdam: North-Holland.

—— (2001) 'Hierarchical models and partial exchangeability', in M.C. Galivotti, P. Suppes and D. Constantini (eds), *Stochastic Causality*, Stanford, CA: CSLI Publications.

Weyl, H. (1952) *Symmetry*, Princeton, NJ: Princeton University Press.

Williams, G.C. (1966) *Adaptation and Natural Selection*, Princeton, NJ: Princeton University Press.

Wittenberger, J.F. (1983) 'Tactics of mate choice', in P. Bateson (ed.), *Mate Choice*, Cambridge: Cambridge University Press.

Zahavi, A. (1975) 'Mate selection – A selection for a handicap', *Journal of Theoretical Biology*, 53: 205–14.

—— (1977) 'The cost of honesty (further remarks on the handicap principle)', *Journal of Theoretical Biology*, 67: 603–5.

11 Constructivist logic and emergent evolution in economic complexity

J. Barkley Rosser, Jr.[1]

> The 'fallacy of composition' that drives a felicitous wedge between micro and macro, between the individual and the aggregate, and gives rise to emergent phenomena in economics, non-algorithmic ways – as conjectured originally by John Stuart Mill…, George Herbert Lewes…, and codified by Lloyd Morgan … in his popular Gifford Lectures – may yet be tamed by unconventional models of computation.
>
> (Velupillai 2008: 21)

Introduction: a plethora of complexities

This chapter will extend further a discussion regarding the relationships between different views of economic complexity, or complexity more generally, that has been going on for some time, with Velupillai and some of his associates (2005) broadly on one side and Rosser (2009) on the other. This earlier round tended to focus on the relative usefulness of various versions of *computational complexity* as contrasted with what Rosser labelled *dynamic complexity*. Here we shall seek to understand more deeply the roots of each of these perspectives in logic and evolutionary theory, particularly the concept of *emergence* associated with certain versions of evolutionary theory. While this discussion will highlight more sharply the contrasts in these views, it will also lead to the position of their possible reconciliation in actually existing economic systems, with this perhaps a fulfilment of the desire stated by Professor Velupilllai in the opening quotation provided above.

Following Day (1994), Rosser (1999, 2009) defined dynamic complexity as being determined by the deterministically endogenous nature of the dynamics of a system: that it does not converge on a point, a limit cycle, or simply expand or implode exponentially. This 'broad tent' definition includes the 'four Cs' of cybernetics, catastrophe theory, chaos theory and the 'small tent' complexity of heterogeneous agent models in which local interactions dominate the dynamics. Curiously, while Horgan (1997: 303) considers chaotic dynamics to be complex (and coined the term 'chaoplexity' to link the two concepts together), the list he provides of 45 definitions gathered by Seth Lloyd does not clearly include anything that fits this view that is so widely used by economists.[2] Indeed, many of the definitions appear to be variations of algorithmic or computational complexity, many of them being information measures of one sort or another. This last is not surprising, as Shannon's information measure as Velupillai (2000) has argued that it is the foundation for the Kolmogorov–Solomonoff–Chaitin–Rissanen varieties of algorithmic and computational complexity. Most of these measures involve some variation on the minimum length of a computer program that will solve some problem.

While there are several of these measures, a general argument in favour of all of them is that each of them is precisely defined, and can provide a measure of a degree of complexity. This has been argued to be favourable aspect of these definitions (Markose 2005; Israel 2005), even if they do not clearly allow for a distinguishing between that which is complex and that which is not. At the same time they allow for qualitatively higher degrees of complexity. In particular, a program is truly computationally complex if it will not halt; it does not compute. The bringing in of the halting problem is what brings in through the back door the question of logic with the work of Church (1936) and Turing (1937) on recursive systems, which in turn depends on the work of Gödel.

In general, one advantage of the dynamic definition is that it provides a clearer distinction between systems that are complex and those that are not, although there are some fuzzy zones as well with it. Thus, while the definition given above categorizes systems with deterministically endogenous limit cycles as not complex, some observers would say that any system with a periodic cycle is complex as this shows endogenous business cycles in macroeconomics. Others argue that complexity only emerges with aperiodic cycles, the appearance of chaos or discontinuities associated with bifurcations or multiple basins of attraction or catastrophic leaps or some form of non-chaotic aperiodicity. So, there is a gradation from very simple systems that merely converge to a point or a growth path, all the way to fully aperiodic or discontinuous ones. In almost all cases, some form of nonlinearity is present in dynamically complex systems and is the source of the complexity, whatever form it takes.[3] This sort of hierarchical categorization shows up in the levels identified by Wolfram (1984; see also Lee 2005) which arguably combine computational with dynamic concepts.

The idea of either emergence or evolution, much less emergent evolution, is not a necessary part of the dynamic conceptualization of complexity, and certainly is not so for the various computational ones. However, it has been argued by many that evolution is inherently a dynamically complex system (Foster 1997; Potts 2000), possibly even the paradigmatic complex system of them all (Hodgson 2006a). Curiously, even as complex dynamics are not necessarily evolutionary, likewise emergence is not always present in evolution or even arguably its core (which is presumably natural selection with variation, mutation and inheritability). But, the most dramatic events of evolution have been those involving emergence, the appearance of higher order structures or beings, such as the appearance of multi-cellular organisms. While most evolutionary theorists reject teleological perspectives that increasing complexity associated with successive emergence events (Gould 2002), the association of emergence with evolution goes back to the very invention of the concept of emergence by Lewes (1875), who was influenced by John Stuart Mill's (1843) study of *heteropathic laws*, and who in turn influenced C. Lloyd Morgan (1923) and his development of the concept of emergent evolution.

While many advocates of computational ideas find the idea of emergence to be essentially empty, we shall see that it reappears when one considers the economy as a computational system (Mirowski 2007a). Whatever its analytic content, emergence seems to happen in the increasingly computational based real economies we observe, with this emergence being a central phenomenon of great importance. Thus, some effort of reconciliation of these ideas is desirable, although this effort will first take us on a journey through the deeper controversies within the logic of computability.

The struggle for the soul of mathematics: constructivism versus formalism

In a discussion in which one side of the argument has been accused of ultimately lacking mathematical foundation, the emergent evolution view, it may seem a distraction to consider a debate within mathematics itself. However, Roy Weintraub (2002) has argued quite convincingly that to understand the evolution of economic theory one must understand the parallel evolution of mathematical theory as well, given the deep reliance upon mathematics that economics indulges in. So, we shall consider a foundational struggle that remains unresolved in mathematics, whose implications have only recently begun to seep into the awareness of mathematical economists. This is the struggle between constructivism and formalism.

Formalist mathematics is also known as classical mathematics, and it is the dominant view within mathematics. While the issues at hand trace back earlier, the first major public disputes between the schools appeared in the mid-to-late nineteenth century, as Leopold Kronecker (1968) attacked the increasing use of infinite sets in formal mathematics, initially against Weierstrass, but eventually against Georg Cantor (1915), who was the main developer of the idea of multiple levels of transfinite sets. Kronecker opposed the use of completed infinities in proofs, and called for an emphasis on the 'intuitively valid' natural numbers in proofs with finite steps, constructive proofs in which the observer can see exactly what is going on and how the proof is arrived at.[4]

The next round of this would be between Luitzen Brouwer, of fixed point theorem fame, and David Hilbert. In addition to calling for constructive proofs, Brouwer (1908) emphasized the intuitionistic idea that the excluded middle should not necessarily be excluded. This fit in easily with the questioning of infinite sets as many of the key theorems of Cantor involved proof by contradiction, including the one establishing that the real numbers constitute a set of a higher level of infinity than the countably infinite natural numbers, along with the theorem establishing that there is no highest level of infinity at all. These theorems were thrown out the window by Brouwer and his intuitionistic followers. This debate became most heated in the 1920s, with Hilbert (Hilbert and Ackermann 1950) supporting the newly emerging ZFC formal axiom system that was developed by Zermelo (1908) and Fraenkel (1961). Hilbert's removal of Brouwer from a leading editorial board pushed intuitionism to the fringes until it would be revived with constructivism by Bishop (1967), supported by the increasing use of computers in mathematics and the sciences more broadly.

Besides criticizing the use of completed infinite sets and the Law of the Excluded Middle in formal mathematical proofs, the constructivists also objected to the 'C' part of the ZFC, the Axiom of Choice, which allows for the ordering of infinite sets and indeed of the real number continuum, and was first proposed by Zermelo. Substantial parts of topology and such useful concepts as Lebesgue measure depend on at least a limited form of the Axiom of Choice applicable to countable infinities to prove things about them, there being different versions of the axiom applying to different levels of infinity (Zorn 1935). Ironically, the ultimate axiom of choice allowing for the well ordering of all infinite sets is false (Specker 1953), although even more ironically this apparently ultimate victory of constructivism depends on a proof by contradiction.[5] Even more ironically, the Axiom of Choice is much less necessary in nonstandard analysis (Robinson 1966) in which infinite real numbers are allowed, and in which one can differentiate the Dirac delta function (Keisler 1976: 230).[6]

The struggle moves to economic theory

It has been Velupillai and his associates (Velupillai 2005; Doria *et al.* 2009) who have brought this constructivist critique of formal, classical mathematics into economics to critique the foundations of much of mathematical economic theory.[7] A general thrust has been to uncover non-constructivist proofs of key theorems underlying many widely accepted results in economic theory. Thus, Velupillai (2006, 2009) focuses on the standard proofs of the existence of general equilibrium. These proofs have generally used fixed point theorems, with that of Brouwer being the most fundamental. However, this theorem and its relatives such as Kakutani's, used in the general equilibrium existence proofs, depend on Sperner's Lemma, which in turn depends on the Bolzano-Weierstrass Theorem, which is proven using a proof by contradiction. Hence, it is nonconstructive.[8] Velupillai notes that this issue was understood at some level by the key developers of modern computable general equilibrium (CGE) models (Shoven and Whalley 1973; Scarf 1993), but that they in the end basically glossed over the issue.

Especially for the latter, the emphasis has been on using CGE models to carry out policy analyses, with presumably the approximate solutions one obtains given that one is operating with strictly countably infinite rational numbers 'good enough'. Velupillai (2005: 164) has questioned this in practice, citing the peculiar finance function of Clower and Howitt (1978), which has its rational number solutions distinctly different from the solutions for the adjacent irrational numbers. He also argues (2005: 186) that round off errors associated with these problems can sometimes lead to wildly divergent outcomes that can lead to real problems, such as the serious misfiring of a Patriot missile during the first Gulf War that missed its target by 700 metres, thereby killing 28 soldiers in 'friendly fire' in Dhahran, Saudi Arabia.

A stream of related papers have shown that when one tries to put various standard results of economic theory into computable forms, they turn out not to be effectively computable in a general sense. These results have been found for Walrasian general equilibria (Lewis 1991; Richter and Wong 1999), Nash equilibria (Prasad 1991; Tsuji *et al.* 1998), more general aspects of macroeconomics (Leijonhufvud 1993) and whether or not a dynamic system is chaotic (da Costa and Doria 2005).

The more purely theoretical problems such as the lack of non-constructivity of basic theorems often involves such issues the law of the excluded middle. However, for these problems of effective non-computability, the issue often revolves around the problem of the fact that computers operate with the countably infinite rational numbers (as are presumably all actual economic data),[9] while much of the theory has been proven assuming the real number continuum. Efforts have been made to overcome the problem of being able to compute with real numbers (Blum *et al.* 1998), but these remain controversial and have not been generally accepted by the advocates of the constructivist approach.

Computing emergence

The re-emergence of the emergence concept was associated with the general emergence of the complexity concept during the 1980s and 1990s, with Kaufmann (1993) in particular associating it with evolution and the emergence of higher order structures in the evolutionary process, indeed pushing this process as potentially more important than the more traditional Darwinian mechanisms associated with natural selection (although presumably the higher order structures that survive and reproduce because they are successful in the evolutionary process of natural selection). Crutchfield (1994) proposed a more computational form of it, and Bak (1996) associated it with self-organization. Some other approaches considered in Rosser (2009) include the hypercyle model of Eigen and Schuster (1979),[10] the multi-level evolution model of Crow (1953), Hamilton (1972) and Henrich (2004), the synergetic model of entrained oscillations (Haken 1983), and the frequency entrainment model of Nicolis (1986) as the anagenetic moment (Rosser *et al.* 1994), which draws on Boulding (1978). McCauley (2004) has criticized these approaches due to their lack of possessing invariance principles, although he recognizes that symmetry breaking may be a way to approach emergence in a more formal manner.[11] This becomes part of a broader debate between physics and biology, which we are not going to resolve here, but recognize that the point must be noted.

While emergence is usually argued to involve hierarchy and the appearance of a new, higher level within a hierarchical structure, some discussion sees it as a pattern appearing out of a more disordered state, somewhat along the lines of self-organization. The frequency entrainment approach of Nicolis can be viewed as an example of this sort of emergence. Examples of this may well be emergence of a common language (Niyogi 2006) or of flocking in animals or herding by agents in a market. This latter has been considered in its general form by Cucker and Smale (2007), drawing ultimately on Viczek *et al.* (1995), in which a set of mobile agents converge on the same velocity, with birds flocking being the canonical example. This convergence depends on the elements of an adjacency matrix whose elements indicate the strength of influences from one bird to another.

However, the more common perspective on emergence is that it involves processes or events at a lower level of a hierarchy that generate the existence of or a phenomenon at a higher level of that hierarchical structure. This is more difficult to pin down in terms of conditions, especially computable conditions. Thus, Lee (2005) considered a formulation in which emergence was said to occur when a transformational function led to one state being changed into another that is more computationally complex as measured by Kolmogorov (1965) complexity, which is the minimum program length that will halt and describe a state on a universal Turing machine. However, Lee notes that determining this minimum length of program is itself not computable (any attempted program to solve it will not halt), a rather basic problem for any computationally defined measure.

Furthermore, it is not at all clear that because state A is more computationally complex than state B, that A is therefore at a higher level of a hierarchy. This problem arises from the very fact that the emergence of a higher (supposedly more computationally complex) level of a nested hierarchy may arise from some sort of entrainment of behaviour or oscillation at the lower level of the hierarchy. As with Haken's slaving principle and adiabatic approximation, the convergence or entrainment at the lower level means that what were viewed as distinct elements requiring individual modelling at the lower level can be aggregated and viewed as a single element at the higher level. This can result in the higher level dynamics being describable by a shorter length program due to this simplification through aggregation. Hence, it may well not be that the higher level must describable by a program of shorter length than the shorter level, even though in reality the lower level is embedded within the higher level.

Lee then proceeds to consider the hierarchy aspect more directly. This leads to following Langton (1992) in comparing the four level Chomsky (1959) hierarchy with the four level hierarchy of Wolfram (1984). Chomsky's categories, each of four levels according to computational power, are regular language, context-free language context-sensitive language, and recursive enumerable language (that is, a Turing machine), which Mirowski (2007a) sees as a natural way to distinguish market forms. That of Wolfram is more closely linked to dynamic conceptualizations and refers to cellular automata systems, moving from systems that converge on a homogeneous state (Class I), ones that evolve towards simple separated structures or periodic structures (Class II), ones that evolve towards chaotic dynamical structures (Class III) and ones that evolve to complex localized structures (Class IV).

Curiously, Langton's formulation seems to invert the latter two categories. He defines an order parameter λ that depends on the number of finite cell states, their neighbourhood size and the number of transition paths. As this parameter rise one sees the system passing from Class I to Class II to Class IV and finally to Class III, with the sharpest jump in the parameter being between the second and third of these. He then suggests that from the computational perspective the first two are halting, the third is undecidable and the fourth is non-halting. It is Crutchfield (1994) who links such a passing through a hierarchy of computational classes as emergence, and Jensen (1998) who ties all this to self-organized criticality, although these formulations have come under much criticism from various quarters, such as McCauley, who suggests the idea of complete surprise and unpredictability following Moore (1990) as a better foundation for the idea of emergence. Returning to Lee's argument, the highest level in which non halting takes place is that of the universal Turing machine.

Emergence in market dynamics

So, much of this has operated at a fairly abstract level. Does it have anything to do with real markets? Vernon Smith (1962, 2007) emphasizes how the experimental evidence (and actual evidence in many constructed markets) has shown that certain kinds of market structures are consistent with very rapid approaches to equilibria, particularly the double-auction form, a result strongly reinforced by Friedman and Rust (1993). What, if anything, does all this discussion of problems of computability and emergence have to do with real markets, where we can see mechanism designs that regularly generate equilibrium outcomes?

A challenging view of this has been provided controversially by Mirowski (2007a) in his theory of markomata, of markets as evolving forms of algorithms that the fundamental essence of markets is that they are algorithms, not merely that they can be simulated by computers. This then suggests that computability issues are deeply inherent in the structure and functioning of markets. The link with emergence is that he sees market forms evolving, and that over time higher Chomskyian hierarchical levels emerge that nest the lower levels, with these higher levels taking the form, for example, of futures markets, markets for derivatives and so forth.

This brings our discussion from the previous section of the chapter into play rather forcefully. There we saw the argument that lower levels of either Chomskyian or Wolframian hierarchies tend to be both 'better behaved' (less dynamically complex) and also more computable. As one moves to the higher level, one eventually moves to the level of a universal Turing machine, but one also approaches the zone of halting problems and other matters of non-computability of one sort or another. The lack of effective computability of general equilibrium begins to loom in a more serious fashion as one considers the possibility that real world markets may be a series of unresolved hierarchies with varying degrees of computability. Lower level spot markets constructed as double auctions may function (compute) very well and rapidly achieve solutions. But, as these become embedded in higher order markets involving derivatives made out of derivatives that agents do not even understand when they are trading them, potential problems can arise, and the difficulties observed in financial markets in recent years may well represent exactly such phenomena playing themselves out, systems breaking down because of their ultimate failure to compute at the highest levels.

Many criticisms were levelled at Mirowski's argument in the symposium accompanying his article, with some focusing on institutional elements and the argument that markets are social processes of exchange between humans within certain institutional setups (Conlisk 2007; Kirman 2007; also separately, Hodgson 2006b). This form of criticism downplays or even denies the idea of a market as an algorithm. However, another vein of criticism came from the other direction (Zambelli 2007), asserting that Mirowski had failed to properly account for issues of computability, in particular that he did not understand that the market structure could well collapse down to universal Turing machine, that he was wrong to assert the finite nature of lower level markets in the hierarchy. While finite mechanisms are computable, there are an infinite set of these finite mechanisms available to a universal Turing machine, and that even though it is finite in a sense, the fact that in effect it is unbounded makes it as if is infinite (Odifreddi 1989).

I find myself substantially agreeing with Mirowski's (2007b) response to this latter argument. He agrees with several critics that the Chomskyian hierarchy may be too simplistic, too 'flat' in its lower levels, and then suddenly jumping up to a much higher level of computational complexity, sort of a '1,2, infinity' story. He states his desire for a more nuanced and fully gradated hierarchy, but then contrasts his view with the usual view that simply reduces all markets and market mechanisms to the same level, especially the general equilibrium view that assumes one big central decision maker that simultaneously solves all markets. This is surely a contrast with the world of Vernon Smith and of Friedman and Rust with their separately solving markets, even if these do quite well all by themselves. The problems arise when they interlink and aggregate and become embedded in the higher order markets. The lower level markets are simpler and finite and easily solved. It is as one moves up the line to the higher levels, to the potential general equilibrium that keeps racing out of one's reach as the market constantly evolves newly emerging forms at the higher levels of aggregations of derivatives upon derivatives upon options upon futures upon spot markets and so on.[12]

Besides the evidence of market malfunctions in collateralized debt obligation markets and other such esoterica, other theoretical work is appearing that is consistent with this form of Mirowski's argument, and especially of its potential for an open-ended non-computing that can lead to all kinds of destabilizing and complex dynamics. In particular, while they avoid the question of hierarchical levels as such, Brock *et al.* (2008) establish that contrary to the usual view that increasing the number of available assets in financial markets stabilize and improve efficiency by spreading risk, they may destabilize markets with heterogeneous agents, especially if those agents engage in trend extrapolating behaviour, which has long been known to be destabilizing in asset markets (Zeeman 1974).

They discuss a variety of cases, including ones where the standard results hold, but it would appear that it is possible for the two results to hold simultaneously with some minor adjustments to their models. Thus, it may be the case under certain circumstances that an increase in the number of assets could both increase efficiency and even local stability in the markets, even as they threaten the broader resilience of the markets and their global stability. This might be manifested in a particularly extreme form if one were to simultaneously observe a decrease in variance coinciding with an increase in kurtosis, increasingly obese fat tails coinciding with a hugging of the mean in the middle. Such an outcome would be an economic equivalent of the 'stability-resilience' trade-off long posited to hold in ecological systems by Holling (1973).

Conclusion

This chapter has reconsidered the argument over the nature of economic complexity as to whether it is best thought of in computational terms or in dynamic terms, taking as the accompanying idea of the latter the idea of emergence in evolutionary processes. The analysis of computational complexity took us into the deeper, revived debates now flowing into economics from logic and metamathematics over constructivism and formalism. The latter was found to be on a somewhat weak footing from the standpoint of computability theory, relying on various theories of hierarchies and the emergence of new levels in them, none of these fully developed or satisfactory, despite the use of such concepts as bifurcation via symmetry breaking.

A possible meeting point of these ideas is seen in the markomata idea of Mirowski, with his vision of markets being simultaneously algorithmic systems that are evolving higher order structures. This evolutionary process drags the system into increasing problems of computability, and this idea may well be a key way of considering the sorts of difficulties observed in recent years in global financial markets.

Notes

1 I wish to thank Cars Hommes, Roy Weintraub, Vela Velupillai and Stefano Zambelli for providing useful materials or comments.
2 The list with the name of the person most associated with the definition in parentheses is: information (Shannon); entropy (Gibbs, Boltzmann); algorithmic complexity, algorithmic information content (Chaitin, Solomonoff, Kolmogorov); Fisher information; Renyi entropy; self-delimiting code length (Huffman, Shanno-Feno); error-correcting code length (Hamming); Chernoff information; minimum description length (Rissanen); number of parameters, or degrees of freedom, or dimensions; Lempel-Ziv complexity; mutual information, or channel capacity; algorithmic mutual information; correlation; stored information (Shaw); conditional information; conditional algorithmic information; metric entropy; fractal dimension; self-similarity; stochastic complexity (Rissanen); sophistication (Koppel, Atlan); topological machine size (Crutchfield); effective or ideal complexity (Gell-Mann); hierarchical complexity (Simon); tree sub-graph diversity (Huberman, Hogg); homogeneous complexity

(Teich, Mahler); time computational complexity; space computational complexity; information-based complexity (Traub); logical depth (Bennett); thermodynamic depth (Lloyd, Pagels); grammatical complexity (position in Chomsky hierarchy); Kullbach–Liebler information; distinguishability (Wooters, Caves, Fisher); Fisher distance; discriminability (Zee); information distance (Shannon); algorithmic information distance (Zurek); Hamming distance; long-range order; self-organization; complex adaptive systems; edge of chaos. These last three potentially fit parts of the dynamic complexity concept, and self-organization in particular suggests emergence.

3 Goodwin (1947) and Turing (1952) studied coupled linear systems with lags that could generate complex dynamics, although the normalized uncoupled equivalent forms of these are nonlinear.

4 See Barrow (1992, Chapter 5) for an account of the disputes and those between Brouwer and Hilbert, with Kleene (1967: 186–98) for a more detailed account of the mathematical issues involved.

5 For a very neat proof of this falsity, see Rosser (1978: 540–1).

6 Velupillai (2007) discusses the mathematical complications associated with the Feynman integral approach to dealing with the difficulties of the Dirac delta function.

7 Although the first to specifically consider the implications of the Gödel theorems for economics was Albin (1982).

8 Needless to say this constitutes yet another irony, that the great intuitionist leader's most famous theorem did not follow the constructs of constructivist intuitionism. Brouwer himself became aware of this and eventually provided an alternative version that did so (Brouwer 1952).

9 It is not necessarily the case that all economic data must be rational numbers. Thus, irrational numbers were first understood from real estate, as in a value that might be based on the length of a diagonal of a square piece of land. However, conveniently, the set of algebraic numbers is still countably infinite, and the only transcendental numbers that might serve as the basis for economic data are probably a small finite set such as π and e.

10 For further development of this idea as a basis of emergence see its application in the form of hypercyclic morphogenesis (Rosser 1991, 1992).

11 McCauley (2005) in particular identified Haken as providing a symmetry breaking approach to emergence, ultimately depending on the work of Turing (1952). Chua (2005) argues that such symmetry breaking (and the origin of true complexity) must be based on local interactions.

12 It must be recognized that despite Mirowski's remark about '1,2, infinity' what is involved here is not a leap to infinity and thus to true undecidability or non-computability. The problem is more one of an increasing complexity that actually existing markets and computers are unable to keep up with in fact, if not in principle.

References

Albin, P.S. (1982) 'The metalogic of economic predictions, calculations and propositions', *Mathematical Social Sciences*, 3: 329–58.

Bak, P. (1996) *How Nature Works: The science of self-organized criticality*, New York: Columbia University Press.

Barrow, J.D. (1992) *Pi in the Sky: Counting, thinking, and being*, Oxford: Clarendon Press.

Bishop, E.A. (1967) *Foundations of Constructive Analysis*, New York: McGraw-Hill.

Blum, L., Cucker, F., Shub, M. and Smale, S. (1998) *Complexity and Real Computation*, New York: Springer-Verlag.

Boulding, K.E. (1978) *Ecodynamics: A new theory of social evolution*, Beverly Hills, CA: Sage.

Brock, W.A., Hommes, C. and Wagener, F. (2008) 'More hedging instruments may destabilize markets', Mimeo, SSRI, University of Wisconsin-Madison; CeNDEF, University of Amsterdam.

Brouwer, L.E.J. (1908) 'De onbetrouwbaarheid der logische principes (The untrustworthiness of the principles of logic)', *Tijdschrif voor wijsbegeerte*, 2: 152–8.

—— (1952) 'An intuitionist correction of the fixed-point theorem on the sphere', *Proceedings of the Royal Society London*, 213: 1–2.

Cantor, G. (1915) trans. P.E.B. Jourdain, *Contributions to the Founding of the Theory of Transfinite Numbers*, Chicago and London: Open Court.

Chomsky, N. (1959) 'On certain formal properties of grammars', *Information and Control*, 2: 11–54.

Chua, L.O. (2005) 'Local activity is the origin of complexity', *International Journal of Bifurcation and Chaos*, 15: 3435–56.

Church, A. (1936) 'A note on the entscheidungsproblem', *Journal of Symbolic Logic*, 1: 40–1, correction 101–2.

Clower, R.W. and Howitt, P.W. (1978) 'The transactions theory of the demand for money: A reconsideration', *Journal of Political Economy*, 86: 449–65.

Conlisk, J. (2007) 'Comment on "Markets come to bits: Evolution, computation, and markomata in economic science"', *Journal of Economic Behavior and Organization*, 63: 243–6.

Crow, J.F. (1953) 'General theory of population genetics: A synthesis', *Cold Spring Harbor Quantitative Symposium on Biology*, 20: 54–9.

Crutchfield, J. (1994) 'The calculi of emergence: Computation, dynamics and induction', *Physica*, D 75: 11–54.

Cucker, F. and Smale, S. (2007) 'On the mathematics of emergence', *Japanese Journal of Mathematics*, 2: 197–227.

da Costa, N.C.A. and Doria, F.A. (2005) 'Computing the future', in K.V. Velupillai (ed.), *Computability, Complexity and Constructivity in Economic Analysis*, Oxford: Blackwell.

Day, R.H. (1994) *Complex Economic Dynamics*, vol. I: *An introduction to dynamical systems and market mechanisms*, Cambridge, MA: MIT Press.

Doria, F.A., Cosenza, C.N., Lessa, C.T. and Bartholo, R.S. (2009) 'Can economic systems be seen as computing devices?' *Journal of Economic Behavior and Organization*, 70(1–2): 72–80.

Eigen, M. and Schuster, P. (1979) *The Hypercycle: A natural principle of self-organization*, Berlin: Springer-Verlag.

Foster, J. (1997) 'The analytical foundations of evolutionary economics: From biological analogy to economic self-organization', *Structural Change and Economic Dynamics*, 8: 427–51.

Fraenkel, A.A. (1961) *Abstract Set Theory*, 2nd edn, Amsterdam: North-Holland.

Friedman, D. and Rust, J. (eds) (1993) *The Double Auction Market*, Redwood City: Addison-Wesley.

Goodwin, R.M. (1947) 'Dynamical coupling with especial reference to markets having production lags', *Econometrica*, 15: 181–204.

Gould, S.J. (2002) *The Structure of Evolutionary Theory*, Cambridge, MA: The Belknap Press of Harvard University Press.

Haken, H. (1983) *'Synergetics:' An introduction. Nonequilibrium phase transitions in physics, chemistry, and biology*, 3rd edn, Berlin: Springer-Verlag.

Hamilton, W.D. (1972) 'Altruism and related phenomena, mainly in the social insects', *Annual Review of Ecology and Systematics*, 3: 192–232.

Henrich, J. (2004) 'Cultural group selection, coevolutionary processes, and large-scale cooperation', *Journal of Economic Behavior and Organization*, 53: 3–35.

Hilbert, D. and Ackermann, W. (1950) *Principles of Mathematical Logic*, New York: Chelsea.

Hodgson, G.M. (2006a) *Economics in the Shadow of Darwin and Marx: Essays on institutional and evolutionary themes*, Cheltenham: Edward Elgar.

—— (2006b) 'What are institutions?' *Journal of Economic Issues*, 40: 1–24.

Holling, C.S. (1973) 'Resilience and stability of ecological systems', *Annual Review of Ecology and Systematics*, 4: 1–24.

Horgan, J. (1997) *The End of Science: Facing the limits of knowledge in the twilight of the scientific age*, New York: Broadway Books.

Israel, G. (2005) 'The science of complexity: Epistemological problems and perspectives', *Science in Context*, 18: 1–31.

Jensen, H. (1998) *Self-Organized Criticality*, Cambridge: Cambridge University Press.

Kaufmann, S.A. (1993) *The Origins of Order: Self-organization and selection in evolution*, Oxford: Oxford University Press.

Keisler, H.J. (1976) *Elementary Calculus*, Boston: Prindle, Weber, & Schmidt.

Kirman, A. (2007) 'The basic unit of economic analysis: Individuals or markets? A comment on "Markets come to bits" by Phil Mirowski', *Journal of Economic Behavior and Organization*, 63: 284–94.

Kleene, S.C. (1967) *Mathematical Logic*, New York: John Wiley & Sons.

Kolmogorov, A.N. (1965) 'Combinatorial foundations of information theory and the calculus of probabilities', *Russian Mathematical Surveys*, 38: 29–40.

Kronecker, L. (1968) *Leopold Kronecker's Werke*, K. Hensel (ed.), New York: Chelsea.

Langton, C.G. (1992) 'Life at the edge of chaos', in C.G. Langton, C.E. Taylor, J.D. Farmer and S. Rasmussen (eds), *Artificial Life II*, Redwood City: Addison-Wesley.

Lee, C. (2005) 'Emergence and universal computation', in K.V. Velupillai (ed.), *Computability, Complexity and Constructivity in Economic Analysis*, Oxford: Blackwell.

Leijonhufvud, A. (1993) 'Towards a not-too rational macroeconomics', *Southern Economic Journal*, 60: 1–13.

Lewes, G.H. (1875) *Problems of Life and Mind, First Series: The foundations of a creed*, vol. II, Cambridge: Riverside Press.

Lewis, A. (1991) 'On Turing degrees of Walrasian models and a general impossibility result in the theory of decision making', Mimeo, School of Social Sciences, University of California-Irvine, CA.

Lloyd Morgan, C. (1923) *Emergent Evolution*, London: Williams and Norgate.

McCauley, J.L. (2004) *Dynamics of Markets: Econophysics and finance*, Cambridge: Cambridge University Press.

—— (2005) 'Making mathematics effective in economics', in K.V. Velupillai (ed.), *Computability, Complexity and Constructivity in Economic Analysis*, Oxford: Blackwell.

Markose, S.M. (2005) 'Computability and evolutionary complexity: Markets as complex adaptive systems (CAS)', *Economic Journal*, 115: F159–92.

Mill, J.S. (1843) *A System of Logic: Ratiocinative and inductive*, London: Longmans Green.

Mirowski, P. (2007a) 'Markets come to bits: Evolution, computation and markomata in economic science', *Journal of Economic Behavior and Organization*, 63: 209–42.

——— (2007b) 'On kicking the habit: A response to the JEBO symposium on "Market come to bits"', *Journal of Economic Behavior and Organization*, 63: 359–71.

Moore, C. (1990) 'Undecidability and unpredictability in dynamical systems', *Physica Review Letters*, 64: 2354–7.

Nicolis, J.S. (1986) *Dynamics of Hierarchical Systems: An evolutionary approach* Berlin: Springer-Verlag.

Niyogi, P. (2006) *The Computational Nature of Language and Evolution*, Cambridge MA: MIT Press.

Odifreddi, P. (1989) *Classical Recursion Theory*, Amsterdam: Elsevier.

Potts, J. (2000) *The New Evolutionary Microeconomics: Complexity, competence and adaptive behaviour*, Cheltenham: Edward Elgar.

Prasad, K. (1991) 'Computability and randomness of Nash equilibria in infinite games' *Journal of Mathematical Economics*, 20: 429–42.

Richter, M.K. and Wong, K.C. (1999) 'Non-computability of competitive equilibrium' *Economic Theory*, 14: 1–28.

Robinson, A. (1966) *Non-Standard Analysis*, Amsterdam: North-Holland.

Rosser, J.B. Jr (1991) *From Catastrophe to Chaos: A general theory of economic discon tinuities*. Boston, MA: Kluwer Academic Publishers.

——— (1992) 'The dialogue between the ecologic and the economic theories of evolution' *Journal of Economic Behavior and Organization*, 17: 195–215.

——— (1999) 'On the complexities of complex economic dynamics', *Journal of Economic Perspectives*, 1: 169–92.

——— (2009) 'Computational and dynamic complexity in economics', in J.B. Rosser J (ed.), *Handbook of Complexity Research*, Cheltenham: Edward Elgar.

Rosser, J.B. Jr, Folke, C., Günther, F., Isomäki, H., Perrings, C. and Puu, T. (1994) 'Dis continuous change in multilevel hierarchical systems', *Systems Research*, 11: 77–94.

Rosser, J.B. Sr (1978) *Logic for Mathematicians*, 2nd edn, New York: Chelsea.

Scarf, H. (1993) 'The computation of equilibrium prices: An exposition', in K.J. Arrow and M.D. Intriligator (eds), *Handbook of Mathematical Economics*, vol. II, 4th edn Amsterdam: Elsevier.

Shoven, J.B. and Whalley, J. (1973) 'General equilibrium with taxes: A computational procedure and an existence proof', *Review of Economic Studies*, 40: 475–89.

Smith, V.L. (1962) 'An experimental study of competitive market behavior', *Journal of Political Economy*, 70: 111–37.

——— (2007) *Rationality in Economics: Constructivist and ecological forms*, New York Cambridge University Press.

Specker, E.P. (1953) 'The axiom of choice in Quine's New Foundations for mathematical logic', *Proceedings of the National Academy of Sciences of the USA*, 39: 972–5.

Tsuji, M., da Costa, N.C.A. and Doria, F. (1998) 'The incompleteness theories of games' *Journal of Philosophical Logic*, 27: 553–68.

Turing, A.M. (1937) 'Computability and λ-definability', *Journal of Symbolic Logic*, 2 153–63.

——— (1952) 'The chemical basis of morphogenesis', *Philosophical Transactions of the Royal Society*, B 237: 37–72.

Velupillai, K.V. (2000) *Computable Economics*, Oxford: Oxford University Press.

——— (ed.) (2005) *Computability, Complexity and Constructivity in Economic Analysis* Oxford: Blackwell.

——— (2006) 'Algorithmic foundations of computable general equilibrium theory' *Applied Mathematics and Computation*, 179: 360–9.

—— (2007) 'Taming the incomputable, reconstructing the nonconstructive, and deciding the undecidable in mathematical economics', *Technical Report, 22*, Economia, University of Trento.

—— (2008) 'Uncomputability and undecidability in economic theory', Invited Lecture in *Workshop on Physics and Computation, 7th International Conference on Unconventional Computation*, Vienna, Austria.

—— (2009) 'A computable economist's perspective on computational complexity', in J.B. Rosser Jr (ed.), *Handbook of Complexity Research*, Cheltenham: Edward Elgar.

Viczek, T., Czirók, A., Ben-Jacob, E. and Shochet, O. (1995) 'Novel type of phase transition in a system of self-driven particles', *Physical Review Letters*, 75: 1226–9.

Weintraub, E.R. (2002) *How Economics Became a Mathematical Science*, Durham, NC, Duke University Press.

Wolfram, S. (1984) 'Universality and complexity in cellular automata', *Physica*, D 10: 1–35.

Zambelli, S. (2007) 'Comments on Philip Mirowski's article: "Markets come to bits: Evolution, computation and markomata in economic science"', *Journal of Economic Behavior and Organization*, 63: 354–8.

Zeeman, E.C. (1974) 'On the unstable behavior of the stock exchanges', *Journal of Mathematical Economics*, 1: 39–44.

Zermelo, E. (1908) 'Unterschungen über die grundlagen der mengenlehre I', *Mathematische Annalen*, 65: 261–81.

Zorn, M. (1935) 'A remark on method in transfinite algebra', *Bulletin of the American Mathematical Society*, 41: 667–70.

12 Remarks on numerical systems, algorithms and economic theory

Richard H. Day

Complexity confounds our ability to comprehend completely the multiple layers of material and organic structures. We do not understand how mind emerges from this intricate evolution or how mind participates as creator in that evolution – except to give the source of novel thought and action a name: the intuition. But once armed with the concepts of number, measurement, causality and logic, reason can advance.

To derive existence and stability properties of equilibria, economists usually ground theoretical work on the real number system. We implicitly assume that 'real' theory is close enough to the truth. In the rationals the task is more difficult, sometimes without answers at all. Still, it is a fact that all monetary and physical calculations in an actual market economy exploit the rationals or the integers (depending, for example, on whether you use a penny or a dollar as numeraire), a fact that most theorists ignore without a qualm. An exception occurred more than half a century ago when optimization theory was extended to the case of integers in order to solve the transportation problem. While considerable applied work was subsequently undertaken in this vein, few economists took note. In the meantime the construction of computer representations of empirical economic processes has gone on apace, living as it were in the rational world of digital numbers.

Now a theorist of note has taken up the fundamental issue implicit in this distinction between 'real' economic theory and 'rational' computational economics. Kumaraswamy Velupillai, in a series of challenging articles and books, calls for a reconstruction of the discipline directly on a computational, numeric basis. Velupillai is a rare, philosophically oriented economist, concerned with the fundamental meaning of theory and the appropriateness of its methods. Central to his analysis is the distinction among the alternative methods of mathematical proof, in particular between constructive proof and proof by contradiction. The central implication of his argument is important: if you have 'proved' that something 'exists', say 'A', but you have no way of representing 'A', then inferences based on 'A' have no practical relevance.

Consider the economist's representation of economizing as the solution of a constrained optimizing problem, that is, as the choice or decision that provides the most preferred alternative among those that satisfy financial and physical constraints. The choice alternatives include contemplated activities such as buying, selling, consuming and producing, while the constraints may involve cash, demand deposits, stocks of durable goods, legal restrictions and so forth. Consumers in a modern economy have a vast array of potential alternatives at any one time and a vast array of potentially relevant information to consider. In various ways they drastically reduce the complexity of the problem by concentrating on a few alternatives at any one time among all those that will arise over a lifetime. Indeed, the same is true for producers, however sophisticated. The more complex their business, the more drastically they must decompose their economizing activity into an interactive structure of individual managerial functions presented over time. In short, real world economizing involves relatively simple decision making and managerial activities that over time arrive at realized decisions to consume and produce.

However simple or complex, alternative ways of thinking and acting arise. The ideas of feasible and best ways of acting emerge in each given situation which guides the agent through time. But termination of the process for arriving at action is required because a decision *must* be made. Common classes of mathematical programming models possess algorithmic sequences of arithmetic computations designed to produce or *converge* to an optimal solution. Such algorithms search – in practice – always among the rational numbers. In some cases a best, real-valued solution can be determined as 'existing' theoretically. This implies in effect that a solution is worth pursuing. But in many cases a best solution can only be approached in the sense that a better solution can be found but only ones for which improvement is negligible from a practical point of view. Especially, when significant nonlinearities and or large numbers of variables and constraints are involved, computation must be terminated short of a 'best' solution. If one accounts for the time and cost of reaching a 'best' decision, however, so-called 'suboptimal decisions' are actually optimal. In any case, real solutions can only be approximated. Indeed, real numbers *only* 'exist' as a limiting concept.

The economic theorist is not usually concerned with solving particular individual consumption or production problems. His problem is to characterize their solution for the purpose of further theorizing: to explain how the actions of individual households and firms add up to market aggregates on the basis of which the operation of the various sectors or the economy as a whole can be understood. For this, it is the *outcome* of algorithmic behaviour, not that computational behaviour itself that is his building block. Any of his results carried out in the real domain are *convenient abstract characterizations* only of the actual phenomena of interest that of necessity exist practically only in the rational numbers.

Let us turn to the analysis of the market economy as a whole, that is, to the Walrasian formulation of general equilibrium in the form based directly on the commodity supply and demand functions. These functions characterize the potential outcomes of the collective of individual households' and firms' algorithmic decisions given a system of commodity prices. They shift attention from the behaviour of individuals to the existence of market clearing prices. The algorithmic behaviour of the participants is subsumed.

Velupillai, here again, makes an important point. The equilibrium existence theory *à la* Arrow–Debreu is not algorithmic. The proofs are all carried out in the real number domain based on non-constructive, fixpoint arguments. Here, however, we should also recognize that Walras did also specify an algorithmic representation of market clearing. It is governed by a '*tâtonnement* process': a sequence of prices each one in the sequence chosen as an adjustment over its predecessor by reducing its value if its corresponding product was in a surplus and increasing it for those for which demand exceeded surplus. Most mid-twentieth century mathematical economists analysed this simple algorithmic scheme. As Goodwin somewhere pointed out, Walras thought of it as a way to prove existence.

Here again, most theorists are not interested in the algorithmic modes by which households and firms arrive at their respective decisions, but rather the properties of the final outcome of those decisions. They implicitly assume that the final outcome can be characterized as the solution to a constrained optimization problem – without worrying about the manner in which that problem has been solved. But suppose now that the *tâtonnement* process does not converge in principle or, even if it does, that it cannot converge in finite time, so that the economy is out–of–equilibrium *all the time*? Then some commodities will be in short supply, others exhibiting a surplus. The process of adjustment will still continue to function out of equilibrium, just as it does in reality *all the time*. *From this point of view it is the* tâtonnement *process itself that must be of greatest interest, not its potential equilibrium.*

Much of what has been discussed above is a kind of defence of standard 'real' but potentially computational economic theory, classic ideas from which we learn something useful: that it contains some algorithmic content and in itself provides a coherent partial understanding of how – in principle – a decentralized private ownership economy is coordinated. One must remember the fundamental problem faced by Adam Smith and that continued to be posed again and again in the succeeding centuries with ever greater symbolic formality: 'Can a system of prices coordinate the exchange of consumption and production goods among a completely decentralized collection of households and firms?' General equilibrium theory finally provided the first completely rigorous answer to this question, one that is purely formal to be sure and not algorithmic. It does not describe *how* an economy can potentially solve this problem. Walras' *tâtonnement* does solve it in the sense of producing a sequence of adjustments that – given the right regularity conditions and given the stationarity of the technology and preferences of the market participants – could approximate a competitive equilibrium ever more closely – and that is the only sense in which real numbers exist.

It is important to understand that the convergence of a dynamic process in general is a limiting concept. Consider the simplest Keynesian model, $y = \alpha y + j + g$ where α is the marginal propensity to consume, $0 < \alpha < 1$, y is income, αy is consumption, j is investment, and g is government expenditure; all in per capita terms and all rational. The solution in terms of income yields the familiar multiplier equation for equilibrium income,

$$\tilde{y} = \frac{1}{1-\alpha}(j+y),$$ (12.1)

which will be rational. However, consider the algorithmic dynamic process,

$$y_{t+1} = \alpha y_t + j + g.$$

Using its recursive structures, we find that from an initial income y_0,

$$y_t = \alpha^t y_0 + (1 + \alpha + \alpha^2 + \ldots + \alpha^{t-1})(j + g),$$

which converges, as $t \to \infty$, in the limit (12.1). Thus, even when a *rational* equilibrium exists, the algorithm only approaches it in the limit.

Let me close with a ringing endorsement of Velupillai's algorithmic point of view. It presents economizing activity as *functioning through* time, that is, as a dynamic process. The economic aspects of life – as in all the biosphere of which it is a part – is always changing, ever evolving. The essence of algorithmic theory and dynamic theory generally is the symbolic and computational representation of this fundamental character of life as we know it. They deserve all the emphasis that Velupillai demands. Surely, the time will come when the self-appointed optimal control 'mainstream' will have surpassed its flood stage with its suffocating purge of any consideration of the out of equilibrium, algorithmic character of real world dynamics. Surely, it will in turn be overcome by a renewed surge of theoretical research into the nature of actual economizing behaviour and market exchange.

13 An experiment on equilibrium selection

The relative unimportance of context

Håkan J. Holm[1]

Introduction

Predicting the equilibrium in economics often involves severe computational problems (see Velupillai 2000). However, even if the set of equilibria is simple to calculate, frequently a coordination problem remains to be solved. Such coordination problems can result in inferior outcomes even in mutual interest games. If we consider the pure coordination game in Figure 13.1 in its existential form (as described by Sugden 1995), then without communication the game theoretical prediction of the average behaviour of a population would be the mixed strategy equilibrium where both players choose each strategy with probability 0.5. The average payoff would be 100 in this equilibrium. However Schelling (1960) has argued convincingly that the expected payoff can be improved upon by letting the players use contextual information about the game like the strategy labels. Thus, for instance by denoting strategies C1 and R1 by 'Heads' and C2 and R2 by 'Tails' experimental results demonstrate that the majority of subjects are able to coordinate in the (Heads, Heads) equilibrium (see e.g. Mehta *et al.* 1994).

Schelling's (1960) theory of focal points has become a standard reference in textbooks in game theory (see e.g. Fudenberg and Tirole 1991; Binmore 1992 and it has been developed further by e.g. Bacharach (1993) and Sugden (1995) It has also been confirmed in various experiments (e.g. Mehta *et al.* 1994; Holm 2000). Thus, few would argue that the ideas put forth by Schelling (1960) are unimportant in coordination situations, especially when one considers that some

		Column player	
		C1	C2
Row player	R1	200,200	0,0
	R2	0,0	200,200

Figure 13.1 A pure coordination game.

contextual information is always present in real strategic situations. This leads to a dilemma: at the same time as contextual information enriches game theory by making it possible to predict a unique focal equilibrium, the importance of contextual information also challenges the very foundation of any theory intended to be applicable to different contexts. It is therefore somewhat strange that so little effort has been directed in trying to find out *how* important this type of information is compared to payoffs which are captured by the existential game form. Our experiment can be seen as a simplistic step in this direction.

The purpose of this chapter is to study the strength of a focal point induced by strategy labels when a small payoff asymmetry is introduced.[2] The asymmetry is designed so that the non-focal equilibrium in the original game becomes payoff salient in the new game by letting it be both Pareto dominant and risk dominant.[3] In this way the subjects are forced to select what principle to believe in (and believe that others believe in, etc.), strategy label saliency or payoff saliency.

Experimental design

In the first experiment we recruited 145 undergraduate students from the introductory course in Economics at Lund University, Sweden. The subjects filled in a questionnaire including four tasks. This chapter concerns the two first tasks.[4] Each subject played the game described in Figure 13.1 where the payoff referred to Swedish crowns and where the strategy labels 'Left' and 'Right' were used.[5] The subjects were told that they were paired with an anonymous co-player. Furthermore, the player and co-player were unable to communicate and contingent upon the players guessing the same direction they earned SEK 200 each (i.e. if both chose 'Right' or if both chose 'Left'). If they chose different directions, nobody earned anything.

The payoff in the equilibrium expected to be non-focal in the first task (i.e. 'Left, Left') was increased by 5 per cent (to SEK 210) in the second task. The subjects could not observe the outcomes from the first game before they made their choices in the second game.[6]

To see if the results were robust we also replicated the experiment with some small changes in the design. In the second experiment 161 new undergraduates of the same category participated.[7] We also replicated the experiment with a subject pool from a different country. In the third experiment 164 undergraduates from the introductory course in Microeconomics at Northwestern University, USA, participated. An experimental session took 10–15 minutes in all three experiments and the expected hourly earnings were US$2.50 in the first experiment, US$7.50 in the second and US$15 in the American study.[8]

Results

We observed two results in the experiments (see Table 13.1):

1   The strategy combination ('Right', 'Right') constituted a focal point in Task 1. We can reject the null hypothesis (that the average probability of a subject to choose 'Right' is 0.5) at a significance level below 1 per cent for all three experiments. This result is rather expected and demonstrates primarily that the experiments are successful in inducing a focal point by strategy labels.
2   The subjects chose the payoff salient equilibrium even if the strategy label induced focal point from Task 1 was optional. Hence, our results strongly support that the principle of payoff saliency is the stronger one and that even small payoff differences eliminate the strategy label effect.

The results indicate a hierarchy of principles where payoff salience is the stronger one for the vast majority. This is also demonstrated by the subjects' answers on both tasks. There are four different possible answers: LR, RL, LL and RR, where LR denotes that the subject has chosen 'Left' in the first task and 'Right' in the second task and so forth.

In all experiments more than 90 per cent of those having chosen 'Left' in the first period continued to choose 'Left' in the second period whereas more than 79 per cent of the subjects that played 'Right' in the first period changed to 'Left' in the second task.

Table 13.1 The number of subjects answering 'right' or 'left' on Task 1 and 2

	Task 1				Task 2			
	Left		Right		Left		Right	
	no.	%	no.	%	no.	%	no.	%
Experiment 1	54	37.2	91	62.8	123	84.8	22	15.2
Experiment 2	60	37.3	101	62.7	141	87.6	20	12.4
Experiment 3	58	35.4	106	64.6	141	86.0	23	14.0

Note
Experiment 1 and 2 refer to the first and second study in Sweden and Experiment 3 refers to the American study.

Table 13.2 The number of answers categorized into the four possible ways to choose in Task 1 and Task 2

	LL		LR		RL		RR	
	no.	%	no.	%	no.	%	no.	%
Experiment 1	51	35.2	3	2.1	72	49.7	19	13.1
Experiment 2	57	35.4	3	1.9	84	52.2	17	10.6
Experiment 3	53	32.3	5	3.0	88	53.7	18	11.0

These results only consider one type of contextual information and it may be that other strategy labels are less sensitive to changes in payoffs. It is also likely that the strategy label effect would have better chances in surviving a payoff asymmetry involving a set of equilibria where Pareto dominance and aspects of security pulled in opposite directions. However, as a benchmark for future research, the figures are strong. Thus, for equilibria that are neutral with respect to security, we can conclude that even if it is true that strategy labels often are exploited to the benefits of the parties in pure symmetric coordination situations, they are relatively irrelevant in the presence of an equilibrium being both Pareto dominant and risk dominant.

Dynamic considerations

The importance of various coordination principles has been extensively studied by van Huyck *et al.* (1991) in a dynamic context. One of their findings is that strong precedents are salient. Thus, the equilibrium historically chosen is likely to be chosen in the future. As a consequence, if two slightly different coordination games are to be played sequentially and if the behaviour in these two games is governed by two different principles, whose relative strengths are studied, then this effect would favour whatever principle governed the first game.

This chapter focuses on the relative strength of coordination principles in a static sense. To isolate the question of the relative strength of strategy labels compared to payoff saliency we designed the game so as to eliminate or minimize the effects from factors whose importance already has been established. Hence, security considerations were eliminated and the effect of strong precedents was reduced by *not* letting the subjects being aware of the history of the other players' choices. The cost of this design is that our results are not applicable for analysis of the stability of focal points (in a dynamic sense).

It should be noted however, that due to the sequence of the tasks in the experiment the effect of strong precedents would magnify the strategy label effect at the cost of the payoff effect since only the former is present in the first task whereas possibly both are present in the second task. This observation consequently reinforces our result on the dominance of the payoff effect even further.

Conclusion

Classical game theory predicts that behaviour will be governed solely by the payoff structure. Hence, the fact that payoff effects dominate strategy label effects should come as no surprise. However, the degree to which the payoff effects dominate the strategy label effects is interesting, since it indicates when strategy labels are of minor importance. Consequently, this result may have a value not only as a descriptive empirical characteristic of how people act, but also as constructive information for those who sometimes worry too much about strategy label effects in their design of economic experiments.

Appendix A

In this appendix we have translated the information about the first Swedish experiment and the text on the questionnaire from Swedish to English. The graphical structure of the text is unchanged from the original.

Information about the experiment

You have been paired with a co-player belonging to a certain category of subjects. If you and your co-player are able to coordinate your choices, then you will earn points in the experiment. The payoff (in terms of points) depends partly on your choices and partly on the co-player's choices. However, your co-player's choices will be unknown to you and she/he will not know your choices.

By your answers you will collect points that will be counted in Swedish crowns. You can earn at most SEK 1110 (and at least SEK 0) depending on how well you succeed, given the choices of your co-player. Three winners will be selected at random of all subjects that answer the questions. The winner of the first prize will get the value he/she has gained (in terms of a bookshop gift voucher or a restaurant gift voucher) in the experiment. The second and third prize winners will get the value corresponding to one-half and one-quarter of the number of crowns earned in the experiment. Hence, your task is to collect as many points as possible by choosing strategically in order to guess your co-player's choices.

By looking at the top of the *Questionnaire* you can see what category your co-player belongs to.

1   Please, check that a category is given for your co-player!
2   Fill in your own name!
    (Your name is needed to make it possible to identify the winners. Your answers will be anonymous for all other purposes.)
3   Please, fill in the questionnaire and remain silent on your place until the experimenter breaks off the session.

Good luck!

Questionnaire

Your name:

The Co-player's Category:
Male student

_____

_____

Instruction. You will confront four strategic situations, where your payoff depends partly on your own choices and partly on your co-player's choices. Your task is to earn as many points (in crowns) as possible. The result will be available as soon as your choices are combined with those of your co-player.

1   You are going to choose between Right and Left.

Points. If you choose the same direction as your co-player, then you will earn 200 crowns each. (That is if you both choose Right or if you both choose Left.) If you and your co-player choose different directions, nobody will earn anything.

Circle *one* alternative!
Alternatives: Left   Right

2   You are going to choose between Right and Left.

Points. The same problem as in Task (1). Thus, you have to choose the same direction as your co-player to gain anything. You will earn 200 crowns each if you both choose Right. If both choose Left, then you will earn 210 crowns each.

Circle *one* alternative!
Alternatives: Left   Right

3   You are going to choose a distribution.

Points. You and your co-player have the opportunity of sharing 500 crowns. In order to get the money you and your co-player have to be in agreement over how to share the money. If both choose the same distribution, you will get the amount prescribed by your part of the distribution and your co-player will get his part of the distribution. If your choices lead to disagreement about how to share the money, both receive zero crowns.

Circle *one* alternative below!
Alternatives:

You get 400 crowns and your co-player gets 100 crowns.

You get 300 crowns and your co-player gets 200 crowns.

You get 250 crowns and your co-player gets 250 crowns.

You get 200 crowns and your co-player gets 300 crowns.

You get 100 crowns and your co-player gets 400 crowns.

Explanation and examples. Notice that when you have chosen one altern
ative there is only one alternative that your co-player can choose if you
agree about how to share the money.

Example:
i   If you have chosen the uppermost alternative, agreement requires that
    your co-player has chosen the lowermost alternative. (In this case, you
    will get 400 crowns and your co-player will get 100 crowns.)
ii If you have chosen the middle alternative, agreement requires that your
    co-player also has chosen the middle alternative. (In this case, both will
    get 250 crowns.)
iii If you have chosen the second lowermost alternative, agreement
    requires that your co-player has chosen the second uppermost altern
    ative. (In this case, you will get 200 crowns and your co-player will get
    300 crowns.)

4   You are going to choose a distribution.

Points. You and your co-player have the possibility of sharing 500 crowns.
The problem is the same as in question (3), but here you and your co-player
have fewer ways to share the 500 crowns.

Circle *one* alternative below!
Alternatives:

You get 300 crowns and your co-player gets 200 crowns.

You get 200 crowns and your co-player gets 300 crowns.

Notes

1 I would like to thank Hans Carlsson at Lund University, participants at the 17th Arne
  Ryde Symposium and seminar participants at the Stockholm School of Economics for
  comments on an earlier version of this chapter. Financial support from Jan Wallander'
  and Tom Hedelius' foundation for research in the social science, and Kellogg Center
  for Strategic Decision Making are gratefully acknowledged.
2 The idea to study different equilibrium selection principles over a class of 2x2 games
  defined by payoff changes can also be found in Carlsson and van Damme's (1993)
  theoretical study.
3 It is fairly well-known from experimental studies that aspects of risk (as captured by
  Harsanyi and Selten's (1988) risk dominance concept) and aspects of security can
  produce coordination failures in terms of causing the subjects not to select the Pareto
  dominant outcome (see Cooper *et al.* 1990; van Huyck *et al.* 1991; Straub 1995). To
  avoid these effects we constructed our games such that both risk dominance and Pareto
  dominance point in the same direction. Furthermore, in our games the equilibria are
  neutral with respect to security.
4 The information given to the subjects and the exact formulations in the questionnaire
  are given in the Appendix.
5 Note that the game was not presented to the subjects in matrix form.
6 This has important implications, which we will return to later on.

7 The information given to the subjects and the exact formulations in the questionnaire for the two latter experiments are very similar to the one in the first experiment.
8 An experimental session also included two additional questions that do not directly relate to the issue of this chapter (see Holm 2000). These questions were presented after the two tasks this chapter focuses on. See tasks 3 and 4 in the Appendix.

References

Bacharach, M. (1993) 'Variable universe games', in K. Binmore, A. Kirman and P. Tani (eds), *Frontiers of Game Theory*, Cambridge, MA: MIT Press.

Binmore, K. (1992) *Fun and Games: A text on game theory*, Lexington, MA: D.C. Heath.

Carlsson, H. and van Damme, E. (1993) 'Global games and equilibrium selection', *Econometrica*, 61: 989–1018.

Cooper, R.W., Dejong, D.V., Forsythe, R. and Ross, T.W. (1990) 'Selection criteria in coordination games: Some experimental results', *American Economic Review*, 80: 218–32.

Fudenberg, D. and Tirole, J. (1991) *Game Theory*, London: MIT Press.

Harsanyi, J. and Selten, R. (1988) *A General Theory of Equilibrium Selection in Games*, Cambridge, MA: MIT Press.

Holm, H.J. (2000) 'Gender based focal points', *Games and Economic Behavior*, 32: 292–314.

Mehta, J., Starmer, C. and Sugden, R. (1994) 'The nature of salience: An experimental investigation of pure coordination games', *American Economic Review*, 84, 658–73.

Schelling, T.C. (1960) *The Strategy of Conflict*, Cambridge, MA: Harvard University Press.

Straub, P. (1995) 'Risk dominance and coordination failures in static games', *Quarterly Review of Economics and Finance*, 35: 339–63.

Sugden, R. (1995) 'A theory of focal points', *Economic Journal*, 105: 533–50.

van Huyck, J., Battalio, R. and Beil, R.O. (1991) 'Strategic uncertainty, equilibrium selection, and coordination failure in average opinion games', *Quarterly Journal of Economics*, 106: 885–910.

Velupillai, K.V. (2000) *Computable Economics*, Oxford: Oxford University Press.

14 The complexity of social choice

Kislaya Prasad

Introduction

The modern theory of social choice is the culmination of two traditions – utilitarianism and the mathematical theory of elections and committee decisions (Sen 1986). From the former comes the idea that the effects of decisions, including public policy decisions, are to be judged in terms of the personal welfare of individuals. In its simplest form, utilitarianism compares two social states by comparing the sum of individual utilities in these states. The second tradition was concerned with the design of elections, and focused heavily on the comparison of alternative voting mechanisms. From here comes the idea that the information base for social welfare decisions is to be the ordinal rankings of alternatives by individuals. As Sen (1986) describes it: 'The union produced modern social choice theory. The big bang that characterized the beginning took the form of an impossibility theorem.' Arrow (1951) showed that, when aggregating individual preference rankings into a social ordering, a small list of mild desirable conditions cannot be fulfilled by any ranking whatsoever. The ensuing literature built upon this, and provided a whole array of negative results. In the face of these results, it is perhaps understandable that the question of the computational feasibility of implementing different social choice rules took back stage. Upon reading Arrow, one takes away the feeling (not entirely justified) that there is not much room for improvement over the rules, such as majority voting, in use today. Since majority voting is computationally simple to implement, and if major improvements are beyond our reach, perhaps there is not much left to say on the subject.

There are both theoretical and practical reasons why impossibility reasons are not a cause for giving up on thinking about computational issues in social choice. For one, as Mas-Colell *et al.* (1995: 799) conclude in their text:

> The result of Arrow's impossibility theorem is somewhat disturbing, but it would be facile to conclude from it that 'democracy is impossible'. What it shows is something else – that we should not expect a collectivity of individuals to behave with the kind of coherence that we may hope from an individual ... In practice collective judgments are made and decisions are taken. What Arrow's theorem tells us, in essence is that the institutional detail and procedures of the political process cannot be neglected

Indeed, the very fact that we cannot devise ideal voting systems explains a large portion of political activity (e.g. conflict over the order in which alternatives are considered by a committee). Even within the realm of what is possible, different rules governing the political process matter, and there is scope for weighing in on the computational properties of alternatives. On the normative side, it may be possible here to make a principled distinction between what is, and what is not, practically feasible. If we want an improvement upon existing procedures, we ought not to neglect the computational dimensions of the problem. On the positive side, it is probably a fair conjecture that prominent rules and procedures have their place in society because of their computational properties. This is to say more than just that 'majority voting is computationally efficient'. The way in which social decisions are made, the way in which rules and institutions evolve, the effect that new technologies such as mass media and the Internet have on political process, are all affected by the complexity inherent in aggregating a large and diverse set of opinions about alternatives before a group. To understand how individuals and groups cope with complexity is to develop a better understanding of the political process.

An appreciation of this point goes back right to the beginning of the discipline. Recall the claim of utilitarians such as Bentham (1789) that social decisions can be made on the basis of calculations involving individual utilities. Objections to this view arose soon after. In his essay 'Bentham', Mill expressed doubts about the form of utilitarianism preached by Bentham, as well as by his father James Mill, and writes:

> We think utility, or happiness, much too complex and indefinite an end to be sought, except through the medium of various secondary ends, concerning which there may be, and often is, agreement among persons who differ in their ultimate standard.

> (Mill 1838: 170)

This anticipates, to some extent, the later distinction between *act* and *rule* utilitarianism. Since the complexity of most situations makes it infeasible to make a reasoned choice among alternatives, people tend to be guided by simple moral rules. These rules suffice for most circumstances, and there is always the possibility of handling exceptions with a more detailed calculation. The idea extends to the sphere of public policy, where decisions also tend to be guided by rules (or simple images and metaphors that are used to derive rules). Much of politics is a negotiation about the rules to apply when choosing among alternatives. This perspective suggests a reorientation of our thinking about social choice, away from an emphasis on actions and their consequences, to rules and their evolution. If rules are a device to allow us to cope with complexity, then a useful starting point would be to think about the place of complexity in social choice.

In this chapter, my focus will be much narrower than the concerns outlined above as motivation. I will be reviewing briefly some results in the complexity of social choice. Attempts to incorporate computational complexity into formal economic models are beset by serious difficulties. These relate, in one way or another, to an inadequate formalization of the notion of complexity. We do not, as yet, have a widely accepted set of axioms for an individual or a group with limited computational abilities. In the present chapter I will adopt a formalization of complexity which was developed in the 1970s and arises as a result of the synthesis of two distinct literatures: (i) the theory of computational complexity, which is concerned with general statements about properties of algorithms for a problem, and (ii) combinatorial optimization, where much of the effort was devoted to finding efficient algorithms for problems that arise in Operations Research. The genealogy may be traced back to Turing (1936) and Dantzig *et al.* (1959) respectively. The two lines of research were combined by Karp (see Karp 1986), who demonstrated that the lack of success in finding efficient algorithms for a number of combinatorial optimization problems (such as the Travelling Salesman problem) was not accidental. Establishing a link with previous results in symbolic logic, Karp presented strong formal evidence to imply that efficient solutions for these problems are unlikely to exist. From these beginnings, over the next several years, the theory of NP-completeness was developed. I will be adopting the definition of an efficient algorithm used in this theory – a problem is computationally efficient if it has an algorithm that computes a solution in a number of steps that is a polynomial function of the size of the problem. A problem is computationally intractable if it has no algorithm that runs in polynomial time. It is sometimes possible to prove that a problem has no polynomial time algorithm. However, the more typical situation is that problems turn out to be NP-complete (which will also be taken to mean that the problem is intractable). These notions will be more formally defined in the next section of the paper. The philosophical implications of such results have perhaps best been stated by Cherniak:

> If complexity theory in some sense 'cuts the computational universe at its joints' – providing a principled basis for a hierarchy of qualitative distinctions between practically feasible and infeasible tasks – then we need to examine the idea that, in at least some interesting cases, rationality models ought not to entail procedures that are computationally intractable.
>
> (Cherniak 1984: 739)

With complexity definitions in place, in the third section of the chapter, I will ask if there are instances of voting rules which are computationally intractable. Then, in the fourth section of the chapter, I will address the question of calculation of indices of power, such as the Shapley value and the Banzhaf value, of weighted majority games. The fifth section then concludes.

Complexity theory

Since any computation which conforms with our notion of what is effectively computable can be performed on a Turing machine (TM), it is reasonable to con-

struct complexity measures on the basis of resources expended by a TM computing a particular function. Suppose a function is known to be computable. We
could measure its complexity by its running time (the number of steps taken by
the TM) or its space requirements (storage requirements of the TM). The typical
function takes an argument, and after the computation is completed, returns
some output. The resources required by the TM will depend on the input. I will,
like much of the literature, focus on the *worst case* performance. Although storage considerations are often important, the focus here will be on time complexity. For this, let TM_i be a Turing machine given input w. Then,

$$T(n) = \max\{m \,|\, TM_i \text{ halts after } m \text{ steps for input } w \text{ of length } n\}.$$

Note that $T(\cdot)$ is a function of n, the length of the input, which will be called the
size of the problem. For instance, we may have a function $T(n) = kn^2$, or $T(n) = e^n$.
As mentioned above, use will be made of the polynomial–super-polynomial distinction in making statements about the hardness of a problem. Polynomial time
complexity (e.g. $T(n) = kn^2$) is taken to imply computational efficiency, while
exponential time complexity (e.g. $T(n) = e^n$) implied intractability. The use of
this distinction is a formalization of actual experience with algorithms in Operations Research and Computer Science. If resource requirements grow exponentially with the size of the problem, a theoretically trivial problem may become
practically impossible to solve. Consider the Travelling Salesman problem – this
is the problem of finding the shortest tour through n cities, visiting each city only
once and in one continuous tour. This problem can easily be solved by hand for
a small number of cities, but even the most ingenious attempts stumble at
instances with a few hundred cities.[1]

An algorithm is said to be polynomially time bounded – by polynomial
$W(n)$ – if $T(n) < W(n)$ for all n. A problem belongs to the class P if it has a polynomially time bounded solution. A related problem is that of checking whether a
candidate is actually a solution to a given problem. For instance, we may be
given a tour through n cities – is this the shortest tour? In case it is possible to
check in polynomial time if a candidate is a solution the problem is said to be in
the class NP. Clearly, $P \subset NP$. It is not, however, known if this containment is
proper. There are problems in NP which have no known polynomially bounded
solution procedures. A problem is said to be NP-*hard* if a polynomial time algorithm for it could be transformed (in a number of steps which is a polynomial in
the length n of the input) into algorithms for any of the other problems in NP. If
a problem is NP-hard and is *in* NP it is said to be NP-*complete*. The Travelling
Salesman problem is NP-complete. These are obviously the hardest problems in
NP.

NP-completeness of a problem is generally considered to imply computational difficulty since a polynomial algorithm for the problem would imply $P =
NP$. This prospect is considered extremely implausible.

A standard technique for proving NP-completeness is to show that (i) the
algorithm for a problem Y can be transformed, in polynomial time, into an

algorithm for an NP-complete problem X ($X \leq_p Y$); and (ii) Y is in $N\,P$. For this approach to work, there would have to be at least one problem which was not proved NP-complete by this method. This is a problem in Logic called Satisfiability (see, for instance, Garey and Johnson 1979). A variant of Satisfiability – also NP-complete – is now presented. Consider formulas in propositional logic constructed out of literals (Boolean variables or their negation). A formula in *Conjunctive Normal Form* (CNF) is a conjunction of clauses C_1, C_2,..., C_r where each clause is formed by a disjunction of literals. For instance,

$$(x^1 \vee x^2 \vee x^4) \wedge (x^1 \vee \neg x^2) \wedge (x^2 \vee \neg x^3).$$

The Satisfiability problem for formulae in CNF: is there an assignment of 1 or 0 (true or false) to each variable that makes the formula true (evaluate to 1)? That this problem is decidable is obvious. Complete enumeration can be used to test every possible assignment. The problem with an enumeration scheme is that the number of assignments to evaluate grows super-polynomially with the number of variables. NP-completeness of the Satisfiability problem for CNF implies that significant speed-ups are not possible unless $P = N\,P$.

There are a number of other sets for which complete problems have been found. One other that will be used here is #P. Problems complete for #P were introduced by Valiant (1979) to characterize the complexity of enumeration. The typical NP-complete problem is a decision question: 'Is there a solution for problem A?' or 'What is the solution for A?' In enumeration questions we ask: 'How many solutions does A have?' or 'What are the different solutions for A?' Some important questions relating to the computation of indices of power will be seen to be #P-complete.

Complexity results in social choice

It is a general rule that elections are held infrequently, relative to the need to make social decisions. The amount of information used is limited, being restricted to ordinal rankings between a small number of alternatives. Complicated procedures are used to reduce the size of the set of alternatives (agenda). These are all attempts to manage the complexity inherent in eliciting information about individual preferences. But are there intractable problems in social choice in the sense of the previous section? The answer, we will see, is in the affirmative.

Suppose a set of alternatives, V, is given. Individual preference orderings R_i are defined over V for each individual i in society. The vector $(R_1,..., R_n)$ is called a preference profile. A social choice rule (SCR) is a function f from the set of all preference profiles to a social ordering R over V. In other words $R = f(R_1,..., R_n)$. The social choice is the top-ranking element of R. I now present an example of a SCR f which is NP-complete. This is drawn from Prasad (1988)

Weak Unanimity

Individual preferences are defined over a set of items $V = \{x^1, x^2, \ldots, x^n\}$ and its negation $\neg V = \{\neg x^1, \neg x^2, \ldots, \neg x^n\}$ with $n > 2$. Individuals submit preference orderings, and group members are allowed to indicate their indifference among agenda items. They are also allowed to express negative preferences and veto alternatives. I will adopt the following convention – individuals submit lists where earlier listed items are more highly preferred, with the use of parentheses indicating indifference. So, for instance, $(x^1 x^3)x^2$ indicates that the individual is indifferent between x^1 and x^3, and both of these are preferred to x^2. Social preferences are constructed by finding a subset X of $(V \cup \neg V)$ such that at least one item from the top of every individual's preference ordering is in it, with the restriction that both x^i and $\neg x^i$ may not be chosen. Let $\neg X$ denote the relative complement of X, i.e. $(V \cup \neg V - X)$. The social preference ordering is $(X)(\neg X)$.

An instance of this SCR is as follows. Let $V = \{x^1, x^2, x^3\}$, and let there be five voters with the following top-ranked items: Voter 1, $(x^1 x^2 x^3)$; Voter 2, $(x^1 \neg x^2)$; Voter 3, $(x^1 \neg x^3)$; Voter 4, $(\neg x^1 x^3)$ and Voter 5, $(\neg x^1 \neg x^2)$. A committee decision to satisfy all members is $X = (x^1 \neg x^2 x^3)$.

Note that X may be empty (for instance, if there are two voters and x^1 is the only thing at the top of individual 1's ordering, while $\neg x^1$ is the only thing at the top of 2's ordering). The following interpretation will help fix ideas. Each member of some committee has some subset of interest in the agenda. This consists of endorsements or vetoes on items from the agenda. A voter is said to be satisfied if at least one of his recommendations is included in X. A committee decision is arrived by making sure that each member is satisfied. In the problem, as stated, the complexity depends upon the size of the agenda. It can be made to depend on the size of the electorate by considering the problem to be one of subcommittee selection.

Weak Unanimity is now shown to be NP-complete (the argument is from Prasad 1988). We saw earlier that the Satisfiability problem for CNF is NP-complete. I will show that CNF $\leq_P$ Weak Unanimity. In other words, if we had a polynomial time algorithm for Weak Unanimity, we could use it determine in polynomial time whether an arbitrary CNF formula was Satisfiable. Consider a TM which solves instances of Weak Unanimity. Given a formula in CNF we construct, in polynomial time, an instance of Weak Unanimity. Let the formula (a conjunction of clauses) be $C_1 \wedge C_2 \wedge \ldots C_m$, where each C_k is a disjunction of literals. Corresponding to each clause C_k, construct an individual preference ordering over all the $x_i \in V$ as follows: voter k has ranking $(X_k)(\neg X_k)$ where X_k is the set of literals in clause C_k and $\neg X_k$ is the set of literals not in C_k. The preference aggregation algorithm returns a social ordering $(X)(\neg X)$ with the property that X contains a literal from each C_k and does not contain both some x^i and its negation $\neg x^i$. Now construct the following assignment of values for the Boolean variables. If $x^i \in X$, assign it value 1. If not, assign x^i value 0. This assigns a value 1 to a literal in each clause, making the CNF formula true. The transformation is polynomial time bounded, involving one scan through the input. This proves that Weak Unanimity is NP-hard. Membership in NP is obvious, so that it is NP-complete. The result does not depend in any significant way upon the fact that the agenda has been increased to include negation. A variation is in terms of sets (Hitting Sets) – given a collection C of subsets of a finite set S, is there a subset of size k or less which contains at least one element from each member of C? So complexity results in social choice are easy obtain, but do they arise for any of the alternatives discussed in the literature?

The decisive results in the complexity of voting problems were provided by Bartholdi *et al.* (1989a, 1989b). They showed that a voting rule devised by Charles Dodgson (better known by his pen name Lewis Carroll) is NP-complete. Dodgson's rule is related to the famous Condorcet paradox. Condorcet had considered the possibility of finding a candidate who could beat all of the other alternatives in pair-wise majority votes. He discovered that even when individual preferences are transitive, the social rankings determined through pair-wise majority voting could be intransitive, displaying cycles. A Condorcet winner is defined as the candidate who would beat every other candidate in a pair-wise contest. If a Condorcet winner does not exist, is there a way of identifying the candidate who is, in some well-defined sense, closest to being a Condorcet winner? Dogson's rule is to award the election to the candidate who requires the minimum number of switches in the voters' preference ordering to become the Condorcet winner. Bartholdi *et al.* (1989a) proved that it is NP-hard to determine whether a given candidate has won the election. They observe that, in his life as Lewis Carroll, Dodgson would have appreciated the fact that for a large election the candidates would have died before the election was decided. Bartholdi *et al.* (1989a) consider some other voting problems that are NP-complete. Their work on the Dodgson rule is refined by Hemaspaandra *et al.* (1997).

A second class of results by Bartholdi *et al.* (1989b) relates to manipulation of elections. The Gibbard–Satterthwaite theorem shows that it is impossible to devise voting rules that are immune to manipulation (given that a small number of additional conditions are satisfied). Typically, there will be instances in which a voter can improve his outcome by *not* voting sincerely. For several common voting rules, such as plurality voting, it turns out to be easy to manipulate elections. Consider, for instance, a voter who most prefers candidate A, then B and finally C. If A is unlikely to win, it may be in the voter's interest to vote for B instead of A to forestall the possibility that C wins. If the intention is to make B win then, under plurality voting, manipulation is easy – the voter should vote for B. For more complicated voting schemes the answer may not be so obvious. The question is whether there are voting rules for which manipulation becomes difficult. If this were the case, then we would have less reason to worry that an election could be manipulated. In fact there are voting schemes that are difficult to manipulate. One such is the *single transferable vote* mechanism. Under this rule, voters rank the candidates, and vote totals for first-place rankings are tallied. If one of the candidates wins more than 50 per cent of the first-place votes, he wins the election. If not, the candidate who garners the lowest first-place vote total is eliminated. Votes for eliminated candidates get transferred to the next most preferred candidate. Vote totals for first-place rankings are totalled again, and so on. For this mechanism, if there is a candidate a voter would like to see win, the problem of finding an optimal manipulation strategy is NP-complete.

There is now an emerging literature that studies the complexity of voting systems. Faliszewski *et al.* (2006) review much of the work that has taken place in more recent years, discuss a range of related problems and point to some interesting directions. It would be a recommended starting point for anyone interested in the subject.

Power indices for voting games

I consider next indices of power, such as the Shapley value and the Banzhaf index, in the context of weighted majority voting. In weighted majority games, individuals have different numbers of votes, and the question is 'what is a measure of the individual's ability to influence the outcome?' In electoral systems where an individual has only one vote, people may form coalitions that vote together as a bloc, making the system one of weighted majority voting with the groups substituting for individuals. It is clear that the power of a player in such games is not proportional to the number of votes. So what is a good measure of power? Such questions arise in problems as diverse as congressional apportionment and cost allocation (e.g. landing fees at airports). An ideal notion of a fair voting system would be one that gives equal influence to all individuals, but such an ideal is very distant from current reality in most electoral systems. For instance, a group that consistently votes for one party can exert different amounts of influence depending on whether everyone is in the same congressional district, or people have been split up into different districts. The latter would diminish the power of the group to influence outcomes. A normative ideal is to devise schemes that bring about a 'fair' distribution of power, and a prerequisite for this is a measure of the power of an individual under different electoral systems. On the positive side, much of politics is an attempt to influence the power of different groups in society. This is what makes the drawing of congressional districts such a controversial topic in the USA.

Power indices have long been known to be difficult to compute, and this is true even when the characteristic function is easy to define (e.g. in a weighted majority game).

The first complexity result for power indices appears to be that of Garey and Johnson (1979) – who state that determining whether the Shapley–Shubik index has a non-zero value is NP-hard. I will now describe some results from Prasad and Kelly (1990), and then point the reader to some of the more recent work along this line. Attention is limited to weighted majority games (this has the advantage that the characteristic function of the game is easy to compute, so that the computational difficulty can be attributed to the power index itself). Assume there is a set $N = \{1, 2,..., n\}$ of players, and a corresponding set $W = \{w_1, w_2,..., w_n\}$ of integer weights (the 'number of votes' for each player). Suppose we are given a positive integer q (the number of votes needed to 'win'). For some specified player i, does there exist a subset S of N such that

$$\sum w_j < q \text{ for } i \in S \text{ and } \sum_{S \cup \{i\}} w_j \geq q.$$

In other words, is there a coalition S such that the inclusion of player i makes it possible for the coalition to win? We call this problem PIVOT. This coalition game can be described in terms of its characteristic function as follows. Let the value $v(S)$ of a coalition S be defined by

$$v(S) = 1 \text{ if } \sum_S w_j \geq q, \text{ and } v(S) = 0 \text{ otherwise.}$$

Alternatively stated, player i is pivotal for S if $v(S) - v(S \cup \{i\}) = 1$. We can think of this difference as the marginal contribution of player i to the coalition S. Power indices can be defined in terms of the number of sets for which for a player i is pivoting. The problem of determining if there is a set for player i is pivotal is NP-complete. The normalized Banzhaf index is

$$\beta_i(v) = \frac{\theta_i}{2^{n-1}}.$$

The Shapley–Shubik index is

$$\varphi_i(v) = \sum_{T \subseteq N} \frac{(t-1)!(n-t)!}{n!}(v(T) - (v(T - \{i\})$$

where $i \in T$ and t is the number of elements in T. Since both of these indices are related to the number of sets for which player i is pivotal, it will be evident that the problem of deciding whether either of these indices is greater than zero is NP-complete. Although this is useful, it doesn't quite characterize the complexity of *computing* power indices. For this we need the concept of #*P*-completeness alluded to earlier. The problem of computing θ_i, the key ingredient in the Banzhaf index, is #*P*-complete. The problem of computing the Banzhaf index also turns out to be #*P*-complete (more precisely, #*P*-parsimonious-complete). Much is now known about the complexity of computations relating to power indices. I refer the reader to Faliszewski and Hemaspaandra (2008) for an up-to-date picture, as well as interesting new results. In particular, they note (ibid: 4): 'Deng and Papadimitriou (1994) established that the (raw) Shapley–Shubik power index is #*P*-metric-complete … The raw Shapley-Shubik power index … is not #*P*-parsimonious-complete.'

Conclusion

The previous sections of this chapter have established the fact that a number of calculations involving voting happen to be intractable. Such results are clearly of interest when devising electoral systems where to the list of desiderata one must add computational tractability. But there is a subtle, and much more interesting, set of questions that I believe deserves greater inquiry. Electoral systems are rarely static, and evolve in response to changes in the composition of the electorate, in technology, in laws and as a response to random events. Congressional apportionment in the USA is just one example. In India, various forms of reservation of Parliament seats are hotly debated. Campaign finance laws change (and people find ways around the new laws). There are frequent changes in rules and procedures governing decision making in all kinds of groups. So while the design paradigm is sometimes useful, what we typically have is incremental changes and redesigns in electoral systems. The evolution of rules follows a dynamic that is influenced by a number of factors – for instance, the ability of different interest groups to influence outcomes and their calculation of costs and benefits of different changes. Are complexity considerations pertinent in determining what is, or is not, feasible to implement? Do they matter for institutional development? Is there any feature of the existing set of institutions that we can attribute to an economizing of costs inherent in the aggregating of preferences?

The complexity results discussed in this chapter continue to be relevant. For instance, consider an individual (or a group) considering whether to support a proposal that would change the current electoral system. Their willingness for this is likely to depend on the effect this would have on the influence they wield. The appropriate guide for such a decision is one of the indices of power discussed above. But we know this comparison can be difficult to make, and this fact ought not to be ignored.

Note

1 In this example, the 'size' of the problem appears are the number of cities visited, and not the length of a tape input given to a TM. For most problems there is a natural measure of size, and this will correspond to the length of the tape input in the TM representation of the problem.

References

Arrow, K.J. (1951) *Social Choice and Individual Values*, New York: Wiley.
Bartholdi III, J.J., Tovey, C.A. and Trick, M.A. (1989a) 'Voting schemes for which it can be difficult to tell who won the election', *Social Choice and Welfare*, 6(2): 157–65.
—— (1989b) 'The computational difficulty of manipulating an election', *Social Choice and Welfare*, 6(3): 227–41.
Bentham, J. (1789) *An Introduction to the Principles of Morals and Legislation*, London: Payne (reprinted, Oxford: Clarendon Press, 1907).
Cherniak, C. (1984) 'Computability, complexity, and the universal acceptance of logic', *Journal of Philosophy*, LXXI(12): 739–58.

Dantzig, G.B., Fulkerson, D.R. and Johnson, S.M. (1959) 'Solution of a large-scale traveling salesman problem', *Operations Research*, 2: 393–410.

Deng, X. and Papadimitriou, C. (1994) 'On the complexity of comparative solution concepts', *Mathematics of Operations Research*, 19(2): 257–66.

Faliszewski, P. and Hemaspaandra, L. (2008) 'The complexity of power index comparisons', Working Paper, Department of Computer Science, University of Rochester, NY.

Faliszewski, P., Hemaspaandra, E., Hemaspaandra, L.A. and Rothe, J. (2006) 'A richer understanding of the complexity of election systems', Technical Report TR-2006–903, Department of Computer Science, University of Rochester, NY.

Garey, M. and Johnson, D. (1979) *Computers and Intractability: A guide to the theory of NP-completeness*, New York: W.H. Freeman.

Hemaspaandra, E., Hemaspaandra, L.A. and Rothe, J. (1997) 'Exact analysis of Dodgson elections', *Journal of the ACM*, 44(6): 806–25.

Karp, R.M. (1986) 'Combinatorics, complexity, and randomness', Turing Award Lecture, *Communications of the ACM*, 29(2): 98–109.

Mas-Colell, A., Whinston, M.D. and Green, J.R. (1995) *Microeconomic Theory*, Oxford: Oxford University Press.

Mill, J.S. (1838) 'Bentham', *London and Westminster Review*, August 1838, reprinted in *Utilitarianism and Other Essays*, by John Stuart Mill and Jeremy Bentham (1987) Harmondsworth, Middlesex: Penguin.

Prasad, K. (1988) 'Three studies: The complexity of social decisions, the complexity of games, and the nonparametric Bayes analysis of duration data', PhD thesis, Syracuse University, NY.

Prasad, K. and Kelly, J.S. (1990) 'NP-completeness of some problems concerning voting games', *International Journal of Game Theory*, 19: 1–9.

Sen, A. (1986) 'Social choice theory', in K.J. Arrow and M.D. Intriligator (eds), *Handbook of Mathematical Economics*, vol. III, Amsterdam: Elsevier Science Publisher B.V. (North-Holland).

Turing, A.M. (1936) 'On computable numbers, with an application to the entscheidungsproblem', *Proceedings of the London Mathematical Society Series 2*, 42: 230–65.

Valiant, L. (1979) 'The complexity of computing the permanent', *Theoretical Computer Science*, 8: 189–201.

Part V

History of thought and methodology

15 Varieties of internal critique

Tony Lawson

> The headlong rush with which economists have equipped themselves with half-baked knowledge of mathematical traditions has led to an un-natural mathematical economics and a non-numerical economic theory. Whether this trend will reverse itself of its own volition is very doubtful. But discerning scholars of mathematical philosophy – including front-ranking mathematical theorists … have seriously speculated, in the last few years, that the trend in mathematics itself may force a change in its methodology and epistemology. If mathematical traditions themselves incorporate the ambiguities of structures that are replete with undecidabilites in their bread-and-butter research, it will only be a matter of time that such habits will rub off on even the obdurate mathematical economist.

> (Velupillai 2005a: 870)

Most serious observers of modern economics accept that the latter is not in a healthy state. It is dominated by a mathematical 'modelling' project whose results repeatedly fail by the usual explanatory and predictive criteria to which project members claim to adhere. Yet the usual response to failure is not to give the methods in question lower priority in the economist toolbox. Rather it is to empty the toolbox of all other methods in order to focus the mind on making progress with the mathematical devices that are so uncritically thought to be the proper tools of any self-respecting science.

What is to be done if this situation is to be transformed? The mathematical modellers dominate the profession. They can be bypassed. But in the academy, at present, this can be meaningfully achieved only by moving elsewhere, to discussions of economics within departments of sociology, human geography, politics, anthropology, business management and such like.

Are there any useful strategies for those who wish to stay in economics and seek to engage those in power? Here the critique must be an internal one. An internal or immanent critique proceeds by way of working from certain internally accepted features of a project or paradigm, and pointing out that they lead to problems, inconsistencies or limits elsewhere within the project or paradigm, conceived on *that project's own terms*. Unless we start from some assumptions or presumptions accepted by, or preconceptions of, the mainstream mathematical modellers, we will not even be in with a hope of engaging. Although by no means sufficient, an internalist approach does seem to be necessitated.

How might an internal critique be effectively executed? There will not be a unique approach. Nor do I think that all possible approaches are likely to be equally effective, or even to carry equal potential to be effective.

Better models?

A first approach, one I am myself rather cautious towards, is that of seeking to adopt the same sort of mathematics as the current mainstream employs, and to use it to indicate a problem with existing models.

I believe this is what Geoffrey Hodgson (2004) has in mind, when, in seeking to undermine my own critique of modern mainstream economics, he advances the idea that formalistic models might be used for making internal critiques. Here Hodgson's goal is not internal critique per se, but to defend the claim that contemporary approaches to mathematical modelling in economics do have some use. And one of the uses, Hodgson suggests, is to facilitate internal critique.

In the context of modern mainstream economics this role for formal models cannot be denied simply because the mainstream is everywhere couched in terms of mathematical formalism; the insistence on mathematical deductive methods is the essence of that project. The possibility, to which Hodgson points, arises just as a consequence of the mainstream problematic insistence on formalistic methods. Indeed, as most mainstream contributions advance by precisely addressing perceived (internal) weaknesses, or inconsistencies or limitations of preceding substantive (specific modelling) contributions, most mainstream efforts themselves constitute or contain internal critiques of what went before them. And yet the enterprise continues, and is perhaps even strengthened by such endless productions.

Of course, heterodox economists will likely employ currently or standard formalistic methods or models for purposes of seeking more destabilising critiques than will mainstream economists themselves. And I do not at all want to belittle their achievements on their own terms. However, I am not optimistic that internal critiques of this sort lead to any necessary advance in terms of illuminating the world in which we actually live. Mostly they lead to the internal shoring up of an irrelevant conceptual system. And even when a conceptual framework is radically transformed or replaced, it almost always is so by an equally irrelevant alternative formalistic system. Witness the recent turn to evolutionary game theory, agent based modelling, complexity theory and so forth. I do not believe that these provide advances in understanding social reality over earlier conceptual schema. Some commentators do seek to interpret such developments as examples of mainstream pluralism. But in spirit they are no such things. And at the methodological level, in particular, they are quite the opposite. At best they are manifestations of the mainstream flexibility to move from one highly questionable conception consistent with the formalisms with which they are familiar to other conceptions employing the same or similar methods.

Is there no scope for progress via this sort of internal critique involving formalistic methods? It seems to me that the best bet for those keen on internal critiques utilising formal models of the sort that mainstream economists themselves employ is precisely to keep plugging away in the hope that mainstream practitioners eventually grow tired of shoring up existing, or seeking new, conceptual systems (for I doubt that the options by way of constructing new systems will run out), and are willing to turn to something else. But, as I say, I am not optimistic it will happen.

Alternatives to mathematical deductivist modelling?

Is there any alternative, and perhaps more promising, way to proceed? If the problem is that, by making an internal critique of (elements of) one mathematical-deductivist approach, mainstream economists merely readjust it or invent an alternative one, the surest way to make real progress, it has seemed to me, is to orient the internal or immanent critique at features *common to (or presupposed by) the variety of mathematical-deductivist methods or projects* associated with the contemporary mainstream economics. It is to carry out an immanent critique of the mathematical-deductivist approach to social theorising itself. This anyway has been my approach (see e.g. Lawson 1997, 2002, 2003).

Mainstream economists recognise that event regularities are required (or need to be posited) if their methods are to have application (see e.g. Allais 1992: 25). It is widely recognised that such regularities (whether deterministic or stochastic) rarely emerge in the social realm. What I have shown is that such regularities, if they are to be guaranteed, require conditions (a closed world of isolated atoms) that are rather unlikely to hold in the social realm. For I have argued for a different social ontology, of openness, structure, process, internal relationality, emergence, emergence, meaning and value, a perspective against which the implicit ontology of the mainstream approach is seen to be highly impoverished, and which if correct, explains the generalised failings of modern economics. For, if the ontology I defend is correct, then methods that presuppose atomism and closure are questionable, and the reason for the continuing failure of a project that insists on them is evident (again see Lawson 1997, 2003).

This is indeed an internal or immanent critique just because (or to the extent that) in footnotes, introductions, public speeches, rhetorical asides and so forth, mainstream economists talk in a manner that presupposes worldviews according to which social reality is anything but closed and atomistic. The problem is an apparent lack of awareness that their methods prohibit the sorts of theorising that conforms to their implicit broader perspectives.

An alternative mathematics?

However, my critique is clearly found to be too radical for some, in particular those who cannot break free from the idea that mathematical methods of sorts are either essential or least capable of providing insight. And in any case my critique only applies to the sorts of mathematics that economists currentl employ. Who knows what the future of mathematics holds?

This is where Vela's work comes in. For as I understand it, in an importan strand of his unique and outstanding research contribution, Vela provide internal critiques of the types of mathematical methods that economists emplo (not of specific models per se), by showing that they cannot achieve what expected of them (and indeed even thought to have been achieved by them). An Vela does this whilst keeping open, and enthusiastically discussing, the possibil ity of a mathematical approach eventually emerging that is free from the sort problems he identifies in existing approaches (see e.g. Velupillai 2005a, 2006).

An example of this approach is Vela's investigation of effectiveness of matl ematics as applied to the project of General Equilibrium Theory (GET), and sp cifically its computational 'subset', Computable General Equilibrium theo (CGE).

A major contribution to GET, of course is Gerard Debreu's (1960) codifyir text, the *Theory of Value*, one in which Debreu claims to treat the theory of val 'with the standards of rigor of the contemporary formalist school of mathem; ics' where, this 'effort toward rigor substitutes correct reasonings and results f incorrect ones' (Debreu 1960: viii).

Following the codification achieved by Debreu, Scarf (1990) began sustained research programme to 'constructivize' one aspect of the mathemati of general equilibrium theory: the problem of existence. Scarf came to belie that proving existence by non-constructive means was unsatisfactory from 1 point of view of economics as an applied subject. This is the research pr gramme that was pursued under the rubric of Computable General Equilibriu theory (CGE).

One question Vela poses is whether Scarf's programme can be carri through successfully. The claim, by leading applied economists, Vela infor us, *is that it has been carried through successfully* and GET is, now, an er nently applicable field, with clear computational and numerical content. Clea if this is the claim then any undermining of it is an internal critique. Does Scarf programme succeed? Vela's answer is clear: 'the Scarf program can succeed in its aim to constructivise the equilibrium existence problem of GI i.e., the constructive and computable content of CGE is vacuous' (Velupi 2005a: 860).

Focusing on GET and CGE, Vela points to 'their mathematically unreas able ineffectiveness'. By ineffectiveness, Vela means being uncomputable non-constructive. By 'unreasonable' he is expressing his assessment that mathematics used – i.e., methods of proof utilized in GET and CGE – and axioms assumed – were not only economically injudicious but also unnecess and irrelevant from every conceivable numerical and computational point view' (Velupillai 2005a: 861).

I do not think I need to cover the technical details of Vela's analysis he Basically Vela isolates certain axioms etc. that are fundamental to Debr results, and interprets them in the light of various other accepted 'theorems, propositions and facts'. The result achieved is striking:

> If the above theorem, propositions and claims are appended to the Theory of Value, or to any later 'edition' of it such as Arrow–Hahn (1971), then it can be shown that none of the propositions, theorems and claims of a mathematical sort would retain their validity without drastic modifications of their economic content and implications. In particular, not a single formal proposition in the Theory of Value would have any numerical or computational content.
>
> (Velupillai 2005a: 862)

Going one step further and examining the theory in the light of the further result that the Uzawa Equivalence Theorem is neither constructively nor computably valid, Vela argues that this insight (in conjunction with the invalidity Proposition of the Bolzano–Weierstrass Theorem) bears the conclusion that 'the constructive content of CGE models, and their computational implications for economic policy analysis, are vacuous'. He adds 'a similar exercise can be carried out for *every* sub-field of economic theory to which the mathematical method has been applied – in particular, game theory' (Velupillai, 2005a: 863).[2]

Is there an alternative mathematics that transcends this internalist constructivist critique? In Vela's view, the quantitative economist's analytical role lies between the work of the Political Arithmetician and the Accountant. He assesses that neither of these requires anything more than arithmetic, statistics and the rules of compound interest, where these in turn 'require nothing more than an understanding of the conditions under which systems of equations can and cannot be solved'.

Getting to the crux of the issue Vela asks:

> But what kind of quantities do these equations encapsulate as parameters, constants and variables? Surely, the kind of quantities that enter the equations of the Political Arithmetician and the Accountant cannot be other than rational or natural numbers – negative and non-negative?... I cannot see any role for real numbers in quantitative economics and, hence, none whatsoever for real analysis and the proof techniques allied to it.
>
> (Velupillai 2005a: 867)

Vela's concludes that 'the only kind of equations that can play any role in the analytical activities of the Political Arithmetician and the Accountant are Diophantine equations' (ibid.).

Vela asks how the problem of solvability of such equations can be studied and what methods are available to systematise and routinise their use? Vela's answer is again striking: 'The paradoxical answer to both of these questions is that the problem of solvability is intractable and their systematic and routinised study is almost impossible' (ibid: 868).

After a mathematical exposition Vela elaborates:

> we are forced to come to terms with the unsolvability of Diophantine equations.... Hence, the best we can do, as Political Arithmeticians and Accountants, and even as behavioural agents, however rational, so long as the constraints are Diophantine, is to act according to the gentle and humble precepts enunciated by George Temple: 'collect specimens, to describe them with loving care, and to cultivate them for study under laboratory conditions'. Clearly, anyone familiar with the work of Charles Sanders Peirce will also realise that this kind of natural historic study fits comfortably with that great man's advocacy of the retroduction in such disciplines. The tiresome dichotomy between induction and deduction, refreshingly banished by Peirce more than a century ago, may well get cremated in economics, once and forever, if we combine the methodology of the natural historian with the epistemology that is implied in retroduction.
>
> (ibid.: 870)

As this passage indicates, Vela's hope for economics lies in the exploration of the properties of alternative forms of economics. It is following this last passage that Vela adds the critical note with which I opened this chapter. Clearly Vela is optimistic that new and more relevant forms of mathematics will evolve. In it the emphasis will change. Proofs will be down played; and undecidable propositions will play a bigger role. It is no coincidence that Vela likes the following assessment of Stanislaw Ulam:

> Mathematics is not a finished object based on some axioms. It evolves genetically. This has not yet quite come to conscious realization....
>
> [T]here might someday be entirely new points of view, even about sets or classes of sets. Sets may someday be considered as 'imaginary'. I think that will come to pass, though at present it is not admissible.
>
> *Mathematics will change. Instead of precise theorems, of which there are now millions, we will have, fifty years from now, general theories and vague guidelines*, and the individual proofs will be worked out by graduate students or by computers.
>
> *Mathematicians fool themselves when they think that the purpose of mathematics is to prove theorems, without regard to the broader impact of mathematical results.* Isn't it strange.
>
> *In the next fifty years there will be, if not axioms, at least agreements among mathematicians about assumptions of new freedoms of constructions, of thoughts.* Given an undecidable proposition, there will be a preference as to whether one should assume it to be true or false. Iterated this becomes: some statements may be undecidably undecidable. This has great philosophical interest.
>
> (Cooper 1989: 310–12; quoted in Velupillai 2005a: 864;
> italics added by Vela)

I do not know if all of Vela's arguments are correct. But assuming that they are (and I certainly have no reason to suppose otherwise) he provides a third, and highly original form of internal critique.

Which of the three approaches to internal critique is the better one? Perhaps it depends on the goal. If the aim is a set of models much like those in existence but producing different results, theorems or whatever, then the first approach discussed above is presumably the most effective. If the goal is to encourage the view that non-mathematical approaches be included, and even given some emphasis, within the economist's toolbox, then I suspect the ontological approach I defend has the advantage. If the aim is to persuade the economics profession to consider alternative and seeming more speculative, less constraining, types of mathematics that promise to be coherent with economists' own requirements of methods of applied economics, then Vela's approach has advantages.

No doubt, the most reasonable position is that all such approaches (and any others not here considered) should be employed side by side. What is clear is that few have the knowledge of mathematical traditions or the ingenuity to take the third path. We thus have to be very grateful that there is at least one person amongst us who able to pull it off. It is thus enormously fitting that such a volume as this has been produced celebrating the enormous contribution of the uniquely gifted scholar that is Vela.

Notes

1 As Vela reminds us Debreu's *Theory of Value* depends rather fundamentally on the axiom of completeness (Debreu 1960: 10); compactness (ibid.: 15), continuity – topologically characterised (ibid.: 15), the maximum-minimum (or Weierstrass) theorem (ibid.: 16), separating hyperplane theorems (ibid.: 24–5) and the Brouwer and Kakutani Fixed Point Theorems (ibid.: 26).

2 He also speculates:

> It will be a tedious exercise but I suspect that, eventually, such an exegesis can even be automated! The general strategy would be to identify the key mathematical axioms, theorems and concepts that underlie any particular mathematics applied to a sub-field of economic theory and, then, to investigate their constructive, computable, nonstandard or real analytic nature. Thus, for example, a seemingly innocuous application of dynamical systems theory in endogenous theories of the business cycle would also be susceptible to such an exegetic exercise. Any use of the Cauchy–Peano Theorem in the existence theory for differential equations will fall foul of the failure of the validity of the Bolzano–Weierstrass Theorem in constructive mathematics. This is because the Bolzano–Weierstrass Theorem is equivalent to the Ascoli Lemma which, in turn, is used to simplify the proof of the Cauchy–Peano Theorem.

(Velupillai 2005a: 863)

References

Allais, M. (1992) 'The economic science of today and global disequilibrium', in M. Baldassarri, J. McCallum and R. Mundell (eds), *Global Disequilibrium in the World Economy*, Basingstoke: Macmillan.

Arrow, K.J. and Hahn, F.H. (1971) *General Competitive Analysis*, San Francisco, CA: Holden-day, Inc.

Cooper, N.G. (ed.) (1989) *From Cardinals to Chaos: Reflections on the life and legacy of Stanislaw Ulam*, Cambridge: Cambridge University Press.

Debreu, G. (1960) *Theory of Value: An axiomatic analysis of economic equilibrium*, London: John Wiley and Sons, Inc.

Hodgson, G. (2004) 'On the problem of formalism in economics', *Post-Autistic Economic Review*, 28: article 1.

Lawson, T. (1997) *Economics and Reality*, London and New York: Routledge.

Lawson, T. (2002) 'Mathematical formalism in economics: What really is the problem?', in P. Arestis and S. Dow (eds), *Methodology, Microeconomics and Keynes: Festschrift for Victoria Chick*, London: Taylor & Francis.

Lawson, T. (2003) *Reorienting Economics*, London and New York: Routledge.

Scarf, H. (1990) 'Mathematical programming and economic theory', *Operations Research*, 38(3): 377–85.

Velupillai, K.V. (2005a) 'The unreasonable ineffectiveness of mathematics in economics', *Cambridge Journal of Economics*, 29(6): 849–72.

Velupillai, K.V. (ed.) (2005b) *Computabiliy, Complexity and Consructivity in Economics Analysis*, Oxford: Blackwell Publishing Ltd.

Velupillai, K.V. (2006) 'Algorithmic foundations of computable general equilibrium theory', *Applied Mathematics and Computation*, 179(1): 360–9.

16 Rational economic man

A centrepiece in social science?

Carsten Heyn-Johnsen

Preface and apology

In the last half of the 1980s the perennial discussion of the scientific justification of rational economic man, REM, to be claimed the relevant and rigorous foundation of economics, addressed the question of aggregating agents in macroeconomics. Insisting on a microfoundation for macroeconomics, and, at the same time, satisfying demands for scientific relevance, pointed at the necessity of breaking the improvised methodological confines of the representative agent. Reviving Arrow's *impossibility theorem*, topically, and the even more fundamental critique of Keynes' in his stringent search for 'The Choice of Units' (Keynes 1936, Chapter iv), was another intellectual barrage delivered against the daily trade in economics.

As this new opening not only addressed macroeconomic methodology, but inevitably had substantial implications for the relevance of REM as a thought construction, one could be in doubt where it would take us in the endless, non-conclusive and perhaps non-concludable, discussion of not only REMs but also of *hominus economicus*' epistemological and ontological status in social science. If it would take us anywhere.

The University of Aalborg, Denmark, enjoyed at that time the academic and intellectual luxury of having Professor K. Velupillai as a member of the social science faculty. The generosity of Professor Velupillai included sharing his visions with the students of economics and those of us who were his colleagues. His research leading to these visions embraced the foundations and philosophy of mathematics. As economists, as unspoiled parochial as they normally come, we heard of and were offered interpretations of Church thesis, Turing machines, decidability, completeness, etc., getting impressions and hints of the relevance and consequences for epistemology and, if understood and taken seriously, for economics. It was exciting days and gave some of us a premonition of a critique that could conclude the perennial, stultifying REM discussion, re-establish the outlook and take us onward to new views and ways in economics.

The premonition materialized in the two works cited in the chapter below. 'Rationality, Computability, and Complexity' (Rustem and Velupillai 1990) demonstrates a REM not to be sure of being able to produce his preferences by any intelligible, systematic procedure. Preferences without which REM would be immobilized as the ass of Buridan's. And in *Computable Economics: the Arne Ryde Memorial Lectures* (Velupillai 2000), the published, elaborated lec tures given in 1994 at a Scanian castle, Trolleborg with Tycho Brahe in the ancestry, Professor Velupillai is circumscribing and opening the forward vista of 'Computable Economics'.

This Festschrift-essay is a backward vista of *homo economicus* in economics starting from the postulated behaviourism of Adam Smith's, without the rationa dimensions emphasized by Augustinus, the church father in North Africa, almos 1500 years in advance. J.S. Mill is rationalizing the figure by taking him into the realm of a philosophy of ethics, utilitarianism. And ensued, till these days, he is mingled with utility as a theory of value. If there will be a logic of reception in accordance with the logic of the discovery of Professor Velupillai's, economics in theory and applied, will have to follow suit for pure epistemological reasons This does not necessarily affect the ethics of utilitarianism. But the consequence affects the theory of economic value and dynamics, and will thereby decisively ramify economics as applied in economic policy.

The economic man, political economy and economics

Producing and consuming *economic* man has been a workhorse in the history o political economy ever since his introduction with his 'propensity to truck barter, and exchange one thing for another' by Adam Smith (1776: 12) in the eighteenth century, as the materialistic foundation of political economy. These propensities are neither located in metaphysics nor mere assumptions. They figure as 'the necessary consequence of the faculty of reason and speech. It is common to all men, and to be found in no other race of animals' (ibid.). As such 'to truck, barter, and exchange one thing for another' are psychological and anthropological universals, according to Smith.

Economic man has transmogrified into *rational* economic man. He is the workhorse in the history of *economics*, from the second half of the nineteenth century till today's workhouses of academic economics. In our times he has been supplemented with quasi psychic faculties in recognizing the future socio- economic constraints on the unfolding of his economy. This faculty is traded as 'rational expectations', as the ability to foresee, e.g. any degree of contra finality his planned economic activities may lead to.[1]

This a priori, nonsociological yet materialistic, foundation of economic theory has been praised and attacked from the very moment it was published. As an introduction to an edition of *The Wealth of Nations*, E.R.A. Seligman cites 'Read Adam Smith as he deserves to be read and you will perceive that before him no political economy existed' as eulogies of Jean Baptiste Say's and the dissenting John Ruskin alluding to Adam Smith as 'the half-bred and half-witted Scotch- man who taught the deliberate blasphemy: "Thou shalt hate the Lord, thy God damn his laws and covet his neighbour's goods".' (Smith 1776: v).

These extremes in the recension and history of reception refer to the material- ism, and ethical radicalism, imbedded in the 'inquiry into the causes of wealth by Adam Smith. A world view, 'Anschauung', with economic man's self-interest, 'self-love', as a final end. Self-interest as motive for creating wealth through interaction, 'truck, barter, and exchange one thing for another', with the degree of fulfilment of the motive as the yardstick for ethical value.

> man has almost constant occasion for the help of his brethren, and it is in vain for him to expect it from their benevolence only. He will be more likely to prevail if he can interest their self-love in his favour, and show them that it is for their own advantage to do for him what he requires of them.
>
> (ibid.: 13)

Interaction as a symmetric or reciprocal social relation involves everyman's motives; making the economic stratum of society self-contained, sociologically as well as ethically. The market economy. With man's natural liberty, as a precondition for the functioning of this self-contained economy, the free market economy follows as an ethical corollary. Adam Smith establishes, thereby, a political economy in accordance with natural law, and the self-interest of economic man as the metaphysical final end of the inquiry. The Smithian political economy is not positive but normative in its teleology.

It is a political economy which does not pretend being a positive descriptive theory of any society in history – at the time it was published it was at best *utopian* – but rather a political critique of existing social conditions. No wonder a social critique inferred from materialism, ethical radicalism of self-interest and natural law, called forth an ideological debate in academia and elsewhere. Not only an ideological debate. The political economy of Adam Smith, imbedding economic man acting as to increase the wealth of nations, has preformed a great part of economic science till our days.[2] Reflected in the epithet 'Adam Smith is the founding father of economics'.

A strong normative element in social philosophy comes as no surprise, and economic wealth as prerequisite for economic and social welfare is not intellectually outlandish. But that does not comprise the philosophical grounding of economic man. To present the *subject* in the philosophy of social welfare, and the *object* of the theory of political economy, as a pure mental artefact, lacks contextual reason.

The artefact, 'economic man', has taken a life of its own beyond the social philosophy in which it originated as an inseparable part. With some faculties added along, e.g. global rationality including the realm of beliefs and the well-ordering of desires, rational economic man has become the *subject* in economics. The metaphysics of Adam Smith are now, *mutatis mutandis*, located in the axioms of rational economic man. From which the choice theoretic base for determining supply and demand in the economy is logically deduced, under mathematical assistance of real analysis and topology.

The casuistical matrix in the recension of the political economy of Adam Smith is dimensionally high. In the chronological ordered columns of authors as well as in the topical rows. For the central topics we find rows of alternating critique and anticritique interspersed with cells of ignore. As for the columns of authors almost every combination of the same cells could be found. The following are samples of topics of relevance in the development of the justification of economic man in economic theory as well as his justifiable homicide. They address methodological as well as substantial issues concerning the predicate and subject of 'economic man'.

To conclude this part, just a few observations on the general view of economic development, the growth of wealth, as the rationale in the writings of Adam Smith. Economic growth is a process ultimately limited by nature, by the economic resources offered by nature. For each nation there is, thus, a maximum attainable total wealth. The reachable degree of and speed towards that maximum is determined by the unfolding political economy. The efficiency in production and consumption allowed by the political economy. But this is just referring to the wealth of nations. Whereas the subject in the philosophy of social welfare is economic man, the individual. The ethical valuation of the growth of wealth refers accordingly to the wealth per capita and not national wealth as such. Here we encounter a *contra finality* in the general view of Adam Smith's.

As Adam Smith is subscribing to the dominating, proto Malthusian, population theory, the growth in wealth per capita leads to a growth in population that eventually, and irrespective of the wealth producing efficiency of the nation, will affect the wealth per capita, bringing us back where we took off on the scale of social welfare. Reaching the limits of the wealth of nations the derived rationale, improving or optimizing the political economy, parts its moorings to ethical radicalism. As the nation now stands out as the object of political economy, and the subject in the philosophy of 'social welfare', we have retrograded to the political economy of *l'ancien régime* which Adam Smith set out to overcome.[3]

An apple of discord – the anthropological economic man

Combining natural law and hypostasized anthropology Adam Smith is rationalizing his counterfactual political economy. This rationalization is focal in the critique of *The Wealth of Nations* that followed. Even critics sympathetic towards materialism and the political economy of liberalism enter the *apparatus criticus* of the recension portfolio. This is an ironic aspect of the history of the portfolio. Without ontologically reified man, natural law would have no subject to proclaim free, they stand and fall together. The ironic part is, as mentioned above, the part played by economic man as a mental artefact in the analysis of the, also and therefore, counterfactual political economy. In shorthand; for Adam Smith the phenotype of man is empirically more substantial than the genotype. In his moral philosophy man is conditioned by the specificity of his social life. And that should, a fortiori, be so for economic man too.[4]

> The difference in natural talent in different men is, in reality, much less than we are aware of, and the very different genius which appears to distinguish

men of different professions, when grown up to maturity, is not upon many occasions so much the cause as the effect of division of labour.

(Smith 1759: 67)

This statement based on material experience shows that Adam Smith could only have reserved a minor scope for 'mans natural given propensities' in a more comprehensive philosophical foundation of political economy.

Hegel and Marx

None the less, the main thrust of Hegel's and Marx's critique ignores this statement and its consequence for the interpretation of the seminal work of Adam Smith. In this respect *The Wealth of Nations*, and the anthropology therein, is taken as a strictly positive theory for their critique.

In the critical matrix according to Hegel's optimistic idealism and the historical materialism of Marx, with imbedded dialectics, focus is on economic man and his propensities. They both dissent. These propensities are socio-phenotypical, not genotypical. The political economy of Adam Smith is not reflecting man's innate propensities. But it could imbed a phase of his societal development. Division of labour enhances productivity and is an organization of social production with wider economic as well as sociological ramifications. Products of distributed production have to be redistributed for consumption. The economic result of the division of labour is recombined in consumption by truck, barter and exchange. As such the division of labour is a social organization in which societal man has to follow suit. Psychologically, socially and politically.

Man is a *zoon politikon* in the most literal sense: he is not only a social animal, but an animal that can be individualised only within society. Production by a solitary individual outside society – a rare event, which might occur when a civilised person who has already absorbed the dynamical social forces is cast into the wilderness – is just as preposterous as the development of speech without individuals who live *together* and talk to one another.

(Marx 1859: 189)

The political economy of Adam Smith is to support the development and unfolding of that organization. Distribution and the sine qua non of redistribution is carried through by economic man in the *market*. Potential gain in efficiency is the watch spring, and political economy the balance. Together they control the growth in wealth of nations. In both markets, the market for the distribution of labour and the market for redistributing the product of divided labour as commodities, self-interest addresses self-interest. Politically unhampered markets, i.e. free interaction of economic men, assure exchange ratios, and quantities exchanged, in accordance with conjoined self-interests of the participants.

The referential natural prices of Adam Smith, circumscribing ethical efficiency and equality, are arguments for his programme of political economy. Natural law and the metaphysics of self-interest come together in economic liberalism.[5]

The unchanging and unchangeable natural core of man, hypostasized economic man, is preconditional in arguing out a materialistic founded ethics of political economy. Were, *a contrario*, the essence of man accommodating the political economy, the justification for liberalism would lose its 'positive' foundation. Economic liberalism would in that case be an idealistic construction with the education of man by man-made institutions of the market as an epiphenomenon, intended or not. A political economy bereft of a scientific base. This is not the contribution of Adam Smith. He proclaims more than just a political programme.

Hegel is welcoming liberalism as a realized, idealistic, construction. Political and economic liberalism *is* civil society (*bürgerliche Gesellschaft*), brought about by the cunning of reason (*die List der Vernunft*). Another word for Providence. Reason as it is located in the closest nearness of God. Civil society is the end of philosophy and history. Not as the result of natural law or the propensities of genotypical man, but as the unification of the worldspirit (*Geist*) and the consciousness of man. The Idea has come to itself. Seemingly the particular, individual man, and the universal, the man in the market, the economic man, seems to have been fallen apart. What could look like the abyss of self-interested particulars of humanity, the chaos of Hobbes, does not prevail. Providence secures that:

> This proliferation of arbitrariness generates universal determinations from within itself, and this apparently scattered and thoughtless activity is subject to a necessity which arises of its own accord. To discover the necessity at work here is the object of political economy.
>
> (Hegel 1991: 227)

A few alterations in the wordings and we have arrived at today's textbook's introduction to economics. As it is stated innocent of any awareness of hegelian dialectics.

Hegel is rejecting the ethical idea of a liberalism, based on natural law, having the individual as a pre-social given. In his world view the project is rather in strict accordance with God's plan to be *revealed* in due time. That is, when man is ready and prepared by the experiences of his own history. Adam Smith is wrong in his premises but gets it right in his felicitous conclusions. The political economy of liberalism serves the common good in the historic progress of mankind. Interaction in the market is seen as a reconciliation of the particular self-interests. Competing economic man with his private and isolated economic aims produces the harmonious outcome, civil society.

> Subjective selfishness turns into a contribution towards the satisfaction of the needs of everyone else. By a dialectic movement, the particular is medi-

ated by the universal so that each individual, in earning, producing and enjoying on his own account, thereby earns and produces for the enjoyment of others.

(Hegel 1991: 233)

The ardent and strictly worldly pupil of Hegel, Marx, is sending in a word of warning against the eschatological reception of Smith and, more to the point, the idealism of Hegel. There is no worldspirit at work as an 'invisible hand'. 'The real point is not that each individual's pursuit of his private interest promotes the … general interest. One could just as well deduce … that each individual reciprocally blocks the assertion of others' interests'. (Marx 1858: 156).

In Marx's view, Smithian political economy is an apology erected on an untenable anthropology.

Classical political economy following upon *The Wealth of Nations* is historically conditioned as 'forms of thought expressing with social validity the conditions and relations of a definite, historically determined mode of production, viz., the production of commodities' (Marx 1872: 76). The economy of modern world is described in classical economic theory, but its ethics are self-referential as rationalizations, not of man's situation in the world and his conditions in life as such, but of economic man as conditioned by the unintended laws of capitalist economy. Neither the conditions nor the ethics implied thereby characterizes the beginning or end of man's history.

This eighteenth-century individual – the product on one side of the dissolution of the feudal forms of society, on the other side of the new forces of production developed since the sixteenth century – appears as an ideal, whose existence they project into the past. Not as a historical result but as a history's point of departure. As the Natural Individual appropriate to their notion of human nature, not arising historically, but posited by nature.

(Marx 1858: 84)

Historical materialism, as a philosophy of history, embraces the development of society and of man in society, individually and collectively, in harmony and conflict. Metaphorically, the developing of man's forces of production (*Produktivkräfte*) is the watch spring, and the relations of production (*Produktionsverhältnisse*) the balance. The dialectical interplay of these two elements establishes the actual mode of production (*Produktionsweise*), retarding or accelerating mans mastering of nature in producing his material and moral life in society.[6]

In this view Marx is criticizing and expanding the metaphysics of Adam Smith. Natural law and man's self-interest is not the final end. The, never attainable, final end is not economic man but man in and for himself. Hegel's logic is included in the materialistic humanism of Marx.

Human history is an integral part of natural history, for it describes the cultivation through time of the external nature of man. The whole of history can be understood as the process through which man is prepared to become th object of his own perception. History produces man as self-determinatio and self-affirmation ... History, therefore embraces into one process th evolution of external nature and the evolution of man from nature.

(Levine 1972: 29?

Political economy or economics, as social science, cannot be derived fror economic man, rational or not, as a prime or starting point. This is an epistem logical conclusion in Marx's critique of economic man of the classics, a critiqu that comprised J.S. Mill.

A congenial critique from a self-declared positivist and nominalist, V. Paret as the homicide of economic man, will be presented below. Following a shc detour into normative *ordo*-theory in nowadays public choice theory.

Homo economicus *as guinea pig in 'constitutional choice': Brennan and Buchanan*

In contradistinction to Hegel and Marx's critical destruction, G. Brennan and Buchanan give a supportive interpretation of economic man in *The Wealth Nations*. 'Our argument is that the homo economicus construction supplies postulate about human behaviour that is in many ways uniquely suited for t comparative institutional analysis that underlies genuine constitutional choic (Brennan and Buchanan 1981: 159). A genus of choice Adam Smith had in mi writing *The Wealth of Nations*. In this confirming interpretation all scienti claims and content is removed from the concept of 'economic man'; i.e. the m aphysics of self-interest and the reciprocity of self-interests is of no intrinsic s entific, ontological or epistemological, value per se.

> Our implied criticism of the over-extended usage of the *homo economi* abstraction in trying to explain human behaviour 'scientifically' lies in • conviction that 'scientific prediction' is *not* what our whole exercise is ab and that this application is not the usage for which the abstraction v intended ... we offer a *methodological*, rather than a predictive ('scientifi defence of the whole construction.
>
> (ib

This absolves Adam Smith from inconsistencies in his 'chosen' metaphys albeit the positive argumentation is somewhat nebulous in its semantics. ˙ defensive logic is along the following line(s). Carrying through normative c• parative institutional studies presupposes a referential to be used uniformly evaluating alternative social orders. 'Simple requirements of methodolog consistency requires this' (ibid.). Modelling man as *homo economicus* is possible choice for the theoretical guinea pig to secure the comparability of outcome of the thought experiments.

Why this choice?

The question we are interested in posing about any particular social order is whether the rules by which individual actions are coordinated are such as to transform actions undertaken by participants in their own *private* interests into outcomes that are in the interests of others.

(ibid.: 160)

Intellectually, the rationalization of the choice is difficult to digest: We know that this curious alchemy is in fact worked by the *market* – that the invisible hand operates, under certain more or less well-defined conditions, to convert private interest into public interest.

(ibid.)

The *market* is the sought for institution. But is this to be understood in a positive empirical sense? Are we situated in the Popperian world of falsification with operational specifications of the private and social interests of *homines economici*? Or are we still in the world of Adam Smith, looking for 'more or less well-defined conditions' for a preferential political economy in accordance with the metaphysics of economic man? Supposed rational or not.

Be that as it may, this stands as an example of economic man surviving more than 200 years and still performing thoughts in the social sciences.

Pareto's join and dissent

If we consult Pareto, the comparative institutional analysis and many of the theorems of public choice theory that is based on the 'believe that homo oeconomicus remains the appropriate model of behaviour in the derivation of normative propositions about the institutions themselves' (Brennan and Buchanan 1981: 165) would be stillborn. Or would at least not be part of social science, proper.

'Science does not attempt to establish any particular method of economic organization, and it is not the business of science to do so' (Pareto 1897: 499). '(Social science) ... has not to give us precepts: it studies first the natural properties of things, then solves the problems attendant on the question: given certain premises, what will the consequences be?' (Pareto 1896: §1).

Topically Pareto accepts the research in 'comparative institutional analysis' of today. In the context of our inquiry the question is what role, in a methodological sense, economic man is to play in that research? On one hand we have that

Science does, however, attempt to solve problems of the following sort: (1) What are the effects of a régime of free competition? (2) What are those of a régime of monopoly? (3) Those of a collectivist régime?... for the purpose of ascertaining what results would follow upon their installation ... but it must be borne in mind that this knowledge will always be approximately only.

(Pareto 1897: 499)

On the other hand, is *homo economicus* the ontological relevant guinea pig in scientific questions as these? The answer depends on the part of Pareto's *oeuvre* consulted. Pareto endeavours to purge economic man of all psychological content, and connotations, implied by the semantics of utility. In the pure economics department of political economy, economic man is acting to maximize his individual advantage, his *ophelimity*, as a strictly individual relation between economic man and his goods. A behaviouristically revealed relation. Ophelimity is the word for a *noumenon* which is not to be qualified or quantified by any psychological interpretations.

Looking for the answer in *Cours d'économie politique* (1890) and the ensuing reply to his critics, 'The New Theories of Economics' (1897), gives us a disturbing *nonconclusion*. In the 'Cours' the view is that 'Hypothetical facts are derived from observed facts' including the hypothesis of *homo economicus*. He is not a scientific derivation from 'theological or telelogical principles or supposed natural rights or metaphysical considerations'. Pareto underlines his methodological demand with a surprising statement concerning Adam Smith, that this is 'the method followed, apart from a few deviations of scarce importance, by classical political economy, from Adam Smith onwards' (Pareto 1896: 574). Pareto's classification of the political economy of Adam Smith as an early example of pure economics is surprising. Nonetheless, even ignoring the metaphysics of man's natural rights, classical political economy is still not serving the following demand of Pareto's:

> It is not enough to assign the characteristic of perfect hedonist to man ... It is also necessary to decide what qualities of foresight and reason and so on are to be granted him. These qualities ... are to some extent assumed to be implicit. This does not appear correct to us: postulates should always be declared explicitly.
>
> (Pareto 1892: 410–11)

Market coordination by the metaphorical 'invisible hand' will not materialize, unless it is supported by a sufficient degree of foresight and reason. To our knowledge these facultative qualities are neither specified nor calibrated by the Masters of classical political economy. Perhaps with the exception of Marx, when he analyses the 'salto mortale' aspect of the circuit of money-capital, i.e. capital proper.

But if these methodological demands are observed, '[t]his method is logically faultless, provided that each time we return to the real world we do not forget to demonstrate that laws found for abstract men do possess real value' (Pareto 1892: 409), a scientific comparative institutional analysis can be carried through. With given specifications of *homo economicus*

> we have been able vigorously to prove that the coefficients of production are determined by the entrepreneurs in a régime of free competition precisely in the same way as a socialist government would have to fix them if it is wanted to realize a maximum of ophemility for its subjects.
>
> (Pareto 1897: 499)[7]

The comparative analysis is undecided at this point.

The use of *homo economicus* as a referential leads to indifference between free capitalistic competition and socialism, a stalemate in this first approximation to solve the problem within the confines of pure economics. In a second approximation the deadlock can be overcome by modifying *homo economicus* who 'acts only as a result of economic forces' (Pareto 1896: 592), but this takes us into unchartered areas, beyond pure economics.

Staying in economics a second approximation could 'take account of the expense of putting the mechanism of free competition into full play, and ... compare this expense with that necessary for establishing some other new mechanism which society may wish to test' (Pareto 1897: 500) and further approximations could be necessary to reach significant conclusions in economics. The *cost–benefit* approach, however, consists of 'pure experiments' performed on the abstractum, *homo economicus.* A final factual test is always necessary, as experience is the only criterion of *truth.*

> This method of approaching the subject differs substantially from that adopted by a large class of economists, who, after giving in their adhesion to a system, put forth all their power in showing its advantages in defending it against all attacks to which it may be exposed.
>
> (ibid.)[8]

In questions of this comparative kind economics has reached its limits, there is no scientific road leading from the experiments in pure economics to a recommendable political economy. No first principles or ideas can help us in this matter. We have to try it out in reality, in politics, economics and sociology. To observe what takes as it unfolds and reconstruct social science according to experience. For Pareto, as can be learned from the chronology of his ouevre, even the scientific relevance of *homo economicus* is limited. As the social implications of the *abstractum* are not empirically tractable.

As a declared, 'good nominalist-empiricist', Pareto addresses the problem of how to establish a correspondence between the terms *individual* and *social* and the phenomena they denominate. In an invited lecture at the International Congress of Philosophy in Geneve, 1905, under the title 'L'Individuel et le Social', Pareto commits homicide on *homo economicus.* The lecture is in a direct mood, 'La signification de ces termes parait évidente; mais ... ils manquent de précision' (Pareto 1905: 125).

As a noun 'Individual' is precisely delimited in time and space, it indicates man seen isolated in his life cycle. 'Society', on the contrary, is *not* precisely delimited. Spatially it is mostly, with a latent circularity, defined implicitly by its members. When it comes to time dimensions, we have to decide on either a cross section of members, at a moment, or all members born, alive or dying within a certain time span.

As adjectives the terms are more vague. For social man, living in society, from a certain point of view we can say all his characteristics are *individual,* from another, all are *social*. 'En définitive, il n'existe aucun moyen sûr de séparer l'un de l'autre ces deux genres de caractères' (ibid.: 126). So *homo economicus* as isolated man with his preferential choices and constrained interaction in society, led by his desire to maximize his strictly individual and non-quantifiable ophelimity in climbing the 'hill of pleasure', is an abstraction with no positive or real value for social science. He is not to be found even as a remote real phenomenon, according to Pareto.[9]

Strictly isolated, individually experienced, 'ophelimity' is of no theoretical interest, and that goes for wealth a fortiori:

> même si nous nous bornons à tenir compte de la richesse, la somme qu'en possède chaque homme ne représente pas entièrement ses intérêts, et il y a lieu de prendre en considération l'importance des sommes possédées par chaque individu. Ainsi il se peut que, même dans les cas où chaque individu don't se compose la société voit sa richesse augmenter, il se produise une opposition d'intérêts.
>
> (ibid.: 127)

Turning 'Pareto improvement' into a criteria devoid of any scientific relevance.

The full thrust of nominalism and positivism dislodges *homo economicus* from social science:

> C'est une observation banale et bien souvent répétée qu'une société n'est pas une simple juxtaposition d'individus et que ceux-ci, par les seul faits qu'ils vivent en société aquierent de nouveaux caractères. Si nous pouvions donc observer des hommes isolés et des hommes vivant en société, nous aurions le moyen de connaitre en quoi ils diffèrent et nous pourrions séparer l'individuel du social, mais le premier terme de cette comparaison nous fait *entièrement default*, et le seconde nous et seul connu.
>
> (ibid.: 126, emphasis mine)[10]

Even as a pure speculative or mental phenomenon, a 'Gedankenexperiment', *homo economicus*' vitality is not enhanced. He does not belong to any thinkable positive *episteme*.

Mill and utilitarism as vehicles bringing economic man from the eighteenth to the twentieth century

Society is a precondition in any theory of political economy. A society populated by economic man can only exist, to be thought of as to subsist, if some cohesive societal force is manifest. It could be a despotic, autocratic, personalized force or some faculty of socialization imbedded in, or in addition to, the self-interest of economic man. Adam Smith coined the force, 'invisible hand'. In the normative political economy of his it could *not* be a despotic force, but it could be suggested as economic man acting aware of an *identity* of interests in the marketplace. The snag involved in the self-contained economic stratum of his political economy is that identity of interests has to reign in *all* relations. A faint possibility in this part of the *oeuvre* of Adam Smith. Natural law comprises man's natural rights, but it does not imply self-constrained or socially conditioned interaction between men. Leaving the market-making of the 'invisible hand' postulated, not demonstrated.

In his *Theory of Moral Sentiments*, as mentioned above, intersecting self-interests is the core of compassionate man. Contrasting economic man, who is distributed on three sociologically defined agencies *competing* for wages, profits and rent in the political economy. Also in this distributional part the postulate is not corroborated, there is no spontaneous harmony of egoism. Identity of interests has to be brought forth as an artificial identity of interests imposed by the 'visible hand' of socially enforced rules of behaviour. 'Economic man' is still economic man, but harnessed in his interactions. If an answer to the question 'How is society possible?' has to be provided, this is a restricting prerequisite in Bentham's economic liberalism.

And, furthermore, if economic liberalism is to be an answer to the related question of 'What is a good society?', maintaining 'the wealth of nations' as the rationale, and the self-interest of economic man as the final end, the political economy of Adam Smith must be supplemented with Bentham's utilitarian theory of law.[11] For Bentham the natural end of human action, its motivation, is gain in pleasure. The metaphysics is hedonism, wherein balancing pleasure and pain commands actions and interactions. That goes *eo ipso* for economic interaction; where we have that exchange is acquisitive as seen from both its poles. A stable system of exchange relations, i.e. a viable political economy, is therefore conditional on proper recompense. A condition fulfilled by law and latent punishment, i.e. deprivation of potential pleasure, in the case of Bentham, and by the postulate of the 'invisible hand' in Smith's case.

The ethical principle of utility is at the end of the conceptual chain: (a) natural law tells man to be free; (b) to be free is to be allowed to pursue own interests; (c) gain in pleasure is in the interest of everybody; (d) experienced pleasure leads to a happy state of mind; (e) happiness is *good*; (f) as utility is an attribute of physical objects or local situations promoting happiness, utility, thus, is *good* – the principle is derived from the axiom that happiness is good. Bentham is explicit on that point, what 'is used to prove every thing else, cannot itself be proved: a chain of proofs must have their commencement somewhere. To give such a proof is as impossible as it is needless' (Bentham 1789: 13). In social philosophy, the metaphysical diversion par excellence, with tellurian or celestial teleologies, the utility principle is the *archimedean point* allowing us to talk normatively about possible social worlds, to discus 'constitutional choices'. 'Is it possible for a man to move the earth?... Yes; but he must first find out another earth to stand upon' (ibid.: 15).

Adam Smith and Bentham are both observing from the same ontological vantage point, but 'although the principle of utility is the common principle of Bentham's juridical philosophy and Adam Smith's economic philosophy, it has not the same sort of application in both cases' (Halévy 1928: 118). Adam Smith is more in tune with modern axiomatized economics. His postulated 'invisible

hand' is part and parcel *in* the core of these economics.[12] Whereas the artificia
alignment of behaviour by the enforced law of Bentham, based on a *natural* cr
teria of what is right or wrong behaviour in the market, has no, should have n
place in modern economics:

> Nature has placed mankind under the government of two sovereign master
> pain and pleasure. It is for them alone to point out what we *ought* to do, a
> well as determine what we shall do. On the one hand the standard of rig
> and wrong, on the other hand the chain of causes and effect, are fastened
> their throne.
>
> (Zeuthen 1965: 31, emphasis min

J.S. Mill sets out to establish an Archimedean point in social philosophy v
the quaternary consisting of his *A System of Logic Ratiocinative and Inductiv
Principles of Political Economy with Some Applications to Social Philosoph
On Liberty* and *Utilitarianism* (Mill 1843, 1848, 1859, 1861). An endeavou
taking the economic man of Smith and Bentham into the twentieth century b
the history of *reception* and *critique* of his, and Bentham's, utilitarian ethics.

The politics of Mill and his amalgamation of logic, inference, experience an
science into methodological conceptualizations such as 'experiential' as 'ratioc
nations' of the 'empirical' in building up and handling syllogistic reasoning, thi
in addition to his prolific *oeuvre*, became the object of sundry interpretations an
nonconclusive critiques of his utilitarianism, its genesis and essence for mo
than 100 years.

On one side we have the obvious controversial subjects of politics and ethic
and, on the other, subjects one could – for the argument – regard as politicall
neutral such as logic and the theory of knowledge. But Mill is essaying to elabo
rate a logic and epistemology that could be entertained in a conclusive practic
support of ethical utilitarianism based on the metaphysics of Bentham, i.
hedonism. It is his endeavour, by politics and eudaemonism as its propaganda,
turn normative utilitarianism of what we ought to do, into descriptive ethics c
what we, as a sociological fact, *believe* ought to be done.

According to Mill, there are two departments in logic, the 'Logic of Consist
ency' and the 'Logic of Truth'. In 'System of Logic' they are characterized a
such and, surprisingly, conjoined in an absorbing critique of intuitionalism. A
he writes to his German interpreter of 'System of Logic':

> The German *a priori* view of human knowledge is likely for some tim
> longer to predominate. But the *System of Logic* supplies what was muc
> wanted, a textbook of the opposite school – that which derived all know
> ledge from experience ... any success in that attempt was chiefly valued b
> me as a necessary means towards placing metaphysical and moral scienc
> on a basis of analysed experience in opposition to the theory of innate prin
> ciples so unfortunately patronised by the philosophers of your country.
>
> (Anschutz 1968: 51

The question is how to base 'metaphysics and moral science' on experience. What inferential steps can be taken conforming with a 'logic of consistency'? And in the case of utilitarianism, not as deontic ethics, an ethic of duty, but as consequential ethics, why should the 'experiential' standard of value be a measure of hedonism, the calculus of pleasure and pain?

The review of Mill's utilitarianism focused on these two questions. The *first*, the analysis of Mill's inferential *syllogism*. From man's positive behaviour as the *major*, to the universal rule of behaviour to be evaluated in accordance with its consequential effects, as the *minor*. The *second*, scrutinizing the ontological status of Mill's standard of value. Universal utilitarianism is *not* a theory of value. The value of an action depends of the value of the consequences of that action, that is, teleological value (cf. Adolphsen 1969: 3).

Mill's 'proof' of hedonistic utilitarianism and economic man

What logic can take us from stated positive observations of man's desire for pleasure to the ethical call for general happiness of man? As a declared experientialist Mill is not subscribing to Kantian categorical imperatives, whether supported by synthetic 'a priories' or not.

> According to the one opinion, the principles of morals are evident *a priori*, requiring nothing to command assent, except that the meaning of the terms to be understood. According to the other doctrine, right and wrong, as well as truth and falsehood, are questions of observation and experience.
>
> (Mill 1861: 2)

From the day it was published, focus has been on the tenability of Mill's logical constructions in the perennial debate on utilitarian ethics. Does it deserve to be beheaded by the guillotine of Humes? Utilitarianism founded on a naturalistic fallacy, an inference from *what is* to *what ought to be*, the normative twin of causal *post hoc ergo propter hoc*, relegates itself to the underwood of ideologies. Not founded on that fallacy, it can serve as a philosophy of ethics, at least logically.[13] In *Utilitarianism*, 1861, Mill states the principle as follows,

> No reason can be given why the general happiness is desirable, except that each person, so far as he believes it to be attainable, desires his own happiness. This, however being the fact, we have not only all the proof which the case admits of, but all which is possible to require, that happiness is a good: that each person's happiness is a good to that person, and the general happiness, therefore, a good to the aggregate of all persons. Happiness has made out its title as *one* of the ends of conduct, and consequently one of the criteria of morality.
>
> (Hall 1968: 155)

Mill's ethics were met with a sympathetic critique by J.E. Cairnes and H. Sidgwick, accepting hedonism as a psychological hypothesis, and later on with its vehement rejection by G.E. Moore and F.H. Bradley, with a renewed Cantabrigian critique of hedonism in the footsteps of W. Whewells. Semantics indicate that something important is at stake, paraphrasing the logic of the sentence above as:

> If many pigs are fed at one through, each desires his own food, and somehow as a consequence does seem to desire the food of all; and by parity of reasoning it should follow that each pig, desiring his own pleasure, desires also the pleasure of all.
>
> (Bradley 1927: 113)

The critique is unanimous Humean, 'ought to be' cannot be deduced from 'what is'; Mill's proof is a naturalistic fallacy, the inference from 'man desires happiness' to 'man ought to be a utilitarian' is invalid. In Moore's phrasing 'Mill has made as naive and artless a use of the naturalistic fallacy as anybody could desire' (1903 66). To which he adds a semantic critique to the effect that Mill is making 'desirable' a *homonym*, thereby producing a *quarternio terminorum* in his syllogism of utilitarianism, as such:

> The good is identical with the desirable.
> The desirable is identical with the desired.
> Therefore, the good is identical with the desired.
> He [Mill] has attempted to establish the identity of the good with the desired, by confusing the proper sense of 'desirable', in which it denotes that which is good to desire, with the sense which it would bear if it were analogous to such words as 'visible'.
>
> (ibid.: 67–8)

Interchanging the major and minor gives a case like: Man X desires to kill Y, to kill Y is desirable(visible), therefore to kill Y is good. The homonym is breaching 'The Logic of Consistency' of the syllogism, implying Mill's utilitarianism to be an *aporia*, irrespective of eventual naturalistic fallacies.

Mill's attempt to produce utilitarianism by experientialism, by positive observation and logical ratiocination, has failed, according to Sidgwick and Moore. They both recommend ethical intuition, in a cartesian and humean sense, to overcome the breaches of logic in Mill's ethical philosophy.[14] At the beginning of the twentieth century the record on the matter is, thus, Sidgwick and Moore both support utilitarianism based on intuition. Although differing by Sidgwick accepting and Moore rejecting psychological hedonism as an adequate theory of value in ethics. Moore's position can thus be characterized as *ideal* intuitional utilitarianism. An ethical utilitarianism not to be based on naturalism and hedonism, as there are more ways and values to be considered.

In the ensuing period, of 40 years, *rational economic man* has the philosophical support of Sidgwick's but not of Moore's.[15] Elsewhere in philosophy, ethical questions played a minor role. Themes of these days were set by *logical positiv-*

ism relegating the fundamental quest in philosophy, *Ontology*, into pure metaphysics out of science. Otto Neurath apart, the participants of '*Der Wiener Kreis*' did not offer economics any special attention, and their ethics were wholly relativistic. In economics, on the other hand, some utilitarian inspired theoretical analyses were presented by Pigou. His thought experiments of maximizing social utility through equalitarian redistributions of income, accepting the psychological hedonism of economic man, had no foundation in logical *empiricism*.[16] Not even if assisted by Weber–Fechner's empirical findings of decreasing psychological response to increasing physical stimuli.

Writing in the same period, Keynes ignored rational economic man. His *theory of monetary production* is inspired by Moore's ethics in defining the object of analysis. It concerns the unequal distributed deficiency of monetary income, and the consequential deprivation of a morally acceptable life for the unemployed. Keynes' epistemology and strictly positive analysis of 'the society in which we happen to live', with its two pivotal institutions, money and private property rights, together forming *the* institution of money-wage labour, is consistent with logical positivism of the time. The empirical, the factual given, *effective monetary demand* is in no need of further value 'ratiocinations' to become 'experiential'. '[Keynes] ... go[es] straight for the real important things. He succeeds in doing so just because he makes free use of his superb intuition and acute observation of the real world' (Hicks 1939: 4).

Reacting on the relativistic ethics of logical empiricism, philosophy of ethics revived in the 1940s. Early in the revitalization there was an *anticritique* in a defence of Bentham and Mill. Scaffolding hedonistic utilitarianism by

> Bentham thinks, by showing that it and it alone of all ethical theories, squares with our unsophisticated moral judgements and reasonings and sets up as morally good something which, by the basic law of human motivation, actually is sought by people.
>
> (Hall 1968: 176)

And by rationalizing the two constituting propositions of Mill's eudeamonism – (1) happiness is desirable, and (2) happiness is the only desirable final end – assuming man is rational, i.e. not accepting contradictions in terms, and his de facto desire of happiness, he has to accept proposition (1). The same goes for proposition (2). Being rational and having happiness as the only desired final end, one can only deny happiness as the only desirable goal at the cost of being irrational (cf. Adolphsen 1969: 28).

The logical critique of Moore's, the homonymic 'desirable', is dissolved. Reinstalling 'utility' as denominating the attribute of 'things' desirable. By these steps, the philosophical support of the ontological *raison d'être* of rational economic man is restored. 'Utility' as behavioural motivation is his founding and grounding. Hence the relevance for political economy and economics of its questioning. Consenting Bentham and Mill's utilitarianism in social philosophy and politics is implicit acceptance of the scientific relevance of economic man.[17]

With just one caveat under the reign of logical *positivism*, the desire of happiness has to be de facto. 'Desire' has to be experiential in Mill's methodological taxonomy, that is, established by induction.

Signing logical *empiricism*, a contrario, involves a priori dispensation of all positive demands on the thought construction, and embracing the *rationalization* of eudeamonism as a philosophy of value, smoothes the path for axiomatizing *rational* economic man, REM. Bringing us to these days theoretical microfoundation of economics as such. Not inferred from positive experience, the theory *is* the well-known set of axioms defining REM.

'Rationality' denotes a maximization principle governing the actions of REM, and rationality connotes, in addition, an attribute of preferences by the axiom of transitivity in the complete weak ordering of all possible bundles of commodities in the economic universe. Furthermore an axiom, as some variety of private property or rights of disposal, is implied in stating the endowments of REM as a constraint on maximizing endeavours in his choice and action. With this theory at hand it is possible to produce a variety of models of economic action and interaction.

Utility, axioms and economics

The main road

Exploiting the maxims of logical empiricism to the full, *Theory of Value: an axiomatic analysis of economic equilibrium* (Debreu 1959) became a beacon for the fairway of economic research. From the preface we take it that the content has been taught in Chicago and Yale since 1953. The analysis is based on a price system or a 'value function defined on the commodity space' (ibid.: vii). Two 'schools' are combined in the work. Topically it is the 'school of Lausanne', a code for Walras and Pareto, and the 'Bourbaki school' of mathematics as the analytical high way.

The theory of value is stated 'with the standards of rigor of the contemporary formalist school of mathematics ... Allegiance to rigor dictates the *axiomatic* form of the analysis where the theory, in the strict sense, is logically entirely disconnected from its interpretations' (ibid.: viii, emphasis mine). Of the two aspects of 'the theory of value' announced to be addressed, '(1) the explanation of the prices of commodities resulting from the interaction of the agents of a private ownership economy through markets, (2) the explanation of the role of prices in an optimal state of an economy' (ibid.: vi), only (2) is actually handled with rigor. An *optimal* state of the economy is defined as an attainable state 'to which no attainable state is preferred'. An *attainable* state is a market equilibrium, satisfying *possible* consumption minus *possible* production equals the endowments of the economy, that is, excess demand equals zero. If a *given* system of prices, *p*, delineating the sets of possible consumption and production for all agents, *allows* an attainable state, this state is an optimum. And vice versa, if the state is attainable and optimal, there will be a system of prices allowing it.

'These two essential theorems of the theory of value thus explain the role of prices in an economy' (ibid.: 90). But they do not 'explain' prices.[18]

As the commodity space is preference-ordered by REM, these theorems reflect eudeamonism in one of the infinite many possible real-valued utility functions:

'Let Xi (consumption set of i) be a connected subset of R^l (l as the number of generic commodities), completely preordered by $\frac{L}{i}$. Under assumption (a) there is on Xi a continuous utility function.' with assumption (a), stating that preferences are continuous too.

(ibid.: 56)

These are well-known welfare theorems connecting 'Pareto-optimality' and prices in a 'private ownership economy'. Theorems, and the role of prices, to be interpreted respecting the restrictions by the assumptions necessitated for their rigorous derivation by mathematics, 'which freed mathematical economics from its tradition of differential calculus and compromises with logic' (ibid.: viii). Preferences have to be continuous, and so has therefore the measure 'in kind' of the commodities. 'A quantity of well-defined trucks is an integer; but it will be assumed instead that this quantity can be any real number. This assumption of perfect divisibility is imposed by the present stage of development of economics' (ibid.: 30). Not because of economics 'tradition of differential calculus and compromises with logic' but necessitated by the demands of rigorous equilibrium analysis of value.

The existence of equilibria for REM in the 'commodity space' is rigorously demonstrated. If one of the equilibrating 'value functions', relatively to the given 'utility functions', are stumbled upon by chance the economy equilibrates (see Note 18 above). 'Stumbled upon' because the analysis does not include market generated dynamics of the price system. Leaving 'Two important problems [that] have not been studied in this chapter: the uniqueness and the stability of equilibrium' (ibid.: 89). Problems topically at the core of the research ensuing this seminal work of Debreu.

To our knowledge that has not been the case for the last of 'Two important and difficult questions ... not answered by the approach taken here: the integration of money in the theory of value ... and the inclusion of indivisible commodities' (Debreu 1959: 36). Divisibility assumed as a *rigorous* precondition, that is. The commodity-space, R^l, is continuously infinite in all dimensions. The number of dimensions, *l*, is assumed finite, but the quantity of a commodity '...can be any real number' (ibid.: 32). Continuity makes the set of *l*-tuples in commodity-space uncountable. And the Ø-set apart, continuity makes subsets uncountable too. Uncountable sets REM has to order by his preferences. In the nature of the matter, this gives rise to 'difficult questions'. Not only, but also, of conceptual consistency and interpretation.

The introduction or definition of 'commodity' seems not to be on par 'with the standards of rigor of the contemporary formalist school of mathematics'.

The semantics are uneasy, going from the tentative: 'It is possible to present in this introduction the essential features of the two concepts in a simplified and slightly imprecise manner' to 'the theory will be developed in terms of the two general, abstract concepts of commodity and price'. And, 'summing up, a commodity is a good or a service *completely* specified physically, temporally, and spatially'. With the mind-boggling addendum 'It is assumed that there is only a *finite* number *l* of distinguishable commodities.' And the conclusion 'From now on the full generality of the concept of commodity, as illustrated by all the examples above, should always be kept in mind' (ibid.: 28–32, emphases mine).

Axiomatizing in the a priori unrestricted mood of logical *empiricism* implies problems of consistency and interpretation of the predicate 'commodity'. Bordering to an impredicative 'commodity space', in our case. Straightforward these problems could be prevented applying the relevant demarcation of generic commodities defined by the actual revealed preferences of REM. Leading us back to Mill's 'experientialism', or the prior inductions demanded by logical *positivism*. And the route of research, from there, would with certainty falsify the 'assumption of perfect divisibility' and thereby destroy the topology of 'commodity space'. It is, thus, counterfactual misleading to state the divisibility assumption to be 'imposed by the present stage of development of economics'.

Rationalizing eudeamonism as a philosophy of value supports the concept of 'utility' and actualizes the 'commodity space' as the locus for REM to maximize his utility. This is the *development* of economics in the 1950s. Its methodology is logical empiricism and 'the contemporary formalist school of mathematics' demanding ubiquitous density and connectedness. Reintroducing 'utility' and real-valued 'utility functions' in general equilibrium economics is pre-Paretian. There is a psychological hedonism in the behaviouristics of REM.

A differing tributary – to become a wadi

Pareto's critique of the metaphysics of economic man had consequential followers. In continuation of 'A Reconsideration of the Theory of Value' (Allen and Hicks 1934) elaborating the value analysis of Pareto/Edgeworth, J.R. Hicks general equilibrium theory in *Value and Capital* (Hicks 1939) is discarding 'utility functions' altogether. The analysis is performed on preference orderings without any arbitrary translation into real-valued functions. 'The quantitative concept of utility is not necessary in order to explain the market phenomena. Therefore, on the principles of Occam's razor, it is better to do without it' (ibid. 18). Hicks is proceeding in a tempered manner. No unnecessary rigour or generalizations to disturb the vision. For example, assuming *locally* decreasing marginal rates of substitution for an equilibrium to be realized, 'is the simplest of the various possibilities before us' (ibid.: 23).

Expanding the coverage of the analysis by similarly argued assumptions 'What begins as an analysis of the consumer's choice among consumption goods ends as a theory of economic choice in general. We are in sight of a unifying principle for the whole of economics' (ibid.: 24). Paretian scales of preferences *cum* an axiom of maximization can, in this way, even lead us into the dynamics of capital accumulation and the trade cycle. All based on the positive theory of Paretian economic man.

> Now of course this does not mean that if any one has any other ground for supposing that there exists some suitable quantitative measure of utility, or satisfaction, or desiredness, there is anything in the above argument to go against it. If one is a utilitarian in philosophy, one has a perfect right to be a utilitarian in one's economics. But if one is not (and few peoples are utilitarians nowadays), one also has the right to an economics free of utilitarian assumptions.
>
> (ibid.: 18)

As sketched above, this did not become the methodological mainstream after 1950, though.

Another off-spring from 'A Reconsideration of the Theory of Value' was 'New Welfare Economics'. An endeavour to exploit the criteria of Pareto-optima and improvement in welfare economics.[19] What are our possibilities of aggregating the scales of preferences of Paretian economic man to be contra posited the production possibilities as an aggregate of the production functions of firms? If possible, potential Pareto improvements in aggregate production and consumption could be exposed as 'scientific' recommendations in accordance with the preferences of aggregated economic man. Recommendations as alternatives or supplements to Keynesian monetary analyses and recommendations.

Disappointingly this line of research was dismantled as a result of the dissemination of Arrow's 'impossibility theorem', summing up the end of an intellectual endeavour:

> If we exclude the possibility of interpersonal comparisons of utility, then the only methods of passing from individual tastes to social preferences which will be satisfactory and which will be defined for a wide range of sets of individual orderings are either imposed or dictatorial.
>
> (Arrow 1951: 59)

Macroeconomics is lost for REM, as from here on 'truck, barter and exchange' between 'Rational Economic Men' is expulsed as intelligible expositions of the ways of 'Wealth of Nations'.[20] Academic history of economics from this point of internal development, is the epistemological micro–macro divide and the perennial essays in bridging that same divide. Inserting *representative* REM as a makeshift for genuine microfoundation of macroeconomics became state of the arts. A state as ubiquitous as intellectually dissatisfying in macroeconomic interpretations and analyses. Taking stock of the situation in the last half of the 1980s, K.J. Arrow, the academic genitor, and Alan Kirman published a variety of devastating interpretations and conclusions regarding the status and role of REM in macroeconomic theory.[21] The main thrust of criticism aims at the methodological rationale for REM as a thought construction.

Arrow 'want to stress that rationality is not a property of the individual alone, although it is usually presented that way' (1986: 385). Outside *fictitious* perfect competition assuming facultative rationality gets involved. The *entelechy* of it comprises not only the assumption regarding preferences, but also rational assessments of choice alternatives embedding 'perceptions of others and, in particular, of their rationality become part of one's own rationality ... it will involve computational and informational demands total at variance with the traditional economic theorist's view of the decentralised economy' (ibid.). An entanglement on par with Keynes' case of beauty-contest conjectures in the general economic case.[22] It has to be traversed to reach the standard referential equilibrium of economic theory. 'What does rational behaviour mean in the presence of disequilibrium? Do individuals speculate on the equilibrating process?... There are no good answers to these questions ... they do illustrate the conceptual difficulties of rationality in a multiperson world' (ibid.: 387, emphasis mine). The good answer demands the preferences of the totality of REM to be 'subjected on to' the data of an eventual equilibrium. For obvious reasons, assuming a total homogenization of REM as 'the representative agent', is just begging the question.

The situation is a logical *fix*, as 'There is no more misleading description in modern economics than the so-called microfoundations of macroeconomics .. If we aggregate over several individuals, such a model is unjustified' and 'attempt(s) to obscure or avoid the aggregation problem is an old one' (Kirman 1989: 138). Scraping along with the representative REM leads to nowhere, so at this point a timely question could be, what, more exactly, is it we are attempting or avoiding to aggregate?

The 'kernel of the poodle' is not there to be found

In conventional microfoundations of economics the physical commodity space including leisure, is defined *uno actu* as it is transformed into an economic space via a valuation by REM. Valuation as a mental process, the result of which is coined the axiom of 'rational preferences', whereby the commodity space is structured according to innate desires and beliefs of REM. The predicate 'rational' signifying a transitive binary relation between all and every subset of the infinite commodity space in l dimensions. The agent specific relation, 'at least as desired as', is *imagined* to establish the individual economic universe of any REM. On this background, in his 'propensity to truck, barter, and exchange one thing for another', REM interacts with all other REM, each imbedded their economic universes, in an acquisitive urge to obtain the highest ranking subset in his ordered commodity space, through exchange.[23]

The aggregation problem concerns the possibility of calculating the l excess demand functions for the aggregated *system* of individual economic universes rational interaction, i.e. when all and every REM is seeking to maximize optimize his utility by ways of commodity exchanges. Arrow and Kirman poi to the logical aporia in this scientific endeavour. But the logical soundness of the critique should not overshadow its lacking in epistemological relevance. Problems in aggregating imagined preordered sets and structures are imaginal too.

A more revealing question pertains the process that could generate these sets and structures representing the desires of socially unbounded individuals. One fundamental answer is presented by B. Rustem and K. Velupillai (Rustem and Velupillai 1990; Velupillai 2000). Granting the convention all its assumptions besides the continuity of the commodity space, for obvious reasons, '[t]he procedure by which an ordering over a countable set of alternatives is conceptualized is by confronting REM with a sequence of binary choices' (Rustem and Velupillai 1990: 423). Looking at REM as a feed-forward neural net, i.e. if bounded by Church thesis it could be operationalized on the most general level as a Turing machine, the question of how or by what procedure the preference ordered commodity space comes into being can be put. 'I ask whether the rational economic agent can effectively generate, as a preference ordering, the relevant series of statements that are choices from sets containing two elements' (Velupillai 2000: 32).

When an algorithmic procedure for computing 'rational preferences' is substituted for the conventional axiom, when effective computation is substituted for unspecified mental processes, the result is conclusive for the 'aggregation problem'. The problem is relegated to the history of economic thoughts on *homo economicus*. If we accept the cognitive consequences of modelling REM as a neural net and a fortiori as a Turing machine, the problem stands out misconceived as an epistemological chimera. Because 'there is no effective procedure to decide whether a preference order can be generated by methodically – i.e. systematically – evaluating alternatives' (ibid.: 39). In addition, this marks an unsurmountable intellectual obstacle for any conventional microeconomic foundation of economics. The seemingly simple posed question of economic man ordering his preferences in a discrete commodity space cannot be reprocicated by intelligible and systematic methods.

The only way to handle the problem is to put more structure, including some measure of heterogeneity, on the characterization of economic agents. Not to keep preferences unspecified, albeit axiomatically rational, in a closure of economic models, but to take decision rules and preferences fully specified or generated endogenously by some specified circumstantial process. 'Anyone who makes significant progress in this direction … by explaining how interaction may yield restrictions on the evolution of the distribution of agents' characteristics, will have made a radical step forward' (Kirman 1989: 138). In this case 'the radical step forward' could be effected by a modest regression in the history of economic thought looking for suggestions. The classics, including Marx, offer more than one proposal for sociological and socio-historical closures. Keynes' offer is to harness the question in the strict monetary logic of 'the society in which we happen to live' and its consequential conditioned psychology. And, of course, Pareto and Veblen could be consulted for richly argued and, therefore, potentially fecund proposals. Finally any im- or explicit historical materialistic approach to social science proposes closures for micro- as well as macroeconomics.

The important, per se not very surprising, conclusion 'that some aspects of behaviour cannot be encapsulated by any formalism at all. It can, so to speak, be studied only as it unfold' (Rustem and Velupillai 1990: 431) is debilitating neither curiosity nor social science. Man's behaviour unfolds in every moment and corner of the empirical world. We observe the outcomes and endeavour to reproduce and 'explain' the same outcomes. The unfolding of a variety of models of the world can be meaningfully investigated by simulations as long as we accept the wide epistemological confines of the algorithm.

This liberated agnosticism is in the same vein as Erwin Schrödinger's in the preface of his *What is Life?* (1955: 1). Divinations on the outcome of the process of life are not accessible by mathematical analysis. But that does not prohibit thoughts to be thought nor stories to be told.

Notes

1 Economic man becomes *rational*, formally, when he is assumed to maximize the value/pleasure of his endowments, and his experienced value/pleasure is a decreasing function of the quantity of any given good in his possession. In the interval of 1814 to 1854 these two axioms were worked out for economics, chronologically as:

  a Many of the questions, both in morals and politics, seem to be of the nature of the problems *de maximis et minimis* in fluxions; in which there is always a point where a certain effect is the greatest, while on either side of this point it gradually diminishes (Malthus 1814: 30)

  b 'We shall invoke but a single axiom … i.e. that each one seeks to derive the greatest possible value from his goods or his labour' (Cournot 1982/1838: 44).

  c 'Increase of the same kind of consumption yields pleasure continuously diminishing up to the point of satiety' (Gossen 1854: 60).

2 Adam Smith cannot have regarded his own work as a positive theory of society. His anti-Hobbesian view on the nature of man would never allow the 'economic man' as a positive, factual, man in history. Without compassion of man there would be no society and a fortiori no political economy to be found. In *lingua economics*, utility functions or preferences are interdependent between men. *The Theory of Moral Sentiments* containing lectures on moral philosophy by Adam Smith and published 1759, 17 years before *The Wealth of Nations*, is the source for this assessment (Smith 1759).

3 The classical conception of economic growth comprises limits to growth. For Smith, Ricardo and Malthus nature sets these limits. For Marx the political economy sets its own limits of growth. The accumulation of capital annihilates the rate of profit per se. Growth will resume in the revolutionized political economy which is not of *l'ancien régime* but of a society governed by the radical ethics of communism. Not growth in exchange value, but growth in social welfare. It is still to be seen which of the envisaged limitations, if any, will finally throttle the accumulation of capital.

4 This is a representative of the socio-phenotype adhered to by Adam Smith:

  The difference between the most dissimilar characters, between a philosopher and a common street porter, for example, seems to arise not so much from nature as from habit, custom and education … By nature a philosopher is not in genius and disposition half so different from a street porter, as a mastiff is from a greyhound, or a greyhound from a spaniel, and this last from a shepherd's dog.

  (Smith 1776: Book I, Ch. ii)

  The citation in the text, above, follows.

5 These rationalizations of liberalism are the prototypical covering law of nowadays economics. With the natural law imbedded in the axioms of independent and complete preferences and self-interest in the same axioms and in the, often only implied assumption, of rational economic choice as not only a mental but also a physical exchange action. It is sometimes traded as 'positive economics'.

6 The metaphor is covering Adam Smith's view on development and growth but is not eschatological, that is, Marx is not a Christian.

7 The term 'vigorously' is verbatim from the text of Pareto's. But it could have been, or perhaps should have been, 'rigorously'? That would be in accordance with the usage of that term in science at the turn of the century. Rigour of theories and in theoretical analysis is the demand of bringing our assumptions in as close accordance with observable facts as possible. It is a neologism of our days to have 'rigour' designating the axiom of utility *maximizing* rational economic man. This is not a logomachy it is a question with epistemo- and ontological ramifications.

8 The phrase 'adhesion to a system' could include conceptual and methodological 'systems' in social science. For Pareto positivism does not belong to the realm of methodology it belongs, with a strong inductive bent, nominalism along, to the epistemology of his. In methodology he is rather a progenitor of Feyerabend (1978) when he states:

> You may adopt the method of reasoning you prefer, you may request help from history, physics, mathematics, you may accept or reject the theories of evolution, and if the old logic does not satisfy you, you may use the *new mathematical* one. Everything is permissible, everything is good, as long as you are able to discover new truths, shed new light on what is already known, rectify errors; in short, increase the quantity and the quality of human knowledge.
>
> (Pareto 1892: 390, emphasis mine)

9 According to U. Ricci the reason Pareto never accepted a reprint of the 'Cours', with its deductions from *homo economicus* to a theory of political economy, was 'because he believed he had progressed beyond this stage of analysis' (Ricci 1933: 10). One could suggest, also to pay homage to Pareto in his heaven, it was a strong intellectually substantiated belief of his.

10 In my translation this conclusive part in Pareto's critique becomes:

> It is an often repeated triviality that society is not a simple juxtaposition of individuals and that these, just by the fact that they live in society, acquire new characters. So if we could observe isolated men and men living in societies, we would have the ways to know by what they differ and we could separate the individual from the social, but the first term in this comparison *is not there to be found*, and the second is the only known to us.

11 Economic liberalism is subscribed to, intellectually, by Smith, Bentham and Hegel. The intellectual emancipation and idea of liberty in the Liberal movement was pan-European but Smith and Bentham endowed it with the idea of utility 'peculiar to the Anglo-Saxon world' (Halévy 1928: 118).

12 In comparative institutional analysis the rationale of Bentham's juridical philosophy is sometimes embraced. But the referential model of man in mainstream microeconomics is not rational economic man in uninhibited acquisitive activity. Equilibria are socially constrained *ab initio*. Exchange ratios between goods and leisure approximating infinity and *forced* upon the market game, as in slavery and robbery, are implicitly 'outlawed'. And the costs of enforcing social constraints are not part of the rational set up, they are 'invisible' too. Conceptually, 'rational' is not located in a reality, is not part of an ontology. It is an idea in which, e.g. rational equilibrium respecting real 'menu costs', equivocates as 'near rational'.

13 In Mill's prolific work Bentham's utilitarianism is pivotal in the ethics and political economy part of it. Mill's assessment is moving from dissent to an elaborated

approval and propagation of the utility principle. This fact alone could explain the sundry interpretations and nonconclusive critique of the principle. It is of some interest that the philosophical critique of Mill has the same movements. Moving from consent, dissent and back to consent over 100 years. The point here and in the sequel is to look at the covariance between these time series of the same 100 years, and the vitality of economic man in economics.

14 There is some irony in this. Moore's critique can be produced by Mill's 'Logic' if the focus is directed towards Mill's position on the epistemological status of 'Universals'. If the major 'The good is identical with the desirable' is denoting a particular proposition on observables, the 'desirable' *is* the actual 'desired':

> All inference is from particulars to particulars ... General propositions are merely registers of such inferences already made, and short formulae for making more ...
> The major premise of the syllogism, consequently, is a formula of this description ... and the conclusion is not an inference drawn from the formula, but an inference drawn according to the formula ... the real logical antecedent or premise being the particular facts from which the general proposition was collected by induction.
>
> ('Logic' cited in Anschutz 1968: 77)

It will not save the natural fallacy in Mill's utilitarianism but it transmits the experiential content to the minor. But, of course, Mill was inviting Moore's criticism:

> Thus although he accepts Locke's contention that the objects of the understanding are all in the last resort ideas, he also regards himself as free to assert with Bacon that they are not ideas but things. And then again although he wishes to say, and mostly does say, that the only thing that exist are the particular things we know in sense experience, he is also tempted to say, and frequently does say, that the behaviour of these things is only explicable by laws of nature which holds independently of them.
>
> (ibid.: 83)

15 W.S. Jevons published *Theory of Political Economy* in 1871. Ten years after Mill's *Utilitarianism* the Anglo-Saxon 'economic man' is coming to age as 'rational economic man' proper. Jevons' economic man seeks pleasure, and stands in front of 'problems de maximis et minimis in fluxions' (Malthus 1814). With the fluxions labelled 'degree of utility' or 'differential coefficient' in the case of an assumed continuous functional relation between utility and commodities. Bentham developed and emphasized the two concepts of 'maximisation' and 'utility' in his political and legal writings but

> As an economist, as today defined, Bentham made no attempt to develop an economic calculus or a theory of relative values and prices. His economic theorising in fact, is of an exactly opposite pattern to that typical of the neo-classicals. It is not mainly abstract, deductive and 'micro-economic', tightly organised around the assumption of a maximising individual; but on the contrary, is rather practical 'macro-economic', concerned with aggregate monetary problems, and if not statistical, at any rate concerned to exploit such crude statistics as were available...
>
> (Hutchison 1956: 290)

16 A distinction between logical positivism, the early 'Wiener Kreis', and logical empiricism, as a later development, is sometimes drawn. The *differentia specifica* being induction – confirmation versus hypothetico/deductive – confirmation/falsification as the methodological steps between theory and empirical evidence. The last *modus* is the modus of the Deduction–Nomological model of scientific explanation of Hempel and Oppenheim from 1948. This brings us back to Mill, (above, note 14) 'the only thing that exist are the particular things we know in sense experience' the *explanan*

dum, and 'the behaviour of these things is only explicable by laws of nature which holds independently of them'. There is the *explanandum*, the particular action, and the *explanans* of the motives of observed behaviour as a natural law. With the disturbing added statement, '[a]ll inference is from particulars to particulars ... the real logical antecedent or premise being the particular facts from which the general proposition was collected by induction' (*idem.*). In this way Mill's ratiocinated induction occupies the same position in the inferential chain as the hypothesis/axiom in the D–N model.

17 Albeit 'utilitarianism' comprises hedonism in common usage, the renewed philosophical debate has 'utilitarianism' as a universal theory. A theory to be combined with any standard for valuing consequences. Rejecting hedonism in social philosophy is a rejection of economic man in economics. But hedonism as a psychological hypothesis in economics does not involve modern utilitarianism per se.

18 The announced 'explanation of the prices of commodities resulting from the interaction of the agents of a private ownership economy through markets' is not there to be found. The analysis is not taking us further than Walras' recipe: 'the attainment of the equilibrium prices requires a rise in the prices of those commodities the effective demand for which is greater than the effective offer ... etc.' (Walras 1954: 72) and

> This hints at a tendency for an increase in the price of a commodity to decrease the corresponding excess demand. It prompts one, when trying to reduce positive excess demands, to put the weight of the price system on those commodities for which the excess demand is the greatest.
>
> (Debreu 1959: 83)

This procedure is not a tendency generated by the market. And as an algorithm forced upon the market by an auctioneer, there is no demonstration, rigorous or not, of its effectiveness in calling forth a market equilibrium.

19 At least the 'improvement' criteria is crypto-utilitarian and could not have been accepted by Pareto post 1909.

20 As there is no unique mapping from equilibrium macro-GDP values on to the set of preferences of the individual REM (Sonnenschein 1972). This constitutes an unsolved problem in the theory of economic value. Aptly characterized as a lack of a *conservation principle* in economics and the social sciences in general (Velupillai 2000: 64–5). One could see it as a logical corollary from the non-existence of natural constants in these fields of inquiry.

21 See Arrow (1986) and Kirman (1989).

22 'We have reached the third degree where we devote our intelligences to anticipating what average opinion expects the average opinion to be. And there are some, I believe, who practise the fourth, fifth and higher degrees' (Keynes 1936: 156).

23 As these processes are intentionally imagined we can ignore the assumption of a continuous physical commodity space. Just as the dimensions of qualities are assumed to be finite and not continuous, the quantities in all *l* dimensions are denumerable by the natural numbers. We are only describing the assumed world not rigging it for mathematical analysis.

References

Adolphsen, J.B. (1969) *Den moderne debat om Utilitarismen* (*The Modern Debate of Utilitarianism*), Aarhus, mimeo.

Allen, R.G.D. and Hicks, J.R. (1934) 'A reconsideration of the theory of value', *Economica*, 1(1): 52–76.

Anschutz, R.P. (1968) 'The logic of J.S. Mill', in J.B. Schneewind (ed.), *Mill: A collection of critical essays*, New York: Macmillan.

Arrow, K.J. (1951) *Social Choice and Individual Value*, New York: John Wiley.

—— (1986) 'Rationality of self and others in an economic system', *Journal of Business*, 59: 385–400.

Bentham, J. (1789) *An Introduction to the Principles of Morals and Legislation*, London: Clarendon Press.

Bradley, F.H. (1927) *Ethical Studies*, Oxford: Oxford University Press.

Brennan, G. and Buchanan, J. (1981) 'The normative purpose of economic 'science': Rediscovery of an eighteenth century method', *International Review of Law and Economics*, 1: 155–66.

Cournot, A.A. (1987/1838) *Researches into the Mathematical Principles of the Theory of Wealth* English edn, New York: Macmillan.

Debreu, G. (1959) *Theory of Value: An axiomatic analysis of economic equilibrium*, New York: Cowles Foundation.

Feyerabend, P.K. (1978) *Against Method*, London: Routledge.

Gossen, H.H. (1854) *Entwicklung der Gesetze des menschlichen Verkehrs, und der darauss fliessenden Regeln für menschliches Handeln*, Braunschweig: Vieweg.

Halévy, E. (1928) *The Growth of Philosophical Radicalism*, London: Faber & Faber.

Hall, E.W. (1968) 'The "proof" of utility in Bentham and Mill', in J.B. Schneewind (ed.), *Mill: A collection of critical essays*, New York: Macmillan.

Hegel, G.F.W. (1991) *Elements of the Philosophy of Rights*, Cambridge: Cambridge University Press.

Hicks, J.R. (1939) *Value and Capital: An inquiry into the some fundamental principles of economic theory*, London: Clarendon Press.

Hutchison, T.W. (1956) 'Bentham as an economist', *Economic Journal*, 66(262) (June): 288–306.

Jevons, W.S. (1970) *The Theory of Political Economy*, 2nd edn, Bungay UK: Richard Clay.

Keynes, J.M. (1936) *The General Theory of Employment, Interest and Money*, London: Macmillan.

Kirman, A. (1989) 'The intrinsic limits of modern economic theory: The emperor has no clothes', *Economic Journal*, 99(395): 126–39.

Levine, N. (1972) 'Humanism without eschatology', *Journal of the History of Ideas*, 33(April–June): 281–98.

Malthus, T. (1814) *Observations on the Effects of the Corn Laws, and of a Rise or Fall in the Price of Corn on the Agriculture and General Wealth of the Country*, London: J. Johnson and Co.

Marx, K. (1858) *Grundrisse* (English edn), Harmondsworth: Penguin.

—— (1859) *A Contribution to the Critique of Political Economy*, Introduced by Maurice Dobb (1970), New York: International Publishers.

—— (1872) *Capital* (*Das Kapital*), vol. I (1967), New York: International Publishers.

Mill, J.S. (1843) *A System of Logic Ratiocinative and Inductive, Collected Works of J.S. Mill*, vii–viii (1973), Toronto: Toronto University Press.

—— (1848) *Principles of Political Economy with Some Applications to Social Philosophy, Collected Works of J.S. Mill*, ii–iii (1965), Toronto: Toronto University Press.

—— (1859) *On Liberty, Collected Works of J.S. Mill*, XVIII (1977), Toronto: Toronto University Press.

—— (1861) *Utilitarianism, Collected Works of J.S. Mill*, X (1969), Toronto: Toronto University Press.

Moore, G.E. (1903) *Principia Ethica*, Cambridge: Cambridge University Press.

Pareto, V. (1892) 'Considerazioni sui principi fondamentali dell' economia politica pura', *Giornale degli Economisti*, 4(May): 201–39.

—— (1896) *Cours d'économie politique*, vol. I, Lausanne: Librairie de l'Université

—— (1897) 'The new theories of economics', *Journal of Political Economy*, 5(September): 485–502.

—— (1905) 'L'individuel et le social', in E. Claparede (ed.), *Congres International de Philosophie 2*, Geneve: Kundig.

Ricci, U. (1933) 'Pareto and pure economics', *Review of Economic Studies*, 1(October): 3–21.

Rustem, B. and Velupillai, K. (1990) 'Rationality, computability, and Complexity', *Journal of Economic Dynamics and Control*, 14(2): 419–32.

Schrödinger, E. (1955) *What is Life?* Cambridge: Cambridge University Press.

Smith, A. (1759) *The Theory of Moral Sentiments* (1976), Indianapolis, IN: Liberty Classics.

—— (1776) *An Inquiry into the Nature and Causes of the Wealth of Nations* (1910), London: Everyman's Library.

Sonnenschein, H. (1972) 'Market excess demand functions', *Econometrica*, 49: 549–63.

Velupillai, K. (2000) *Computable Economics: The Arne Ryde Memorial Lectures*, Oxford: Oxford University Press.

Walras, L. (1954) *Elements of Pure Economics: Or the theory of social wealth* trans. W. Jaffé, New York: Routledge.

Zeuthen, F. (1965) *Videnskab og Velfærd i Økonomisk Politik*, Copenhagen: G.E.C. Gads Forlag.

17 Resisting the sirens of realism in economic methodology

A Socratic odyssey

Thomas A. Boylan and Paschal F. O'Gorman

A festschrift should not simply promote detailed argumentative disputation; it should also offer the opportunity to get clear about thematic motives in the thinking of an outstanding colleague – and, in the mirror of an extraordinary path of thought, observed with respect and admiration from a distance marked by friendship, it also offers the opportunity to arrive at a better understanding of one's own thematic motives.

(Habermas 1995: 10)

Introduction

Current debates in the methodology of economics can be characterized as lying on either side of a fault-line dividing the adherents of realism, or at least certain variants of it, from those who advocate anti-realist positions as being the most appropriate methodological basis for economics. The path by which the methodology of economics has arrived at this situation has been a tortured and indeed tortuous journey, embracing most, if not all, of the major developments in philosophy, and specifically in the philosophy of science during the course of the twentieth century. From the emergence of logical positivism in the early part of that century to its transmogrification into logical empiricism, the latter becoming essentially identified with the Received View (Suppes 1977), through the Popperian interlude of falsificationism, along with its associated Kuhnian and Lakatosian responses, all of which influenced and preoccupied methodological reflections in economics to various degrees. The breakdown of the putative Received View gave rise to what Caldwell (1982) termed the 'post-positivist' era. While it is difficult to assign precise dates to developments in the movement of ideas, the 1974 Nafplion Colloquium on Research Programmes in Physics and Economics and the publication of the proceedings in a seminal volume edited by Spiro Latsis could be canvassed as marking the beginning of a new and vibrant phase in economic methodology (Latsis 1976). While the shadow of Kuhnian paradigms and Lakatosian research programmes hung over the Latsis volume, the next 30 years witnessed the proverbial 'explosion' in the literature on economic methodology (Hands 2001a).

By the 1990s it was clear that the main contending methodological frameworks in economic methodology gravitated around realism on the one hand and rhetoric, which had been introduced by McCloskey (1983, 1986), on the other. In 1995 we attempted to negotiate a methodological *via media* between realism and rhetoric, arising from our dissatisfaction with aspects of both of these positions (Boylan and O'Gorman 1995). We termed our position 'causal holism' and it represented a fusion of Van Fraassen's constructive empiricism (Van Fraassen 1980) with Quine's holism (1981). Causal holism was motivated by our concern with what we perceived to be the 'epistemic cost' to the empirical content of economics arising from the excessive preoccupation with a particular form of formalization in economics, something we shared with Tony Lawson's critical realism. While we do not propose to rehearse the arguments of causal holism here, beyond emphasizing a central tenet which underlay our position: that while we took an extremely liberal view of the intellectual resources that could be permitted in the construction of theory, when it came to theory selection and evaluation, our criterion was informed by the concept of descriptive adequacy. This we argued had significant implications for economics. The malaise in economics remains, we believe, centrally concerned with this question and its related issues. Causal holism took issue with the epistemological fundamentals of realism, and found rhetoric either unwilling or unable to provide a satisfactory analysis of a number of issues.

Arising from our work on causal holism, our research efforts developed in a number of different directions. One direction pursued was the exploration of a Wittgensteinian interpretation of rationality as a potential source of modification of the conceptual basis of rationality as used in mainstream (neoclassical) economics (Boylan and O'Gorman 2003a). Another direction, and one we considered to be as fundamental, if not more urgent, was the need to address the relationship between developments in the philosophy of mathematics and theoretical economics, in the context of major developments in philosophy in the twentieth century, in this case the 'linguistic turn' (Boylan and O'Gorman 2007). These were issues which received, in our view, seriously inadequate attention in the literature of economic methodology. Our methodological position was interpreted as being a sophisticated form of empiricism but anti-realist in orientation. Certainly our position as causal holists, when extended to the philosophy of mathematics, led us to the need to address the issue of realism and anti-realism in mathematics. It was clear to us that within the literature on economic methodology, neither the realists nor the anti-realists addressed the implications of the distinction between realism and anti-realism in the philosophy of mathematics and more significantly to the implication of this distinction for economic theorizing.

In the summer of 1995, in the inspiring surroundings of the beautiful city of Florence, during the course of the Tenth International Congress on Logic, Methodology and Philosophy of Science, we articulated a book-length study of these developments and their implications for economics. However, circumstances conspired against us which prohibited our pursuit of this project, when one of us became involved in senior management within our University between 1997 and 2001. By 2000, however, Vela arrived in Galway, and after his term as a Fellow of Peterhouse College in Cambridge during 2000–2001 was completed, he took up the John Elliot Cairnes Professorship of Economics, a part-time position that was especially created for him at the National University of Ireland, Galway. Vela's arrival in Galway and the opportunity to speak to him of his innovative and challenging research agenda, with its implications for the fundamental reconsideration of theory construction and evaluation at the most sophisticated technical level of analysis, revitalized our interest in our earlier project, in what was a more philosophical approach to aspects of the same project as Vela was pursuing. This offering represents our modest contribution to celebrate the sixtieth birthday of a gifted theorist, and a unique human being, whom we have had the great privilege and pleasure of having as a colleague and friend for the last nine years.

The structure of the remainder of the chapter is as follows: in the second section we outline the dominance of realism in economic methodological thinking as represented in the work of Lawson and Mäki; this is followed in the third section, where we examine a number of aspects of realism in the philosophy of mathematics which have significance for economic methodology. In the fourth section we address anti-realism in the philosophy of mathematics, and the emergence of constructive mathematics and its methodological implications for economics. The final section addresses the issue of the kind of mathematics to be used in theory construction in economics, and re-engages with our opposition to current realist positions in economic methodology.

The dominance of realism in economic methodology

With the breakdown of the Received View, the stability that characterized the period of dominance under logical empiricism gave way to the vibrancy and instability of the 'post-positivist era'. As part of the response to the mounting critique of the Received View, both instrumentalism and realism emerged as rather different philosophical and methodological alternatives. The former, instrumentalism, found its way into economics through Friedman's celebrated essay (Friedman 1953). Later in the 1970s, realism, and more specifically scientific realism, emerged as a serious contender as the dominant philosophy of science in the face of a plethora of competing methodological positions. In its historical emergence, scientific realism, viewed against the background of a variety of interpretations of realism, was seen as a powerful alternative to various empiricist-positivist approaches to science at this time, and also presented an equally potent alternative to varieties of relativism which were gathering increasing momentum.

Not that realism presented a unified, much less a monolithic, structure of fixed dogmas. As Mäki has noted, realism 'is used as the name for a variety of doctrines about things such as science, sense perception, universals, other minds, the past, mathematical objects, truth, moral values, possibilities and so on' (1998: 404). This merely confirms Hooker's earlier observation, referring to the varieties of realism on offer, that there is 'a certain taxonomic disarray at present

(1987: 258). It was this 'taxonomic disarray' that presumably prompted Wade Hands to describe the debates on realism in economics as 'a many splendoured thing' (2001b: 53). By the time Hands wrote the above, however, the work on realism in the methodology of economics had progressed from raking over the coals of the debates which were derived largely from arguments between instrumentalists and scientific realists in the philosophy of science. Referring to the writings that had emerged in the 1980s and 1990s, Hands could correctly note that 'Those writing on economic methodology have cut the philosophical umbilical cord to the Received View and the many different faces of "realism" are now emerging within the methodological literature' (ibid.: 53).

In our earlier work we did not attempt to sort out 'the taxonomic disarray', but rather we deployed Putnam's concept of 'stereotypes' in an attempt to capture the salient characteristics of scientific realism, noting with Putnam that propositions expressing stereotypical characteristics are not analytic truths (Boylan and O'Gorman 1995). In other words, any particular scientific realist may not accept the full array of stereotypes, but would presumably accept a number of them or at best some reasonable modifications thereof. We identified four such 'stereotypes' that captured, we believe, some of the principal features of scientific realism in the contemporary philosophy of science. First, all scientific realists share a minimal common position, namely, that contrary to philosophical instrumentalism, the sentences of a theory are either true or false; second, and contrary to relativism in its various guises, these sentences are true or false by virtue of how the world is deemed to exist independently of ourselves (Newton-Smith 1981: 21); third, and by way of elaboration of the above, a central ontological thesis is articulated, namely, that the actual world exists independently of every or any knowing subject. In Hooker's very apt and succinct phrase, 'existence is logically and conceptually independent of epistemic conditions' (1987: 156). Finally, and contrary to Kantian idealism, where the object(s) in themselves are not knowable, the independently existing world is indeed knowable. Indeed for many realists their commitment is to knowable, unchanging objects or natural kinds, where these natural kinds have essential properties which exist independently of us and we are capable of knowing them. The above stereotypes do not purport to constitute a comprehensive or exhaustive list of the themes of realism, much less the variegated subtleties which underlie the differences within realism. Rather our focus on a number of the key stereotypical features of scientific realism is to provide a reference frame which conveys something of the richness and heterogeneity of this increasingly dominant philosophy of science, thereby providing the broader background to the scientific realist approach to emerge in the philosophy of economics by its two leading contemporary exponents, Tony Lawson and Uskali Mäki respectively.

While sharing the commitment to a realist philosophy of economics, the disposition to realism by Lawson and Mäki are different in many respects. While Mäki is a philosopher by training who developed an interest in the philosophy of economics, Lawson went to Cambridge to study mathematics, but later reoriented his career to economics. As he describes it, 'Having come to economics by way of first studying mathematics I was immediately impressed by, as I saw it, the widespread and rather uncritical application of formalistic methods and systems to conditions for which they were obviously quite unsuited' (Lawson 1997: xiii). This dissatisfaction turned his interest 'to questions of ontology, and specifically to the study of how methods and modes of reasoning might be fashioned to insights concerning the nature of social being' (ibid.: xiii). With Lawson's ensuing work, 'the ontological turn' in the philosophy of economics was underway. Since the 1980s Lawson has produced an impressive corpus of work developing, refining and extending an economic methodology under the rubric of 'critical realism'. This work includes two major book-length studies, *Economics and Reality* (1997) and *Reorienting Economics* (2003).

Lawson initially drew on the work of Roy Bhaskar (1978, 1979, 1986) and the latter's transcendental realism to provide this philosophical launching pad for the development of critical realism. We have elsewhere criticized the use of transcendental realism and its role in critical realism (Boylan and O'Gorman 1997). While Lawson himself is not particularly enamoured with the title of 'critical realism', which he points out differs in a number of important aspects from that of Bhaskar's original formulation, he is happy 'to persist with the label of critical realism ... in full recognition that it is an ascription for which numerous conceptions may eventually equally qualify' (Lawson 1997: 158). But it is arguably transcendental realism which provides him with his unique philosophical arsenal with which he attacks the methodological underpinnings of mainstream economics, while also supplying him with the building blocks for his alternative approach. Transcendental realism provides the ontological basis for Lawson's approach which he juxtaposes with the mainstream theorizing of reality, which he labels 'empirical realism'. It is the seriously inadequate nature of this latter conceptualization of reality by mainstream economics and the methods of analysis which follow from it, which is the principal target of Lawson's critical realism.

Unlike Mäki's realism, Lawson's critical realism is not just the articulation of an alternative philosophical position, but is in fact highly prescriptive in orientation with respect to providing a foundational critique of mainstream economics. This is reflected in his claim that research into socio-economic life and institutions should be based on the nature of the socio-economic phenomenon being investigated. To this end the arguments derived from his philosophical ontology, which will deploy such constructs as open/closed systems; the structured nature of social reality into the empirical, the actual and the real and its theory of causal mechanism; the separability of the ontological structure under investigation; the transformational model of social activity which captures the complex interaction of structure and agency in social systems, along with a relational model of social structure. From these, and other constructs, critical realism develops a challenging and complex account of the ontological nature of socio-economic reality. From this analysis, critical realists attempt to derive methods deemed more appropriate for the study of socio-economic life than what is available in mainstream economics. Central to the method of critical realism is that of abduction (or retroduction), derived from C.S. Peirce (1867), which proceeds from 'a conception of some phenomenon of interest to a conception of some totally different types of thing, mechanism, structure or condition that at least in part, is responsible for the given phenomenon' (Lawson 1997: 24).

Since the 'ontological turn' is the pivotal point of departure for critical realism, a brief treatment of Lawson's analysis of ontology conveys the centrality of ontology in his overall analytical frame. Lawson distinguishes between two concepts of ontology: one he terms *scientific ontology*, which refers to what is, or exists, in the form of entities or things. Since the study of everything that exists is unmanageable, for purposes of focus and within the particular domain under study, attention is directed to what is considered to be the most important and fundamental for analysis. This aspect of ontology is distinguished from *philosophical ontology*, which is concerned with the common features that are shared by the entities or things that exists within a particular domain of study. This concept of ontology is of necessity more tentative and speculative in nature, with the primary function of identifying, classifying and providing a grammar which describes the common and essential features of what may appear as different and unconnected and may in fact be concealed from observation. Central to this analysis is Lawson's view that neither of these categories are immutable, depending as they do on the specificity of context and historical circumstances.

A further distinction, at the core of his analysis, arises from the above. Not only should ontology be viewed as in the above categories, but a further differentiation trust be made between this view of ontology and the study of theories and the knowledge claims they purport to support. What is central here for Lawson, are the presuppositions of theorists which are implied by their advocacy or commitment to a particular theory or research programme. Study of theories in this view, which Lawson would claim has been the predominant preoccupation of the philosophy of science, entails such issues as: theory selection; the plausibility of theory on grounds as tractability, simplicity, aesthetics; and the claims to knowledge by these theories about the entities or things in the world. A stringent criticism proffered by Lawson is that to confuse these two types of analyses, i.e. to subsume the concern with the ontological into concern with theories, is to commit the 'epistemic fallacy'. As he states it, 'To suppose that the study of being can be reduced to the study of theories and their presuppositions (about being) is to commit the epistemic fallacy, to reduce ontology to epistemology' (Lawson 2004: 2). Therefore the primacy of ontology over epistemology is defended and its implication for the reconsideration of economic methodology and ultimately the reorientation of economics has become the dedicated programme of critical realism.

The prolific contribution of Uskali Mäki reflects the approach of the trained philosopher to issues of interest to him in economic philosophy and methodology. There is clearly evident throughout his work a commitment to realism. For instance in his study of Austrian economics, he was at pains to point out that his analysis was 'built upon realist and essentialist premises' (Mäki 1990).

In our assessment of Mäki's early work we analysed in detail his approach to the reconstruction of economic methodology on realist grounds (Boylan and

O'Gorman 1995). This included an overview and critique of his complex network of intricate and nuanced distinctions within the parameters of realism. It also included the complex manner in which these distinctions – including his concept of realisticness as distinct from realism – may be applied in economics. Arising from the apparently discrete array of topics of concern to Mäki, it was not easy to contextualize his work, or to identify the philosophical sources that have influenced his work, but his commitment to an essentialist realism was never in doubt. In this context, as in the case of Lawson, Mäki has produced a prolific and challenging corpus of work.

More recently, however, Mäki has provided a welcome, if succinct insight into his approach to the philosophy and methodology of economics (Mäki 2002). He argues that much of the recent philosophy and methodology has pursued a 'top-down' approach. This has involved the adoption of a particular philosophy of science, and applying its 'descriptive categories and prescriptive rules' to economics. Frequently, based on this approach, economics comes up short, appearing to perform badly in the light of the chosen criteria and is thereby deemed to be in poor scientific shape.

Mäki's own approach is different and there are two aspects to it. The first arises from his insight that 'the peculiar characteristics of economics' throws up particular challenges to any adopted philosophy of science. In fact, Mäki makes the interesting claim that his study of the vast philosophical literature on realism over the last quarter century has 'not revealed to me any single version of realist philosophy that would fit with economics without major modifications' (ibid.: 91). From this he has come to 'appreciate a critical and creative attitude', believing that the philosophical resources available have 'to be adjusted and tailored so as to do justice to the specificities of the target of study, economics'. The second aspect is his declared empirical attitude, in which our philosophical account of economics should focus on, and be informed by, 'the actual theories, methods, and meta-theories that practicing economists hold' (ibid.: 91). In contrast to the conventional 'top-down' approach of the dominance of existing philosophy of science on economic methodology, Mäki would invoke a 'bottom-up approach' as a better descriptor of the empirical dimension of his approach. More generally, however, he suggests that a more accurate way to view 'the totality of my research on the topic' would be as a 'dialectical approach', in which 'philosophical concepts are adjusted and created in the light of empirical information concerning the actualities of economics' (ibid.: 91).

On this account, Mäki conveys his commitment to what is in practice an empirical approach to sorting out the actual philosophical approaches of practising economists and their actual theories. This is clearly contained in Mäki's 'bottom-up' approach as an integral part of his more general 'dialectical approach'. However, it should be noted, that at the outset of this contribution, where Mäki identifies the central question being addressed as being, 'whether realism about economics is a viable position', he lays down a rather definitive and generalized condition, when he states that any 'genuine controversy over the factuality of *any particular* strand or piece of economics requires realism as a *general* interpretation of economics – or at any rate requires debunking the anti-realist arguments discussed below' (ibid.: 90). Mäki proceeds to address in this contribution a number of 'nonreasons for nonrealism about economics'. While this is not the occasion to interrogate Mäki's position, the ubiquity and absolute necessity of realism is clearly manifest in Mäki's position. This combined with Lawson's comprehensive and systematic development of critical realism and its challenging implications for economic theory and method, had made realism, whether critical or dialectical, a presiding if not the dominant presence in contemporary methodology of economics.

In our view, despite the sophistication of these realist approaches, they fail to address the relevance of the realist/anti-realist debate in the philosophy of mathematics for economic methodology. This is surprising given the central role of mathematics in economics.

Realism in philosophy of mathematics and economic methodology

Realism in the philosophy of mathematics is a vast subject, containing an extensive agenda of issues on ontology, semantics and epistemology. In this section we focus, albeit briefly, on three critical dimensions of realism in the philosophy of mathematics which are significant for economic methodology. These are Frege's linguistic turn, platonism and Cantorian set theory. The Fregian linguistic turn is rarely discussed in economic methodology. Numerous Fregian scholars, especially Dummett, see Frege as the founding father of twentieth century philosophy of language (Dummett 1991). In particular, a paradigm shift occurred in philosophy at the turn of the twentieth century at the hands of Frege and the early Wittgenstein. In his early work, *The Foundations of Arithmetic*, Frege enunciates three fundamental principles:

> Always to separate sharply the psychological from the logical, the subjective from the objective;
> never to ask for the meaning of a word in isolation, but only in the context of a proposition;
> never to lose sight of the distinction between concept and object.
>
> (1968: x)

The first two principles mark the paradigm shift, which is frequently referred to as the 'linguistic turn' in philosophy. This turn has both negative and positive dimensions. The negative dimension is known as Frege's anti-psychologism (Potter 2000). One could say that modern philosophy from the seventeenth to the nineteenth centuries, whether in its empiricist, rationalist or Kantian versions, all agreed on the central importance of psychology for philosophy. Humean empiricists start their philosophizing with sense perceptions, images, ideas as vague images and finally the external expression of these in the terms of natural languages. Cartesian rationalists, with their mind–body dualism, see entities such as ideas or concepts and judgements as pertaining to the non-spatial, non-temporal private, mental world. According to some commentators, empiricist psycholo gism 'cannot justify more than a fragment of arithmetic as it is generally under stood and practised' (ibid.: 8). In empiricists' eyes we can only experience finitely many objects. Consequently, any philosophical account of arithmetic compatible with empiricism will fail to give an account of the potentially infinite sequence of natural numbers and of arithmetical quantification over that domain In short, empiricist psychologism leads to some version or other of strict finitism (ibid.: 8). In our view, this line of argument needs significant interrogation and development. However, an indispensable part of the Fregian objection to empiri cist psychologism is on a different footing: namely any empiricist account of numbers in terms of mental images, fails to adequately address the objective information conveyed by number statements (Frege 1968). Moreover, Fregian objections to Cartesian psychologism are not based on strict finitist considera tions: the Cartesian mind is not subject to any empiricist constraints. Rather the Fregian objection is on the grounds of Cartesian privacy: what is going on in the Cartesian private mind is of no concern to the logical analysis of arithmetical truths. The logician is primarily concerned with what is objectively communi cated by language, the basic unit of which is the proposition, i.e. a sentence which is true or false. In short, for Frege the starting point of a logically rigorous philosophy of mathematics is not the psychologistic terrain of post seventeenth century philosophy; rather it is the logic–language nexus of which he himsel was a pivotal pioneer.

However, as is well known, Frege was a severe critic of natural languages syntactically and semantically they left a lot to be desired and hence were inade quate for the construction/formulation of a rigorous mathematical proof. Frege was among the first to appreciate the indispensable role of a formal, rigorou language to any mathematico-logical account of a valid proof. To this end particularly in his early *Begriffschrift*, he attempted to furnish logicians with a rigorous language capable 'of bringing into sharp focus those elements which are essential for the validity of proof' (Kenny 2000: 13). In short, for Frege before we engage in proving a theorem, we must first outline the formal linguis tic structure required. Moreover, as we have explained elsewhere (Boylan and O'Gorman 2007), this Fregian approach to a rigorous formal language is not a Bourbaki, formalist one.

In recent work (Boylan and O'Gorman 2003a) we have explored some of the implications of the linguistic turn for economic methodology in general. Here our concern is more specific: namely computable economics. In our view com putable economics is centrally located in the spirit of the Fregian linguistic turn It is not an exaggeration to say that Velupillai is the Frege of computable eco nomics. In the spirit of logical rigour and clarity set by Frege, he specifies both the formal language and the formal mathematics required for his original and challenging research programme for theoretical economics. Thus the logico syntactical-semantical characteristics of Velupillai's proofs are explicitly stated in the spirit which animated Frege.

The second dimension or 'cornerstone' of realism in the philosophy of mathematics is platonism, which has undergone a number of sophisticated articulations in the course of the twentieth century (Benacerraf and Putnam 1983). Platonism is frequently presented as an ontological thesis: 'for a platonist, mathematical statements are about an objective reality ... existing independently of ourselves' (Dummett 2000: 264). In this connection Geach distinguishes between 'actual' and 'non-actual' objects. In his piece 'What Actually Exists', he gives a 'provisional explanation' of actual objects as follows: 'x is actual if and only if x either acts or undergoes change or both' (Geach 1969: 65). Material objects are actual. Numbers, however, lack this characteristic. Nonetheless by virtue of the way we use the logical apparatus of identity and quantification in arithmetic, mathematicians are ontologically 'committed' to numbers as real but non-actual objects.

Part of the rationale informing this ontological dimension of platonism is the correspondence theory of truth as applied to arithmetic: if an arithmetical statement is true, there must be something in virtue of which it is true. For our purposes, it is useful to divide the correspondence theory of truth into three principles. The first principle, just mentioned, is sometimes called 'the truthmaker principle' (Green 2001: 29). The second principle is frequently called the bivalence principle, i.e. there are only two truth values, namely what Frege called the True and the False. The third principle we will call the independence principle: statements are true or false 'independently of the means available to us of recognizing their truth value' (Dummett 2000: 3). For instance, Goldbach's conjecture that every even number greater than two is the sum of two primes is either true or false. Mathematicians may never prove or disprove this conjecture. For the realist that is beside the point: Goldbach's conjecture is in reality true or false.

In economic methodology, numerous methodologists, especially those of a realist persuasion, accept these principles. Indeed it is not unusual for realist methodologists to insist that these principles are indispensable for any rational being who wishes to avoid both incoherence and relativism. Realist indispensability arguments for these principles in economic methodology range from Kantian-type transcendental arguments, as advocated by critical realists, to Mäki-type analyses showing how specific anti-realists in economic methodology presuppose either these principles or principles closely allied to them. We have already explained our reasons for opposing Kantian-type transcendental arguments (Boylan and O'Gorman 1997). More recently we have suggested why we are not impressed by Mäki-type arguments for realism (Boylan and O'Gorman 2008). In our view, it is legitimate for economic methodologists to take an anti-realist position. In particular, anti-realism in mathematics does not end up either in irrationality or relativism. This theme will be taken up in the next section of the chapter.

Finally, we turn to the third dimension of realism, namely Cantorian set theory. In Frege's logicist programme, the ontological commitment to numbers as objects, implies the ontological commitment to *the actual* infinities of Cantorian set theory. More generally, according to both Fregian logicism and the altogether different Hilbertian formalism, 'the deepest insight into the nature of the infinite' is furnished by Cantorian set theory, which includes Cantor's theory of transfinite numbers (Hilbert 1983: 188). To show to the non-mathematician what is involved in Cantorian set theory, Hilbert draws on the distinction between potential infinity and actual infinity. Prior to Cantor's innovative work, mathematicians looked on infinity as potential or Aristotelian. In a potential infinite sequence there is no final term. In this sense it is incomplete. This incompleteness is shown by the phrase 'and so on'. According to realists 'potential infinity is not the true infinite'. We encounter 'the true infinite when we regard the totality of numbers itself as a completed unity ... This kind of infinity is known as actual infinity' (ibid.: 188). As Dummett puts it, Cantorian set theory 'treats infinite structures as if they could be completed and then surveyed in their totality, in other words, as if we could be presented with the entire output of an infinite process' (2000: 41). In Poincaré's metaphor, '(actual) infinity exists before the finite; the finite is obtained by cutting out a small piece from (actual) infinity' (1963: 66). Cantor systematically developed the concept of actual infinity into his theory of transfinite numbers. In short, as claimed by Hilbert, with due rhetorical flourish and mixed metaphors, 'thanks to the Herculean collaboration of Frege, Dedekind and Cantor, the actual infinite was made king and enjoyed a reign of great triumph. In daring flight, the (actual) infinite had reached a dizzy pinnacle of success' (1983: 190).

However, the Fregian logicist programme encountered a number of paradoxes. Various solutions to these were offered within the logicist camp. Moreover, Hilbert's own non-logicist programme was also inspired by his commitment to Cantorian mathematics summed up in his famous claim 'no one shall drive us out of the paradise which Cantor has created for us' (1983: 191).

How are realist developments in the foundations of mathematics relevant to economic methodology? Weintraub maintains that the formalization of economic theory in the course of the twentieth century occurred in two phases (Weintraub 2002). The first phase, based on analogies to theoretical classical mechanics, as distinct from experimental physics, was dominated by calculus. The second phase, initiated by Debreu and others, was dominated by recourse to Cantorian set theory, which, for short, we follow Dummett and others by calling it classical (realist) mathematics (Dummett 1973). The relevance of classical mathematics to economic methodology rests on numerous factors. In the context of computable economics, we here focus on one such factor, namely the distinction between constructive and non-constructive proofs. As Dummett points out, 'the distinction between constructive and non-constructive proofs arises within classical mathematics, and is perfectly intelligible from a completely platonistic standpoint' (Dummett 2000: 6). The platonist fully endorses constructive proofs: in non-technical terms the platonist, to prove the existence of something, is absolutely satisfied with any proof which actually constructs the thing in question. However, platonists are not limited to such methods of proof. Platonists also embrace non-constructive proofs. An elementary example of a non-constructive method of proof acceptable to the platonist is the use of the *reductio ad absurdum* method, which fundamentally presupposes the realist principle of the excluded middle and, in our view, more fundamentally, the principle of bivalence. (For a finite set, it is in principle possible to turn a *reductio ad absurdum* proof into a constructive one, but not for an infinite set.)

We now turn to economic methodology. Velupillai proves that the solution to the so-called economic problem of the existence, uniqueness and stability of a decentralized economy given in general equilibrium theory is not a constructive one: it uses the non-constructive Brouwerian fixed point theorem (Velupillai 2002b). However, recalling Dummett's point in the previous paragraph, this, on its own, does not mean, from a realist/platonist point of view, that one may not be able to find a constructive proof for this non-constructive result. According to Dummett 'a classical mathematician may spend a considerable amount of time looking for a constructive proof of a result for which he already has a non-constructive one' (2000: 7). Indeed some 'practitioners of applied CGE modelling, Shoven and Whalley, claiming that Scarf had devised a constructive proof of a fixed point theorem' (Velupillai 2002b: 315). In this connection Velupillai shows that such a so-called constructive proof is non-constructive. In short, as things stand, methodologically we can claim that general equilibrium theory depends on the indispensable use of a non-constructive proof, in the domain of Cantorian, actual infinity, set theory. *So what?* The difficulty arises when eminent theoretical economists, such as Arrow and Hahn (1971) and others claim that general equilibrium has made a case to 'establish that for the economy here described [i.e. a Walrasian exchange economy] there exists a set of signals, market prices, that will lead agents to make decisions that are mutually compatible' (ibid.: 311). In view of the fact that the mathematical proof supplied presupposes the domain of Cantorian actual infinity and that the proof is non-constructive, the claim made by Hahn and Arrow 'is unwarranted' (Velupillai 2002b: 311). Non-technically, we may say that the so-called equilibrium point exists in Cantor's infinite Paradise located in a non-spatial and non-temporal, platonist world and, since the method of proof is non-constructive, there is no good reason to suppose that such a point could be given any economic interpretation in the socio-economic world subsisting in real historical time. To make this claim more precise, we need to look at anti-realist developments in twentieth century philosophy of mathematics. This topic is addressed next.

Anti-realism in the philosophy of mathematics, the emergence of constructive mathematics and computable economics

Anti-realism in philosophy of mathematics is normally associated with Brouwer's intuitionism. As Dummett has pointed out,

> the name 'intuitionism' is due to Brouwer's acceptance of the Kantian thesis that our concept of the natural number series is derived from temporal intuition, our apprehension of the passage of time ... from the a priori form of that experience as involving temporal succession.
>
> (2000: 22)

We agree with Dummett that this Kantian-type approach 'is by no means essential for the acceptance of an intuitionistic conception of arithmetic' (ibid.: 22).

Leaving Kantianism aside, the distinction between platonism and intuitionism is usually drawn in terms of the correct understanding of mathematical infinity. As we have already seen, for platonists the real infinity is Cantorian actual infinity. For intuitionists 'all infinity is potential infinity: there is no completed infinite' (ibid.: 40). Under the influence of Poincaré, whom Benacerraf and Putnam call 'a quasi-intuitionist' (Benacerraf and Putnam 1983: 2), Brouwer saw the platonist ontological commitment to Cantorian completed infinity as a significant source of the paradoxes endemic to the Frege–Russell platonist, logicist programme.

In particular, in intuitionism, the infinite sequence of natural numbers is determinate, but not in the platonist sense of forming a completed structure. Rather it is determinate in two other senses. First, 'there is never any choice about how to extend any given initial segment of the sequence' (Dummett 2000: 22). Second, it is determinate in the sense that 'given any mathematical object we can always effectively recognize whether or not it can be reached by repeated application of the successor to 0 and hence whether or not it belongs to the sequence' (ibid.: 22). According to Dummett, the intuitionist claim that there is no actual infinity means 'that to grasp an infinite structure is to grasp the process which generates it, that to refer to such a structure is to refer to that process, and to recognize the structure as being infinite is to recognize the process will not terminate' (ibid.: 40). In this way, intuitionist mathematics is ontologically committed to potential infinity, whereas realist platonist mathematics is committed to Cantorian completed infinity.

When giving a preliminary survey of developments in twentieth century philosophy of mathematics, Benacerraf and Putnam distinguish between two broad categories. The first group is made up of mathematicians and philosophers who accept mathematics, including Cantorian set theory, as it is. These maintain that 'existing mathematics is used as a touchstone for the formation of an epistemology, one of whose conditions of adequacy will be its ability to put *all* of mathematics in proper perspective' (Benacerraf and Putnam 1983: 3, emphasis added). The other group also includes mathematicians and philosophers. Unlike members of the previous group, these 'don't take existing mathematics and mathematical activity as sacrosanct and immune from criticism' (ibid.: 2). They, as it were, want to prune existing mathematics in light of some external epistemological criteria. Clearly intuitionists belong to this category: in their view 'any part of real analysis that cannot be obtained by intuitionist methods ought to be discarded' (ibid.: 2).

Thus in addition to their respective divergent ontological commitments to potential infinity and to actual infinity, intuitionists and platonists disagree on the proper methods to be used in mathematics. Intuitionists limit the methods to be used in a proof to constructive ones, whereas the platonist is not so limited. Dummett expresses the intuitionist requirement as follows: the intuitionist 'must have a constructive proof because the intuitionistic interpretation of the conclusion is always such that no non-constructive proof could count as a proof of it' (2000: 7).

This point was nicely illustrated by Poincaré at the turn of the twentieth century before Brouwer's intuitionism emerged. Poincaré called anti-Cantorians, like himself, pragmatists, not intuitionists.

> Let us take for example Zermelo's theorem according to which space is capable of being transformed into a well-ordered set. The Cantorians will be charmed by the rigour, real or apparent, of the proof. The pragmatists will answer:
>
> 'You say that you can transform space into a well-ordered set. Well! Transform it!'
>
> 'It would take too long.'
>
> 'Then at least show us that someone with enough time and patience could execute the transformation.'
>
> 'No, we cannot, because the number of operations to be performed is infinite, it is even greater than aleph zero.'
>
> 'Can you indicate how the law which would permit space to be well-ordered can be expressed in a finite number of words?'
>
> 'No.'
>
> And the pragmatists conclude that the theorem is devoid of meaning, or false or *at least not proved*.
>
> (1963: 67, emphasis added)

Moreover, for the intuitionist the demand that a proof be constructive necessitates the rejection of the principle of the excluded middle in any proof concerning a potential infinite domain. Prior to intuitionism and the axiomatization of truth-functional logic, the law, or principle, of the excluded middle was a cornerstone of traditional logic. While the principle is not among the axioms of truth-functional logic, it is a theorem. However, the closely allied principles of bivalence and independence noted in the previous section are presupposed by truth-functional logic. Truth-functional logic presupposes that there are only two truth values and that a proposition is either true or false irrespective of our knowledge of it. In this sense the dispute between the intuitionist and the realist philosophically hinges on the notion of truth. Without getting involved in the details, Dummett sums up this difference as follows:

> From an intuitionistic standpoint, therefore, an understanding of a mathematical statement consists in the capacity to recognize a proof of it when presented with one; *and the truth of such a statement can consist only in the existence of such a proof.* From a classical or platonistic standpoint, the understanding of a mathematical statement consists in a grasp of what it is for that statement to be true, *where truth may attach to it even when we have no means of recognizing the fact* ... Hence the platonistic picture is of a realm of mathematical reality, existing objectively and independently of our

knowledge which renders our statements, true or false. On an intuitionistic view, on the other hand, the only thing which can make a mathematical statement true is a proof of the kind that we can give ... *It is for this reason that the intuitionistic reconstruction of mathematics has to question even the sentential logic employed in classical reasoning.*

(2000: 4–5, emphasis added

With the emphasis on the notion of a constructive proof, the mathematical spotlight begins to shift away from the detailed specifics of intuitionistic mathematics on to the range of notions used by logicians and mathematicians when speaking about constructive proofs. For instance, when discussing proofs logicians frequently say that a proof must be an effective, mechanical procedure carried out in a finite number of steps. This procedure is rule governed, all the rules are explicitly stated in an unambiguous language and each rule must be applied one step at a time. The logico-mathematical challenge was to rigorously formalize this constellation of notions. One rationale for this challenge is fairly basic. Mathematicians had to address the issue of whether or not there is an algorithmetic solution for some mathematical problems. To do this mathematicians must rigorously formalize the notion of an effective mechanical procedure. In the 1930s this objective was achieved in a variety of ways by Turing machines Church's λ–calculus, Post's machine and Kleene's modification of the Herbrand-Gödel notion of recursiveness.

According to Wang, and re-echoed by Epstein and Carnielli, while Turing machines were very influential, the concept of recursive functions, which 'first appeared historically as more or less a cumulation of extensions of the simple recursive definitions of addition and multiplication' (Wang 1974: 77), could be used much more easily (Epstein and Carnielli 2000: 86). However, irrespective of the pragmatic advantage of facility of use – a priori what is easier to use solving one problem may be more difficult for solving another – what is now called the Church or the Church–Turing thesis is crucial. Velupillai's articulation of this thesis, which is indispensable to his project of computable economics, is very clear and concise:

Many different, independent attempts were made in the formative years of recursive function theory to formalize the intuitive notion of effectively calculable or computable function, number, object, etc. Thus, there was Turing's device of a machine...; there was the Gödel-Herbrand notion of general recursiveness coming down from Dedekind, Peano and others who used mathematical induction and iteration to build up the number system there was Church's attempt ... leading to the λ–calculus; and so on Church's thesis is a statement encapsulating the phenomenological fact – or as Emil Post called it, a natural law – that all of these independent attempts ultimately yielded one and the same class of functions, numbers and objects as effectively calculable or computable.

(Velupillai 2000: 1

In other words these various systems proposed as rigorous formulations of the intuitive, informal notion of computable are equivalent. For instance 'given a definition of a partial recursive function $\varnothing$, we will produce a Turing machine which calculates that function; and given a Turing machine which calculates a function $\varnothing$, we will produce a partial recursive definition of $\varnothing$' (Epstein and Carnielli 2000: 144).

It should be noted that the Church–Turing thesis is not a mathematical theorem which can be proved or disproved in the exact mathematical sense, for it states the identity of two notions only one of which is mathematically defined. Moreover, much has been written for and against various interpretations of the Church–Turing thesis. Whatever position one adopts, there appears to be consensus on one thing, namely that the thesis is not part of mathematics. For instance, the mathematics of Turing machines and recursion theory stand, even if one has reservations about the thesis. Moreover, in our view, Epstein and Carnielli are surely correct in noting that 'whatever else the Most Amazing Fact establishes, it shows that the notion which is stable under so many different formulations must be fundamental' (ibid.: 230).

The mathematical outcome of these and other related developments is that anti-realist inspired, constructive mathematics has a variety of forms. Historically the first to emerge was Brouwer's intuitionism and which is given a logico-linguistic turn by Dummett. Another version is the Russian school of Markov. This version 'develops Turing's ideas based on the acceptance of Church's thesis' (ibid.: 249). Another version is due to Bishop which sees Brouwer's intuitionism as too idealistic and too infinitist, while recursive analysis is too formal and limited. Our concern here, however, is not with the 'internal' debate about constructive mathematics per se. There is a voluminous literature on the technical development of constructive mathematics – useful guides are provided by Bridges and Richman (1987) and Bridges and Vîta (2006). Rather our focus is on the philosophical and methodological limitations of the realist framework for economic methodology.

It is now time to sum up some of the differences between platonists, constructivists and strict finitists. In terms of infinity, the platonist is ontologically committed to Cantorian, completed infinity, the constructivist is ontologically committed to potential infinity, whereas the strict finitist rejects these and is ontologically committed to what can be constructed in actual practice. Moreover, following Dummett, the differences may also be expressed in terms of their respective philosophies of meaning. For Dummett the constructivist:

> holds that the expressions of our mathematical language must be given meaning by reference to operations which we can *in principle* carry out. The strict finitist holds that they must be given meaning by reference only to operations which we can *in practice* carry out. The platonist, on the other hand, believes that they can be given meaning by reference to operations which we *cannot even in principle* carry out, so long as we can conceive of them as being carried out by beings with powers which transcend our own.
>
> (2000: 43, emphasis added)

In short, anti-realist philosophy of mathematics, in resisting the temptation to enter into Cantor's paradise, contributed to the emergence of constructive mathematics. Velupillai's research programme of computable economics is located in these developments. It emerges from 'the confluence of events that led to the fundamental results of Gödel, Kleene, Church, Post and Turing – the fashioning of recursion theory' (Velupillai 2000: 8). We have already noted how Weintraub reads the process of the mathematization of economics as consisting of two major phases. Clearly computable economics is opening up a third phase. This new phase will entail theoretical economists, becoming not only familiar with, but being at home with the mathematical techniques of Gödel numbering, Cantorian diagonalization, universal Turing machines, basic recursion theory, applied recursion theory, i.e. computational complexity theory, diophantine complexity theory and algorithmetic complexity theory and so on. Like any revolutionary research programme, computable economics furnishes us with a novel ontological-epistemological picture of an economy and economic agents. Economic agents are Turing machine problem solvers 'with their "rich" repertoire of incompletenesses, uncomputabilities, and undecidabilities' (ibid.: 151). The economist is also a problem solver. In investigating an economic problem, the economist encodes the relevant issues in a recursion-theoretic way and from the outcome 'draws the ensuing economic implications' (ibid.: 3). In this novel research programme 'questions about decidability replace the traditional emphasis on optimization' (Velupillai 2002b: 325). In particular, Velupillai concurs with Lewis that:

> It is obvious that any choice function ϑ that is not *at least computationally viable* is in a very strong sense *economically irrational*. Unless the computation is trivial, i.e., involves no computation at all, and thus is both complete and accurate without the use of any Turing Machine, the choice prescribed by a *computationally non-viable* choice function can only be implemented by computational procedures that do one of two things: either (a) the computation does not halt and fails to converge, or (b) the computation halts at a non-optimal choice.
>
> (Lewis 1985: 45 as quoted in Velupillai 2000: 42–3)

Obviously computable economics provides us with a novel and challenging research programme with its third phase in the mathematization of economics, phase closely aligned to the anti-realist philosophy of mathematics outlined in this section.

Concluding remarks: the challenge to economic methodology

Based on our earlier work, we have consistently advocated resistance to the alluring sirens of scientific realism in economic methodology (Boylan and O'Gorman 1995). We argued in that work for the need to develop a methodological middle ground between the platonic certainties of realism and the post modern anti-realism of rhetoric. While economics is much more than metaphoric poetry or Aristotelian-inspired rhetoric, its realist reading has an inbuilt tendency to locate economic theory in some remote cosmic exile, inaccessible to us fallible human beings. For causal holism, economic theory today is firmly rooted in the scientific tradition which emerged post the seventeenth century scientific revolution. Of course, like scientific realists, we do not interpret this scientific tradition in either a Humean or a logical positivist framework. Because of this, some realists have made brave, but failed, attempts to colonize causal holism within the framework of realism (Fleetwood 2002; Boylan and O'Gorman 2006). These realists do not pay sufficient attention to our distinction between the methodological issues that surround the construction of an economic model and those which arise in connection with the testing of such models.

In connection with the issue of the construction of an economic model, realists failed to appreciate how we attempted to liberate economic theorizing from the realist reading of economic theory as fundamentally explanatory (Boylan and O'Gorman 1995). For causal holists, economic theorizing provides the economist with the mathematico-linguistic 'apparatus' to be used in the construction of specific economic models. In our view computable economics is a clear example of this: computable economics is providing the economist with novel mathematico-linguistic resources in its efforts at modelling various aspects of economic agents, institutions and so on. This theoretical dimension is quite distinct from the other pillar of causal holism: ascertaining whether or not models so constructed are 'descriptively adequate' (Boylan and O'Gorman 1995).

In particular, Mäki-type realists as well as critical realists are preoccupied with the correspondence theory of truth. This theory obtains its plausibility from simple examples which apply to the observable world. For instance, no one will deny that the proposition 'The moon orbits the earth' is true because that proposition corresponds to the fact. Moreover, the moon and the earth exist independently of us knowing anything about them. However, when we move into the potential infinite domain of arithmetic, the correspondence theory is neither self-evident nor obvious. Does the potentially infinite sequence of natural numbers exist independently of the method of generating it? These are fundamental philosophical questions. In this context we have clearly signalled how causal holism has its origins in a later Wittgensteinian philosophy of language (Boylan and O'Gorman 2003a). In this context we can only here hint at our reasons for questioning the realist, correspondence theory of truth by referring the reader to the Wittgensteinian, anti-realist position noted by Dummett, 'The language that we use when we are engaged in mathematics ... is *our* language' (2000: 263). As Poincaré insisted at the turn of the twentieth century, we 'refuse to argue on the hypothesis of some infinitely talkative divinity capable of thinking an infinite number of words in a finite length of time' (1963: 67). Thus in our language 'meaning must be connected with our own capacities: it cannot be derived from the hypothetical conception of capacities we do not have' (Dummett 2000: 263). But the supposition that the condition for the truth of a mathematical statement as specified by realists does not infer 'that it is one which a human being need be supposed to be even capable of recognizing as obtaining ... The solution is to abandon the principle of bivalence' (ibid.: 260). Such an anti-realist position is neither incoherent nor relativist. However, this anti-realism is either totally ignored or deemed to be relativist by realist economic methodologists.

Our insistence that economic methodologists should address the realist/anti-realist debate in the philosophy of mathematics is not just based on the general philosophical considerations noted in the last paragraph. Our insistence is also based on the nature of contemporary economics. A core activity in economics is the construction of economic models and these models are predominantly mathematical ones. In *Beyond Rhetoric and Realism*, we put the methodological spotlight on the construction of economic models, as distinct from the quest for realist explanations, à la critical realists. Since economists are in the business of constructing specific mathematical models, the issue of what kind of mathematics is best suited for this endeavour needs to be addressed. The realist/anti-realist debate is significant here, but unfortunately it is ignored by both realist and postmodern economic methodologists.

According to causal holism there is no simple, a priori answer to the question of what kind of mathematics should be used in economic modelling. In this connection we re-echo the position advocated in computable economics namely 'there is no given, *a priori*, single formal framework that is natural, in any sense, for the formalization of economics' (Velupillai 2000: 2). In our view Velupillai is absolutely correct when he emphasizes Solow's dictum 'problems must dictate methods not vice versa' (ibid.: 1). However, the matter does not rest there. Clearly, from the foregoing presentation of the realism/anti-realism debate in philosophy of mathematics, if an economist is an anti-realist, the nonconstructive techniques of classical mathematics will not be acceptable. In particular, if an economist is an intuitionist, anti-realist à la Dummett, she will never entertain realist, non-constructive proofs. Thus the whole Arrow–Debreu exercise would be deemed to be *not* a proof at all. On the other hand if an economist is a realist, then anti-realist restrictions would not apply in the construction of economic theory and models. The whole range of constructive and non-constructive methods of proof would be at the economist's disposal in constructing economic models. Thus the Arrow–Debreu project would be unobjectionable, philosophically, at least at the level of construction.

But surely it is unrealistic to expect that either economists or economic methodologists should become expert on the vast range of challenging issues raised in the realist/anti-realist debate? Even if they did, as Benacerraf and Putnam point out, eminent mathematicians and philosophers fall on both sides of the divide: there is no consensus. Thus perhaps economic methodologists should adopt the principle that the pure mathematics should look after itself. In other words economic methodologists do not need to take a stand on this realist/anti-realist debate.

Causal holism is more than sympathetic to this methodological stand. Rather what the realist/anti-realist debate shows is that realist methodologists are naive in not acknowledging this divide and its consequences for economic methodology. Moreover, the debate draws attention to the ranges of mathematical methods available and especially the merits of constructive methods for the application of mathematics in theoretical economics. In addition, adhering to Solow's thesis that problems dictate methods, we would argue that when it is a question of proving the economic existence of a theoretical entity, the use of the purely non-constructive methods of classical mathematics is methodologically questionable. A classical, purely non-constructive, existence proof guarantees the existence of the object in the domain of Cantorian infinity and, because the proof is purely non-constructive, there is nothing to support the hypothesis that this mathematical object has an economic interpretation. For all we know, the point could be transfinite. Without a constructive proof, mathematical existence in Cantor's paradise does not *ipso facto* transform into existence in real historical time. In short we have no evidence to show that it is not an economical fiction subsisting in the platonic world of Cantor's paradise.

Economic models, however, deal with much more than existence claims. Can we impose any kind of restrictions on the mathematics to be used in these cases? Prima facie, an eclectic position suggests itself: in some cases classical mathematics can be used, in others, one will use constructive methods. Against this, on the grounds of simplicity, one could argue that all modelling should be limited to constructive methods. If one uses classical mathematics, the constructive/non-constructive divide will often not be apparent in the conclusions. Then how is one to give the conclusion an economic interpretation? Will the 'logic' of modelling for existence, outlined in the last paragraph, apply here? If one uses classical mathematics, one will have to go back through the proof, find the non-constructive part and then try to find ways of 'constructivizing' it. If one merely used constructive mathematics there would be no need for all of this. In this sense, one favours constructive mathematics on the grounds of simplicity. That is certainly plausible. However, under the influence of Quine, scientific decisions in causal holism depends on a number of considerations, such as usefulness for prediction, coherence, simplicity, 'a taste for old things' and the bar of experience. Moreover, as Putnam points out, for Quine 'success in satisfying these desiderata simultaneously is a matter of trade-offs rather than formal rules' (Putnam 1995: 10). Causal holism has embraced this Quinean thesis (Boylan and O'Gorman 2003b). Hence simplicity alone will not decide the issue. The spirit of Solow's dictum 'problems must dictate methods not vice versa' is central to causal holism.

To conclude, we have attempted to briefly indicate how causal holism is a more nuanced and more sophisticated methodology of economics than those suggested by either post-modern or realist methodologies. Our hope is that, within a Socratic inspired debate that should inform economic methodology, we have moved beyond the confines of so-called indispensability arguments for realism that are currently dominating much of economic methodology. We trust that Velupillai's extraordinary innovative work in mathematical economics will also encounter that hospitable environment, informed by the same Socratic tradition of critical interrogation and constructive debate, which alone will ensure the creative progress of our discipline.

References

Arrow, K.J. and Hahn, F.H. (1971) *General Competitive Analysis*, San Francisco, CA Holden Day.

Benacerraf, P. and Putnam, H. (eds) (1983) *Philosophy of Mathematics: Selected read* ings, 2nd edn, Cambridge: Cambridge University Press.

Bhaskar, R. (1978) *A Realist Theory of Science*, Hemel Hempstead, UK: Harvester Press.

—— (1979) *The Possibility of Naturalism*, Hemel Hempstead, UK: Harvester Press.

—— (1986) *Scientific Realism and Human Emancipation*, London: Verso.

Boylan, T.A. and O'Gorman, P.F. (1995) *Beyond Rhetoric and Realism: Towards a refor* mulation of economic methodology, London: Routledge.

—— (1997) 'Critical realism and economics: A causal holist critique', *Ekonimia*, 1 9–21; reprinted in S. Fleetwood (ed.) (1999) *Critical Realism in Economics: Develop* ment and debate, London: Routledge.

—— (2003a) 'Economic theory and rationality: A Wittgensteinian interpretation', *Review* of Political Economy, 15: 231–44.

—— (2003b) 'Pragmatism in economic methodology: The Duhem–Quine thesis revis ited', *Foundations of Science*, 8: 3–21.

—— (2006) 'Fleetwood on causal holism: Clarification and critique', *Cambridge Journal* of Economics, 30: 123–35.

—— (2007) 'Axiomatization and formalism in economics', *Journal of Economic Surveys* 21: 426–46; reprinted in D.A.R. George (ed.) (2008) *Issues in Heterodox Economics* Oxford: Blackwell Publishing.

—— (eds) (2008) *Popper and Economic Methodology: Contemporary challenges* London: Routledge.

Bridges, D.S. and Richman, F. (1987) *Varieties of Constructive Mathematics*, Cambridge Cambridge University Press.

Bridges, D.S. and Vîta, L.S. (2006) *Techniques of Constructive Analysis*, New York Springer.

Caldwell, B. (1982) *Beyond Positivism: Economic methodology in the twentieth century* London: George Allen & Unwin.

Dummett, M. (1973) 'The philosophical basis of intuitionist logic', in H.E. Rose and J.C Shepherdson (eds), *Logic Colloquium*, Amsterdam: North-Holland; reprinted in M Dummett (1978) *Truth and Other Enigmas*, London: Duckworth.

—— (1991) *Frege and Other Philosophers*, Oxford: Clarendon Press.

—— (2000) *Elements of Intuitionism*, 2nd edn, Oxford: Clarendon Press.

Epstein, R.L. and Carnielli, W.A. (2000) *Computability*, 2nd edn, London: Thomson Learning.

Fleetwood, S. (2002) 'Boylan and O'Gorman's causal holism: A critical realist evalu ation', *Cambridge Journal of Economics*, 26: 27–45.

Frege, G. (1968) *The Foundations of Arithmetic*, trans. J.L. Austin, Oxford: Basil Blackwell.

Friedman, M. (1953) 'The methodology of positive economics', in M. Friedman (ed.) *Essays in Positive Economics*, Chicago, IL: University of Chicago Press.

Geach, P. (1969) *God and the Soul*, London: Routledge and Kegan Paul.

Green, K. (2001) *Dummett: Philosophy of language*, Cambridge: Polity Press.

Habermas, J. (1995) *Postmetaphysical Thinking: Philosophical essays*, trans. W.M Hohengarten, Cambridge: Polity Press.

Hands, D.W. (2001a) *Reflection without Rules: Economic methodology and contempor* ary science theory, Cambridge: Cambridge University Press.

—— (2001b) 'Economic methodology is dead – long live economic methodology: Thirteen theses on the new economic methodology', *Journal of Economic Methodology*, 8: 49–63.

Hilbert, D. (1983) 'On the infinite', in P. Benacerraf and H. Putnam (eds), *Philosophy of Mathematics: Selected Readings*, 2nd edn, Cambridge: Cambridge University Press.

Hooker, C.A. (1987) *A Realistic Theory of Science*, Albany, NY: State University of New York.

Kenny, A. (2000) *Frege*, Oxford: Blackwell Publishers.

Latsis, S. (ed.) (1976) *Method and Appraisal in Economics*, Cambridge: Cambridge University Press.

Lawson, T. (1997) *Economics and Reality*, London: Routledge.

—— (2003) *Reorienting Economics*, London: Routledge.

—— (2004) 'A conception of ontology', website of Cambridge Social Ontology Group, Cambridge University. Online, available at: www.csog.group.cam.ac.uk/A_Conception_of_Ontology.pdf (accessed 14 November 2009).

Lewis, A.A. (1985) 'On effectively computable realization of choice functions', *Mathematical Social Science*, 10: 43–80.

McCloskey, D. (1983) 'The rhetoric of economics', *Journal of Economic Literature*, 22: 481–517.

—— (1986) *The Rhetoric of Economics*, Brighton, UK: Wheatsheaf Books.

Mäki, U. (1990) 'Scientific realism and Austrian explanation', *Review of Political Economy*, 2: 310–44.

—— (1998) 'Realism', in J.B. Davis, D.W. Hands and U. Mäki (eds), *The Handbook of Economic Methodology*, Cheltenham: Edward Elgar.

—— (2002) 'Some nonreasons for nonrealism about economics', in U. Mäki (ed.), *Fact and Fiction in Economics: Models, realism and social construction*, Cambridge: Cambridge University Press.

Newton-Smith, W.H. (1981) *The Rationality of Science*, London: Routledge and Kegan Paul.

Peirce, C.S. (1867) in C. Hartshorne and P. Weiss (eds), *Collected Papers of Charles Sanders Peirce, 1931–35*, vols 1–6, Cambridge, MA: Harvard University Press.

Poincaré, H. (1963) *Mathematics and Science: Last essays*, trans. J.W. Bolduc, New York: Dover Publications Inc.

Potter, M. (2000) *Reason's Nearest Kin: Philosophers of arithmetic from Kant to Carnap*, Oxford: Oxford University Press.

Putnam, H. (1995) *Pragmatism*, Oxford: Basil Blackwell.

Quine, W.V.O. (1981) *Theories and Things*, Cambridge, MA: Harvard University Press.

Suppes, F. (ed.) (1977) *The Structure of Scientific Theories*, 2nd edn, Urbana, IL: University of Illinois Press.

Van Fraassen, B. (1980) *The Scientific Image*, Oxford: Clarendon Press.

Velupillai, K. (2000) *Computable Economics*, Oxford: Oxford University Press.

—— (2002a) 'The wisdom and wit of Sen's contributions to capital theory: Some sketches', *Review of Development and Change*, 5: 1–23.

—— (2002b) 'Effectivity and constructivity in economic theory', *Journal of Economic Behaviour and Organization*, 49: 307–25.

Wang, H. (1974) *From Mathematics to Philosophy*, London: Routledge and Kegan Paul.

Weintraub, E.R. (2002) *How Economics became a Mathematical Science*, Durham, NC: Duke University Press.

18 Who, in Scandinavian economic theoretic literature, picked up major threads from Wicksell's writings?

B. Thalberg[1]

The major Wicksellian ideas

Wicksell was indeed an economist who advanced a number of seminal ideas, thus creating opportunities for pupils to develop important theoretical issues. The most prominent Swedish economist building on Wicksell was Erik Lindahl.

However, it has been asserted by the Swedish economist Göran Ohlin[2] that Wicksell did not get the appreciation he deserved from his Swedish contemporaries in the form of pupils and observance.[3] One reason was, Ohlin argues, that many Swedes were at the time absorbed by the writings of Gustav Cassel. In Oslo the situation was not quite the same; Wicksell's 'Lectures' I and II were early central books on the students' required reading list, and particularly was the young student Ragnar Frisch most enthusiastic about Wicksell, considering him his foremost teacher.

What were Wicksell's seminal ideas? Paul Samuelson gave, I think, an adequate summary of Wicksell's major scientific ideas in his lectures 'Wicksell, The Economist' (Samuelson 1963). Samuelson emphasized Wicksell's works (and ideas) on:

1 capital and general equilibrium
2 marginal productivity
3 the impact of technological change
4 marginal cost pricing and imperfect competition
5 business cycle rhythm generated by random shocks of innovation which impinge on an endogenous system geared to produce quasi-regular rhythms
6 the proper role of government expenditure in an affluent or less-than-affluent society
7 the relationship between interest rates set by the central bank and cumulative trends of inflation or deflation.

Samuelson mentions the names of theorists who, in particular, worked on and developed the said Wicksellian themes further. His list includes just two Scandinavian economists: Lindahl as to the proper role of government expenditures, and Frisch as to Wicksell's suggested explanation of the cycle.[4]

Erik Lindahl

Wicksell certainly got a prominent and devoted pupil in Erik Lindahl (1891–1960) whose doctorate thesis was basically built on Wicksell's *Finanztheoretische Untersuchungen* (1896). Wicksell read (1919) most parts of Lindahl's thesis in proof.[5] In December 1919 Wicksell acted as the faculty's opponent at Lindahl's public defence of his thesis. Wicksell's assessment of the thesis was very positive.[6]

Lindahl's scientific works have been commented upon by a number of well-known economists. Particularly, *The New Palgrave. A Dictionary of Economics* (Eatwell *et al.* 1987) contains three articles assessing Lindahl's contributions to economic theory.[7] All three articles stress his connection with Wicksell, and in particular his elaboration of Wicksell's *Finanztheoretische Untersuchungen*.

Lindahl's theory of taxation and public expenditure, as he presented in his thesis and later elaborated on, was based on the 'benefit approach' as suggested by Wicksell. Lindahl's single most important contribution is, Bohm writes,

> perhaps his treatment of the problem of 'just taxation'. He showed that, by systematic application of the so-called benefit principle, a significant part of this problem could be subjected to scientific analysis. Furthermore, his work on public finance paved the way for integrating public goods into general equilibrium models of the market economy.
>
> (Eatwell *et al.* 1987: 200)

Elaborated versions of Lindahl's public-sector equilibrium were later called *Lindahl Equilibrium*, which became a celebrated concept in economic theoretic literature.

While Lindahl's name is chiefly associated with his works in the field of taxation and public expenditure, his influence can be traced also in other areas. He was a central member of the 'Stockholm School', and his work in this connection on 'intertemporal' and 'temporary' equilibrium inspired, for example, Hicks' analysis in *Value and Capital* and *Capital and Growth* (Siven 2002).

The Stockholm School

Looking for Swedish pupils of Wicksell other than Lindahl we may of course consider also the other members of the famous Stockholm School. Following Björn Hansson (1991) we may define the school as a team of Swedish economists[8] who, in the period 1927–1937 worked closely together to develop a dynamic method. Stages in their struggle to develop an original dynamic method were *inter alia*: Myrdal's work on 'anticipations', Lindahl's constructions 'intertemporal' and 'temporary' equilibrium, Lundberg's disequilibrium sequence analysis, Hammarskjöld's idea of windfall profit as a link between periods and the systematic use of the concepts *ex ante* and *ex post*. None of these ideas and concepts were developed with reference to Wicksell. In fact, Björn Hansson writes that while 'it is commonly thought that the "Swedishness" of the Stock-holm School arose from their presumed Swedish ancestry: Wicksell and Cassel,... Wicksell's and Cassel's influence on the distinctive feature of the Stockholm School, their dynamic method, is negligible' (Hansson 1991: 169).

Otherwise, the members of the Stockholm School wrote much about macro-economics and economic-political issues, and since Wicksell's 'cumulative-process' is an early and celebrated macroeconomic theory (in fact it has been described by Blaug as the macrotheory of the nineteenth century), they were cer-tainly inspired by Wicksell in the area. But this influence was of a general kind.[9]

Johan and Gustaf Åkerman

Johan Åkerman wrote his doctorate thesis on the rhythm of economic life (Åker-man 1928) in Lund a few years after Wicksell had left for Stockholm. Still, Wick-sell did advise Åkerman on his thesis. In his foreword, Åkerman acknowledged that Wicksell had looked through a first draft of the thesis, and that his criticism caused him to rewrite important parts of it. While the aim to develop principally a general cycle theory was a central theme of both Wicksell and Åkerman, their suggested model differed significantly. Åkerman commented in his thesis on Wicksell's idea about the central role played by random shocks of innovation. He argued (ibid.: 97) that the weight given to the force of external irregular impulses in Wicksell's model leads us to a theory that is not very concise. While, we may say, Wicksell saw it as a main problem to explain the irregularity of the cycle and the difficulty to predict its next phases, Åkerman held that the task of a cycle theory was primarily to explain the, after all, basic regularity of the cycle. The force that provided this basic regularity was, Åkerman argued, to be found in the yearly recurrent seasonal swings.[10] The starting point of an upturn, or a downturn, is, according to Åkerman, always a seasonal variation.[11]

Many of Åkerman's later publications deal with cycle theory in some way, and other works of him are as a rule also characterized by his own original ideas, different from Wicksell.

We may, furthermore, ask whether Johan Åkerman's older brother Gustaf may be considered a pupil of Wicksell.[12] His thesis 'Realkapital und Kapitalzins' (Åkerman 1923), was inspired by Wicksell who wrote a thorough review of it. Wicksell had, he writes, been very attracted by Åkerman's thesis already when he read some drafted chapters of it. Wicksell's review, while critical on minor points, was on the whole very laudatory. In fact, Wicksell found what he denoted 'Åkerman's problem' so fascinating and important that he added a 23 pages long appendix to his review, entitled 'Mathematical treatment of the Åkerman prob-lem' (Wicksell 1923). An example of a Professor who elaborates on the work of his pupil, and not the other way round.

While Gustaf Åkerman's thesis on capital theory was theoretical, his later works are of an empirical and popular kind. He did not pursue other Wicksellian issues. Thus, one can hardly speak of him as a pupil of Wicksell in the sense Göran Ohlin uses the word.

An ardent Norwegian pupil

Wicksell's works, in particular 'Lectures I' and 'Lectures II' (1901, 1906), were important parts of the students' curriculum in Norway. Ragnar Frisch, who studied Economics in Oslo 1916–1919, has described the study there as not very advanced at the time. It was, he said, only the Wicksellian works, which he studied with uttermost interest and care, that really gave him something.

In 1926 Frisch started his venture into theoretical research by attempting – in the tradition of Mitchell and others – to develop methods to extract cyclical and trend components from economic time-series. He was fascinated with the technique, and expressed over the years steadfast faith in some of its main results (such as the existence of persistent cycles of *various* lengths, and the 'Harvard A-, B-, and C-curves'). However, later Frisch turned to a more genuinely theoretic approach, attempting to develop a truly dynamic theory that could explain the cycle phenomenon generally, and account for the cycle's various components. Instrumental to the development of his cycle theory, and to the development of his dynamic analysis generally, was the methodological idea of Wicksell as indicated by his 'rocking-horse' analogy (the impulse–propagation dichotomy).[13] In his essay in the Cassel Festschrift (Frisch 1933), Frisch attempted to demonstrate how a specific structural and stable macroeconomic model (defining his propagation mechanism) might generate realistic fluctuations when exposed to a series of erratic impulses.

It was part of Frisch's vision that not only should the 'disturbed solution' (i.e. including erratic impulses) involve fluctuations, but the model of the propagation itself should imply an oscillating return to equilibrium. However, according to a recent study (Zambelli 2007), Frisch's explicit propagation model does not generate oscillations. Nevertheless, Frisch's 1933 essay was praised by a number of great economists; for example Samuelson who in his *Foundations of Economic Analysis* (1958: 284) stressed its importance for the development of dynamic economic theory generally.[14]

Frisch readily acknowledged that he owned the basic idea of his cycle theory to Wicksell. Besides the dichotomy, Frisch also stressed that Wicksell was 'the first who has formulated explicitly the theory that the source of energy which maintains the economic cycles are erratic shocks' (Frisch 1933: 197). A reason why Frisch attached so great significance to the energy matter is that he strongly believed that the world is stable in the sense that when an economic system gives rise to oscillations, these will most frequently be damped. A main problem is therefore to explain the maintenance of the cycle. But, Frisch stated, Wicksell did not take up 'a closer mathematical study of the mechanism by which irregular shocks or impulses may be transferred into cycles' (ibid.: 198). This task happened to be left to his Norwegian pupil.

Frisch did also, among several others, attempt to give a formal interpretation of Wicksell's famous 'cumulative process', which sketches how the bank rate of interest – through price movements – tends to gravitate towards the 'normal rate'[15] and overshoots. The solution of Frisch's specific and fairly simple mathematical model of the process involves undamped sinusoidal oscillations.

However, Frisch argued, adding forces of friction to this simplified model, i
would certainly generate damped movements (Frisch 1952).

Frisch's admiration of Wicksell, and assessment of him as a teacher is, in par
ticular, evident from his introduction to an article on Wicksell (ibid.). It may b
fitting to quote the following two passages:

> Personally, I never met Knut Wicksell, I saw him once when he delivered
> lecture in Oslo, but being an unassuming student at the time, I did not hav
> the courage to talk to him. So my knowledge of his theory came onl
> through his writings. That, however, was a very intense and absorbing forr
> of making his acquaintance. Already from my early student days, I read hi
> writings (in German and Swedish) avidly. And I continued to do so later.
>
> When I started my study on Wicksell, I found that his works were nc
> easy reading. Often it was only at the third or fourth reading that I graspe
> his ideas. Invariably, each new reading made me more and more enthusias
> tic. Sometimes it happened that I thought I had finally caught him in a
> inconsistency or in unclear thinking. Every time this happened, it turned ou
> however, that the error was mine.
>
> (Frisch 1952: 654–5

Frisch's enthusiasm about Wicksell's works left its marks on his students. Fc
example, in his monograph on the probability approach in econometrics, eve
Frisch's most outstanding student, Haavelmo (1944: 34), dwells on Wicksell'
model of the 'cumulative process'. He derives a simplified equation for Wick
sell's theorem about the price effect of a bank rate of interest that differs fror
the natural rate, a relationship which is interesting per se. But Haavelmo did nc
discuss the validity of the theory, but applies, for illustration, the Wicksellia
equations in a general analysis on the degree of autonomy of the relations.

Conclusion

This chapter tends, I think, to confirm Göran Ohlin's assertion (cf. Note 3) tha
considering his many seminal ideas, Wicksell did not get the appreciation h
deserved from his Swedish contemporaries in the form of pupils and observance
While the Swedes often stressed the heritage from Wicksell, only Lindahl too
up one of his major ideas and developed it further. Wicksell was, it may b
added, neglected in spite of the fact that a number of very talented young Swede
were at the time engaged in economic theoretic research. A reason may be, a
Göran Ohlin suggested, that many young Swedes were then absorbed by th
writings of Gustav Cassel. Moreover, the Stockholm School group was, withou
building on Wicksell, strongly concentrated on their aim to develop, generall
and originally, a dynamic method.

In retrospect it can be said that the kind of dynamic model to explain the cycle
that was suggested by Wicksell and developed mathematically by Frisch, is aliv
and well. Much modern analysis is conceptually in accordance with this form o

dynamics, and discussions often focus upon the nature of impulses behind observed macroeconomic variability, studied within an impulse–response type of analysis.

What about the Stockholm School and its endeavour to develop a dynamic method? In a book, *The Stockholm School of Economics Revisited*, the editor Lars Jonung concludes that 'the Stockholm School has not survived as a continued "live" tradition of research' (Jonung 1991: 34). But he adds, 'elements of the School have been absorbed in mainstream economics, and continue to have an influence' (ibid.).

Notes

1 One day in 1971 Vela appeared at my lectures in Lund. A few days later we met in the street and talked together a long time. I was fascinated by his story. He had arrived in Sweden (22 years old) in 1970, where he for his living worked as a labourer at a cement factory, and did at the same time attend classes in Swedish. Before coming to Sweden he had graduated from the Faculty of Engineering at Kyoto University, concentrating on Applied Mathematics. One day in Kyoto he came across Gunnar Myrdal's *Asian Drama* and became so fascinated that he decided to go to Sweden. Many years later Myrdal got wind of the story and they had several long conversations in Stockholm. Vela took for credit a few of my courses and was also my assistant a short time. In January 1973 he finished his Master's in Economics on a thesis on economic control-theory. Later that year he went to Cambridge, England, where he was accepted at their doctorate programme. All years since 1973 I have been in contact with Vela, and more so than with any other of my students. In 1990, on the occasion of my retirement, he organized a conference to my honour. The proceedings from the conference, edited by Vela, were published in 1992. In 1994 he delivered in Lund an Arne Ryde Memorial Lecture on computable economics (Velupillai 2000).
2 Professor of Economics at Uppsala University 1969–1992. A nephew of Bertil Ohlin.
3 In an address to the Arne Ryde Symposium on the Theoretical Contributions of Knut Wicksell, Lund 19–20 September 1977; published in Thalberg (2002: 26).
4 As to other great economists who developed Wicksellian ideas Samuelson mentions Joan Robinson on capital and general equilibrium, Solow on marginal productivity, Hicks on impact of technological change and Hotelling and Chamberlin on marginal cost pricing and imperfect competition.
5 'Die Gerechtigkeit der Besteuerung', Lund 1919.
6 Lindahl inserted into his thesis some equations and an adherent figure suggested by Wicksell.
7 By Otto Steiger, John Roberts and Peter Bohm. Few other theorists are given that much attention in *The New Palgrave*.
8 Including G. Myrdal, E. Lindahl, E. Lundberg, D. Hammarskjöld, A. Johansson, B. Ohlin, I. Svennilson.
9 Cf. Schumpeter's remark that Wicksell's 'Swedish disciples never ceased to call themselves Wicksellians, even when they criticized and surpassed him' (Schumpeter 1961: 1085).
10 If we consider seasonal variations as part of the impulse side in the type of model suggested by Wicksell, we may say that the impulses are, following Åkerman, dominated by the fairly regular seasonal variations.
11 I do not know of any cycle theorist who has adopted Åkerman's idea of the decisive importance of seasonal variations.
12 Gustaf was born in 1888 and Johan in 1896 (while Wicksell was born in 1851).
13 See Wicksell's review of Karl Petander's book *Goda och dåliga tider* (Wicksell 1918: 71, note 1).

288   B. Thalberg

14 Another example is Hicks who did, however, criticize Frisch's specific model of the cycle. A high degree of dampening, he writes, 'leaves us with fluctuations which are mainly random'; and a low degree of dampening would ensure that a regular cycle 'would follow even from a single disturbance' (Hicks 1950: 90–1).
15 Rate of interest at which the demand for loan capital and the supply of savings exactly agree.

References

Åkerman, G. (1923) 'Realkapital und Kapitalzins', doctoral thesis, University of Lund.

Åkerman, J. (1928) 'Om det ekonomiska livets rytmik', PhD thesis, Stockholm.

Eatwell, J., Milgate, M. and Newman, P. (eds) (1987) *The New Palgrave: A Dictionary of Economics*, Basingstoke: Palgrave Macmillan.

Frisch, R. (1933) 'Propagation problem and impulse problem in dynamic Economics', in *Essays in Honour of Gustav Cassel*, London: Allen & Unwin.

Frisch, R. (1952) 'Frisch on Wicksell', in H.W. Spigel (ed.), *The Development of Economic Thought*, New York: Wiley.

Haavelmo, T. (1944) 'The probability approach in econometrics', *Econometrica*, 12 (Supplement): 1–118.

Hansson, B. (1991) 'The Stockholm School and the development of dynamic method', in B. Sandelin (ed.), *The History of Economic Thought*, London: Routledge.

Hicks, J.R. (1939) *Value and Capital: An Inquiry into some Fundamental Principles of Economic Theory*, Oxford: Clarendon Press.

Hicks, J.R. (1950) *A Contribution to the Theory of the Trade Cycle*, Oxford: Oxford University Press.

Hicks, J.R. (1965) *Capital and Growth*, Oxford: Clarendon Press.

Jonung, L. (1991) *The Stockholm School of Economics Revisited*, Cambridge: Cambridge University Press.

Myrdal, G. (1968) *Asian Drama: An Inquiry into the Poverty of Nations*, New York: Twentieth Century Fund.

Samuelson, P. (1958) *Foundations of Economic Analysis*, Cambridge, MA: Harvard University Press.

Samuelson, P. (1963) *Wicksell Lectures 1962*, Uppsala: Almquist & Wiksell.

Schumpeter, J. (1961) *History of Economic Analysis*, London: Allen & Unwin.

Siven, C-H. (2002) 'Analytical foundations of Erik Lindahl's monetary analysis 1924–30', *History of Political Economy*, 34(1): 111–53.

Thalberg, B. (2002) *Arne Rydes Stiftelse 1971–2001*, Lund: Media-Tryck, Lunds Universitet.

Velupillai, K. (2000) *Computable Economics*, Oxford: Oxford University Press.

Velupillai, K. (ed.) (1992) *Essays in Honour of Björn Thalberg*, London: Macmillan.

Wicksell, K. (1896) *Finanztheoretische Untersuchungen nebst Darstellung und Kritik des Steuewesans Schwedens*, Jena: Verlag von Gustav Fisher.

Wicksell, K. (1901) *Föreläsningar i nationalekonomi I*, Lund: C.W.K. Gleerups Förlag.

Wicksell, K. (1906) *Föreläsningar i nationalekonomi II*, Lund: C.W.K. Gleerups Förlag.

Wicksell, K. (1918) 'Review of Goda och dåliga tider by Karl Petander', *Ekonomisk tidskrift*, 19: 66–75.

Wicksell, K. (1923) 'Review of Gustaf Åkerman', *Ekonomisk Tidskrift*, 25: 145–80.

Zambelli, S. (2007) 'A rocking horse that never rocked: Frisch's "Propagation problem and impulse problems" ', *History of Political Economy*, 39(1): 145–66.

Part VI

Capital, viability and growth

19 *The Accumulation of Capital* over 50 years on

G.C. Harcourt and Prue Kerr[1]

The Accumulation of Capital, Joan Robinson (1956), was intended to be Joan Robinson's *magnum opus*. It grew out of the advances she was making on many fronts in the years of World War II and afterwards. The major influences on her were Keynes (of course); her work on Marx placed within a fruitful setting and approach by Kalecki;[2] Harrod's seminal work on dynamic theory just before (1939) and soon after the end of the war (1948); pressing real world problems associated with the postwar reconstruction of Europe; and the emergence of consciousness about development in under-developed societies in the economics profession of the developed societies.

Keynes's revolution was increasingly being accepted in both academia and government. Attention was turning from the employment – creating effects of accumulation to its capacity-creating effects. Keynes had conquered the short period in a macroeconomic sense, at least as far as his immediate colleagues and disciples in Cambridge were concerned, so it was natural that they, when account is taken of these other influences as well, should turn their attention to the long period and so to the generalization of *The General Theory* to the long period, see, for example Robinson (1952a and 1956: vi).

Piero Sraffa, virtually unknown to even his closest colleagues and friends, was following his own revolutionary new path in economic theory, criticizing the conceptual and logical bases of the supply and demand theories in all their forms while simultaneously rehabilitating classical and Marxian political economy. His influence would not come fully into the public domain until the publication of *Production of Commodities* ... in 1960. Hints of what was to come were in the Introduction in 1951 to the Sraffa with Dobb edition of the works and correspondence of David Ricardo. Indeed, for Joan Robinson, the Introduction to the Ricardo volumes brought a great flash of illumination about the nature and role of profits in advanced capitalist economies. When reprinting her 'Essays 1953' (originally published as 'a little known pamphlet ... by the Students Bookshop, Cambridge, in 1953' (Robinson 1973: v)) in volume IV of her *Collected Economic Papers* (1951–1979) in 1973, she wrote:

These essays were written in a hilarious mood after reading Piero Sraffa's Introduction..., which caused me to see that the concept of the rate of profit

on capital is essentially the same in Ricardo, Marx, Marshall and Keynes
while the essential difference between these, on the one side, and Walras
Pigou and the latter-day textbook writers, on the other, – is that the Ricardi
ans are describing an historical process of accumulation in a changing world
while the Walrasians dwell in a timeless equilibrium where there is no dis
tinction between the future and the past.

(247

As well as these positive developments in the making of theory there was also
considerable attention given to methodological issues, again stimulated by Har
rod's desire to replace static by dynamic analysis, or at least make the latter jus
as important, as a natural complement to the revived interest in distribution and
growth over time, reinterpreted in the light of Keynes's and, in Joan Robinson's
case, Kalecki's new theories. For Harrod this new and exciting way of seeing
and doing economics made 'the old static formulation of problems [seem] stale
flat and unprofitable' (Harrod 1939: 15). These concerns, the original province
of classical political economy and Marx, were suppressed by the rise of neoclassical economics with its concentration on price formation and resource alloca
tion in mostly competitive and static settings. Joan Robinson is typically
forthright about this. In the Preface to her 1956 volume, she writes:

> Economic analysis, serving for two centuries to win an understanding of the
> Nature and Causes of the Wealth of Nations, has been fobbed off with
> another bride – a Theory of Value ... deep seated political reasons for the
> substitution ... also a purely technical reason ... excessively difficult to con-
> duct an analysis of over-all movements of an economy through time, involv
> ing changes in population, capital accumulation and technical change, at the
> same time as an analysis of the detailed relations between output and price
> of particular commodities ... Economists for the last hundred years have
> sacrificed dynamic theory in order to discuss relative prices ... unfortunate
> [because] such a drastic departure from reality [makes verification of results
> impossible and rules out] discussion of most of the problems that are actu-
> ally interesting [condemning] economics to ... arid formalism.

(v

This led her to reappraise what equilibrium meant in the short period and the
long period, especially in a macroeconomic setting. She coupled this with her
increasing dissatisfaction with both neoclassical concepts and methods, as she
saw them, especially in the theory of distribution and its accompanying relev
ance for a discussion of the choice of technique in the economy as a whole in
analysing the process of growth. The outcome was both a sustained attack on
neoclassical and neo-neoclassical results and procedures and the development of
distribution and growth theory in a classical Marxian–Kaleckian–Keynesian set
ting. These developments may be judged as innovative, revolutionary in their
effects, perhaps even so shocking that, now all the principal first generation

pioneers are dead, much of the profession, following good economic practice, seem to assume that they and their ideas never existed in the first place.

With such a background it is not surprising that *The Accumulation of Capital* was published when its author was the same age as Keynes when he published *The General Theory*. Again, just as she wrote *Introduction to the Theory of Employment* (1937), her 'told-to-the-children' book (Keynes 1973: 148), to help to explain his new theory, so she wrote her *Essays in the Theory of Economic Growth* (1962a) to explain *The Accumulation of Capital* to those who were mystified, or irritated, or both by the 1956 volume. The 1962 volume was a great help in extracting messages that had been overlaid or were not brought out clearly in her 'big book' (though the *Essays. . .* too are not always easy going).

All the above themes may be found in a number of articles and chapters in books preceding the publication of *The Accumulation of Capital*. In *The Rate of Interest and Other Essays* (1952a) we are told immediately that

> the *theme* of these essays is the analysis of a dynamic economic system [– dynamic analysis in the sense] that it cannot explain how an economy behaves in given conditions, without reference to past history; . . . static analysis purports to describe a position of equilibrium which the system will reach ... if the given conditions remain unchanged for long enough no matter where it started from.
>
> (ibid.: v)

She adds:

> Short-period analysis is concerned with the equilibrium of a system with a given stock of capital and ... given expectations about the future. Past history is thus put into the initial conditions, so the analysis is static in itself ... yet part of a dynamic theory. [Thus] Keynes' General Theory, [though] strictly static in form,... opened the way for a great outburst of analysis of dynamic problems.
>
> (ibid.)

After the introductory title essay we have 'Notes on the economics of technical progress', 'The Generalisation of the General Theory' and 'Acknowledgments and disclaimers', in which Marx, Marshall, Rosa Luxemburg, contemporaries Kalecki and Harrod, and two concepts, the acceleration principle and general, are named. The collection was preceded by her long introduction to the English translation of Rosa Luxemburg's *The Accumulation of Capital* in 1951. Following it were her very important 1953 essays *On re-reading Marx*, to which we have already referred and which contain her Cambridge economist visit to Oxford essay where some of her methodological critiques about time and space in economic analysis are presented in a stark and compelling manner (especially when read with hindsight) and, of course, her 1953–1954 *Review of*

294 G.C. Harcourt and P. Kerr

Economic Studies paper which first brought the Cambridge–Cambridge debates in capital theory into the public domain.

There are in addition an *Economic Journal* article, 'The model of an expanding economy' (1952b) and her Delhi School of Economics lecture on 'Marx, Marshall and Keynes'. These are reprinted in volume II of her *Collected Economic Papers* (1960), the Preface of which is dated in December 1959. Significantly the author writes that the essays belong 'to the field of what is sometimes called post-Keynesian economics' (Robinson 1960: v). To this we add her difficult but profound essay, 'The philosophy of prices', 'Notes on the theory of economic development' and 'Population and development'. The second section of the volume, 'highly scholastic ... consists of various chips from the block from which [she] hacked [*The*] *Accumulation of Capital*' (ibid.).

It is quite extraordinary on how many fronts she was advancing virtually simultaneously. The interconnectedness between them was certainly clear in her own mind though, naturally, when taking stock at various points in time, she felt that clarity, emphasis, proportion and perspective had not always been attained. Especially, as we noted, is this true of *The Accumulation of Capital* and her perception of its reception, which led her to publish *Essays* ... in 1962 in order to provide readers with a clearer perspective. In the Preface, she writes:

> The essays ... might be regarded as an introduction rather than ... a supplement to [her] *Accumulation* ... [which] was found excessively difficult. The main fault [was] too terse an exposition of the main ideas ... and a failure to mark sufficiently sharply the departure from the confused but weighty corpus of traditional teaching ... required when ... a Keynesian approach to long-period problems [was adopted]. [She offered] the present volume with apologies to readers whose heads ached over the earlier one.
>
> (Robinson 1962a: v)

Nevertheless, it could be argued that, as ever, she may have been too hard on herself; for, if we read Tibor Barna's review of the 1956 volume (1957) it is apparent that serious readers could absorb both the big picture, and the minutiae of what she presented. Barna wrote:

> The object of Mrs. Robinson's analysis is to clarify the consequences and the proximate causes of differences in, and changes in, the rate of accumulation ... Mrs. Robinson works with a dynamic two-sector linear model, and in ... Book II, without the use of mathematics or diagrams, squeezes all the answers out of her model ... [Her] achievement is [to have] written a full-scale textbook on what is probably the most important post-war subject by making use of an efficient dynamic theory.
>
> (Barna 1957, quoted in Kerr with Harcourt 2002: vol. III, 30–1, 33)

In contrast, we have Abba Lerner's rather perplexed review (1957). For him the volume is 'a pearl whose most conspicuous product is irritation' (ibid., quoted in Kerr with Harcourt 2002: vol. III, 34).

[T]he most useful parts of the book are the errors and the ingenious confusions the search for which can give such first-class exercise in economics to graduate students (and to professors) who could do with a tough work out and who can stand the tough cuteness of Mrs. Robinson's style.

(ibid.: 40)

He covers himself by a rueful reference to his chastening experience with Joan Robinson (and friends) concerning *The General Theory* whereby he had come to scoff but remained to pray, his 'disturbing memory of ... feeling similarly supercilious about queer things going on in Cambridge ... before Mrs. Robinson and her friends so patiently educated [him] on the incipient Keynesian revolution' (ibid.: 34–5).

Be that as it may, her most enthusiastic and sympathetic readers regard the *Essay* ... as the best place to go in order to understand and build on her contributions as far as positive economic analysis of the dynamic processes at work in modern capitalist economies are concerned. This comes out clearly in Athanasios (Tom) Asimakopulos (1969, 1970; reprinted in Kerr with Harcourt 2002: vol. III, 119–43), and in his last assessment after her death and sadly, just before his own, Asimakopulos (1991; reprinted in Kerr with Harcourt 2002: vol. III, 144–63). He concluded that her 'extension of Keynes's General Theory to the long period is faithful to the essential features of that theory' (ibid.: 160).

Again, if we examine Harvey Gram and Vivian Walsh's superb evaluation in the 1983 *Journal of Economic Literature* (reprinted in Kerr with Harcourt 2002: vol. V, 365–406) on her economics in retrospect, an evaluation based principally on their reading of her five volumes of *Collected Economic Papers*, we find that most of their evidence for the masterly account they give of her approaches and achievements comes from sources other that *The Accumulation of Capital* itself (though it clearly is one, often the most important, starting point for the issues discussed and interconnections brought out).

As we noted above, in the Preface to *The Accumulation of Capital*, Joan Robinson looked at the broad sweep of development in our discipline from Adam Smith to the Keynesian revolution and after. Having outlined the preoccupation of the classical economists and Marx with distribution, accumulation and growth, underwritten by the need for a theory of value, she mentions the 100 years or so of neoclassical dominance where the principal propositions related to explanations of prices and the allocation of scarce resources between competing ends, usually in a static setting, so ignoring growth and technical progress but not the welfare implications. The trade cycle and other issues were often banished to an underworld until historical events and the Keynesian revolution brought them again into focus, with Keynes ultimately as interested in explaining sustained unemployment in capitalist economies as in explaining cyclical processes.

Now Joan Robinson's object was to move neoclassical preoccupations off stage and return to classical issues in the light of the advances associated with Keynes and Kalecki. In a Preface to a later edition of her book, probably written in or after 1959 but never published, she explained very clearly the four main issues and questions with which she was concerned.

She considers a model of an unregulated free enterprise economy in which firms 'within the limits set by their command of finance' determine the rate of accumulation, while the members of the public, constrained 'by their command of purchasing power, are free to make the rate of expenditure what they please ... [a] model ... not unrealistic in essential respects'.

The model may be used 'to analyse the chances and changes of an economy as time goes by' by considering 'four distinct groups of questions':

1   We make comparisons of situations, each with its own past, developing into its own future, which are different in some respect (for instance, the rate of accumulation going on in each) to see what the postulated difference entails.
2   We trace the path which a single economy follows when the technical conditions (including their rate of change) and the propensities to consume and to invest are constant through time.
3   We trace the consequences of a change in any one of these conditions for the future development of the economy.
4   We examine the short-period reaction of the economy to unexpected events.

The first group of questions is more naturally handled in terms of comparisons of steady states (including stationary states). The conditions for steady states to be achieved are set out with no implication that the unregulated behaviour of decision makers will ever bring them about.

The second set of questions concerns what happens when one of the conditions for steady growth is not satisfied. The third set relates to the path which the economy will follow when, having been in a steady state, a basic change, for example, 'an increase in monopoly which causes profit margins to increase', occurs.

The fourth set concerns the reactions of the inducement to invest to current events in an uncertain world and relates to the possibility of oscillation in the transition from one state of affairs to another, or even to the generation of a trade cycle by 'mere uncertainty' without any change in basic conditions. In principle, the author claims, 'this type of analysis enables us to deal with all the possible vicissitudes of a developing economy and prepare the way for discussions of public policy'.

What tended to obscure these objectives set out so starkly was the simultaneous development of a concentration on the conditions for steady growth, especially with technical progress going on, which preoccupied both Joan Robinson and mainstream writers on these issues. Though she and Kahn clearly thought of Golden Age analysis as a preliminary to the real business of exploring dynamic processes in historical time, the way she presented the analysis in *The Accumulation of Capital*, with 'reality' often breaking through, tended to blur the analytical boundaries between the two. It is not until we get to the *Essays* and the developments built on them that we see that analysis of the medium term with short-period situations growing out of those that preceded them becomes centre stage. Even then, it was Goodwin and Kalecki more than Joan Robinson who were to make the most substantial advances on this front. Asimakopulos was not that far behind these other two; he used her approach but differed starkly from her in one respect. Increasingly, Joan Robinson was inclined to see the short period as a point in time, as an adjective not a noun, not a defined period. This was Asimakopulos's most serious criticism of her contributions and, in his own work, he always used the short period in the sense of a definite stretch of time which he believed to be faithful to Keynes's legacy and also to be the proper setting in which to develop Joan Robinson's insights and conjectures.

Nevertheless, if we use the unpublished preface as our map, we may see more clearly the nature and purpose of the structure of her book and of the other papers that preceded and followed it.

Kahn was probably even more clear in his own mind than Joan Robinson about this distinction. Thus, in his 1959 article in *Oxford Economic Papers*, he provided extremely clear statements of the principles involved. The article explains succinctly and clearly all that can be said and done within the confines of Golden Age analysis in which use is made of heroic assumptions because 'for [his] own part, [he desired] to learn to walk before he tried to run' (Kahn 1972: 195). Kahn is especially clear on the use and abuse of identities – in this case, saving equals investment – and on the definitions of different classes of income which are implied by them. He also brings out beautifully the two-sided relationship between the rate of profits and accumulation which is a (Kaleckian) feature of the analysis; the correct definition of the rate of profits as an expected variable; the nature of technical progress and how it may be tackled within this framework; and the distinction between a bastard Golden Age, in which unemployment may exist and worsen over 'time', and a 'true' Golden Age, truly mythical, in which the labour force and the stock capital goods are fully employed over 'time'. (In Harrod's terms the first case implies that g_w is less than g_n, the second, that they are equal.) Kahn stresses that the analysis is *entirely* confined to differences (comparison), that it does not relate to changes (processes). Thus:

> When one speaks of a Golden Age being preferred [to another one], it means it would be preferable to be in it. But to be in it involves *having* been in it for a long time past, and enjoying the legacy of the past in terms of the accumulated stock of capital and the degree of mechanisation. The desirability of a movement from one ... to the other, and the manner in which it might be smoothly negotiated, is ... [an] important and difficult [problem],... This paper is ... no more than prolegomena to the solution of real problems.
>
> (Kahn 1972: 206–7, emphasis in original)

Joan Robinson herself was searching for fundamental and simple principles which underlie the process of growth. In particular, she investigated the creation of the surplus in the consumption goods sector for use in the investment goods sector as wages of labour there, concentrating on what determined how much *potential* accumulation could be obtained from a given potential surplus. The surplus itself depended on employment and the productivity of labour in the consumption goods sector and the real wage. Between them, they determined the potential buying power over labour in the investment goods sector. How much accumulation this potentially made possible was determined by the technique of production in force there. In her first run through she supposed there to be only one method of production known at any moment of time and technical progress was handled by asking how the one dominant method could be changed from period to period. This was a short-hand way of overcoming the problem of the choice of technique at a moment of time. (This was analysed in great detail later on in the book.)

By using this approach the links between real saving and real investment could be made crystal clear while their interconnections in a capitalist economy could come in later on by using the Keynes/Kalecki analysis of the determination of planned investment expenditure, planned saving and the distribution of income and their effects on the overall level of output and employment. This served to provide the link between potential surplus creation and its realization now set in an analysis of distribution, accumulation and growth rather than in a one-period analysis of employment and unemployment.

By page 84 she has completed her analysis of the story of accumulation with one technique of production and, as yet, no technical progress.[3] Reading the chapters leading up to this over 50 years later, it is easier to see both the influence of Kalecki on her approach and her impatience to get to the second strand of the overall project, analysis of accumulation in historical time. This leads at times to her being inconsistent with her views about the nature of equilibrium in growth models and the incoherence of a story of getting into equilibrium. She covers herself to some extent by discussing the nature of tranquil conditions which create an atmosphere and environment akin to those of a true Golden Age equilibrium state where expectations are assumed always to be realized so that the stock of capital goods currently in existence is always in accord with what was expected to happen when each part of it was first installed. We do not think though that, at this time, she had faced up fully to the question of fossils from the past being inappropriate for today's conditions and how they could be scrapped over time from the capital stock without bursting even surrogate Golden Age conditions.

With these provisos, she concisely states on pages 83–4 her previous arguments in four propositions. She concludes that though many of her

> conclusions will have to be extensively modified as the assumptions of one technique and no rentier consumption are relaxed ... the argument [nevertheless] holds good in all essential respects, and provides a picture of the basic characteristics of accumulation under the capitalist rules of the game

(94

The propositions are:

> In an economy with only one technique, and no consumption out of profits, when the supply of labour adapts itself to demand, starting from any given situation (produced by past history), the future rate of accumulation is limited:
>
> 1   By the technical surplus available above the subsistence wages for the workers employed.
> 2   Within that limit,... by the surplus above the level of real wages that the workers are willing to accept and able to enforce (by creating an inflation barrier against a fall in real wages).
> 3   Within that limit,... by the energy with which entrepreneurs carry it out.
> 4   When the size of the labour force is independent of the ... demand for workers, a maximum is set to the ... rate of accumulation by the rate of increase of the labour force. When accumulation fails to reach this rate there is growth of long-period unemployment.
>
> (83–4)

Joan Robinson was an admirer of Wilfred Salter's work (1960, 1965) in which he sharpened up the vagueness of Marshall's analysis by showing how, by accumulation, technical progress could be embodied in the stock of capital goods without the need to scrap all previous vintages. The latter could be used for current production provided that they could be expected to cover their variable costs; the latest vintages would only be embodied if they were expected to cover their expected *total* costs, including the normal rate of profits, by their expected proceeds. A temporary equilibrium (in a competitive situation) would be attained when, for each, separated in time, burst of technical advances, capacity had so increased that the prices of products produced only allowed the normal rate of profits to be received on the latest vintage. Salter also included an analysis of the choice of technique alongside the analysis of the determination of total investment expenditure in the firm, the industry and, ultimately, the economy as a whole.

Salter's influence is implicitly present in Joan Robinson's discussion of the diffusion of techniques in Chapter 9 ('Technical progress'), though, unlike Salter, she discusses first the case in which there is only one possible method of production for each commodity which is 'superior to all older ones at every level of wages' (85). The analysis of 'a spectrum of technical possibilities [with] different ratios of labour to capital in a given phase of knowledge' (ibid.) is left to the next chapter.

She discusses the diffusion of techniques, referring, again implicitly, to Schumpeterian innovators taking the lead and to laggards being driven out by competitive (in a Marxian sense) forces. This allows her to discuss a leap frog effect which depends partly on the physical durability of new capital goods and partly on the strength of competition, which, in turn, often leads to scrapping, or, at least, retirement, long before the physical lives of machines have come to an end. She refers to the paradox of patents: '[a] patent is a device to prevent the diffusion of new methods before the original investor has received profits adequate to induce the requisite investment' (87). The justification of the system 'is that by slowing down the diffusion of new techniques it ensures that there will be more progress to diffuse [clearly] a system rooted in a contradiction' (87).

Joan Robinson sets out the conditions for stability, movements in accumulation and wages over time to ensure a matching of overall demand and supply (and their compositions) in the economy as a whole. She reproduces in words much the same conditions as those Marx set out in more formal terms in the schemes of reproduction. As with Marx, she points out that '[it] is only necessary to set out the conditions required for stability [steady advance] to see how precarious [its] preservation is under the capitalist rules of the game' (89). She lists the conditions for the 'smooth development of a progressive economy' (89):

First, the stock of machines (in terms of productive capacity) must grow at the rate appropriate to the increase in output per worker that is taking place, while competition must ensure that prices so move relatively to money–wage rates as to keep equipment working at normal capacity, that is to say, real wages rise with output per worker so that sufficient demand occurs to absorb the ever-growing output of the ever-growing stock of equipment.

Second, any chance discrepancy between available labour and equipment must be quickly eliminated. If there is surplus labour the real wage must rise less fast than output per head but outlay in the investment goods sector must be such as to speed up accumulation in terms of productive capacity. If labour is scarce real wages must rise more than output per head and the rate of accumulation must slow down. 'When this mechanism is operating the supply of capital goods is continuously adjusted to the supply of labour ... any tendency to surplus or scarcity ... is promptly corrected' (89).

She proceeds by narratives concerning two economies, Alaph and Beth, that momentarily are alike as far as their labour forces and phase of technical development are concerned, but which have reached this position by different histories with regard to past development, giving their decision makers different expectations. Rates of accumulation have differed and therefore the distribution of their work forces and levels of real wages are different also. She then looks for the conditions which should prevail if the conditions in one economy change to those of the other so as to allow the first economy to follow a path of smooth development, one akin to that followed in the other economy. Such gradual transitions technically could take place 'but there is no mechanism provided by the capitalist rules of the game that can be relied upon to steer the economy on to the appropriate course' (92).

This analysis is followed by sections on under consumption, weak and strong accumulation and biased technical progress, culminating in her definition of the existence of a Golden Age:

When technical progress is neutral, and proceeding steadily, without any change in the time pattern of production, population growing ... at a steady rate and accumulation going on fast enough to supply productive capacity for all available labour, the rate of profit[s] tends to be constant and the level of real wages to rise with output per man [*sic*] ... no internal contradictions in the system ... [if] entrepreneurs have faith in the future and desire to accumulate at the same proportional rate as they have been doing in the past, there is no impediment to prevent them [and] the system develops smoothly [with output and the stock of capital (valued in terms of commodities) growing at a rate compounded of the rate of increase in the labour force and the rate of increase in output per worker].

(99)

Joan Robinson adds: 'We may describe those conditions as a *golden age* (thus indicating that it represents a mythical state of affairs not likely to obtain in any actual economy)' (99, emphasis in original).

Moreover, if the rate of technical progress and of population increase are given by nature, the *golden age* is a state of bliss since consumption increases at the maximum feasible rate compatible with maintaining such a rate. In Joan Robinson's view this is the equivalent to $g_n = g_w = g_a$ in Harrod's analysis. But it is far away from reality because '[t]he limit to the rate of growth of wealth, over the long term, is set not by technical boundaries but by the lethargy which develops when the goad of competition and rising wage rates is blunted' (ibid.: 100).

In section II of Book II entitled 'The technical frontier', we start on the analysis which would have been most familiar to readers because of Joan Robinson's 1953–1954 article, 'The production function and the theory of capital', which, as we noted above, brought into the public domain what subsequently came to be known as the Cambridge–Cambridge debates in the theory of capital. Chapter 10 is entitled 'The spectrum of techniques' and at the end of the final paragraph the author has a footnote which reads: 'The reader is warned that the argument ... is difficult out of proportion to its importance [that] we shall return to conclusions substantially the same as those of the last chapter' (Robinson 1953–1954: 101). She tells us that the diagrams illustrating the argument are to be found below at page 416 (actually page 411 when we get there). In the third edition, published in 1969, as well as reproducing the sections from the previous editions, she added a postscript containing '[an] alternative form of the foregoing diagrams, which may be easier to follow [and which] had been developed from the analysis of Piero Sraffa's *Production of Commodities by Means of Commodities*' (426).

Then off we go, analysing the choice of technique in the economy as a whole, inspired by Knut Wicksell and using what became known as a book of blueprints containing different known ways of producing consumption goods. Joan Robinson discusses how and why one technique over a range of possible values of either the wage rate (w) or the rate of profits (r) will be dominant, and how, because of discreteness in techniques, there are unique w, r values at which adjacent techniques are equi-profitable (or, for a given value of the rate of interest equal to the value of the economy-wide *r*, allow the same *w* to be paid). On pages 109–10 the Ruth Cohen curiosum (capital-reversing) is explained. In a footnote Joan Robinson writes that what she has called 'a perverse relationship' was pointed out to her 'by Miss Ruth Cohen … a somewhat intricate piece of analysis which is not of great importance' (109)!

Here Joan Robinson was basically explaining *differences* – what technique(s) would dominate in possible Golden Ages according to the values postulated for one of the factor prices – rather than *changes*, processes occurring in historical time, though she sometimes writes as if the latter is being considered as well. As we noted, in later years she rejected this way of looking at the choice of technique in the investment decision when she brought the analysis of technical progress into the picture. That is to say, she subsequently rejected the traditional neoclassical distinction between moving *along* the production function in response to different values of the relative factor prices, on the one hand, and movements *of* the production formation itself – new books of blueprints – as a result of technical change occurring, on the other (see Robinson 1971: 103–4). In this she was joined by Kaldor who from 1957 to 1962 produced a number of versions of his technical progress function, see Kaldor (1957, 1959a, 1959b, 1961), Kaldor and Mirrlees (1962). Kaldor was explicitly dealing with processes in (he hoped) historical time whereby new advances in knowledge and known alternative input ratios were simultaneously embodied in the stock of capital goods in the processes of accumulation and growth, with their accompanying effects on the distribution of income and the immediate levels of activity and income, see Harcourt (2006: 114–19) for a critical evaluation of Kaldor's approach.

Joan Robinson's description of business people's behaviour is a strange mixture of real world practice and pure theory, dare we say it, neoclassical theory at that? At one point she is near suggesting the use of the pay-off or pay-back criterion in order to determine in which technique to invest (as well as to stave off the effects of inescapable uncertainty). At another point she writes as if she were a bright graduate of a leading business school, describing in words what is happening in the DCF procedures taught there.

The chapter closes with some sensible remarks about some special cases which could 'deflect [entrepreneurs] from using the technique that (at the ruling wage rate) yields the highest obtainable rate of profit on capital' (110). The constraints/cases include finance, management, monopoly and monopsony. Always she contrasts the behaviour most appropriate for a world of tranquility with that in the more real world of uncertainty and attendant risks. In the latter, flexibility is at a premium and this explains, amongst other things, 'the success of many small businesses using simple techniques in competition with highly mechanised giants' (113).

The next major issue Joan Robinson tackled was the analysis of technical progress (Chapters 16–18). She examined in isolation, as it were, from what went before what types of technical advance could, at least in principle, be consistent with Golden Age conditions being achieved and sustained. At the same time she warned readers that the analysis and results were far from what actually would be observed in growing economies. She wrote before Salter, for example, had published his 1960 book and 1965 IEA chapter (the latter was a simultaneous analysis of choice of technique and technical advance, taking in both movements along the *ex ante* production function induced by factor prices *and* movements of the *ex ante* production function itself due to technical advances, for the economy as a whole). Joan Robinson was familiar with his earlier analysis at the level of the firm and industry of the same processes.[4]

It is fair to say that Joan Robinson did not succeed in her 1956 book in integrating the analyses of these separate issues as well as she could have wished when she gathered her main findings together in Chapter 18, 'Synopsis of the theory of accumulation in the long run' (173–6). She did feel, as we have noted, that while these added details, they did not lead materially to a departure from the main thrust of her findings in the first major section of the volume. There are 20 major findings gathered together. The author indicates in which chapters the analysis that led to the propositions stated may be found. Reading with hindsight through her synopsis it is relatively easy to see the major influences on her procedures in the preceding pages.

First, Marx's schemes of production and reproduction, together with conditions that have to be satisfied for each period's potential output in all sectors (departments) and their compositions to be absorbed, that is to say, for aggregate demand to equal aggregate supply and for their compositions to match up. It was Marx's contention, of course, that it would only be a fluke if the acts of individual decision makers when taken together resulted in these systemic conditions being met; and that the failure to meet them would cause instability and possibly crisis in the behaviour of competitive economies. As Claudio Sardoni (1981) has made clear, Marx's schemes were not forerunners of modern steady-state constant growth models, for in Marx's analysis, the rates of growth could vary from period to period provided that in each period aggregate demand and supply and their compositions matched. Joan Robinson does not mention this explicitly, probably because she was intent on establishing the conditions which Golden Ages have to meet and sustain though she was well aware of the consequences of this not occurring. Especially was this so because she had a clear understanding of the possible volatility of accumulation plans in capitalist societies so that the distinction between the potential surplus which techniques and the conditions of the class war made possible, on the one hand, and the possibility of its realization in the sphere of distribution and exchange, on the other, was very much an explicit part of her thinking.

Also underlying her analysis is her attempt to solve the two problems thrown up by Harrod's seminal work. First, the stability or otherwise of the warranted rate of growth (g_w) – the rate of growth which if attained would persuade business people that they had made the correct decisions concerning accumulation and production so that they should continue the same rate of increase of accumulation in the future. As we know, if their decisions taken together do *not* put the economy on g_w, the economy is most likely to give out misleading signals which lead to decisions that take the economy further and further away from attaining g_w, see Harcourt (2006: 102–9).

Second, Harrod distinguishes between the potential rate of growth of the economy, its natural rate defined by growth in the labour force together with the rate at which the representative worker's productivity improves over time, and the expected, warranted and actual rates of growth (g_a). Work by Harrod himself and subsequently by Solow, Swan and Meade as neoclassicals, on the one hand, and Kaldor, Kahn and Joan Robinson as post-Keynesians, on the other, have examined whether there are forces potentially available in the economy which would take g_w (and g_a) towards g_n. In the neoclassical case this is achieved (in simple models) by changes induced in the capital–output ratio (v), in the post-Keynesian case, it is achieved by induced changes in the saving ratio, s: ($g_w = s/v$).

A weakness in all these analyses, up to which Joan Robinson faces but does not, we think, solve satisfactorily, is Harrod's assumption that g_n may be regarded as independent of the values of g_w and g_a. This assumption cannot be sustained once it is recognized that improvements in labour productivity are the direct outcome of the rate at which technical advances are embodied in the stock of capital goods by actual rates of accumulation and that the growth of the labour force is endogenous, not exogenous, see Harcourt (2006: 109–13).

She also takes from the classicals and Marx, usually through Sraffa's revival of their approach, the concept of the rate of profits, where it comes from and what determines its size. When she wrote *The Accumulation of Capital* she had already said that she was inspired by Sraffa's introduction to volume one of the Ricardo volumes, as we noted above.

Finally, the influence of Kalecki (and Keynes) is clear when Joan Robinson considers how aggregate supply and aggregate demand match up to one another in the growth process and in a Golden Age, especially when account is taken of rates of accumulation over time and the effects of macroeconomic processes on the distribution of income between profits and wages, when the marginal propensities to save from these two categories of income differ. Joan Robinson's analysis is thus an overarching, original synthesis of all these strands set within the context of Golden Age conditions and the effects of lapses from them.

We now move to the remaining six books, (Chapters 19–37), with Book III 'The short period'. She deals more sketchily with nevertheless relevant topics The chapters contain as would be expected shrewd insights and contributions but are more in the nature of minor additions to her main task, tidying up, as it were When she wrote her sequel volume (1962a) she more successfully integrated the various strands she had analysed in her 'big book'. Nevertheless, as we noted for sympathetic readers with eyes to see and ears to hear, it was possible to see what she was attempting and to applaud how well she had done it.

Chapter 19 is concerned with 'Prices and profits'. The author discusses non-Golden Age conditions. She starts with a section on long and short periods. For her the short period in an analytical sense is not any definite period of time but a convenient abstraction meaning a period in which changes in the stock of capital goods can be neglected (179). Asimakopulos does not disagree with this (see Asimakopulos 1984, reprinted in Kerr with Harcourt 2002: vol. V).

> Although she does not attach a definite length to the short period here, it clearly encompasses some interval of time ... long enough to enable decisions to be made and carried out to change the degree of utilization of the relatively unchanged productive capacity.
>
> (ibid.: 448)

It was only when she changed Marshall's short period to meaning a point in time, 'a moment in a stream of time ... a state of affairs, an adjective not a substantive' (Robinson 1971: 17–18), so doing away with period analysis, that he and Joan Robinson parted company. There was now 'no time available to permit variations in the utilisation of productive capacity in response to changing short-term expectations' (Asimakopulos op. cit.: 448).

Joan Robinson makes utterly clear that 'everything that happens in an economy happens in a short-period situation, for an event occurs or a decision is taken at a particular time [when] the physical stock of capital is what it is' (180). But there are long-period as well as short-period aspects of all happenings, for example, the short-period aspect of accumulation is to be a major determinant of aggregate demand, while the long-period aspects concern the rate of growth of productive capacity – the rate of accumulation – and the technique of production. Moreover, long-period effects bring about the transformation of one short period into another.

Golden Ages and quasi-Golden Ages are

> imaginary situations ... an analytic device, not a description of reality. In reality to-day is a break in time. Yesterday lies in the past, ... has ceased to be relevant to what happens today, except in so far as experience of it colours expectations about what will happen next. Tomorrow lies in the future and cannot be known. The short-period situation ... is like a geological fault; past and future developments are out of alignment. Only in ... a golden age do the strata run horizontally from yesterday to to-morrow without a break at to-day.
>
> (181)

Having given concise descriptions of what may happen she adds that 'when we descend from the clear air of a golden age, where normal prices always rule, into the fogs of historical time, our analysis cannot but be blurred and imprecise' (190).

> The rate of profit on capital, in a short period situation, is an even more foggy notion than the level of profits earned by given equipment, for to express profits at a rate we must know the value of capital ... In reality, to find the expected return which governs investment decisions is like ...

> looking in a dark room for a black cat ... not there, and to give a true
> account of realized returns is like the ... chameleon on a plaid rug. [Never-
> theless] the long-period influences ... are working themselves out through
> the fog of uncertainty in which short-period situations develop [but] ...
> cannot be seen with any great precision.
>
> (190–2)

In chapter 20, 'Wages and prices', Joan Robinson considers the interaction
between a number of possible short-period situations and the underlying long-
period situation of, in effect, tranquility approximating to Golden Age conditions. She discusses different market structures – competitive, monopolistic
and oligopolistic ones – and examines the impact of buyers and sellers markets
on the likely course of prices vis-à-vis wages, effective demand in the short term
and planned accumulation in the short term. In some situations, the initial starting point supposes there to be near to over full capacity working; in others there
is surplus capacity. As well there may be a long-term tendency to an over supply
of labour on which may be imposed either additional unemployment due to
short-term fluctuations or a temporary rise in employment relative to the long-
term tendency. Within this framework she considers buyers' and sellers' markets
for both consumption and investment goods, paying special attention to the setting of prices in the short term relative to expectations about long-period subjective normal prices.[5] In this way her analysis may be seen as an up-date of Adam
Smith's discussion of market prices and their movements around (or converging
on) underlying natural prices.

She analyses the overall effects on effective demand of changes in prices and
wages in different situations, taking into account the feedback on planned accumulation and the relative strengths of labour and capital in the particular class
wars of the given situations. Always she is on the look out for asymmetries in
responses. For example, in the section on the adjustment of capacity to available
labour she writes at the end of three paragraphs of analysis: 'This strongly reinforces the conclusion that a deficiency of demand for labour relatively to supply
is much less likely to be self-correcting than a deficiency of supply relatively to
demand' (197).

The opening paragraphs of chapter 21, 'Fluctuations in the rate of investment'
are pure Kalecki.

> The accumulation of capital over the long run takes place as a result of
> decisions to invest made in a succession of short-period situations ... every
> day the sun rises upon a economy which has ... a particular who's who of
> capital goods ... and a particular state of expectations based upon past
> experience and the diagnosis of current trends. In ... a seller's market cur-
> rent experience indicates that more productive capacity could be profitably
> used and is likely to cause decisions to invest ... A high level of employ-
> ment in the investment sector means high quasi-rents in the consumption
> sector ... high profits cause profits to be high ... in a buyer's market there is

excess capacity ... investment is discouraged. Low profits cause profits to be low.

This double interaction between investment and profits is the most troublesome feature of the capitalist rules of the game, both from the point of view of entrepreneurs who have to play it and of economists who have to describe it.

(198)

She tells a story of an investment boom due, say, to an innovation, concluding:

The essential character of a boom (as opposed to golden-age accumulation) is that it is based on a contradiction. Investment is going on under the influence of the seller's market which investment ... creates ... there is some extra investment due only to the high level of demand (relative to capacity) induced by the investment. The seller's market [could] continue only if the rate of investment (and ... demand for commodities) continued to expand ... in proportion to the increase in capacity ... and since the rate of increase in investment cannot continue indefinitely while the rise in capacity goes on continuously ... the seller's market cannot continue. Investment due to a seller's market is sawing off the bough that it is sitting on by bringing the seller's market to an end.

(201)

The author then sketches a typical trade cycle and closes by comparing two views of why cycles repeat themselves: one is entirely endogenous leading to the four phases of the cycle, the other needs an exogenous event to overcome the argument that 'the internal power of recovery ... is too weak to overcome the shock of the slump ... the apparent regularity of the cycle is accidental ... something always has turned up to cause a revival' (212).

Many years later, this came to be called the real business cycle view.

The last chapter in this book is entitled 'Cycles and trends'. She argues that the 'trend which emerges *ex post* from the operation of the trade cycle is not the same thing as the growth ratio of a golden age, but is an imperfect reflection of it' (213). Here we are reminded that Kalecki's initial analysis of the cycle was of a trendless cycle, i.e. the trend was due to another, independent set of factors so justifying the statistical procedure of detrending time series. However, by the end of his life, he had scrapped this view and developed a theory of cyclical growth (as did Goodwin independently) in which the trend and cycle are indissolubly mixed. Kalecki's classic statement of this was: 'The long-term trend [is] but a slowly changing component of a chain of short-period situations ... [not an] independent entity' (Kalecki 1968: 165). This later view is consistent with Joan Robinson's statement:

The short period is here and now ... incompatibilities in the situation will determine what will happen next. Long-period equilibrium is not at some date in the future; it is an imaginary state of affairs in which there are incompatibilities in the existing situation here and now.

(1962b: 690)

However, she had not yet reached this view in *The Accumulation of Capital* where the Golden Age is a reference point for various possible scenarios, depending in part on the level of competition in market structures, on the nature of technical progress going on and on what is happening to the labour supply, the rate of increase of which is, for the most part, treated as exogenous.

Her concept of the inflation barrier, the situation in which wage-earners will no longer accept the implied level of consumption of wage goods associated with the existing level of production of investment goods by creating a wage-price spiral, plays a role as does the structure of vintages in the stocks of capital goods of both sectors. Much of her analysis in this chapter has been influenced, as she acknowledges, by a now little known article by Kaldor (1954), 'The relation of economic growth and cyclical fluctuations'.

One of her more fanciful scenarios is entitled 'The approach to bliss' (the state, not the economist). It involves what she called elsewhere moving down a well-behaved production function with decreasing rates of investment and of profits until a given total level of employment is attained in the consumption goods sector, bar that which is needed to allow replacements for the constant stock of capital goods employed in the sector. With fluctuating investment, investment boom by boom gets less and consumption in depressions gets greater and greater. Total employment is constant over the long run, that is to say, on average – all this is 'a logical possibility ... most unlikely to be realized under the capitalist rules of the game' (219). A tendency for the rate of profits to fall, 'combined with cyclical fluctuations ... undermine[s] the urge to accumulate and promote [s] defensive monopolies. An economy heading towards bliss is never likely to be able unaided to pass through the slough of stagnation to arrive there' (219).

Five more books complete the main part of the volume. There is a prescient conclusion:

> The reader must draw his [*sic*] conclusions for himself. On parting I only beg him to glance back to Chapter 2 and recall that the outputs of saleable goods ... are not co-extensive with economic wealth, let alone with the basis of human welfare.

(386)

The spirits of Marshall and Pigou shine through.

Book IV on 'Finance' is written at a high level of abstraction. There is a well-behaved banking system but no central bank. There are notes (issued by respectable banks) for transaction purposes, both to buy consumption goods and pay wage bills, there are short-term bills and long-term bonds. At any moment of time entrepreneurs fall into two groups – those keen to accumulate beyond their available receipts associated with their activities, those who are saving because their current accumulation plans do not absorb all their current receipts. Through the banks and the bond market, finance is redistributed from the second group to the first group, not always without hitches.

Generally speaking, in this abstract world, provision of finance tends more to be a drag on accumulation than a boost, partly because of liquidity preference conditions, partly because of swings between euphoria and pessimism in the banking system which tend to amplify fluctuations in the 'animal spirits' of entrepreneurs. (There are shades of Hyman Minsky's later work here.)

The conclusion of her detailed and careful analysis is rather disappointing: 'over the long run, the rate of accumulation is likely to be whatever it is likely to be' (244).

Introducing a rentier class complicates but leaves the analysis of accumulation basically unchanged. The most important result is that the rate of profits no longer equals the rate of growth but exceeds it. There are some nice paradoxes arising from the Kaleckian proposition that profits now equal net investment *plus* rentier expenditure, for example, 'the double-sided relation between entrepreneurs and rentiers'.

> Just as each entrepreneur individually gains by paying his workers less, but suffers through a loss of markets from others paying their workers less, so each entrepreneur would like his wife and his shareholders to be content with little, so that he can use the bulk of his profits for investment (or for reserves to finance future investment) while he gains from the expenditure of other wives and other shareholders, which makes the market for commodities buoyant.
>
> (256)

Rentiers also complicate the narrative of the trade cycle without affecting the main lines of former arguments. In particular, rentier expenditure may be an important buffer in the slump because of inertia in both the change in the money rate of interest and in rentier consumption itself. Joan Robinson refers to Robin Matthews's (1954–1955) article on the saving function and the problem of trend and cycle in which Matthews related the ratchet effect in Duesenberry's (1949) model to unemployment levels rather than to output and income per head levels, i.e. Matthews took into account the effects of productivity rising over time. Joan Robinson points out that

> [c]onsumption out of profits plays an important part in the mechanism by which a long-run trend of accumulation emerges from the trade cycle. Each boom leaves behind it an increase in rentier wealth and consuming power due to … savings … while the boom was going on … the drop in each slump is checked at a higher level of demand for consumption goods, and provided … additional rentier wealth [is not wiped out by bankruptcies], each revival starts from a higher level of output than the last.
>
> (269)

Rentiers affect the nature of finance because a large part of wealth is now 'outside the direct control of entrepreneurs [and this influences] accumulation through its effect upon the control over finance' (274).

Book VI is entitled 'Land'. Historically, the author argues, land should be discussed before capital because it 'is of the greatest importance as a factor of production, and the development of a technical surplus of food is the first prerequisite for accumulation' (283). Moreover, the 'rules of the game' with respect to land tenure and inheritance and the habits and traditions of landowners affect the subsequent behaviour in the industrial sector and society at large.

Following a rather stylized discussion of the reasons for historical diminishing returns in terms of the marginal products of labour and land, and modifications due to the actions of improving landlords, Joan Robinson discusses the vital role of the agricultural surplus in the process of accumulation.

Chapter 30 is concerned with factor ratios and techniques. In this and the succeeding chapters Joan Robinson discusses separately the relationships between possible factor prices and techniques chosen and then varieties of technical progress with factor prices held constant, before attempting to bring the two analyses together to provide an overall picture. She is carefully explicit about the simplifying assumptions she invokes in order to make the analysis tractable (for her, if not always for the reader!) and is painfully honest about how far away even her most detailed narratives are from real world happenings. In order to make precise what is meant by marginal products in the analysis of labour and land, she uses a tranquil static state, finding

a separate picture for each degree of mechanisation and for each overall ratio of land to labour when total output consists of commodities. There is a corresponding three-dimensional jigsaw puzzle for each ratio of investment to consumption.

And the whole complex alters through time as technical knowledge changes.

(306)

'In principle', she adds, 'the whole of [the] formal analysis [could be repeated] in terms of this scheme ... a most formidable task [upon which would have to be superimposed] all the short-period complications [smudged] over with the uncertainties of an untranquil world' (306). She does not embark on such an undertaking, preferring to take a couple of problems to illustrate how the analysis might be tackled.

Needless to say, by the time the reader gets to the end of the book a tremendous amount has had to be digested, and many evidently were not up to the task. Joan Robinson followed up first with a symposium published in *Oxford Economic Papers* in 1959 in which David Worswick presented his stockade dictum model of her volume (a reading with which she was not that pleased) and Kahn contributed, as we noted, his extremely clear and helpful 'Exercises...'. Solow, for one, found Worswick's construction of value when he gave his de Vries tures on *Capital Theory and the Rate of Return* (Solow 1963). Harcourt unknowingly[6] reproduced some of Worswick's analysis when he wrote a comment on Harry Johnson's 1962 article, 'A simple Joan Robinson model of accumulation with one technique' (see Harcourt 1963 and 2006: 16–20). These papers illustrate her claim that the model of the second Book in her 1956 volume allows the major, most fundamental propositions of her analysis to be established. Nevertheless, as we noted, Joan Robinson felt it necessary to provide a (very adult) 'told-to-the-children' guide to her volume, resulting in the publication in 1962 of *Essays in the Theory of Economic Growth*.

Finally, we briefly discuss three other reactions to her book which contributed to her decision to write *Essays*. These are Worswick's (1959) 'comment with algebra', Kelvin Lancaster's review article (1960) and Ronald Findlay's 'Robinsonian model of accumulation' (1963).

Worswick's principal object was to reproduce in algebra (with an accompanying economic explanation and intuition) the propositions of Joan Robinson's model with one technique. He uses the device of a (benevolent) dictator within a stockade to direct production and plan accumulation. Within the stockade there are advanced production techniques and the stockade is surrounded by a hinterland from which unlimited supplies of labour may be obtained. (Unlike Solow (1963) who adopted Worswick's model, the labourers in the hinterland play little part in determining the level of real wages.) For most of the analysis production is concentrated on and assumptions are set up so as to be able to have physical units in which to measure the outputs of consumption goods and machines.

Worswick works out the conditions which decide the distribution of employment between the production of consumption goods and machines, given the initial inherited stock of machines, and with a constraint of full employment sometimes imposed. Towards the end of the article Worswick introduces something akin to profits and asks how they are created (realized) by expenditure, being potentially there as a surplus of consumption goods in the consumption goods sector.

Worswick concludes that the discussion may appear to be a sustained attack on Joan Robinson's model of accumulation with one technique. It was certainly not his intention, adding that the main difference in presentation was his introduction of the planning dictator. This may be why Joan Robinson was *not* that pleased with the article. Worswick claims that their respective conclusions mostly overlap but that his exposition brings out 'certain points more clearly … not remarkable. We all know that the best approach to Ricardo or Keynes is not to read their original work' (Kerr with Harcourt 2002: vol. III, 67).

This leads Worswick to question whether using the dictator to arrange the economy may be more than a mere trick of presentation. It is: 'the system [will] only "break down"' if the dictator goes mad' (ibid.), whereas the conditions for a Golden Age will only be met in an unregulated capitalist economy by the uncoordinated actions of individual business people in a competitive situation by a fluke.

Findlay (1963) drew on Lancaster's (1960) model of *The Accumulation of Capital* to go over in algebra (and geometry) the same ground on Golden Ages as that which Joan Robinson covered in her book. His is a comprehensive and helpful article, reaching many of the same conclusions as Joan Robinson had and explicitly relating the findings to the other principal contributors at the time – Harrod and Domar, Solow and Swan, Kaldor – and at the end of the article to antecedents – Keynes (Harrod/Domar), Wicksell (Solow/Swan) and Marx (Joan Robinson), with Kaldor possibly drawing on all five. He gives Keynes a relatively low input at what was then the present state of play but suggests that when money and finance are introduced, as they must be, Keynes will play a much larger role – 'it is almost certain that liquidity preference, and perhaps even the ideas of the "mysterious" Chapter 17 ... will play a central role' (Kerr with Harcourt 2002: vol. III, 84).

Before discussing Joan Robinson's response to Worswick and Findlay we note Lancaster's stringent critique in his review article. He tries to soften the blow by writing that 'any work of Mrs. Robinson must command respect' (Lancaster 1960: 63). Moreover, when it is a book which is meant to do for growth what *The Economics of Imperfect Competition* did for price theory, her book must be judged only by the highest standards, 'judged as a whole in terms of its fabric, method and its general sweep: in terms of these, it does not succeed' (ibid.). Lancaster thought that the chief fault was 'failure of communication', and he quotes her reply to Worswick that she was 'very sorry that my book should be so difficult. What I meant is quite simple, but I evidently failed to make it clear' (Robinson 1959: 141).

The chief reason is that the comparative statics method that is so appropriate for *The Economics of Imperfect Competition* (not that Joan Robinson subsequently thought so) is 'not at all well suited to handling dynamic problems of capital' (Lancaster 1960: 64) – because the 'words and pictures' tradition is 'inadequate to the task of dynamic analysis in economics' (ibid.). He adds that 'The "arts" tradition of jumping straight from a simplified abstract analysis to a Grand conclusion about the real world proves too strong for the more austere scientific caution' (ibid.). (Lancaster should have known for his first degree was in English Literature.)

He concentrates on Joan Robinson's basic model and shows it is fine when the provision of equilibrium conditions is the task set it (as Joan Robinson made explicit anyway). But she was after process and the materials have not been provided, as it becomes absolutely clear to Lancaster when attempts to set up any dynamic equations for the model are attempted. He is explicitly harsh about this.

> In the section of her book in which she has a more or less clearly defined equilibrium model, that of long-run accumulation, her discussion of processes consists either of a reiteration of the equilibrium conditions, or the arbitrary selection of one possible process from an infinity of possibilities, with no particular attempt to justify the selection.
>
> At best one can *describe* verbally a process which has been traced out by other methods, just as we can describe the course of the planets and the sun without being able to show verbally why the course is as it is.
>
> (Lancaster 1960: 69 emphasis in original)

He concludes that 'what is little more than a two-by-two linear equilibrium model (and well deserving of discussion as such) can be dressed in a woolly cloak of words to appear to be a full-blooded economy' (ibid.: 70).

As we noted, Joan Robinson did lay herself open through some of her asides to such a critique. But what is also clear from Kahn's paper, her aims were in general much more modest, at that stage, than Lancaster implies. Moreover, when she gets to grips with Worswick's and Findlay's versions of her model, she more than holds her own because of her superb intuition concerning the driving forces at work in capitalism. Findlay anticipates her response by making explicit his MIT credentials so suggesting that he does not find her ideas very plausible 'because [he] went to the Massachusetts Institute of Technology' (Findlay 1963: 412).

In her comment on Worswick's article (Robinson 1959) she takes up two points, one minor, one major. She wonders why he makes such heavy weather about what happens when there are no machines in the capital goods sector. If there is literally no capital there, employers have no hold over workers and a different economic system would be relevant. If we use Worswick's own algebraic expression, as capital becomes vanishingly smaller, the cost of machines tends to their wage costs and the quantity of profit in the sector tends to zero (in competitive conditions) but the *rate* of profit remains at the overall rate – a typical example of Joan Robinson's analytical mind at work.

The major point concerns the limitations imposed by setting the wages in terms of treacle, the homogeneous consumption good. Joan Robinson prefers to set the wage in money terms, sell treacle to workers and allow the market to set the price, responding to the expenditure of the wages bill from the capital goods sector. Then the larger is the labour force in that sector, the higher will be the price set and the lower will be the treacle wage (a variant of Kalecki's model, of course).

If too many people are called to make machines, the real wage will fall below the level tolerated outside the stockade, wage demands will rise inside it, the inflation barrier will bite (Joan Robinson does not claim this to be the *only* cause of inflation). If the wage is too low to attract workers a shortage of labour will appear. If the dictator's equivalent of animal spirits is sluggish, few are called to make machines, the price of treacle will be lower and treacle wages in the stockade will be higher.

From this starting point the analysis can be extended to analyse a basket of consumption commodities, and the dictator as a planning authority adjudicating between the interests of those inside and outside the stockade. Worswick's analysis gives only limited illumination 'so long as he leaves the dictator stuck in the treacle' (142).

Joan Robinson (1963) was worried about being 'ungracious' by complaining about 'a reader [Findlay] who [had] taken so much trouble on her behalf' (408). Her main complaint was that Findlay had set up her model in such a way that by standing it on its head he had emptied causality out of the model. In particular she objected to the real wage determining accumulation in his accumulation function. This is alright in a Ricardian corn model but not in one – hers – when the wage bargain is in terms of money so that the real wage depends upon price. In her model the rate of accumulation and the marginal propensity to save out of profits determine the rate of profits and it, in conjunction with technical conditions, determine the real wage. The prime mover in the whole affair is the overall rate of accumulation emerging from the struggles of individual firms to increase productive capacity.

Findlay parts company with her here, arguing that it is unfortunate that Joan Robinson like Keynes adopts a uni-linear conception of causation whereas his model, a feedback mechanism used to relate the rate of accumulation, the rate of population growth and real wages, is one of mutual determination. He illustrates this by an analogy. If the temperature of a room is regulated by a thermostat it makes little sense to ask whether the supply of heat governs temperature or the other way around – the values of the variables are mutually determined. He adds that his Figure 1 illustrating this bears the same relation to *The Accumulation of Capital* as the *IS/LM* diagrams do to *The General Theory* (ouch).

Findlay tries to reconcile propositions common to the neoclassical model and his version of Joan Robinson's model. A rate of accumulation in excess of population growth drives up real wages and reduces the rate of accumulation. (Both authors pitch their discussion in terms of reconciling discrepancies between the values of g_n and g_w.) Joan Robinson wants animal spirits to dominate and so uses feedback from rising real wages on to the nature of technical progress as the mechanism, just as Marx did. Findlay hoped that after thesis and antithesis, his synthesis finally had Joan Robinson's ideas right even though as an MIT person he did not find them very plausible.

Notes

1 This chapter arises from our volume *Joan Robinson*, which we are writing for Tony Thirlwall's series 'Great thinkers in economics' to be published by Palgrave Macmillan, by whose kind permission we reproduce this text. All references containing only page numbers refer to Joan Robinson (1956) or, when indicated, later editions thereof.
   May we say how delighted we are to contribute to this volume in honour of Vela long a friend and inspiration, whose contributions cover so many areas and are characterized by deep scholarship and analysis.
2 Piero Sraffa teased her that she seemed to regard 'Marx as a little-known forerunner of Kalecki', see Joan Robinson (1956: vi).
3 The table of contents contains seven books: 'Introduction', 'Accumulation in the long run', 'The short period', 'Finance', 'The rentier', 'Land', 'Relative Prices' and 'International Trade'. Book II 'Accumulation in the long term', has as well three sections 'Accumulation with one technique', 'The technical frontier' and 'Accumulation with technical progress'. There are 37 chapters in all, followed by 'Notes on various topics' 'Diagrams' and 'The value of invested capital', written by David Champernowne and Richard Kahn. By the third edition the volume was 444 pages long.
4 Though Salter's book on these themes was not published until 1960, the dissertation on which it was based was examined in 1955 and its results were already well known in Cambridge at that time.

5 In her world even competitors are price-makers who act together, not collusively, but because they know that all their rivals are experiencing similar conditions, for example, a rise in costs.

6 In the sense that only after he had worked out his results did he realize that they looked familiar – so he reread Worswick's paper and found two identical paragraphs in it.

References

Asimakopulos, A. (1969) 'A Robinsonian growth model in one-sector notation', *Australian Economic Papers*, 8: 41–58; reprinted in P. Kerr with the collaboration of G.C. Harcourt (2002) *Joan Robinson: Critical assessments of leading economists*, 5 vols, London and New York: Routledge, vol. III.

—— (1970) 'A Robinsonian growth model in one-sector notation. An amendment', *Australian Economic Papers*, 9: 171–6; reprinted in P. Kerr with the collaboration of G.C. Harcourt (2002) *Joan Robinson: Critical assessments of leading economists*, 5 vols, London and New York: Routledge, vol. III.

—— (1984) 'Joan Robinson and economic theory', *Banca Nazionale del Lavoro Quarterly Review*, 37: 380–409; reprinted in P. Kerr with the collaboration of G.C. Harcourt (2002) *Joan Robinson: Critical assessments of leading economists*, 5 vols, London and New York: Routledge, vol. V.

—— (1991) *Keynes's General Theory and Accumulation*, Cambridge: Cambridge University Press.

Barna, T. (1957) 'Review of Joan Robinson's The Accumulation of Capital (1956)', *Economic Journal*, 67: 490–3; reprinted in P. Kerr with the collaboration of G.C. Harcourt (2002) *Joan Robinson: Critical assessments of leading economists*, 5 vols, London and New York: Routledge, vol. III.

Duesenberry, J.S. (1949) *Income, Saving and the Theory of Consumer Behaviour*, Harvard, MA: Harvard University Press.

Findlay, R. (1963) 'The Robinsonian model of accumulation', *Economica*, 30: 1–12; reprinted in P. Kerr with the collaboration of G.C. Harcourt (2002) *Joan Robinson: Critical assessments of leading economists*, 5 vols, London and New York: Routledge, vol. III.

Gram, H. and Walsh, V. (1983) 'Joan Robinson's economics in retrospect', *Journal of Economic Literature*, 21: 518–50; reprinted in P. Kerr with the collaboration of G.C. Harcourt (2002) *Joan Robinson: Critical assessments of leading economists*, 5 vols, London and New York: Routledge, vol. V.

Harcourt, G.C. (1963) 'A simple Joan Robinson model of accumulation with one technique: A comment', *Osaka Economic Papers*, 9: 24–8.

—— (2006) *The Structure of Post-Keynesian Economics: The core contributions of the pioneers*, Cambridge: Cambridge University Press.

Harrod, R.F. (1939) 'An essay in dynamic theory', *Economic Journal*, 49: 14–33, reprinted in P. Kerr with the collaboration of G.C. Harcourt (2002) *Joan Robinson: Critical assessments of leading economists*, 5 vols, London and New York: Routledge, vol. III.

—— (1948) *Towards a Dynamic Economics: Some recent developments of economic theory and their application to policy*, London: Macmillan.

Johnson, H.G. (1962) 'A simple Joan Robinson model of accumulation with one technique', *Osaka Economic Papers*, 10: 28–33.

Kahn, R.F. (1959) 'Exercises in the analysis of growth', *Oxford Economic Papers*,

II: 143–56; reprinted in R.F. Kahn (1972) *Selected Essays on Employment and Growth*, and P. Kerr with the collaboration of G.C. Harcourt (2002) *Joan Robinson. Critical assessments of leading economists*, 5 vols, London and New York: Routledge vol. III.

—— (1972) *Selected Essays on Employment and Growth*, Cambridge: Cambridge University Press.

Kaldor, N. (1954) 'The relation of economic growth and cyclical fluctuations', *Economic Journal*, 64: 53–71.

—— (1957) 'A model of economic growth', *Economic Journal*, 67: 591–624.

—— (1959a) 'Economic growth and the problem of inflation: Part I', *Economica*, 26 212–26.

—— (1959b) 'Economic growth and the problem of inflation: Part II', *Economica*, 26 287–98.

—— (1961) 'Capital accumulation and economic growth', in F.A. Lutz and D.C. Hague (eds), *The Theory of Capital*, London: Macmillan.

Kaldor, N. and Mirrlees, J.A. (1962) 'A new model of economic growth', *Review of Economic Studies*, 29: 174–92.

Kalecki, M. (1968) 'Trend and business cycles reconsidered', *Economic Journal*, 78 263–76; reprinted in Kalecki (1971) *Selected Essays on the Dynamics of the Capitalist Economy, 1933–1970*, Cambridge: Cambridge University Press.

Kerr, Prue (ed.) (2002) with the collaboration of G.C. Harcourt, *Joan Robinson: Critical Assessments of leading Economists*, 5 vols, London and New York: Routledge.

Keynes, J.M. (1936) *The General Theory of Employment, Interest and Money*; *Collected writings*, vol. VII (1973), London: Macmillan.

—— (1973) *The General Theory and After. Part II: Defense and development*; *Collected writings*, vol. XIV, London: Macmillan.

Lancaster, K. (1960) 'Mrs. Robinson's dynamics', *Economica*, 27: 63–9.

Lerner, A.P. (1957) 'Review of Joan Robinson's *The Accumulation of Capital*', *American Economic Review*, 47: 693–9; reprinted in P. Kerr with the collaboration of G.C. Harcourt (2002) *Joan Robinson: Critical assessments of leading economists*, 5 vols, London and New York: Routledge, vol. III.

Matthews, R.C.O. (1954–1955) 'The saving function and the problem of trend and cycle', *Review of Economic Studies*, 22: 75–95.

Robinson, J. (1937) *Introduction to the Theory of Employment*, London: Macmillan (2nd edn 1969).

—— (1942) *An Essay on Marxian Economics*, London: Macmillan (2nd edn 1966).

—— (1951–1979) *Collected Economic Papers*, five vols (1951, 1960, 1965, 1973, 1979), Oxford: Basil Blackwell.

—— (1951) 'Introduction', to R. Luxemburg, *The Accumulation of Capital*, London: Routledge and Kegan Paul; reprinted in J. Robinson (1951–1979) *Collected Economic Papers*, five vols, Oxford: Basil Blackwell, vol. II.

—— (1952a) *The Rate of Interest and Other Essays*, London: Macmillan.

—— (1952b) 'The model of an expanding economy', *Economic Journal*, 62: 42–53; reprinted in J. Robinson (1951–1979) *Collected Economic Papers*, five vols, Oxford: Basil Blackwell, vol. II.

—— (1953) *On Re-reading Marx*, Cambridge: Student's Bookshop; reprinted in J. Robinson (1951–1979) *Collected Economic Papers*, five vols, Oxford: Basil Blackwell, vol. IV.

—— (1953–1954) 'The production function and the theory of capital', *Review of*

Economic Studies, 21: 81–106; reprinted in J. Robinson (1951–1979) *Collected Economic Papers*, five vols, Oxford: Basil Blackwell, vol. II.

—— (1956) *The Accumulation of Capital*, London: Macmillan (2nd edn 1965, 3rd edn 1969).

—— (1959) 'A comment', *Oxford Economic Papers*, 11: 11–12.

—— (1962a) *Essays in the Theory of Economic Growth*, London: Macmillan (2nd edn 1963).

—— (1962b) 'Review of H.G. Johnson *Money, Trade and Economic Growth* (1962)', *Economic Journal*, 72: 690–2; reprinted in J. Robinson (1951–1979) *Collected Economic Papers*, five vols, Oxford: Basil Blackwell, vol. III.

—— (1963) 'Findlay's Robinsonian model of accumulation', *Economica*, 30: 408–11; reprinted in J. Robinson (1951–1979) *Collected Economic Papers*, five vols, Oxford: Basil Blackwell, vol. III.

—— (1971) *Economic Heresies: Some old-fashioned questions in economic theory*, London: Macmillan.

Salter, W.E.G. (1960) *Productivity and Technical Change*, Cambridge: Cambridge University Press (2nd edn 1966).

—— (1965) 'Productivity growth and accumulation as historical processes', in E.A.G. Robinson (ed.), *Problems in Economic Development*, London: Macmillan.

Sardoni, C. (1981) 'Multisectoral models of balanced growth and Marxian schemes of expanded reproduction', *Australian Economic Papers*, 20: 383–97.

Solow, R.M. (1963) *Capital Theory and the Rate of Return*, Amsterdam: North-Holland.

Sraffa, P. (ed.) (1951–1973) with the collaboration of M.H. Dobb, *Works and Correspondence of David Ricardo*, 12 vols, Cambridge: Cambridge University Press.

Worswick, G.D.N. (1959) 'Mrs. Robinson on simple accumulation: A comment', *Oxford Economic Papers*, II: 125–41; reprinted in P. Kerr with the collaboration of G.C. Harcourt (2002) *Joan Robinson: Critical assessments of leading economists*, 5 vols, London and New York: Routledge, vol. III.

20 The means of subsistence and the notion of 'viability' in Sraffa's surplus approach[1]

Guglielmo Chiodi

As is well known, there are two basic approaches in contemporary economic theory: the Classical approach (which the Marxian and the Sraffian ones belong to) and the Postclassical (or Neoclassical) approach. One important feature of the former, which is relevant in the present context, is that the prices and the quantities appearing in the corresponding frameworks are respectively determined by *distinct* forces, instead of their being determined by the same set of forces, as within the Postclassical framework.

The most important consequence of that specific feature of the Classical approach is that it allows the coming into being of the notion of 'viability' of an economic system, a fundamental property – as will be shown in the sequel – which indicates the *possibility* of the system to *reproduce itself* over time.

As a preliminary, let us suppose an extremely simple economy producing wheat by means of wheat, part of the latter being used as means of sustenance for the workers and the rest as means of production. Let us call $a \in (0, 1)$ the quantity of wheat used as means of production per unit of wheat produced, per unit of time, and $c \in (0, 1)$ the quantity of wheat used as means of sustenance for the λ units of labours employed per unit of wheat produced per unit of time. Thus, the economy considered could be represented through these alternative compact forms:

$$a \rightarrow 1 \qquad\qquad (20.A)$$

$$A + c \rightarrow 1 \qquad\qquad (20.B)$$

$$a \oplus \lambda \rightarrow 1 \qquad\qquad (20.C)$$

A 'viability' condition for the economy which refers to representation (20.A) is:

$$1 - a > 0 \qquad\qquad (20.1)$$

an *alternative* 'viability' condition to (20.1), referring to representation (20.B), is:

$$1 - (a + c) \geq 0 \qquad\qquad (20.2)$$

The 'viability' conditions (20.1) and (20.2) differ one from each other very profoundly.

In fact, taking into account representation (20.A), for the economy to be 'viable' it is *sufficient* that condition (20.1) be verified; in other words, it is sufficient that from each unit of the wheat produced per unit of time *any* quantity left over for consumption (and, in the case, for investment and exports also) would do. In this case one could affirm that the economy is 'productive'. For example, if $a = 0.8$, the economy is 'viable', for $1 - 0.8 > 0$.

By contrast, taking as a reference representation (20.B), and supposing $c = 0.4$, formula (20.2) leads to $1 - (0.8 + 0.4) < 0$, and therefore the economy is obviously '*non*-viable', simply because each unit of the wheat produced per unit of time would not be sufficient to replace *all* the quantity of the wheat used for its own production, that is quantity a (used as means of production) *plus* quantity c (used as means of sustenance for the labourers).

The crucial difference between the two alternative criteria for ascertaining 'viability' – by comparing (20.1) and (20.2) – lies in the inclusion or not of the workers' subsistence in defining the condition of the economy 'viability', or, which turns out to be the same thing, in considering essential or not the quantity of labour necessary for the production of wheat – as can be seen at a glance by comparing (20.A) with (20.B) or (20.C). At the basis of these alternative approaches there exist radically different *conceptions* of the economy and of its functioning – as will be seen in the sequel.

The above preliminary considerations might be put also in a different way.

By supposing condition (20.1) verified, the equation $(1 - a)x = y$ has a unique solution $x \geq 0$ *for any* $y \geq 0$, where $x =$ total quantity of wheat produced, $y =$ net quantity of wheat produced.

The practical problem to solve, in this respect, consists in the choice of the net quantity of wheat y that society would like to have at its disposal. In general, such a quantity could be fixed at any level whatsoever, and the above equation would continue to have an economic meaningful solution. The fixing of this quantity, however, while it encounters the obvious limit of the *total* amount of the labour force as well as of the available 'productive capacity' of the economy at any given point of time, does appear absolutely unconnected with the quantity of labour required *per unit of product* and, as a consequence, it does appear unconnected also with the corresponding subsistence for the workers. In fact, the 'viability' condition expressed by (20.1), by making reference to a representation of the economy which straightforwardly puts out of the picture the quantity of labour required per unit of product, puts *out* of the picture at the same time the subsistence for the workers. As the net product y could be fixed at a level *independently* of these subsistence, the former might in general be fixed at a level *inferior* to the latter, with the uneasy consequence that the economy could be considered 'viable' according to condition (20.1) but, *at the same time*, 'unable' to secure workers' subsistence – as is plainly evident from the simple numerical example given above. In such a circumstance workers' subsistence should be forced to be *reduced* within the limits imposed by the *technological constraint* – as expressed by the quantity *a* of wheat used as means of production. This result is the mere reflection of having taken into account the *technological* constraint only, leaving out the notion of 'viability' the *social* constraint, given by the subsistence for the workers. On reflection, however, the exclusion of workers' subsistence appears quite strange – suffices it to notice that labour is needed in each and every process of production.

The 'viability' condition (20.1) could *formally* be modified by simply substituting *a* + *c* for *a* in the corresponding expression. In this way, one might be induced to think that workers' necessary productive consumption has found its proper place. However, this is an illusion. In fact, in such a circumstance condition (20.1) would not be a *general* condition of 'viability' any more, for it would *ipso facto* exclude from the set of 'viable' systems those producing with no surplus – let alone the fact that all the formulas considered above are based on the implicit assumption of constant returns to scale.

The notion of 'viability' – in the form which will be considered in the present chapter – has been explicitly and consistently put forward by Sraffa (1960). Before examining it in some detail, however, it may worth considering the analogous notions, originally given at different times, by others, specifically by Hawkins and Simon (1949), by Gale (1960) and by Pasinetti (1977).

Hawkins and Simon's paper (1949) can conventionally be taken as the starting point in the study of the notion of 'viability' in economic analysis. The publication of that paper originated from a mathematical mistake contained in a lemma stated by Hawkins in his previous (1948) paper. The proof of that lemma, in fact, was 'defective'. It referred to a system of n linear homogeneous equations of the type $\mathbf{Bx} = \mathbf{0}$, which was actually the 'closed' Leontief system (1941),[2] with the square matrix $\mathbf{B}$ of rank $n - 1$ and determinant equal to zero, the elements of the matrix $\mathbf{B}$ being $b_{ij} = a_{ij}$, for $i \neq j$, and $b_{ii} = a_{ii} - 1$, for $i = j$, with the 'technical' coefficients of production $a_{ij} \geq 0$, $\forall\, i, j$, with $1 - a_{ii} > 0$, $\forall\, i$; whereas vector $\mathbf{x}$ represented the quantities of the commodities produced. The lemma asserted that the system of equations $\mathbf{Bx} = \mathbf{0}$ could be satisfied by a solution with *all* values of equal sign. This was true, however, only for systems composed of three equations at most, but it failed, in the most general case, with systems composed by more than three equations – as was demonstrated through a counter-example produced by Hawkins and Simon (1949: 246).

A fundamental feature of the 'closed' Leontief model – which Hawkins and Simon in their joint paper were referring to – should be noted: the nth column and the nth row of the matrix of the production coefficients refer to 'final demand' (consumption, investment, exports) and to labour coefficients respectively. Thus, each of them is *formally* assimilated, respectively, to any column representing *input* and to any row representing *output*. The *transition* to the 'open' Leontief model is operationally made by 'detaching' from the original matrix of the 'closed' model the column of the 'final demand' coefficients and the row of the labour coefficients.[3] It should also be noted that this transition implies not only a *formal* manipulation of the type referred to now, but it also implies a *substantive* change in the representation of the economy, to the effe that in the 'open' model a neat separation is definitely established between the 'technical' coefficients of production, which reflects the actual technical knowledge existing in the economy at a given point of time, and the heterogeneous elements composing the 'final demand', such as exports, investments and consumption, each one of them essentially influenced by distinct forces. At the basis of that separation – it is worth noticing – it lies a well defined *theoretical* approach, in which the *objective* data of the technology are given the crucial role of representing the essential 'core' of the productive system.

The 'open' Leontief model can then be formally treated as a non-homogeneous system of $n - 1$ linear equations of the type $(\mathbf{I} - \mathbf{A})\mathbf{x} = \mathbf{y}$, where $\mathbf{I}$ = identity matrix, $\mathbf{A} = (n - 1) \times (n - 1)$ matrix of the 'technical' coefficients of production, $\mathbf{x} = (n - 1) \times 1$ output vector, $\mathbf{y} = (n - 1) \times 1$ 'final demand' vector. Within this context, Hawkins and Simon (1949: 247), established a necessary and sufficient condition for the solution to the equation $(\mathbf{I} - \mathbf{A})\mathbf{x} = \mathbf{y}$ to be positive,[4] with the immediate implication for the economy, characterized by a 'technical' matrix satisfying the condition referred to now, of being able to produce *any* list of goods, and, in particular, any list of *consumption goods*. In the simple economy of the first section of the chapter, above, condition (20.1) corresponds to the Hawkins and Simon 'viability' condition.

It is worth noticing, therefore, the *exclusive priority* attributed by Hawkins and Simon to the 'technical' coefficients of production in determining the 'viability' of the system, in contrast with the *subordinate* role attributed instead to consumption. This is plainly evident from the structure of the equations given by Hawkins and Simon and explicitly admitted by themselves in stating the last equation of the 'closed' Leontief system being 'linearly dependent on the first m equations' (ibid.: 246) – these m equations actually correspond to the $n - 1$ equations of the system $(\mathbf{I} - \mathbf{A})\mathbf{x} = \mathbf{y}$, due to the symbols used by Hawkins and Simon in the transition from the 'closed' to the 'open' model. (It must be added that if it is necessary that the determinant of the matrix of the 'closed' Leontief model must be equal to zero for the system to have a solution, it is also true that *any* row (or *any* column) can be considered linearly dependent on the remaining ones.)[5]

The 'open' Leontief model remains also the basic reference in the far more refined analysis subsequently made by Gale (1960), though he introduces – as will be presently seen – the crucial distinction between a 'simple Leontief model' characterized by the 'technical' coefficients of production only *and independently of the labour coefficients*, and a 'simple Leontief model' *with labour explicitly considered*.

Gale (1960: 294) initially takes into account a linear single-production model having equal number of goods and processes. He then puts the *feasibility* question: given a non-negative square matrix of technical coefficients $\mathbf{A}$, does a program exist which actually makes it possible for the production of given quantities of goods? The problem consists in ascertaining whether the equation

$$\mathbf{x}T\,(\mathbf{I} - \mathbf{A}) = \mathbf{y}T$$

has a meaningful solution; in other words, if there exist levels of activity (given by the vector **x**) which allow for the *net* production of quantities of goods (given by the vector **y** $\geq$ **0**).

As a preliminary, Gale defines as *productive* the above 'simple linear production model' if there exists a non-negative vector x' such that $x'T > x'TA$, and consequently he defines as *productive* the same matrix **A**. He is then in a position to prove (ibid.: 296–7), the following theorem:

If the matrix **A** *is productive, then for any vector* **y** $\geq$ **0** *the equation*

$$xT\,(I - A) = yT$$

has a unique non-negative solution.

Compared with the notion of 'viability' stated by Hawkins and Simon, Gale's notion asserts once again that the 'viability' of a system is *exclusively* based upon the 'technical' conditions of production, though a different formal procedure is pursued and different analytical tools are thereby utilized.[6] Moreover, it is confirmed that an economy is 'viable' if it is capable of producing a *net* physical flow of commodities, over and above the requirements dictated by the 'technology' matrix.[7] But the very novelty of Gale's analysis in that respect lies, as mentioned above, in the explicit introduction of labour that he makes in his second model. The taking into account of the labour means two things at the same time: (i) the introduction of a *definite* time-horizon within which the goods must be available for consumption, (ii) the recognition of the unavoidable *limited* amount of resources available at a given point of time, in particular the *existing* amount of labour force. His notion of 'viability' is thus far more restrictive than Hawkins and Simon's, although he leaves the implications of the matter without further investigation.

It is only with Sraffa (1960), however, that the notion of 'viability' takes on a completely different characterization with respect to those so far considered.

From the very beginning of his book, Sraffa introduces the notion of 'viable economic system', that is a system capable of being reduced to a self-replacing state 'by changing the proportions in which the individual equations enter it' (1960: 5). A self-replacing state (within a single-product industries framework) is a state in which the quantity produced of each commodity is not less than the quantity totally employed all over the system (both as means of production as well as consumption for the workers).[8]

The first numerical table given by Sraffa on the opening pages of his book is hereafter reproduced to make discussion easier:

280 qr. wheat + 12 t. iron → 400 qr. wheat

120 qr. wheat + 8 t. iron → 20 t. iron

It represents an economic system in a self-replacing state with no surplus, whose main features are the following:

1   Each quantity of the commodities appearing on the left side of the arrows is *jointly* used 'in part as sustenance for those who work, and for the rest as means of production' (ibid.: 3). For each of them, therefore, it is not necessary to know the *proportion* of the quantities corresponding to the two distinct possible uses.
2   Sraffa defines 'methods of production and productive consumption', called simply 'methods of production', the whole set of the numerical relations given by the quantities of the commodities used and produced in the system.

Exchange values exclusively spring from those numerical values which, were they adopted, would allow each industry to obtain back, after the exchange, the necessary amount of the commodities needed to start production again.

It is important to stress this very feature of the exchange values of the commodities: they have to be regarded as the basic reference *for making the reproduction of the whole system actually realizable*. The property of 'viability' is then the other side of the coin, for it expresses the *possibility* of the system to continue production over time. That possibility, it must be emphasized, is the reflection of the specific numerical relations existing among *all* the commodities used and produced in the economy which, in turn, are not only the result of a particular technological state existing in the economy at a given point of time; rather, they are the result of the far more important *entire history* which has been characterizing the society considered, namely, the complex *social and political relations among the people* which have progressively come into being over time.[9] By looking back at the above numerical table representing the economy, it is worth noticing that *no distinction* has been made between the quantity of each commodity used as a means of production and the quantity of it used for the sustenance of the workers. *Both* types of commodities used for production are situated on the same footing, for they exert the same function. This way of representing the economy does not undergo any substantial change in the case a surplus were produced. In this circumstance, even when the workers would share with the surplus, no reason would exist in separating out the means of production from the means of sustenance for the workers. It is just for not 'tampering with the traditional wage concept' (and thus for the necessity of treating the subsistence wage and the surplus wage as a whole) that Sraffa (1960) separates out the two different components of the commodities used for production, at the crucial condition, however, that the means of sustenance for the workers still continue to exert 'their influence on prices and profits', though 'in devious ways' (ibid.: 10).

The crucial point worth noting here is that the commodities used as sustenance for the workers are part and parcel in defining the 'viability' of the system. In terms of the simple economy of the first section of the chapter, above, Sraffa's 'viability' condition would be expressed by formula (20.2). This marks the very difference between the Sraffian notion of 'viability' on the one hand, and the analogous notion put forward by Hawkins and Simon and Gale, on the other. The definition of 'viability' of the latter rests exclusively confined to the *technology* of the economy, with the social and political aspects put out of the picture, and the 'viability' of the economy manifests itself in the potential existence of a *surplus* of commodities on which consumption goods can find their place *as a residue*, heavily depending upon the tenet of the technology. By contrast, 'viability' within the Sraffian framework is synonymous of *survival* of the system as a whole – a characteristically *holistic* goal to be pursued by *any* human community.[10]

It is worth noticing, in this connection, the different meaning to be attached to the notion of 'surplus' within Sraffa's representation of an economy. The specificity of the Sraffian notion of 'surplus' – contrasted with analogous notions of 'surplus' which can be found in the literature – clearly emerges once the necessary commodities for workers' subsistence are *systematically* inserted into the picture, making in this way their role to be directly exerted on the *reproduction* of the system. The economy represented by the numerical table already referred to above is actually an economy with *no surplus*. Virtually, the economy there represented might possibly have a 'surplus' were subsistence proportionally reduced or the methods of production were 'improved', or both things at the same time. But this is another way of saying that a 'surplus' *does not exist as such*.[11] Rather, it is essentially a *social* construction, an ultimate reflection of *ethical, religious and political values* existing in the system and shaping, in a more or less stable way, the relationships among people.[12]

With or without a surplus the Sraffa models so far considered have in common the same key feature: the labour income (or the subsistence wage, in the surplus economy) is determined from *outside the system of production*. This means, more specifically, that the commodity composition of the subsistence bundle is determined *independently of and prior to any economic valuation*. What is more, the economic valuation of the system, through the production prices, is *based*, among the other data given by the means of production and the commodities produced, also on the set of commodities necessary as sustenance for the workers.

It is interesting to compare Sraffa's treatment of labour consumption with the analogous treatment of consumption (in which labour consumption is obviously included) made by Hawkins and Simon (1949) and by Gale (1960) in their respective analyses. In Sraffa, as has been seen, the set of commodities necessary for the workers is included among the initial data of the model; it can be seen as a sort of 'constraint' for the system to be respected, neither more nor less than the existing methods of production. It should also be noted that the services of labour are *not* considered as a commodity.

On the contrary, in the treatment of 'viability' made by Hawkins and Simon and by Gale – as has been made clear in the previous sections of the chapter – consumption appears merely as a *determined* amount of commodities instead of being a *determining* variable.

In a pure competitive framework, a way is open to the *market* to be the ultimate responsible for the determination of *real* wages: the law of supply and demand will thus govern the price structure, which means that *any* commodity will be valued according to its *relative scarcity* as is 'objectively' displayed in the market. As a consequence, labour force – treated as a commodity like any other – will be priced according to the same criterion (relative scarcity) and the corresponding real wage will be fixed at a level which, in general, will result *independent of any standard of subsistence* generally recognized in the economy considered. As a matter of fact, real wages 'arbitrarily' fixed at levels different from the 'equilibrium' level are considered a 'hindrance' to the 'smooth working' of the market, before, or independently of, any consideration be put forward as regards the necessity or the 'social reasonableness' of fixing *some* minimum level.[13]

From the above picture it would thus *seem* that the market, in determining the commodity prices, worked in the most 'objective' way, in so far as it treats *any* commodity on the same footing as any other, by applying to each of them the same basic principle of 'relative scarcity'. However, it would be incorrect to attribute that kind of 'objectivity' to the working of the market. In fact, behind that market mechanism a subtle *value judgement* has crept in, that of considering the 'labour force' just a commodity like any other.[14] This particular value judgement is indeed absolutely and unequivocal non-existent within the Sraffa framework, where even non-labour incomes (such as profits, for example) are *not* determined on the basis of the 'relative scarcity' principle either.

It seems quite natural to conclude, up to this point, that the far more 'stringent' definition of 'viability' (in the sense specified above, because workers' sustenance is included in the definition) is that provided by Sraffa, as compared with the analogous notion provided instead by the authors so far considered. It still remains the more 'stringent' notion of 'viability', as will be seen in a moment, even in comparison with that provided by Pasinetti (1977).

In the part of his analysis, relevant to the notion of 'viability' here discussed, Pasinetti (1977: 36), starts by taking into account an input-output table (Table 20.1): in which the symbols *w*, *i* and *t* stand respectively for the commodities wheat, iron and turkeys – wheat and iron are measured in tons, whereas turkeys are measured in grosses.

Table 20.1 Flow of commodities in physical terms

	w		*i*		*t*		
w	240	+	90	+	120	=	450
i	12	+	6	+	3	=	21
t	18	+	12	+	30	=	60
	↓		↓		↓		
	450 (*w*)		21 (*i*)		60 (*t*)		

Source: Pasinetti (1977:36).

As can be easily recognized, the quantity of each commodity used in production *jointly* refers to the means of production and to the means of sustenance for the workers. What Pasinetti does immediately afterwards, however, is just to provide a different table, by starting from the previous one, in order 'to distinguish the *technical* relations between the different industries from the relations between these industries and the final demand (consumption and investment)' (ibid., italics added). The Table 20.1 is thus modified as Table 20.2, in which the final row shows the annual flow of labour services to each industry (measured in man-years), whereas the final column shows the total consumption.

What Pasinetti has actually done is an operation similar to that usually made in the transition from the 'closed' to the 'open' Leontief model – putting in this way the very premise for a definition of 'viability' in which the consumption of the workers are evidently put out of the central representation of the economy, in opposition to the analogous definition of 'viability' which can instead be attributed to Sraffa.

In fact, by taking as the initial reference the 'closed' Leontief model (in the form already seen at the beginning of the present chapter, that is $\mathbf{Bx} = \mathbf{0}$), Pasinetti explicitly emphasizes the strict *dependency* of consumption on the techniques of production:

> the first $(n - 1)$ columns represent the technical coefficients of the production processes. These coefficients are given by technology. In general, then, we cannot expect to find among the first $(n - 1)$ columns one that just happens to be linearly dependent on the others...
>
> Only the nth column remains to be considered. This column clearly *can* be linearly dependent on the others, since it contains a set of magnitudes concerning consumption which are not technically given and which can be adjusted. Condition [according to which the determinant of the matrix $\mathbf{B}$ must be equal to zero for the system to have solutions other than zero] therefore simply amounts to stating that this column *must* be linearly dependent on the others ... And this is fairly obvious. There can be no economic system in which per capita consumption levels are independent of the matrix of technical coefficients.
>
> (Pasinetti 1977: 56)

Table 20.2 Flow of commodities and labour services

	w	i	t	Final sector		
w	186	54	30	180	=	450
i	12	6	3	–	=	21
T	9	6	15	30	=	60
Final sector	18	12	30			
	↓	↓	↓			
	450	21	60			

Source: Pasinetti (1977:376).

Then, in his comment on the economic meaning of the solution to the 'open' Leontief model $(\mathbf{I} - \mathbf{A})\mathbf{x} = \mathbf{y}$ – according to which the maximum eigenvalue of matrix $\mathbf{A}$ should be less than unity – he says:

> It implies [...] that the technical properties of the economic system must be such as to permit the production of *at least* some commodity in addition to those needed for the replacement of the means of production used up in the production process. If an economic system were technically so backward that it was not even capable of reproducing the inputs which it had used up, then it could not survive (i.e., it would not be *viable*).
>
> (ibid.: 63)

In this way Pasinetti made a neat distinction between the strictly 'technological' aspect of the production system and the necessary productive consumption of the workers – that distinction being perfectly in line with the less 'stringent' notion of 'viability' provided by authors like Hawkins and Simon and Gale previously discussed but plainly in opposition to the analogous 'stringent' definition given by Sraffa.[15]

The means of subsistence are considered, within the Sraffian framework, an indispensable premise for production. Their inclusion into the formal model is of the utmost importance both from an *analytical* as well as from a *substantial* point of view.

As regards the former, Sraffa successfully provided a *consistent* framework of representing an economy centred upon the unavoidable and basic core of any economy, that is its production system. Although a similar attempt was already made by the old classical economists and by Marx, nonetheless their models, as is well known, were *partially* ruined by the respective theories of value they maintained. Sraffa, by incorporating many features of the Classical and Marxian approach within his own model (like the fundamental notion of 'subsistence', for example),[16] provided in addition a renewed function to production prices, that of allowing the reproduction of the system as a whole.

As regards the substantial point of view, the inclusion of the means of subsistence into the framework can be regarded as a real breakthrough for a generalization and for an extension of the main results.

A generalization, and an extension at the same time, can be suggested by considering alternative *profiles* of 'viability'. In the original Sraffian model, the subsistence bundle that a unit of labour receives can be thought, in the first instance, to *exclusively* meet the necessities of a *single* worker. But any worker, in general, can be regarded as belonging to a *household*. The subsistence can thus obviously be 'enlarged' so as to cover also some or all components of the household. The question is: which members of the household? Quite naturally the extension should be first reserved to the 'non-working' wife/husband, then to sons and to old parents. The reasons for this extension can be found not only on social grounds but also on economic ones: although the wife/husband is supposed not to work *directly* in a production process, nevertheless she/he is *indirectly* involved in production, for she/he provides services to the worker Moreover, if production is seen as a process taking place over time cycle by cycle, then the sons for the future and the old parents for the past can be seen a *instrumental* for the *reproduction* of the system. Apart from the strictly eco nomic reason of reproduction, subsistence can be also extended to the *disable* people of the family, who by definition cannot be 'productive' in the economi sense. On social and political ground, the 'extension' can continue as to include people other than members of the 'family' traditionally conceived.

The point is that whoever the 'beneficiaries' are the model can accommodat their inclusion so as to have a set of alternative profiles of 'viability'. It is wortl noting that each will be based on the circumstance that the commodities that fea ture as inputs to production comprise in part an appropriate or *decent* standard o subsistence, for if a society is to reproduce itself, then it must be such as t permit its members to appear in public without shame.

Notes

1 The author is much grateful to Enrico Bellino, Leonardo Ditta, Peter Edwards an Giorgio Gilibert for the highly valuable suggestions given. The usual caveats apply.
2 The original Leontief models are in Leontief (1941) and (1951).
3 It should be noted, however, that the transition referred to in the text can be seen as a 'application' of the 'closed' model made by some economists other than Leontief - see, for example, Dorfman *et al.* (1958) and Pasinetti (1977).
4 The condition was that all the principal minors of the matrix $(I - A)$ be positive Nikaidô (1970: 13–17), proved a theorem according to which the Hawkins–Simo 'viability' condition is equivalent to the two following conditions: (i) for some posit ive vector y the equation $(I - A)x = y$ has a non-negative solution x, (ii) for any non negative vector y the equation $(I - A)x = y$ has a non-negative solution x.
5 There is no space in the present context to discuss the disputable application made b Fujimoto and Fujita (2006) of the Hawkins and Simon condition in their criticism o the so-called 'commodity exploitation theorem'. Further reflections on the Hawkin and Simon condition can be found in Jeong (1982, 1984), and Fujita (1991).
6 In opposition to Hawkins and Simon, but without explicitly mentioning them, Gal (1960: x) says:

> It is a true theorem that a Leontief model is capable of producing a positive bill o goods if and only if the principal minors of the production matrix are all positive This fact, however, gives us no new economic insight into the properties o Leontief models because there is no economic interpretation to be attached to th principal minors.

7 Schwartz (1961), following the tradition of Hawkins and Simon (1949) and of Gal (1960) (who consider 'viable' an economy if it is capable of producing a *physical sur plus*), expresses some ambiguity in his regarding the workers' consumption 'as *socially determined* "living wage"' (Schwartz 1961: 14, italics added), while making at the same time, explicit reference to the Walrasian tradition (which makes consump tion demand dependent upon prices and income distribution). The latter position i functional to Schwartz in order to justify the legitimacy in separating the workers consumption goods from the other 'technological' elements of the Leontief matrix.
8 A constructive method of ascertaining the 'viability' of a system in the Sraffa frame work can be found in Chiodi (1992). Chiodi (1998) deals with some problems con

nected with the 'non-self-replacing' states. On the origin of the first equations in Sraffa (1960) see de Vivo (2004) and Gilibert (2004).

9 The importance of the history for the humanistic disciplines is evaluated by Moog (1964). On this work cf. Chiodi and Ditta (2004).

10 Reflections on the holistic feature of Sraffa's 1960 work are contained in Chiodi (2008).

11 On this specific point cf. Pearson (1957).

12 Reflections on ethical aspects in Sraffa can be found in Edwards (2008). Cf. also Chiodi and Ditta (2008).

13 Dorfman *et al.* (1958: 359), for example, assert that in the case of absolute redundancy of labour 'only the obvious social and sociological reasons explain why positive wages are paid'.

14 Though in a different context, some ethical implications of considering a good as commodity are worked out in Chiodi and Edwards (2006).

15 In his mathematical formulation of the Ricardian system, Pasinetti (1960) had instead inserted the inequality $f'(0) > \bar{x}$, $\bar{x}$ = natural real wage rate, as a property of the technical production function $X_1 = f(N_1)$, X_1 = physical quantity of corn produced in one year, number of workers employed in the corn production.

16 In this respect cf. Stirati (1992), Pivetti (2000) and Picchio (2004).

References

Chiodi, G. (1992) 'On Sraffa's notion of viability', *Studi Economici*, 46: 5–23.

—— (1998) 'On non-self-replacing states', *Metroeconomica*, February: 97–107.

—— (2008) 'Beyond capitalism: Sraffa's economic theory', in G. Chiodi and L. Ditta (eds), *Sraffa or An Alternative Economics*, Basingstoke: Palgrave Macmillan.

Chiodi, G. and Ditta, L. (2004) 'Economia e processi di sviluppo: la sorprendente lezione di Vianna Moog', *Sociologia e Ricerca Sociale*, 74: 12–36.

—— (2008) 'Introduction', in G. Chiodi and L Ditta (eds), *Sraffa or An Alternative Economics*, Basingstoke: Palgrave Macmillan.

Chiodi, G. and Edwards, P. (2006) 'Economics, ethics, commodities, alienation and the market: Reflections on issues raised by Titmuss', *Quaderni di Ricerca* n. 5, Dipartimento Innovazione e Società, Università di Roma 'La Sapienza', Rome: Aracne Editrice.

De Vivo, G. (2004) 'Da Ricardo e Marx a Produzione di merci a mezzo di merci', *Convegno Piero Sraffa (Roma, 11–12 Febbraio 2003), Atti dei Convegni Lincei 200*, Rome: Accademia Nazionale dei Lincei.

Dorfman, R., Samuelson, P.A. and Solow, R.M. (1958) *Linear Programming and Economic Analysis*, Tokyo: McGraw-Hill, Kogakusha.

Edwards, P. (2008) 'Sraffa: Notes on moralizing, money, and economic prudence', in G. Chiodi and L. Ditta (eds), *Sraffa or An Alternative Economics*, Basingstoke: Palgrave Macmillan.

Fujimoto, T. and Fujita Y. (2006) 'Refutation of the commodity exploitation theorem', *CAES Working Paper series*, WP-2006–003, Fukuoka University.

Fujita, Y. (1991) 'A further note on the correct interpretation of the Hawkins–Simon conditions', *Journal of Macroeconomics*, 13(2): 381–4.

Gale, D. (1960) *The Theory of Linear Economic Models*, New York: McGraw-Hill.

Gilibert, G. (2004) 'Le equazioni svelate. Breve storia delle equazioni di Produzione di merci a mezzo di merci', *Convegno Piero Sraffa (Roma, 11–12 Febbraio 2003), Atti dei Convegni Lincei 200*, Rome: Accademia Nazionale dei Lincei.

Hawkins, D. (1948) 'Some conditions of macroeconomic stability', *Econometrica*, 4(16): 309–22.

Hawkins, D. and Simon, H.A. (1949) 'Note: Some conditions of macroeconomic stability', *Econometrica*, 3/4(17): 245–8.

Jeong, K. (1982) 'Direct and indirect requirements: A correct economic interpretation of the Hawkins–Simon conditions', *Journal of Macroeconomics*, 4(3): 349–56.

—— (1984) 'The relation between two different notions of direct and indirect input requirements', *Journal of Macroeconomics*, 6(4): 473–6.

Leontief, W. (1941) *The Structure of American Economy, 1919–1939. An Empirical Application of Equilibrium Analysis*, Cambridge, MA: Harvard University Press.

—— (1951) *The Structure of American Economy, 1919–1939. An Empirical Application of Equilibrium Analysis*, 2nd edn, New York: Oxford University Press.

Moog, V. (1964) *Bandeirantes and Pioneers*, trans. L.L. Barrett, New York: George Braziller.

Nikaidô, H. (1970) *Introduction to Sets and Mappings in Modern Economics*, Amsterdam: North-Holland.

Pasinetti, L. (1960) 'A mathematical formulation of the Ricardian system', *Review of Economic Studies*, February: 78–98.

—— (1977) *Lectures on The Theory of Production*, London and Basingstoke: Macmillan.

Pearson, H.W. (1957) 'The economy has no surplus: A critique of a theory of development', in K. Polanyi, C.M. Arensberg and H.W. Pearson (eds) (1971), *Trade and Market in the Early Empire. Economies in History and Theory*, Chicago, IL: Gateway Edition, Henry Regnery Company (originally published in 1957).

Picchio, A. (2004) 'Hay, carrots, bread and roses: Subsistence and surplus wage in Sraffa's papers', unpublished paper.

Pivetti, M. (2000) 'Il concetto di salario come "costo e sovrappiù"', in M. Pivetti (ed.), *Piero Sraffa. Contributi per una biografia intellettuale*, Rome: Carocci editore.

Schwartz, J.T. (1961) *Lectures on the Mathematical Method in Analytical Economics*, New York: Gordon and Beach.

Sraffa, P. (1960) *Production of Commodities by Means of Commodities. Prelude to a Critique of Economic Theory*, Cambridge: Cambridge University Press.

Stirati, A. (1992) 'Unemployment, institutions and the living standard', *Contributions to Political Economy*, 11: 41–66.

21 A disequilibrium growth cycle model with differential savings

Serena Sordi

Introduction

Over the last four decades a significant body of literature has emerged inspired by Goodwin's (1967, 1972) approach to growth cycle modelling. Vela K. Velupillai (see, for example, Velupillai 1979, 1982a, 1982b, 1983, 2006 and Fitoussi and Velupillai 1987) – in his path to developing an approach to macrodynamic modelling rooted in the Cambridge tradition and in particular in Goodwin's model and Kaldor's theory of income distribution and technical progress – has contributed importantly to this literature. With respect to Goodwin's model, he has among other things concentrated on how to relax the extreme ('classical') assumption about savings behaviour originally made by Goodwin and on how to remove from the model the assumption of equilibrium in the goods market (an assumption in contrast with the spirit of previous contributions by Goodwin himself, e.g. Goodwin 1948, 1951). In doing this, he has also strongly emphasised the importance of bifurcation theory – in particular of the Hopf bifurcation theorem – for a qualitative analysis of macrodynamic models with three-dimensional – or higher – dynamical systems.

This chapter builds on these basic recurring themes of Vela's work with the purpose of highlighting their relevance for growth cycle modelling. My purpose is in particular to build a growth cycle model with both differential savings propensities and disequilibrium in the goods market. This is done in order to show (1) that both modifications of the model entail an increase of the dimensionality of the state-space of its dynamical system and (2) that the resulting four-dimensional, nonlinear dynamical system has a structure such that the existence part of the Hopf bifurcation theorem can be easily applied.

The remainder of the chapter is organised as follows. In the first section we give a brief overview of the modified version of the model. The next section discusses the dynamics of the model, giving both conditions for limit cycle solutions and some numerical evidence. A few concluding and summarising results are finally given in the last section.

The model

I shall consider, as a starting point for further modifications, the generalisations of Goodwin's growth cycle model presented in Sordi (2001, 2003). The unifying element of the latter contributions is the attempt to relax one or another of the simplifying assumptions introduced by Goodwin in order to obtain a dynamical system of the Lotka–Volterra type. In Sordi (2001) it is shown that the relaxation of the classical assumption about savings and the consideration of the differential savings hypothesis à la Kaldor-Pasinetti causes the dynamical system of the model to become of the third order.[1] In Sordi (2003), on the other hand, assuming for simplicity that the workers' propensity to save is equal to zero, I have considered a different generalisation – which is obtained by introducing into the model an independent investment function and an adjustment mechanism to goods market disequilibrium – and shown that this modification too causes the dynamical system of the model to become of the third order. In both cases, the steps required to apply the Hopf bifurcation theorem to prove the possibility of periodic solutions for the model are simple ones. In the present contribution I intend to put together the two generalisations by considering a version of the model with the assumption of both differential savings and disequilibrium in the goods market. To concentrate on these two modifications, I use a version of the model that is otherwise as close as possible to Goodwin's simple original formulation.

The notation and basic assumptions I use throughout the chapter are listed in Table 21.1.

In addition to the assumptions of a constant exponential growth of both labour force and productivity of labour I borrow from Goodwin (1967), the building blocks of the present version of the model can be briefly described as follows:

Real-wage dynamics:

$$\hat{w} = f(v, \hat{v}) = h(v) + \lambda \hat{v}, \; h(v) > 0, \; h(v) > 0, \; h(0) < 0 \forall v, \; \lim_{v \to 1} h(v) = \infty, \; \lambda > 0 \quad (21.1)$$

This more general formulation of the Phillips curve-type dynamics for the real wage is intended to incorporate Phillips' original idea that labour's bargaining power will be higher in phases where the employment is high, and the more so the more the employment rate tends to rise (see Phillips 1958: 299). To the best of my knowledge, this formulation was first introduced into a modified version of Goodwin's model by Cugno and Montrucchio (1982: 97–8) and then employed by other authors, for example by Sportelli (1995: 42–3). In order to simplify and concentrate on the two above mentioned modifications of the model, I retain the original formulation in real terms of wage dynamics.

Savings behaviour:

$$S_c = s_c P_c = s_c r k_c = s_c(1 - u)q\varepsilon \quad (21.2)$$

$$S_w = s_w(wl + P_w) = s_w(wl + rk_w) = s_w q - s_w(1 - u)q\varepsilon \quad (21.3)$$

Table 21.1 Notation and basic assumptions

for any variable x, $\dot{x} = dx/dt$, $\hat{x} = \dot{x}/x$
q, output
q^e, expected output
l, employment
$q/l = a = a_0 e^{\alpha t}$, $\alpha > 0$, labour productivity
$n = n_0 e^{\beta t}$, $\beta > 0$, labour force
$g_n = \alpha + \beta$, natural rate of growth
g, rate of growth of output
w, real wage
$u = wl/q$, share of wages
$v = l/n$, employment rate
$k = k_c + k_w$, capital stock
$k_c = \varepsilon k$, capital stock held by capitalists
$k_w = (1 - \varepsilon)k$, capital stock held by workers
k^d, desired capital stock
$\sigma = k/q$, capital-output ratio
$\varepsilon = k_c/k$, proportion of capital held by capitalists
P_c, capitalists' profits
P_w, workers' profits
$P = P_c + P_w$
$r = P/k = (1 - u)q/k = (1 - u)/\sigma$, rate of profit
s_w, S_w, workers' propensity to save and workers' savings respectively
s_c, S_c, capitalists' propensity to save and capitalists' savings respectively
$0 \leq s_w < s_c \leq 1$
$S = S_w + S_c$

This formulation incorporates Kaldor's (1956) differential savings hypothesis according to which both capitalists and workers save a fixed proportion of their incomes with the propensity to save of the latter strictly less than the propensity to save of the former.[2]

Investment equations:

$$\dot{k}_w = s_w(wl + P_w) = s_w q - s_w(1 - u)q\varepsilon \tag{21.4}$$

$$\dot{k} = \xi(k^d - k), \quad \xi > 0 \tag{21.5}$$

$$\dot{k}_c = \dot{k} - \dot{k}_w \tag{21.6}$$

This formulation incorporates the idea that, with regard to investment, capitalists and workers behave in rather different ways.[3] It appears reasonable to assume that workers own their shares of the stock of capital only indirectly, through loans to the capitalists for a return of interest (Pasinetti 1962: 171). To simplify, in equation (21.4) I have assumed that workers loan out to the capitalists the full amount of their savings, this influencing the number but not the logic of my exercise. Capitalists, on the other hand, decide how much to invest bearing

in mind the amount of output they want to produce. Thus, once they have estab
lished the desired level of production and consequently also the desired stock o
capital, they decide their investment – on the basis of a flexible accelerato
mechanism – in order to close the gap between the desired stock of capital and
the actual stock (see Goodwin 1948). This is formalised in equation (21.5) where
k^d is related to expected output and I have assumed that expectations are of the
extrapolative type so that (see Gandolfo 1997: 219):

$$k^d = \overline{\sigma}q^e = \overline{\sigma}(q + \tau\dot{q}), \ \tau > 0$$

Thus, (21.5) becomes:

$$\dot{k} = \xi(\overline{\sigma} + \overline{\sigma}\tau\dot{q} - \sigma)q, \ \xi > 0 \tag{21.7}$$

Eventually, as specified in equation (21.6), the variation of the amount of the
stock of capital held by capitalists simply follows as a residual, after the amoun
of total investment has been decided by them on the basis of the flexible acceler
ator and workers have decided how much to save and 'loan' to capitalists.

Goods market adjustment mechanism:

$$\dot{q} = g_n q + \eta(\dot{k} - S) \tag{21.8}$$

According to this formulation, the dynamics of output is governed by ar
error-adjustment mechanism such that output reacts to excess demand taking
account also of a trend component.[4] Choosing the time-unit in such a way tha
$\xi = 1$ and substituting from (21.7), equation (21.8) becomes:

$$\hat{q} = g_n + \eta[\overline{\sigma} + \overline{\sigma}\tau\hat{q} - \sigma - s_w - (s_c - s_w)(1 - u)\varepsilon]$$

from which:

$$\hat{q} = \frac{g_n + \eta(\overline{\sigma} - s_w)}{1 - \eta\overline{\sigma}\tau} - \frac{\eta}{1 - \eta\overline{\sigma}\tau}[\sigma + (s_c - s_w)(1 - u)\varepsilon] \tag{21.9}$$

Derivation of the dynamical system of the model

We are now in a position to derive the reduced form dynamical system of the
model. First, from the definition of the variable v, equation (21.9) and the
assumptions about the dynamics of n and a (see Table 21.1) it follows that:

$$\hat{v} = \frac{\eta(\overline{\sigma} - s_w + \overline{\sigma}\tau g_n)}{1 - \eta\overline{\sigma}\tau} - \frac{\eta}{1 - \eta\overline{\sigma}\tau}[\sigma + (s_c - s_w)(1 - u)\varepsilon] \tag{21.10}$$

Second, from the definition of the variable u and equation (21.1), we obtain:

$$\hat{u} = h(v) + \lambda \hat{v} - \alpha \tag{21.11}$$

Moreover, from (21.7) and (21.9):

$$\hat{k} = \left(\frac{\bar{\sigma} - \sigma}{\sigma}\right) + \frac{\bar{\sigma}\tau}{\sigma}\left[\frac{g_n + \eta(\bar{\sigma} - s_w)}{1 - \eta\bar{\sigma}\tau} - \frac{\eta}{1 - \eta\bar{\sigma}\tau}[\sigma + (s_c - s_w)(1 - u)\varepsilon]\right] \tag{21.12}$$

so that:

$$\hat{\varepsilon} = \hat{k}\left(\frac{k}{k_c} - 1\right) - \frac{\hat{k}_w}{k_c} = \hat{k}\left(\frac{1 - \varepsilon}{\varepsilon}\right) - \left[\frac{s_w - s_w(1 - u)\varepsilon}{\varepsilon\sigma}\right]$$

$$= \frac{(\bar{\sigma} - \sigma)(1 - \varepsilon)}{\sigma\varepsilon} + \frac{\bar{\sigma}\tau(1 - \varepsilon)}{\sigma\varepsilon}\left[\frac{g_n + \eta(\bar{\sigma} - s_w)}{1 - \eta\bar{\sigma}\tau} - \frac{\eta}{1 - \eta\bar{\sigma}\tau}[\sigma + (s_c - s_w)(1 - u)\varepsilon]\right]$$

$$- \left[\frac{s_w - s_w(1 - u)\varepsilon}{\varepsilon\sigma}\right] \tag{21.13}$$

Finally, (21.9) and (21.12) imply that:

$$\bar{\sigma} = \left(\frac{\bar{\sigma} - \sigma}{\sigma}\right) + \left(\frac{\bar{\sigma}\tau - \sigma}{\sigma}\right)\left\{\frac{g_n + \eta(\bar{\sigma} - s_w)}{1 - \eta\bar{\sigma}\tau} - \frac{\eta}{1 - \eta\bar{\sigma}\tau}[\sigma + (s_c - s_w)(1 - u)\varepsilon]\right\} \tag{21.14}$$

Equations (21.10), (21.11), (21.13) and (21.14) form a complete 4D-dynamical system in the four endogenous variables v, u, ε and σ:

$$\dot{v} = \frac{\eta}{1 - \eta\bar{\sigma}\tau}\{\bar{\sigma} - s_w + \bar{\sigma}\tau g_n - \sigma - (s_c - s_w)(1 - u)\varepsilon\}v \tag{21.15}$$

$$\dot{u} = [h(v) + \lambda\hat{v} - \alpha]u = [G(v, u, \varepsilon, \sigma) - \alpha]u \tag{21.16}$$

$$\dot{\varepsilon} = \frac{(\bar{\sigma} - \sigma)(1 - \varepsilon)}{\sigma} + \frac{\bar{\sigma}\tau(1 - \varepsilon)}{\sigma(1 - \eta\bar{\sigma}\tau)}\{g_n + \eta(\bar{\sigma} - s_w) - \eta[\sigma + (s_c - s_w)(1 - u)\varepsilon]\}$$

$$- \left[\frac{s_w - s_w(1 - u)\varepsilon}{\sigma}\right] \tag{21.17}$$

$$\dot{\sigma} = (\bar{\sigma} - \sigma) + \frac{(\bar{\sigma}\tau - \sigma)}{1 - \eta\bar{\sigma}\tau}\{g_n + \eta(\bar{\sigma} - s_w) - \eta[\sigma + (s_c - s_w)(1 - u)\varepsilon]\} \tag{2.18}$$

where the function $G(v, u, \varepsilon, \sigma)$ in equation (21.16) is such that:

$$G_v(v, u, \varepsilon, \sigma) = h'(v) > 0, \quad G_u(v, u, \varepsilon, \sigma) = \frac{\lambda\eta(s_c - s_w)\varepsilon}{1 - \eta\bar{\sigma}\tau}$$

$$G_\varepsilon(v, u, \varepsilon, \sigma) = -\frac{\lambda\eta(s_c - s_w)(1 - u)}{1 - \eta\bar{\sigma}\tau}, \quad G_\sigma(v, u, \varepsilon, \sigma) = -\frac{\lambda\eta}{1 - \eta\bar{\sigma}\tau}$$

Letting $E^+ \equiv (v^+, u^+, \varepsilon^+, v^+)$ stand for the unique positive equilibrium point of the model, from (21.16) it follows that:

$$v^+ - h^{-1}(\alpha)$$

Moreover, we must have:

$$\bar{\sigma} - s_w + \bar{\sigma}\tau g_n - \sigma^+ - (s_c - s_w)(1 - u^+)\varepsilon^+ = 0 \tag{21.19}$$

$$(\bar{\sigma} - \sigma^+)(1 - \varepsilon^+) + \frac{\bar{\sigma}\tau(1 - \varepsilon^+)}{1 - \eta\bar{\sigma}\tau}\{g_n + \eta(\bar{\sigma} - s_w)$$
$$- \eta[\sigma^+ + (s_c - s_w)(1 - u^+)\varepsilon^+]\} - [s_w - s_w(1 - u^+)\varepsilon^+] = 0 \tag{2.20}$$

$$(\bar{\sigma} - \sigma^+) + \frac{(\bar{\sigma}\tau - \sigma^+)}{1 - \eta\bar{\sigma}\tau}\{g_n + \eta(\bar{\sigma} - s_w) - \eta[\sigma^+ + (s_c - s_w)(1 - u^+)\varepsilon^+]\} = 0 \tag{21.21}$$

Substituting from (21.19), (21.20) and (21.21) gives

$$(\bar{\sigma} - \sigma^+)(1 - \varepsilon^+) + \bar{\sigma}\tau(1 - \varepsilon^+)g_n - [s_w - s_w(1 - u)\varepsilon] = 0 \tag{21.22}$$

$$(\bar{\sigma} - \sigma^+) + (\bar{\sigma}\tau - \sigma^+)g_n = 0 \tag{21.23}$$

Thus, from (21.23):

$$\sigma^+ = \frac{\bar{\sigma}(1 + \tau g_n)}{(1 + g_n)} \tag{21.24}$$

Then, substituting (21.24) in (21.19) and (21.22),

$$\bar{\sigma} - s_w + \bar{\sigma}\tau g_n - \frac{\bar{\sigma}(1 + \tau g_n)}{(1 + g_n)} - (s_c - s_w)(1 - u^+)\varepsilon^+ = 0$$

$$\left[\bar{\sigma} - \frac{\bar{\sigma}(1 + \tau g_n)}{(1 + g_n)}\right](1 - \varepsilon^+) + \bar{\sigma}\tau(1 - \varepsilon^+)g_n - [s_w - s_w(1 - u^+)\varepsilon^+] = 0$$

we get the equilibrium values for ε and u, which are given by:[5]

$$\varepsilon^+ = \frac{1 - s_w[s_c(1 + g_n) - \bar{\sigma}g_n(1 + \tau g_n)]}{(s_c - s_w)g_n\bar{\sigma}(1 + \tau g_n)} = \frac{s_c[g_n\bar{\sigma}(1 + \tau g_n) - s_w(1 + g_n)]}{(s_c - s_w)g_n\bar{\sigma}(1 + \tau g_n)} \tag{21.25}$$

and

$$u^+ = \frac{1 - g_n\bar{\sigma}(1 + \tau g_n)}{s_c(1 + g_n)} \tag{21.26}$$

All these expressions simplify notably when expectations are such that $\tau = 1$, which we assume to be the case from now on. Thus, the positive equilibrium point of the dynamical system is given by:

$$E^+ \equiv (v^+, u^+, \varepsilon^+, \sigma^+) = \left(h^{-1}(\alpha),\ 1 - \frac{g_n\bar{\sigma}}{s_c},\ \frac{s_c(g_n\bar{\sigma} - s_w)}{(s_c - s_w)g_n\bar{\sigma}},\ \bar{\sigma} \right)$$

where, given the economic meaning of the variables, we must have:

$$0 < h^{-1}(\alpha) < 1 \quad 0 < 1 - \frac{g_n}{s_c} < 1 \quad 0 < \frac{s_c(g_n\bar{\sigma} - s_w)}{(s_c - s_w)g_n\bar{\sigma}} < 1 \quad 0 < \bar{\sigma}$$

The first and the last of these conditions are always satisfied. Thus, the crucial conditions are the second and the third one. It is straightforward to show that they are both satisfied when

$$0 \le s_w < \bar{\sigma}g_n < s_c \le 1 \tag{21.27}$$

It is a matter of simple algebra to show that the positive equilibrium point E^+ guarantees results that, as should be expected, have both a Pasinettian–Kaldorian and a Goodwinian flavour. First, substituting in (21.9) and (21.12), it is easy to show that the coordinates of E^+ are such to guarantee a steady-state growth of output and of the capital stock at a rate equal to the natural rate:

$$(\hat{q})^+ = (\hat{k})^+ = \frac{g_n}{1 - \eta\bar{\sigma}} - \frac{\eta g_n\bar{\sigma}}{1 - \eta\bar{\sigma}} = g_n$$

Second, substituting in the definition of the rate of profit, we have that in the steady state the Cambridge equation is satisfied:

$$r^+ = \frac{1 - u^+}{\sigma^+} = \frac{g_n}{s_c}$$

Third, substituting in (21.1), it follows that in the steady state the real wage grows at the same rate as labour productivity:

$$(\hat{w})^+ = h(v^+) = \alpha$$

Fourth, in order to be economically meaningful it requires that condition (21.27) is satisfied and this guarantees that the 'Pasinetti case' holds. Finally, and most importantly, it is possible to show that there exist parameter values for which E^+ becomes locally unstable and that, when this happens, the model may have a limit cycle solution. This final result can be easily illustrated by using the Hopf bifurcation theorem. In order to do that, as a preliminary step, we need to carry out a local stability analysis.

Local stability analysis and the emergence of limit cycle behaviour

The Jacobian matrix $\mathbf{J}|_{E^+}$ of the dynamical system (21.15)–(21.17) linearised at E^+ is:

$$\mathbf{J}|_{E^+} = \begin{bmatrix} 0 & j_{12} & j_{13} & j_{14} \\ j_{21} & j_{22} & j_{23} & j_{24} \\ 0 & j_{32} & j_{33} & j_{34} \\ 0 & 0 & 0 & j_{44} \end{bmatrix}$$

where:

$$j_{12} = \frac{\partial \dot{v}}{\partial u}\bigg|_{E^+} = \frac{\eta(s_c - s_w)\varepsilon^+ v^+}{1 - \eta\bar{\sigma}} = \frac{\eta s_c(g_n\bar{\sigma} - s_w)v^+}{(1 - \eta\bar{\sigma})g_n\bar{\sigma}}$$

$$j_{13} = \frac{\partial \dot{v}}{\partial \varepsilon}\bigg|_{E^+} = \frac{\eta(s_c - s_w)(1 - u^+)v^+}{1 - \eta\bar{\sigma}} = \frac{\eta(s_c - s_w)g_n\bar{\sigma}v^+}{(1 - \eta\bar{\sigma})s_c}$$

$$j_{14} = \frac{\partial \dot{v}}{\partial \sigma}\bigg|_{E^+} = \frac{\eta v^+}{1 - \eta\bar{\sigma}}$$

$$j_{21} = \frac{\partial \dot{u}}{\partial v}\bigg|_{E^+} = h'(v^+)u^+ = \frac{h'(v^+)(s_c - g_n\bar{\sigma})}{s_c}$$

$$j_{22} = \frac{\partial \dot{u}}{\partial u}\bigg|_{E^+} = \frac{\lambda\eta(s_c - s_w)\varepsilon^+ u^+}{1 - \eta\bar{\sigma}} = \frac{\lambda\eta(g_n\bar{\sigma} - s_w)(s_c - g_n\bar{\sigma})}{(1 - \eta\bar{\sigma})g_n\bar{\sigma}}$$

$$j_{23} = \frac{\partial \dot{u}}{\partial \varepsilon}\bigg|_{E^+} = \frac{\lambda\eta(s_c - s_w)(1 - u^+)u^+}{1 - \eta\bar{\sigma}} = \frac{\lambda\eta(s_c - s_w)g_n\bar{\sigma}(s_c - g_n\bar{\sigma})}{(1 - \eta\bar{\sigma})s_c^2}$$

$$j_{24} = \frac{\partial \dot{u}}{\partial \sigma}\bigg|_{E^+} = \frac{\lambda\eta u^+}{1 - \eta\bar{\sigma}} = \frac{\lambda\eta(s_c - g_n\bar{\sigma})}{(1 - \eta\bar{\sigma})s_c}$$

$$j_{32} = \frac{\partial \dot{\varepsilon}}{\partial u}\bigg|_{E^+} = \frac{\eta}{1 - \eta\bar{\sigma}}(s_c - s_w)(1 - \varepsilon^+)\varepsilon^+ - \frac{s_w}{\bar{\sigma}}\varepsilon^+ = \frac{s_w s_c(g_n\bar{\sigma} - s_w)(\eta s_c - g_n)}{(1 - \eta\bar{\sigma})(s_c - s_w)g_n^2\bar{\sigma}^2}$$

$$j_{33} = \frac{\partial \dot{\varepsilon}}{\partial \varepsilon}\bigg|_{E^+} = g_n - \frac{\eta(s_c - s_w)}{1 - \eta\bar{\sigma}}(1 - \varepsilon^+)(1 - u^+) + \frac{s_w(1 - u^+)}{\bar{\sigma}}$$

$$= \frac{(s_c - s_w)g_n - \eta s_c(g_n\bar{\sigma} - s_w)}{(1 - \eta\bar{\sigma})s_c}$$

$$j_{34} = \frac{\partial \dot{\varepsilon}}{\partial \sigma}\bigg|_{E^+} = -\left[\frac{1 + (1 - \eta\bar{\sigma})g_n}{\bar{\sigma}(1 - \eta\bar{\sigma})}\right](1 - \varepsilon^+) + \frac{[s_w - s_w\varepsilon^+(1 - u^+)]}{(\bar{\sigma})^2}$$

$$= \frac{s_w(s_c - \bar{\sigma}g_n)}{(1 - \eta\bar{\sigma})(s_c - s_w)g_n\bar{\sigma}^2}$$

$$j_{44} = \frac{\partial \dot{\sigma}}{\partial \sigma}\bigg|_{E^+} = -(1 + g_n)$$

Under the following two assumptions, which can be shown to hold for a wide range of plausible parameter values,

Assumption 1. The desired capital–output ratio is high enough and such that:

$$\bar{\sigma} > 1/\eta$$

Assumption 2. The natural growth rate is high enough to satisfy:

$$g_n > -\frac{\eta s_w s_c}{s_c(1 - \eta\bar{\sigma}) - s_w} > 0$$

the signs of all non-zero elements of $\mathbf{J}|_{E^+}$ are uniquely determined and such that:

$$j_{12} < 0 \, j_{13} > 0 \, j_{14} > 0$$
$$j_{21} > 0 \, j_{22} < 0 \, j_{23} > 0 \, j_{24} > 0$$
$$j_{32} < 0 \, j_{33} < 0 \, j_{34} > 0$$
$$j_{44} < 0$$

Then, simple calculation shows that the characteristic equation is given by:

$$(\lambda - j_{44})[\lambda^3 + A\lambda^2 + B\lambda + C] = 0$$

where

$$A = -(j_{22} + j_{33}) > 0$$
$$B = j_{22}j_{33} - j_{23}j_{32} - j_{12}j_{21} > 0$$
$$C = j_{12}j_{21}j_{33} - j_{13}j_{21}j_{32} > 0$$

Thus, one characteristic root is certainly negative and equal to

$$\lambda_1 - j_{44} < 0$$

whereas the other three are the roots of:

$$\lambda^3 + A\lambda^2 + B\lambda + C = 0$$

Given that A, B and C are all positive, from the necessary and sufficient Routh–Hurwitz conditions for all characteristic roots to be negative if real or have a negative real part if complex it follows that the equilibrium point is locally asymptotically stable if and only if:

$$AB - C > 0$$

Selecting the propensity to save out of wages as the bifurcation parameter, it is possible to show that:

$$A(s_w)B(s_w) - C(s_w)$$

$$= \frac{1}{(1 - \eta\bar\sigma)^2 g_n^2 \bar\sigma^2} \{ -[s_w(\eta s_c - g_n)(1 - u^+) - \lambda\eta(g_n\bar\sigma - s_w)u^+$$

$$+ (1 - \eta\bar\sigma)g_n^2\bar\sigma]\eta s_c(g_n\bar\sigma - s_w)u^+[\lambda g_n + v^+h'(v^+)]$$

$$+ (1 - \eta\bar\sigma)g_n^2\bar\sigma\eta s_c(g_n\bar\sigma - s_w)v^+h'(v^+)u^+ \}$$

so that

$$A(s_w)B(s_w) - C(s_w) \gtreqless 0$$

according to whether:

$$-[s_w(\eta s_c - g_n)(1 - u^+) - \lambda\eta(g_n\bar\sigma - s_w)u^+$$

$$+ (1 - \eta\bar\sigma)g_n^2\bar\sigma]\eta s_c(g_n\bar\sigma - s_w)u^+[\lambda g_n + v^+h'(v^+)]$$

$$+ \eta s_c(g_n\bar\sigma - s_w)(1 - \eta\bar\sigma)g_n^2\bar\sigma v^+h'(v^+)u^+ \gtreqless 0$$

which simplifies to:

$$F(s_w) \equiv [-s_w(\eta s_c - g_n)(1 - u^+) + \lambda\eta(g_n\bar\sigma - s_w)u^+][\lambda g_n + v^+h'(v^+)] - (1 - \eta\bar\sigma)g_n^3\bar\sigma\lambda \gtreqless 0$$

When workers do not save, so that $s_w > 0$, Assumption 1 guarantees that we have:

$$F(0) > 0 \leftrightarrow A(0)B(0) - C(0) > 0$$

namely, that all the Routh–Hurwitz conditions for stable roots are satisfied. The same holds for sufficiently small $s_w > 0$ by continuity. We have thus proved the following:

Proposition 1. Under Assumptions 1 and 2, if the propensity to save out of wages is sufficiently low and such that

$$F(s_w) > 0$$

the positive equilibrium E^+ of the dynamical system (21.15)–(21.18) is locally asymptotically stable.

The function $F(s_w)$ is a decreasing function of s_w. As a consequence, when s_w is further increased, the difference $A(s_w)B(s_w) - C(s_w)$ sooner or later becomes negative so that there exists a parameter value s_{wH} such that $A(s_{wH})B(s_{wH}) - C(s_{wH}) = 0$ and $F'(s_{wH}) \neq 0$. We have thus established the possibility of persistent cyclical paths of the variables of the model:

Proposition 2. Under Assumptions 1 and 2, there exists a value of the propensity to save out of wages

$$s_{wH} = \frac{g_n\bar{\sigma}\lambda\eta u^+[\lambda g_n + v^+h'(v^+)] - (1 - \eta\bar{\sigma})g_n^3\bar{\sigma}\lambda}{[\lambda g_n + v^+h'(v^+)][(\eta s_c - g_n)(1 - u^+) + \lambda\eta u^+]} > 0$$

at which the dynamical system (21.15)–(21.18) undergoes an Hopf bifurcation.

Proposition 2, however, proves only the existence part of the Hopf bifurcation theorem and says nothing about the uniqueness and stability of the closed orbits. With the help of numerical simulation, however, it is not difficult to find values of the parameters of the model that satisfy all conditions required by the analysis we have performed and that are such that when the positive equilibrium point loses local stability a stable closed orbit emerges. For example, using for simplicity a linear generalised Phillips curve-type dynamics for real wages, such that:

$$\hat{w} = h(v) + \lambda\hat{v} \approx -y + \rho v + \lambda\hat{v}$$

and the following set of parameter values:

$$\eta = 1 \quad s_c = 0.8 \quad \bar{\sigma} = 2.57 \quad \alpha = 0.0221$$
$$\beta = 0.0037 \quad \gamma = 0.92 \quad \rho = 1 \quad \lambda = 0.1$$

such that:

$$v^+ \approx 0.9421 \quad u \approx 0.9171 \quad \varepsilon^+ \approx 0.5389$$
$$s_{wH} \approx 0.0349$$

and choosing $s_w = 0.0354$, all trajectories converge to a limit cycle. More precisely, as appears from Figures 21.1 and 21.2, and as was to be expected from local analysis, the capital–output ratio converges monotonically and rapidly to its equilibrium value, whereas the other three variables persistently fluctuate around their equilibrium values.

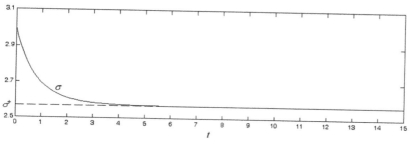

Figure 21.1 Dynamics of the capital–output ratio.

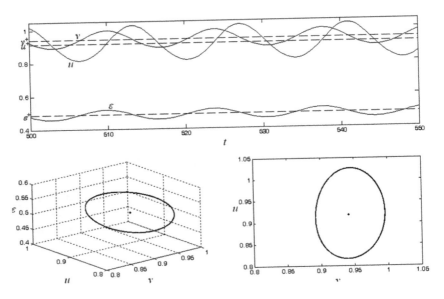

Figure 21.2 Visualization of the growth cycle in 2D and 3D.

Conclusions

In this chapter we have investigated a generalisation of the growth cycle model obtained by taking a lead from some of Vela's suggestions. We have arrived at a version of the model with a four-dimensional dynamical system in the employ ment rate, the share of wages, the proportion of capital held by capitalists and the capital–output ratio. First, we have utilised the Hopf bifurcation theorem to prove the existence of persistent and self-sustained growth cycles and, second we have given numerical evidence that the emerging limit cycle is stable. Thus we can conclude that our modification of the growth cycle model represents novel case in which that model gives rise to persistent fluctuations of the vari ables (to be added to those already existing in the economic literature).

What we have done in this chapter, however, provides only a basic under standing of the dynamics of the model. Much remains to be done both in term of local and global bifurcation analysis. Moreover, to concentrate on the effect of the introduction into the model of the differential savings hypothesis and dis quilibrium in the goods market, I have used the simple linear flexible accelerate as an explanation of investment and neglected many other possible extensions the model, well established in the existing literature. However, given that bot the existence part of the Hopf bifurcation theorem and some useful numeric techniques such as two-parameter bifurcation diagrams and chaos plots can b applied to higher dimensional dynamical systems as well, there seems to b room for a closer analysis of the dynamics of the present model and for furth generalisation along the lines here suggested and sketched.

Notes

1 This is a basic fact that appears to have been overlooked in the literature. Balducci and Candela (1982: 111f.), for example, after having assumed the classical hypothesis, justify their assumption by writing that 'the different assumptions like the Kaldor-Pasinetti one do not substantially modify the content of the analysis'. As far as I am aware, the only other contribution that hints at the fact that a proper consideration of workers' saving along Kaldor-Pasinetti lines leads to a model with a higher-dimensional dynamical system is the article by van der Ploeg (1984) where, however, the resulting dynamics are not analysed in detail.
2 To obtain (21.3), ignoring risk and uncertainty, I have assumed, following van der Ploeg (1984: 8), that the rate of interest is equal to r.
3 In doing this, I am following Vela's suggestion (1983: 248) according to which in a macrodynamic model in which we allow savings out of wages in addition to savings out of profits we should modify the concept of a single investment function. The two investment equations I consider, however, are different from the ones introduced by him.
4 In making this assumption I am again following a suggestion by Vela (see, for example Velupillai 1982b: 81 or 2006: 754–5) according to which any proper generalisation of the growth cycle model should concentrate on relaxing Goodwin's assumption of equi-librium in the goods market. As in the previous case, however, the formulation I have chosen to work with is different from the one suggested by Vela and is instead the one used in the growth cycle model advanced by Glombowski and Krüger (e.g. 1988).
5 When $s_w = 0$, we obtain $\varepsilon^+ = 1$, i.e. all the capital stock is held by capitalists whereas the opposite case, with $\varepsilon^+ = 0$, is obtained when $s_c = 0$.

References

Balducci, R. and Candela, G. (1982) 'A model of growth cycle with its application to the Italian case', *Economic Notes*, 4: 108–29.
Cugno, F. and Montrucchio, L. (1982) 'Cyclical growth and inflation: A qualitative approach to Goodwin's model with money prices', *Economic Notes*, 3: 93–107.
Fitoussi, J.-P. and Velupillai, K.V. (1987) 'Growth cycles in distributive shares, output and employment', in J.-P. Fitoussi and P.A. Nuet (eds), *MacroDynamique et Disequili-bres*, Paris: Economica.
Gandolfo, G. (1997) *Economic Dynamics*, Study Edition, Berlin: Springer-Verlag.
Glombowski, J. and Krüger, M. (1988) 'A short-period growth cycle model', *Recherches Economiques de Louvain*, 54: 425–38.
Goodwin, R.M. (1948) 'Secular and cyclical aspects of the multiplier and the accelera-tor', in L.A. Metzler and others (eds), *Income, Employment and Public Policy. Essays in Honour of Alvin H. Hansen*, New York: W.W. Norton & Company.
—— (1951) 'The nonlinear accelerator and the persistence of business cycles', *Econo-metrica*, 19: 1–17.
—— (1967) 'A growth cycle', in C.H. Feinstein (ed.), *Socialism, Capitalism and Eco-nomic Growth*, Cambridge: Cambridge University Press.
—— (1972) 'Growth cycle', in E.K. Hunt and J.G. Schwartz (eds), *A Critique of Eco-nomic Theory*, London: Penguin Books.
Kaldor, N. (1956) 'Alternative theories of distribution', *Review of Economic Studies*, 23: 83–100.
Pasinetti, L.L. (1962) 'Rate of profit and income distribution in relation to the rate of eco-nomic growth', *Review of Economic Studies*, 29: 267–79.

Phillips, A.W. (1958) 'The relation between unemployment and the rate of change of money wage rates in the United Kingdom, 1861–1957', *Economica*, 25: 283–99.

Ploeg, F., van der (1984) 'Implications of workers' savings for economic growth and the classical struggle', in R.M. Goodwin, M. Krüger and A. Vercelli (eds), *Nonlinear Models of Fluctuating Growth*, Berlin: Springer-Verlag.

Sordi, S. (2001) 'Growth cycles when workers save: A reformulation of Goodwin's model along Kaldor–Pasinetti lines', *Central European Journal of Operations Research*, 9: 97–117.

—— (2003) 'The interaction between trend and cycle in macrodynamic models of the economy', in N. Salvadori (ed.), *The Theory of Economic Growth: A 'Classical Perspective'*, Aldershot: Edward Elgar.

Sportelli, M.C. (1995) 'A Kolmogoroff generalized predator–prey model of Goodwin's growth cycle', *Journal of Economics*, 61: 35–64.

Velupillai, K.V. (1979) 'Some stability properties of Goodwin's growth cycle', *Zeitschrift für Nationalökonomie/Journal of Economics*, 39: 245–57.

—— (1982a) 'When workers save and invest: Some Kaldorian dynamics', *Zeitschrift für Nationalökonomie/Journal of Economics*, 42: 247–58.

—— (1982b) 'Linear and nonlinear dynamics in economics: The contributions of Richard Goodwin', *Economic Notes*, 3: 73–92.

—— (1983) 'A neo-Cambridge model of income distribution and unemployment', *Journal of Post-Keynesian Economic*, 5: 454–73.

—— (2006) 'A disequilibrium macrodynamics model of fluctuations', *Journal of Macroeconomics*, 28: 752–67.

Part VII

Markets and their behaviours

22 Evolution of FX markets and new financial economics

Joseph L. McCauley

Introduction

The notion of equilibrium is deeply ingrained in the culture of academic economics. Market equilibrium is the benchmark against which real markets are supposed to be measured, and an implicit, unstated assumption of both stability and computability is made. Typical academicians assume uncritically and implicitly that free markets could somehow self-organize into a dynamically stable system and thereby approach statistical equilibrium. A stationary stochastic process would then describe fluctuations about equilibrium. *Empirical evidence shows rather that price processes in deregulated markets, left to traders' actions, are nonstationary.*

There is no empirical evidence for an approach to market equilibrium, market clearing is not observed. Countries that protect their own industry and currency and if necessary, effectively impose tariffs, know this. But academicians have not realized that a stationary market is not an efficient market. Arrow and Debreu first created the illusion that uncertainty/probability could be banished from microeconomic theory, and Lucas later created the illusion that nonstationarity could be banished from both macroeconomic reality and modelling. *We show below that, in contrast with those standards, erroneous ideas, an efficient market is a martingale process, and a stationary process is in conflict with a martingale process.* We will provide empirical evidence that current foreign exchange (FX) markets are martingales, to within observational error, after a ten-minute trading time lag. We will focus on the pair correlations of returns necessary to understand the underlying finance market dynamics. *Efficient markets and stationary markets generate completely different, conflicting pair correlations.*

As our first example, we present a case where currency speculation was apparently self-stabilizing as the consequence of stiff regulations. The theme of this chapter can be understood as market stability and inefficiency from regulations, market instability and efficiency from deregulation. We will argue that, compared with the stability observed under the gold standard, deregulation of money has made markets more efficient in the sense that the markets become noisy in a way that makes them hard or impossible to beat, and with great risk.

That is, finance market noise is unstable noise, dynamically seen. Of particular interest on the theme of making mathematics more effective in economics, we contribute a new, fundamental analysis of the limitations on the discovery of mathematical models from time series, and provide a mathematically effective model of FX market dynamics. The explanation how an equilibrium market contradicts an inefficient market is also new. This chapter is dedicated to my invaluable and very close friend Vela Velupillai, in the spirit of making mathematics more effective in economics, both in theory and practice (Velupillai 2005). Perhaps as a first in the social sciences, we present hard empirical evidence, described and interpreted by an identified nonstationary model, of how FX traders systematically repeat their random daily behaviour on successive trading days during the week. The systematic repetitiveness is seen in the mean square fluctuations in returns.

Especially interesting is that Eichengreen (1998) argues that FX speculation was stabilizing before the First World War. Empirical analysis shows that FX markets are unstable and efficient in our present era. Our empirically deduced FX market model explains the observed behaviour, and we can model the pre-First World War non-efficient equilibrium FX dynamics as well. Our main point is that deregulated markets are dynamically unstable, stable equilibrium is mutually exclusive with free, so-called efficient markets. The history of the dollar since the gold standard provides the illuminating example.

There are three central points in what follows: (i) markets are dominated by noise, albeit not white noise, and the job of the theoretical economist is to find out what kind of noise the traders make. As Fischer Black argued (1986), it's the 'noise traders' who dominate normal markets and thereby provide liquidity. (ii) 'Value' can only be identified falsifiably as consensus value, the price where the 1-point returns density peaks (McCauley et al. 2009). 'Value' is therefore whatever price most traders assign to an asset at a given time t. Unless one can gaze into a crystal ball and foresee the price the largest fraction of traders will independently assign later, notions of 'overvalued' and 'undervalued' are effectively subjective. And, (iii) unregulated markets are nonstationary/unstable, so if we want stability then we must impose 'regulations with teeth'. To explain these points and more, it's most useful first to explain an efficient market, then to explain the characteristics of a hypothetical stationary market and then to provide a historic example of the latter. We restrict our discussion to normal liquid markets, markets where the trading is so frequent and the volume so great that bid/ask spreads are very small relative to the last sale price, so that trading is effectively reversible (McCauley et al. 2008). Finance markets, excepting crashes, satisfy this requirement; cars, housing, etc. do not. Fat tails and Hurst exponent scaling, if they occur at all, describe normal liquid markets, not crashes. The idea of a gradually inflating bubble, like the US stock market bubble of 1990–2001, belongs to a normal, liquid market.

Eichengreen (1998) has presented a very stimulating history of the evolution of FX markets from the gold standard of the late nineteenth century through the Bretton Woods Agreement (post-Second World War to 1971) and beyond to the freely traded (i.e. 'deregulated') currencies of our present market globalization era. He effectively asserts a change from stability to instability over the time interval of the First World War and gives the qualitative reasons for that change. Adding equations to his discussion, we show how speculators can extract money systematically from a hypothetical market in statistical equilibrium with little risk. An 'efficient market' is in contrast very hard if not impossible to beat. We will explain in two related ways why an equilibrium market is not an 'efficient market' but is instead, in principle, a beatable market. The present era normal liquid FX markets are in contrast impossible to beat at the level of simple averages and pair correlations, are 'efficient', and consequently are described as 'martingales' (McCauley *et al.* 2008). The ideas of martingales and options/hedging were irrelevant in the pre-First World War era. Next, we define our notation.

Stochastic processes

Let $(x_1, \ldots, x_n)$ be the observed points in a time series at times $(t_1, \ldots, t_n)$. We want to understand/describe the underlying and a priori unknown dynamics that generated the time series. That is, we want to extract the dynamics from the empirical data. Finance market dynamics are stochastic: trades on the shortest time scale, $\Delta t \approx 1$ seconds, cannot be predicted deterministically. A stochastic process $x(t)$ is specified/defined by its n-point densities

$$f_{n-1}(x_1, t_1; \ldots; x_{k-1}, t_{k-1}, x_{k+1}, x_{k+1}; \ldots; x_n, t_n) = \int dx_k f_n(x_1, t_1; \ldots; x_n, t_n) \tag{22.1}$$

so that, e.g.

$$f_1(x, t) = \int dy f_2(y, s; x, t) \tag{22.2}$$

and

$$f_n(x_1, t_1; \ldots; x_1, t_1) = p_n(x_n, t_n | x_{n-1}, t_{n-1}; \ldots; x_1, t_1) f_{n-1}(x_{n-1}, t_{n-1}; \ldots; x_1, t_1)$$
$$= p_n(x_n, t_n | x_{n-1}, t_{n-1}; \ldots; x_1, t) \ldots p_2(x_2, t_2 | x_1, t_1) f_1(x_1, t_1) \tag{22.3}$$

In finance, $x(t) = ln(p(t)/p_c(t))$ is the log return where $p(t)$ is the price of the underlying asset (stock, bond or foreign exchange) at time t and $p_c(t)$ is consensus value, or just 'value', the location of the peak of the 1-point returns density $f_1(x, t)$ at time t (McCauley *et al.* 2009). The use of the 1-point density has been overrated in the literature, and we have explained in detail why the log increment $x(t, T) = ln(p(t + T)/p())$ generates spurious results in data analysis (Bassler *et al.* 2008).

The 1-point density carries no information whatsoever about the underlying stochastic process (Hänggi *et al.* 1978; McCauley 2007a, 2007b). Pair correlations provide the lowest level of specification of a specific processor or class of processes, so we need at least the two-point density f_2 or the two-point conditional density p_2, to have any hope of $\langle x(t + T)x(t)\rangle$. Both Gaussian processes and Markov processes are completely specified by pair correlations, and while FX markets behave Markovian at the level of pair correlations (because they are efficient), they are never Gaussian.

Efficient markets

Here and in all that follows we assume a normal liquid market, a market where the noise traders trade frequently so that bid/ask spreads are small relative to price. A crash is not a normal liquid market. Fat tails and scaling, if they occur at all, describe normal liquid markets, not crashes (McCauley 2005). In a normal liquid market one can reverse a small trade within seconds with little or no loss (McCauley 2004).

By the efficient market hypothesis (EMH), we mean a *normal liquid market* that is either very hard or perhaps impossible to beat. This means that there are no *easy to find* correlations or patterns that can be exploited systematically for profit. A Markovian market would be unbeatable in this sense. However, real liquid markets may be merely very hard but not impossible to beat. Such markets are described by martingale process, and martingales permit memory that cannot be detected at the level of simple averages or pair correlations, martingales look Markovian at the level of pair correlations (McCauley *et al.* 2008). But we don't want to assume any of this, we want next to deduce it from the condition that the past provides no knowledge of the future at the level of pair correlations. Higher order correlations are then left unspecified.

To formulate the dynamics of hard to beat markets we assume that the increment autocorrelations vanish, where by increments we mean $x(t, T) = x(t + T) - x(t)$, $x(t,-T) = x(t) - x(t - T)$. The statement that trading during an earlier time interval provides no signals for traders in a later nonoverlapping time interval *at the level of pair correlations is simply*

$$\langle (x(t_1) - x(t_1 - T_1))(x(t_2 + T_2) - x(t_2))\rangle = 0 \qquad (22.4)$$

if there is no time interval overlap, $[t_1 - T_1, t_1] \cap [t_2, t_2 + T_2] = \varnothing$, where $\varnothing$ denotes the empty set on the line. This is a much less restrictive condition than assuming that the increments are statistically independent, or that the market is Markovian. The condition (22.4) is necessary but insufficient for a drift-free Markov process (we assume here that the average drift has been subtracted from empirical time series). This insufficiency permits market memory at a level beyond pair correlations, in principle, but the necessity makes the market look Markovian (unbeatable) at the level of pair correlations.

Consider any stochastic process $x(t)$ where the increments are uncorrelated where (22.4) holds. From this condition we obtain the autocorrelation function for positions (returns). Let $t > s$, then

$$\langle x(t)x(s)\rangle = \langle (x(t) - x(s))x(s)\rangle + \langle x_2(s)\rangle = \langle x^2(s)\rangle > 0 \qquad (22.5)$$

since $x(s) - x(t_o) = x(s)$, so that $\langle x(t+T)x(t)\rangle = \langle x^2(s)\rangle$ is simply the variance in x at the earlier time t. *This condition is equivalent to a Martingale process*:

$$\int dy\, y p_2(y, t + T | x, t) = x, \tag{22.6}$$

$$\langle x(t+T)x(t)\rangle = \iint dx\, dy\, xy p_2(y, t + T); x, t) f_1(x, t)$$
$$= \int x f_1(x, t) dx (\int y dy\, p_2(y, t + T); x, t)) = \int x^2 f_1(x, t) dx \tag{22.7}$$

At the level of pair correlations a martingale cannot be distinguished from a drift-free Markov process. Mandelbrot proposed the martingale as a model for the EMH on the basis of simple averages in x (Mandelbrot 1966), but we have deduced the martingale property from a two-point condition, the lack of increment autocorrelations. Note also that (22.5) can be interpreted as asserting that earlier returns have no correlation with future gains.

Next, we discover an extremely important point for data analysis and modelling. Combining

$$\langle (x(t+T) - x(t))^2 \rangle = + \langle (x^2(t+T)) \rangle + \langle x^2(t) \rangle - 2\langle x(t+T)x(t)\rangle \tag{22.8}$$

with (22.5) we get

$$\langle (x(t+T) - x(t))^2 \rangle = \langle x^2(t+T) \rangle - \langle x^2(t) \rangle \tag{22.9}$$

which depends on both t and T, excepting the rare case where $\langle x^2(t)\rangle$ is linear in t. *Uncorrelated increments are generally nonstationary.* Notice further that (22.5) states that

$$\sigma^2(t + T) = \langle x^2(t + T) \rangle - \sigma^2(t). \tag{22.10}$$

i.e. $\sigma^2(t + T) > \sigma^2(t)$, the variance increases with time, statistical equilibrium cannot be approached unless $\sigma(t)$ approaches a constant limit, so the process is nonstationary, is dynamically unstable. *An efficient market is nonstationary, far from equilibrium.* This has not been understood in financial economics.

A martingale process is a generalization of the idea of a fair game. Next, we contrast an efficient market with an equilibrium market, which is not a fair game process.

Stationary markets

A neoclassical equilibrium deterministic market is a barter system, money/liquidity does not exist. There, 'value' is the 'price-label' at which goods and services are exchanged. Undervalued and overvalued are well-defined ideas but profit is disallowed by lack of money. Real markets are noisy, uncertainty dominates real life. The generalization of neoclassical equilibrium to a noisy market is a stationary process. A stationary process describes fluctuations about statistical equilibrium (or a steady state), which is described by a *normalizable* time-invariant 1-point density of returns $f_1(x)$. All averages calculated from the equilibrium density, e.g. the mean and variance, are constants. Nothing changes with time at the level of simple averages. Any other definition of 'equilibrium' that contradicts this does not describe equilibrium (time translational invariance with an invariant, normalizable 1-point density).

Here's an example from the literature where equilibrium was seriously misidentified. Muth (1961) writes demand/consumption and supply (using our notation) as

$$D = r\delta p(t)$$
$$S = \gamma\langle\delta p(t)\rangle + \varepsilon(t) \qquad (22.11)$$

where δp is supposed to be the deviation from an equilibrium price, $\langle\delta p(t)\rangle$ is the expected price deviation at time t, and $\varepsilon(t)$ is noise representing uncertainty. The idea is to try to understand how producers' expectations correspond to future prices. Setting $D = S$ Muth obtains

$$\delta p(t) = \gamma\langle\delta p(t)\rangle/r + \varepsilon(t)/r. \qquad (22.12)$$

This is called the 'rational expectations' model and is self-contradictory: from an equilibrium assumption $D = S$ we cannot consistently derive a time-varying price δp! The inconsistency in the notion of 'local price equilibria' (McCauley 2004) is related. The correct procedure would be to write $dp/dt = D - S$, locate an equilibrium price using $D = S$ and then linearize to get an equation of motion for $d\delta p/dt$, to which demand noise could be added. Then, one would study the stability of the resulting stochastic differential equation. Variation of price with time 'in equilibrium' is mathematical nonsense. Fama misidentified time varying market averages as representing 'market equilibrium' in his discussion of martingales and the EMH (McCauley 2004; Fama 1970), and Sharpe misidentified the time-varying averages in CAPM as 'market equilibrium (McCauley 2004; Sharpe 1964). From self-contradictory models can only follow the confusion of the false financial expectations. McCann wrote (1994) that rational expectations in the hands of Lucas effectively redefined equilibrium so that 'disequilibrium becomes a vacuous concept'. That effort failed. Nonstationarity was merely masked in economic theorizing by self-organized confusion. We've elsewhere (McCauley 2008b) provided a fairly complete critique of rational expectations (Sargent and Wallace 1976), including Lucas' policy advice.

In neoclassical economics value is the price label where barter occurs, and 100 per cent of all agents agree on value. We can generalize this in a useful way. 'Value' in an uncertain (fluctuating, noisy) market is the price assigned by the largest fraction of traders to an asset, is consensus value or most probably value, the price where the returns density $f_1(x, t)$ peaks, and this holds whether a market is stationary or nonstationary. In a stationary market value so-identified is constant. In a nonstationary market value is not constant and will shift unpredictably. We can refer to this as 'Value under uncertainty'. Noise represents agents' uncertainty, and only a small fraction of traders (those with price expectations near the peak of f_1) agree on 'value'. In a hypothetical stationary market overvalued and undervalued are useful, observable ideas because value stands still and the process is ergodic, what goes up must come down and vice versa. It is exactly this feature that makes such a market inefficient, makes the market beatable, as we will now show. All earlier economic theorizing about stationary and ergodicity (McCann 1994; Sargent and Wallace 1976) missed this key point.

More generally, in a stationary process densities f_n and transition densities p_n of all orders n are time translationally invariant,

$$f_n(x_1, t_1 + T; \ldots; x_n, t_n + T) = f_n(x_1, t_1; \ldots; x_n, t_n) \tag{22.13}$$

and $p_2(x_n, t_n|x_{n-1}, t_{n-1}) = p_2(x_n, t_n - t_{n-1}|x_{n-1}, 0)$ as well. A stationary process also requires time translational invariance of a *normalizable* 1-point density $f_1(x)$, so that the mean $\langle x(t) \rangle$, variance $\sigma^2 = \langle x^2(t) \rangle - \langle x(t) \rangle^2$, and all higher moments are constants, independent of t. The 1-point density describes fluctuations about statistical equilibrium where the equilibrium values of the process are the averages calculated using that density. In equilibrium nothing changes with time. But there is a subtle point that must be appreciated. Stationary processes may be Markovian, but time translationally invariant Markov processes are generally not stationary.

For a time translationally invariant Markov process a stationary 1-point density f_1 can be derived via the Fokker–Planck *pde* (partial differential equation) (McCauley 2004), but the stationary density generally is not normalizable unless the process is confined to a box of finite size, $\infty < a \leq x \leq b < \infty$. The lognormal price process provides the simplest example (McCauley 2004). In the case of an infinite or semi-infinite interval ($b = \infty$) a time translationally invariant Markov process is generally not stationary because the stationary 1-point density is not normalizable, and this is the rule, not the exception. Such a process does not describe fluctuations about statistical equilibrium. In this case a time dependent mean and the moments are calculated from $f_1(x, t) = p_2(x, t|0, 0)$ with initial condition $f_1(x, 0) = d(x)$. Again, the lognormal process is the canonical example of a time translationally invariant nonstationary Markov process. Next we explain how and why a stationary market would contradict the efficient market hypothesis (EMH).

Consider a stationary process $x(t)$. Here, $f_1(x, t) = f_1(x)$ is normalizable and time translational invariance of the transition density $p_2(y, t + T|x, t) = p_2(y, T|x, 0)$ yields pair correlations

$$\langle x(t + T)x(t) \rangle = \langle x(T)x0 \rangle \tag{22.14}$$

depending on T alone, independent of t, or $\sigma^2 = \langle x^2(t) \rangle. = \langle x^2(0) \rangle = $ constant with $x(0) = 0$. This result does *not* follow for a time-translational invariant Markov process where $f_1(x)$ is not normalizable, and contradicts the martingale condition

(22.5), where for a martingale the pair correlations depend on t alone independent of the time lag T (a drift-free Markov process is always a martingale). For a time translationally invariant martingale

$$x(t + T) = x(t) + \int_t^{t+T} \sqrt{D(x(s))dB(s)} \tag{22.15}$$

we obtain

$$\sigma^2 = \langle x^2(t) \rangle = \int_0^t ds \int_{-\infty}^\infty dy D(y) p_2(y, s|0, 0) \tag{22.16}$$

which depends unavoidably on t. A martingale is a nonstationary stochastic process. *This means that an efficient market (a hard to beat market) cannot be stationary.*

The increment correlations of a stationary process do not vanish,

$$\langle x(t, T)x(t, -T) \rangle = \langle x(2T)x(0) \rangle - \sigma^2, \tag{22.17}$$

yielding pair correlations that can be traded on for profit. We will describe below how to 'vacuum' money systematically out of a hypothetical stationary market, and also will discuss how this was apparently done in FX markets on the gold standard before the First World War.

Why FX trading may have been stable under the gold standard

The gold standard became widely accepted around 1890. But even then the 'quantity theory of money' (conservation of money) did not apply. With a strict gold standard, and no new mining production or coinage of existing gold, money would be conserved in the absence of credit. But credit has played a strong role in finance and economics since at least the renaissance in Europe, and dominates all markets today: with any credit card purchase money is created with the tap of a computer key. Today, the 'amount of money' in the world is an ambiguous notion.

The interesting point is that before the First World War stable currency values were maintained by the threat of central bank intervention. This led speculators to bid up a weak currency with the expectation of a profit, and thereby strengthened the currency via a self-fulfilling process: speculation in that era tended to stabilize FX markets. After the First World War the central bank threat either fell by the wayside or else no longer carried sufficient weight, and FX markets became unstable: weak currencies were bid lower by speculators. The historic reasons for the change are discussed. This chapter can be understood as adding equations to Eichengreen's history (Eichengreen 1998) of the globalization of capital.

Adhering to a gold standard means tight money. Credit cards didn't exist, consumer credit was sparse, generally on the level of a running bill at a local grocery store. Banks in the gold standard era did not easily make loans for consumption. The level of economic activity was correspondingly much less than in our present era, and the price level was correspondingly lower. Markets were relatively illiquid, meaning that items were not frequently traded. Credit and the explosion of dollars changed all of this. Economic expansion/consumption requires easy money via credit. We begin with the pre-First World War era in which credit was not the overwhelmingly dominant factor in finance.

First, there was competition between silver and gold to set the monetary standard. For a while both metals were used, but the bimetallic monetary standard was largely eliminated in the late nineteenth century when silver became cheap in terms of gold. Great Britain's reliance on silver was an exception. According to Eichengreen's history of the gold standard and its eventual replacement as international standard by the post-Second World War Dollar under the Bretton Woods Agreement (Eichengreen 1998), *we can infer that there was a fundamental shift in the foreign exchange (FX) noise distribution after the First World War*. Until the Great Depression, the Western countries followed the gold standard within bounds set by central banks.

The main job of western central banks and parliaments was seen as keeping the national currency from falling outside chosen gold standard bands. Eichengreen claims that before the First World War the currency speculators, confident that governments could be relied on eventually to react to maintain the gold-value of the currency, bid a weak currency up, expecting a profit in the long run. Unfortunately, the older FX data are too poor to test this idea but, if true, that would mean that financial markets were asymptotically stationary in the pre-First World War era. This is interesting, because we know empirically that FX markets at least since 1958 are dynamically unstable. Eichengreen's claim is that the onset of the instability coincided with social changes due to the First World War.

Here's how the pre-First World War FX market presumably worked. Imagine a USD (United States dollar) equivalent to 25.9 grains of gold. Take the Reichsmark (RM) (we may think of it as the 'euro' of that time) as the foreign currency of interest, and focus on trade with Germany. Assume that credit (money creation without gold backing) doesn't change the money supply significantly inside the USA. A trade deficit means too many dollars outside the country, therefore too few inside the country so that economic activity within the USA falls, i.e. the trade deficit reduces liquidity inside a country on the gold standard (meaning deflation, unless more money is printed). Less money means lower prices (deflation), so the trade deficit is eventually reversed via cheaper exports. The latter brings money back into the country. This increases the USD against the RM without the need for a devaluation of the weak USD by the central bank. Incidentally, the central bank in the USA was created late, in 1913. By reducing the money supply (weakening demand further), a central bank could speed up this process. We can describe this stabilization process mathematically.

Consider the logarithmic return $x(t) = ln(p(t)/p_c)$ where p is the price of one currency in units of another (e.g. the Reichsmark in 1913, or the euro today, in USD), and p_c is the consensus price fixed in the pre-First World War case by gold. In a *stationary* process, the 1-point returns density $f(x, t)$ is time independent: the average return, the variance and all other moments of the 1-point distribution are constants. A market in statistical equilibrium reflects a stationary process $x(t)$. We can easily model an asymptotically stationary market. With the usual stochastic supply–demand equation

$$dp = rpdt + \sigma_1 pdB(t) \tag{22.18}$$

where $B(t)$ is the Wiener process (dB/dt is white noise), we obtain (via Ito calculus)

$$dx = (r - \sigma_1^2/2)dt + \sigma_1 dB(t). \tag{22.19}$$

Let $R = r - \sigma_1^2/2$ denote the expected return, $\langle x \rangle = Rt$. For FX markets we know empirically (Bassler *et al.* 2007) that $R \approx 0$. If $-\infty < x < \infty$, then (22.2) is the lognormal model introduced by Osborne in 1958 (Osborne in Cootner 1964) and used by Black and Scholes in 1973, and is unstable/nonstationary. The reference price p_c is the price at which the returns distribution peaks and defines what we mean by 'value'. 'Value', or most probable price, is the price agreed on by the largest fraction of speculators. The speculators' behaviour generates the noise distribution, which in the case of (22.19) is white. But central bank intervention means that $-\infty < x < \infty$ is the wrong boundary condition. A Brownian particle on the unbounded line is nonstationary, but its motion becomes stationary if we put the particle in a box of finite length. On a gold standard, the reference price is set by gold. Without a gold standard, the reference price is set by speculators' expectations.

With the pre-First World War USD supported within a gold band $b_1 < x < b_2$, we can set the equilibrium probability density $f(x)$ = constant except at the boundaries and then we obtain an approach to statistical equilibrium: $f(x, t)$ approaches $f(x)$ as t increases (see Stratonovich 1963 for the mathematical details), i.e. the market is asymptotically stationary. Here's how speculators could systematically suck money out of a stationary market. Consider the price distribution $g(p, t) = f(x, t)dx/dp$ with price variance σ_p^2. One buys, e.g. if $p < p_G + \sigma_p$, and one sells if $p > p_G + \sigma_p$. Such fluctuations are guaranteed because a stationary process is ergodic (Yaglom and Yaglom 1962), and the first passage (or 'hitting') time for a specific fluctuation can easily be calculated (Stratonovich 1963; Durrett 1984; McCauley 2010, forthcoming). So we understand how speculators could systematically have made money, as Eichengreen claims, with little risk in the pre-First World War era. The main risk is that the trader must have enough cash to sit on his bet until the price passes through equilibrium again and goes up, which is guaranteed to occur in finite, predictable (hitting) time. *FX options, hedging against foreign currency risk, was not demanded in that era.*

In a stationary market, returns merely fluctuate about the statistical equilibrium return $x = 0$, with constant variance. The two-point and all other higher order densities are time translationally invariant, e.g. the conditional two-point density obeys $p_2(y, s{:}x, t) = p_2(y, s - t{:}x, 0)$. Time translational invariance alone is a necessary but not sufficient condition for statistical equilibrium (McCauley *et al.* 2008), because time translational invariance does not guarantee the existence of a normalizable time independent 1-point density $f(x)$. This point is not appreciated in the economics and finance literature, where stationarity in empirical data is generally merely assumed without first testing for it.

We must interpret the boundary conditions in order to understand how stability worked: it was not the gold standard, which is superfluous, but rather the serious threat of punishment combined with reward that stabilized the system. The band, $b_1 < x < b_2$ represents the threat of government intervention. The process is asymptotically stationary *if* both b_1 and b_2 are finite (particle confined between two walls), so that $\langle x \rangle = (b_1 + b_2)/2 = $ constant represents the gold value of the USD. The central bank would threaten to intervene to buy/sell USD if x would hit b_1 or b_2, so speculators would confidently buy dollars if $\sigma < x < b_1$, e.g. where $\sigma^2 = \langle x \rangle = $ constant. Ergodicity of a stationary process guarantees that profitable fluctuations occur with average first passage time $\tau = \sigma^2/2\sigma_1^2$. *So it was the boundary conditions, and not the gold standard alone, that provided stability.* Setting boundaries, establishing 'threats, of punishment with teeth', made the difference. Having more gold than speculators gave the central bank threats of intervention 'teeth'.

In the language of the Ultimatum Game (Hauert 2008), the boundary conditions/government regulations were threats of financial punishment. Those threats of punishment were effective ('had teeth') if the central banks had gold reserves large enough to beat the speculators, if necessary. A related social analogy is the old saying 'kids like boundaries'. Also related is the old problem of 'The Tragedy of the Commons (*Allmende*)': with free farmers sharing a common meadow the tendency is for each farmer to add 'one more cow'. This is an example of an unregulated free market system. Adam Smith wrote earlier that moral restraint is required for a free market system to function. Moral restraint is inadequate, 'regulations with teeth' are required for stability. Even during the depression, the gold reserves of the USA, France and Germany were more than adequate compared with the paper currency in circulation.

The system worked, that speculators created stabilizing self-fulfilling prophecies before the First World War, was because governments (i) had adequate gold reserves and (ii) saw their job as maintaining the stability of the currency, instead of guaranteeing high employment. The First World War changed that. The rise of socialism and labour unions after the First World War meant that social spending, *inflation via printing paper money, had to be given priority.*

Eichengreen asserts that post-First World War FX markets were both volatile and (in my words) nonstationary: speculators, expecting any sign of devaluation of a currency to reflect the inability of a government to maintain the gold value of the currency, bid the currency lower. That shift in agents' expectations is attributed in part to the fact that government spending on social programmes was largely negligible before the First World War, but had to be taken seriously by 1930. We have no evidence for volatility prior to 1987, but we do know empirically that by 1958 the stock market was well described by dynamically a nonstationary model, lognormal pricing (Osborne in Cootner 1964). 'Volatility' in a diffusive model like (22.2) requires an x-dependent diffusion coefficient (McCauley 2004, 2008a; Bassler et al. 2007), the diffusion coefficient is the volatility, locally seen. The model of the 1958–1987 stock market, Osborne's Gaussian returns model, is not volatile.

Eichengreen's thesis can be stated mathematically as the claim of a shift in the form of the noise distribution as a consequence of strongly felt socialist union pressures after the First World War. Summarizing, central bank intervention to devaluate was largely unnecessary before 1914, because if the USD fell to the gold export arbitrage point b_2 then speculators, believing the bank would intervene and maintain the gold value of the USD, bought the weak currency with the assurance of a later gain, pre-empting the necessity for the bank to devalue. *Derivatives (FX options) were unnecessary as hedge against foreign currency risk.*

FX markets from the First to the Second World War

Inflation of the money supply via credit is necessary (but not sufficient) for a boom or bubble (Kindelberger 1996). Banks and the government saw the avoidance of inflation, not high employment, as their main job. Because of this particular social orientation, the stock market crash of 1929 caused a financial crisis deflation occurred because there was no 'lender of the last resort' to provide liquidity. Margin trading in the 1920s, as in the 1990s, was a major source of running up stock prices, and when so the crash affected the lenders, banks in that era were allowed to lend money for stock speculation, and many banks went bankrupt and closed after the Crash. Depositors withdrew money from remaining banks for fear of losing it, and so there was a liquidity drought. The depression/deflation followed from the lack of money in circulation: many people were unemployed, and those with money tended to hoard instead of spending it because *bank deposits were not insured in that time.* Franklyn D. Roosevelt (FDR) was elected President in 1932 based on his promise/threat to abandon past social policies and institute a 'back to work' policy, therefore to restore liquidity. People with money knew what that meant, inflation via social spending, and stored to convert their USD into gold.

FDR's famous Bank Holiday in 1933 was partly the consequence of a run on gold by speculators getting rid of the USD: they expected social spending and consequent inflation (government spending was Keynes's recommendation for getting out of a slump). So, in 1935 FDR outlawed the ownership of gold by Americans, recalled all gold coins (excepting those held by coin collectors) and fixed the price of gold artificially at US$35/oz, thereby guaranteeing that Americans could not depreciate the USD by buying gold. Fear of bank failures was widespread. In a further effort to control the dollar, bank deposits were insured, and the Glass–Steagal Act was passed to keep banks out of the stockbrokerage business. After a long time these acts eventually restored confidence in the banking system, but the hangover/fear from the Depression lasted into the 1950s. With Roosevelt's acts in place as law, the USA government could then spend freely on public works projects like TVA, which was and still is a very effective socialist project, and WPA and get away with it, because the US then had the largest gold reserves in the world. France and surprisingly, Germany, were second and third.[1] The Second World War brought new pressures into play.

The post-Second World War era of 'adjustable pegged' FX rates

We can summarize this era without the details, which have been discussed elsewhere (McCauley 2009, forthcoming), by stating that (i) the gold standard was replaced by the Bretton Woods Agreement of 'fixed adjustable exchange rates' and (ii) the inflation due to military spending and rebuilding Western Europe, especially Germany, was so great that the number of USD in circulation outside the USA matched the gold supply in Fort Knox by about 1960. No detailed calculation is required to know that a devaluation was necessary, but gold was still hypothetically fixed at \$35/oz. In the face of lack of controls, FX markets are unstable.

Destabilizing speculative behaviour is described by the Gaussian returns model that Osborne proposed empirically to describe stock returns (FX returns were not tested) in 1958 (Osborne in Cootner 1964)

$$dx = (r\sigma_1^2/2)dt + \sigma_1 dB(t), \qquad (22.20)$$

subject to no boundary conditions. *Even with* r < *0 this model allows no approach to statistical equilibrium* (McCauley 2004), is inherently nonstationary/unstable. Presumably, FX markets were like this since the end of the First World War. This model was used by Black and Scholes in 1973 to price options falsifiably (McCauley 2008b), and presumably worked until 1987, i.e. option pricing from 1973–1987 and beyond is described by a model that describes the market as nonstationary/unstable.

Emergence of deregulation

Modern credit, based on fractional reserve banking, is an effectively uncontrolled form of money creation. Credit became important after 1971. By 1971 France held enough USD and demanded payment in gold that, if met, would have emptied Fort Knox.

There was a seemingly politically painless way out, let inflation do the job. So Nixon deregulated the dollar in 1971. He first superficially raised the official price of gold to US\$38 but financial reality rapidly took over. Significantly,

Forex was also created in 1971, and the Chicago Board of Options Exchange (CBOE) was created in 1973, the year that the Black–Scholes solution was published. The trading of derivatives/options/hedging exploded, because without a standard and without 'boundaries with teeth' derivatives were now needed to hedge currency bets. By 1973 gold had hit US$800/oz and OPEC, correctly understanding the implicit USD devaluation, raised the price of oil drastically. Several countries nationalized their oilfields. A VW Beetle that had cost US$700–800 in 1968 cost US$1600 by 1974, and the gasoline price had doubled in dollars as well, after first hitting US$1.20/gal.

We can identify the USD deregulation as the beginning of the philosophy and practice of deregulation in American and therefore in Western politics. That programme, globalization via privatization and deregulation, is now worldwide. Americans got rid of dollars in favour of anything and everything (e.g. art, collectible coins) and ran up credit card bills with the expectation that tomorrow's USD would be worth much less than today's. In the 1980s Savings and Loans were 'deregulated' and went bankrupt, unable to compete with bond houses that split principle and interest into separate derivatives for sale to the public. Leveraged buyouts financed by junk bonds emerged and became the order of the day on Wall Street. Monetization of everything began in earnest, derivatives being a form of monetization and with credit/leverage providing the required pseudoliquidity. FX transactions, on the order 10^8/min. *circa* 1981, decoupled from economic growth. With no certainty about currency at home or in international trade, physicists were hired on Wall St. to model derivatives. The inflation rate became so high ('stagflation', inflation combined with unemployment) that the (Carter-appointed) US Federal Reserve Bank Chairman Paul Volcker let interest rates float to 13.5 per cent in 1981, reducing inflation to 3.5 per cent by 1983. Friedman's free market policies began their (until recently) unchallenged heyday.

In 1994 an extremist free market Congress took power in the USA and the stock bubble grew correspondingly: the DJA quadrupled 1994–2000 (1987–1994 it had doubled, and had doubled earlier 1973–1987). The signs of the bubble were everywhere: working people quit their jobs to 'momentum trade' dot.com stocks on margin. *The bubble was popped in exactly the same way as in 1929*: the Federal Reserve, seeing the bubble, tried to deflate it slowly via a systematic sequence of many small quarterly interest rate increases. The difference with 1929 is that, with lenders of the last resort in place to avoid a crash, the air never completely came out. Stocks still sell at very high price/earnings ratios because there are so few other places to park all the money in circulation. But as we've pointed out elsewhere, ideas of 'overvalued' and 'undervalued' are effectively subjective (McCauley et al. 2009).

In 1998 the world finance market was saved from a crash by providing liquidity (Dunbar 2000). Following two ideas, the Modigliani–Miller 'theorem' (McCauley 2004; Modigliani and Miller 1958) and the expectation that market equilibrium will prevail after large deviations, the hedge fund Long Term Capital Management (LTCM) had achieved a debt to equity ratio approaching infinity, with leveraging supplied by nearly every major bank in the world. Not admitting that markets are nonstationary, and ignoring that the money/liquidity bath is absolutely necessary for the application of Brownian models, they literally 'became the market' in Russian bonds (with trading rules based on the nonstationary Black–Scholes model), so that when they wanted to sell, they suffered the Gamblers' Ruin. Modigliani and Miller had considered only small changes in returns, where there is no need to worry about the Gamblers' Ruin. The Modigliani–Miller argument is wrong when extrapolated to large debt to equity ratios, but Americans borrow, spend and consume as if Modigliani and Miller would have been incorporated into the American psyche. This is only since the deregulation of the USD and the corresponding great inflation of the 1970s.

Today, instead of gold and central bank 'sticks' (with corresponding 'carrots' for speculators), we have the International Monetary Fund and other non democratic, supra-governmental agencies like the World Bank and the World Trade Organization that try to play a regulatory role in the world economy. The European Union is not a confederated democracy like Switzerland, but is top-down bureaucracy or administration (*Verwaltung*), with rules made in Brussels handed down by edict. A currency remains strong when an economically strong enough country pays higher interest rates, which is a deflationary mechanism. A weak currency like the Bush dollar, with trade and budget deficits running through the ceiling since 2001, can finance its debt only through attracting foreign money via high enough interest rates. A small country like Argentina cannot do that: the US gets away with it only because speculators have not believed that the US government will allow the USD to collapse, and then came more (and necessary) inflation due to pumping in liquidity to prevent a financial crash after the Sub-Prime Mortgage Debacle of autumn 2007. But in contrast with the gold standard, there's no enforcement mechanism. The entire financial edifice is built on belief, and as Soros (1998) has correctly emphasized there is always a perception gap between economic belief and market reality.

There is in any case not enough gold in the world even to think about financing modern consumption and economic growth. The number of USD in the world had increased about 55 per cent from 1945–1965, *and by about 2000 per cent 1971–2001*. Inflation via fast, cheap credit is absolutely necessary for what we call modern prosperity, but the value placed on the USD relative to other currencies is a matter of faith, and when confidence is lost, as it now is lost by the world in the Bush/neo-conservative policies, then there is no bottom to catch the USD as it falls. The crisis is severe enough that both the Chinese and some oil suppliers consider pricing oil in euros, not dollars.

For the USA, the traditional method of remedying a trade imbalance (devaluation of the currency) no longer works. With the Bush deficit made worse by war spending, the USD fell from US$0.87/euro in 2000 to US$1.33/euro today, but China, beyond control by the West, pegs the yuan to the USD, guaranteeing that cheap production in China will always win. The West exports manufacturing to China, increasing unemployment and simultaneously increasing inflation via increasing oil prices due to a weak USD.[2] At the same time, USA must pay high enough interest rates to attract foreign capital (via sale of Treasury Bills and

Bonds) to finance the enormous deficit. China had enough dollars to buy Chevron in 2005, but the free market congress nixed the deal. A central bank's method of trying to control the money supply is simple: selling bonds and bills reduces the money supply (banks are required to participate), while buying them back increases the money supply. With fractional reserve banking, necessarily required for the inflation via credit for economic growth and consequent consumption, a bank need keep on hand only a certain fraction of what it lends (again, without full backing by gold, credit is money creation). The story with China now is similar to the story with Europe in the 1950s: the US sacrificed its currency (and now jobs as well) for strategic reasons, but then lost control of its own currency (it's a free market in FX!). A trade tariff combined with rebuilding some of the American industry that was lost first to the Mexican Border and then to Asia would be the correct alternative.

The history of globalizing capital can be understood systematically as the history of the increase in liquidity and deregulation internationally. It was, in fact, only a few years ago that the Glass–Steagal act was eliminated by the believers in completely unregulated free markets who dominate the US Congress, allowing banks to go back into the stock market business. The entire programme in deregulation is based on an uncritical belief in a nonexistent stability of unregulated markets, in the face of empirical evidence that unregulated markets are unstable.

The empirical basis for modelling in the social sciences

The irrelevant dilemmas created for themselves by economists who wish to begin theorizing either on the basis of shaky assumptions about agents' intentions, or by imposing postulates a priori on the behaviour of the market is described by McCann. Those of us who want to understand markets cannot use such confusion. Instead of wallowing communally in the unnecessary mire, we present next the foundation for modelling in the social sciences, although truth be known the same rules apply to the analysis of time series in physics or in any science. This section is dedicated especially to Vela.

Consider a one dimensional stochastic process and coarsegrain the x-axis into bins. The number and size of bins must be such that, excepting the region for large enough $|x|$ where no points are observed, the number of points/bin is large compared with unity. Obviously, this will fail when x is large enough in magnitude: 'good statistics' means having a lot of points in each bin.

One needs many runs of the same identical experiment in order to obtain good histograms/statistics and averages. This means that for data analysis we need N different realizations of the time series $x_k(t)$, $k = 1,\ldots$, where for good statistics $N \gg 1$. At time t each point in each run provides one point in a histogram. The average of a dynamical variable $A(x, t)$ is then given by

$$\langle A(x, t) \rangle = \frac{1}{N} \sum_{k=1}^{N} A(x_k(t), t) \qquad (22.21)$$

where the N values $x_k(t)$ are taken from different runs *at the same time* t. Assume that the variable x takes on n discrete values x_m, $m = 1,2,\ldots$, and assume that x_m occurs W_m times during the N runs, falls into the mth bin, and denote

$$w_m = W_m/N, \sum_{m=1}^{n} w_m,$$

with,

$$N = \sum_{m=1}^{n} W_m. \tag{22.22}$$

Then

$$\langle A(x, t) \rangle = 1\backslash N \sum_{m=1}^{n} w_m A(x_m(t), t). \tag{22.23}$$

The w_m are what we mean by the histograms for the 1-point density. If the histograms can be approximated by a smooth density $f_1(x, t)$, then (22.23) becomes

$$\langle A(x, t) \rangle = \int dx f_1(x, t) A(x, t). \tag{22.24}$$

This is the unconditioned average. In finance, for calculating option prices, e.g. we always want instead the conditional average starting from a specific initial condition (x_0, t_0). This would require histograms for $f_2(y, t{:}x, s)$, whereby the transition density $p_2 = f_2/f_1$ could then be constructed. In practice this is hard. What one does instead is first to check the increment autocorrelations. If the increment autocorrelations vanish then we have a martingale. Martingales obey diffusive dynamics. If $f_1(x, t)$ has been extracted, and extracting the time dependence is nontrivial, then the diffusion coefficient $D(x, t)$ can in principle be found by solving the inverse problem in the diffusion *pde* (Bassler *et al.* 2006, Alejandro-Quinones *et al.* 2006). Both p_2 and f_1 satisfy the same *pde* for Ito processes. As noted, this procedure requires that one has discovered the time dependence of f_1. If scaling holds then this is easy, one need only find the Hurst exponent H for the variance. But scaling generally does not hold. FX data are traded 24 hours a day. In that case, when we analyse one market, e.g. the London market, then we must be able to reset the clock and take an arbitrary time, say 9 a.m., as the starting time each day (Bassler *et al.* 2007).

A single time series provides no statistics, no histograms: there is only one point at each time t. Dynamics cannot be deduced from a single time series unless very special conditions are first met. There are exactly three cases where this is possible. If one of the cases cannot be applied then no theory can be derived from the observed time series. Here, we meet the requirement for some underlying degree of statistical regularity in the time series. We will now classify the possible regularities.

First, if the time series is stationary then the 1-point density and all absolute averages of all not explicitly time dependent functions $A(x)$ are t-independent (Stratonovich 1963). In this case we have the ergodic theorem (Yaglom and Yaglom 1962),

$$\langle A(x) \rangle = \frac{1}{N} \sum_{k=1}^{N} A(x_k(t)) = \int dx A(xt) f_1(x) \tag{22.25}$$

where the 1-point density is obtained from the time series from ergodicity: equally sized regions in the one dimensional phase space x are visited with frequency proportional to $f_1(x)$, so we can coarsegrain the interval $x_{min} < x < x_{max}$ into cells and obtain f_k by counting how often x_k occurs in the time series. If there is no drift and the motion is bounded (takes place in a box) then $f_1(x) =$ constant if there is no probability current through the system (e.g. solve $\partial f / \partial t = (\partial^2 f / \partial x^2)/2 = 0$ in a box). But finance markets are nonstationary, are very far from statistical equilibrium. The equations that describe finance markets do not even admit statistical equilibrium as a possibility.

Second, if the increments are stationary, if $x(t, T) = x(t + T) - x(t) = x(T)$ 'in probability', then we can obtain $f_1(x, T)$ from a single, long time series by sliding a window. We start at a point t, read the value of x at the point $t + T$ and thereby construct a histogram that yields $f_1(x, T)$. In this case the log increment $x(t, T) = lnp(t + T)/p(t) = lnp(T)/p(0) = x(T)$ is a 'good' variable, and a single long time series yields 'good statistics'. We may test for stationary increments by breaking the time series up into N 'runs' of equal length, and then calculating the mean square fluctuation

$$\langle (x^2(t, T)) \rangle = \frac{1}{N} \sum_{k=1}^{N} x_k^2(t, T) \tag{22.26}$$

for all different times $t_{min} < t < t_{max}$ in a single run. If the increments are stationary then the mean square fluctuation is constant, independent of starting time t, as in the case of solutions of $\partial f / \partial t = (\partial^2 f / \partial x^2)/2$ on the unbounded interval generally do not have stationary increments.

The reader is now referred to a discussion in Chapter 1 of McCauley (2004) where it's implicitly argued that nothing can be discovered unless something is periodic, or is in *some* sense systematically repeated, or is invariant (period zero). The repetitiveness in ergodicity (quasiperiodicity), and with stationary increments $x(T) = x(t, T)$ the 2-point density (but not the 1-point density!) is time translationally invariant.

What can we do if we have a single, long time series and the increments are nonstationary and uncorrelated? In this case we can only start by making an *ansatz*. We assume, e.g. that the traders repeat the same stochastic dynamics each day. This is equivalent to assuming that the same diffusion coefficient $D(x, t)$ describes the trading day after day. So each day is regarded as a rerun of the same 'experiment'. This may or may not be true: once the data analysis has been performed, we can check for its validity as follows. Calculate the mean square fluctuation $\langle x^2(t, T) \rangle$ for one day. Then, calculate the same quantity on the time scale of a week. If the *ansatz* is true then the weekly plot of the mean square fluctuation will look like five repetitions of the daily plot.

If this fails, then there is no need to write finance or economics texts because there is no empirical basis, or any other basis, for discovering any lawful behaviour whatsoever. The same argument applies to other social sciences. We would then be in the situation described by Wigner (1967) where there may be laws of motion but we would have no way to discover them.

We've noted elsewhere that 'no arbitrage' between geographically different markets is an analogue of rotational invariance (McCauley 2004), but there is no accompanying conservation law even in the most idealized case because market dynamics are driven-dissipative, are therefore not described by a Lagrangian. In addition, we do not find FX market statistics to be independent of geographical location.

FX markets today

In the 1980s FX transactions decoupled from economic growth, with US10^8/min. traded. There was a 55 per cent increase in USD 1945–1965. There was a 2000 per cent increase in USD 1971–2001. What we identify as modern prosperity is impossible without high liquidity/credit/inflation. With no gold standard or any stiff regulations to stabilize one currency against another, the foreign currency bets via derivatives have become standard market procedure.

For the USA, the traditional method of remedying a trade imbalance, devaluation of the currency, no longer works. The USA borrows and consumes too much and produces too little. This is a consequence of deregulation, moral restraint does not work. With the increasing US deficit made worse by war spending, the USD fell from US$0.87/euro in 2000 to US$1.33/euro today. China, beyond control by the West, pegs the yuan to the USD, guaranteeing that cheap production in China will always win. Both the Chinese and oil producers now consider abandoning the weakening dollar in favour of the euro.

The philosophy of the West since the stagflation era is the philosophy of the Chicago School of Economics, whose main protagonist is Milton Friedman. We can paraphrase Friedman's (Friedman and Friedman 1980) advice as: if someone else can produce it cheaper, then let them produce it. That argument makes an invalid assumption of liquidity in inventiveness and consequent demand for labour. Jacobs (1995) advocated something entirely different: to replace imports by local production, and to use local currency and laws to support that production. It's as if Asia follows Jacobs, even if Asia has not read her.

We can compare the present era of USD weakness, 2001–2008, with the 1970s, but aside from the weakness of a USD that has flooded the world, the circumstances are different. US production has been much reduced since 1971 while US consumption has exploded. We don't know when the worldwide inflationary bubble will pop, but we can make an order of magnitude prediction.

The bubble will pop when a liquidity crunch, like the present sub-prime mortgage crisis, involves bets so large that a consortium of banks can no longer cover the lost bets. In that case there are two clear alternatives: deflation and depression, or further degradation of the currency by outlandish money creation.

We want to contrast real FX market behaviour with what is widely believed, namely, 'stylized facts'. The so-called 'observed stylized facts' of FX markets have been stated by Hommes (2002): (i) 'asset prices are persistent and have, or are close to having, a unit root and are thus (close to) nonstationary'; (ii) 'asset returns are fairly unpredictable, and typically have little or no autocorrelations' and (iii) 'asset returns have fat tails and exhibit volatility clustering and long memory. Autocorrelations of squared returns and absolute returns are significantly positive, even at high-order lags, and decay slowly.' These three statements reflect a fairly standard set of expectations in financial economics. Next, we contrast those expected stylized facts with the hard results of our recent FX data analysis (Bassler *et al.* 2007). Our analysis is based on six years (1999–2004) of euro/USD exchange rates taken at one minute intervals.

In point (i) above 'unit root' means that in $p(t + T) = ap(t) +$ noise, $a = 1$. That is a necessary condition for a martingale, an efficient market. That condition rules out persistence or anti-persistence like fractional Brownian motion (fBm), and prices are not 'close to nonstationary', prices are far from stationary. (ii) Increment autocorrelationsin FX market returns will vanish after about ten minutes of trading, and a simple coordinate transformation $x(t) = ln(p(t)/p_c)$ cannot erase persistence, whatever 'persistence' might be. Both prices and returns have positive autocorrelation, and autocorrelations in increments are approximately zero after ten minutes of trading. (iii) We find no evidence for fat tails in intraday trading, and no evidence for the persistence of Hurst exponent scaling on the time scale of a day. Because of nonstationarity of the increments, a seven year FX time series is far too short (the histograms have too much scatter due to too few points) to indicate what may happen on a time scale of a month. The proof will be presented in a later paper that volatility clustering does not indicate 'long memory' but can be understood as a purely Markovian phenomenon for variable diffusion processes, stochastic processes with diffusion coefficients $D(x, t)$ where the (x, t)dependence is inherently nonseparable (Bassler *et al.* 2006; Alejandro-Quinones *et al.* 2006).

We've recently explained elsewhere that the data analyses used to arrive at the expected stylized facts have generally used a technique called 'sliding windows' (Bassler *et al.* 2007; Gallucio *et al.* 1997; Borland 1998). Sliding windows produce spurious, misleading results because FX data are nonstationary processes with nonstationary increments. The spurious results are fat tails and Hurst exponent scaling (Bassler *et al.* 2007; Borland 1998).

Next, we describe our study of a six year time series of euro–dollar exchange rates from Olsen & Associates (Bassler *et al.* 2007). The increments $x(t, T) = x(t + T) - x(t) = ln(p(t + T)/p(t))$ are nonstationary, *as is shown by the root mean square fluctuation in increments plotted against* t *in Figure 22.1*, where $T =$ ten minutes to ensure that there are no autocorrelations in increments. Second, note

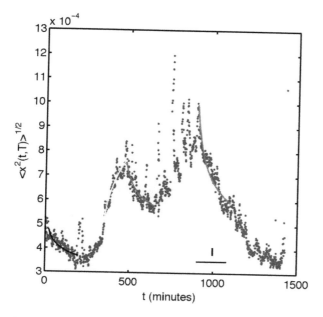

Figure 22.1 The root mean square fluctuation of the daily euro–US$ exchange rate.

Notes

$A_T(t_1,t_2) = \langle x(t_1,T)x(t_2,T)\rangle/(\langle x^2(t_1)\rangle\langle x^2(t_2)\rangle)^{1/2}$ for two nonoverlapping time intervals $[t_1,t_1 + T]$, decay rapidly toward zero for $T \geq$ ten minutes of trading. The root mean square fluctuation $\langle x^2(t, T)^{1/2}\rangle$ of the daily euro–USD exchange rate, the unconditioned average of the diffusion coefficient of the martingale process, is plotted against time of day t, with $T =$ ten minutes to insure that auto-correlations in increments have died out. For either a stationary process or a process with station-ary increments, the plot would be a flat line. The four continuous lines drawn in represent regions where scaling with four different Hurst exponents can be used to fit the data.

that the returns data do not scale with a Hurst exponent H or even with several different Hurst exponents over the course of a trading day (we define a trading day in a 24 hour market by resetting the clock at the same time each morning). Figure 22.2 shows that the same stochastic process is repeated on different days of the week, so that we can assume a *single*, definite intraday stochastic process $x(t)$ in intraday returns. In Figure 22.1 we see that scaling can be used to fit the data only within four disjoint time intervals during the day, and even then with four different Hurst exponents ($H < 1/2$ in three of the intervals, $H > 1/2$ in the other). *That is, the intraday stochastic process* x(t) *generally does not scale and instead will exhibit a complicated time dependence in the variance.* The variance does not approach a constant, the process is nonstationary and far from equilib-rium. If we would dare to extrapolate on the basis of Figure 22.2, then we would roughly estimate $\sigma^2(t) \approx t$ for a time lag of $T \approx 1$ day.

We investigated only one of the four intervals marked in Figure 22.1 because the other three present us with much sparser histograms. Within that interval a data collapse $F(u) = t^H f(x, t)$ with $H \approx 0.35$ can be used to fit the data, and we

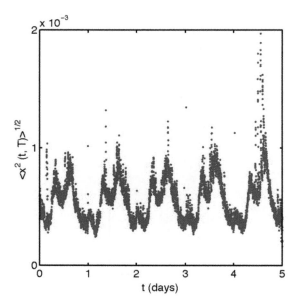

t (days)

Figure 22.2 The root mean square fluctuation of the daily euro–US$ exchange rate: intraday stochastic process.

Notes
We observe that the same intraday stochastic process occurs during each trading day. Both of the plots (a) and (b) would be flat were the increments $x(t, T)$ stationary. Instead, the *rms* fluctuation of $x(t, T)$ varies by a factor of three each day as t is varied, exhibiting strongly nonstationary increments.

see that the scaling function $F(u)$ has no fat tails, is instead approximately a two-sided exponential (Figure 22.3). For martingale dynamics the transition density obeys McCauley (2007b) and Stratonovich (1963)

$$\frac{\partial p_2(x, t|x_o, t_o)}{\partial t} = \frac{1}{2}\frac{\partial^2}{\partial x^2}(D(x, t)p_2(x, t|x_o, t_o)) \tag{22.27}$$

$p_2(x, t|x_o, t) = \delta(x - x_o)$, where volatility is described by the inseparable (x, t) dependence in the diffusion coefficient $D(x, t)$, and the 1-point density obeys the same *pde*

$$\frac{\partial f_1(x, t)}{\partial t} = \frac{1}{2}\frac{\partial^2}{\partial x^2}(D(x, t)f_1(x, t)) \tag{22.28}$$

The lognormal pricing model has a diffusion coefficient linear in p and is nonvolatile, is topologically equivalent to a Wiener process $x(t)$ (McCauley *et al.* 2008), where $D(x, t)$ = constant. For the region in Figure 22.3 where the 1-point density scales (Bassler *et al.* 2006, 2007),

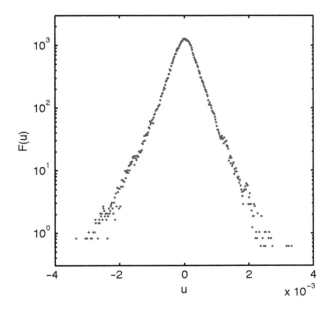

Figure 22.3 Scaling function $F(u)$.

Notes
Our scaling analysis uses the data for the longest curve drawn in Figure 22.1 above $t = 1000$ minutes. Here, we exhibit the data collapse by plotting the scaling function $F(u) = t^{-H}f_1(x, t)$ for $H = 0.35$ with ten minutes $\leq T \leq 160$ minutes. Note that $F(u)$ is slightly asymmetric and is approximately exponential, showing that the variance is finite.

$$f_1(x, t) = t^{-H}F(u), \quad u = x/|t|^{H} \tag{22.29}$$

we obtain from (22.28)

$$2H(uF)' + (\hat{D}F)'' = 0 \tag{22.30}$$

where (Bassler *et al.* 2006)

$$D(x, t) = |t|^{2H-1}\hat{D}(u). \tag{22.31}$$

From this we obtain

$$\hat{D}(u)F(u) = \hat{D}(0)F(0) - 2H\int_0^u uF(u)du \tag{22.32}$$

For a two-sided exponential density

$$F(u) = \begin{cases} A_+e^{-vu}, & u > 0 \\ A_-e^{-\gamma u}, & u > 0 \end{cases} \tag{22.33}$$

we obtain

$$\hat{D}(u) = \begin{cases} 2H[1 + vu]/v^2, u > 0 \\ 2H[1 - \gamma u]/\gamma^2, u < 0 \end{cases}.$$ (22.34)

We can calculate the transition density numerically but not analytically, so we understand the dynamics of the nonstationary variable diffusion processes that describe FX markets.

FX market instability is characterized as follows. First, we have a martingale process (uncorrelated increments), and we explained in the fourth part of the chapter above why martingales are inconsistent with a stationary process. The mean square fluctuation does not stabilize on the time scale of a day so the variance does not approach a constant. Using

$$\sigma^2(t + T) = \langle x^2(t, T) \rangle + \sigma^2(t),$$ (22.35)

if we use Figure 22.2 and take the time lag to be one day we see that the mean square fluctuation is t-independent, the increments are approximately stationary. This means that the variance is linear in the time on that time scale, which is expressed in (22.29) as

$$\langle x^2(t, T) \rangle \approx T \langle x^2(1) \rangle.$$

We've explained elsewhere (Bassler et al. 2008) why nonstationary processes generally cannot be transformed into a stationary Gaussian process. A stationary process cannot be used to describe or understand financial markets in our era. In the past, financial economists stuck to stationary models for lack of knowledge how to model nonstationary processes, and how to extract information on nonstationary processes from raw data. Neither excuse holds any longer, we can treat nonstationary market dynamics precisely.

Spurious stylized facts

Our main point here is: *the data analyses used to arrive at the expected stylized facts have generally used a technique called 'sliding windows'* (Bassler et al. 2007). The aim of this section is to explain that sliding windows can produce spurious, misleading results because FX data are nonstationary processes with nonstationary increments. Only one previous FX data analysis (Gallucio et al. 1997) that we are aware of showed that sliding windows lead to a spurious Hurst exponent $H_s = 1/2$, and correctly identified the cause as nonstationarity of the increments. We explain the occurrence of $H_s = 1/2$ theoretically below. It must be realized that there are three separate 1-point densities under consideration. First, there is the empirically correctly obtained density $f_1(x, t)$. Second is the increment density $f_{incr}(z, t, T) \neq f_1(x, t)$ (22.35) because the increments are nonstationary. Third, there is the 'spurious density' $f_s(z, T)$ obtained from a sliding window analysis which equals neither of the first two densities, and cannot even be calculated analytically because the ergodic theorem cannot be applied.

Here's what's meant by the sliding window method: one treats the increment $z = x(t, T)$ as if it would be independent of time of day t, and attempts to construct histograms $f_1(z, T)$ for increments at different lag times T by reading a time series of returns $x(t)$. There, one starts at initial time t and forms a window at time $t + T$. One assumes that the increment $z = x(T, t) = x(t + T) - x(t)$ generates a 1-point density that is independent of t by sliding the window along the entire length of the time series, increasing t by one unit at a time while holding T fixed. For a long time series, one of at least $t_{max} \approx$ several years in length, $t_{max} >> T$, this method is expected to produce good statistics because it picks up a lot of data points. The histograms generated from varying t in the *increments* $x(t, T)$ yield $f_1(z, T)$ independently of t if the increments are stationary, *otherwise the assumption generally is false*. In our case the assumption is false: first, Figure 22.1 shows that the increments are uncorrelated after about ten minutes. Second, Figure 22.2 shows that the mean square fluctuation $\langle x^2(t, T) \rangle$ with T fixed at ten minutes depends very strongly on t throughout the course of a trading day. This means simply that the traders' noisy behaviour is not independent of time of day. *Our conclusion is that FX data, taken at ten minutes (or longer) intervals are described by a martingale with nonstationary increments in log returns.*

To illustrate how spurious stylized facts are generated by using a sliding window in data analysis, we apply that method to a time series with uncorrelated nonstationary increments, one with no fat tails and with a Hurst exponent $H = 0.35$, namely, a time series generated by the exponential density (22.24) with $H = 0.35$ (Figure 22.3) and linear diffusion (22.39). The process is Markovian. Figure 22.3 was generated by taking 5,000,000 independent runs of the Ito process, each starting from $x(0) = 0$ for $T = 10$, 100 and 1000. The sliding window result is shown as Figure 22.3. In this case, the sliding windows appear to yield a scale free density $F_s(u_s)$, $u_s = x_s(T)/T^{H_s}$, from an empirical average over t that one cannot even formulate analytically, *because for a nonstationary process there is no ergodic theorem*. Not only are fat tails generated artificially here, but we get a Hurst exponent $H_S = 1/2$ that disagrees with the Hurst exponent used to generate the time series. *This is the method that has been used to generate stylized facts in nearly all existing finance data analyses.*

Next, we describe our study of a six year time series of euro–USD exchange rates from Olsen & Associates (Bassler *et al.* 2007). The increments $x(t, T) = x(t + T) - x(t) = ln(p(t + T)/p(t))$ are nonstationary, *as is shown by the root mean square fluctuation in increments plotted against* t *in Figure 22.1*, where $T = $ ten minutes to ensure that there are no autocorrelations in increments (Figure 22.1). Second, note that the returns data do not scale with a Hurst exponent H over the time scale of a trading day (we define a trading day in a 24 hour market by resetting the clock at the same time each morning). Figure 22.2 shows that the same stochastic process is repeated on different days of the week, so that we can assume a *single*, definite intraday stochastic process $x(t)$ in intraday returns.

In Figure 22.1 we see that scaling can be used to fit the data only within four disjoint time intervals during the day, and even then with four different Hurst exponents ($H < 1/2$ in three of the intervals, $H > 1/2$ in the other). *That is, the intraday stochastic process x(t) generally does not scale and will exhibit a complicated time dependence in the variance $\langle x^2(t) \rangle$.*

Within the trading interval where we checked a collapse $F(u) = t^H f(x, t)$ can be used to fit the data, we see that the scaling function $F(u)$ has no fat tails, is instead approximately exponential Figure 22.4. Here, we investigated only one of the four intervals because the other three are generated by much fewer points. If we apply the method of sliding windows to the finance time series within the interval *I* shown in Figure 22.1, then we get Figure 22.4, which has artificially generated fat tails and also a Hurst exponent $H_S = 1/2$, just as with our numerical simulation using time series generated via the exponential density to generate a Markov time series Figure 22.3. *This shows how sliding windows can generate artificial fat tails and spurious Hurst exponents of 1/2 in data analysis.* That is, the use of sliding windows generates 'spurious stylized facts' when the increments are nonstationary. This observation has far reaching consequences for the analysis of random time series, whether in physics, economics/finance or biology.

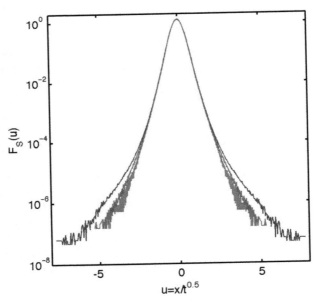

Figure 22.4 The 'sliding interval scaling function'.

Notes
The 'sliding interval scaling function' $F_s(u_s)$, $u_s = x_s(T)/T^{H_s}$, is constructed using a slidi window time average for the same time interval as in Figure 22.3 for $T = 10$, 20 and 40 m utes. Note that fat tails have been generated spuriously by the sliding window, and that a Hu exponent $H_s = 1/2$ has been generated, contradicting the fact that the correct scaling functi shown as Figure 22.3 has $H = 0.35$.

With uncorrelated, nonstationary increments, in an interval where scaling fits then the mean square fluctuation (Bassler *et al.* 2006) is

$$\langle x^2(t, T)\rangle = \langle (x^2(t + T) - x(t))^2 \rangle = \langle x^2(1)\rangle[(t + T)^{2H} - t^{2H})] \tag{22.36}$$

In most existing data analyses we generally have $T/t \ll 1$ (where $T =$ ten minutes and t ranges from opening to closing time over a day), so

$$\langle x^2(t, T)\rangle \approx \langle x^2(1)\rangle 2Ht^{2H-1}T. \tag{22.37}$$

A sliding window then (illegally, because the process is not ergodic so that time averages cannot be replaced by ensemble averages) averages empirically over t,

$$\langle x^2(t, T)\rangle_S \approx \langle x^2(1)\rangle 2H\langle t^{2H-1}\rangle_S T \tag{22.38}$$

yielding $\langle x^2(t, T)\rangle \approx T^{2H_S}$ with $2H_S = 1$. Sliding window Hurst exponents $H_S = 1/2$ have been reported often enough in the literature (see, e.g. Borland 1998), but without any correct explanation of how they arise from self similar models where increments are uncorrelated with $H \approx 1/2$. That $H_S = 1/2$ is a consequence of using sliding windows was first reported by Galluccio *et al.* in 1997 in a paper that we did not appreciate at all until we rediscovered the implications of nonstationary increments for ourselves. In 1996 there was no theory available as guide.

Finally, we speculate that stock prices, in contrast, may exhibit fat tails (but not Hurst exponent scaling) in intraday trading. That case remains to be analysed correctly, taking into account the nonstationarity of the increments. We've shown elsewhere (McCauley 2008b) that arch/garch methods are falsified by FX market data.

We emphasize the importance of Figures 22.1 and 22.2, both of which illustrate different aspects of the instability of FX trading in our era. Figure 22.1 shows the erratic behaviour of traders' intraday behaviour as the average of the diffusion coefficient (Bassler *et al.* 2008)

$$\langle x^2(t, T)\rangle \approx T\int dx D(x, t) f_1(x, t), t \gg T. \tag{22.39}$$

The 'noise' in Figure 22.1 is not volatility, it's instead due to the fact that with a lag time of $T =$ ten minutes, for each time t there are only 1500 points in a six year time series from which to obtain statistics. In principle, as is shown by (22.39), that plot Figure 22.1 should be piecewise smooth as a function of t, allowing for slope discontinuities in $D(x, t)$. Figure 22.2 also shows something entirely new: that the intraday behaviour is repeated with the mathematical precision of a statistical law on an interday basis. This is perhaps the first example of hard evidence of regularity in behaviour, discovered on an empirico-theoretic basis, in economics and psychology in particular, and in the social sciences in general.

Acknowledgements

This chapter is based in part on my lecture given at the 2007 Geilo NATO-ASI on Evolution, and relies strongly on references (Bassler *et al.* 2008; McCauley 2008a), and on other papers written with my close colleagues Kevin Bassler and Gemunu Gunaratne. My wife/partner and former *Schwarzwälder Bote* local editor, Cornelia Küffner, read and suggested improvements in the presentation. I have dedicated this chapter to my very good friend and colleague Vela Velupillai, an expert on both economic history and computability, a colleague with such fine and broad tastes that he appreciates Wigner's essays on the reasons for the effectiveness of mathematics in physics and is also one of the few who appreciates Moore's work on the computational capabilities of dynamical systems. I wish to add that very few physicists have read and appreciated Wigner's essays, and fewer still have studied and understood Turing's ideas. I might wish for more colleagues like Vela, but he's unique, and I'm very fortunate to have benefited from his deep friendship and interests, and his extensive knowledge of the history of economic thought. We also have in common a love of wasting our time reading *krimis* written in Scandinavian by Swedish and Icelandic writers.

Notes

1 A myth is that the Nazis came to power in 1933 because the Allies drained Germany via reparations. In fact, Germany successfully resisted reparations but had high unemployment for the same reason as did the US. Hitler's Finance Minister Hjalmar Horace Greely Schacht got the ball rolling via Keynsian-style inflationary public spending. That was the era when the Autobahns began to be built, e.g. the wild German inflation of 1923 was a Berlin ploy to deflect France's demands for reparations payments.
2 According to Milton Friedman, 'if they can make it cheaper then let them make it'. That extremist free market position makes an invalid assumption about 'liquidity' namely, that via inventiveness enough new jobs will be found to replace those lost. But economists have rarely worried about empirical inconsistencies in their assumptions.

References

Alejandro-Quinones, A.L., Bassler, K.E., Field, M., McCauley, J.L., Nicol, M., Timofeyev I., Török, A. and Gunaratne, G.H. (2006) 'A theory of fluctuation of stock prices' *Physica*, 363ª: 383–92.
Bassler, K.E., Gunaratne, G.H. and McCauley, J.L. (2006) 'Hurst exponents, Markov processes, and nonlinear diffusion equations', *Physica*, 369a: 343–53.
Bassler, K.E., Gunaratne, G.H. and McCauley, J.L. (2008) 'Empirically based modelling in the social sciences and beyond and spurious stylized facts', *International Review of Financial Analysis*, 17: 767–88.
Bassler, K.E., McCauley, J.L. and Gunaratne, G.H. (2007) 'Nonstationary increments scaling distributions, and variable diffusion processes in financial markets', *PNAS*, 104 172,287–90.
Black, F. (1986) 'Noise', *Journal of Finance*, 3: 529–43.
Black, F. and Scholes, M. (1973) 'The pricing of options and corporate liabilities' *Journal of Political Economy*, 8: 637–54.

Borland, L. (1998) 'The microscopic dynamics of the nonlinear Fokker-Planck equation: A phenomenological model', *Physical Review*, E57: 6634.

Dunbar, N. (2000) *Inventing Money, Long-Term Capital Management and the Search for Risk-Free Profits*, New York: Wiley.

Durrett, R. (1984) *Brownian Motion and Martingales in Analysis*, Belmont, CA: Wadsworth.

Eichengreen, B. (1998) *Globalizing Capital: A History of the International Monetary System*, Princeton, NJ: Princeton University Press.

Fama, E. (1970) 'Efficient capital markets: A review of theory and empirical work' *Journal of Finance*, 25: 383–417.

Friedman, M. and Friedman, R. (1980) *Free to Choose*, New York: Harcourt, Brace, Janovitch.

Gallucio, S., Caldarelli, G., Marsilli, M. and Zhang, Y.-C. (1997) 'Scaling in currency exchange', *Physica*, A245: 423–36.

Hänggi, P., Thomas, H., Grabert, H. and Talkner, P. (1978) 'Note on time evolution of non-Markov processes', *J. Stat. Phys.*, 18: 155–9.

Hauert, C. (2008) 'Evolutionary dynamics', in A. Skjeltorp and A.V. Belushkin (eds) *Evolution from Cellular to Social Scales*, Dordrecht: Springer, Proceedings of 2007 Geilo NATO-ASI.

Hommes, C.H. (2002) 'Modeling the stylized facts in finance through simple nonlinear adaptive systems', *PNAS*, 99(Suppl. 3): 7221–8.

Jacobs, J. (1995) *Cities and the Wealth of Nations*, New York: Vintage.

Kindleberger, C.P. (1996) *Manias, Panics, and Crashes: A History of Financial Crises*, New York: Wiley.

Mandelbrot, B. (1966) 'Forecasts of future prices, unbiased markets, and "martingale" models', *Journal of Business*, 39: 242–55.

McCann, C.R. Jr (1994) *Probability Foundations of Economic Theory*, London: Routledge.

McCauley, J.L. (2004) *Dynamics of Markets: Econophysics and Finance*, Cambridge: Cambridge University Press.

—— (2005) 'Making mathematics effective in economics', in K.V. Velupillai (ed.), *Computability, Complexity and Constructivity in Economic Analysis*, Oxford: Blackwell.

—— (2007a) 'Markov vs. non-Markovian processes: A comment on the paper "Stochastic feedback, nonlinear families of Markov processes, and nonlinear Fokker–Planck equations" by T.D. Frank', *Physica*, A382: 445–52.

—— (2007b) 'The Fokker-Planck equation and Chapman-Kolmogorov equation for Ito processes with finitely many states of memory', in A. Skjeltorp and A.V. Belushkin (eds), *Evolution from Cellular to Social Scales*, Dordrecht: Springer, Proceedings of 2007 Geilo NATO-ASI.

—— (2008a) 'Evolution of FX markets via globalization of capital', in A. Skjeltorp and A.V. Belushkin (eds), *Evolution from Cellular to Social Scales*, New York: Plenum, Proceedings of Geilo NATO-ASI.

—— (2008b) 'Nonstationarity of efficient markets, FX evolution from stability to instability', *International Review of Financial Analysis*, 17: 820–37.

—— (2009 forthcoming) *Rational Expectations as Empirically Based Modelling*.

—— (2010 forthcoming) *Stochastic Processes for Physics, Economics, and Finance*, Cambridge: Cambridge University Press.

McCauley, J.L., Bassler, K.E. and Gunaratne, G.H. (2009) 'On the analysis of time series with nonstationary increments', in B. Rosser (ed.), *Handbook of Complexity Research*, Cheltenham: Edward Elgar.

—— (2008) 'Martingales, detrending data, and the efficient market hypothesis', *Physica* A387: 202–16.

Modigliani, F. and Miller, M. (1958) 'The cost of capital, corporation finance, and the theory of investment', *American Economic Review*, 48: 261–97.

Muth, J.F. (1961) 'Rational expectations and the theory of price movements', *Economerica*, 29: 315–35.

Osborne, M.F.M. in Cootner, P. (1964) *The Random Character of Stock Market Price* Cambridge, MA: MIT Press.

Sargent, T.J. and Wallace, N. (1976) 'Rational expectations and the theory of economi policy', *Journal of Monetary Economics*, 2: 169–83.

Sharpe, W.F. (1964) 'Capital asset prices: A theory of market equilibrium under. con ditions of risk', *Journal of Finance*, 19: 425–42.

Soros, G. (1998) *The Crisis of Global Capitalism*, New York: Little, Brown & Co.

Stratonovich, R.L. (1963) *Topics in the Theory of Random Noise*, vol. I, (trans. R.A. Si verman), New York: Gordon & Breach.

Velupillai, K.V. (2005) 'The unreasonable ineffectiveness of mathematics in economics *Cambridge Journal of Economics*, 29: 849–72.

Wigner, E.P. (1967) *Symmetries and Reflections*, Bloomington, IN: Indiana Universi Press.

Yaglom, A.M. and Yaglom, I.M. (1962) *An Introduction to the Theory of Stationa Random Functions*, (trans. and ed. R.A. Silverman), Englewood Cliffs, NJ: Prentic Hall.

23 Elasticity puzzle

An inquiry into micro–macro relations

Shu-Heng Chen, Ya-Chi Huang and Jen-Fu Wang

Introduction and motivation

In this chapter, an agent-based computational capital asset pricing model is applied to address the issue, known as the *elasticity puzzle*, originating from a famous reciprocal relation between the *elasticity of intertemporal substitution* and the *relative risk aversion coefficient*. Based on this reciprocal relation, the implied relative risk aversion coefficient can be unexpectedly, and possibly unacceptably, high when the estimated elasticity of intertemporal substitution is very low and even close to zero.

Existing studies on the elasticity puzzle, be they theoretical or empirical, are largely confined to the conventional framework built upon the devices of rational expectations and representative agents. A number of recent empirical studies, however, have documented that agents are heterogeneous in their elasticity of intertemporal substitution.[1] Two questions immediately arise. The first one concerns the aggregation problem. If the intertemporal elasticity is heterogeneous among agents, then what is the relation between the aggregate elasticity and its individual counterparts? This leads us to the very basic issue raised by Alan Kirman (1992), 'whom or what does the representative individual represent?' The second one is to do with why the rich and the stockholders tend to have to high intertemporal elasticities, and their counterparts tend to have low ones. Why is such a behavioural parameter so critical in determining the wealth share of individuals?[2]

Empirical studies also find that the Euler consumption equation applies well only to the stock market participants, and not to all individuals. It is certainly plausible that not all individuals can be good at optimizing. So, here comes the third question. Is it possible for some agents who happen to be good at optimizing and hence behave closer to what the Euler equation predicts to eventually become wealthier, and for those who do not and hence fail to meet the Euler equation to eventually become poor? Do the rich really have different intertemporal elasticities as opposed to their opposites, or are they just 'smarter' or endowed with better luck? Is it possible for the 'observed' heterogeneity in intertemporal elasticity to be just *spurious*? In sum, what is the relationship between the observable elasticity and the true one, considering that agents are *boundedly rational*?

Using an agent-based computational model, we develop a consumption capital asset pricing model (CAPM, hereafter) composed of boundedly rational interacting heterogeneous agents. These agents are heterogeneous in their forecasts (the way in which they learn from the past), saving and investment decisions, and are driven by an adaptive scheme, specifically, genetic algorithms. Their preferences can be homogeneous or heterogeneous, depending on what we are asking. Simulating the model can generate a sequence of time series observations of individuals' profiles, including beliefs, consumption, savings and portfolios. Unlike most theoretical or empirical studies of the consumption CAPM model, the agent-based computational model does not assume an exogenously given stochastic process of returns and consumption. Instead, aggregate consumption, asset prices and returns are also endogenously generated with agents under specified risk preferences and intertemporal elasticities. With these endogenously generated aggregate and individual data, we are better equipped to answer the three questions posed above in relation to survival dynamics.

The rest of the chapter is organized as follows. We shall first give a little technical review of the elasticity puzzle, followed by a literature review on the reflections upon the puzzle. There are basically two kinds of reflections, namely, the one from the econometric viewpoint, and the one from the theoretic viewpoint. For the latter, we further distinguish the relaxation of the assumption of the power utility function and the relaxation of the assumption of the representative agent. This background knowledge helps us define the departure of this chapter, which has an agent-based consumption Capital Asset Pricing Model as its core. The technical details of the model are left for Appendix A and Appendix B. Based on the proposed agent-based consumption CAPM model, we propose two experimental designs to examine the effect of bounded rationality on the estimated elasticity, and the results are shown and analysed in equation (23.5). The analysis is econometric and is based on the Euler consumption equation, whose derivation is briefly reviewed in Appendix C. We then end the chapter with a few concluding remarks.

The puzzle and the reflections

Elasticity puzzle

The elasticity of intertemporal substitution (EIS, hereafter), as a technical characterization of economic behaviour and a basic parameter of economic models, plays a pivotal role in economic analysis. To mention a few of its characteristics, its magnitude can determine the sensitivity of saving to the interest rate, the effect of capital income taxation (King and Rebelo 1990; Summers 1981) and the impact of uncertainty on the rate of economic growth (Jones et al. 1999). Given its significance, a great deal of effort has been devoted to the empirical study of its magnitude.

An early influential empirical finding was established in Hall (1988), who provided evidence of a low or, in fact, an almost zero intertemporal elasticity:

All the estimates presented in this paper of the intertemporal elasticity of substitution are small. Most of them are also quite precise, supporting the strong conclusion that the elasticity is unlikely to be much above 0.1, and may well be zero.

(ibid.: 340)

This result implies that consumption growth is completely insensitive to changes in interest rates. Hall's estimation is built upon the *consumption capital asset pricing model*, originally put forwarded by Breeden (1979). A typical assumption in this model is that preference is *intertemporally separable*. A significant consequence of making this assumption is that the EIS and the risk attitude, the two distinct aspects of preference, are intertwined. In actual fact, the EIS and the risk aversion parameter are *reciprocals* of one another. If we further assume that a representative agent maximizes the expectation of a time separable *power utility function*:

$$u_t = E\left\{\sum_{r=0}^{\infty} \beta^r \frac{c_{1-\rho}^{t+r}}{1-\rho} | \Omega_t\right\} \tag{23.1}$$

where β is the rate of time preference, c_t is the investor's consumption in period t and ρ is the coefficient of relative risk aversion, then the mathematical expectation $E(\cdot|)$ is conditional upon information available to agents at time t, Ω_t. Then the reciprocal relation simply becomes

$$\psi = \frac{1}{\rho'} \tag{23.2}$$

where . is the elasticity of intertemporal substitution.

This reciprocal relation puts Hall (1988) in sharp contrast to Hansen and Singleton (1982, 1983), which is commonly cited for evidence that the (constant) coefficient of relative risk aversion is small. Hall's estimates suggest that the value of the intertemporal elasticity of substitution, i.e. the reciprocal of the parameter estimated by Hansen and Singleton, is much smaller than that implied by any of the Hansen–Singleton estimates. The disparity defines an '*elasticity puzzle*' as phrased by Neely *et al.* (2001), by asking 'is the risk aversion parameter in the simple intertemporal consumption CAPM small as in Hansen and Singleton (1982, 1983), or is it that its reciprocal, the intertemporal elasticity of substitution, is small, as in Hall (1988)?'[3]

In a technical way, the *elasticity puzzle* can be summarized as the conflicts of estimating the same coefficient in two regression equations. The one used in Hall (1988) and many follow-ups is the consumption Euler equation,

$$\Delta c_t = \tau + \psi_r + \xi_t, \tag{23.3}$$

where Δc_t is the consumption growth at time t, r_t is the real return on the asset at t and τ is a constant. As is well discussed by Hall (1988), the *time aggregation* problem, e.g. using quarterly data instead of monthly data, can cause the error ξ_t to be no longer white noise. Instead, it is linear in the innovation to consumption growth and asset returns, and is correlated with the regressor r_t. However, given a vector of instruments Z_{t-1} that is uncorrelated with the error, ψ can be identified by the moment restriction

$$E[Z_{t-1}\xi_t] = 0 \tag{23.4}$$

Here Z_{t-1} typically consists of economic variables known at time $t-1$, such as lagged consumption growth and asset returns. Equation (23.3) can be estimated using *two-stage least squares* (2SLS) if the error is homoskedastic, or by the *linear generalized method of moments* (GMM) if the error is heteroskedastic.

Alternatively, the regression equation considered by Hansen and Singleton (1983) is the reversed form of (23.3):

$$r_i = \mu + \frac{1}{\psi}\Delta c_t + \eta_t = \mu + \rho c_t + \eta_t \tag{23.5}$$

where μ is a constant and η_{t+1} is the error. The reciprocal of the EIS, which is also the coefficient of the relative risk aversion ρ under CRRA utility, is then identified by the moment restriction

$$E[Z_{t-1}\eta_t] = 0. \tag{23.6}$$

The moment restrictions (23.4) and (23.6) are equivalent up to a linear transformation.

The elasticity puzzle can then be exemplified by a comprehensive study by Campbell (2003), who gives a very extensive comparison between the estimates of the two equations (23.3) and (23.5) by using many different countries' data. He reports in his Table 9 the results. In considering the case of using quarterly US data (1947–1998) on non-durable consumption and T-bill returns, the 95 per cent interval for ψ is [−0.14, 0.28], and for

$$\frac{1}{\psi} [−0.73, 2.14].$$

Therefore, one rejects the null hypothesis $\psi = 1$ using equation (23.3), which instruments for the T-bill return, but fails to reject $\psi = 1$ using equation (23.5), which instruments for consumption growth.[4]

Reflecting on the puzzle

Econometrics

Given this technical description, a natural way to reflect upon the elasticity puzzle is to assume an econometric essence of the puzzle, and the instruments Z_t seem to attract the wide attention of econometricians. There are at least two major observations made regarding Z_t. The first observation is related to the choice of normalization for the moment restriction. Although equations (23.4) and (23.6) correspond to the same moment restriction up to a linear transformation, GMM is not invariant to such transformations. Therefore, the choice of normalization for the moment restriction can affect point estimates and confidence intervals. Nonetheless, the conventional asymptotic theory may make the choice of normalization negligible in large samples, leading to the same inference of the EIS. Therefore, the puzzle may be more than just a debate over whether normalization of the key structural equation matters.

The second observation was pioneered by Neely *et al.* (2001), which attributes the disparate estimates of this fundamental parameter to failures of *instrument relevance*. Instruments which are insufficiently correlated with endogenous variables, also known as *weak instruments*, can cause estimators to be severely biased and the finite-sample distribution of test statistics to depart sharply from the limiting distribution, leading to large size distortions in hypothesis tests. Neely *et al.* (2001) noted that weak instruments are a problem in estimating the EIS because both consumption growth and asset returns are notoriously difficult to predict. Because of weak identification, it is imperative, as they suggested, to use prior beliefs grounded in *economic theory* to settle the debate over small versus large risk aversion.

Economic theory: preferences

Coming back to *economic theory*, what seems to be immediately relevant is the *utility function* or *risk attitude* upon which the reciprocal relation (23.2) is built. Consumption asset pricing models typically assume a power utility function in which the elasticity of intertemporal substitution cannot be disentangled from the coefficient of relative risk aversion. Despite the use of a power utility function, Hall (1988) still argued that this specification is inappropriate because the EIS deals with the willingness of an investor to move consumption between time periods and is well defined even in the absence of uncertainty. By contrast, the coefficient of relative risk aversion concerns the willingness of an investor to move consumption between states of the world and is well defined even in a one-period model.

Epstein and Zin (1991) suggested an alternative specification for preference which can disentangle risk aversion from intertemporal substitution. Specifically, the utility function can be defined recursively as follows:

$$u_t = (1 - \beta)c_t^{\frac{1-\rho}{\theta}} = \beta(E_t(u_{t+1}^{1-\rho})^{\frac{\theta}{1-\rho}} \tag{23.7}$$

for $\theta \equiv (1 - \rho)/(1 - 1/\psi)$ where ψ is the elasticity of intertemporal substitution and ρ and β, as before, are the coefficient of relative risk aversion and the rate of time preference, respectively. When $\theta = 1$, or alternatively, when $\rho = 1/\psi$, this specification reduces to a time-separable power utility model.

This specification retains many of the attractive features of the power utility function but is *no longer time separable*. Nonetheless, in spite of the theoretical appeal of the Epstein–Zin specification, empirical tests, such as Epstein and Zin (1991) and Smith (1998), have not been successful in disentangling the elasticity of intertemporal substitution from the coefficient of relative risk aversion.

Economic theory: heterogeneity

In addition to preference, *heterogeneity* provides another possibility to reflect upon the puzzle. This is so because one feature common to all the studies which we go through above is their reliance on the *representative-agent assumption*. The representative-agent assumption says that one can treat the aggregate data as the outcome of a single 'representative' consumer's decisions. However, as Kirman (1992) argued, the conditions regarding the individual preference necessary for the representative agent to be an exact representation of the behaviour of underlying agents are quite stringent, so much so as to be implausible. Therefore, while the representative agent model is still considered to be useful for analysing behaviour from aggregate data, the recent research tendency does indicate a gradual movement towards *models of heterogeneous agents* by abandoning this device. On the elasticity puzzle, Guvenen (2002) was the one pioneering this direction.

In his analysis, Guvenen showed that the elasticity puzzle arises from ignoring two kinds of heterogeneity across individuals, namely, heterogeneity in wealth and heterogeneity in the EIS. For the first type of heterogeneity, there is substantial wealth inequality in the US, and 99 per cent of all the equity is owned by 30 per cent of the population. Obviously, a large fraction of US households do not participate in stock markets. On the other hand this group's contribution to total consumption is much more modest: the top 10 per cent of the wealthy account for around 17 per cent of aggregate consumption. As to the second type of heterogeneity, a variety of microeconomic studies using individual-level data conclude that *an individual's EIS increases with his wealth*.

Putting these two kinds of heterogeneity together, we can conclude that there is a small group of wealthy households who have significantly higher EIS than the rest, but their preferences are largely not revealed in aggregate consumption. Instead, aggregate consumption data mainly reveals the low elasticity of the poor who contribute substantially. Put differently, the representative-agent assumption implies that the average consumer and the average investor are the same and thus different macroeconomic time series should yield comparable estimates of the EIS. However, the two kinds of heterogeneity fail the representative-agent assumption by distinguishing the average consumer (the poor) from the average investor (the rich).

Guvenen (2002) did not attempt to solve the elasticity puzzle as the conflicts between (23.3) and (23.5), because his use of the Epstein–Zin recursive utility function disentangles these two conceptually different aspects of preferences. For example, in his model ρ for the poor and rich are assumed to be equal and they are calibrated to be three, whereas ψ is 0.1 for the poor and 1 for the rich. This setting is largely motivated by another branch of the literature involved in the elasticity puzzle, namely, the real business cycle model. Therefore, his main concern is to reconcile the difference between the estimated EIS in the econometric models, such as Campbell and Mankiw (1989), Hall (1988) and Patterson and Pesaran (1992), with that in the real business cycle model. In other words, his concern is more with the elasticity itself rather than the puzzle regarding the two reciprocals. Consequently, his models of heterogeneous agents are not directed towards solving the puzzle, if there is one.

In this chapter, we would like to continue to play with the idea of *heterogeneity*. As Guvenen himself said, 'we believe that a view of the macroeconomy based on heterogeneity across agents in investment opportunity sets and preferences provides a rich description of the data as well as enabling a better understanding of the determination of aggregate dynamics' (2002: 30), it is also our conviction that *heterogeneity* plays a key role in pushing forward the frontier of this research area. Our confidence is further strengthened by a series of empirical studies which deviate from the device of the representative agent, such as Attanasio *et al.* (2002), Vissing-Jørgensen (2002), and Vissing-Jørgensen and Attanasio (2003). These studies show the existence of large difference in the EIS between the stockholders and non-stockholders. Moreover, using the Epstein–Zin recursive utility function, Vissing-Jørgensen and Attanasio (2003) further showed the difference in the risk aversion among groups of different individuals.

Our departure: an agent-based computational thinking

Heterogeneity has already been well incorporated into the asset pricing model for more than a decade. In the literature, it is known as the *asset pricing model of interacting heterogeneous agents* (Brock and Hommes 1998; Chiarella and He 2002, 2003a, b; Ganuersdorfer 2000; He and Chiarella 2001; Lux and Marchesi 2000; Westerhoff 2003, 2004). However, to the best of our knowledge, none of these studies has been devoted to tackling the elasticity issue. There are two main reasons for this. First, many of these heterogeneous models are not directly comparable to the standard homogeneous consumption CAPM model. While they also have infinitely lived agents in their models, these agents are assumed to be *myopic* in the sense that they only maximize their expected utilities for the next period. Maximizing lifetime utility is still not typical in this family of models. Second, as a result of this myopic setting, the utility function only takes wealth explicitly into account, and consumption is simply absent. Hence, these models are not able to generate time series of consumption, and are not suitable for the study of intertemporal elasticity.

Usually, introducing heterogeneity, complex heterogeneity in particular, and the associated interaction can severely weaken the analytical tractability of models. This is why most asset pricing models of interacting heterogeneous agents have difficulty being regarded as heterogeneous consumption CAPM model. A way to make a breakthrough on this is to make the model *computational*. The *agent-based computational asset pricing models* initiated by the Santa Fe research team on economics are indeed a response to such an analytically daunting task (Chen and Yeh 2001, 2002; LeBaron 2000, 2001; LeBaron *et al.* 1999; Palmer *et al.* 1994).

Chen and Huang (2008) were the first to extend the conventional homogeneous consumption CAPM model to its agent-based counterpart. This extension was originally motivated by another famous debate in finance literature, i.e. the relevance of risk attitude to wealth share dynamics (Blume and Easley 1992, 2004; Sandroni 2000). They simulated a multi-asset financial market with agents who are heterogeneous in risk preference, including CARA, CRRA and many others. They found that wealth share dynamics, portfolio dynamics and saving behaviour are inextricably interwoven with populations of risk preferences. Specifically, this model can *endogenously* generate a positive relation between the degree of risk aversion and the wealth share, a similar result found in Vissing-Jørgensen and Attanasio (2003). Furthermore, an 'empirically' efficient frontier is also generated *endogenously*, even without the usual Markowitz assumption of the linear mean-variance preference (Markowitz 1952; Tobin 1958). The wealth density along the efficient frontier is not uniform, a phenomenon that has not been noticed or discussed either in the theoretical or empirical literature.

As a follow-up to Chen and Huang (2008), this chapter is the first application of the *asset pricing model of interacting heterogeneous agents* to examine the elasticity puzzle. What then is the significance of this?

First of all, empirical studies already indicate the need to bring heterogeneity into the consumption capital asset pricing model. It is generally found that different individuals may actually have different elasticities of intertemporal substitution and possibly different degrees of risk aversion. Therefore, to have a model that communicates better with these 'stylized' facts, it is desirable to have a heterogeneous version of consumption CAPM, and the agent-based computational consumption CAPM has greater flexibility in dealing with complex heterogeneity.

Second, in addition to heterogeneity, *bounded rationality* is another important feature widely shared by agent-based computational economic models. That agents are boundedly rational is no longer a peculiar assumption in the current economics literature (Evans and Honkapohja 2001). This is particularly so in agent-based computational finance, partially due to the advent of behavioural finance (Chen and Liao 2004). Models of financial markets which assume that the mean and variance of wealth are not known in advance to agents, but have to be estimated by agents, are prevalent in the literature. Using microstructure simulation, Adriaens *et al.* examined the impact of adaptive behaviour to the CAPM model, and concluded 'an assumption of rational expectations which is normally made within the CAPM model does not seem to be justified' (2004: 14).

As to the consumption CAPM model, the implications of bounded rationality have rarely been addressed. This is actually a little odd given the fact that all empirical studies of the EIS are based on the *consumption Euler equation*, which is derived under the assumptions that agents know all conditional means and variances of their portfolio returns, and hence they are able to solve an infinite-time horizon utility maximization problem. The question arising is certainly not whether these assumptions are true or not. (They are trivially not.) Instead, it is, to what extent, the assumptions will do harm for the prediction made is based on the Euler equation, such as the EIS and the associated elasticity puzzle. As a matter of fact, Vissing-Jørgensen and Attanasio (2003) already found from their *Consumer Expenditure Survey* data that a large number of households did not follow the Euler equation, and suggested that these households be removed from the sample. This is what we plan to explore in this chapter. Specifically, we ask:

If agents are boundedly rational, and we still use consumption and returns data generated by these boundedly rational agents to estimate the Euler regression equation, can we actually uncover the underlying ψ (or ρ) of these boundedly rational agents?

The question posed above asks whether we can *recover* the true values of ψ (or ρ) when agents are boundedly rational. To tackle this question, one can simulate consumption CAPM models which are composed of boundedly-rational agents with exogenously given values of ψ (or ρ), and then derive the estimated values $\hat{\psi}$ (or $\hat{\rho}$) by applying the *standard econometric procedure* to the data generated from the model. By comparing ψ and $\hat{\psi}$ (or ρ and $\hat{\rho}$) among many repetitions, one can then answer whether the standard econometric procedure is able to uncover the true value.[5]

Agent-based computational consumption CAPM model

Consider a complete securities market. Time is discrete and indexed by $t = 0, 1, 2, \ldots$ There are M states of the world indexed by $m = 1, 2, \ldots, M$, one of which will occur at each date. States follow a stochastic process. Asset m pays dividends $w_m > 0$ when state m occurs, and 0 otherwise. At each date t, the outstanding volume of each asset is exogenously fixed at *one unit*, so that the total wealth in the economy at date t, W_t, will equal

$$w_m \sum_{m=1}^{M} p_{m,t},$$

where $p_{m,t}$ is the price of the asset m at time t. The dividends will be distributed among the investors proportionately according to their owned share of asset m. The distribution received by each agent i, $W_{i,t}$, can be used to consume and reinvest.

There is a finite number of agents with *homogeneous* or *heterogeneous* temporal preferences in this economy, indexed by $i \in \{1, 2, \ldots I\}$. Each agent i has their subjective beliefs about the future sequence of the states. Each of these subjective beliefs is characterized by a probabilistic model, denoted by B^i. Since B^i may change over time, the time index t is added as B_t^i to make such a distinction. The agent's objective is to maximize their lifetime expected utility, and there are two decisions that are involved in this optimization problem. First, they have to choose a sequence of saving rates starting from now to infinity, and second a sequence of portfolios to distribute their saving over M assets. Let us denote these two sequences of decisions by

$$\{\{\delta_{t+r}^i\}_{r=0}^\infty, \{\alpha_{t+r}^i\}_{r=0}^\infty\},$$

where δ_t^i is the saving rate at time t, and

$$\alpha_t^i = (\alpha_{1,t}^i, \alpha_{2,t}^i, \ldots \alpha_{M,t}^i)$$

is the portfolio comprising the M assets. The two sequences of decisions will be optimal and are denoted by

$$\{\delta_{t+r}^{i,*}\}_{r=0}^\infty \text{ and } (\alpha_{t+r}^i\}_{r=0}^\infty\},$$

if they are the solutions to the following optimization problem.

$$\max_{\{\delta_{t+r}^i\}_{r=0}^\infty,(\alpha_{t+r}^i\}_{r=0}^\infty} E\left[\sum_{r=0}^\infty (\beta^i)^r u^i(c_{t+r}^i)|B_t^i\right] \tag{23.8}$$

subject to

$$c_{t+r}^i + \sum_{m=1}^M \alpha_{m,t+r}^i \cdot \delta_{t+r}^i \cdot W_{t+r-1}^i \leq W_{t+r-1}^i, \forall r \geq 0 \tag{23.9}$$

$$\sum_{m=1}^M \alpha_{m,t+r}^i = 1, \alpha_{m,t+r}^i \geq 0, \forall \geq 0 \tag{23.10}$$

In equation (23.8), u^i is agent i's temporal utility function, and β^i, also called the discount factor, reveals agent i's time preference. The expectation $E()$ is taken with respect to the most recent belief B_t^i. Equations (23.9) and (23.10) are the budget constraints.[6] By combining constraint (23.10), constraint (23.9) can also be written as (23.12),

$$c_{t+r}^i \leq (1 - \delta_{t+r}^i) W_{t+r-1}^i, \tag{23.12}$$

where c_t^i denotes consumption. These budget constraints do not allow agents to consume or invest by borrowing.

Given the saving rate $\delta_t^{i,*}$, agent i will invest a total of $\delta_t^{i,*} \cdot W_{t-1}^i$ in the M assets according to the portfolio $\alpha_t^{i,*}$. In other words, the investment put into each asset m is $\alpha_{m,t}^{i,*} \cdot \delta_t^{i,*} \cdot W_{t-1}^i$. By dividing this investment by the market price of asset m at date t, $p_{m,t}$, we derive the share held by agent i of that asset, $q_{m,t}^i$.

$$q_{m,t}^i = \frac{\alpha_{m,t}^{i,*} \cdot \delta_t^{i,*} \cdot W_{t-1}^i}{p_{m,t}}, \, m = 1, 2, \ldots, M \tag{23.13}$$

The equilibrium price $p_{m,t}$ is determined by equating the demand for asset m with the supply of asset m, i.e.

$$\sum_{i=1}^{I} \frac{\alpha_{m,t}^{i,*} \cdot \delta_t^{i,*} \cdot W_{t-1}^i}{p_{m,t}} = 1, \, m = 1, 2, \ldots, M \tag{23.14}$$

Rearranging equation (23.14), we obtain the market equilibrium price of asset m:

$$p_{m,t} = \sum_{i=1}^{I} \alpha_{m,t}^{i,*} \cdot \delta_t^{i,*} \cdot W_{t-1}^i \tag{23.15}$$

Agents' shares of assets will be determined accordingly by equation (23.13).[7] Afterwards, state m occurs, and is made known to all agents at date t. The dividends w_m will be distributed among all stockholders of asset m in proportion to their shares, and their wealth will be determined accordingly as

$$W_t^i = \sum_{m=1}^{M} (w_{m,t} + p_{m,t}) \cdot q_{m,t}^i.$$

The date moves to $t + 1$, and the process then repeats itself.

The departure from the conventional consumption CAPM model is the relaxation of the stringent assumptions: *homogeneous* and *rational expectations*. With this relaxation, the discrete-time stochastic optimization problem defined by equations (23.8), (23.9) and (23.10) are no longer analytically solvable.[8] Therefore, we assume that all agents in our model are *computational*. They cope with the optimization problem with a numerical approximation method, and the specific numerical method used in this chapter is the *genetic algorithm*. In this chapter, we use the genetic algorithm to evolve both agents' *investment strategies* and *beliefs* simultaneously. The two-level evolution proceeds as follows:

- At a fixed time horizon, investors update (evolve) their beliefs of the states coming in the future.
- They then evolve their investment strategies based on their beliefs.

The two-level evolution allows agents to solve a *boundedly rational* version of the optimization problem (23.8). First, the cognitive limit of investors and the resultant adaptive behaviour free them from an infinite-horizon stochastic

optimization problem, as in equation (23.8). Instead, due to their limited perception of the future, the problem effectively posed to them is the following:

$$\max_{\{\{\delta^i_{t+h}\}^{H-1}_{h=0}, \{\alpha_{t+h}\}^{H-1}_{h=0}\}} E\left[\sum_{h=0}^{H-1} (\beta^i)^h u^i(c^i_{t+h})|B^i_t\right] \qquad (23.16)$$

Here, we replace the infinite-horizon perception with a finite-horizon percep-
tion of length H, and the filtration (σ-algebra) induced by S_{t-1} with B^i_t, where B^i_t
is investor i's *belief* at date t. In a simple case where m_t is *independent* (but not
necessarily stationary), and this is known to the investor, then B^i_t can be just the
subjective probability function, i.e. $B^i_t = (b^i_{1,t}, \dots b^i_{M,t})$, where $b^i_{M,t}$ is investor i's
subjective probability of the occurrence of the state m in any of the next H peri-
ods. In a more general setting, B^i_t can be a *high-order Markov process*. With the
replacement (23.16), we assume that investors have only a vague perception of
the future, but will continuously adapt when approaching it. As we shall see in
the second level of evolution, B^i_t is *adaptive*.

Furthermore, we assume that investors will *continuously* adapt their investment strategies according to the *sliding window* shown in Figure 23.1. At each
point in time, the investor has a perception of a time horizon of length H. All
their investment strategies are evaluated within this reference period. They then
make their decision based on what they consider to be the best strategy. While
the plan comes out and covers the next H periods, only the first period,
$\{\delta^{i,*}_t, \alpha^{i,*}_t\}$, will be actually implemented. The next period, $\{\delta^{i,*}_{t+1}, \alpha^{i,*}_{t+1}\}$, may not
be implemented because it may no longer be the best plan when the investor
receives the new information and revises their beliefs.

With this sliding-window adaptation scheme, one can have two further simplifications of the optimization problem (23.8)–(23.10). The first one is that the
future price of the asset m, $p_{m,t+h}$ remains unchanged for each experimentation
horizon, namely, at time t,

$$p^i_{m,t+h} = p_{m,t-1}, \forall h \in \{0, H-1\}, \qquad (23.17)$$

where $p^i_{m,t+h}$ is i's subjective perception of the h-step-ahead price of asset m.
Second, the investment strategies to be evaluated are also time-invariant under
each experimentation horizon, i.e., $\delta^i_t = \delta^i_{t+1} = \delta^i_{t+2} = \dots \delta^i_{t+H-1}$, and $\alpha^i_t = \alpha^i_{t+1} = \alpha^i_{t+2} = \dots \alpha^i_{t+H-1}$.

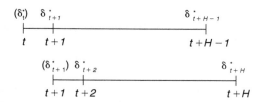

Figure 23.1 A sliding-window perception of the investors.

With these two simplifications, we replace the original optimization problem, (23.8)–(23.10), that is presented to the infinitely-smart investor, with a modified version which is suitable for a boundedly-rational investor.

$$\max_{\{\{\delta_t^i\},\{\alpha_t^i\}\}} E\left[\sum_{h=0}^{H-1}(\beta^i)^h u^i(c_{t+h}^i)|B_t^i\right] \tag{23.18}$$

subject to

$$c_{t+h}^i + \sum_{m=1}^{M}\alpha_{m,t}^i\cdot\delta_t^i\cdot W_{t+h-1}^i \le W_{t+h-1}^i, \forall h \in \{0, H-1\}, \tag{23.19}$$

$$\sum_{m=1}^{M}\alpha_{m,t}^i = 1,\ \alpha_{m,t}^i > 0,\ \forall m, \tag{23.20}$$

$$c_{t+h}^i = (1 - \delta_t^i)W_{t+h-1}^i, \forall h \in \{0, H-1\}. \tag{23.21}$$

Autonomous agents

One of the mainstays of agent-based computational economics is *autonomous agents* (Tesfatsion 2001). The idea of autonomous agents was initially presented in Holland and Miller (1991). Briefly, these agents are able to learn and to adapt to the changing environment without too much external intervention, say, from the model designer. Their behaviour is very much endogenously determined by the environment with which they are interacting. Accordingly, sometimes their behaviour can be very difficult to trace and to predict, and is known as *emergent behaviour*.

In this chapter, we follow what was initiated in Holland and Miller (1991), and equip our agents with the genetic algorithm (GA) to cope with the finite-horizon stochastic dynamic optimization problem, (23.18)–(23.21). The GA is applied here at two different levels, a high level (learning level) and a low level (optimization level). First, at the high level, it is applied as a *belief-updating scheme*. This is about the B_t^i appearing in (23.18). Agents start with some initial beliefs of state uncertainty, which are basically characterized by parametric models, say, Markov processes. However, agents do not necessarily confine themselves to just stationary Markov processes. Actually, they can never be sure whether the underlying process will change over time. So, they stay alert to that possibility, and keep on trying different Markov processes with different time frames (time horizons). Specifically, each belief can be described as 'a kth order Markov process that appeared over the last d days and may continue'. These two parameters can be represented by a binary string, and a canonical GA is applied to evolve a population of these two parameters with a set of standard genetic operators. Details are given in Appendix B.

Once the belief is determined, the low-level GA is applied to solve the stochastic dynamic optimization problem defined in (23.18)–(23.21). Basically, we use Monte Carlo simulation to generate many possible ensembles consistent with the given belief and use them to evaluate a population of investment plans composed of a saving rate and a portfolio. GA is then applied to evolve this population of candidates. Details are given in Appendix A.

In sum, the high-level GA finds an appropriate belief, and under that belief the low-level GA searches for the best decisions in relation to savings and portfolios. This style of adaptive design combines *learning how to forecast* with *learning how to optimize*, a distinction made in Bullard and Duffy (1999). These two levels of GA do not repeat with the same frequency. As a matter of fact, the belief-updating scheme is somewhat slow, whereas the numerical optimization scheme is more frequent. Intuitively, changing our belief of the meta-level of the world tends to be slower and less frequent than just fine-tuning or updating some parameters associated with a given structure. In this sense, the idea of *incremental learning* is also applied to our design of autonomous agents.

Summary

Figure 23.2 is a summary of the agent-based artificial stock market.

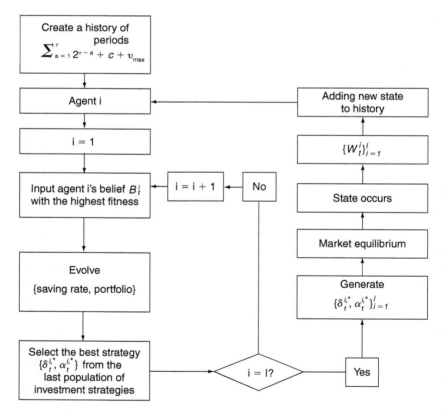

Figure 23.2 A summary of agent-based artificial stock markets.

Experimental designs and data generating processes

Experimental designs

Two series of experiments are conducted in this chapter. Each design can be summarized by the design table, Table 23.1, which characterizes Experiment I. Each experimental design may differ in only few parameter values, and share the same for the rest. Therefore, we can use Table 23.1 to state the common structure of the two experiments. The parameters used to control the experiments can be classified into two categories. Parameters in the top half of Table 23.1 correspond to the market and its participants, whereas those in the bottom half pertain to the adaptive scheme (i.e. genetic algorithms) associated with the autonomous agents.

To examine the influence of bounded rationality on the observed elasticity, in the first experiment, we distinguish agents by their forecasting accuracy. As has been shown in Chen and Huang (2008), this can be done by endowing agents with different validation horizon (v).[9] Chen and Huang (forthcoming) have shown that a longer validation horizon implies higher forecasting accuracy, and, other things being equal, a higher wealth share. In the first experiment, we consider agents with three different values of v, namely, $v = 25, 50, 100$. These three types of agents are evenly distributed among a market of 30 participants; so there are ten agents associated with each v (see Table 23.1).

Table 23.1 Experimental design

Market and participants	
Number of market participants (I)	30
Number of types of agents	3 (5)
Number of each type of agent	10 (6)
Number of assets (states) (M)	5
Dividends paid by asset m	6-m
Stochastic processes	iid or first-order Markov
Number of market periods (T)	100
Type of utility function	Power function
Discount rate (β)	0.45
Coefficient of relative risk aversion (ρ)	1 (0.5, 1, 2, 3, 4, 5)
Elasticity of Intertemporal Substitution (ψ)	1
Autonomous agents	
Agents' perception of the time horizon (H)	25
Number of ensembles (L)	5
Population size (number of strategies) (N)	100
Number of generations (G)	50
Validation horizon (v)	25, 50, 100 (100)
Population size (number of beliefs) (J)	100
Frequency of running GA on the belief set (Δ)	2
Number of bits for beliefs ($\tau_1 + \tau_2$)	10

Notes
Experiment I and Experiment II share the values for most parameters. For those they do not, we put the values used in Experiment I outside the parentheses, whereas we leave the values used in Experiment 2 inside the parentheses.

Agents in the first experiment share the same utility function, i.e. the log utility function, which implies $\rho = \psi = 1$ (Table 23.1). The purpose of the first experiment is to examine whether we can discover these coefficients by using the standard econometric procedures with the artificial data on consumption and returns.

The second experiment assumes agents share the same perception parameter (validation horizon), while distinguishing them by risk preferences. Motivated by Chen and Huang (2007), we vary the value of ρ from 0.5, 1, 2,..., to 5, as shown in Table 23.1. As shown in Chen and Huang (2007), risk aversion contributes to the wealth share in a positive way: the higher the coefficient, the higher the wealth share. The purpose of this experimental design is then to see whether we are able to discover the true value for each of the six values of ρ or their reciprocals (ψs).

For each design of the two experiments, 100 runs are conducted, and each lasts for 100 periods. For 50 of these 100 runs, we employ *iid* as the state-generation mechanism, whereas, for the other 50 runs, the first-order Markov process is used.

Data generated

Based on the theoretical model presented in the previous section, the simulation counterpart can generate a number of time series observations, including individual behaviour and aggregate outcomes. Since these variables will be then be used in the econometric analysis for the later stage, we shall first briefly summarize them here.

Let us start with individual profiles. The individual behaviour as described by equations (23.8) to (23.13), and with the modifications (23.18) to (23.21), covers the following time series:

- $\{c_t^i\}$, $(i = 1, 2,..., I)$: individual consumption
- $\{\delta_t^i\}$, $(i = 1, 2,..., I)$: individual saving rate
- $\{\alpha_{m,t}^i\}$, $(m = 1, 2,..., M$ and $i = 1, 2,..., I)$: individual portfolio
- $\{q_{m,t}^i\}$, $(m = 1, 2,..., M$ and $i = 1, 2,..., I)$: individual holding share of each asset.

Then, for the aggregate data, we have the following series:

- Time series of aggregate consumption ($\{c_t\}$)
- Time series of asset price ($\{p_{m,t}\}, m = 1, 2,..., M)$.

Econometric analysis of the simulation results

Experiment I

Estimation using the individual data

The main econometric equation or the system of equations which we shall build upon to estimate the parameter of EIS is mainly based on Hall (1988).[10]

$$\Delta c_t^i = \tau^i + \psi^i r_{t-1}^i + \xi_t^i (i = 1, 2, \ldots I), \tag{23.22}$$

where

$$\Delta c_t^i = \log\left(\frac{c_t^i}{c_{t-1}^i}\right). \tag{23.23}$$

Notice that the heterogeneity of individuals in terms of the elasticity of intertemporal substitution makes equation (23.22) also heterogeneous among agents. Therefore, all estimated coefficients, such as τ and ψ, are heterogeneous among agents as they are denoted by τ^i and ψ^i. Furthermore, the heterogeneity in terms of investment behaviour also makes the rates of return r_t facing agents heterogeneous, which are denoted by r_t^i in equation (23.22).

The return facing each individual is determined by their chosen portfolio α_t^i, and can be calculated as follows.

$$r_t^i = \log(R_t^i) \tag{23.24}$$

where

$$R_t^i = \sum_{m=1}^{M} \alpha_{m,t}^i R_{m,t}, \tag{23.25}$$

and

$$R_{m,t} \equiv \frac{p_{m,t} + w_{m,t}}{p_{m,t}}. \tag{23.26}$$

Equation (23.26) gives the rate of return of the asset m, and equation (23.25) is the rate of return of the portfolio α_t^i.[11] Following the derivation of the Euler consumption equation (see Appendix C), we do not use the rate of return (R_t^i) but its logarithm (r_t^i) as the dependent variable.

To estimate the coefficients ψ_i, we may start with equation (23.22), and estimate each of the 30 equations individually. Alternatively, we may consider the set of 30 individual equations as one giant equation, and estimate the 30 ψ_is altogether. The latter approach is the familiar seemingly unrelated regression estimation (SURE). SURE can be useful when the error terms (ξ_t^i) of each equation in

(23.22) are related. In this case, the shock affecting the consumption of one agent may spill over and affect the consumption of the other agents. Hence, estimating these equations as a set, using a single large equation, should improve efficiency. In this chapter, we do find the error terms among different agents to be correlated; therefore, SURE is applied. To do so, we rewrite the set of equations (23.22) into a single equation as (23.27).

$$\Delta c = \Gamma + r\Psi + \Xi \tag{23.27}$$

where

$$\Gamma = \begin{pmatrix} \tau^1 \\ \tau^2 \\ M \\ \tau^{30} \end{pmatrix}, \Delta c = \begin{pmatrix} \Delta c^1 \\ \Delta c^2 \\ M \\ \Delta c^{30} \end{pmatrix}, r = \begin{pmatrix} r^1 & 0 & K & 0 \\ 0 & r^2 & K & 0 \\ M & M & O & \\ 0 & 0 & K & r^{30} \end{pmatrix}, \Psi = \begin{pmatrix} \psi^1 \\ \psi^2 \\ M \\ \psi^{30} \end{pmatrix}, \Xi = \begin{pmatrix} \xi^1 \\ \xi^2 \\ M \\ \xi^{30} \end{pmatrix}.$$

Here, we remove the subscript t, so each Δc^i, r^i and ξ^i are column vectors which represent, respectively, the dependent and independent observations and error terms at each period t ($t = 1, 2, ..., T$). Ordinary least square (OLS) cannot be directly applied to equation (23.27) because, as we mentioned earlier, the consumption residuals (ξ_t^i) among different agents are correlated. Furthermore, based on the White test, evidence of heteroskedasticity is also found in each of the equations (23.22). This evidence together indicates that we should use the generalized least squares (GLS) approach rather than OLS to estimate equation (23.27).

The GLS estimation of the vector Ψ is given in Table 23.2. The estimate contains the elasticity of the intertemporal substitution of 30 agents, who, under Experiment I, differ only in the parameter validation horizon (v). In Table 23.2, we cluster the agents with the same validation horizon together, and number them accordingly. So, we number from one to ten the agents with the longer

Table 23.2 The estimated elasticity of intertemporal substitution, individuals

$v = 100$		$v = 50$		$v = 25$	
Agents	ψ^i	Agents	ψ^i	Agents	ψ^i
1	0.382712	11	0.351886	21	0.381981
2	0.359462	12	0.36754	22	0.359424
3	0.391014	13	0.378627	23	0.377209
4	0.398979	14	0.375977	24	0.387241
5	0.405536	15	0.375729	25	0.368271
6	0.392223	16	0.338635	26	0.388041
7	0.400596	17	0.36601	27	0.368864
8	0.374271	18	0.400018	28	0.349934
9	0.38577	19	0.380438	29	0.327249
10	0.381275	20	0.326659	30	0.394376

validation horizon ($v = 100$), from 11–20 the agents with the middle validation horizon ($v = 50$), and from 21–30 the agents with the shortest validation horizon ($v = 25$).

While the true value of ψ^i is identically one for all agents, the estimated counterpart is numerically different among agents. It ranges from a minimum of 0.326 (Agent 20) to a maximum of 0.405 (Agent 5). This range is also very much less than one, and the average 0.374 is just about one-third of the true value. As a result, we fail to discover the agents' true intertemporal substitution preference; instead, it is dramatically underestimated, which means, on the other hand, that if we take its reciprocal as the estimate of the coefficient of risk aversion then, obviously, it is overestimated.

To give a further examination of the estimated EIS ($\hat{\psi}^i$) among agents with different perception (v), Figure 23.3 depicts the box-whisker plot of the $\hat{\psi}^i$ of each group. It can be seen that agents with the long validation horizon ($v = 100$) tend to have a higher value of $\hat{\psi}^i$, while the distribution associated with the medium horizon ($v = 50$) and the short horizon ($v = 25$) is almost the same.

At this stage, it is still too early to infer whether our simulation results can shed light on the empirical evidence on the heterogeneity in either the risk aversion or the intertemporal substitution, as we have shown above. However, it does question whether the observed heterogeneity, either in ψ or ρ, is just spurious,

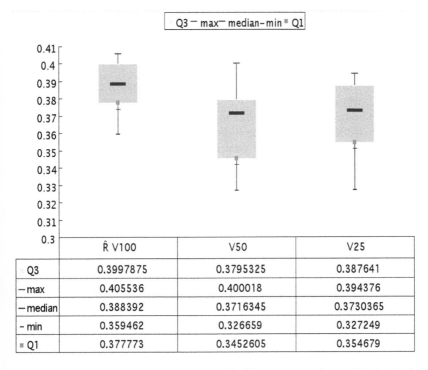

	Ř V100	V50	V25
Q3	0.3997875	0.3795325	0.387641
—max	0.405536	0.400018	0.394376
—median	0.388392	0.3716345	0.3730365
- min	0.359462	0.326659	0.327249
▪ Q1	0.377773	0.3452605	0.354679

Figure 23.3 The estimated EIS of agents with different perception (validation horizons).

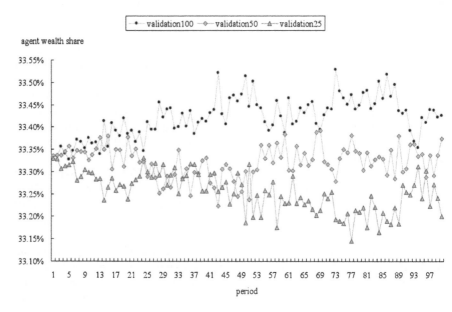

Figure 23.4 Wealth share of the three groups of agents.

including the empirically positive relation between ψ and wealth. Having said that, we shall compare the estimated ψ^i of the 'rich' people with that of the 'poor' people by using our simulation results.

Figure 23.4 shows the wealth share of the three groups of agents. As Chen and Huang (2008) already showed, the agents with a long validation horizon tend to have a higher wealth share than those with a short one, which is consistent with what we have here. In our Experiment I, the richest group of agents (agents with $v = 100$) own 0.7 per cent more in terms of their share than the poorest group of agents (agents with $v = 25$), and the 'middle class' (agents with $v = 50$) own 0.4 per cent less than the richest ones, but 0.3 per cent more than the poorest ones. These differences are numerically slight, but are statistically significant. By combining this result with that of Figure 23.3, we find that the richest group of agents is also the one with the highest $\hat{\psi}$. However, from our setting, these agents, be they eventually poor or rich, share the same EIS, which is one. As a result, the observed heterogeneity may be spurious. Alternatively speaking, in our agent-based simulation, both the wealth share and the observed relation between consumption and the return are endogenously generated. Agents with a better forecasting accuracy may be able to behave closer to the optimizing behaviour (Euler consumption equation); hence, they are not only richer but their observed EIS, $\hat{\psi}^i$, is also closer to the true value.

Estimation using the aggregate data

As we mentioned above, the early econometric work on the estimation of the elasticity of intertemporal substitution mainly used only aggregate data. The result which we have in the previous section, however, uses the individual data instead. Therefore, to conduct experiments in parallel to the early work and to examine the effect of aggregation upon the estimation of the EIS, in this section we also estimate the EIS based on the aggregate data.

The data generated by the agent-based simulation are flexible enough to allow for different levels of aggregation. We consider two different levels of aggregation. At the first level, we employ the device of the representative agent for each group of agents, i.e. agents with the same validation horizon. We then derive the consumption and return data for this representative agent, and estimate the Euler consumption equation based on the derived (aggregated) data. At the second level, we then consider the whole economy as a unit, and repeat the same process above with the device of the single representative agent. This leads to the following two modifications of equation (23.27), namely, equations (23.28) and (23.31).

$$\Delta c = \Gamma + r\Psi + \Xi \tag{23.28}$$

where

$$\Gamma = \begin{pmatrix} \tau^L \\ \tau^M \\ \tau^S \end{pmatrix}, \Delta c = \begin{pmatrix} \Delta c^L \\ \Delta c^M \\ \Delta c^S \end{pmatrix}, r = \begin{pmatrix} r^L & 0 & 0 \\ 0 & r^M & 0 \\ 0 & 0 & r^S \end{pmatrix}, \Psi = \begin{pmatrix} \psi^L \\ \psi^M \\ \psi^S \end{pmatrix}, \Xi = \begin{pmatrix} \varsigma^L \\ \varsigma^M \\ \varsigma^S \end{pmatrix}.$$

and

$$\Delta c_t^L = \log \left(\frac{\sum_{i=1}^{10} c_t^i}{\sum_{i=1}^{10} c_{t-C}^i} \right), \Delta c_t^M = \log \left(\frac{\sum_{i=11}^{20} c_t^i}{\sum_{i=11}^{20} c_{t-1}^i} \right), \Delta c_t^S = \log \left(\frac{\sum_{i=21}^{30} c_t^i}{\sum_{i=21}^{30} c_{t-1}^i} \right), \tag{23.29}$$

$$\Delta r^L = \log \left(\frac{\sum_{i=1}^{10} R_t^i}{10} \right), \Delta r^M = \log \left(\frac{\sum_{i=11}^{20} R_t^i}{10} \right), \Delta r^S = \log \left(\frac{\sum_{i=21}^{30} R_t^i}{10} \right) \tag{23.30}$$

Equation (23.28) is the Euler consumption equation with the assumption that treats each group of individuals as a single representative agent. Equation (23.29) is the growth rate of the group consumption, and the group consumption is simply defined as the sum of the individual consumption. Equation (23.30) is the logarithm of the return facing each representative agent, and this return is defined as the simple average of the returns facing each individual within the

group. The superscripts L, M and S refer to the long, medium and short validation horizons. As in the case of equation (23.27), the subscript t is not shown
here, since each of the three-group components in Δc, r and $\varXi$ are considered to
be column vectors composed of time series observations.

Likewise, equation (23.31) is the Euler consumption equation that is based on
the assumption of treating the whole economy as a single representative agent.
This version is the one frequently used in macroeconometrics. Equations (23.32)
and (23.33) are the further aggregation in parallel with equations (23.29) and
(23.30).

$$\Delta c_t = \tau + \psi_{t-1} + \xi_t, \tag{23.31}$$

where

$$\Delta c_t = \log \left| \frac{\displaystyle\sum_{i=21}^{30} c_t^i}{\displaystyle\sum_{i=21}^{30} c_{t-1}^i} \right|, \tag{23.32}$$

and

$$r_t = \log \left(\frac{\displaystyle\sum_{i=1}^{30} R_t^i}{30} \right). \tag{23.33}$$

SURE with GLS is then applied to the aggregate Euler consumption equation
(23.28), whereas GLS alone is applied to equation (23.31). The estimation
results are presented in Table 23.3. The estimated EIS of the three groups of
agents, $\hat{\psi}^L$, $\hat{\psi}^M$ and $\hat{\psi}^S$, are given in the upper panel of Table 23.3, whereas that
of the economy-wide counterpart, $\hat{\psi}$, is given in the lower panel. These estimates
are in a sharp contrast to those estimates based on individual data (see Table
23.2). In Table 23.2, we have seen that the EIS has been underestimated, and the
estimate is about one-third of the true value. However, here it is further underes
timated and is even less than one-tenth of the true value.

Table 23.3 The estimated elasticity of intertemporal substitution, groups

Parameter	Estimate	Std err.	t value	Pr > |t|	R^2
Aggregation level I: equation (23.28)					
$\hat{\psi}^L$	0.05427	0.0017	31.99	<0.0001	0.0925
$\hat{\psi}^M$	0.05388	0.0017	31.31	<0.0001	0.0895
$\hat{\psi}^S$	0.02829	0.0011	25.07	<0.0001	0.0013
Aggregation level II: equation (23.31)					
$\hat{\psi}$	0.08678	0.0024	35.06	<0.0001	0.1115

Among the three groups of agents, agents with better forecasting accuracy (longer validation horizons) are still found to be ones with higher estimated EIS: $\hat{\psi}^L > \hat{\psi}M^m > \hat{\psi}^S$. In particular, for the agents with the short validation horizon, the estimated EIS is only 0.028, and the respective R^2 is barely above zero. Therefore, the general finding from using individual data is that the observed heterogeneity in the EIS is spurious. So is the observed positive relation between the wealth share and the EIS.

One interesting question frequently asked in agent-based modelling is: what is the relation between the micro and macro? By comparing the $\hat{\psi}$ from the aggregate data (Table 23.3) and the $\hat{\psi}^i$ for the individual data (Table 23.2), one may find that the representative agent of the whole economy constructed using the aggregate data does not well represent the distribution of individuals. An $\hat{\psi}$ of 0.086 is far below the entire distribution of $\hat{\psi}'s$, not to mention being the mean or median of it.

Experiment II

Estimation using the individual data

The second experiment assumes that agents differ in their risk preference. While all of them have the CRRA-type risk preference, their ρs are different and range from 0.5, 1, 2,…, to 5. Five agents correspond to each of the six values of ρ. We number these agents from 1 to 30 based on the value of ρ as shown in Table 23.4. As before in (23.27), SURE is applied to estimate the intertemporal elasticity of each agent, and the results are given in Table 23.4.

Table 23.4 The estimated elasticity of intertemporal substitution (experiment II), individuals

Agents	$\hat{\phi}^i$	Agents	$\hat{\phi}^i$	Agents	$\hat{\phi}^i$
$\rho = 0.5,$	$\varphi = 2$	$\rho = 2,$	$\varphi = 0.5$	$\rho = 4,$	$\varphi = 0.25$
1	0.241	11	0.290	21	0.321
2	0.245	12	0.295	22	0.326
3	0.242	13	0.300	23	0.327
4	0.245	14	0.298	24	0.326
5	0.230	15	0.302	25	0.322
APE	0.879	APE	0.405	APE	0.299
$\rho = 1,$	$\varphi = 1$	$\rho = 3,$	$\varphi = 0.3$	$\rho = 5,$	$\varphi = 0.2$
6	0.250	16	0.317	26	0.319
7	0.249	17	0.322	27	0.318
8	0.246	18	0.319	28	0.319
9	0.249	19	0.322	29	0.322
10	0.247	20	0.318	30	0.317
APE	0.751	APE	0.030	APE	0.597

Table 23.4 presents the estimated elasticity of the six groups of agents; each is associated with a different ρ (ψ). Since the utility function is the CRRA type the true ψ is just the reciprocal of the corresponding ρ. In Table 23.4, we also lis the value of the ψ in parallel. This makes it easier for us to compare $\hat{\psi}^i$ with ψ^i.

From Table 23.4, a few observations can be made. First, while the ψs vary from 0.2 to 2, their estimated counterparts are distributed within a much narrower range, namely, around 0.25 to 0.3. Within this range, most of the estimated ψs miss their true values. The ψ of less risk-averse agents are underestimated, whereas the ψ of more risk-averse agents are overestimated. To see this, the average percentage error (APE) for each ψ is also given in Table 23.4. It is clear that, starting from the less risk-averse agents ($\rho = 0.5$), the APE starts to decline, and further down to the minimum when ρ approaches 3. It then increases again when ρ moves away from 0.3. Second, associated with this APE pattern, there is a positive relation between the $\hat{\psi}^i$ and ρ. If the positive relation between the wealth share and ρ still exists as in Chen and Huang (2007), then we have again found a positive observed relation between the wealth share and estimated intertemporal elasticity.

Estimation using the aggregate data

In the vein of the previous section, we also examine an aggregate version of the Euler consumption equation, which in structure is very similar to equation (23.31). Due to the very usual econometric consideration, the generalized method of moments is applied to estimate the aggregate Euler consumption equation, and the result is shown is Table 23.5. By comparing this result with the previous one, we can see the sharp decline in the estimated intertemporal elasticity. Remember that we have agents with elasticities from 0.2 to 2; however, the estimated elasticity is almost nil, while being still significantly different from zero. Therefore, the representative agent does not represent the society at all: i is not the centroid (average) of them.

In addition, by comparing this result with that from the earlier aggregate Euler consumption equation (Table 23.3), we may gauge the possible implication of the degree of heterogeneity on the estimated elasticity. In the early case (Experiment I) all agents share the same degree of risk aversion, and now they are divided into six groups of risk aversion. The $\hat{\psi}$ decreases from the early 0.0867 to only 0.0072 currently, and R^2 also drops from the original 11.15 per cent to only 1.38 per cent. Therefore, by using aggregate data, the intertemporal elasticity may be further underestimated when agents' risk preferences are heterogeneous.[12]

Table 23.5 The estimated elasticity of intertemporal substitution, groups

Parameter	Estimate	Std err.	t value	Pr > |t|	R^2
$\hat{\psi}$	0.0072	0.0005	14.04	<0.0001	0.0138

Concluding remarks

One of the main attractions of using the agent-based model is its ability to demonstrate the so-called *micro–macro relation*. Sometimes it may not be easy to track, step by step, from the bottom (micro interactions) to the top (macro outcomes), and hence one may not be able to have a full grasp of the causes and the consequences. Nevertheless, it does allow us to gauge how serious a misleading conclusion one may draw when the analysis is entirely based on the aggregate outcomes. In this chapter, an illustration based on the famous *elasticity puzzle* is demonstrated.

Our results based on the agent-based simulation show that the puzzle may come from our ignorance of a fundamental issue: *can we use econometrics to discover the individuals' profiles while they are boundedly rational and are placed in an interacting and evolving environment?* Both of the two experiments show that the intertemporal elasticity of individuals is underestimated, and the degree of underestimation is even more severe when only aggregate data are used. Furthermore, we also find that agents who have better forecasting ability and are hence wealthier tend to have a higher 'observable' intertemporal elasticity than those with less forecasting accuracy, even though they both share the same intertemporal elasticity. Therefore, the observed positive relation between the wealth share and the intertemporal elasticity can be spurious.

There are a number of points which are open for further research. First of all, the robustness of some of the results observed in this chapter should be further examined by using different econometric procedures. In this chapter, we do not use OLS because of the econometric reason. However, we have found that if one uses OLS, the already underestimated intertemporal elasticity (found in Experiment I) can be even biased away, and the results can nicely match many empirical results, such as Hall (1988) and Campbell (2003).

Second, the independent variable, the return, only considers dividends. The capital gain is not included for the reason given in Appendix C. However, it is still interesting to see the results by 'blindly' trying the version with capital gains. Third, all individuals know their own returns, but these personal data are not easy to obtain in empirical studies. So it would also be interesting to see the relation between consumption and returns, when the latter is defined by only the observable market data.

Acknowledgements

The chapter is devoted to a Festschrift in honour of Prof. Velupillai (Vela). The acknowledgement first goes to Prof. Velupillai, who has been the greatest teacher in many disciplines for the authors, not just in economics, but also computation theory, mathematics and cognitive sciences. His several visits to National Chengchi University during late 1990s also helped shaping the current AI-ECON Research Center, a centre devoted to the economic research paradigm advocated by Vela. The authors are also grateful to Prof. Stefano Zambelli for his profound coordination efforts to make us have a chance to demonstrate some humble work which we have done under Vela's influence. An earlier version of this chapter was presented at the Thirteenth International Conference on Computing in Economics and Finance (Montreal, Canada), 2007 ESHIA Conference (Fairfax, USA) and 2007 Econophysics Colloquium (Ancona, Italy). Thanks also go to the participants for their comments to our presentations. Research support in the form of NSC grant No. NSC. 94–2415-H-004–003 is gratefully acknowledged.

Appendix A

Evolution at the low level: investment strategies

Appendix A.1: coding and initialization

The implementation of the genetic algorithm starts with a representation (coding) of solutions. Here, we employ the real coding. The saving rate (δ_t^i) and the portfolio (α_t^i) are coded as real-valued numbers: $\{\delta_t^i | \alpha_{1,t}^i, \alpha_{2,t}^i, \ldots, \alpha_{M,t}^i\}$. To solve (23.18), an initial population of investment strategies with *population size N* is first generated for each investor i, $GEN_{t,0}^i \equiv \{\delta_{t,n}^i(0), \alpha_{t,n}^i(0)\}_{n=1}^N$. The number inside the parentheses refers to the generation number in the GA cycle. Population $GEN_{t,0}^i$ is generated as follows:

- $\delta_{t,n}^i(0)$ is randomly generated from the uniform distribution $U(0, 1)$.
- To generate a portfolio $\alpha_{t,n}^i(0)$, a set of numbers $(Q_1, Q_2, \ldots, Q_M)$ are randomly generated from $U(0, 1)$. Then, to make sure that their sum is equal to 1, they are rescaled as follows:

$$\left(\frac{Q_1}{\sum_{q=1}^{M} Q^q}, \frac{Q_2}{\sum_{q=1}^{M} Q_q}, \ldots, \frac{Q_M}{\sum_{q=1}^{M} Q_q} \right). \tag{23.34}$$

Appendix A.2: fitness evaluation: **Eval** $\{GEN_{t,g}^i\}$

Corresponding to (23.18), the fitness measure f is simply the H-horizon discounted expected utility:

$$f_t(n, g) \equiv f(\delta_{t,n}^i(g), \alpha_{t,n}^i(g)) \equiv E\left\{ \sum_{h=0}^{H-1} (\beta^i)^h u^i(c_{t+h}^i) | B_t^i \right\}, \tag{23.35}$$

where $f_t(n, g)$ refers to the fitness of the nth investment strategy in the population $GEN_{t,g}^i$ (i.e., the gth generation of the GA cycle). The Monte Carlo simulation technique is used to evaluate the fitness (23.35). The way to do this is to simulate a certain number, say L, of H-horizon histories of the states based on investor i's belief, B_t^i. For each *simulated history* $l(l \in [1, L])$, we can obtain a realization of (23.35), i.e.

$$\sum_{h=0}^{H-1} (\beta^i)^h u^i(c_{t+h}^i)|l), \, l = 1, 2, \ldots, L.$$

Then, we estimate $f_i(n, g)$ by taking the sample average,

$$\hat{f}_i(n, g) = \frac{\displaystyle\sum_{l=1}^{L}\sum_{h=0}^{H-1} (\beta^i)^h U^i(c_{t+h}^i)}{L} |l).$$

(23.36)

Appendix A.3: genetic operation: $GEN_{t,g}^i \to GEN_{t,g+1}^i i$

Once the procedure **Eval** $\{GEN_{t,g}^i\}$ is completed, all investment strategies are associated with a fitness which is the output of (23.36).

Eval: $\{\delta_{t,n}^i(g), \alpha_{t,n}^i(g)\}_{n=1}^{N} \to \{f_i(n, g)\}_{n=1}^{N}$

(23.37)

Based on their fitness, we shall revise and renew these investment strategies based on investor i's belief B_t^i. This revision and renewal procedure involves the use of four standard genetic operators, namely, *selection, crossover, mutation* and *election*.

Selection: The *tournament selection* with tournament size four is employed. For each selection, four investment strategies are randomly selected from $GEN_{t,g}^i$. Of them, the best two will be chosen as the parents (mating pool). We denote them by $I_x \equiv \{\delta_{t,x}^i(g), \alpha_{t,x}^i(g)\}$, and $I_y \equiv \{\delta_{t,y}^i(g), \alpha_{t,y}^i(g)\}$, where $x, y \in [1, N]$.

Crossover: With probability p_{cross} (*crossover rate*), the two parents chosen above will generate an offspring by taking a weighted average of the two investment strategies, and the weights will be determined by the relative fitness of the two strategies.

$$I_Z \equiv \{\delta_{t,z}^i(g), \alpha_{t,z}^i(g)$$

$$= \frac{f_i(x, g)}{f_i(x, g) + f_i(y, g)}(\delta_{t,x}^i(g), \alpha_{t,x}^i(g)) + \frac{f_i(y, g)}{f_i(x, g) + f_i(y, g)}(\delta_{t,y}^i(g), \alpha_{t,y}^i(g)) \quad (23.38)$$

Mutation: The offspring I_z will then have a small probability (*mutation rate*) to mutate. If mutation happens, it will proceed as follows. For the saving rate, a number randomly selected from the $U[0, 1]$ will be used to replace $\xi^i(g)$. For the portfolio, a set of numbers, $\varepsilon \equiv (\varepsilon_1, \varepsilon_2, \ldots, \varepsilon_M)$, randomly generated from $U(0, 1)$, will replace $\alpha_{t,z}^i(g)$. Then the rescaling technique described in (23.34) will be applied. We call the resultant strategy $I_{z'}$.

Election: The use of the election operator examines whether the new investment strategy is expected to perform better than the one it replaced. In election, we shall use (23.36) to evaluate the potential fitness of I_z, and compare it with the fitness of the two parents, I_x and I_y. Then, only the one with the highest fitness will be retained for the next generation, $GEN^i_{t,g+1}$.

Appendix A.4: loops

Once a new investment strategy is generated, a *loop* leads us back to selection, which is then followed by crossover, mutation and election and then the next new investment strategy is generated. The loop will continue until all N strategies of $GEN^i_{t,g+1}$ are generated. $GEN^i_{t,g+1}$ will be evaluated based on the **Eval** procedure, and based on the evaluation, genetic operators will be applied to $GEN^i_{t,g+1}$ to generate $GEN^i_{t,g+2}$. This loop will also be repeated over and over again until a termination criterion is met, e.g. when g reaches a prespecified number G.

When the renewal and revision process is over, the investor will select the best strategy from the last population of investment strategies, say, $GEN^i_{t,G}$.

$$(\delta^{i,*}_t, \alpha^{i,*}_t) = \arg \max_{GEN^i_{t,G}} \{f_i(n, G)\}^N_{n=1} \tag{23.39}$$

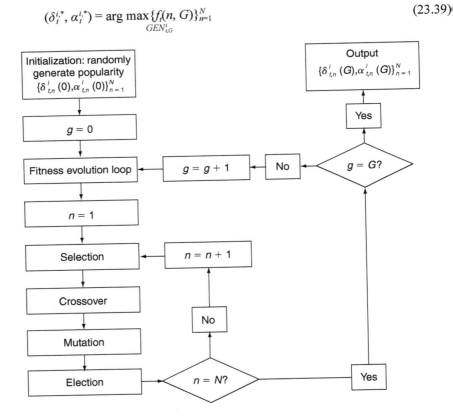

Figure 23.5 Flowchart of the low-level GA.

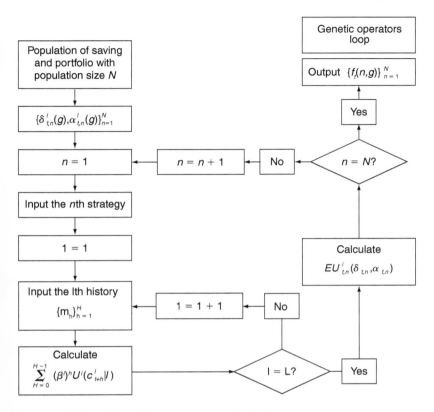

Figure 23.6 Flowchart of the investment optimization.

Appendix B

Evolution at the high level: beliefs

At the low level of evolution, the investor revises and renews his investment strategies with respect to a specific belief selected from a *population of beliefs* $\{B^i_{j,t}\}^J_{j=1}\{Bi\}$. .In other words, at each point in time, the investor may have more than one model of uncertainty in the world. The idea that each agent can simultaneously have several different models of the world, which are competing with each other in a co-evolving process, is a distinguishing feature of the *population learning models* (Arifovic and Maschek 2003; Arthur *et al.* 1997; Chen and Yeh 2001; Holland and Miller 1991; Vriend 2000). Of course, these models are not equally promising, and the investor tends to base his decision (investment strategies) on one of the most promising ones. However, as time goes on, his beliefs of the world will be revised and renewed in light of the newly incoming information. In this section, we shall describe how genetic algorithms can be applied to modelling the beliefs updating process.

Appendix B.1: coding and initialization

In our agent-based consumption CAPM, each investor's perception of the uncertainty (finite-state stochastic process) of the market can be characterized by two elements: first, the *dependence structure* (k) and, second, the *sample size* (d). Based on this characterization, the investor believes that the market over the last d days follows a kth-order Markov process. According to this belief, they would use a part of the historical data $\{m_{t-s}\}_{s=v+1}^{v+d+1}$, referred to as the *training period*, to estimate the Markov transition matrix, and the rest of the data $\{m_{t-s}\}_{s=v+1}^{v}$, referred to as the *validation period*, to validate the estimated model. As a result, each belief can be represented by a binary string, of length $\tau_1 + \tau_2$,

$$\underbrace{a_1 a_2 \ldots a_{\tau_1}}_{\tau_1 \text{ bits}} \underbrace{a_{\tau_1+1} a_{\tau_1+2} \ldots a_{\tau_1+\tau_2}}_{\tau_2 \text{ bits}}, \; a_1 \in \{0, 1\}, \forall 1 \le i \le \tau_1 + \tau_2$$

that has the following interpretation: the states follow a Markov process of the order

$$k = \left(\sum_{i=1}^{\tau_1} 2^{\tau_1-i} a_i \right) \tag{23.40}$$

over the last

$$d = \left(\sum_{i=\tau_1+1}^{\tau_1+\tau_2} 2^{\tau_1+\tau_2-i} a_i \right) + c \tag{23.41}$$

days. To facilitate estimation, d cannot be too small, and that demands an additional constant of c. In our current model, we simplify and limit the *dependent structure* (k) to 0 or 1, that is, we only assume the stochastic process to be *iid* or first-order Markov.

At the initial date $(t = 0)$, all investors are endowed with a population of J beliefs, which are randomly generated. Then, every Δ day, this population of beliefs will be reviewed and revised based on the fitness function, which is a kind of likelihood function to be specified below.

Appendix B.2: belief updating scheme

Agents in our model follow the practice of machine learning. They are supposed to care about the risk of over-fitting, and hence use data in the validation period to perform model selection. One way of ensuring that our agents behave in this way is to set the fitness function as the fitting error in the validation set, rather than the training set. The belief updating scheme is outlined in Figure 23.7.

The essence of the belief updating scheme is to maintain a style of online learning, while not to overload the computational intensity. As we can see from

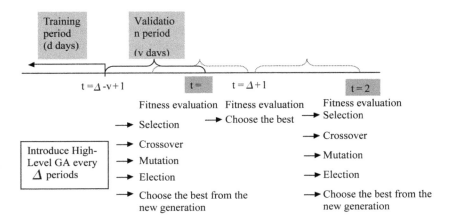

Figure 23.7 Belief updating scheme.

Figure 23.7, at each time t agents retain the most recent v days as the validation period. They use the data before the validation period, that is, the data of the training period, to estimate the parameters of each belief. Then a fitness measure for a belief $B^i_{j,t}$ is its associated *likelihood*, evaluated by the validation set $\{m_{t-s}\}^v_{s=1}$,

$$L^i_{j,t} = L(\{m_{t-s}\}^v_{s=1}|B^i_{j,t}). \tag{23.42}$$

Equation (23.42) is the likelihood of the observations $\{m_{t-s}\}^v_{s=1}$ in the validation period under the belief $B^i_{j,t}$. Every Δ period, after they finish the evaluation of each belief's fitness, they apply the genetic operation to update their belief set (see Appendix B.3), and the belief with the highest fitness will be chosen. Even in the period that the genetic operation is not applied, say, when $t \in [\Delta + 1, 2\Delta - 1]$, they evaluate the fitness of beliefs in their current belief set using the newest data and choose the best from it.

Appendix B.3: genetic operation

Once the procedure for evaluating each belief's fitness (**Eval** $\{B^i_{j,t-1}\}^J_{j=1}$) is completed, all beliefs are associated with a fitness which is the output of (23.42).

$$\textbf{Eval}: \{B^i_{j,t-1}\}^J_{j=1} \rightarrow \{L^i_{j,t-1}\}^J_{j=1} \tag{23.43}$$

Based on this fitness evaluation, we will revise and renew investor i's beliefs by using the following four genetic operators: selection, crossover, mutation and election.

Selection: A tournament selection with tournament size four is adopted. The best two beliefs will be chosen as the parents (mating pool).

Crossover: With probability p_{cross}, the two parents chosen above will generate an offspring by the *uniform crossover*. With this crossover, each bit position of the offspring will be taken randomly either from the father or the mother with a one-half chance for each. For an illustration, let us consider the pair of parents to be $B^i_{x,t-1} = 00101010$, corresponding to a belief of $(k_x, d_x) = (0,170)$, and $B^i_{y,t-1} = 0111110010$, corresponding to $(k_y, d_y) = (0,498)$. Then, an offspring, B^i_z, can be

$$B^i_z = 0011100010 \rightarrow (k_z, d_z) = (0,226).$$

Mutation: There is a small probability p_{mutate} (mutation rate) by which each bit of B^i_z may encounter a change. For example, the mutation which changes the fifth bit from '1' to '0', and the last bit from '0' to '1' will result in a new string:

$$B^i_z = 0011100010 \rightarrow (k_z, d_z) = (0,195).$$

Election: Finally, B^i_z will also be evaluated by the observations $\{m_{t-s}\}^v_{s=1}$, and the likelihood will be figured out. We will then compare the likelihood from B^i_z, with

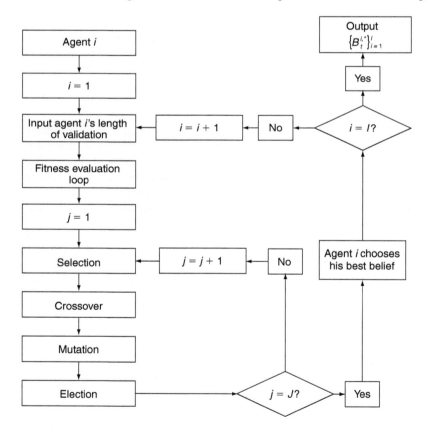

Figure 23.8 Flowchart of the high-level GA.

the likelihood from the parent models, and the best one will be passed on the next generation, $\{B^i_{j,t-1}\}^J_{j=1}$.

Appendix B.4: loops

Once a belief is generated, a loop in Figure 23.8 will lead us back to selection, which is then followed by crossover, mutation and election before the next belief is generated. The loop will continue until all J beliefs of $\{B^i_{j,t-1}\}^J_{j=1}$ are generated. One of the beliefs, $B^{i,*}_{j,t}$, will be chosen based on the likelihood criteria,

$$B^{i,*}_t = \arg \max_j L(\{m_{t-s}\}^v_{s=1}|B^i_{j,t}) \tag{23.44}$$

The belief set will remain unchanged for the next Δ periods, when another loop of revision and renewal process is conducted, and $B^{i,*}_{t+\Delta}$ is brought about.

Appendix C: Euler consumption equation

The data generated from the agent-based computational consumption CAPM model is then used to fit the Euler consumption equation, which is derived from the assumption of homogeneous agents under rational expectations.[13] Below we shall follow Hansen and Singleton (1983) to re-derive this equation to fit our specific context.[14]

Consider the representative consumer with a CRRA (constant relative risk aversion) utility function:[15]

$$u(c_t) = c_t^{1-\rho}/1 - \rho, \rho > 0. \tag{23.45}$$

The representative consumer in this economy is assumed to choose a consumption plan so as to maximize the expected value of his time-additive utility function,

$$E\left[\sum_{r=0}^{\infty} \beta^r u(c_{t+r})|\Omega_t\right], 0 < \beta < 1. \tag{23.46}$$

The mathematical expectation $E(\cdot|)$ is conditioned on information available to agents at time t, Ω_t. Current and past values of real consumption and asset returns are assumed to be included in Ω_t.

Agents substitute present for future consumption by trading the ownership rights of M assets. As above, the vector $\vec{q}_t$ denotes the holdings of the M assets at date t, $\vec{p}_t$ denotes the vector of prices of the M assets, and $\vec{w}_t$ denote the vector of M values of the dividends at date t. Then the agents' consumption and investment plan (c_t, q_t) maximize (23.46) subject to the sequence of budget constraints,

$$c_{t+1} + \vec{p}_{t+1} \cdot \vec{q}'_{t+1} \leq (\vec{p}_t + \hat{w}_t) \cdot \vec{q}'_t. \tag{23.47}$$

The first-order necessary conditions, that involve the equilibrium price of the M assets, are

$$u'(c_t) = \beta \cdot E[u'(c_{t+1})|\Omega_t] \cdot R_{m,t}; \ m = 1, \ldots, M, \tag{23.48}$$

where

$$R_{m,t} = \frac{p_{m,t} + w_{m,t}}{p_{m,t}}$$

is the return on the mth asset expressed in units of the consumption good.

The definition of asset returns here is different from the usual derivation. This is because we have a different time line for agents. Due to computational hardness for the fixed point, our temporal equilibrium is not Walrasian. Agents submit their orders based on their estimated price $p^i_{m,t}$, which in general is different from the realized temporal equilibrium price $p_{m,t}$. In other words, the equilibrium prices only happen after their submission. By this time line, when they are making the decision for the period $t + 1$ the effective return is actually the $R_{m,t}$ defined above.[16]

Substituting (23.45) to (23.49) and rearranging gives

$$E[\beta \left(\frac{c_{t+1}}{c_t}\right)^{-\rho} \cdot R_{m,t}|\Omega_t] = 1; \ m = 1, \ldots, M, \tag{23.49}$$

Assuming that the joint distribution of consumption and returns is lognormal, from (23.49), a restricted linear time series representation of the logarithms of consumption and asset returns can be derived. Let

$$x_t \equiv c_t/c_{t-1}, \ U_{m,t} \equiv x_t^{-\rho} R_{m,t-1}.$$

Then (23.49) can be rewritten as

$$E(U_{m,t}|\Omega_{t-1}) = 1/\beta, \ m = 1, \ldots, M. \tag{23.50}$$

Next, let

$$\Delta c_t \equiv \log x_t, \ r_{m,t} \equiv \log R_{m,t},$$
$$Y_t \equiv (\Delta c_t, r_{1,t-1}, \ldots, r_{M,t-1}),$$
$$u_{m,t} \equiv \log U_{m,t} = -\rho \Delta c_t + r_{m,t-1}(m = 1, \ldots, M),$$

and Ω^y_{t-1} denote the information set $\{Y_{t-s}: s \geq 1\}$. Furthermore, assume that Y_t is a stationary Gaussian process. This distributional assumption implies that the distribution of $u_{m,t}$ conditional on Ω^y_{t-1} is normal with a constant variance σ^2_m and a mean $\mu_{m,t-1}$ that is a linear function of past observations on Y_t.

Hence,

$$E(U_{m,t}|\Omega^y_{t-1}) = E(\exp[u_{m,t}]) = \exp[\mu_{m,t+1} + (\sigma^2_m/2)], \ m = 1, \ldots, M. \tag{23.51}$$

Since $\Omega^y_{t-1} \subseteq \Omega_{t-1}$, we can take expectations of both sides of (23.50) conditional on Ω^y_{t-1} to obtain

$$E(U_{m,t}|\Omega^y_{t-1}) = 1/\beta. \tag{23.52}$$

Equating the right-hand sides of equations (23.51) and (23.52) and solving for $\mu_{m,t-1}$ yields $\mu_{m,t-1} = -\log\beta - (\sigma^2_m/2)$. Define

$$V_{m,t} \equiv u_{m,t} - \mu_{m,t-1} = \rho\Delta c_t + r_{m,t-1} + \log\beta + (\sigma^2_m/2), \tag{23.53}$$

Then,

$$E(V_{m,t}|\Omega^y_{t-1}) = 0$$

and

$$E(r_{m,t-1}|\Omega^y_{t-1}) = \rho E(\Delta c_t|\Omega^y_{t-1}) - \log\beta - (\sigma^2_m/2), \tag{23.54}$$

because

$$r_{m,t-1} = E(r_{m,t-1}|\Omega^y_{t-1}) + \varepsilon_{m,t-1} \tag{23.55}$$

$$\Delta c_t = E(\Delta c_t|\Omega^y_{t-1}) + v_t \tag{23.56}$$

Substituting (23.55) and (23.56) with (23.54) and rearranging, we obtain

$$r_{m,t-1} = \rho\Delta c_t - \rho v_t + \varepsilon_{m,t-1} - \log\beta - (\sigma^2_m/2). \tag{23.57}$$

Define

$$\eta_t = -\rho v_t + \varepsilon_{m,t-1},$$

and

$$\mu = \log\beta - (\sigma^2_m/2),$$

then equation (23.57) becomes

$$r_{m,t-1} = \mu + \rho\Delta c_t + \eta_t, \tag{23.58}$$

where μ is a constant, and η_t is the random term.[17] Similarly, one could follow Hall (1988) to derive the inverse form of (23.58).

$$\Delta c_t = \tau + \psi r_{m,t-1} + \xi_t. \tag{23.59}$$

Notes

1 For example, it is found that the intertemporal elasticity is different between the poor and the rich, and is also different between stockholders and non-stockholders. See the literature review later in this chapter.
2 The question becomes even more puzzling given the irrelevance theorem of preferences to wealth share (Sandroni 2000; Blume and Easley 2004).
3 Depending on the exact formulation, it is sometimes also known as the *risk-free rate puzzle* (Weil 1989).
4 Actually, these numbers are provided by Yogo (2004), and are not directly available from Campbell (2003).
5 The simulation study proposed here is very different from the usual empirical study in which the true value of ψ (ρ) is unknown, and hence there is no basis to gauge the possible bias due to bounded rationality.
6 Given agent i's expected future prices $p^i_{m,t+r}$ and their wealth W^i_{t+r-1}, $\forall r \geq 0$, this constraint can also be written as

$$c^i_{t+r+1} + \sum_{m=1}^{M} p^i_{m,t+r+1} q^i_{m,t+r+1} \leq \sum_{m=1}^{M} (p^i_{m,t+r} + w_{m,t+r}) q^i_{m,t+r}, \quad \forall r \geq 0, \quad (23.11)$$

where $q^i_{m,t+r}$ is the number of shares m held by agent i at time $t + r$.
7 The realized price $p_{m,t}$ in general is not the same as the expected $p^i_{m,t}$. As a result, the *ex post* realized share is not the same as the *ex ante* realized share. This can further cause the agent's deviation from the optimizing behaviour. The fundamental cause of this difference is that agents are not able to trade in 'equilibrium' prices. Quite often they trade in the disequilibrium price unless they have perfect foresight. Also see the main text below and the associated Note 8.
8 Spear (1989) shows that for markets composed of complex heterogeneous agents, the rational expectations equilibria may not even be computable. Also, see Velupilla (2000).
9 See Appendix B.2 for the discussion of this parameter. Also see equation (23.42) and Figure 23.7.
10 The derivation of the Euler consumption equation is briefly reviewed in Appendix C.
11 The rate of return defined here (23.26) is not conventional. Appendix C discusses the reason for using this particular rate. See also Note 16.
12 Of course, determining how far or how generally that we can extend the finding here requires more work.
13 There is also an assumption about the joint distribution of consumption and returns. We shall be back to this issue later.
14 Hall's (1988) derivation is similar, and, therefore, is skipped.
15 The CRRA utility function is what we need here. In fact, our agent-based simulation is further restricted to the case where $\rho = 1$, i.e. the log utility function. See Table 23.1.
16 In fact, an alternative measure which can capture the capital gain is

$$R_{m,t} = \frac{p_{m,t} + w_{m,t}}{p^i_{m,t}} = \frac{p_{m,t} + w_{m,t}}{p_{m,t-1}}.$$

The second equality is based on the random-walk assumption, equation (23.17). This discussion of different measures of returns points out the relevance of *trading mechanisms*. Is the asset traded with a *continuous double auction*, or traded with a *Walrasian auctioneer*, or traded with *a rationing scheme*? Obviously, the empirical literature may not be interested in this distinction because the Euler consumption equation is only applied to the *low-frequency* data, and never to the daily data, not to mention the *high-frequency* data. It, therefore, raises the question: which time frame is actually the most appropriate one to examine the Euler consumption regression? The issue may not be that important as far as the aggregate data is concerned. Nonetheless, when we move to individual data, as the current empirical research indeed is doing, this issue is no longer irrelevant. The advantage of agent-based modelling is that it allows us to explore the possible existence of *heterogeneity in the time frame*.

17 Notice that the dependent variable is $r_{m,t-1}$, which is different from the Hansen–Singleton derivation of the Euler consumption equation. This is due to the different time frame to which we refer. See Note 16 for the explanation.

References

Adriaens, H., Donkers, B. and Melenberg, B. (2004), 'Extending the CAPM model', Paper presented at the Tenth International Conference of the Society for Computational Economics: Computing in Economics and Finance, University of Amsterdam, Amsterdam, the Netherlands, 8–10 July.

Arifovic, J. and Maschek, M. (2003) 'Expectations and currency crisis: An experimental approach', Paper presented at the ninth International Conference on Computing in Economics and Finance, University of Washington, Seattle, 11–13 July.

Arthur, W.B., Holland, J., LeBaron, B., Palmer, R. and Tayler, P. (1997) 'Asset pricing under endogenous expectations in an artificial stock market', in W.B. Arthur, S. Durlauf and D. Lane (eds), *The Economy as an Evolving Complex System II*, Reading, MA: Addison-Wesley.

Attanasio, O.P., Banks, J. and Tanner, S. (2002) 'Assets holding and consumption volatility', *Journal of Political Economy*, 110: 771–92.

Blume, L. and Easley, D. (1992) 'Evolution and market behavior', *Journal of Economic Theory*, 58: 9–40.

—— (2004) 'If you're so smart, why aren't you rich? Belief selection in complete and incomplete markets', unpublished working paper.

Breeden, D.T. (1979) 'An intertemporal asset pricing model with stochastic consumption and investment opportunities', *Journal of Financial Economics*, 7: 265–96.

Brock, W.A. and Hommes, C.H. (1998) 'Heterogeneous beliefs and routes to chaos in a simple asset pricing model', *Journal of Economic Dynamics and Control*, 22: 1235–74.

Bullard, J. and Duffy, J. (1999) 'Using genetic algorithms to model the evolution of heterogeneous beliefs', *Computational Economics*, 13: 41–60.

Campbell, J.Y. (2003) 'Consumption-based asset pricing', in G.M. Constantinides, M. Harris and R.M. Stulz (eds), *Handbook of the Economics of Finance*, vol. IB, Amsterdam: Elsevier.

—— and Mankiw, N.G. (1989) 'Consumption, income, and interest rates: Reinterpreting the time series evidence', NBER Working Paper No. 2924.

Chen, S.-H. and Huang, Y.-C. (2007) 'The relationship between relative risk aversion and survivability', in T. Terano, H. Kita, H. Deguchi and K. Kijima (eds), *Agent-Based Approaches in Economic and Social Complex Systems IV. Agent-Based Social Systems*, Vol. III, Tokyo: Springer.

—— (2008) 'Risk preference, forecasting accuracy and survival dynamics: Simulations based on a multi-asset agent-based artificial stock market', *Journal of Economic Behavior and Organization*, 67(3): 702–17.

Chen, S.-H. and Liao, C.-C. (2004) 'Behavioral finance and agent-based computational finance: Toward an integrating framework', *Journal of Management and Economics*, 8. Online journal.

Chen, S.-H. and Yeh, C.-H. (2001) 'Evolving traders and the business school with genetic programming: A new architecture of the agent-based artificial stock market', *Journal of Economic Dynamics and Control*, 25: 363–93.

—— (2002) 'On the emergent properties of artificial stock markets', *Journal of Economic Behavior and Organization*, 49: 217–29.

Chiarella, C. and He, X. (2002) 'Heterogeneous beliefs, risk and learning in a simple asset pricing model', *Computational Economics*, 19(1): 95–132.

—— (2003a) 'Dynamics of beliefs and learning under aL-processes: The heterogeneous case', *Journal of Economic Dynamics and Control*, 27(3): 503–31.

—— (2003b) 'Heterogeneous beliefs, risk and learning in a simple asset-pricing model with a market maker', *Macroeconomic Dynamics*, 7(4): 503–36.

Epstein, L.G. and Zin, S.E. (1991) 'Substitution, risk aversion, and the temporal behavior of consumption and asset returns: An empirical analysis', *Journal of Political Economy*, 99: 263–86.

Evans, G.W. and Honkapohja, S. (2001) *Learning and Expectations in Macroeconomics, Series on Frontier of Economic Research*, Princeton, NJ: Princeton University Press.

Ganuersdorfer, A. (2000) 'Endogenous fluctuations in a simple asset pricing model with heterogeneous agents', *Journal of Economic Dynamics and Control*, 24: 799–831.

Guvenen, M.F. (2002) 'Reconciling conflicting evidence on the elasticity of intertemporal substitution: A macroeconomic perspective', Working Paper No. 491, Department of Economics, Rochester University, NY.

Hall, R.E. (1988) 'Intertemporal substitution in consumption', *Journal of Political Economy*, 96: 339–57.

Hansen, L.P. and Singleton, K.J. (1982) 'Generalized instrumental variables estimation of nonlinear rational expectations models', *Econometrica*, 50: 1269–86.

—— (1983) 'Stochastic consumption, risk aversion, and the temporal behavior of asset returns', *Journal of Political Economy*, 91(2): 249–65.

He, X. and Chiarella, C. (2001) 'Asset price and wealth dynamics under heterogeneous expectations', *Quantitative Finance*, 1(5): 509–26.

Holland, J. and Miller, J. (1991) 'Artificial adaptive agents in economic theory', *American Economic Review*, 81: 365–70.

Jones, L.E., Manuelli, R. and Stachetti, E. (1999) 'Technology (and policy) shocks in models of endogenous growth', NBER Working Paper No. 7063.

King, R.G. and Rebelo, S.T. (1990) 'Public policy and economic growth: Developing neoclassical implications', *Journal of Political Economy*, 98(5): S127–50.

Kirman, A. (1992) 'Whom or what does the representative individual represent?' *Journal of Economic Perspectives*, 6(2): 117–36.

LeBaron, B. (2000) 'Agent-based computational finance: Suggested readings and early research', *Journal of Economic Dynamics and Control*, 24(5–7): 679–702.

—— (2001) 'Evolution and time horizons in an agent based stock market', *Macroeconomic Dynamics*, 5: 225–54.

——, Arthur, W.B. and Palmer, R. (1999) 'Time series properties of an artificial stock market', *Journal of Economic Dynamics and Control*, 23: 1487–516.

Lux, T. and Marchesi, M. (2000) 'Volatility clustering in financial markets: A microsimulation of interacting agents', *International Journal of Theoretical and Applied Finance*, 3: 675–702.

Markowitz, H. (1952) 'Portfolio selection', *Journal of Finance*, 7: 77–91.

Neely, C.J., Roy, A. and Whiteman, C.H. (2001) 'Risk aversion versus intertemporal substitution: A case study of identification failure in the intertemporal consumption capital asset pricing model', *Journal of Business and Economic Statistics*, 19: 395–403.

Palmer, R.G., Arthur, W.B., Holland, J.H., LeBaron, B. and Tayler, P. (1994) 'Artificial economic life: A simple model of a stockmarket', *Physica D*, 75: 264–74.

Patterson, K.D. and Pesaran, B. (1992) 'The intertemporal elasticity of substitution in consumption in the U.S. and in the U.K.', *Review of Economics and Statistics*, 74(4): 573–84.

Sandroni, A. (2000) 'Do markets favor agents able to make accurate predictions?' *Econometrica*, 68(6): 1303–41.

Smith, D.C. (1998) 'Finite sample properties of tests of the Epstein–Zin asset pricing model', *Journal of Econometrics*, 93: 113–48.

Spear, S. (1989) 'Learning rational expectations under computability constraints', *Econometrica*, 57(4): 889–910.

Summers, L.H. (1981) 'Tax policy, the rate of return, and savings', NBER Manuscript, No. 995.

Tesfatsion, L. (2001) 'Introduction to the special issue on agent-based computational economics', *Journal of Economic Dynamics and Control*, 25: 281–93.

Tobin, J. (1958) 'Liquidity preference as behavior towards risk', *Review of Economic Studies*, 25: 65–86.

Velupillai, K.V. (2000) *Computable Economics*, Oxford: Oxford University Press.

Vissing-Jørgensen, A. (2002) 'Limited asset market participation and the elasticity of intertemporal substitution', *Journal of Political Economy*, 110: 825–53.

Vissing-Jørgensen, A. and Attanasio, O. (2003) 'Stock-market participation, intertemporal substitution, and risk aversion', *American Economic Review*, 93(2): 383–91.

Vriend, N.J. (2000) 'An illustration of the essential difference between individual and social learning, and its consequences for computational analyses', *Journal of Economic Dynamics and Control*, 24: 1–19.

Weil, P. (1989) 'The equity premium puzzle and the *risk-free rake puzzle*', *Journal of Monetary Economics*, 24(3): 401–21.

Westerhoff, F. (2003) 'Heterogeneous traders and the tobin tax', *Journal of Evolutionary Economics*, 13: 53–70.

—— (2004) 'Multi-asset-market dynamics', *Macroeconomic Dynamics*, 8: 596–616.

Yogo, M. (2004) 'Estimating the elasticity of intertemporal substitution when instruments are weak', *Review of Economics and Statistics*, 86(3): 797–810.

24 Bubbles and crashes

A cyborg approach

*Ralph Abraham, Todd Feldman and
Daniel Friedman*

Introduction

Our goal in this contribution is to introduce the basic assumptions and features of our market models, and to give some early results of one of our "cyborg" experiments – that is, experiments involving human as well as robotic agents. But we will begin with a brief history of the project, written by Ralph.

In 1968, after moving from the math department of Princeton University to that of the University of California at Santa Cruz, I met Dan, then a grad. student. After Dan's PhD and some early positions, he became professor of economics at UCLA. During the 1980s I visited frequently at UCLA, and we used to meet for lunch at the faculty club. While I had no actual involvement in mathematical economics, I nevertheless kept up on the news through Dan. Then in 1985, Dan moved to UC Santa Cruz, and we continued meeting for the occasional lunch at the faculty club.

Meanwhile, chaos theory was heating up as a new style of applied math, and the economics community was becoming curious. Richard Goodwin, as assistant professor at Harvard, fellow of Peterhouse College (Cambridge) and professor in Siena, had led a long-term project on non-equilibrium economics, nonlinear dynamics and so on. He became an early adopter and harbinger of chaos theory. His 1988 lectures in Siena appeared as a book in 1990, spreading his enthusiasm.

All this led to my invitation to give the Jacob Marshak Lecture at UCLA in January, 1987. After my talk on "Nonlinear Systems, Complex Dynamics, and the Social Sciences" there followed a lively Q&A, during which there were several questions from an Indian gentleman revealing a deep knowledge and understanding of dynamical systems theory. At the end, I went up to him to inquire, "Who are you?" – and thus met Vela Velupillai.

Shortly thereafter, I received an invitation to a Workshop on Mathematical Economics at the Certosa di Pontignano, Siena (May 1991). This was the occasion of my meeting the wonderful Richard Goodwin, having a ride in his pet car, seeing Vela again and also meeting Lionello Punzo, both former students of Goodwin. In addition, I met a group of mathematical economists reporting exciting research in bifurcations of iterated mappings of the plane, especially Laura Gardini of Urbino, with whom I did joint work in the 1990s.

After 2000, Dan began telling me of his work in evolutionary game theory, and an opportunity arose early in 2004 to jointly apply for a grant from the National Science Foundation. The NSF program involved was aimed at new mathematical methods for the social and behavioral sciences. After reading a special issue of *Nonlinear Dynamics, Psychology, and Life Sciences* on agent-based modeling, we saw a way to apply agent-based modeling to extend evolutionary game theory. In our grant application we wrote:

> Our proposed research will extend the class of models called evolutionary games by allowing the set of strategies (actions) of each player (trader, agent) to be a continuous space, rather than just a finite set. This continues a line of study begun in joint work of Dan Friedman and Joel Yellin in 1997. The central concept of this work is the adaptive landscape.

This grant proposal was funded, and since mid 2004 we have used NetLogo – an agent-based modeling software system – to create a sequence of financial market models. Next, we will explain the basic concepts as they have evolved to date. Later, we will describe the cyborg experiment and its results.

The basic model: math

Our project website, www.vismath.org/research/landscapedyn/, presents several models. Here we describe the simplest one, Market Model 9.0. These concepts are basic to all of our market models.

We envision a number of money market managers (typically 20 to 100 in our simulations) trading in a financial market with two kinds of assets, riskless (safe) and risky. Each manager has a choice from a continuum of strategies characterized by a nonnegative real number, u. This is her *risk parameter*, and defines the division of her portfolio between the two kinds of assets. The minimum value, $u = 0$, indicates no risk (all assets are riskless), the value, $u = 1$, indicates all risk (all assets are risky), and $u > 1$ indicates leveraged investment (borrowing on the safe asset).

Further, each manager has a portfolio of total worth, z, which we normally assume to be between 0 and 4, with $z = 1$ indicating a typical starting value. With each step, each portfolio's worth is adjusted according to its risk parameter. The safe portion u earns at rate R_0, which we have fixed at $R_0 = 0.03$, while the risky portion $(1 - u)$ earns at rate R_1, with typically $R_1 \geq R_0 \geq 0$. The manager's gross annual return is thus,

$$R_G = (1 - u)R_0 + uR_1 \tag{24.1}$$

Financial math leads us to pose,

$$R_1 = R_s/\bar{u}^2 + 2\dot{\bar{u}}/\bar{u} \tag{24.2}$$

where $R_s = R_0 + R_d$ and $R_d = 0.03$, or $R_s = 0.6$; $\bar{u}$ is the mean value of u choices for all managers; and $\dot{\bar{u}}$ is the time rate of change of $\bar{u}$. Full details may be found in (Friedman and Abraham 2006).

Also, we assume that the gross return is decreased by a risk cost,

$$c(u) = c_2 u^2/2$$

where $c_2 = 0.02$. (In the research version of this basic model, Model 8.0, the constant c_2 may be varied by a slider.) Then the net return is,

$$R(u) = u(R_1 - R_0) - c_2 u^2/2 \tag{24.3}$$

Combining (24.1) and (24.2) we obtain the payoff function,

$$\varphi(u, F) = u(R_s/\bar{u}^2 + 2\dot{\bar{u}}/\bar{u} - R_0) - c_2 u^2/2 \tag{24.4}$$

where $F(u)$ denotes the dependence of net payoff on the distribution of u choices of all managers.

The simulation proceeds in steps of discrete time intervals of size "stepsize", which the operator may choose as days, weeks and so on. With each step, each manager's worth, z, is adjusted (depending on the stepsize) according to the net annual return $R(u)$ according to her current choice of risk, u. Additionally, her strategy choice, u, is adjusted according to the assumption of landscape dynamics, a gradient rule. That is, we assume that each manager is hill-climbing up the gradient of the payoff function (24.3) which depends on the current strategy choices of all managers (and their changes) through $\bar{u}$ and $\dot{\bar{u}}$ in (24.3).

The basic model: NetLogo

We now explain the graphical user interface of our simplest NetLogo model, Market 9.0, shown in Figure 24.1. The "population" slider (default setting, 30) determines the number of managers for the simulation. The "center" slider (default 20 percent) determines the mean u for the initial distribution of managers. The "setup" button creates the chosen number of managers with chosen mean u, and with random values of (u, z) within a medium-sized rectangle in the upper half of the black graphics window. The "frequency" drop down menu (default 52, or weekly steps) determines the number of updates per year. The "go" button begins the simulation, which continues until the "go" button is pushed once more. The small triangles in the upper half of the graphics window indicate the managers, each positioned according to its (u, z) coordinates, so they are seen to move smoothly about as the simulation progresses.

The other features of the interface shown in Figure 24.1 are three plots and three monitors, that collectively show the position of managers, the landscape function, the market price as a ticker-tape and as current value, the total elapsed time in years and the current value of net risky yield, R_1.

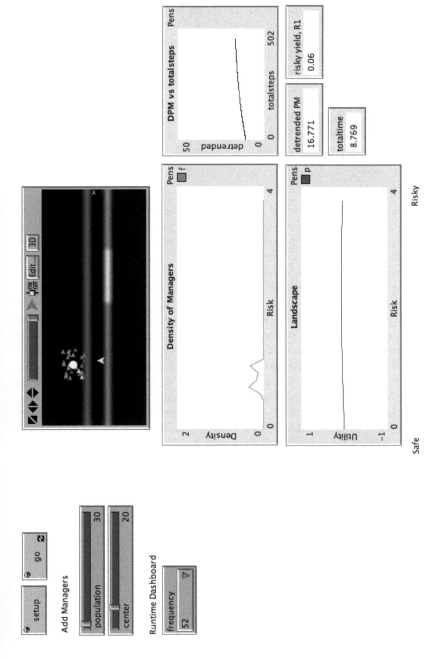

Figure 24.1 Interface of NetLogo Market Model 9.0.

It has been proven (Friedman and Abraham 2006) that this model always converges to a heap of managers all in one spot, and indeed, that is we what we observe as the simulation progresses. To obtain bubbles and crashes we need a more sophisticated model, such as Market Model 9.1. It implements two innovations: *surprise* (stochastic variations in payoff) and the c_2-*dynamic* (varying the c_2 coefficient in the gradient rule in response to losses, as explained below).

All of our models are posted on our website with documentation. The NetLogo models posted there function as applets, that is, you may run the model within your web browser. In addition, the NetLogo models may be downloaded and run in the NetLogo programming environment, which may be freely downloaded from the NetLogo website, http://ccl.northwestern.edu/netlogo. We encourage you to try out the applets.

The advanced models

In the course of our project, we made a succession of extensions to the basic model, in search of dynamical features underlying the bubble and crash behavior of real financial markets. Our more sophisticated models have provided many insights into market forces contributing to bubbles and crashes, as reported in our articles published on our website. Three successive extensions, called Model 8.1, 8.2 and 8.3, extend the research version of the basic model, Model 8.0. In parallel, we prepared simplified models of two of these, Models 9.0 and 9.1.

The first of these extensions was successful in exhibiting bubble and crash behavior, and most of our research (reported in the papers mentioned in our bibliography below) has been done with this extension, Model 8.1. The chief dynamical feature of this extension, the c_2-dynamic, has the coefficient c_2 in the risk cost (see equation 24.2 above) controlled by an algorithm, rather than by a slider. Unlike the basic model, here we have endogenous perturbations affecting each manager's payoff separately, that we call *surprise*. Our model determines surprise by an Ornstein-Uhlenbeck process. Due to the occasional negative surprise, the managers accrue losses, from which we calculate (for each manager independently) a weighted sum, $\hat{L}$, with higher weights for recent losses, and declining weights for older losses. Our algorithm for the c_2-dynamic makes use of all the individual $\hat{L}$ values, combined in a global, z-weighted mean, L_m. Recall that z is a variable (for each manager) measuring the current worth of that manager's portfolio. The rule to update c_2 is $c_2 = \beta L_m$, where β is a constant.

The user interface for Model 9.1 is shown in Figure 24.2. Note there are several additional sliders, one of which is "beta", which sets the constant β. The others are described in the User Manual for Model 8.1.

The cyborg experiment using Hubnet

The arrival in the 1980s of agent-based modeling in general, and NetLogo in particular, has stimulated a new wave of simulation research in economics, and more generally in the social and behavioral sciences. And it is in this context that

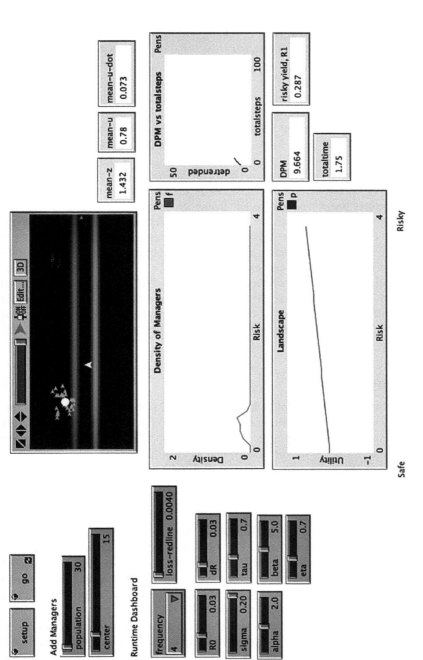

Figure 24.2 Interface of NetLogo Market Model 9.1.

we have situated the work performed under our recent NSF grant. However, during our work with NetLogo we discovered that it has various unique features that extend beyond the spectrum of other agent-based modeling systems. One of these unique extras is the HubNet system. This provides NetLogo client interfaces, so that a local net of computers may share control of the graphical user interface of a simulation as it runs. Originally developed for classroom use, we have found it useful for experiments involving human subjects interacting with a market of robot managers, and in other experiments as well. We feel that this work advances the programs initiated by Richard Goodwin and his students into new levels, and that many future agent-based simulations and experiments will follow.

Despite their intrinsic interest, financial bubbles and crashes as yet have no widely accepted theoretical explanation. In response, we developed an out-of-equilibrium agent-based model focusing on portfolio managers who adjust their exposure to risk in response to a payoff gradient, as described above. Bubbles and crashes occur for a wide range of parameter configurations in our advanced models incorporating an endogenous market risk premium based on investors' historical losses and exponential averaging. Even though the simulations confirm bubbles and crashes, simulation models are more valuable when they work in tandem with empirical studies and/or laboratory experiments with human subjects. Therefore, we devised an experiment where human subjects interact with automated robots to test the assumptions driving our NetLogo models.

Experimental design

We conducted an experiment at the University of California at Santa Cruz Learning and Experimental Economic Projects (LEEPS) lab using the Hubnet feature of NetLogo. In a participatory simulation, a group of human subjects can take part in enacting the behavior of a system as each human controls a part of the system by using an individual interface, the HubNet client. The LEEPS laboratory has 14 computers each linked to Hubnet via a server where subjects interact in a virtual market as seen in Figure 24.3.

A typical experiment lasted 90 minutes and involved five inexperienced human subjects recruited by email from a campus-wide pool of undergraduate volunteers. Humans silently read the instructions and then listened to an oral summary by the conductor. After a couple of practice rounds, they played about 12 periods. Human subjects are paid based on the average of their wealth achieved at the end of each trading period which is redeemed at a couple of cents of real money, typically between $15 and $25.

During the trading period each human acts as a trader in a stock market alongside other humans and automated robots. Their objective is to maximize their wealth by buying and selling shares of a single stock at price P,

$$P = V\bar{u}^{\alpha}, \tag{24.5}$$

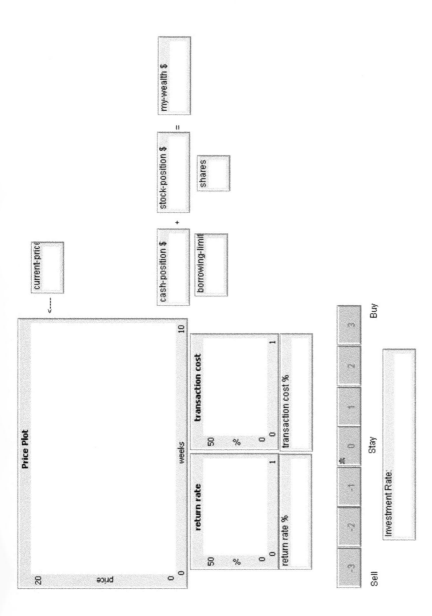

Figure 24.3 Human interface.

where V is the fundamental value, $\bar{u}$ is the mean distribution of allocation choice among robots and humans and α is a positive parameter that measures sensitivity to buying pressure. See equations (24.1) and (24.2) above. Humans do not know the price equation (24.1) nor the values of V, $\bar{u}$ or α. However, as shown in Figure 24.3, they can see the current price and price plot. We do tell them that price is determined by the growth rate, interest rate and buying and selling pressure. More specifically, we tell them the growth rate is zero, the interest rate is 3 percent, and that no one individual can move the stock price, but collectively, net buying pressure increases the price and net selling pressure decreases the price.

Each trading period consists of 20 "years," where the computer screen updates the trades and wealth on a weekly basis as shown in Figure 24.3. Before each trading period begins humans are endowed with $500 and 70 shares of stock. Their wealth at any point in time is equal to their cash plus their number of shares owned times the stock price. Human cash and wealth change based on several factors. First, humans earn interest on cash savings as well as pay interest if they borrow. Margin buying is allowed up to a limit that depends on their current wealth. Second, a buy reduces their cash position by the amount purchased times the stock price plus a transaction cost. A sell increases their cash position by the amount sold times the current stock price minus a transaction cost. Third, human shares grow based on the growth rate.[1] In addition, humans can go bankrupt. If a human goes bankrupt, they are banned from trading and incur a loss of $500 for the period. However, they are allowed to resume trading in the next period.

Humans view events on the monitor screen and respond by clicking one of seven buttons called adjustment-rates. Of the seven adjustment-rates, 3 accumulates shares at a very fast rate, 2 accumulates at a medium rate, 1 accumulate shares at a slow rate, 0 refrains from trading, –1 sells at a slow rate, –2 sells at a medium rate and –3 sells at a fast rate. A message box reminds them which button is active. In addition, there exists monitors to view their holdings of cash, shares, wealth, transaction cost and rate of return.

Treatments

We use two types of treatments. The first type varies the number of traders who participate in a market. The second type involves information about the other participants:

- Number of humans and robots. As the population size declines price volatility and the frequency of crashes increase. The three different population treatments include (one human and 29 robots), (five humans and 25 robots) and (five humans and five robots). Each experiment runs four blocks. We run three blocks of each treatment where the fourth block repeats the treatment run in the first block. For every experiment we rotate block order so the final data set contains the same number of observations per treatment. In addition, all blocks are known to everyone.

• Information. Depending on the experiment, humans are able to see (or not see) a graphics window, density of traders plot and a landscape plot as shown in Figure 24.4 (or not, as in Figure 24.3). The graphics window displays automated robots as small triangles and human traders as round dots where humans can identify themselves by a specified color. The graphics window allows humans to see the ratio of stock position to wealth of every human and robot. The density of managers chart is a histogram of the horizontal position of all traders, automated and human. The landscape chart shows the return rate (profit before transactions costs) each week for traders at every horizontal position (stock position relative to wealth).

The baseline configuration values in the simulated model are $R0 = dR = 0.03$, $g = 0.0$, $\sigma = 0.2$, $\tau = 0.7$, $\eta = 0.7$, $\beta = 2$, $\alpha = 2$, $\lambda = 1$, $d = 1$, rate $= 1.3$ and $c = 1$. We use the same parameter values for the sessions except we increase σ to 0.3 to induce sufficient variability so that humans cannot predict future price movements. Humans are not specifically told parameter values. The meanings of these parameters are described on our websites.

Integrating robots and humans

The humans' shares and wealth are translated into an appropriate u and z. Humans' risk allocation, u_j, equals one minus the ratio of their cash to wealth and the portfolio size, z_j, changes based on their gross return, inflow rate and outflow rate,[3]

$$u_j = 1 - \left(\frac{cash_j}{wealth_j}\right), \tag{24.6}$$

$$\dot{z}_j = [R_o + (R_1 - R_o - t_j - \delta \hat{L}_j + \rho z_o e^{\lambda \hat{R}_j}]z_j. \tag{24.7}$$

where j refer to humans and t refers to the transaction cost. The humans' initial z_j is equal to 1 and subsequently changes based on equation (24.3). The robots receive their initial risk allocation, u_i, and portfolio size, z_i, randomly via a uniform distribution in the (u, z) rectangle $[0.2, 1.4] \times [0.4, 1.6]$, set via the sliders. The u and z possible range is between 0 and 4. The distinction between how portfolio size changes for a robot and a human is that robots receive an idiosyncratic shock and do not pay transaction costs whereas humans pay transaction costs and do not receive an idiosyncratic shock. The transaction cost is determined as,

$$t_j = c(adjustment\text{-}rate_j)^2, \quad c = constant. \tag{24.8}$$

As in real markets humans face transaction costs where larger orders incur larger trading costs. The constant, c, is set to 1 such that trading at a fast rate incurs

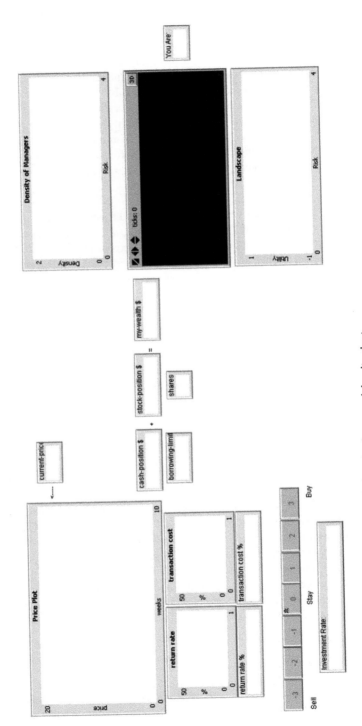

Figure 24.4 Human interface with graphics window, landscape and density chart.

a transaction cost of 25 percent, a medium rate incurs a cost of 6.25 percent, and a slow rate incurs a cost of 1.6 percent. Humans are able to see a monitor that tracks their transaction costs. For every trade transaction costs reduce humans' cash savings. We use transaction costs for humans in order to analyze whether humans are sensitive to market frictions or whether they thrash between buying and selling at fast rates. Another integration issue involves buying and selling. The buttons –3, –2, –1, 0, 1, 2, 3 shown on the interface were chosen for ease of viewing. The actual rates are 0.125 for a slow rate, 0.25 for a medium rate and 0.5 for a fast rate. These rates were chosen based on the standard deviation of the robot's chosen gradient, 0.125, in an all robot simulation using a baseline configuration. We then scale the adjustment rates up in order to accurately affect human cash and share holdings.

Results

To investigate these assumptions from Friedman and Abraham (2006), and to check their robustness, we analyze data from all nine sessions. We define a crash as a decline in price P of at least 50 percent from its highest point within the last half year.

Do humans react to an exponential average of their losses?

In order to investigate whether humans react to an exponential average of their losses we run the following regression,

$$adjustment\text{-}rate_{j,t} = \beta_0 + \beta_1 * cash_{j,t} + \beta_2 * shares_{j,t} + \beta_3 * wealth_{j,t} + \beta_4 * return_t +$$
$$\beta_5 * h5\text{-}r25 + \beta_6 * h1\text{-}r29 + \beta_7 * \hat{L}_{j,t} + beta_8 * \hat{L}_{j,t}\text{-}h5\text{-}r25 +$$
$$\beta_9 * \hat{L}_{j,t}\text{-}0.15cm\text{-}h1\text{-}r29 + \beta_{10} * crash\text{-}period + \varepsilon$$

where the dependent and explanatory variables have the following meanings,

- the dependent variable, $adjustment\text{-}rate_{j,t}$, is the trading rate of human j at time t,
- $cash_{j,t}$ represents the level of cash holdings of human j at time t,
- $shares_{j,t}$ represent the number of shares of human j at time t,
- $wealth_{j,t}$ represents the level of wealth of human j at time t,
- $return_t$ is the log first difference in price,
- $h5\text{-}r25$ is an indicator variable that assigns a 1 to the (five human, 25 robot) treatment and 0 otherwise,
- $h1\text{-}r29$ is an indicator variable that assigns a 1 to the (one human, 29 robot) treatment and 0 otherwise,
- $\hat{L}_{j,t}$ is the humans' exponential average of losses of human j at time t,
- $crash\text{-}period$ is an indicator variable that assigns a 1 to the time period of a crash and 0 otherwise,
- the intercept represents the base treatment (five human, five robot),

- the $\hat{L}_{j,t}$ is determined by setting η equal to 0.7. The interaction variables, $\hat{L}_{j,t}$-h5-r25 and $\hat{L}_{j,t}$-h1-r29 tells us how humans respond to an exponential average of losses relative to the $\hat{L}_{j,t}$, (five human, five robot) baseline treatment.

The results in Table 24.1 indicate humans do respond to losses. However, how they respond to losses depends on the treatment. Humans responded to losses by selling less in the (five human, five robot) treatment and selling more in the (five human, 25 robot) and (one human, 29 robot) treatments. The theory says that as losses accumulate humans should sell. Results from all treatments confirm the theory. One reason why humans respond less to losses in the the (five human, five robot) treatment is possibly due to the number and predictability of crashes. After the first period in (five human, five robot) block, humans realized that a crash was inevitable and therefore waited for a crash in order to accumulate shares at low prices. Lastly, the crash-period estimate reveals humans bought slightly during crashes.

Do humans follow a gradient?

Figure 24.5 shows how frequently humans choose one of the seven adjustment rates. The distribution of choices is relatively symmetric with humans choosing to hold 45 percent of the time. This provides evidence that humans are sensitive and aware to market frictions. Humans do not jump back and forth between buying at a fast rate and then selling at a fast rate which confirms gradient dynamic behavior versus adaptive dynamic behavior.

In order to test whether humans follow a gradient similar to robots we assume humans see the same gradient as do robots, and regress their choices, *adjustment-rate$_j$*, on the gradient evaluated at the humans' current u_j, called *gradient^h_j*. Theoretically, if humans are exactly following a gradient then the *gradient^h_j*

Table 24.1 Human OLS regression: all sessions

Parameter	Estimate	Standard error	$Pr > |t|$
Intercept	−0.008	0.0009	<0.0001**
Cash$_{j,t}$	0.00008	0.0000012	<0.0001**
Shares$_{j,t}$	0.0015	0.000022	<0.0001**
Wealth$_{j,t}$	−0.0001	0.00001	<0.0001**
Return$_t$	0.625	0.012	<0.0001**
h5-r25	0.033	0.0007	<0.0001**
h1-r29	0.054	0.0007	<0.0001**
$\hat{L}_{j,t}$	−0.047	0.004	<0.0001**
$\hat{L}_{j,t}$-*h5-r25*	−0.633	0.016	<0.0001*
$\hat{L}_{j,t}$-*h1-r29*	−1.137	0.021	<0.0001*
Crash-period	0.013	0.001	<0.0001*

Notes
* significant at 5%; ** significant at 1%.

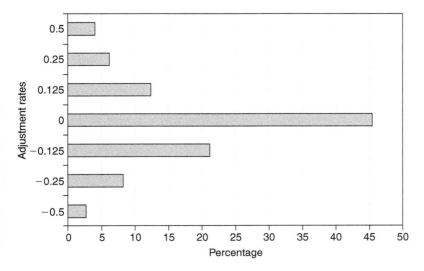

Figure 24.5 Frequency of adjustment-rates.

estimate should equal 1.00. However, comparing the *gradient*^h_j estimate to 1.00 is not appropriate in our study. By design the *gradient*^h_j estimate will be less than 1.00 because humans can only choose seven different adjustment-rates and not a continuous set of adjustment-rates. In order to find a more appropriate comparison estimate, we run the same regression using robot data where the explanatory variable is the robots' actual chosen gradient, *gradient*^r_i, and the dependent variable is the robots' actual gradient translated into one of the seven adjustment-rates humans face. We translate the robots' gradient by using mid-points to construct seven ranges that correspond to the seven adjustment-rates. We then assign an adjustment-rate to each of the robots' gradient depending on which of the seven ranges their gradient falls into.[4] Results from Table 24.2 report the appropriate comparison estimate, *gradientt*^h_j, is 0.87 and not 1.00. Therefore, the closer the estimated coefficient using human data is to the coefficient using robot data, 0.87, the more evidence that humans follow a gradient. According to Table 24.2 humans are not exactly following a gradient but are very close.

Table 24.2 Humans' adjustment rate vs humans' gradient

Parameter	Estimate	Standard error	$Pr > |t|$	R^{sq}
gradient^h_j	0.32	0.0017	<0.0001**	0.11
gradient^r_i	0.87	0.0004	<0.0001**	0.91

Notes
* significant at 5%; ** significant at 1%.

We also ran an additional regression to the one in equation (5) using robot data in order to compare estimates between the human and robot regressions. The regression results indicate the signs and level of significance for all esti mates are the same. Robots and humans only differ in the magnitude of the esti mates. For example, humans actually respond stronger to losses than do robots and robots sell ten times more aggressively that humans during crashes.

Conclusion

We conduct one of the first studies to integrate agent-based modeling and exper imental economics. The experiment consists of a virtual financial market that includes automated robots who follow a gradient (but are distinct in that each receives an idiosyncratic shock) and human subjects. We use the experimenta data to test two important questions: do humans react to market frictions by fol lowing a gradient, and do humans perceive risk by reacting to an exponentia average of their losses? From our analysis we can conclude several results. First humans do respond to losses by selling. However, when crashes are more fre quent and predictable, humans respond less to losses. Overall, since bubbles and crashes are not predictable the analysis of experimental data provides evidence that an exponential average of losses can be used as a way to measure the per ception of risk. Second, humans do not exactly follow a gradient as compared to robots but are very close to following one. In addition, humans follow a gradien more closely when allowed to view all market participants in the graphics window. Lastly, sessions where humans are able to view other market particip ants in the graphics window tend to herd around each other and hardly ever dis perse very far from the group. It is interesting how humans do not follow the robots, who drive the majority of the price dynamics in two of three population treatments.

There is still more work to be done. We would like to use the experimenta data to test the assumptions of other agent-based financial models in order to determine which agent-based model fits the experimental data better. In addition we would like to ask whether humans are a stabilizing or destabilizing force Moreover, we would like to run more sessions with different constants on the transaction costs to see how human behavior changes as we reduce transaction costs.

Acknowledgments

We are grateful to the National Science Foundation for support under grant SES 0436509. Pablo Viotti, our first graduate research assistant, has been a great asset in all aspects of the project, including the NetLogo programming. He was instru mental in the development of our human subject software based on the HubNe feature of NetLogo, which has been marvelously adapted by our graduate student Todd Feldman, to a test of our model assumptions with human managers. Also we have been ably assisted by Andy Sun, Matt Draper and Don Carlisle.

Notes

1 Shares do not grow in the base case where the growth rate is zero.
2 For example, the first experiment ran (one human and 29 robots), (five human, five robots), (five human and 25 robots), and (one human, 29 robots). The second experiment ran (five human, five robots), (five human and 25 robots), (one human and 29 robots) and (five human, five robots). And the third experiment ran (five human and 25 robots), (one human and 29 robots), (five human, five robots) and (five human and 25 robots).
3 See Friedman and Abraham (2006) for an explanation of the inflow and outflow rate.
4 For example, if a robot chose a gradient of 0.1 then that choice would be defined as a slow buy, 0.125, since it is between 0.0625 and 0.1875.

Bibliography

Abraham, Ralph, Dan Friedman and Paul Viotti. Complex Dynamical Systems and the Social Sciences. Online, available at: www.ralph-abraham.org/articles/MS%23123. Agents/agents07a.pdf (accessed April 22, 2009).

Cherkashin, D., J.D. Farmer and S. Lloyd.(2007) A Simple Evolutionary Game with Feedback between Perception and Reality. Santa Fe Institute Working Paper 07–08-032, Santa Fe, NM.

Elliot, Euel and L. Douglas Kiel. Agent-based modeling in the social and behavioral sciences. Nonlinear Dynamics, Psychology, and Life Sciences 8(2) (April 2004): 121–30.

Farmer, J.D. Market force, ecology and evolution. *Industrial and Corporate Change* 11(5) (2002): 895–953.

Friedman, Daniel. (2005) Conspicuous Consumption Dynamics. UCSC working paper. Online, available at: www.vismath.org/research/landscapedyn/articles/ (accessed July 1, 2008).

Friedman, Daniel, and Ralph Abraham. (2006) Bubbles and Crashes: Escape Dynamics in Financial Markets. UCSC working paper. Online, available at: www.vismath.org/research/landscapedyn/articles/ (accessed July 1, 2008).

Friedman, Daniel and Yin-Wong Cheung. Speculative Attacks: A Laboratory Study in Continuous Time. *CESifo Working Paper Series*, CESifo Working Paper No. 2420, CESifo Group Munich.

Friedman, Daniel and Joel Yellin. (1997) Evolving Landscapes for Population Games. University of California, Santa Cruz draft manuscript. Online, available at: www.vismath.org/research/landscapedyn/articles/dan/ (accessed November 15, 2009).

Goodwin, Richard M. (1990) *Chaotic Economic Dynamics*, Oxford: Clarendon Press.

25 Is there gold in Taylor's rule?

A note on the treasure hunt

Francesco Luna

In sum, many of the most interesting issues in contemporary monetary theory require an analytical framework that involves learning by private agents and possibly the central bank as well.

(Bernanke 2007)

a policy rule need not be a mechanical formula.... A policy rule can be implemented and operated more informally by policymakers who recognize the general instrument responses that underlie the policy rule, but who also recognize that operating the rule requires judgment and cannot be done by computer.

(Taylor 1993: 198)

no central bank (that I am aware of) uses a Taylor rule as the main guide to its instrument-rate setting or has committed itself to a similar instrument rule.

(Svensson 2003: 14)

Introduction

Captatio benevolentiae

Like Picasso's, Vela's prolific work has seen several 'periods', as browsing through this volume will have already revealed. In the 'computable economics' period, he has elegantly and convincingly argued that a reasonable[1] benchmark for the rationality of the perfectly rational economic agent could be a Universal Turing Machine. I will not try to argue in favour of or against Vela's perfect rationality, but I will be contented, as a 'working hypothesis', to assume that some Turing Machine ticks between his occipital and temporal bones. This not an application of learning in the sense of inductive inference, was inspired by my mentor, friend and thesis co-director at UCLA (a.k.a. Kumaraswamy Velupillai) who, a few years back, suggested the topic of my dissertation: 'computable' learning in macroeconomics. If I were to attempt to identify (in a similar exercise) Kumaraswamy's Turing Machine so as to determine a name for the function responsible for his output, I would suggest to start the induction experiment from a *text* composed of all the quotes he has chosen, over the years. The method of information presentation would serve at least two purposes. On the one hand, it would show how Vela has superbly managed to introduce, exemplify, support and subliminally transmit the wealth of his ideas, his multifaceted results, his dynamic messages and consistently robust criticisms of inaccuracies and of approximate analysis. On the other hand, Velupillai's evident pleasure with appropriate quotes from the classics reveals his indomitable commitment to learn, harness and ultimately master the Language (with a capital 'L'). Not surprisingly, this second aspect clearly shows how hopeless the suggested exercise would be. It would amount to ask whether, in principle, the learner can learn itself .. Or, perhaps, it might be trivial to get the answer: I should simply ask Vela.

In the matter of learning, memory has an eminent role and some of the results I will employ in this scribble[2] have been generalized and expanded[3] to introduce explicitly memory constraints in the learner. It appears that the sense of smell is the most powerful of the senses in recording and triggering the retrieval of precise memories – not very dissimilar from Proust's Madeleine. Kumara Vela Swamypillai's memory is recognized as nearly prodigious, but, I am told, is not photographic. However, it may be of the olfactory variety. In this case, it will have certainly helped in developing his unerring judgement on what is relevant and interesting if we accept Richard Goodwin's position on the intellectual approach of the good researcher as reported by Robert Solow:

> The unspoken message was that if a thing was worth doing it is worth doing playfully. Do not misunderstand me: 'playful' does not mean 'frivolous' or 'unserious'. It means, rather, that one should follow a trail the way a puppy does, *sniffing the ground*, wagging one's tail, and barking a lot, because it *smells interesting* and it would be fun to see where it goes.
>
> (Solow 1990: 33, italics added)

Kuswamillai's fascination with smell is also betrayed by the signature he has chosen for his email messages and I hope he is not annoyed at me for divulging an imperfect translation of it:

> Men who cannot communicate their knowledge to others
> Resemble a bouquet of un-fragrant flowers in full bloom.
>
> (*Thirukkural* 650)

So to conclude, and employing another of Kuvelamy's favourite quotations:

> What's in a name? That which we call a rose
> By any other name would smell as sweet.
>
> (Romeo and Juliet II, ii, 1–2)

Of course, unless Raveswillai smells even sweeter…

Why computable learning

Computable learning appears quite appropriate in this context for at least two reasons: (i) for institutional restrictions, in many important cases, the policy rate is quite 'granular': the minimum change is limited to a quarter of a per cent; and (ii) the need for transparency, advocated in large part of the recent literature on monetary policy and inflation targeting in particular, can be interpreted as translating into rules that can eventually be codified using some finite alphabet so as to be explained. Both these elements suggest that a procedural approach is called for. Furthermore, how else rigorously and meaningfully to represent a rule if not with a Turing Machine without transcending the Church–Turing thesis?

The learnability framework

I refer to the approach proposed, for example, in Gold (1965, 1967) on inductive inference in general and language identification in particular. In its most general form, an *identification situation* comprises three elements:

1   a *class of objects*;
2   a *method of information presentation*;
3   a *naming relation*.

I will focus only on the learnability results of the following 'objects': (i) time functions and (ii) black boxes. A *time function* takes positive integers (time) into positive integers. A *black box* receives an input and returns an output determined by the all the inputs that have been applied to the black box up to that moment. More precisely: we will consider a black box as a function $o_t = b(i_1, \ldots, i_t)$ where i stands for input and o is the output. Both *i*s and *o*s are taken as integers. Of course, a time function is a special case of a black box where the output depends only on t and not on previous inputs.

The method of information presentation is going to be a *text*.[4] The naming relation for this exercise is chosen to be a *generator*,[5] and the *name* it will guess at each point in time will be a Turing Machine that defines a function from positive integers to positive integers. The 'learnability' concept will be 'identification in the limit', i.e. the time function *TF* or black box *BB* will be said to be identified in the limit if, after some finite time, the guesses are all the same and are indeed a name for *TF* or *BB*. The learnability results can be summarized as in Table 25.1. Time functions can be identified in the limit only if they are at most primitive recursive, while black boxes can be identified if they are generated by finite automata (ultimately, only periodic functions).

The set up

For the time function, at each point in time t, a learner is presented with one instance (an integer for simplicity)[6] belonging to the range of the function and

Table 25.1 Dividing lines between learnability and nonlearnability for time functions and black boxes

Type of object	Class of objects
Time functions ⸻⟶	Recursive
	Primitive recursive
Black boxes ⸻⟶	Finite automata

will guess the name (or one of the equivalent names) of the function that generated the sequence observed so far. The learner will be successful in her attempt if, after a finite number of instances, she converges (that is, her guess doesn't change any longer) on the name of the function which indeed generated the sequence.

In the case of a black box identification, at each point in time the learner will (i) input a value in the black box, (ii) observe the output, (iii) form her guess. In the case of a black box, the learnability concept must be somewhat weakened, since there is the possibility that the input may trigger a 'structural change' that constrains the function to a subset of its initial range. So *weak learnability* implies that only the future behaviour of the black box is to be inferred.

Twin problems

Taylor's quote about 'rules' is based on a rather narrow and quite widespread conception of what a rule is and of the idea it transmits in the context of monetary economics. As a matter of fact, earlier in the same paper Taylor mentions Friedman's proposed constant rate of money creation and clearly wants to distance 'his' rule from such a simplistic mechanism.

On the other hand, it is surprising to read that a computer, according to Taylor, would not be able to implement his envisioned monetary policy rule. Of course, Taylor in this case does not refer to the famous 'Taylor rule' as generally known, but to a rule 'operated more informally by policymakers .. ho also recognize that operating the rule requires judgement' (Taylor 1993: 198). It is interesting to ask whether the impossibility would derive from the large number of contingencies that the policy makers would face. However, if that is what Taylor had in mind, I would be tempted to retort that computer programs that play chess have been famous if not widely popular for more than 20 years,[7] and they certainly can deal with 'astronomically' large sets of options. So there could be more to Taylor's statement.

Interestingly enough, the effort of freeing the idea of 'rule' from a crude and limited mechanical procedure was still called for ten years after Taylor's 1993 influential contribution. In fact, Svensson feels necessary to refer to Taylor's paper to reinforce the message and stress further the need for flexibility and 'judgement' encapsulated in the modern conceptualization of monetary policy:

'[g]ood monetary policy should not be modelled with ad hoc reaction functions that are not structural, but instead as optimizing policy, with the help of optimal targeting rules' (Svensson 2003: 15). If this 'simply' translates into 'a more complex reduced-form reaction function in which the instrument rate is a function of all the inputs in the forecasting process' (ibid.: 14), the only result, as stated, is to increase the complexity of the rule or the *reaction function* without affecting its inherent nature of algorithm, procedure.

However, Svensson insists that 'it is better to model monetary policy as optimizing in the same way we model the private sector' and that 'central banks are at least goal-directed, rational, and optimising as the average household or firm' (ibid.: 14–15). This, indeed, may introduce a novel element that could be problematic. If, for example, we were to follow the lead and describe the central bank choices as based on a rational preference ordering the way economists in general model consumers' behaviour, the choice process itself would, in principle, be ineffective. The result, contained originally in Rustem and Velupillai (1990) and painstakingly worked out in Lilly (1993) was later streamlined in Velupillai (2000) in the ampler context of economic rationality. The scope of this chapter is however limited so I will overlook this problem, which, however, I believe is related more to the way economists tend to 'think' of economic behaviour rather than to the way in which policy makers 'design' economic measures. I will get back to it in the concluding remarks to assess the possible implications for the more general induction exercise. For the rest of my study, I will maintain that the best way to characterize a rule is through a procedure as flexibly implemented as a Turing Machine can do. At the same time, it is interesting to note, the learning approach I follow is quite similar to the one presented by Spear (1989) who suggested a computability framework to address the question whether economic agents could learn how to form rational expectations. Such a framework would indeed have to accommodate optimizing (and, if the induction process is successful, eventually 'perfectly rational') actors, be they consumers, entrepreneurs or the central bank, hence utterly in line with Svensson's recommendation.

I can see two inference problems related to Taylor's rule. First and obvious is the original one faced by Taylor himself: identify the function (rule) mapping output gap and inflation rate to policy rate from the observation of the relevant data. We can assume that at least the original exercise was not having an impact on the way the system was behaving. Using an expression from anthropology, Taylor is a *participant observer* whose actions are not affecting the observed phenomenon.

The twin problem is to study whether it would be possible for the monetary authorities to identify, that is, to learn inductively in a process of observation plus trial and error, a function linking its policy-making process (including inflation and unemployment expectations) plus policy instrument (the policy interest rate in particular) to the variables of interest: growth and inflation.

As mentioned above, the granularity of the policy rate and the very concept of a rule makes the exercise in computable learning quite appropriate in this context. However, even though we may agree to adopt or consider only *effective* policy measures, we may still doubt that the economy itself be a computable object. In case the economy is uncomputable, Gold's exercise could still give an answer to the question 'is Taylor's rule learnable through computable inductive inference procedures?' The answer, in general, would be in the negative, but, of course, it would not imply that specific exercises could not be solved. As an aside, let me note that Gold's approach encompasses arguably all learning mechanisms or strategies as applied in the literature, including, for example, the one based on the 'Cognitive Consistency Principle' proposed by Evans and Honkapoja specifically in the context of monetary economics. According to this principle, 'economic agents should be as smart as (good) economists' (Evans and Honkapoja 2008: 40), hence learning is modelled through econometric techniques[8] available to the professional economist with which the economic agent is endowed.

Taylor's problem

As mentioned, the fundamental hypothesis in this case, is that 'Taylor', the learner, does not affect the object in his attempt to identify it. Hence, the framework is quite 'simple' and immediately linked to the results above: Taylor is dealing with a time function. At each point in time t, he is presented with one instance (an integer for simplicity)[9] belonging to the range of the function and will guess the name (one of the equivalent names) of the function which generated the sequence observed so far. Taylor will be successful in his attempt if, after a finite number of instances, he converges (that is, his guess doesn't change any longer) on the name of the function which indeed generated the sequence. The formulation would be:

$$i = \varphi_T(\omega)$$

where i is the nominal interest rate and ω is an integer[10] obtained univocally combining u, a measure of the output gap (or unemployment gap) and π the inflation rate. The problem is to identify the 'name' T of the function (Turing Machine) underlying the Taylor rule 'used' by the central bank.

According to Table 25.1, as long as the function is *primitive recursive*, such an exercise is in principle feasible. Needless to say, this result reveals nothing on the complexity of the task, that is, no hint is given on how long it may take or what resources it may require. Rather, it fixes some impassable border: classes of more complex functions cannot be identified.

The central bank's problem

A minister is he who can conceive a great enterprise, rightly choose the ways, The means and the time, then successfully accomplish it.

(*Thirukkural* 631)[11]

[A] reaction function in which the real funds rate changes by roughly equal amounts in response to deviations of inflation from a target of 2 percent and to deviations of actual from potential output describes reasonably well what this committee has done since 1986.

(Yellen 1995)

Philosophy Master (PM): Because, sir, there is no other way to express one-self than with prose or verse.

Monsieur Jourdain (MJ): There is nothing but prose or verse?

PM: No, sir, everything that is not prose is verse, and everything that is not verse is prose.

MJ: And when one speaks, what is that then?

PM: Prose.

MJ: What! When I say, 'Nicole, bring me my slippers, and give me my nightcap', that's prose?

PM: Yes, Sir.

MJ: By my faith! For more than forty years I have been speaking prose with-out knowing anything about it, and I am much obliged to you for having taught me that.

(Molière, *Le Bourgeois Gentilhomme*, II: 4)

Whether or not Ms Yellen was indeed obliged to Taylor for having identified the prose the committee had been speaking for many years, the assumption about the abstract nature of the observer (the absolute disconnect between the learning process and the object to be learned) does not hold any more. This has essential implications for the learnability of the function. Assume that indeed the central bank wants to use a Taylor rule. Then, it wants to make sure that it will 'choose' a rule that is 'consistent' with the economy. Let me elaborate: the economy will take as *input* the rule P (which could be interpreted as including also the expectation mechanism applied by the central bank) and data i. Based on this input it will consequently *output* inflation and unemployment functions that are consistent with the rule adopted by the central bank. Using the typical recursive function notation we can summarize the above 'prose':

$$\omega = \varphi_P(i)$$

ω is the integer representation of u and π, φ_P is the policy rule adopted that is supposed to map i into u and π. However, the economy will map

$$\omega = \varphi_{g[P]}(i)$$

This implies that the central bank is looking for a fixed-point rule:

$$P = g[P]$$

Note that P is the inverse of the T rule that Taylor is trying to infer.

One way to model the central bank's learning process is through a two-step procedure:

1   the central bank, holding the rule *P* fixed, observes ω and tries to infer $\varphi_{g[P]}$,
2   by changing its policy rule *P* the central bank tries to infer g[·].

In case of full information:

Proposition 1: If the economy mapping $\varphi_{g[P]}$ from integers to integers is primitive recursive it can be learned in the limit.
Proof. By the learnability results of time functions.

Proposition 2: If the function g[·] is periodic (generated by a finite automata), it can be learned in the limit.
Proof. By the learnability results of black boxes.

Proposition 2 deviates from Spear's (1989) results in a similar context. According to Spear also g[·] could be inferred in case it is primitive recursive. However, as argued above, I think that this would require quite a heroic assumption. In practice, it implies that the impact of the monetary policy framework on the economy is nil and the insistence on modelling the central bank's behaviour in structural form would be quite irrelevant.

Concluding remarks

In a full information context, the Taylor-like researcher should be able to identify up to the class of primitive recursive Taylor rules.[12] As mentioned above, the function to be inferred by the researcher would be the inverse of the monetary policy rule implemented by the authorities. This implies that, were the policy rule itself primitive recursive, the complexity of its inverse could in principle transcend this level making the Taylor-like quest unfeasible.

As for the monetary authorities, their task would be more daunting and they could infer the economy's behaviour – hence successfully implement a Taylor-like monetary policy rule – only in case the economy is well represented by a finite-automata black box.

In case information is incomplete, Velupillai (2000) synthetically shows how the positive results do not hold anymore and I refer the interested reader to that book. However, I would like to point at a specific source of noise that has been stressed quite recently in the literature on monetary policy, prompted by the ever more popular inflation targeting 'revolution'. It relates to the issue of transparency and effective communication by central banks.[13] The recurring preoccupation with contradictory signals contained in the official communication of the central bank, may be interpreted as introducing yet another source of noise in the sequence of information (on the 'text') from which the learner is to infer the underlying function. On such 'noisy texts', as shown by Osherson *et al.* (1986), the learnability results fail in case the contradictory elements, even though from a finite set, may be repeated an infinite number of times. Of course, this has dramatic implications from a policy perspective calling for not only transparent, but also consistent communication. On the other hand, invoking another result from Osherson *et al.* we can state that the learnability results will hold even though a finite portion of the information set is never presented. This seems quite important as it suggests that it would be possible to infer what the central bank would do in extreme situations even though those cases have not presented themselves during the 'successful' learning process.

Notes

1 Alas, I cannot use the term 'rational' to avoid self-referentiality.
2 One of Vela's favourite words to describe his works when he allows me a sneak preview before they are published.
3 While I was working on my dissertation, Vela pointed at Osherson *et al.* (1986) as something I may want to read.
4 Another option would be the *informant*, which gives both positive and negative pieces of information. In other words, at each time it specifies whether the integer presented does or does not belong to the range of the function to be identified.
5 Again there is another possible naming relation; a *tester*, which is a decision procedure. For each integer, it will output a 1 whether the number belongs to the range of the function to be identified and a 0 otherwise. Not surprisingly, this implies that the functions that can be learned by using a tester naming relation have to be recursive.
6 Of course a rational number will also work.
7 After Shannon's (1950) writing about the problem, a rather famous match between man and computer took place in 1978 between David Levy and *Chess 4.7*, developed at Northwestern University, and well before Kasparov's duel with IBM Deep Blue.
8 It is curious to note that the 'Principle of Cognitive Consistency' is derived from psychology and used, for example to explain decision making under stressful conditions .. the question is who is under stress: the economic agent or the economist modelling the behaviour?
9 A rational number will work too. Also multiple inputs can be reduced to a single integer through bijective functions similar to the one in the next footnote.
10 For example, $\omega = \langle i, \pi \rangle = \frac{1}{2}(i^2 + 2i\pi + \pi^2 + 3i + \pi)$, as I learned in Rustem and Velupillai (1990).
11 I would like to draw the reader's attention on the procedural content of this verse. This is a fraction of Vela's background and in part explains his fascination with routines, algorithms and eventually Turing Machines.
12 In the broader sense than the simple 'reaction function in which the real funds rate changes by roughly equal amounts in response to deviations of inflation from a target of 2 percent and to deviations of actual from potential output' (Yellen 1995).
13 See for example Dennis and Williams (2007). Bulir *et al.* (2008a), and Bulir *et al.* (2008b) propose a way to quantify how 'clear' or without contradiction a central bank's communication is.

References

Bernanke, Ben (2007) 'Inflation expectations and inflation forecasting'. Remarks at NBER Summer Institute, Cambridge, MA. Online, available at: www.federalreserve. gov/newsevents/speech/bernanke20070710a.htm (accessed 10 October 2008).

Bulir, A., Smidkova, K., Kotlan, V. and Navratil, D. (2008a) 'Inflation targeting and communication: It pays off to read inflation reports', IMF Working Paper No. 08–234, Washington, DC: International Monetary Fund.

Bulir, A., Cihak, M. and Smidkova, K. (2008b) 'Writing clearly: ECB's monetary policy communication', IMF Working Paper No. 08/252, Washington, DC: International Monetary Fund.

Dennis, R. and Williams, J.C. (2007) 'Monetary policy, transparency, and credibility: Conference summary', FRBSF Economic Letter 2007–12 San Francisco: Federal Reserve Bank of San Francisco, CA. Online, available at: www.frbsf.org/publications/economics/letter/2007/el2007–12.pdf (accessed 10 October 2008).

Evans, G. and Honkapoja, S. (2008) 'Expectations, learning and monetary policy: An overview of recent research', *Centre for Dynamic Macroeconomic Analysis Working Papers Series*, CDMA 08/02, University of St Andrews, UK.

Gold, M.E. (1965) 'Limiting recursion', *Journal of Symbolic Logic*, 30: 28–48.

—— (1967) 'Language identification in the limit', *Information and Control*, 10: 447–74.

Lilly, G. (1993) 'Recursiveness and preference orderings', *Journal of Economic Dynamics and Control*, 17(5–6): 865–76.

Osherson, D.N., Stob, M. and Weinstein, S. (1986) *Systems That Learn*, Cambridge, MA: MIT University Press.

Rustem, B. and Velupillai, K. (1990) 'Rationality, computability, and complexity', *Journal of Economic Dynamics and Control*, 14(2): 419–32.

Shannon, C. (1950) 'Programming a computer for playing chess', *Philosophical Magazine*, Ser. 7, 41(314). Online, available at: http://archive.computerhistory.org/projects/chess/related_materials/text/2–0%20and%202–1.Programming_a_computer_for_playing_chess.shannon/2–0%20and%202–1.Programming_a_computer_for_playing_chess.shannon.062303002.pdf accessed 10 October 2008).

Solow, R. (1990) 'Goodwin's growth cycle: Reminiscence and rumination', in K. Velupillai (ed.), *Nonlinear and Multisectoral Macrodynamics: Essays in Honour of Richard Goodwin*, London: Macmillan, 31–41.

Spear, S. (1989) 'Learning rational expectations under computability constraints', *Econometrica*, 57(4): 889–910.

Svensson, L.E.O. (2003) 'Monetary policy and learning', *Economic Review of the Federal Reserve Bank of Atlanta*, 3: 11–16.

Taylor, J.B. (1993) 'Discretion versus policy rules in practice', *Carnegie–Rochester Conference Series on Public Policy*, 39: 195–214.

Velupillai, K.V. (2000) *Computable Economics*, Oxford: Oxford University Press.

Yellen, J. (1995) Remarks at the FOMC January meeting, quoted in C.T. Carlstrom and T.S. Fuerst, 'The Taylor Rule: A guidepost for monetary policy?', Federal Bank of Cleveland. Online, available at: www.clevelandfed.org/research/commentary/2003/0703.pdf. (accessed 10 October 2008).

26 The economics of Keynes in an *almost* stock-flow consistent agent-based setting

Charlotte Bruun

Introduction

In recent years stock-flow consistent Keynesian models have received increasing attention. Typically applying simulation of difference/differential equations, this strand of literature focus on long run equilibria. Although unsatisfactory from a Keynesian point of view, Dos Santos and Zezza (2008: 472) argue that short run dynamics, e.g. in the form of unsatisfied expectations, is too complex to handle within *formal models of "complete" monetary economies*. Agent-based models, however, pose an alternative to mathematical equations, while retaining the ability to model complete monetary economies. When an *almost* stock-flow consistent approach is chosen here, it is not due to limitations in the method applied, but a positive choice of diverging from the usual accounting principles of stock-flow consistent modelling, in order to capture what is regarded as essential dynamics in the interaction between real and financial spheres.

The model is *almost* stock-flow consistent – following the path of e.g. Godley and Lavoie (2007) and Dos Santos (2006), but choosing the micro-convention of equity revaluations rather than following the macroeconomic convention (Patterson 1990). This option is crucial since it undermines the long period equilibria of stock-flow consistent Keynesian models, and allows finance a more decisive role.

In the following we shall employ a three-step analysis; first we shall present the macrofoundation of Keynes in the terminology of stock-flow consistent modelling, next we shall discuss his microfoundation and finally we shall attempt to unify the two in an agent-based computational model. Experiments are performed on some of the behavioural parameters of the model relating stock and flow magnitudes.

Stock-flow consistency as the macrofoundation of Keynes

In his Tilton papers (Keynes 1933) and the first six chapters of *The General Theory* (1936), Keynes introduced the idea of a monetary production theory. Taking this starting point, the liquidity preference theory of the rate of interest is not vital to Keynesian economics. What is central is the fact that we live in a monetary economy and that, given fundamental uncertainty, we have no way of reconciling monetary and real magnitudes. Keynes' option for monetary magnitudes is motivated from a value-theoretic perspective as well as from a behavioural perspective. In his *choice of units*, Keynes addresses the value problem: how do we measure "the community's output of goods and services [which] is a non-homogeneous complex?" (Keynes 1936: 37). Real magnitudes may be chosen for partial analysis, but for macroeconomic analysis Keynes' well known solution was to apply two fundamental units: money volumes and labour hours. This brings him to national income accounting and the macroeconomic logic of the system. Entrepreneurs hold the power to determine effective demand since the wages they pay out in their production process are also the sum available for purchasing the final product.

This is the flow of funds and income perspective of stock-flow consistency. Every expenditure has a recipitor. Stock magnitudes, on the other side, are often ignored by Keynes' interpreters. The real world is short-sighted and the stocks accumulated by the flow magnitudes may be ignored. This, however, also implies ignorance of the financial markets and, it shall be argued here, the profit calculation performed by entrepreneurs which is vital to Keynes' behavioural motivation for choosing monetary magnitudes:

> He [Karl Marx] pointed out that the nature of production in the actual world is not, as economists seem often to suppose, a case of C-M-C' i.e. of exchanging commodity (or effort) for money in order to obtain another commodity (or effort). That may be the standpoint of the private consumer. But it is not the attitude of business which is a case of M-C-M', i.e. of parting with money for commodity (or effort) in order to obtain more money.
>
> (Keynes 1933: 81)

The consequences of having an M-C-M' circuit is crucial with respect to the level of production. Hiring all labour offered at a wage equal to the marginal product of labour would be the obvious thing to do, if maximizing profits was a question of producing as many goods as possible. Once it is a question of making money rather than making goods, it may be more profitable to leave workers idle.[1] For the entrepreneurs the question is one of getting back at least the money that they paid the workers as wages, and preferably more – a monetary profit. This question must be addressed at the macrolevel. There is only one way of getting back this money for the entrepreneurs as a class without entering new debt; by selling consumption goods. If workers prefer to save some of their wages, whether they hoard the money, open a savings account or purchase a financial asset, entrepreneurs will end up with a larger debt, and an apparently negative monetary profit.[2]

If the M' is to be perceived as actual money it is clear that entrepreneurs as a group cannot obtain a monetary profit unless another group in the economy accepts the necessary debt. This follows from the fact that entrepreneurs cannot produce money. Since the system cannot generate monetary profits, it follows that to the extent that wage-earners do not spend their current wages on purchasing current output, entrepreneurs are forced to accept a monetary position that is below the monetary position they had before they started up production. But this does not necessarily mean that the M-C-M' condition is not fulfilled. Keynes is not very clear on this, but for the system to work, entrepreneurs must assign a monetary value to their real assets. If this subjective evaluation is allowed to enter the profit calculation, then entrepreneurs as a group may experience a positive monetary profit.

Following the stock-flow consistent literature, another alternative is to interpret M and M' as net worth before and after production. Firms will only produce if they expect their net worth to increase. The next question thus concerns the definition of net worth. The stock-flow consistent literature has as the only component in the aggregate net worth of an economy, the real term K for capital goods, which is valued at the production cost and thus equal to household savings (Dos Santos and Zezza 2008: 448). But this appear to be a reminiscence from the C-M-C' nature of production – not M-C-M'! Where is the entrepreneurial motivation for starting up production in this world?

Although certainly consistent, the stock-flow consistent literature ignores the ability of K to generate future income – an ability that is constantly revalued at financial markets. If we combine this information with the stock-flow consistent approach, and use the praxis of the corporate sector in valuing equity, we end up with a behavioural definition of net worth. This allows us to estimate, how the aggregate of economic units perceive their own net worth.

> There are, however, some distinctions between conventions that should be adopted when dealing with national accounts, on the one hand, and corporate sector accounts on the other. Emphasising the importance of constructing income and balance sheet accounts on a sectoral consistent basis leads us to the usual national accounting convention of treating equities as a liability of the corporate sector. [...] On the other hand, it is usual in interpreting corporate sector accounts *not* to treat equities as liabilities.
>
> The concept of wealth which is likely to be of economic interest excludes (some part of) equity as a liability of the corporate sector.
>
> (Patterson 1990: 289, 293)

Equity issued and equity held is *not* valued at the same price, since we follow the corporate literature at this point rather than the macroeconomic literature. Equity held is valued at the current market price whereas equity issued is fixed at its issuing price. For the net worth of the economy as a whole this implies a dependence on equity prices. Since we retain the definition of aggregate income as consumption plus investment, this is also what makes this model *almost* stock-flow consistent. Changes in aggregate wealth is *not* equal to the flow of savings – revaluations of the stock of capital must be added!

If an assumption that all investment is financed by issuing equity were to be imposed on the model, the net worth of the economy would be equal to the stock of equity measured at current market price. Recognizing the importance of this, profits are not defined as the difference between the flow of sales and the flow of costs, but as the difference between the net worth of the company in the beginning and the end of the period. The market determines the stock magnitudes and from this we deduce profits as a flow, in opposistion to the conventional view that would have the net worth of a company determined as accumulated profits.

This makes the profit calculation and thus the production decision depend upon the moods of the financial markets. Financial markets are not only mediators between investors and savers, they also evaluate future returns on equity, and thus its monetary value. For the individual entrepreneur owning capital to which a monetary value is attached may appear to be just as good as holding money, but for the entrepreneurs as a whole, capital cannot be realized in the form of money – they cannot all sell at the same time. In this sense monetary production systems rest on an illusion that make them fragile.

The balance sheet matrix (Table 26.1) follows the tradition of stock-flow consistent modelling and the notation of Dos Santos and Zezza (2008), except for the treatment of equities as described above. Equity emissions are entered at face value as a liability and equity holdings are entered at market value as an asset. As has been emphasized by the financialization literature (e.g. Skott and Ryoo 2008), firms also hold equity. They may buy back their own equity, or choose to hold equity issued by other firms. Equity held by firms is therefore treated symmetrically to equity held by households.

If a firm issues equity in order to finance an investment, this operation will be neutral with respect to its net worth, i.e. capital goods (K) and equity issued (E^s) will rise by the same magnitude. The net worth of the aggregate community thus depends on any deviation in the way the market evaluates K, i.e. the stock of real capital from the original price of K. Expectations enter the model as a magnitude that may be read at the market for equity. This also allows for the possibility that aggregate movements of equity prices are independent of the sum of the prospects for individual firm. Stock-flow interactions may give financial markets a life of their own, which feeds back into the decisions to produce, invest and consume. In this case we do not have to model how agents form expectations on the performance of a specific firm.

Since, opposite most stock-flow consistent literature, we operate, not only with different institutional sectors, but also with individual households, and

Table 26.1 The balance sheet

	Households	Firms	Bank	Government	Totals
Bank deposits	+Dh	+Df	−D	+Dg	0
Bank loans	−Lh	−Lf	+L	−Lg	0
Equities held	+pEh	+pEf			+pE
Equities issued		−E^s			−E^s
Capital goods		+K			+K
Net worth Σ	Vh	Vf	V$b \approx 0$	V$g \approx 0$	K + pE − E^s

Table 26.2 Current transaction flow matrix

	Households	Firms		Bank	Government	Row totals
		Current	Capital			
Consumption	$-C$	$+C$				0
Investment		$+\Delta K$	$-\Delta K$			0
Wages	$+W$	$-W$				0
Transfers	$+G$				$-G$	0
Taxes	$-T$				$+T$	0
Interest on deposits	$+i_d Dh$	$+i_d Df$		$-i_d D$	≈ 0	0
Interest on loans	$-i_l Lh$	$-i_l Lf$		$+i_l L$	≈ 0	0
Dividends	$+Fh$	$-F^s + Ff$				0
Bankruptcy loss		$+B$		$-B$		0
Σ	$+SAVh$	$+SAVf$	$-\Delta K$	≈ 0	≈ 0	0

individual firms, the model does not conform to all usual assumptions of stock-flow consistent modelling (e.g. Dos Santos 2006: 544). Households as well as firms both have bank deposits and bank loans. In this model, the individual unit either holds deposits or loans, but in a more diversified model, units may hold both deposits and loans. Both households and firms hold equity, but only firms issue equity. The individual unit may finance purchase of equity through bank loans.

In this model the government plays a very neutral role. It is there to transfer purchasing power to households without income or wealth, so they can consume a minimum. The tax rate is on wage income, and is not fixed but adjusts to the need for transfer income. Thus the net worth of the government is approximately zero.

The banking sector is also a neutral intermediary in the economy. All non-bank agents are provided with a banking account that they freely dispose of up to a credit limit. The bank takes losses equal to the the bank loans of agents that go bankrupt. Such losses are covered by a difference in the banks' lending and borrowing rates. This difference is not fixed but varies with the losses of the bank such that the net worth of banks approximates zero.

The microbehaviour: rules of thumb rather than optimization

Throughout his career Keynes took an interest in measurement, and this also influenced the way he looked at human behaviour. His interest was first and fore-most in the unmeasurable; the fact that we cannot have a perfect measure of value, or of probability. Keynes realized that it is not only theorists that must deal with such problems; economic agents must also find ways of getting around the measurement problems. If agents use imperfect "statistical" measures and economic theorists want to say something about behaviour, they need to take into account the statistical measures as well, and the theoretical and behavioural

Table 26.3 Flow of funds

	Households	Firms	Bank	Government	Totals
Current savings	$+SAVh$	$+SAVf$	≈ 0	≈ 0	SAV
ΔBank deposits	$-\Delta Dh$	$-\Delta Df$	$+\Delta D$	$-\Delta Dg$	0
ΔBank loans	$+\Delta Lh$	$+\Delta Lf$	$-\Delta L$	$+\Delta Lg$	0
ΔEquities held	$-p\Delta Eh$	$-p\Delta Ef$			$-p\Delta E^s$
ΔEquities issued		$+p\Delta E^s$			$+p\Delta E^s$
Bankruptcy loss		$+B$	$-B$		0
ΔCapital		$-\Delta K$			$-\Delta K$
Σ	0	0	0	0	$SAV = \Delta K$
Revaluations					
Equities held	ΔpEh_{t-1}	ΔpEf_{t-1}			ΔpE_{t-1}
Bankruptcy	$-b(pEh)$	$b(E^s) - b(pEf)$			$-b(pE - E^s)$
Equities issued		$p\Delta E^s - \Delta E^s$			$p\Delta E^s - \Delta E^s$
ΔNet worth	$\Delta Vh = SAVh + \Delta pEh_{t-1} - b(pEh)$	$\Delta Vf = SAVf + \Delta pEf_{t-1} + $ $p\Delta E^s - \Delta E^s - b(pEf - E^s)$	$\Delta Vb \approx 0$	$\Delta Vg \approx 0$	$\Delta K + \Delta pE - \Delta E^s - b(pE - E^s)$

measurements become inseparable. One could call this reversed rational expectations! That Keynes was primarily concerned with the measures used by economic agents may be illustrated by the fact that he, after stating the insolubility
of the value problem notes that:

> Nevertheless these difficulties are rightly regarded as "conundrums". They
> are "purely theoretical" in the sense that they never perplex, or indeed enter
> in any way into, business decisions and have no relevance to the causal
> sequence of economic events, which are clear-cut and determinate in spite
> of the quantitative indeterminacy of these concepts. It is natural, therefore
> to conclude that they not only lack precision but are unnecessary.
>
> (Keynes 1936: 39)

Due to measurement problems economic agents cannot tame uncertainty.
What then, do economic agents do? They use methods of decision making that
are not concerned with evaluation of consequences but stems from habit,
instincts etc. Economic agents are not paralysed, but find ways around the
problems.

> Generally speaking, in making a decision we have before us a large number
> of alternatives, none of which are more "rational" than the others, in the
> sense that we can arrange in order of merit the sum aggregate of the benefit
> obtainable from the complete consequences of each. To avoid being in the
> position of Buridan's ass, we fall back, therefore, and necessarily do so, on
> motives of another kind, which are not "rational" in the sense of being con-
> cerned with the evaluation of consequences, but are decided by habit,
> instinct, preferences, desire, will, etc.
>
> (Keynes 1938: 294)

These arguments for using simple decision rules rather than optimization is
the most important micro-property from the work of Keynes to be used in our
model building. Combining rules of thumb with a macrofoundation adds up to
the complexity dictum of our time; the rationality may lie with the system and
not with the individual. It may not be important how exactly we specify the
investment decision of the entrepreneur or the consumption decision of the
worker – what is important is that we look for answers in the real world rather
than in the ideal world. When economic agents in the real world have invented
money as a way of dealing with uncertainty and unmeasurability, why should we
remove the money and pretend that agents have no problems with uncertainty
and lack of an invariable standard of value? Rather than assuming complex
behaviour in a simple world we model simple rule-based behaviour in a complex
world.

The agent-based Keynesian model

The model is of a cellular automaton type since consumers as well as consumption goods are distributed on a two-dimensional grid, in the following called consumer space. One consumer inhabits every cell, and producers, who are outside the grid, can place produced consumption goods where they please on the grid. The grid is used for determining consumption locally as neighbour dependent, inspired by Duesenberry (1949). In order to produce consumption goods, producers must have capital goods, produced by a subsector of producers. Production and purchase of capital goods must be financed by the issuance of equity or bank loans.

The model runs by randomly picking an agent for action. The action to be taken may be consumption, production decision by producer of consumption goods, production decision by producer of investment goods or financial action. Production decisions are only taken once within a statistical period whereas consumption and financial decisions are performed more frequently. When all producers have acted once, the statistical period has ended and all relevant statistics are collected. Payment of interest, dividend and taxes as well as social benefit also follows the statistical period.

Production of consumption goods

There are two main determinants of the production decision; last period's sales and last period's monetary profits. As indicated earlier, monetary profits are calculated according to the following rule:

$$\pi_{it} = (M_{it} - M_{it-1}) + (p_t E_{it} - p_{t-1} E_{it-1}) + (K_{it} - K_{it-1}) - (E^s_{it} - E^s_{it-1})$$

where M_{it} is money holdings (positive or negative banking account, or in our earlier terminology deposits (D) minus loans (L)) of producer i in period t, E_{it} is equity held, K_{it} is capital goods and E^s_{it} is equity issued. p_t is the average price of traded equity in the previous statistical period. Monetary profit affects the production decision in the following way:[3]

$$Y^{initial}_{it} = \begin{cases} Y^{sold}_{it-1} * 1.1 & if \ \pi_{it} > 0 \\ Y^{sold}_{it-1} * 0.9 & otherwise \end{cases}$$

The producers' holding of production capital may limit this initial production decision:

$$Y^{max}_{it} = \alpha_{it} K_{it}$$

where α_{it} is capital productivity. There is no substitution between capital and labour so Y^{max} is the maximum a producer can produce given his capital K_{it} – no matter how much labour he employs.

$$Y_{it}^{intermediary} = \begin{cases} Y_{it}^{max} & \text{if } Y_{it}^{initial} > Y_{it}^{max} \\ Y_{it}^{initial} & otherwise \end{cases}$$

Since Y_{it} is monetary volume of output, labour requirement is calculated as a residual based on a markup factor, μ. The markup factor determines how much of Y_{it} is dedicated to labour and capital costs. Since producers markup both their capital costs and their labour costs, required labour can be found as:

$$L_{it}^{initial} = \mu_{it}\left(Y_{it}^{intermediary} - \frac{K_{it}}{\tau} \right)$$

where μ is the markup factor and τ is the lifetime of one unit of capital, so that

$$\frac{K_{it}}{\tau}$$

is the cost of capital. The producer puts a markup on all his capital, whether it is currently employed or not.

The producer may also be limited by available labour, L^{final}:

$$Y_{it}^{final} = \begin{cases} \dfrac{L^{final}}{\mu} + \dfrac{K}{\tau} & \text{if } L_{it}^{initial} > L_{it}^{final} \\ Y_{it}^{intermediary} & otherwise \end{cases}$$

Once produced, Y is distributed to the consumer space in accordance with previous sales and a random factor. There is no price mechanism equilibrating the market for consumption goods. Goods that are not sold within the period do not perish but remain at the market as unsold stock.[4]

Production of investment goods

The guiding principles of production of consumption goods also applies to production of investment goods. There are, however, some differences due to the fact that investment goods are only produced to order, and a unit of investment goods is much larger that a unit of consumption goods, which is set to one. Since the number of investment projects that a producer of investment goods takes in is smaller, the number of projects is allowed to vary more:

$$Y_{it}^{initial} = \begin{cases} projects_{it-1}*1.5 & \text{if } \pi_{it} > 0 \\ projects_{it-1}*0.5 & otherwise \end{cases}$$

The constraint of labour and capital described above for the producer of consumption goods, also applies to the producer of investment goods.

The market of investment goods is a first in–first out list where investing firms place their orders and from where producers of investment goods pick the desired number of projects. Following from this, producers of investment goods may also be limited by the number of orders at the list.

Investment

There are four major determinants to the investment decision; experienced capital constraint in last period, monetary profit, equity prices and money holdings.

$$K_{it}^* = \frac{Y_{it-1}^{initial}}{\alpha_{it-1}}$$

where K_{it}^* is the desired volume of production capital given last periods possible experience of capital constraint.

$$I_{it}^{initial} = K_{it}^* - K_{it}$$

Furthermore, there is a Tobin's q effect in the investment decision. Thus high equity prices, or large money holdings may induce the producer to expand further or, in the opposite case, reduce the initial investment decision:

$$I_{it}^{intermediary} = \begin{cases} I_{it}^{initial} + 2 & \text{if } p_{it} > \rho \text{ and } M_{it} > I^0 \\ I_{it}^{initial} + 4 & \text{if } p_{it} > 1.25\rho \text{ and } M_{it} > I \\ I_{it}^{initial} + 4 & \text{if } M_{it} > 2I^0 \text{ and } p_{it} > \rho \\ I_{it}^{initial} - 2 & \text{otherwise} \end{cases}$$

where I^0 is a constant denoting also the size of investment in the initial three runs of the simulation, p is the fixed price of capital goods and p_t is the average price of traded equity.

Finally the producer deducts from his desired investments, any investment orderings placed at the market but not yet effectuated:

$$I_{it}^{final} = I_{it}^{intermediary} - I_{it}^{placed\ orders}$$

Consumption

Consumption is neighbour dependent with neighbours defined as Moore neighbourhood in the two-dimensional consumer space. This implies that whenever a consumer gets to act, he will address his neighbours and calculate their average consumption, and this will be the initial consumption set by agent i.

$$C_{it}^{initial} = C_{neighbours}^{average}$$

The consumption decision is, however, also under the influence of the net worth of the consumer (Vh_i) as well as windfall losses or gains (W_i).

$$Vh_{it} = M_{it} + p_t E_{it}$$

where equity is evaluated at current equity prices. Again we use M to denote deposits D – loans L.

$$W_{it} = (p_t - p_{t-1})E_{it-1} + F_{it} - B_{it} - i_d(p_{t-1}E_{it-1}) \qquad (26.1)$$

Windfall is any gain (rise in equity price or dividend payment, F) minus loss due to bankruptcy, B, minus opportunity cost, i.e. lost interest payments from holding equity rather than money.[5]

Financial position and windfalls affect the consumption decision in the following way:

$$C_{it}^{intermediary} = \begin{cases} C_{it}^{initial} * 1.25 & if\,(Vh_{it} > \gamma\,SUB)\ and\ (W_{it} > \gamma\,SUB) \\ C_{it}^{initial} * 1.75 & if\,(Vh_{it} < \delta\,SUB)\ and\ (W_{it} < \delta\,SUB) \\ C_{it}^{initial} * 1.25 & otherwise \end{cases}$$

where SUB is an fixed volume defined as the level of subsistence, and γ and δ are simulation parameters defining how *rich* or how *poor* consumers must be before they start differing from their neighbours. The size of γ and δ thus reflect the stock impact on flows. In the following we shall refer to δ as the credit squeeze, i.e. how much do we squeeze debtors in order to bring down their debt?, and γ the wealth squeeze, i.e. how much do we squeeze creditors in order to bring down their wealth? Through a tax on labour, all consumers are allowed to consume SUB – the level of subsistence.

Once the consumption decision is taken, consumers start searching for the desired goods. All consumer goods are homogeneous except for the fact that they are situated at different cells in the two-dimensional consumer space. Consumers can only purchase goods placed in their own or their neighbouring cells. A consumer may thus be limited by the availability of goods before C^{final} is determined.

Labour market

Since the money wage is fixed, there are no price changes clearing the labour market. Consumers supply a fixed amount of hours, H, and may or may not be hired for the full number of hours.

Demand for labour is determined by the production decision already described. Producers of consumption goods prefer to hire labour in the areas of the consumer space where they sell the most. Remaining labour, and labour for the production of investment goods, is randomly hired.

Credit market

The credit market is probably the most simple market of the model, since the banking sector adapts to demand for loans and deposits – the model simply has bookkeeping entries as a clearing device. All agents, producers as well as consumers are provided with a banking account, and all accounts start out at zero. All transactions are registered with both a payer and a recipient, and thus the M accounts always add up to zero. The volume of aggregate money is measured as the sum of all positive money holdings (deposits D). The interest on deposits i_d is a fixed rate whereas i_l varies with the bank's cost of bankruptcy.

Producers have unlimited access to loans as long as they stay below a bankruptcy limit, β, which is related to their holding of capital and equity as well as their current level of production (Y_{it}) in order to allow firms with a large turnover a larger credit:

$$bankruptcy_{it} = \begin{cases} true & if\ M_{it} + p_t E_{it} + K_{it} < \beta(Y_{it}) \\ false & otherwise \end{cases}$$

The equity issued by the producer declared bankrupt will lose its value, and only the agents holding this particular equity will bear the burden of bankruptcy together with the bank bearing the burden of loans. This implies a risk of bankruptcies spreading in the system. As a compensation to the bank, i_l will rise over i_d until its account balances again. The place of a bankrupt producer will be taken over by a new producer.

Equity market

At the equity market consumers and producers buy and sell equity – but only producers can issue new equity. Except for this difference, the behaviour of consumers and producers is similar. All equity is treated as homogeneous from the perspective of the trader, and all equity pay a fixed dividend.[6] Supply and demand for equity is treated symmetrically so that a negative demand for equity, E^d represents a supply of equity.

In the initial demand for equity, agents transfer half of their deposits or loans into equity. Deposit holders will buy equity for half the value of their deposits and lenders will sell or issue equity in order to cover half of their bank debt. Last period's average price of equity (p_t) reflects the expected price of equity.

$$E_{it}^{d\ initial} = 0.5\left(\frac{M_{it}}{p_t}\right)$$

This initial demand, $E_{it}^{d\ initial}$ is then regulated according to the agents subjective idea of the current pricelevel of equity. The idea of Keynes that agents have a subjective sense of the *normal rate of interest* is transformed to a *normal level of equity prices* p_{it}^n, calculated as the simple average of the minimum and the maximum price experienced by the individual agent:

$$p_{it}^n = \frac{p_{it}^{max} + p_{it}^{min}}{2}$$

Prices affect the initial decision in the following way:

$$
E_{it}^{d\ intermediary} = \begin{cases}
E_{it}^{d\ initial}*0.9 & if\ (p_t > 1.1(p_{it}^n)) \\
E_{it}^{d\ initial}*0.9 & if\ (p_t > 1.3(p_{it}^n)) \\
E_{it}^{d\ initial}*0.9 & if\ (p_t > 1.5(p_{it}^n)) \\
E_{it}^{d\ initial}*0.9 & if\ (p_t > 2(p_{it}^n)) \\
E_{it}^{d\ initial}1.1 & if\ (p_t > 0.9(p_{it}^n)) \\
E_{it}^{d\ initial}1.1 & if\ (p_t > 0.7(p_{it}^n)) \\
E_{it}^{d\ initial}1.1 & if\ (p_t > 10.5(p_{it}^n)) \\
E_{it}^{d\ initial} & otherwise
\end{cases}
$$

Finally the agent takes a bear or bull position based on the windfall gain/loss defined in equation (26.1). If dividend payment minus losses exceeds the opportunity cost measured by the rate of interest, a bull position is taken.

$$
E_{it}^{d\ final} = \begin{cases}
2(E_{it}^{d\ initial}) & if\ bear\ and\ E_{it}^{d\ initial} < 0 \\
0.5(E_{it}^{d\ initial}) & if\ bear\ and\ E_{it}^{d\ initial} < 0 \\
E_{it}^{d\ initial} & otherwise
\end{cases}
$$

Behaviour of agents on the equity market holds both stabilizing and trend following aspects. They only follow trends to the extent that it affects their conception of normal equity prices and their bear/bull position. Apart from that they try to sell high and buy low, thus stabilizing the market.

The equity market is modelled as a linked list of equity through which the agent can search for options to buy or sell, or place options to buy or sell at a reservation price. If an agent gets no response to a placed equity option, he will change the price of the option next time he gets to act at the equity market, unless the option is cancelled by the agent. p_t is calculated for each period as the average price of traded equity during the last period.

Simulation results

Many different simulations can be performed with the model. A full Monte Carlo analysis of robustness has not yet been performed, but in the following we shall present a base run and a number of simulations varying the parameters of this base run. These experiments will focus on stock-flow relationships.

A few things should be noted on the base run. Parameters have been chosen so that the simulation may run for many periods. Here only 1000 periods are presented, but the model may run for longer than that without changing its characteristics. This however is not the case for all possible parameter values. Especially the equity market has a risk of running into an "eternal boom" which will stop the market. As our simulations will show, the model is however stable over a wide range of parameter values.

Table 26.4 Parameter values of the base run

	Parameter	Value
	Number of agents	1800
	Producers of consumption goods	160
	Producers of investment goods	40
	Consumers	1600
SUB	Level of subsistence	50
I^0	Size of initial investment	3
E	Principal of equity	100
ρ	Price of one unit of production capital	100
α	Productivity of capital	20
τ	Lifetime of one unit of capital	10
μ	Inverted mark up rate	0.9
H	Maximum number of working hours per agent	200
β	Credit limit	10
i	Interest rate	1%
f	Dividend	2%
γ	Credit squeeze	5
δ	Wealth squeeze	5

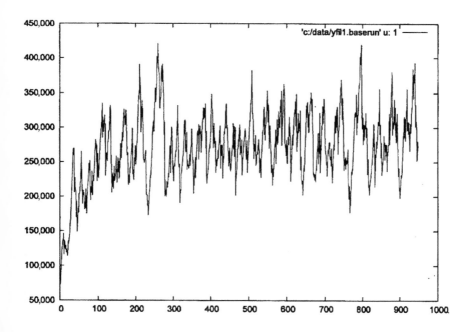

Figure 26.1 National income in the base run.

Notes
National income defined as production of investment goods plus production of consumption goods.
Parameter values as specified in Table 26.4.

Another thing to be noted about the base run is the tendency for the model to generate business cycles without there being any fixed upper or lower bound for the turning points. Neither are there any turning points hidden in the decision rules of the model. Thus the cycle may be regarded as an emergent property of the model.

The business cycle

For some parameter values the model generates cyclical patterns. As illustrated by Figure 26.2 the cycles appear to be set off by an increase in equity prices which results in increasing investments. With a time lag the boom in equity prices and investment causes a rise in consumption. Equity prices do, however, not increase forever. The supply of equities (including emission of new equities) increases due to entrepreneurs needing to finance their investment expenditures, and at the same time consumers start spending more money on consumption goods. This causes a fall in equity prices, and again with a time lag investment and consumption decrease.

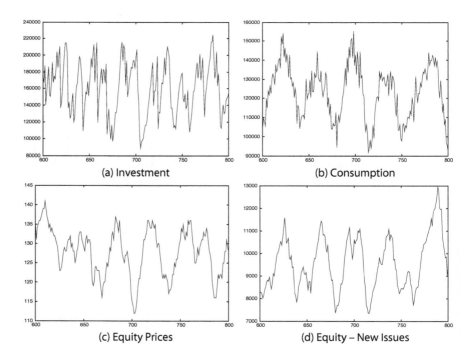

Figure 26.2 The business cycle.

Notes

Parameter values as specified in Table 26.4.

Many aspects of the cyclical pattern should be expected from the way decision rules are specified. The rise in equity prices is, however, not all that obvious. The decision states that agents with positive money holdings will move into holding equities unless the equity price is high compared to the lowest equity price observed by the agent. Agents with negative money holdings will sell equities or possibly emit new equities if they are producers, unless the equity price is very low compared to the highest equity price observed by that agent. For very high equity prices, agents with positive money holdings may choose to sell equities and for very low equity prices agents with negative money holdings may choose to buy equities. An additional rule states that agents who have experienced low payoff from their equity holdings (due to lack of dividend or losses from bankruptcies) will be more careful in their purchase of equities or more ready to sell equities. These rules should not result in a very volatile equity market, but an equity market that smoothly accommodates economic activity.[7] Furthermore, the behaviour of surplus units is approximately symmetric to the behaviour of deficit units, and thus there is no built-in tendency for increasing or decreasing equity prices. There is, however, a built-in stabilizer since high prices will stimulate supply and depress demand.

Squeezing consumers

The agent-based method makes possible a study of distributional aspects. Here we shall experiment with parameters affecting the distribution of wealth between consumers to learn how this affects the aggregate flows of our model. The parameters we shall change are γ and δ – the parameters that may be called the *wealth squeeze* and the *credit squeeze*. The credit squeeze δ determines how poor consumers must be before it affects their consumption, i.e. before they start consuming less thant their neighbours. The wealth squeeze, γ, determines how wealthy consumers are before they start increasing their consumption beyond their neighbours' consumption. In the base run both parameters are set to 5, but here we shall vary them from 1 to 10 to see how it affects aggregate production, equity prices, distribution measured by the Gini coefficient[8] and the volume of money.

From a Keynesian perspective one would expect the highest income with a large γ and a low δ, i.e. in a situation where consumers are allowed to build up a large debt before they are forced to cut back on consumption, and where wealthy consumers are forced to spend their wealth on consumption. This is also what our simulation shows (Figure 26.3). More surprising is the fact that we also get the highest Gini coefficient when we force the wealthy to consume, as well as allowing the poor to consume ($\gamma = 10$ and $\delta = 1$). One would expect the highest Gini where wealthy consumers are allowed to build up more wealth and poor consumers are allowed to accumulate more debt.

To explain this, let us have a look at the relation between income and the Gini over the cycle (Figure 26.4). There is a clear positive relation between income

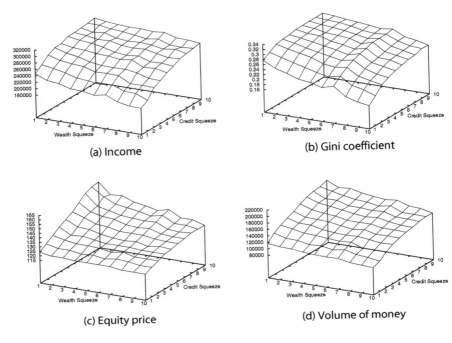

Figure 26.3 Squeezing consumers.

Notes
Effects of varying the credit squeeze and wealth squeeze from 0 to 10 on (a) national income, (b) Gini coefficient, (c) equity price and (d) volume of money. Average value over 1000 periods.

and the Gini coefficient. But what is cause and what is effect? Does income increase as a result of the larger differences, or is the larger difference a side effect to increasing income? It is often concluded that there is a trade-off between income and equality, but with the cycles generated in our model, one cannot talk about a trade-off, since allowing, or promoting, increased inequality will not increase income.

Squeezing producers

There are several parameters one can vary in order to make it more or less easy for producers to obtain a monetary profit, and thus affect their decision to produce and to invest. Here we have chosen three parameters; the markup rate, the dividend rate and the bankruptcy limit.

The (inverted) markup rate tells us how much of the total output producer will pay out as wages. In the base run we had a markup of 0.9 meaning that producers will keep 10 per cent of the monetary value of output. In Figure 26.5 we varied the markup rate from 0.8–1 with an interval of 0.02.

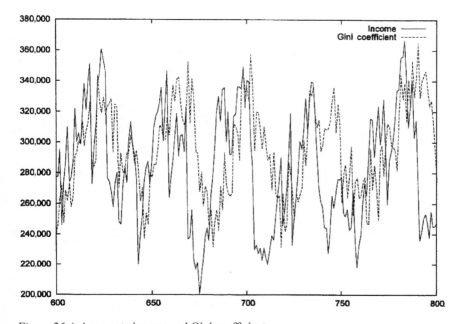

Figure 26.4 Aggregate income and Gini coefficient.

Notes
Gini coefficient multiplied by one million. Parameter values as specified in Table 26.4.

The dividend rate sets the dividend that producers must pay to the holders of their issued equity. In the base run the dividend rate was set to 2 per cent. Here it was varied from 0–5 with an interval of 0.5.

The bankruptcy limit relates the monetary wealth and the turnover of producers to their monetary debt. A low bankruptcy limit will result in more bankruptcies whereas a high bankruptcy limit will allow producers to accumulate large debts. In the base run bankruptcy limit was set to ten. In Figure 26.5 it was varied from one to 20 with an interval of two.

In general the model behaves very much as expected. The bankruptcy limit does not have very much impact on any of the output data chosen – not even on bankruptcy losses! Squeezing producers on their markup, on the other hand, has a very big impact on their profits as well as the level of production. Introducing a dividend has a positive impact on profits as well as production. This may seem paradoxical, but the explanation is to be found in the equity market. The absence of a dividend has a negative impact on the demand for equity, and the resulting low equity prices does not only mean a lower return from issuing new equity, but depresses the whole system. Dividends above 2 per cent however have a negative impact on the system.

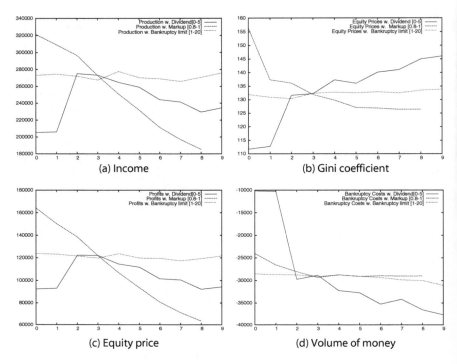

Figure 26.5 Squeezing producers.

Notes
Effects of varying (i). dividends from 0–5, (ii) markup from 0.8–1.0 and (iii) bankruptcy limit from 1–20 on (a) aggregate income, (b) Gini coefficient, (c) equity price and (d) volume of money. Average value over 1000 periods.

Conclusion

Our method of analysis has been first to study the macro-properties of a Keynesian system, then its micro-properties and, finally, to relate the two by building an agent-based model. The purpose of this exercise has been one of building a framework for integrating real and financial spheres in economic modelling following the ideas of Keynes. Although interaction between stocks and flows is modelled consistently, the model is only claimed to be *almost* stock-flow consistent since there are important deviations from usual assumptions of stock-flow consistent economic modelling. The net worth of society does not only stem from the flow of savings out of income, but also from the expectational value of capital, which may be read at financial markets.

Allowing the continuing revaluation of real capital performed by financial markets to enter the calculation of net worth for agents as well as society, opens a gate between real and financial spheres – a gateway that is capable of replicat-

ing situations as the current financial and economic crisis. In fact cyclical behaviour appears to be an emergent property in the model.

Notes

1 In Keynes' words; "For in an entrepreneur economy [...] the volume of employment,
  the marginal disutility of which is equal to the utility of its marginal product, may be
  'unprofitable' in terms of money" (1933: 79).
2 This conclusion is drawn under the assumption that no other sector in the economy,
  public sector or foreign countries, changes its debt position.
3 Rather than describing the final decision in one relation, a notation of initial, intermediary and final decision is chosen.
4 Notice that unsold stock does not enter the profit calculation – with respect to monetary
  profit it is regarded as a loss.
5 Dividend is not necessarily a rate multiplied by the number of equities held, since dividend payments may be set to depend on the profits of the issuing producer.
6 In reality equity is heterogeneous, since in the case where a producer is declared bankrupt, the agents holding the particular equity of this producer, will lose it.
7 For later experiments it will be interesting to see how the model will react to a more
  volatile financial market.
8 Due to the fact that wealth in our model both takes negative and positive values, we
  have had to normalize wealth before calculating the Gini coefficient.

References

Dos Santos, C.H. (2006) Keynesian theorising during hard times: stock-flow consistent
  models as an unexplored "frontier" of Keynesian macroeconomics. *Cambridge Journal
  of Economics*, 30: 541–65.
Dos Santos, C.H. and Zezza, G. (2008) A simplified, benchmark, stock-flow consistent
  post-Keynesian growth model. *Metroeconomica*, 59: 441–78.
Duesenberry, J.S. (1949) *Income, Saving and the Theory of Consumer Behaviour*, Cambridge, MA: Harvard University Press.
Godley, W. and Lavoie, M. (2007) *Monetary Economics: An Integrated Approach to
  Credit, Money, Income, Production and Wealth*, Basingstoke: Palgrave Macmillan.
Keynes, J.M. (1933) The Tilton Papers in *Collected Writings of J.M. Keynes XXIX*,
  London: Macmillan, 76–106.
—— (1936) *The General Theory of Employment, Interest and Money*, in *Collected Writ-
  ings of J.M. Keynes VII*, London: Macmillan.
—— (1938) Letters from Keynes to Hugh Townshend in *Collected Writings of J.M.
  Keynes XXIX*, London: Macmillan, 293–4.
Patterson, K.D. (1990) Stock flow consistent income for industrial and commercial com-
  panies. *Review of Income and Wealth*, S. 36(3): 289–308.
Skott, P. and Ryoo, S. (2008) Macroeconomic implications of financialisation. *Cambridge
  Journal of Economics*, 32: 827–62.

27 Minsky's 'financial instability hypothesis'

The not-too-Keynesian optimism of a financial Cassandra

Elisabetta De Antoni

Introduction

The current financial turmoil has brought the thought and the writings of Hyman Minsky into the limelight, and reflection on his contribution becomes more topical than ever. This chapter focuses on how Minsky's work relates to Keynes. Minsky proposed his 'financial instability hypothesis' as an authentic interpretation of *The General Theory*, so it is not by chance that he is generally seen as a leading post-Keynesian economist. A careful reading of their work nevertheless brings out subtle but crucial differences.

Our comparison refers to H.R. Hudson's representation of the trade cycle (Hudson 1957).[1] On the basis of the interaction between the money market and the goods market, this representation envisages a succession of phases of excess investment and of excess saving, with a simple and plausible transition mechanism from one to the other. Hudson's representation serves as our litmus paper. When 'dipped' in the writings of Minsky and of Keynes, it will reveal important analogies and – above all – some crucial differences.

This chapter is organized as follows. The next three sections set out Minsky' own thought. Specifically, the second and third sections will focus on the two main pillars of Minsky's view, namely the 'financial theory of investment' and cumulative processes. The fourth section then presents Minsky's 'financial instability hypothesis'. The fifth and sixth sections introduce Hudson's litmus paper and 'dip' it into the writings of the two authors, focusing respectively on the analogies and on the differences. Lastly, the final section strikes a concluding balance.

Minsky's 'financial theory of investment'

The first cornerstone of Minsky's thought is his 'financial theory of investment' which considers the ways in which investment is financed.[3] Minsky's starting point is that the basic characteristic of a capitalist economy is the existence of two prices: the market value of capital assets (which reflects volatile and uncertain profit expectations) and the price of current production. The rate of investment, which belongs to both categories, is what aligns the two prices. In a doing, however, it attracts volatility and uncertainty and passes them on to the rest of the economy.

The two prices underpinning Minsky's analysis are shown by the broken lines in Figure 27.1, which recall Tobin's 'q theory'.[4] The broken horizontal line P_k gives the demand price of capital assets – by analogy, also the demand price for investment goods – equal to the present value PV of expected profits Π^e. The rising broken curve P_i gives the supply price of investment goods, coinciding with the price of current production. It is composed of the technologically determined cost (which, given production capacity, from a certain point curves upwards) plus the interest on the short-run financing required by the production of investment goods plus the mark-up. The intersection between the broken lines P_k and P_i determines the level of profitable investments I_p.

At this point, firms have to determine how they will finance new machinery. The solid equilateral hyperbola $Q_i = P_i I$ in Figure 27.1 gives the combinations of P_i and I that are compatible with the internal funds Q_i (gross profits minus taxes and debt servicing) that firms expect to accumulate during the gestation period of investment. The intersection of the equilateral hyperbola Q_i and the supply price curve P_i gives the level of investment I_i that can be financed with these expected internal funds. For investment levels greater than I_i, firms need external finance, whose supply is assumed endogenous. Indebtedness, however, involves the risk – borrower risk (Br) for firms and lender risk (Lr) for their financiers – that expectations could go wrong and that, once in operation, investment might generate profits less than the debt commitments incurred. This risk obviously increases with the amount of indebtedness.

For investment levels exceeding I_i in Figure 27.1, the original demand and supply prices of investment goods (P_k and P_i) have to be adjusted for the increasing risks. The result is shown by the solid lines P_k' and P_i'. The risk-adjusted demand price curve, $P_k' = P_k - Br$, is obtained by subtracting the borrower's risk premium Br from the original demand price P_k.[5] The risk-adjusted supply price curve, $P_i' = P_i + Lr$, is obtained by adding the lender's risk premium Lr to the original supply price P_i.[6] The intersection between the risk-adjusted curves P_k' and P_i' determines the effective level of investment, I_e. The excess over internally financed

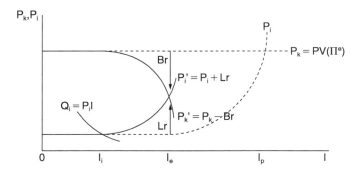

Figure 27.1 The determination of investment.

investment I_i is the level of borrowing. The gap between the original demand price P_k and the original supply price P_i, corresponding to I_e, gives the safety margins required by firms and their financiers against the risks related to indebtedness.

If realized profits turn out to be less than expected, these safety margins will increase firms' capacity to meet debt commitments and reduce banks' losses. If realized profits are as expected or greater, these safety margins represent the compensation to firms and their financiers for their respective risks. As we have seen, the gap $P_k - P_i$ reflects the degree of confidence of firms and their financiers. In Minsky's view, it thus acquires a more general significance as proxy for the whole set of safety margins existing within the financial system. As an example, a reduction in the gap $P_k - P_i$ not only reflects a decrease in borrowers' and lenders' risk premium, but also signals a fall both in liquidity as a proportion of wealth and in the time synchronization between cash receipts and debt commitments at the basis of Minsky's well-known distinction (Minsky 1986: 206–7) between hedge, speculative and ultra-speculative (or Ponzi) finance.[7] Mirroring an overall decrease in safety margins, the narrower gap $P_k - P_i$ signals that the financial system has become more fragile.[8]

Let us now come back to Figure 27.1. In the presence of a general increase in interest rates, the original demand price (consequently also the adjusted demand price) for investment goods falls as long as long-term interest rate rises, while the original (hence the adjusted) supply price of investment rises with short-term interest rates. The overall effect is a fall in effective investment. Minsky's analysis thus confirms the standard negative relationship between investment and the interest rates. However, in his scheme interest rates play a secondary role. Dominating the scene are the other determinants of investment, i.e. profit expectations (Q_i, Π^e) and confidence (Br, Lr). The future being unknown, Minsky assumes that expectations and confidence are myopically based on recent experience.[9] Without much explanation, he then relates them to current profits.

Starting with the initial situation represented by the solid lines in Figure 27.2, Minsky (1986: 193–4) then posits an unexpected increase in current profits. To start

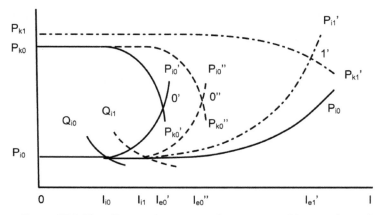

Figure 27.2 The effects on investment of an unexpected increase in profits.

with, such an increase gives rise to an increase in the expected internal funds Q_i. The result is an equivalent rightward shift of the equilateral hyperbola (from Q_{i0} to Q_{i1}), of the level of internally financed investments (from I_{i0} to I_{i1}), and of borrower and lender risk starting from I_i. The adjusted demand and supply price curves become P_{k0}'' and P_{i0}''. As shown by point $0''$, the consequence is an internally funded increase in effective investment (from I_{e0}' to I_{e0}''). This is not yet the end of Minsky's story, though. By increasing profits expected after the installation of the investment goods Π^e, the rise in current profits has two further effects. First, it raises the original demand price – the intercept of the adjusted demand price curve – from P_{k0} to P_{k1}. Second, it increases confidence in the future repayment of debt commitments, thus reducing borrower and lender risk. Consequently, the new adjusted demand and supply price curves become P_{k1}' and P_{i1}'. The result is a further increase in effective investment (from I_{e0}'' to I_{e1}'), this time externally financed.

Figure 27.2 has significant implications. From the standpoint of the real economy, it tells us that profits stimulate investment. As we shall see, this link is at the basis of Minsky's cumulative processes. From the financial standpoint, both internally and externally financed investment grows. Higher indebtedness in turn is associated with lower safety margins. As investment grows, the financial system becomes more fragile.

Minsky's investment theory subtends some crucial assumptions that are anything but granted. Let us start with the investment gearing ratio between external and internal financing. Minsky implicitly assumes that the actual ratio aligns itself with the desired, thus rising pro-cyclically in the upswing and falling in the downswing. As investment increases, external financing grows faster than internal. As a consequence, the incidence of debt commitments on profits rises: finance becomes less hedge and more speculative. Minsky's line of reasoning here is questionable.[10] After all – unless speculative phenomena prevail – the good performance of the real sector (profits included) might strengthen rather than weaken the financial sector.

Other important implicit assumptions lurk in Figure 27.2. To start with, it presupposes that the unexpected rise in current profits is perceived as permanent. If it were not so, it would not affect Q_i and Π^e. As a result, investment would not grow. Profits would not be reinvested. Instead of stimulating debt, they might be used to reduce it. The Minskian link from profits to internally and externally financed investment would break down. Equally important are the implicit assumptions concerning expectations and confidence. On expectations, Minsky's firms seem to foresee unlimited outlets for their future production. Not by chance, the original demand price curve $P_k = PV(\Pi^e)$ is horizontal line. On confidence, Minsky's firms consider exclusively the 'financial' risks connected with the fulfilment of debt commitments. They totally ignore the 'real' risk of zero or negative profits, which would also affect internally funded investment.

An alternative situation is shown in Figure 27.3, where – as a consequence of decreasing profit expectations and/or increasing 'real' risk – the adjusted demand price curve P_k' slopes downward from the start. In this case, the effective level of investment (I_e) determined by the intersection between the P_k' and P_i' curves is

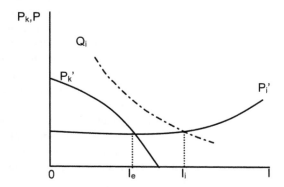

Figure 27.3 Minsky's post-crisis situation.

lower than what can be internally financed (I_i). Investment is so low that it does not require borrowing. Unless it is perceived as permanent, the increase in profits translates into the accumulation of financial and not real assets, and again the Minskian link from profits to internally and externally financed investment would break down. On rare occasions, Minsky takes into account both the case shown in Figure 27.3 and the case in which P_k' is less than P_i' so that investment collapses to zero.[11] In his opinion, however, these are the exceptional post-crisis situations considered in *The General Theory* (Minsky 1975: 115, 1986: 195). Under normal conditions, the investment function is the one described in Figures 27.1 and 27.2.

If Figures 27.1 and 27.2 represent the normal situation, what is the economy that Minsky has in mind? It seems to be one that confidently foresees unlimited output markets and plenty of profitable investment opportunities. In this economy, an increase in profits is not merely reinvested, but – by improving profit expectations and confidence – it also stimulates externally financed investment. What worries investors is the 'financial' risk associated with meeting debt commitments, not the 'real' risk for profits. As we have seen, however, this does not appear to be the economy considered in *The General Theory*.

Minsky's cumulative processes

Minsky rejects the conventional postulate of stability, according to which prices (instantaneously or eventually) clear all the markets. More generally, he rejects the 'crutch' of equilibrium,[12] whether general[13] or under-employment.[14] In Minsky's view, the traditional re-equilibrating price mechanism has to be replaced by quantity mechanisms that exert cumulative effects on one another. After reaching their maximum development, the resulting tendencies wane and reverse. Advanced capitalist economies thus cyclically fluctuate in a permanent disequilibrium.

The cornerstone' of Minsky's cumulative processes is the interdependence between investment (I) and profits (Π).[15] Shown by the solid lines in Figure 27.4.

this assumes an initial (as we shall see, externally financed) increase in investment. Through income fluctuations, the latter tends to generate an equal increase in profits.[16] By Minsky's investment theory, the increase in profits has three effects: (i) it raises expected internal funds Q_i; (ii) it raises expected profits from investment Π^e and their present value $P_k = PV(\Pi^e)$ and (iii) it raises the degree of confidence (Conf), thus reducing borrower and lender risks (Br&Lr). The result is the second increase in investment – financed in part internally (I_i) and in part externally (I_{ind}) – at the centre of the figure, which brings us back to the starting point on the extreme left. The interdependence between investment and profits then becomes the basis of an upward spiral involving all the variables (with the exception of Br&Lr, which fall with expansionary effects on investment).

The upward spiral based on the interdependence between investment and profits is accentuated by its own repercussions on the money market, shown by the broken and dotted arrows in Figure 27.4. The upward-sloping broken arrow leading to M^s refers to the supply side of the money market. In Minsky's view, money is created endogenously and affects the demand for non-monetary assets, not consumption goods. Insofar as the increase in indebtedness implies an increase in bank credit, it also entails an increase in the money supply M^s. This in turn drives up the prices of real capital (as well as financial) assets, which represent the fulcrum of Minsky's transmission mechanism. The new rise in P_k thus generates a new (externally financed) increase in investment on the extreme right of Figure 27.4, which brings us back to the starting point on the extreme left.

The horizontal broken arrow leading to M^d refers to the demand side of the money market. According to Minsky (1986: 180), money's main characteristic is to permit the fulfilment of the obligations connected with indebtedness and economic activity. Money is demanded mainly because it offers insurance services (as a safety margin) against bankruptcy. Thus, in Figure 27.4 the greater confidence due to the initial rise in profits lowers the demand for money in favour of other assets. The result is a further rise in the prices of real capital (as well as financial) assets and an additional increase in externally financed investment (extreme right). Lastly, the dotted arrows describe the contribution of the financial markets. That below P_k indicates that the increase in capital (and financial) asset prices feeds itself by fuelling expectations of capital gains. That above

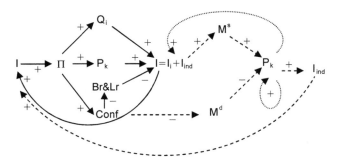

Figure 27.4 Minsky's cumulative processes.

P_k indicates that – by raising firms' and financial intermediaries' net wealth – the rise in capital (and financial) asset prices increases the availability to borrow and to lend and thus further stimulates externally financed investment. If we consider Figure 27.4 as a whole, the initial increase in investment triggers an upward spiral that embraces most of the variables. Only Br&Lr and M^d fall. The increasing debt is thus associated with decreasing safety margins. As the real sector grows, the financial system becomes more and more fragile.

A crucial question remains to be answered. What causes the initial increase in investment (extreme left)? The answer lies in Minsky's 'upward instability proposition' that 'stability – or tranquillity – is destabilising' and 'the fundamental instability is upward'.[17] A period of tranquillity (in which profits are systematically greater than inherited debt commitments) fosters greater confidence in the future, giving rise to a wealth reallocation from money to non-monetary assets, which in turn drives up asset prices (real as well as financial). The result is the initial externally financed increase in investment that triggers the cumulative processes shown in Figure 27.4.[18]

Minsky applies his upward instability proposition to every 'coherent' situation, be it under-employment equilibrium,[19] full-employment equilibrium[20] or steady growth.[21] This proposition raises two objections. The first questions its validity. Coming back to the investment function, let us consider an after-crisis situation where the demand price for investment goods has fallen below the supply price, thus implying the collapse of investment and profits. Following Minsky, we assume that tranquillity decreases the value of the insurance embodied in money, thus decreasing the interest rate used to discount expected profits. What Minsky neglects is that if expected profits were zero, this would not increase the demand price for investment goods. Alternatively, the stimulus might not be strong enough to drive the demand price above the supply price. In both these cases, tranquillity alone would not be sufficient to trigger recovery, and Minsky's upward instability proposition would not hold. Evidently, in his economy expected profits are never that low. The second objection is that Minsky actually attributes the upward instability proposition to Keynes (1936).[22] As we shall see, however, there seems to be nothing of this kind in *The General Theory*

The 'financial instability hypothesis'

Minsky's starting point, then, is that stability itself is destabilizing. A period of tranquillity (in which the financial system is robust and there are not unusual shocks, so that profits are systematically greater than debt commitments) strengthens confidence in the future. The consequent reallocation of wealth from money to non-monetary assets raises the prices of the latter, leading to an increase in investment financed by debt. Owing to the cumulative processes described above, this increase turns into a debt-financed investment expansion and then boom.

At this point, Minsky (1975, 1978, 1982a, 1982b, 1986) points to two drawbacks to the investment boom. First is its increasingly speculative nature. In the general euphoria, firms' debt commitments increase faster than profits and eventually exceed them. Expecting a future bonanza, firms start financing their principal by resort to debt (speculative financing) and then even interest payments (ultra-speculative or Ponzi financing). Thus an initially robust financial system becomes fragile.[23] Second is that the persistence of the boom inevitably creates either bottlenecks in the financial system or inflationary pressures in the goods market that end up requiring a monetary restriction. In either case, the result is a rise in the rate of interest.[24]

The higher interest rate ends the boom, and the investment-profit-investment chain reverts to a downward spiral. The unexpected rise in the cost of funds is thus associated with an equally unexpected fall in (already insufficient) profits. Given financial fragility, honouring inherited debt commitments would require an increase in indebtedness, but this is not only undesirable but actually impossible as confidence in the future ebbs. Firms' debt commitments can no longer be honoured in the ordinary way, i.e. by drawing on liquidity balances, profits or borrowing. This is Minsky's definition of the financial crisis (1982b).

With the outbreak of the crisis, firms' only solution is the sale of assets, which by now are mainly illiquid. The resulting fall in asset prices is strengthened by the expectation of capital losses. The decrease in the net wealth of firms and financial intermediaries further reduces the availability to borrow and to lend. The falling degree of confidence raises liquidity preference and desired safety margins. All of this aggravates the need to lower debt by selling assets. Asset prices plummet. The fall in capital asset prices worsens the contraction of investment and profits and vice versa.[25] The financial crisis thus turns into a debt deflation, which in Minsky's view (1982b) involves asset price and profit deflation. In the end, the debt deflation makes it impossible to honour debt commitments and there is a wave of bankruptcies, leading ultimately to deep depression. According to Minsky, however, depression has also a cathartic role: only the hedge units will survive. Under these circumstances, Minsky's upward instability proposition comes back into play: a new phase of tranquillity increases confidence and reactivates investment. The system again experiences debt-financed expansion, speculative boom, financial crisis, debt deflation and depression.[26]

Minsky (1982a, 1986) found empirical confirmation for his analysis. The financial instability of the American economy – which he had foreseen in advance (Minsky 1963) – surfaced in the mid-1960s, provoking the crises of 1966, 1970, 1974–1975, 1979 and 1982. And financial instability had also marked the periods preceding – and between – the two world wars. According to Minsky (1991), this confirms that financial crisis is systemic. To his own question *Can 'It' Happen Again?* (1982a), Minsky answered that another Great Depression was indeed possible. Under these presuppositions, the task of stabilizing the economy has to be assigned to the government and to the central bank as a lender of last resort. Moreover, the financial system has to be carefully regulated. This is the main message of his *Stabilizing an Unstable Economy* (1986).

As we have seen, the 'financial instability hypothesis'[27] subtends many implicit and questionable assumptions. Minsky himself may well have realized this, as is indicated by his choice of the term 'hypothesis' rather than financial instability 'theory'. Such objections aside, an interesting question is: what is the relationship between Minsky and Keynes? Many economists see Minsky's 1975 book as one of the most authentic interpretations of Keynes, and in fact Minsky himself presented his 'financial instability hypothesis' as an interpretation of *The General Theory*. In Minsky's view, Keynes had lived through the Great Depression and was properly concerned with the case of severe economic slump, consequent financial crisis and debt deflation. Under these circumstances, the demand price for investment falls below the supply price, and investment and profits collapse. According to Minsky, however, Keynes saw the Great Depression only as an extreme case: though he did not develop it, what Keynes actually had in mind was a cyclical perspective.[28]

Minsky's cyclical rereading of *The General Theory* clashes with authoritative alternative interpretations, according to which it has an essentially static nature.[29] To see who is right, let us leave the last word to Keynes himself, who in the introduction to his chapter on the trade cycle expressly states that his theory, though not a business cycle theory, can be extended in that direction.[30] Minsky's 'financial instability hypothesis' must thus be considered as an extension or a reformulation, not an 'interpretation', of Keynes.

This, however, raises a new problem: to what extent does Minsky's extension or reformulation follow the 'line of investigation' suggested by Keynes himself? To answer this question, we turn to Hudson's litmus paper, whose immersion in the writings of Minsky and Keynes will bring to light important analogies and crucial differences.

Hudson's litmus paper: some important analogies between Minsky and Keynes

This section refers to the graphical representation proposed by Hudson (1957) to introduce monetary forces into the cyclical framework proposed by Kaldor (1940). His starting point is the short-run IS-LM model with given money wages and prices.[31] Needless to say, the richness of Keynes' and of Minsky's analysis cannot be captured in a two-curve graph, least of all in the controversial IS-LM model. From our purposes, though, the relevant aspect of Hudson's IS-LM model is its unconventional features. By introducing Kaldorian nonlinearity of the investment function and making a few specific dynamic assumptions, Hudson gets an endogenous cycle that seems to be essentially compatible both with Minsky's 'financial instability hypothesis' and with Keynes' Chapter 22.

Hudson's model is shown in Figure 27.5. The upward slope of the LM_0 curve reflects the usual assumption that the increase in income stimulates the transactions demand for money (more than money supply) and thus implies a higher equilibrium interest rate. But we could also reread the LM_0 curve from a more convincing credit perspective. A higher level of investment and income would then imply greater demand for credit, satisfied endogenously by the financial system at a rising interest rate that in turn mirrors increasing lender's risk. After

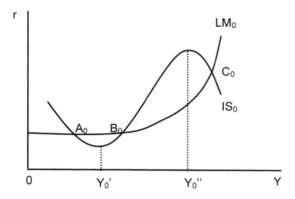

Figure 27.5 Hudson's IS-LM model.

all, the latter is a concept that Minsky (1975: 106) borrows from Keynes (1936: 144) and so is common to both our authors.

The unconventional shape of Hudson's short-run IS_0 curve mirrors the introduction of a nonlinearity in the investment function. In Hudson's view, saving and investment are both positive functions of income. However, while the income sensitivity of saving is constant, that of investment varies with the level of income itself. Specifically, it is small at low levels of income and (after growing with income) falls again at high levels. This is because of the underutilization of the given capital stock at low activity levels and because at high rates of resources utilization the supply price of capital is no longer constant but increasing. The result is that at income levels outside the range $Y_0'Y_0''$ (Figure 27.5) the income sensitivity of saving is greater than that of investment. Starting from an initial equilibrium, the rise in income generates an excess of saving over investment, thus implying a lower equilibrium interest rate. Outside the range $Y_0'Y_0''$, the IS_0 curve therefore has the usual negative slope. Inside that range, however, as on the contrary the income sensitivity of saving is lower than that of investment, it is positively sloped.[32]

The intersection between the IS_0 and LM_0 curves identifies three short-run equilibrium points in Figure 27.5. A_0 and C_0 represent locally stable equilibriums. The reason for this is evident, if we assume that the interest rate clears the money market instantaneously while income clears the goods market only gradually. Starting from these premises, on the left of A_0 and C_0, the interest rate determined by the LM_0 curve is lower than required by IS_0 (on the right, higher). The goods market thus experiences an excess of investment over saving that stimulates income towards the corresponding equilibrium value (or else a saving excess that depresses it). By analogous reasoning, B_0 represents a locally unstable equilibrium: income tends to fall to its left and rise to its right.[33] The upshot is that if in the short run the system is out of equilibrium, any change in income will be away from B_0, towards either A_0 or C_0. According to Hudson, however, in the neighbourhood of locally unstable equilibrium B_0 the zero net investment income level lies. In the long run, A_0 and C_0 thus both imply a changing capital stock. As we shall see, it is precisely this incompatibility between the local stability of short-run equilibriums and the long-run steadiness of the capital stock that originates Hudson's trade cycle.

Let us start with the locally stable short-run equilibrium point A_0 in Figure 27.6, given by the intersection between IS_0 and LM_0. By assumption, at A_0 investment is so low that it fails to replace the existing capital stock. In the long run, the progressive decline in capital will cause a shortage of productive capacity that in turn will stimulate investment. The IS curve will thus gradually shift upwards from IS_0 to IS_1, expanding the economy from A_0 to the tangency point $A_1 = B_1$. Here, however, upward local instability is triggered. To the right of $A_1 = B_1$, the interest rate given by LM_0 is always lower than that required by IS_1. This denotes a chronic excess of planned investment over saving, which stimulates the economy. Other things being equal, the rise in income will be proportional to the imbalance in the goods market denoted by the vertical distance between IS_1 and LM_0. Income will thus rise first at an increasing and then at a decreasing rate finally reaching the new locally stable short-run equilibrium point C_1.

Starting from the peak C_1, the right-hand panel of Figure 27.6 now shows the downswing. By assumption, this time a high level of investment increases the capital stock. In the long run, this expansion will create excess capacity, which in turn depresses investment. The IS curve thus gradually shifts downwards from IS_1 to IS_2, depressing the economy from C_1 to the tangency point $B_2 = C_2$. But here downward local instability comes into play. To the left of $B_2 = C_2$, the interest rate determined by LM_0 is constantly higher than that required by IS_2. This denotes a chronic excess of saving over planned investment, depressing the economy. *Ceteris paribus*, the fall in income will be proportional to the imbalance in the goods market, shown by the vertical distance between LM_0 and IS_2. Income thus falls first at an increasing and then at a decreasing rate, finally reaching the locally stable short-run equilibrium point A_2 (the new trough) from which the upswing starts again.

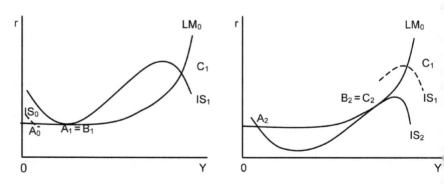

Figure 27.6 Upswing and downswing à la Hudson.

As a graphical representation, Hudson's scheme does not specify all its analytical aspects adequately.[34] For our purposes, though, it has the considerable merit of simplicity. In its immediacy, it brings out the following analogies between Keynes' Chapter 22 and Minsky's 'financial instability hypothesis'.

i   Hudson's cycle arises endogenously from the structural characteristics of the system. It requires no exogenous shocks, nor does it depend on specific time lags and parameter values. All this is in line both with Keynes' and with Minsky's approach.[35]

ii   Hudson's cycle relies on quantity rather than price mechanisms. Specifically, what causes cyclical fluctuations in income is the cyclical fluctuation in investment. Again, these aspects are crucial both in Keynes and in Minsky.[36]

iii   The fluctuations in investment in Hudson mirror changing profit expectations. If income has a positive influence on induced investment according to any given short-run IS curve, this is because it stimulates current and hence expected profits.[37] If in the long run the capital stock has a negative effect on autonomous investment and hence on the position of the IS curve, this is because it depresses current and therefore expected profits.[38] The upswing and downswing shown in Figure 27.6 thus respectively reflect rising and falling profit expectations. So, Hudson's cycle is compatible with the waves of optimism and pessimism envisaged both by Keynes and by Minsky.[39]

iv   The cumulative processes envisaged by Hudson seem to be in line both with Keynes' and with Minsky's views. By introducing the income sensitivity of investment, Hudson strengthens Keynes' multiplier processes. By assuming that income affects investment through profits while investment in turn affects income and profits, Hudson's framework is also compatible with the Minskian link investment-profit-investment. As far as turning points are concerned, the effect of the capital stock on investment is explicitly recognized both by Keynes and by Minsky.[40]

v   Hudson only keeps his traditional LM curve unchanged in order to simplify the exposition. But he expressly recognizes (1957: 382 and 384) that liquidity preference is powerfully affected by expectations and confidence. As profit expectations improve or worsen, the upward or downward shift of IS in the left or right panel of Figure 27.6 may be thus associated with a downward or upward shift of LM. According to our credit interpretation of LM curve, the fall or increase in the lenders' risk would lead to the same results. This means that monetary and financial markets might accentuate fluctuations. Such a destabilizing role seems perfectly in line with Chapter 22 of *The General Theory* and with Minsky's analysis.[41]

The differences between Minsky and Keynes

Now let us focus on the differences between our two authors. A careful reading of their works suggests that – whilst both are at the mercy of the trade cycle – Minsky 'combats' the upswing, Keynes the downswing. What mainly worries

Minsky is the tendency of his economy to an over-indebted investment boom.[42] Not by chance, most of his writings are devoted to this problem.[43] On the opposite side, what mainly worries Keynes is the tendency to the stagnation of investment and high, long-lasting unemployment. Thus, Chapter 22 of *The General Theory* stresses the precariousness of full employment owing to the depressive effect of accumulation on the marginal efficiency of capital,[44] the tendential inadequacy of investment with respect to full employment[45] and the need to support the economy always and anyhow.[46]

As shown by his upward instability proposition, Minsky expressly refers to an economy whose 'fundamental instability is upward'. At the extreme, the relevant curves may then be IS_1 and LM_0 in the left-hand panel of Figure 27.6. The expected profitability of investment tends to be high with respect to the money market interest rate. The result is an excess of investment over saving that stimulates the economy to the peak C_1. On the contrary, the economy described in Chapter 22 of *The General Theory* tends to be characterized by a low marginal efficiency of capital relative to the money market interest rate.[47] At the extreme, the relevant curves may then be LM_0 and IS_2 in the right-hand panel of Figure 27.6. The result is an excess of saving over investments, driving the economy down to the trough A_2.

The subject of the two analyses, then, appears to be quite different. Minsky's economy seems to be dominated by the upswing, Keynes' by the downswing.[48] Can this disparity be reduced to a unitary framework? A possible solution is suggested by Figure 27.7, where the solid lines show an economy *à la* Minsky, the broken lines *à la* Keynes. Other things being equal, Minsky's might be an optimistic economy in the aftermath of a burst of innovation, where the upswing implies a greater improvement and the downswing a milder deterioration in profit expectations. In this economy, profit expectations are systematically more optimistic. The result is a higher IS curve in both panels.

As the vertical distance between IS and LM shows the intensity of the cycle, the figure carries two main implications. For one thing, an economy *à la* Minsky will experience comparatively stronger upswings in the first panel and smaller

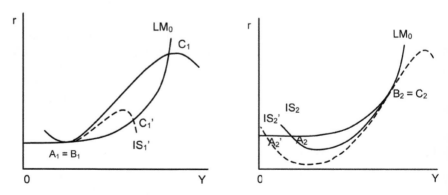

Figure 27.7 Upswing and downswing *à la* Keynes and *à la* Minsky.

downswings in the second. But chiefly, comparing the two panels, we see that the dominant in terms of intensity may be the upswing in Minsky[49] and the downswing in Keynes. The overall greater growth of the upswing-dominated economy would confirm and sustain its higher degree of optimism.

By 'dipping' Figure 27.7 in the writings of Keynes and Minsky, we discover enlightening differences. Let us start with the upswing in the left-hand panel. In Minsky, the excess of planned investment over saving (even more so, over firms' saving) is so great that it inevitably requires business indebtedness.[50] Finance is at the centre of Minsky's architecture. In his Chapter 22, by contrast, Keynes does not even mention firms' indebtedness. Given the smaller excess of planned investment, producers may have sufficient own resources to finance it. This difference, then, engenders disparate concerns about growth. What threatens Minsky's boom is increasing financial fragility due to incessant growth of indebtedness and debt commitments. In Keynes, the problem is not indebtedness but the sharpening divergence between the rising expected yield on investment and the falling actual yield.

This brings us to the peak. As Figure 27.7 shows, what interrupts Minsky's upswing is the rise in the interest rate.[51] In the speculative financial system inherited from the boom, the higher rate triggers the financial crisis. Keynes expressly rejects any such diagnosis.[52] In his view, the excess of the expected return to investment over the actual cannot grow infinitely, so it is the inevitable disappointment of expectations to provoke the crisis. The crisis, then, is financial in Minsky and real in Keynes. Its implications, too, are different. In Minsky, the rise in the interest rate that triggers the crisis reflects the bottlenecks, financial or real, created by the boom. His upswing, in fact, may attain or even surpass full employment. According to Keynes (1936: 322), on the contrary, income growth tends to stop before that point. The marginal efficiency of capital is generally insufficient to ensure full employment.

Let us now turn to the right-hand panel of Figure 27.7. In Minsky's economy, the crisis brusquely reveals the need to reduce indebtedness, which the rise in interest rates has made unsustainable. Under this perspective, the resulting downswing also performs a cathartic role: it restores the robustness of the financial system, paving the way for the ensuing recovery.[53] In Keynes' economy, the crisis turns the boom's over-optimistic profit expectations into a contrary 'error of pessimisms'.[54] This explains the fall in investment underlying the downturn. But here there is no cathartic or beneficial effect. Sweeping away even sound and promising economic activities, recessions and depressions cause permanent damage. In Keynes' words, they belong 'to the species of remedy which cures the disease by killing the patient' (1936: 323).

A last difference between our two authors concerns the weakest turning point, the one in which the interruption of the cycle is most likely.[55] On this issue again, Minsky and Keynes differ. According to Minsky's upward instability proposition, the lower turning point is not open to question. After the storm comes the calm, and tranquillity inevitably leads to recovery. Rather, Minsky's 'obsession' is the upper turning point. Why does his vibrant economy turn downwards, instead of embracing a steady growth path?[56] As we have seen, Minsky finds his answer in the financial sphere of the economy.

Keynes, in Chapter 22, takes the opposite tack. Here, it is the upper turning point that is unquestionable: the over-optimism of the boom is inevitably destined to clash with reality. Keynes' perplexities instead focus on the lower turning point.[57] He admits that the decline in the capital stock tends to stimulate investment and thus the economy, but he worries that this stimulus may be too slow and above all too weak to spark recovery.[58] In his view, 'it is highly improbable that all fluctuations ... in investment ... will be of a cyclical character' (1936: 314). Recessions and depressions do not always imply recovery. Minsky's own assertions notwithstanding, the upward instability proposition seems totally foreign to Keynes' work. The main message of the first 21 chapters of *The General Theory* is precisely that the persistence of the slump is perfectly possible.

Conclusion

Judging by his actual work, however, Minsky was not the interpreter of Keynes that he supposed himself to be. Experiencing the post-war renaissance instead of the tragedy of the Great Depression, he unaware applied Keynes' economics to a system whose fundamental instability is upward. In so doing, he discarded some important issues in *The General Theory*: for instance, the endemic nature of unemployment, the persistent damage of depression and above all the precariousness of recovery. As Velupillai (2008) teaches us, one of the main problems of nonlinear trade cycle theories has been to explain the lower turning point. Minsky's upward instability proposition sweeps this crucial problem aside, and with it the central message of *The General Theory*.

In spite of the not-too-Keynesian optimism of his upward instability proposition, however Minsky had the indisputable merit of questioning the myth of growth, which in his view – instead of converging to a uniform and steady rate – tends to lead to financial fragility and thus to be shaken by financial crises, debt deflations and deep depressions.[59]

Notes

1   We are grateful to Velupillai (2008) for signalling this interesting article.
2   For the 'financial theory of investment', see Minsky (1972, 1975: 114, 1978, 1980, 1986: 193–4).
3   To quote Tobin's review of Minsky's (1986) book: 'He is right to stress that monetary and financial institutions and market make a big difference and to reject the Modigliani–Miller theorem that assets and debts which wash out in accounting aggregations wash out in economic effects as well.' See Tobin (1989: 107).
4   On the 'q theory', see Brainard and Tobin (1968) and Tobin (1969).
5   Minsky (1986: 190):

> Borrower's risk shows up in a declining demand price for capital assets. It is no reflected in any financing charges; it mirrors the view that increased exposure default will be worthwhile only if there is a compensating potential capital gain.

6 Minsky (1986: 192):

> However, lender's risk imparts a rising thrust to the supply conditions for capital assets independent of technological-supply conditions. This rising thrust takes a concrete form in the financing conditions that bankers set. In loan and bond contracts, lender's risk is expressed in higher stated interest rates, in terms to maturity, and in covenants and codicils.

7 In the case of hedge finance, creditors and debtors foresee cash receipts greater than debt commitments in every single period of the life of the loan. In the case of non-hedge finance, such a relationship only holds in the distant future. Given the expectation of a future bonanza, the plan concerning the present and the near future is to fulfil debt commitments by borrowing. This concerns principal in the case of speculative units and also interest payments in the case of ultra-speculative or Ponzi units. Thus, initially, the debt of speculative units is rolled over while that of ultra-speculative units automatically grows with interest payments. Given their dependency on credit, non-hedge units are more fragile. A negative shock (not necessarily an uncommon one) represented, for instance, by an unexpected credit restriction or fall in profits would throw them into financial crisis. Unable to meet their debt commitments in the normal ways, i.e. by profits or by further borrowing, they would be forced to liquidate assets with the risk of selling them off, going insolvent and failing.

8 As a consequence of its over-optimism, a fragile financial system allows its safety margins to fall below the danger level. In the presence of even a not unusual unexpected shock, it is thus prone to financial crises, debt deflations and insolvencies. See Minsky (1964). Under the just-mentioned circumstances, firms have insufficient liquidity, profits and borrowing capacity to discharge inherited debt commitments. Their only alternative would be to reduce debt and debt service through the sale of non-monetary assets. The fall in asset prices, however, would make them insolvent. The result would be a wave of failures, and so deep depression.

9 According to Minsky (1996: 2): 'The uncertainty that permeates the economics of Keynes and the economics of bounded rationality is due to the unsureness about the validity of the model that enters in the decision process.' Under these circumstances, what matters is not only the expectation about the future, but also the degree of confidence in it. Given the ignorance of the future, expectations and confidence are based on recent experience. They consequently generate positive feedbacks. To quote Minsky (1986: 187): 'A history of success will tend to diminish the margins of safety that business and bankers require and will thus tend to be associated with increased investment; a history of failure will do the opposite.'

10 Steindl (1952: 107–21), for instance, sets out a radically different view. According to him, internal funds have a higher income elasticity than external. As income grows, the rise in the desired gearing ratio is thus associated with a fall in the actual one. In the attempt to bridge this gap, firms will increase investment, strengthening the income expansion. The latter, however, will further widen the excess of the desired over the actual gearing ratio. The implications of Steindl's analysis are twofold. First, contrary to Minsky's theses, this time the actual gearing ratio moves counter-cyclically. Second, this behaviour leads to the paradox of debt: the attempt to increase the gearing ratio leads to an expansion of income that instead decreases it. Lavoie (1995) and Hein (2006) trace back Minsky's and Steindl's views to a unitary framework. Assuming that firms fulfil their debt commitments before investing, however, these works seem to neglect the speculative financing that was so central to Minsky.

11 About these two cases, see Minsky (1975: 127, 1986: 195).

12 According to Minsky, there are forces for change in every situation and therefore also in equilibrium, which has to be considered as a moving target (1975: 61) achieved, if ever, but for a fleeting instant. The behaviour of the economy is thus characterized by

equilibrating tendencies (1975: 68) rather than any achieved equilibrium. Minsky's conclusion is that:

> The use of the term equilibrium … may be misleading. It may be best to borrow a term from Joan Robinson and call situations in which rapid disruptive changes are not taking place *periods of tranquillity*, noting that tranquillity is disrupted by investments booms, accelerating inflations, financial and monetary crises, and debt deflations.
>
> (Minsky 1986: 176)

13 With regard to general equilibrium, Minsky (1975, 1978, 1986) rejects the 'Patinkin resolution' that flexible prices end up coordinating all the markets. Let us consider a situation of unemployment. Insofar as wage and price deflation is associated with a fall in profits, it decreases firms' ability to fulfil inherited debt commitments. In this way it jeopardizes the robustness of the financial system, with depressing effects on long-term expectations and investment. In conformity with the experience of 1929–1933 and the 'true' thought of Keynes, the fall in prices can thus further depress aggregate demand and accentuate unemployment instead of reabsorbing it.

14 With regard to Keynes' under-employment equilibrium, Minsky (1975: 68) writes 'During each short-period equilibrium, in Keynes's view, processes are at work which will "disequilibrate" the system. Not only is stability an unattainable goal, whenever something approaching stability is achieved, destabilizing processes are set off.'

15 Minsky (1972) first introduced the link from profits to investment based on his investment theory. Subsequently (1975: 114), he added the causal relation from investment to profits. This allowed him (1980, 1986) to focus on the interdependence between the two variables.

16 Minsky adopts a conception à la Levy–Kaleki–Kaldor by which income distribution mirrors the level and composition of aggregate demand rather than input productivity. Aggregate saving S is the sum of workers' saving (S_w) and capitalists' saving (S_c) equal to the difference between profits (Π) and capitalists' consumption (C_c). This means that $S = S_w + (\Pi - C_c)$. By substituting into the goods market equilibrium condition $S = I + DF + NX$ and rearranging, we get: $\pi = I + DF + NX + C_c - S_w$. Profits Π are therefore determined by investment I, government deficit DF, net exports NX and capitalists' consumption C_c net of workers' saving S_w. *Ceteris paribus*, an increase in investment thus tends to induce an equivalent increase in profits.

17 For the two quotations see, respectively, Minsky (1975: 127, 1978: 37) and Minsky (1974: 272, 1975: 165). Analogously, in Minsky (1986: 219) we read: 'Any transitory tranquillity is transformed into an expansion.' A similar concept is repeated many times in Minsky (1980).

18 To put it in Minsky's words (1986: 183):

> [B]ut tranquility diminishes the value of the insurance (liquidity) embodied in the dollar, so that a rise in the absolute and relative prices of capital and financial assets that are valued mainly for income will take place. Tranquility therefore leads to an increase in acceptable debt to equity ratios even as it raises the value of inherited capital assets. The endogenously determined value of liquidity means that each possible equilibrium of the economy contains disequilibrating forces.

19 With regard to under-employment equilibrium, Minsky says (1978: 36–7):

> For the economy to sustain a virtual equilibrium of employment … profit flows must be sufficient to validate debts … But such fulfilment of debt commitments will affect the willingness to finance debts by bankers and their customers: the value of the insurance embodied in money decreases as the economy functions in

a tranquil way. Stability – or tranquillity – in a world with a cyclical past and capitalist financial institutions is destabilizing.

An analogous concept can be found in Minsky (1975: 61, 127, 165).

20 With regard to full-employment equilibrium, Minsky says (1986: 177): 'The ongoing processes tend to rupture a full-employment equilibrium in an upward direction; that is, once full employment is achieved and sustained the interaction among units tends to generate a more than full-employment speculative boom.' An analogous concept can be found in Minsky (1974: 268, 1980: 26, 1986: 183).

21 With regard to steady growth, Minsky writes (1974: 267): 'The fundamental instability is the way in which a period of steady growth evolves into a speculative boom.'

22 'Thus, recent experience is consistent with the interpretation of Keynes' views that has been put forth here: 'we are dealing with a system that is inherently unstable, and the fundamental instability is "upward" '. See Minsky (1975: 165).

23 According to Minsky, a fragile financial system is dominated by speculative and ultra-speculative (or Ponzi) units. In expectations of a future bonanza, they allow their safety margin to fall below the danger level. Faced by even an ordinary negative shock like a rise in the interest rate or a fall in profits, they have insufficient liquidity, profits and borrowing capacity to meet inherited debt commitments. The only solution left is reducing indebtedness and debt commitments by liquidating non-monetary assets, but with the risk of having to sell them out and of becoming insolvent.

24 Minsky (1978: 45) puts it as follows: 'However, the internal workings of the banking mechanism or Central Bank action to constrain inflation will result in the supply of finance being less than infinitely elastic leading to a rapid increase in short term interest rates.' In Minsky's view, this increase will then spread from the short to the long run, with depressive effects on P_k and I.

25 In Minsky's view, while the fall in the demand price for investment goods depresses investment and profits, the consequent fall in profit expectation reduces the demand price for investment goods.

26 To quote Minsky (1975: 126–7):

> A relatively low-income, high-unemployment, stagnant recession of uncertain depth and duration will follow a debt-deflation process. As the subjective repercussions of the debt-deflation wear off, as disinvestment occurs, and as financial positions are rebuilt during the stagnant phase, a recovery and expansion begins.

27 The hypothesis has given rise to numerous formalizations focusing on one aspect or another. See, for instance, Taylor and O'Connel (1985), Lavoie (1986–1987), Franke and Semmler (1989), Delli Gatti *et al.* (1994) and Skott (1994).

28 Minsky (1975: 58):

> The evidence that it is legitimate to interpret *The General Theory* as dealing with an economy that is cyclical by reason of its essential institutions is spread throughout the volume. References to cyclical phenomena occur not only in Chapter 22 of *The General Theory*, 'Notes on the Trade Cycle', which explicitly deals with business cycles, and in the rebuttal to Viner in *The Quarterly Journal of Economics* of February 1937, but throughout his book. When *The General Theory* is read from the perspective that the subject matter is a sophisticated capitalist economy, whose past and whose future entail business cycles, the ratifying references for an interpretation within a cyclical context are everywhere evident.

29 According to Haberler (1958: 249), for instance: 'Mr. Keynes's theory has still another characteristic which distinguishes it from all business-cycle theories: it is essentially static.'

30   Since we claim to have shown in the preceding chapters what determines the volume of employment at any time, it follows, if we are right, that our theory must be capable of explaining the phenomena of the Trade Cycle.... To develop this thesis would occupy a book rather than a chapter, and would require a close examination of facts. But the following short notes will be sufficient to indicate the line of investigation which our preceding theory suggests.

(Keynes 1936: 313)

31   Using the conventional notation, the expressions for Hudson's IS and LM curves are the usual ones represented, respectively, by $I(Y, r, K) = S(Y, r)$ and by $L(Y, r) = M(Y)$. The signs of the corresponding partial derivatives are also the traditional ones: $S_y > 0$, $S_r > 0$, $I_y > 0$, $I_r < 0$, $I_k < 0$, $L_y > M_y > 0$, $L_r < 0$. With regard to the time behaviour of endogenous variables, Hudson as usual assumes (i) that the time derivatives of income and of the interest rate are positive functions, respectively, of the excess of planned investment over saving and of the excess demand for money and (ii) that the time derivative of the capital stock is zero in the short run and equal to net investment in the long run.

32   The slope of Hudson's IS curve is $dr/dY = (S_y - I_y)/(I_r - S_r)$. Since the denominator is negative, the slope is negative if $S_y > I_y$, positive if $S_y < I_y$.

33   As Hudson (1957: 381) maintains, local stability requires that the slope of IS be lower than that of LM. The model is thus locally stable in A_0 and C_0 (where IS is negatively sloped) and locally unstable in B_0 (where the slope of IS is positive and greater than that of LM).

34   A model analogous to Hudson's has been formalized by Schinasi (1981). Here, however, the effect of flows on stocks consists in the repercussions of government budget financing on financial wealth, not in the impact of net investment on the capital stock. Not by chance, the LM curve is what shifts over the cycle, rather than the IS curve. Schinasi's cycle is thus originated by the behaviour of government instead of the structural characteristics of the economy.

35   To quote Minsky (1986: 172): 'instability is determined by mechanisms within the system, not outside it; our economy is not unstable because it is shocked by oil, wars or monetary surprises, but because of its nature'. Analogous considerations hold for Chapter 22 of *The General Theory*, in which Keynes (1936: 321), for instance, claims: 'The situation, which I am indicating as typical, is ... where investment is being made in conditions which are unstable and cannot endure, because it is prompted by expectations which are destined to disappointment.'

36   Minsky (1978: 30) expressly defines his theory as 'an investment theory of the business cycle'. Analogously, in Keynes (1936: 313) we read:

The Trade Cycle is best regarded, I think, as being occasioned by a cyclical change in the marginal efficiency of capital, though complicated and often aggravated by associated changes in the other significant short-period variables of the economic system.

37   To quote Hudson (1957: 379): 'Alternatively, at higher levels of income ... the consequent rise in profits induces entrepreneurs to plan additional investment.'

38   Hudson (1957: 384) writes: 'It is the growing surplus capacity that is crucial, for it implies that the current rate of profit falls and that expectations as to the future profitability of investment projects are now less favourable for further investments.'

39   With regard to the illusions of the boom and to the disillusion of the slump, see Keynes (1936: 321–2) and Minsky (1975, 1982a, 1982b, 1986).

40   To quote Keynes (1936: 317): 'The disillusion comes because doubts suddenly arise concerning the reliability of the prospective yield, perhaps because the current yield shows signs of falling off, as the stock of newly produced durable goods steadily increases.' Analogous considerations can be found, for instance, in Minsky (1975: 126).

41 To quote Keynes (1936: 316):

> Moreover, the dismay and uncertainty as to the future that accompanies a collapse in the marginal efficiency of capital naturally precipitates a sharp increase in liquidity-preference – and hence a rise in the rate of interest. Thus the fact that a collapse in the marginal efficiency of capital tends to be associated with a rise in the interest rate may seriously aggravate the decline in investment.

In Minsky, finance is the primary source of instability: 'the capitalist market mechanism is flawed, in the sense that it does not lead to a stable price-full employment equilibrium, and ... the basis of the flaw resides in the financial system' (Minsky 1974: 267).

42 Minsky (1986: 173):

> The spectacular panics, debt deflations, and deep depressions that historically followed a speculative boom as well as the recovery from depressions are of lesser importance in the analysis of instability than the developments over a period characterized by sustained growth that lead to the emergence of fragile and unstable financial structures.

43 One of the very few exceptions is Minsky (1982b), which deals with debt deflation.

44 Keynes (1936: 325): 'Whilst aiming at a socially controlled rate of investment, with a view to a progressive decline in the marginal efficiency of capital, I should support at the same time all sorts of policies for increasing the propensity to consume.'

45 Keynes (1936: 322): 'Except during the war, I doubt if we have had any recent experience of a boom so strong that it led to full employment.'

46 Keynes (1936: 322): 'Thus, the remedy for the boom is not a higher rate of interest but a lower rate of interest. For that may enable the so-called boom to last.'

47 In Chapter 22 of *The General Theory*, the concern for the excessively high interest rate compared with the marginal efficiency of capital emerges, for instance, in the comment on the under-consumption school:

> In existing conditions – or, at least, in the conditions that existed until lately – where the volume of investment is unplanned and uncontrolled, subject to the vagaries of the marginal efficiency of capital as determined by the private judgment of individuals ignorant or speculative, and to a long-term rate of interest which seldom or never falls below a conventional level, these schools of thought are, as guides to practical policy, undoubtedly in the right.... If it is impracticable materially to increase investment, obviously there is no means of securing a higher level of employment except by increasing consumption.
>
> (Keynes 1936: 324–5)

48 Accordingly, the description of cumulative processes in Keynes (1936: 317–19) dwells upon the downswing, in Minsky (1975, 1980, 1986) upon the upswing.

49 This might explain why the 'Agenda for Reform' that closes Minsky's famous 1986 book does not question the compatibility between (i) the fiscal stabilization (1986: 297) and support (1986: 308) of the economy and (ii) the constraint (1986: 302) of a government budget balanced over the cycle or in surplus. In an economy dominated by the upswing, this compatibility is more likely.

50 Minsky's reference is always to advanced capitalist economies with large and costly long-term investment that is debt financed. This explains the crucial role of the incidence of debt commitments on profits and of the consequent distinction between hedge, speculative and ultra-speculative finance.

51 For a variety of reasons – the limited equity base of banks, internal and foreign drains of bank reserves, and, in modern times, central bank (Federal Reserve)

actions to restrain the money supply – the supply of finance from banks eventually becomes less than infinitely elastic.

(Minsky 1986: 195)

52   Now, we have been accustomed in explaining the 'crisis' to lay stress on the rising tendency of the rate of interest under the influence of the increased demand for money both for trade and for speculative purposes. At times this factor may certainly play an aggravating and, occasionally perhaps, an initiating part. But I suggest that a more typical, and often the predominant, explanation of the crisis is, not primarily a rise in the rate of interest, but a sudden collapse in the marginal efficiency of capital.'

(Keynes 1936: 315)

53   'However, it is worth noting that during the liquidation phase of a deep depression the financial "stage" is set for a long-wave expansion as debts are reduced, equity assets decline in value, and the stock of ultimate liquidity increases' (Minsky 1964: 325).

54   But over and above this it is an essential characteristic of the boom that investments which will in fact yield, say, 2 per cent in conditions of full employment are made in the expectation of a yield of, say, 6 per cent, and are valued accordingly. When the disillusion comes, this expectation is replaced by a contrary 'error of pessimism', with the result that investments, which would in fact yield 2 per cent in conditions of full employment, are expected to yield less than nothing; and the resulting collapse of new investment then leads to a state of unemployment in which the investments, which would have yielded 2 per cent in conditions of full employment, in fact yield less than nothing.

(Keynes 1936: 321–2)

55   After all, if in Hudson's model the zero net investment income level ended up close to the peak (or the trough), the local stability of short-run equilibrium might become compatible with the steadiness of the capital stock, and the business cycle would break down.

56   Thus, we read: '[T]he main emphasis will be on the upper turning point and the possibility of generating steady growth' (Minsky 1957: 859) ... 'in this paper the lower turning point is essentially unexplained' (ibid.: 867). The same considerations can be found in Minsky (1965).

57   '[T]he substitution of a downward for an upper tendency often takes place suddenly and violently, whereas there is, as a rule, no such sharp turning-point when an upward is substituted for a downward tendency' (Keynes 1936: 314).

58   We read:

[I]t is not so easy to revive the marginal efficiency of capital, determined, as it is, by the uncontrollable and disobedient psychology of the business world. It is the return of confidence, to speak in ordinary language, which is so insusceptible to control in an economy of individualistic capitalism.

(Keynes 1936: 317)

59   An economy that aims at accelerating growth through devices that induce capital-intensive private investment not only may not grow, but may be increasingly inequitable in its income distribution, inefficient in its choices of techniques, and unstable in its overall performance.

(Minsky 1986: 292)

References

Brainard, W.C. and Tobin, J. (1968) 'Pitfalls in financial model building', *American Economic Review*, 58: 99–122.

Delli Gatti, D., Gallegati, M. and Minsky, H.P. (1994) 'Financial institutions, economic policy and the dynamic behaviour of the economy', Working Paper No. 126, Jerome Levy Economic Institute of Bard College, Annandale-on-Hudson, NY.

Franke, R. and Semmler, W. (1989) 'Debt dynamics of firms, stability and cycles in a dynamical macroeconomic growth model', in W. Semmler (ed.), *Financial Dynamics and the Business Cycles: New Perspectives*, Armonk, NY: Sharpe.

Haberler, G. (1937; 5th edn 1958) *Prosperity and Depression: A Theoretical Analysis of Cyclical Movements*, London: George Allen & Unwin.

Hein, E. (2006) 'Interest, debt and capital accumulation: A Kaleckian approach', *International Review of Applied Economics*, 20: 337–52.

Hudson, H.R. (1957) 'A model of the trade cycle', *Economic Record*, 33: 378–89.

Kaldor, N. (1940) 'A model of the trade cycle', *Economic Journal*, 50: 78–92.

Keynes, J.M. (1936) *The General Theory of Employment, Interest and Money*, London: Macmillan.

—— (1937) 'The general theory of employment', *Quarterly Journal of Economics*, 51: 209–23.

Lavoie, M. (1986–1987) 'Systemic fragility: A simplified view', *Journal of Post Keynesian Economics*, 9: 258–66.

—— (1995) 'Interest rates in post-Keynesian models of growth and distribution', *Metroeconomica*, 46: 146–77.

Minsky, H.P. (1957) 'Monetary systems and accelerator models', *American Economic Review*, 47: 859–83.

—— (1963) 'Can "It" happen again?', in D. Carson (ed.), *Banking and Monetary Studies*, Homewood, IL: R.D. Irwin.

—— (1964) 'Longer waves in financial relations: Financial factors in the more severe depressions', *American Economic Review*, 54: 325–35.

—— (1965) 'The integration of simple growth and cycle models', in M. Brennan (ed.), *Patterns of Market Behaviour*, Providence, RI: Brown University Press.

—— (1972) 'An exposition of a Keynesian theory of investment', in G.P. Szego and S. Shell (eds), *Mathematical Methods in Investment and Finance*, Amsterdam: North-Holland.

—— (1974) 'The modelling of financial instability: An introduction', in Instrument Society of America (ed.), *Modelling and Simulation Vol. 5.* Proceedings of the Fifth Annual Pittsburg Conference, PA.

—— (1975) *John Maynard Keynes*, New York: Columbia University Press.

—— (1978) 'The financial instability hypothesis: A restatement', Thames Papers in Political Economy, North East London Polytechnic; reprinted in P. Arestis and T. Skouras (eds) (1985) *Post Keynesian Economic Theory: A Challenge to Neoclassical Economics*, Brighton: Wheatsheaf Books.

—— (1980) 'Capitalist financial processes and the instability of capitalism', *Journal of Economic Issues*, 14: 505–22.

—— (1982a) *Can 'It' Happen Again? Essays on Instability and Finance*, Armonk, NY: M.E. Sharpe.

—— (1982b) 'Debt deflation processes in today's institutional environment', *Banca Nazionale del Lavoro-Quarterly Review*, 143: 375–95.

—— (1986) *Stabilizing an Unstable Economy*, New Haven and London: Yale University Press.

—— (1991) 'Financial crises: Systemic or idiosyncratic?', Working Paper No. 51, Jerome Levy Economics Institute of Bard College, Annandale-on-Hudson, NY.

—— (1996) 'Uncertainty and the institutional structure of capitalist economics', Working Paper No. 155, Jerome Levy Economic Institute of Bard College, Annandale-on-Hudson, NY.

Schinasi, G.J. (1981) 'A nonlinear dynamic model of short run fluctuations', *Review of Economic Studies*, 48: 649–56.

Skott, P. (1994) 'On the modeling of systemic financial fragility', in A. Dutt (ed.), *New Directions in Analytical Political Economy*, Cheltenham, UK and Northampton, MA: Edward Elgar.

Steindl, J. (1952) *Maturity and Stagnation in American Capitalism*, Oxford: Basil Blackwell.

Taylor, L. and O'Connel, S. (1985) 'A Minsky crisis', *Quarterly Journal of Economics*, 100: 871–85.

Tobin, J. (1969) 'A general equilibrium approach to monetary theory', *Journal of Money, Credit and Banking*, 1: 15–29.

—— (1989) 'Book review of "Stabilizing an unstable economy" by Hyman P. Minsky', *Journal of Economic Literature*, 27: 105–8.

Velupillai, K.V. (2008) 'A perspective on a Hicksian non-linear theory of the trade cycle', in R. Scazzieri, A. Sen and S. Zamagni (eds), *Markets, Money and Capital: Hicksian Economics for the Twenty First Century*, Cambridge: Cambridge University Press.

28 Organizational capabilities and industry dynamics

A computational model

Marco Corsino, Roberto Gabriele and Enrico Zaninotto

Introduction

During the last decade, a huge amount of work has revitalized the debate on a set of well recognized regularities concerning the distribution of firm size and the strictly related distribution of growth rates. This research effort (Stanley *et al.* 1995; Axtell 2001; Fu *et al.* 2005; Bottazzi and Secchi 2006) has been directed primarily to designing the stochastic process that better approximates the steady state distribution of firm size that emerges from empirical observations (de Wit 2005).

Taking as a reference the three stage law finding process described by Ijiri and Simon (1977) this study focuses on the first two: 'finding simple generalizations that describe the facts to some degree of approximation'; 'finding limit conditions under which deviations of the facts from generalization might be expected to decrease'. Unfortunately, despite the growing sophistication of the last generation of models, it is difficult to dismiss the idea that

> there is no obvious rationale for positing any general relationship between a firm's size and its expected growth rate, nor is there any reason to expect the size distribution of firms to take any particular form for the general run of industries.
>
> (Sutton 1997: 42)

If the general rule is a skewed size distribution, then both the level of approximation and the limit conditions under which deviations are expected to decrease remain unclear. We know that some versions of stochastic growth processes reproduce the limit size distribution in some industries better than others (see the case of pharmaceuticals described in Fu *et al.* 2005), but we cannot make predictions about whether and how they can be applied to other industries.

Moreover, a common feature of those models is that they are compatible with a minimal role of differences among firms. Such a characteristic stems from the idea underlying the Law of Proportional Effects (Gibrat 1931) that, since its formulation, cast serious doubts about the theory of optimal size. However, even if we dismiss optimal size theory, we cannot dispose of differences among firms in driving the pattern of industry evolution (Nelson 1991). Indeed, a parallel set of empirical regularities concerning the economic performances of business companies, outlines persistent differences in profitability even within narrow defined industrial sectors. The appearance of long-lasting profit differentials among firms has been interpreted as indicating that firm specific organizational capabilities do actually exist. Nonetheless, persistent heterogeneity among firms can barely be reconciled with a law postulating equal chances of growth behind the observed regularities in firm size distribution.[1]

The difficulty of refining a simple generalization (the skew distribution of size), and the problem of accommodating different sets of regularities, demands new theoretical approaches. One such might be the third step advocated by Ijiri and Simon (1977: 116): 'explaining why the generalization "should" fit the facts', or 'discover simple mechanisms that would produce the [empirical regularity]'. A generation of models in which the random growth process was replaced by the introduction of stochastic elements in conventional maximizing models has pioneered this road (Sutton 1997). Likewise, in what follows we try to open the way to explanatory models that do not rest on the assumption of maximization. Our starting point, instead, will be the idea of 'organizational capabilities' as a basic constituent of firms' decision-making processes. In a nutshell, we propose a model of organizational behaviour in which decisions about growth are driven or constrained by organizational capabilities.

Two reasons underpin the choice of putting organizational capabilities at centre stage. On the one hand, the peculiar characteristics in the observed patterns of firm growth (e.g. the Laplace probability density function describing growth rates and the upper tail of firm size which follows a power law distribution)[2] compel further advances on theoretical grounds. This piece of evidence calls for the existence of self-reinforcing mechanisms that are in accordance with the hypothesis that differences among firms play some role in drifting growth. On the other hand, the already mentioned evidence of high and persistent interfirm differences in economic performance casts doubt on the assumption of the optimizing behaviour of organizations, while being compatible with different internal structures of firms acting in imperfect markets.

The model focuses on the interplay between the internal structure of the firm (organizational capabilities) and the structure of the environment as the main determinants of the emerging patterns of growth that may eventually lead to slightly different steady state distributions of size and profitability among firms. The model we design is aimed at building artificial worlds with respect to which we can formulate precise hypotheses. Obviously, to go a step further would require identification of the empirical counterparts of our artificial worlds.

The chapter is organized as follows. In the second section we discuss the most widely accepted regularities concerning the size, growth and profitability of business firms. In the third section we review some recent contributions that provide theoretical underpinnings to the observed patterns of firm profitability and growth. The fourth section presents a simulation model that addresses the role of organizational capabilities in shaping the evolution of industrial structure. In the fifth section we provide some preliminary results of the simulation model that seem to endorse the viability of our approach for a microfoundation of emergent phenomena. The final section provides conclusions and highlights a strategy for future research.

Patterns of firm performance

Firm size and growth rates

The concern of antitrust policy for the implications of high degrees of market concentration, and the observation that firm size distributions are skewed across the general run of industries (Hart and Prais 1956) led to a prominent strand of research in the Industrial Organization field, the literature on Growth of Firms. Classical economic theory relies on the shape of long-run average cost curves as the underlying mechanism influencing the degree of industry concentration. However, it cannot predict the observed shape of the size distribution whether or not the assumption of a U-shaped cost curve is maintained (Simon and Bonini 1958). This limitation stimulated the search for an alternative theory of the firm that could predict the observed patterns of size distribution and provide reliable indicators of business concentration.

Stochastic growth models (Ijiri and Simon 1977) emerged in the 1950s as a promising option for the accomplishment of this task. One crucial assumption allows this class of models to approximate with great accuracy the observed distribution of firm size, that is Gibrat's Law (Gibrat 1931).[3] Gibrat's Law involves three propositions: (i) that average growth rates are independent of firm size;[4] (ii) that there is no heteroskedasticity in the variance of growth rates; (iii) that there is no autocorrelation in growth rates (Kumar 1985). According to Gibrat's conjecture, unexpected shocks drive changes in firm size, an observation that can be analytically formulated as:

$$\Delta \log S_i(t) \equiv \log S_i(t) - \log S_i(t-1) = \mu_i(t) \tag{28.1}$$

where $S_i(t)$ is a measures of firm size (sales, employees, valued added, assets) and $\mu_i(t)$ is usually assumed to be a normally distributed *iid* random variable. A few remarks on the economic implications of equation (28.1) are worthwhile. Equation (28.1) states that the unexpected shocks affecting corporate growth have a permanent effect on firm size. It also suggests that the corporate growth rates of any two firms, picked at random, are likely to be uncorrelated and therefore idiosyncratic. Moreover, equation (28.1) also points to a lack of any dynamics associated with past growth, evidence that is consistent with the hypothesis that companies budget for fixed adjustment costs rather than variable ones (Geroski 2000). A final prescriptive implication of Gibrat's Law is that the size distribution of firms does not provide useful guidance to policy makers keen to endorse the expansion of business enterprises (Boeri 1989).

Unlike stochastic growth models, a later strand of the empirical studies directly addresses Gibrat's conjecture by exploring the size–growth relationship for samples of large firms observed over successive years (Hymer and Pashigian

1962; Mansfield 1962; Singh and Whittington 1975). This stream of applied research transformed the Law of Proportionate Effects into a benchmark for theoretical and empirical studies dealing with the growth of business companies. More recently, a number of econometric studies (Hall 1987; Evans 1987a, b; Dunne *et al.* 1989) and contributions to the econophysics literature (Stanley *et al.* 1996; Axtell 2001) have revived the interest in the Growth-of-Firms literature by drawing attention to certain statistical regularities across industries and over time. The emerging regularities (ER) discussed below summarize two major patterns revealed by both these streams of applied research.

> *ER 1.* Although there is no single form of size distribution that can be considered as typical for the general run of industries, observed distributions of firm size are highly skewed.

Gibrat's Law would imply a distribution of firm size that approaches a log normal with mean and variance that increase indefinitely[5] as time goes by. Extant research regards it as a first approximation of the observed patterns of firm size (Hall 1987), particularly for companies whose accounting data are publicly available (Cabral and Mata 2003). However, departures from the theoretical benchmark have emerged, providing indirect evidence that a simple Gibrat model does not accurately describe the growth of business firms.

Observed frequencies have been found either to exceed (Simon and Bonini 1958; Growiec *et al.* 2008) or to be lower than (Stanley *et al.* 1995) the expected values in the upper tail of the log normal. Indeed, the upper tail behaviour in total manufacturing distribution seems to be the outcome of aggregation of fairly heterogeneous distributions of firm size at the sectoral level (Bottazzi *et al.* 2007). Moreover, the measurement of skewness and kurtosis often deviates from the values of a true log normal distribution (Hart and Oulton 1996; Cabral and Mata 2003; Reichstein and Jensen 2005; Angelini and Generale 2008). The Yule and Pareto distributions are regarded as suitable alternatives to overcome these deviations and guarantee a better fit than the log normal for the observed frequencies in both tails (Axtell 2001). These advantages notwithstanding, none of the distributions considered appears typical for all countries and all industries (Schmalensee 1989). And most scholars take the view that firm size distribution will be skewed, but without any expectations as to the degree of skewness, or the exact form that the distribution might take (Sutton 1997).

> *ER 2.* The distribution of (logarithmic) growth rates displays a tent-shaped (exponential) form.

According to Gibrat's Law, the idiosyncratic shocks driving the evolution of firm size (equation 28.1) generate growth rates,

$$R_T \equiv \frac{S_{t+T}}{S_t}$$

which, for sufficiently large time intervals, are log-normally distributed. However, a strand of studies drawing on the early tradition of stochastic growth models, have portrayed a different picture. These contributions point out that the observed distribution of growth rates departs from the expected Gaussian shape implied by Gibrat's Law, and instead displays a 'tent-shaped' (exponential) form. Stanley *et al.* (1996) pioneered this stream of research investigating data for all publicly traded US manufacturing companies over the period 1975–1991. The authors find out that a symmetric exponential (Laplace) distribution, well describes the pattern of annual (logarithmic) growth rates, evidence confirmed by later studies that explore the growth performance of US companies over a longer period (Amaral *et al.* 2001). The 'tent-shaped' form of the growth rate distribution emerges as an invariant property that holds among manufacturing firms in other countries (Reichstein and Jensen 2005; Fagiolo and Luzzi 2006; Coad 2007), as well as in narrowly defined industrial sectors (Fu *et al.* 2005).

Sources and dynamics of profitability

Economists and management scholars have shown great interest in two intertwined issues concerning the economic performance of business firms: (a) the existence of persistent differences in accounting profitability between firms; (b) the identification of factors responsible for such differences.

Spurred by Mueller's (1977) seminal contribution, the first line of inquiry tests the competitive environment hypothesis claiming that market forces in each product area are effective in bringing profits in line with competitive rates of return. Several studies explored the behaviour of profit, for large companies in developed countries, during the second half of the 1980s (Mueller 1990), providing broad evidence contesting the competitive environment hypothesis.

In all countries, permanent differences across firms are observed, implying that firms enjoying above (below) normal profits at a given time can be expected to gain above (below) normal profits in the future. In addition, short run deviations from company specific equilibrium rates of return were found to erode in the space of three to five years, with dynamic forces producing their major impacts on excess profits within a single year, and rarely lasting for more than one year (Geroski and Jacquemin 1988). Firm characteristics emerge as key drivers of long run company profits levels, while industry factors appear to be more important for explaining the speed of adjustment across firms (Waring 1996; Goddard and Wilson 1999; Wiggins and Ruefli 2002).

The second stream of analysis focuses on the sources of observed variations in accounting profitability (McGahan and Porter 2002; Hawawini *et al.* 2003; Misangyi *et al.* 2006). Strategy scholars took up this investigation following Schmalensee's (1985) questioning of the relevance of corporate factors in explaining persistent heterogeneity in firm performance, which contrasted with the predictions from the resource-based theory of the firm. Disregarding identification of the factors driving superior performance and suppressing concerns over causal mechanisms, the major interest of those studies has been 'the existence and relative importance of time, corporate, industry, and business-unit effects, *however generated*, on the total dispersion of total rates of returns' (Rumelt 1991: 169).

A handful of important conclusions emerge from this far-reaching body of investigations: (a) business-specific effects account for a large portion of profit variation; (b) corporate and industry effects are equally important sources of variation; (c) industry, corporate and business-specific effects are related both in cross-section and intertemporally. Overall, the relatively low fraction of profit variation associated with industry effects compared with business-specific effects, and the significant fraction attributed to corporate effects, have been interpreted as supporting the resource-based view of the firm and the central role of organizational competences that this perspective calls for. To summarize:

> *ER 3.* Heterogeneity in firms' profitability persists in the long run and is significantly influenced by corporate factors.

Heterogeneity, capabilities and firm performance

The patterns emerging from data on firm performance puzzled scholars for some considerable time. For instance, Geroski argued that the large random component of empirically observed corporate growth rates undermines the notions of core competence and learning as drivers of corporate growth:

> The idea of core competencies has emerged largely to help explain both differences in profitability between firms within the same industry and between industries. The basic idea is that there are certain core, team-based activities that help make their possessors distinctive. These skills are thought to be durable and difficult to imitate, and they can, therefore, give rise to persistent competitive advantages which, in the end, lead to persistent profit differences between firms, even those apparently engaged in the same lines of activity. Attractive and interesting as it is, this line of argument is, however, difficult to reconcile with the random variations in corporate growth rates that we observe over time. A firm that possesses real and substantial core competencies should, one would have thought, find itself systematically able to outgrow its rivals year in and year out. And yet, this rarely happens: firms grow fast in one year, but rarely every year over a three or four year period.
>
> (2005: 136)

Recent contributions that draw upon the early stochastic growth models (Ijiri and Simon 1977) reveal a series of statistical properties in the distributions of firm size and growth rates that may go some way to help reconciling the foregoing evidence on profitability and growth, with the notion of organizational capabilities. In particular, the fat tails observed in the growth rate distribution, at different levels of sectoral aggregation, hint at the existence of a self-reinforcing mechanism in the process of corporate growth that a simple Gibrat type model would rule out (Bottazzi *et al.* 2007). Whereas the newer stochastic growth models reprise the notion that the market consists of exogenous investment opportunities, they account for the sources of such correlating mechanisms that might entail a richer structure in the growth dynamics than commonly assumed.

Sutton's (1998) model assumes the market to consist of many independent submarkets, all of the same size and all able to accommodate exactly one firm. This island model differs from the early tradition because it avoids the assumption that firms grow according to Gibrat's Law. It assumes instead that the relation between a firm's size and its growth rate satisfies a weaker restriction claiming that 'the probability that the next market opportunity is filled by any currently active firm is non-decreasing in the size of that firm' (Sutton 1998: 246). Although this modified Simon model correctly predicts the skewed distribution of firm size, it fails to account for the observed tent-shaped patterns of growth rates.

Further extensions of the island model have been proposed, which allow for self-reinforcing mechanisms in the growth process and predict a growth rates distribution that accurately fits the observed data. Fu *et al.* (2005) introduce a self-reinforcing mechanism that depends on two intertwined processes concerning the number and size dynamics of the constituent components of business firms. The processes at work require that the number of constituent units in a firm grow in proportion to the number of existing opportunities, and the size of each constituent unit swings in proportion to its attained size. Their joint operation, conditional on the entry rate of new firms, the number of constituting elements, the time horizon over which the process unfold, leads to a probability density function of growth rates that is Laplace in the centre with power-law tails. In Bottazzi and Secchi (2006), the self-reinforcing mechanism driving the growth process originates from a relaxing of the assumption of equal probabilities in the assignment of emerging opportunities to existing firms. By modelling the probability for incumbents to capture new opportunities according to Polya's urn scheme, the authors introduce in the model a competitive mechanism that rests on the idea of 'competition among objects whose *market success* [is] cumulative or self-reinforcing' (Arthur 1994: xiv). Unlike the traditional island model in which competition operates through the entry of new firms, such an approach is consistent with empirical investigations in which the entry process is switched off and only balanced panels of firms are considered.

While the stochastic growth models presented above are able to reproduce emerging regularities concerning industry dynamics, much is left unexplained. How can these models of growth be justified? Is there any connection with the firm's decision-making process? In this chapter we try to extend the stochastic framework by proposing a model of bounded rational organizations that incorporates behavioural assumptions on: (a) the interactions between the firm and the business environment; and (b) the mechanism by which firms sense and seize business opportunities. The model is meant to show that *the self-reinforcing mechanisms alleged to account for the observed distributions of firm size and growth can be understood as resulting from the joint effect of organizational capabilities and the structure of the environment.*

Our perspective has strong ties to capabilities-based theories of the firm (Dosi and Marengo 2007) as well as the theory of the 'artificial' proposed by Simon (1996). Drawing on their terminology, we describe a firm as a system that purposefully trails goals and functions, and opportunely adapts to fulfil them. The firm, therefore, can be thought as an 'interface' between an inner environment, that is, the organizational capabilities with which it is endowed, and an outer environment, that is, the surroundings in which it operates. Accordingly, the degree of concurrence between the substance and organization of the firm and the context in which it operates will directly influence its profitability and indirectly (through costly mutations of the organizational structure) drive its growth.[6] The achieved outcomes, in turn, will feed a process of search and mutation that make this framework intrinsically evolutionary.

Another feature that distinguishes our contribution from earlier work in the Simonian tradition concerns the way in which we model the taking-up of opportunities by incumbents. Rather than imposing any specific probability density function that might eventually well describe the partition of opportunities across entities, we try to identify and simulate a set of behaviours that might be expected to shape the allocation process. To accomplish this task we borrow from the dynamic capabilities framework which proposes an analytical separation between (1) the capacity to sense opportunities and (2) the capacity to seize opportunities (Teece 2007).[7] Such a reference scheme entails the identification of those elements, interactions and stages an enterprise has to manage in order to successfully address a business opportunity. We incorporate this idea in our simulation model through a two-step procedure. In the first step firms search the environment and detect opportunities. Two factors impinge on their effectiveness in these searching and sensing activities: (i) their current endowment of organizational capabilities; (ii) their relative size. The former establishes the boundaries of the business environment that the firm can explore. The latter determines the ranking of firms according to their sensing ability. In the second step the firm that outperforms its rivals in sensing new opportunities has the chance to seize an opportunity and, eventually, earn a profit. In the next section we detail our strategy to formalize these ideas in the simulation experiment.

A model of growth driven by organizational capabilities

The building blocks

We conceive *the inner system* of the firm as a repertoire of organizational capabilities which supposedly influence a firm's ability to take up the business opportunities populating the neighbouring environment. An explicit model of organizational capabilities is the most important feature of our model. The aim is to disentangle the relationship between firms and technologies. Were technologies freely available to firms, all observed heterogeneity would be explained by the external environment, that is, by the structure of input markets (that give access to resources) or by the nature of the competition in output markets.[8] A long tradition of organizational studies has demonstrated that access to technologies requires particular organizational assets. Therefore, not all technologies are equally available to firms, and complementarities between technology and the organizational features of the firm are quite common. Moreover, some organizational features are not freely disposable to firms: changing organization is costly and requires more than simply acquiring a new technology.

The tradition we refer to dates back to Babbage, who demonstrated the strict correspondence between technical solution and the organization. In particular, he characterized the firm as a *structure of knowledge* that 'enables [the firm] to purchase and apply to each process precisely that quantity of skill and knowledge which is required for it' (Babbage 1835: 201). The correspondence between available knowledge and adopted technologies implies that new technical opportunities are available only if they mirror the internal structure of knowledge.[9]

The empirical work of Joan Woodward (1965), and the theoretical work of James D. Thompson (1967) offer a comprehensive framework to investigate the relationship between technology and organization. In particular, these authors claim that organization matters in cushioning the fixed structure of technology against the variable states of the internal and external environment. In other words, organizational capabilities are a mix of tools aimed at making the technology work in a specific situation.

Finally, it is important to bear in mind that organizational capabilities are embedded in the firm, which amounts to saying that

> [t]he initial conditions ... in which institutions or organizations are formed, can become enduring constraints. They can result in the selection of a particular solution for what is then perceived at the time to be the crucial generic function, for example, recruitment of participants and this can limit the design of other rules and procedures, so that even if the original rationale were to become irrelevant, altering the organisation's recruitment policy would possibly disturb many other aspects of its operations and so impose considerable readjustment costs. In this way the organisational structure can become 'locked in' to a comparatively narrow subset of routines, goals and future work trajectories.
>
> (David 1994: 214)

The above passage recalls the same stickiness of organizational capabilities that Arrow underlines in saying that

> [s]ince the code is part of the firm's or more generally the organization's capital ... it will be modified only slowly over time. Hence, the codes of organizations starting at different times will in general be different even if they are competitive firms.
>
> (Arrow 1974: 56)

Assuming the inner system is the repository for organizational capabilities that can mutate only episodically at high cost, implies that firms may not be able to exploit, or even sense, all technological opportunities in their surroundings.

The outer system is described, *à la* Simon, by two aspects: richness and complexity. Richness is related to the number of opportunities available in the environment. A rich environment is – among others – one in which technological progress gives birth to a large number of new products and processes, or opens up new markets for the existing products. It offers many opportunities, which firms can exploit with no risk of their depletion. Satisfactory solutions are easily achieved and the 'slack', that is, the numerous opportunities in the environment that are not exploited (March 1994), is always high. Complexity represents the difficulty to predict the outcome of an alternative, given the set of already exploited opportunities. This could also be seen as the ruggedness of the environment (Kauffman 1993). In a smooth, non-complex environment, the outcomes of the nearest opportunities are highly correlated. In a complex environment, the outcome of an exploited opportunity does not carry information about the value of other near ones. Complexity translates in the difficulty of environment exploration.

The *exchange between the inner and the outer environment* is guided by two fundamental mechanisms: search[10] and feedback of information on performance. Search determines the way firms capture new opportunities. For the incumbents, we design a two-stage mechanism in which firms: (a) sense opportunities on the basis of their relative sizes; and (b) seize only those opportunities that appear in the neighbourhood of their current position in the landscape. The boundaries of such a neighbourhood, in turn, are a function of the endowment of organizational capabilities of each entity. In a nutshell, firms can only pick up opportunities that are close to their organizational capabilities.

In terms of entry, we assume that newcomers capture opportunities generated in the outer environment with a given probability. At the time of entry, their endowment of organizational capabilities perfectly matches the nature of technological opportunity with which they are associated. As a consequence, whenever an entry occurs a new combination of organizational capabilities appears in the market.

Feedback comes through performance which depends on the value of the opportunities a firm is able to seize and manage. The value of the opportunities is to some extent predictable given the structure of the environment. In a correlated environment, the value of a near opportunity should be not far from that associated with previously captured opportunities. In a rugged landscape, picking up an opportunity whose structure fits the current set of organizational capabilities does not necessarily lead to similar performance in term of profitability. Two outcomes may arise from the mechanism of feedback: when profitability reaches unsatisfactory levels, the firm can either exit or, at a cost, reconfigure its organizational capabilities.

Finally, we need to highlight the evolutionary nature of this scheme: evolution can be interpreted as the change in the set of organizational capabilities that populate the environment. This set evolves through entry and exit (the phylogenetic aspect of evolution) and the mutation of incumbents (ontogenetic evolution).

Details of the model

Consider an industry evolving in a sequence of periods 0, 1,..., t,... T, where 0 is the period in which the variables are initialized. In each period a number of firms F^t is active.[11] Each firm i is endowed with a set of organizational capabilities: OC_i^t are represented as a vector of 1s and 0s of length L. As organizational capabilities can evolve, they are indexed over time. Firm i can be active in different submarkets: this means that, during its life, the firm captures one (which is the condition for its existence), or more opportunities.

We denote BO_i^t as the business opportunity captured by the firm i at time t. The set of all business opportunities available in the market up to time $t > 0$ is given by

$$^0BO^t = \sum_{\tau=0}^{t} \sum_{i \in F^t} BO_i^\tau.$$

Business opportunities are described as a Boolean vector of the same length as the vector representing OC_i^t. Each opportunity has a given value, $v^t(BO)$, that can be thought of as the size of the potential market for that opportunity. The initial value of an opportunity is a random variable whose realization depends on a set of rules defining the environmental setup. In the case of a rugged environment, randomly drawn values are associated with each binary vector describing a BO. In the case of a smooth environment, a set of values is extracted randomly and ordered from the lowest to the highest score. Such values are subsequently associated with vectors of BOs which have been previously ranked by the number of 1s they contain (vectors with equal numbers of 1s are randomly ranked). In this way, BOs with a near structure have near values.[12] The value of an opportunity evolves along time as we will describe below.

We define the following measures of firm performance:

- firm activities, the number of business opportunities a firm has taken up to time t is

$$^0BO_i^t = \sum_{\tau=0}^{t} BO_i^\tau;$$

- firm turnover, the total revenue a firm earns in period t from all the activities in which it is involved:

$$V_i^t = \sum_{\tau=0}^{t} v^\tau(BO_i^\tau);$$

- market share, the ratio between firm turnover and the total revenue of the firms existing at time t: V_i^t/V^t, where:

$$V^t = \sum_{i \in F^t} V_i^t;$$

- firm profits, total turnover net of costs. There are three categories of costs. The first is the cost of a mismatch between organizational capabilities and business opportunities. The value of each opportunity decreases proportionally with the Hamming distance between the two, that is, with the number of the ordered elements in the two vectors that differ.[13] Formally, we can define $m_i^t = |OC_i^t - BO_i^t|$ as the L length vector of the absolute value of the differences between organizational capabilities and business opportunities. This will contain as many 1s as the non-equal elements. Let $d_i^t = \mathrm{I}(m_i^t)$ be the scalar product of the unitary vector and the vector of distances, that is, the sum of the 1s of vector m_i^t. The mismatch between organizational capabilities and business opportunities implies a cost of

$$\frac{d_i^t}{L} v^t(BO_i^t),$$

so that the net value of the business opportunity will be

$$nv^t(BO_i^t) = \left(\frac{L - d_i^t}{L}\right) v^t(BO_i^t).$$

The total net value of business opportunities for firm i at time t is then:

$$NV_i^t = \sum_{\tau=0}^{t} nv^\tau(BO_i^t).$$

The second category of costs involves expenditures associated with organizational change born at time t, $c_i^t(OC_i)$. Finally, in each period, firms bear a fixed production cost f_i for each opportunity at hand: the height of f defines the threshold for opportunity survival in the market. Firm profits at time t are then defined as: $R_i^t = NV_i^t - c_i^t(^{t-1}OC_i^t) - f_i$ (if fixed production costs are equal for all opportunities, $f_i = f \, \forall i \in I$, the third term on the right hand side would be written as $^0BO_i^t f$).

Indicators of market performance can be defined accordingly as: (a) the number of firms operating at time t, F^t; (b) the total number of business opportunities available at time t,

$$^0BO^t = \sum_{\tau=0}^{t} \sum_{i \in F^t} BO_i^\tau;$$

(c) the average size of firms in terms of business opportunities,

$$ABO^t = \frac{1}{F^t} {}^0BO^t;$$

(d) turnover,

$$AV^t = \frac{1}{F^t} \sum_{i=1}^{F^t} V^t_{i};$$

(e) profits,

$$AR^t = \frac{1}{F^t} \sum_i^{F^t} R.$$

The market is initialized at period 0 as follows. An initial number of firms F^0 is created as strings of OC^0. To each firm is attached a BO^0_i with the same structure as OC^0_i (i.e. with the 0s and 1s in the same position) and a value is extracted for each opportunity according to the procedure devised for the specific environment (smooth vs rugged) we are considering. In each subsequent period the following events occur.

a   *Arrival of new opportunities.* A group of business opportunities is extracted from the population of opportunities and assigned to either an entrant or an incumbent firm, according to the following rule. When an opportunity is selected it is assigned with probability p_E to a new entrant: in this case the number of existing firm is increased by 1, $F^t = F^{t-1} + 1$. With the complementary probability $(1 - p_E)$ the opportunity is assigned to an incumbent. Among all existing firms, incumbents are selected according to their market share. The firm extracted first evaluates the newly available opportunities and retains from them, the one whose structure is closer to its set of organizational capabilities (in terms of the Hamming distance between the two Boolean vectors). The firm can also skip the choice whenever the mismatch between its organizational capabilities and all the business opportunities extracted is too high, that is, whenever $d^t_i > d^*$, with d^* defining the maximum distance that allows a firm to seize an opportunity (hereafter, seizing distance). In this case, all new opportunities are lost. Once the opportunity is selected, the firm knows its value $v^t(BO^t_i)$, and the net value $nv^t(BO^t_i)$ can be calculated. This procedure reflects the fact that a firm does not know the exact market value of the business opportunities it chooses.

b   *Updating opportunity values.* The second event occurring each period is the updating of the value of opportunities already taken. A rate of growth g_t $(-1 < g_t < 1)$ is extracted from a normal distribution $(0, \sigma_g)$. The value of each business opportunity is updated according to the rule: $v^t(BO^t_i) = (1 + g^t_i) \cdot v^{t-1}(BO^{t-1}_i)$.

c   *Organizational change.* Firms which, after the allocation of new opportunities and the updating of old business opportunities, present a strong decrease in profitability, $R_i^t \ll R_i^{t-1}$, can, with probability p_{OC}, proceed to organizational change. In this case OC_i^{t-1} are updated at a cost $c_i^t({}^{t-1}OC_i^t)$: that is, a single bit is changed such that the net value of business opportunities is maximized, all other bits remaining fixed (note that this corresponds to a backward looking process of adaptation).

d   *Exit of opportunities and firms.* If in period t, $nv^t(BO_i^t) < f_i(BO_i^t)$, the opportunity is abandoned. If in period t, $R_i^t \le 0$, firm i exits the market.

A comment is needed on the way that competitive dynamics enter our framework. The primary channel through which competition occurs is by the entry of new firms, a standard mechanism since the early generation of stochastic growth models (Simon and Bonini 1958). Competition, however, can implicitly underpin the updating of opportunity values described above. The shrinking and expansion of business opportunities, which we represent as random draws from a $N(0, \sigma_g)$, can be conceived as the outcome of underlying processes concerning pricing behaviour and technological advances.

The absence of an explicit modelling of strategic interactions is by no means a limitation in our model. It has been convincingly argued elsewhere that this feature, albeit in an extreme way, captures the idea that 'most conventionally defined industries exhibit both some strategic interdependence within submarkets, and some degree of independence among submarkets' (Sutton 1997: 49).

Simulation setting and results

Simulation protocol

A comprehensive simulation plan would consider three sets of parameters:

a   Two factors that describe the outer environment are richness and complexity. Complexity is defined by the smoothness or ruggedness of the environment (Kauffman 1993). The environment is smooth when the values of opportunities lying within a given neighbourhood (defined in terms of Hamming distance) are highly correlated. It is rugged in the opposite case. Richness is given by the number of opportunities available in each step.

b   One parameter describing the effect of organizational capabilities on the search process. It corresponds to the seizing distance, d^*, as defined above. For example, a parameter d^* equal to three implies that a firm cannot seize those business opportunities whose structure differs by more than three bits from the structure defining the organizational capabilities of that firm.

c   Two parameters representing feedback and evolution: entry and costs of organizational change. If entry is easy, a high number of new opportunities translates into a growing number of firms and an enrichment of the set of capabilities in the market. If the costs of organizational change are low, firms can easily modify their structure in order to adapt their endowment of organizational capabilities to the structure of the market in which they are operating.

In what follows we focus on the impact of the first two classes of parameters, keeping the rate of entry fixed and disregarding the role of organizational change. We aim at showing how organizational capabilities shape the growth and profitability of firms in different environments, ignoring concerns about the evolutionary properties of the model which, in turn, depend on the parameters regulating feedback and mutation.

Simulation parameters

We initialize the model with a population of 400 firms. Preliminary simulations show that above a minimal threshold, changes in the number of firms existing at the initial stage do not generate qualitatively different results. The support of the distribution of business opportunities values is in the interval [25,100]. It is important to note that the larger the support the fatter the 'potential' tails in the distribution of firm size predicted by the model. Here, 'potential' underlines that the existence of fatter tails also depends on other model characteristics. Or, in other words, that fat tails are 'activated' by the nonlinear interactions of several features of the model.

The length of the vectors representing business opportunities and organizational capabilities is set to 7. Although the results seem to be robust to changes in the value of this parameter, it should be emphasized that, in general, the longer the string the clearer are the differences between alternative scenarios. Usually, longer strings amplify the dissimilarities between the smooth and the rugged worlds. The initial number of opportunities that firms capture is set at a value of 1 in order to mimic the typical assumption made in the literature. The birth rate is exogenous and in all scenarios analysed it is set at 0.1. This choice is spurred by the need to disentangle the dynamics associated with either the evolution of business opportunities picked up by incumbents, or with the ability of entrants to bring new business opportunities into the market.

The fixed cost is set at a value of 10. It represents the cost firms have to pay to be able to produce in each time step. Note that this parameter indirectly establishes a minimal size below which firms are forced to exit the market. The magnitude of adjustment of business opportunity value over time, σ_g, is set at 0.02. This is the pseudo-Gibrat process involving business opportunities that incumbents have already captured and are exploiting to earn profits. The choice seems to be neutral, in the sense that a too high rate of evolution can cancel out other dynamics in the model, while a smaller adjustment will collapse the distribution of growth rates towards zero.

Before presenting the simulation results, we should evaluate the possibility that a steady state (SS) exists in our model. The literature dealing with industry dynamics discusses a wide range of models with different dynamic character-istics leading to different 'limit' distributions of firm sizes (de Wit 2005). The most important assumptions for an SS to exist concern the entry and exit processes and the mechanism governing the growth of firms. By playing with these assumptions one can get a wide range of size distributions, from log normal to Pareto.

Therefore, the possibility for our model to reach an SS is related to the magnitude of the processes governing the demography of the industry. The entry mechanism in our model is assumed to be exogenous; the birth rate is parametrically given. The exit mechanism is endogenous but is strongly influenced by the magnitude of fixed costs (exogenous). If, to some extent, the two processes are balanced out, we end up with a fixed number of firms in the industry. This represents a kind of necessary condition for an SS to exist.

Some results

Our simulation exercise analyses eight scenarios generated by different combinations of parameters concerning on the one side the richness and complexity of the outer environment, and on the other side the seizing distance. As we have already seen the parameter concerning complexity can take the value *smooth* or the value *rugged*. The parameter describing the richness of the environment can take the value 1 (*poor* environment) or the value 3 (*rich* environment). In the first case firms can only decide whether or not to take up the emerging opportunity. In the second case firms can choose among all newly available opportunities the one that best matches their endowment of organizational capabilities. With respect to the seizing distance, d^*, we alternate a value of 7 (organizational capabilities and business opportunities may differ in terms of their constituting bits) with a value of 3 (organizational capabilities and business opportunities may differ by no more than three bits for a firm to grab an opportunity). The eight scenarios are defined as: PRU7, PSM7, RRU7, RSM7, PRU3, PSM3, RRU3, RSM3.

Figure 28.1 shows the distributions of firm size and growth rates in a typical simulation run for three different scenarios. The upper box presents the histograms of the logarithmic size distribution together with a kernel estimation of the density function. A log normal distribution seems to well approximate the pattern of firm size generated in the three scenarios, a finding consistent with the empirical evidence discussed in the literature (Hall 1987; Stanley *et al.* 1995; Cabral and Mata 2003; Growiec *et al.* 2008). A closer look at the plots, however, reveals departures in the upper tail of the distributions that would suggest a poor fit of the log normal distribution for larger firms. These deviations (see descriptive statistics in Tables 28.1 and 28.2) lead to asymmetric (positive values of skewness) and leptokurtic (positive values of kurtosis) distributions.

The middle box in Figure 28.1 emphasizes the deviations referred to above. It presents the Zipf plot (double logarithmic plot of size vs rank) for surviving firms. The three graphs show that for small and medium sized firms the plotted data are concave in relation to the origin, as one would expect for a log normal

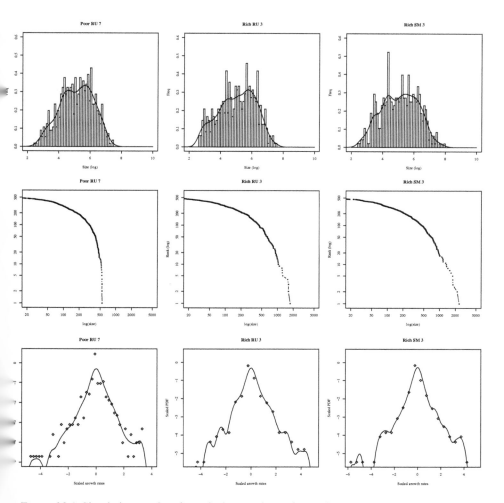

Figure 28.1 Simulation results of a typical run – size and growth.

Notes
Upper box, frequency distribution of logarithmic size; middle box, log rank–log size plot of logarithmic size; lower box, distribution of growth rates (log on the y-axis) with kernel density estimation. Results are obtained with: fixed costs = 10; $d* = 3$, *birth rate* = 0.1; no organizational flexibility; initial number of firms equal to 400. All the pictures refer to time step 2000.

distribution. For larger firms the curvature disappears and a straight line resembling the Zipf plot for the Pareto distribution seems to provide a better fit. Beyond that, as we move towards a rich and smooth landscape with organizational capabilities playing a selective role, the support of the distribution widens and the downward slope of the straight line alleged to fit the observations for larger firms becomes less steep. Overall, this is a first confirmation that the interaction between firms' characteristics and the external environment plays a role.

The lower box in Figure 28.1 shows the distributions of growth rates along with kernel density estimations. The distribution takes a tent-shaped form which is consistent with the pattern described in the empirical studies. In addition, the support of the distribution is fairly constant throughout the scenarios, signalling a certain degree of homogeneity which also emerges in the empirical investigations on narrowly defined industrial sectors.

When organizational capabilities are ineffective for seizing opportunities, $d^* = 7$, changes in the degrees of richness and complexity of the external environment do not impinge on the number of surviving firms or their average size (Table 28.1). However, as we move from a poor and rugged environment (PR7) towards a rich and smooth one (RS7), monotonic changes appear in the higher moments of the firm size distribution. Such changes are noticeable when we compare extreme cases.

The increasing standard deviations in the fourth row of Table 28.1 suggest that differences among surviving firms increase as we move across scenarios. A decreasing median implies that for half of the surviving firms the size decreases as the environment becomes richer and less complex. Also, a higher kurtosis suggests that the distribution becomes more peaked. These results point to a clustering of small firms on the left hand side of the distribution. Nonetheless, as the environment gets richer and the degree of autocorrelation in the value of opportunities rises, the skewness of the distribution increases. Therefore, firms starting off in the simulation with valuable opportunities will grow larger as outside conditions improve.

Table 28.1 Monte Carlo statistics on the firm size distributions – scenarios with $d^* = 7$

Parameters MC mean	Scenarios			
	Poor environment		Rich environment	
	RU7	SM7	RU7	SM7
Number of firms in the industry	602.24	602.24	602.24	602.24
	14.83	14.83	14.83	14.83
Mean size	250.54	250.62	249.17	251.56
	9.73	8.50	11.83	12.13
Median size	148.00	143.40	134.59	131.95
	11.44	9.11	10.48	12.66
Standard deviation of size	277.04	281.87	292.08	322.95
	13.29	14.44	17.38	19.46
Skewness	2.15	2.23	2.30	2.65
	0.31	0.32	0.28	0.45
Kurtosis	6.51	7.04	7.20	10.09
	3.00	3.32	2.88	4.72

Notes
Monte Carlo sample size = 200. MC standard errors in italics.

Although firms can take whatever opportunity they sense in the four scenarios analysed, organizational capabilities may still be operating in a rich environment when the degree of complexity declines. One can reasonably expect that a firm's ability to order new business opportunities and to choose the one that best fits its structure will have non-trivial effects on the size distribution. Indeed, variations in the higher moments of the distribution when shifting from the RR7 to the RS7 scenario, support this idea.

Once the parameter for seizing distance is activated ($d^* = 3$) the selective power of organizational capabilities can directly affect the steady state distribution of firm size. Comparisons with the previous four cases can be done, holding constant the degree of richness and complexity of the external environment. Although no significant change occurs in the support of the distribution, the standard deviations reported in the fourth row of Table 28.2 are close to those presented in Table 28.1, a composite picture emerges if we look at other statistics.

The figures in the first row of Table 28.2 show that whatever the external conditions, a tight seizing distance results in a lower number of surviving firms. Furthermore, a binding seizing distance determines a decline in both average and median firm size in a poor environment. On the other hand, firms operating in a rich environment show a higher average size, with even larger differences appearing when the landscape is smooth. Likewise, the median size of these firms is higher than that observed in Table 28.1.

The skewness and peakedness of the distribution react in different ways to changes in the seizing distance. In the context of a poor and rugged landscape no

Table 28.2 Monte Carlo statistics on the firm size distributions – scenarios with $d^* = 3$

Parameters MC mean	Scenarios			
	Poor environment		Rich environment	
	RU3	SM3	RU3	SM3
Number of firms in the industry	490.7	490.28	489.54	488.28
	15.88	*10.66*	*10.81*	*8.03*
Mean size	218.65	227.99	266.96	277.28
	10.03	*8.08*	*10.60*	*9.48*
Median size	116.51	109.52	166.34	157.76
	11.27	*9.26*	*10.60*	*12.37*
Standard deviation of size	271.75	287.08	285.22	324.60
	12.35	*16.62*	*17.16*	*17.41*
Skewness	2.12	2.48	2.06	2.47
	0.26	*0.42*	*0.31*	*0.42*
Kurtosis	6.10	1.07	5.68	1.77
	2.44	*4.61*	*2.38*	*4.49*

Notes
Monte Carlo sample size = 200. MC standard errors in italics.

divergences emerge when we move towards a scenario with binding seizing distance (from PR7 to PR3). Major differences emerge when we consider the computed values of the kurtosis for smooth landscapes, irrespective of the degree of richness. The figures in the final row of Table 28.2 show a quite low kurtosis (1.07 and 1.77) for cases PS3 and RS3, implying a flatter size distribution than in all other scenarios. Beyond that, the values of skewness under $d^* = 3$ seem to suggest that fatter upper tails in the size distribution are mainly related to the complexity rather than the richness of the environment.

In summary, the model generates firm size distributions that are right skewed and heterogeneous across sectors. We find that the higher the selective power of the firm's organizational capabilities, the more the SS distribution deviates from a log normal. Moreover, the interaction between the external environment and the internal structure of the firm (through the seizing distance) amplifies the selective power of organizational capabilities. In particular: (a) the richer the environment, the wider the set of choices firms have, the stronger the self-reinforcing mechanisms in the growth process that, eventually, lead to a higher skewness in the size distribution; (b) the smoother the environment, the more the values of neighbouring opportunities are correlated, and the larger those firms that start off the simulation process with high value opportunities will become. This process makes the whole distribution flatter and its tails fatter. Beyond that, a high selective power of organizational capabilities in a rugged environment may prevent firms from exploiting the chances of growth that new opportunities bring. This happens in the absence of any compensation for an increased probability of choosing a good opportunity having achieved a good one in the past: in a poor rugged environment the selective action of organizational capabilities seems to cause a sort of 'competence trap'.

The simulation model replicates a skewed distribution of the number of opportunities per firm (Figure 28.2b) that is consistent with the typical patterns in empirical investigations. Such a shape implies that most firms seize a small number of opportunities, while a very few entities account for a large fraction of the business opportunities arising throughout the simulation period. The interaction between the external environment and the internal structure of the firms also influences the heterogeneity in the value of the opportunities they capture. In order to assess the importance of this phenomenon we categorize the total variation in the value of seized opportunities into two components, 'between' and 'within' variation. The former reflects between firm differences in the portfolios of opportunities; the latter reflects the degree of variability in the portfolio of a typical firm.

The analysis we conducted points out (Table 28.3) that, irrespective of the complexity and richness of the outer environment, about three-quarters of the total variability in the value of opportunities is accounted for by heterogeneity in the portfolio of a typical firm. The lowest degree of heterogeneity within the portfolios of opportunities that firms own (i.e. within deviance = 70.4 per cent) arises when the selective power of organizational capabilities is high and the environment is smooth and poor. In such a scenario, relatively fewer opportunities appear along the simulation periods and firms are also more likely to

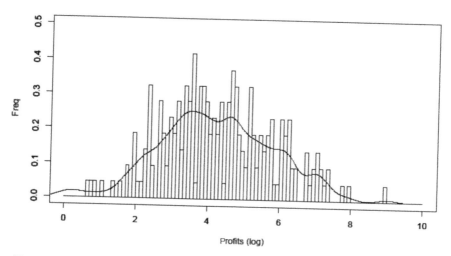

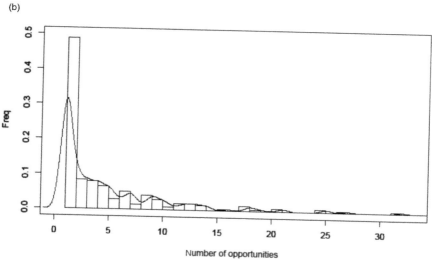

Figure 28.2 Simulation results of a typical run – profits and BOs.

Notes

(a) frequency distribution of profits; (b) frequency distribution of number of opportunities. Results are obtained with: fixed costs = 10; $d* = 3$, *birth rate* = 0.1; no organizational flexibility; initial number of firms equal to 400. All the pictures refer to time step 2000.

Table 28.3 Decomposition of the total variability in the value of opportunities

Parameters	Poor environment			
	RU7	SM7	RU3	SM3
	Total deviance			
MC mean	2507849.8	2573432.8	1834270.6	1874614.8
Standard error	*266485.71*	*303046.13*	*179498.76*	*223559.96*
	Within deviance			
MC mean	2120664.2	2169373.4	1330070.7	1320236.2
Standard error	*47040.98*	*52744.03*	*67596.26*	*87079.33*
Contribution to total deviance (%)	84.56	84.30	72.51	70.43
	Between deviance			
MC Mean	387186.14	404058.86	504199.76	543891
Standard error	*297022.27*	*343794.02*	*216564.85*	*267678.25*
Contribution to total deviance (%)	15.43	15.70	27.49	29.01
	Rich environment			
	RU7	SM7	RU3	SM3
	Total deviance			
MC mean	2741798.2	2524869	2533595.2	3018092.5
Standard error	*325280.76*	*302788.87*	*299542.91*	*357478.36*
	Within deviance			
MC mean	2258267.60	1966505.60	2046910.60	2290772.5
Standard error	*279260.20*	*254108.58*	*261163.76*	*299107.13*
Contribution to total deviance (%)	82.36	77.89	80.79	75.90
	Between deviance			
MC Mean	483529.90	558364.14	486684.88	757322.5
Standard error	*56870.75*	*74842.75*	*59740.43*	*82383.47*
Contribution to total deviance (%)	17.64	22.11	19.21	25.09

Notes
Monte Carlo sample size = 200.

discard a number of opportunities they come across. Besides, the autocorrelated landscape triggers a self-reinforcing process that makes each firm capturing a great deal of equally valued opportunities.

Important differences emerge when comparing the eight scenarios. Assuming the seizing distance is ineffective ($d^* = 7$), as the environment gets richer the between component of total variability increases, with a clearer upsurge in the case of a smooth landscape (from 15.7 per cent to 22.1 per cent). Moreover, when the seizing distance is ineffective a higher degree of relatedness in the landscape impinges on the share between deviances only in a rich environment (from 17.6 per cent to 22.1 per cent). Overall, when organizational capabilities do not play a role in seizing opportunities richness and smoothness seem to have a complementary effect that ultimately amplifies the differences in the portfolios of opportunities across firms.

On the contrary, when the selective power of organizational capabilities is at work ($d* = 3$) richness and smoothness of the outer environment seem to exercise an opposite effect on the degree of interfirm differences. Indeed, a lower degree of complexity intensifies the differences across firms' portfolios (from 19.2 per cent to 25.1 per cent in a rich environment). Vice versa, as we move from a poor to a rich environment the between deviance in the total variability of opportunity values shrinks (from 27.5 per cent to 19.2 per cent in a rugged landscape).

Finally, by holding constant the outer environment we can appreciate how a shift in the seizing distance affects the relative share of the within and between components. Our results show that in all cases, the more organizational capabilities influence the grabbing of new opportunities (from $d* = 7$ to $d* = 3$), the greater are differences in the value of portfolios of opportunities across firms. Such differences are almost twofold in the case of a poor and smooth environment where a tougher seizing distance causes a rise in the between deviance from 15.7 per cent to 29.1 per cent.

The distribution of (logarithmic) profits displays an approximately bell-shaped form (Figure 28.2a) with minor departures from a normal distribution than observed for firm size. In order to appreciate the persistence of profits and the impact of organizational capabilities on long lasting differences across firms, we estimate the autoregressive model in equation (28.2) over the simulated data of surviving firms:

$$\pi_{i,t} = \alpha_i + \beta_i \pi_{i,t-1} + \varepsilon_{i,t} \quad t = 1900, \ldots, 2000 \tag{28.2}$$

In the above regression β_i reflects the persistence with which profits differ period by period from their long run level; α_i captures idiosyncratic differences that may cause the long run profits,

$$\pi_{ip} = \frac{\alpha_i}{1 - \beta_i},$$

that firms earn to diverge from the zero excess profits conjectured in neoclassical economic theory; $\varepsilon_{i,t}$ is an error component which summarizes the influence that unsystematic shocks have on profitability.

Earlier research (Geroski and Mueller 1990) found that firm characteristics are more important than industry factors in explaining the long run equilibrium value of company profits. Accordingly, we expect our capabilities-based simulation model to predict a non-negligible fraction of α_i coefficients different from a zero value. Indeed, the figures in Table 28.4 show that the average estimated α is significantly different from the null profit level in about 30 per cent of the series. Furthermore, the coefficient increases when organizational capabilities play a selective role ($d* = 3$) and the external environment is smooth. The average value of the β coefficient is quite high and constant across the four scenarios, thus signalling that, whatever the environmental conditions, competitive forces do not wipe out extra profits in the short run.

Table 28.4 Monte Carlo statistics on the persistence of profits

Parameters MC mean	Scenarios			
	RU3	SM3	RU7	SM7
β	0.894	0.895	0.927	0.906
	0.02	*0.03*	*0.02*	*0.1*
Percentage of series with a significant β coefficient	99.79	99.57	99.81	99.82
α	21.582	21.660	17.131	16.798
	0.62	*0.71*	*0.41*	*0.62*
Percentage of series with a significant α coefficient	29.019	27.542	31.091	25.573
R^2	0.812	0.817	0.806	0.820
	0.073	*0.100*	*0.041*	*0.018*

Notes
Monte Carlo sample size = 200. MC standard errors in italics. Coefficients α and β in the table refe
to the estimation for each firm i of the linear equation: $\pi_{i,t} = \alpha + \beta\pi_{i,t-1} + \varepsilon_{i,t}$ $t = 1900,\ldots, 2000.$

Conclusions

In this chapter we proposed an approach to analyse firm size, growth rates and
profitability, aimed at reconciling the idea of stochastic models of growth with
the role of organizational capabilities in shaping performance differences among
firms. This was done by building a model that conceives firms as bounded
rational organizations that adapt to the structure of the environment.

A first set of simulation exercises helped us highlight the role of organizational capabilities in shaping the growth and performance of firms. The more
interesting results lie in the different findings that emerge when organizational
capabilities selectively act in the environment either because of the richness of
the environment, or due to the constraint capabilities imposed on the ability to
seize opportunities. The selective power of organizational capabilities also
depends on a second environmental characteristic, that is, the degree of complexity of the landscape in which firms operate. When the landscape is smooth
and correlated, firms that are better placed at the beginning of the process tend to
reinforce their position as time goes by; in such a context organizational capabilities drive the capture of new, highly valued opportunities. This implies a higher
dispersion of limit size, correlation of growth rates, high persistence of performance and high heterogeneity among firms (high between components of the variance of opportunity value). In such an environment, organizational capabilities
represent the core of the behavioural mechanism generating a self-reinforcing
process of corporate growth. By contrast, when organizational capabilities are
used as a selection device in a rugged landscape, we find a case for the 'curse of
capabilities': firms are trapped by their own capabilities, even when they are of
no value for the exploitation of good opportunities.

Despite the preliminary nature of this work, we believe that the present chapter, by opening the way to explanatory models that complement the refinement of a general law, enriches the debate on growth and performance. We sense that a few extensions could make the model more generalizable. First, competition could be modelled explicitly, making the value of investment opportunities sensitive to the number of firms that choose them. Second, it is desirable to activate the evolutionary component of our model, that is, the process of organizational change which may lead firms to modify their positions in the landscape.

Further work is required to define an empirical counterpart for the 'artificial worlds' we built, a necessary step in order to test the predictive power of the model. This should allow us to classify the environmental conditions in which firms operate, and to capture the role of organizational capabilities in seizing business opportunities. Historical data on patents, new products and the volatility of sales and market shares would provide some empirical content to concepts such as environmental richness and complexity.

Notes

1 Moreover, both views contrast with textbook popularization according to which size depends on technology and demand, and profits are the result of market structure (i.e. number of competitors).
2 Palestrini (2007) proposes a unifying framework that relates the double exponential distribution of growth rates and the power-like behaviour of size distribution.
3 Gibrat's Law is a property compatible with a range of models of corporate growth (Boeri 1989) some of which are difficult to reconcile with the bulk of empirical evidence discussed in the econometric literature on the evolution of business size (Geroski 2000).
4 This proposition, known as the Law of Proportionate Effects, implies that 'the probability of a given proportionate change in size during a specified period is the same for all firms in a given industry – regardless of their size at the beginning of the period' (Mansfield 1962: 1030). Furthermore, note that Gibrat's Law can be formulated in three different ways. One could argue that it holds: (1) for all firms in the industry, including those that fail and leave the industry during the period of observation; (2) for all firms in the industry, apart from those that exit the industry; (3) only for firms in the industry that are larger than the minimum efficient size.
5 Hence, the model has no real steady-state distribution. To obtain a stability condition alternative devices that restrict the random walk of firm size are needed (de Wit 2005).
6 Note the analogy with technology studies which explain the failure of innovating firms on the basis of the mismatch between the firm's system of coordination and control and the nature of available technological opportunities (Pavitt 1998).
7 Teece (2007) also mentions the capacity to maintain competitiveness through reconfiguring the firm's tangible and intangible assets, an aspect that we do not explicitly take into account in this version of the model. Besides describing the nature of these three capacities, he extensively specifies the microfoundations that underpin such enterprise-level capabilities.
8 This was precisely the tenet in Bain's industrial economics: tell me where you live, and I will tell you who you are.
9 A modern version of the same idea is Cohen and Levinthal's (1990) concept of 'absorptive capacity'.
10 Our model can easily accommodate finer processes of search, such as that described by Gavetti and Levinthal (2000) in which firms have partial representation of opportunities.

11 In what follows we use the right superscript to denote the period to which the variable
    refers; when left and right superscript are used, this means 'from the period of the left
    superscript to the period of the right superscript'. The subscript i ($i = 1,\ldots, F^r$) refers
    the variable to a firm.
12 While this way of generating the landscape differs from Kauffman (1993), it respects
    the same structure and, at the same time, enables higher variability.
13 Recall Heiner's definition of uncertainty as a competence-difficulty gap, where the
    environmental variable determines the complexity of the environment, and compe-
    tence is defined by the perceptual variables 'which characterise an agent's compe-
    tence in deciphering relationships between its behaviour and the environment' (Heiner
    1983: 564).

References

Amaral, A.N., Gopikrishnan, P., Plerou, V. and Stanley, H.E. (2001) 'A model for the
    growth dynamics of economic organizations', *Physica A*, 299: 127–36.
Angelini, P. and Generale, A. (2008) 'On the evolution of firm size distributions', *Ameri-
    can Economic Review*, 98: 426–38.
Arrow, K.J. (1974) *The Limits of Organization*, New York: Norton.
Arthur, B. (1994) *Increasing Returns and Path Dependence in Economics*, Michigan, MI:
    University of Michigan Press.
Axtell, R.L. (2001) 'Zipf distribution of U.S. firm size', *Science*, 293: 1818–20.
Babbage, C. (1835) *On the Economy of Machinery and Manufactures*, London: Knight.
Boeri, T. (1989) 'Does firm size matter?', *Giornale degli Economisti e Annali di Econo-
    mia*, 48: 477–95.
Bottazzi, G. and Secchi, A. (2006) 'Explaining the distribution of firm growth rates',
    RAND Journal of Economics, 37: 235–56.
Bottazzi, G., Cefis, E., Dosi, G. and Secchi, A. (2007) 'Invariances and diversities in the
    patterns of industrial evolution: Some evidence from Italian manufacturing industries',
    Small Business Economics, 29: 137–59.
Cabral, L.M.B. and Mata, J. (2003) 'On the evolution of the firm size distribution: Facts
    and theory', *American Economic Review*, 93: 1075–90.
Coad, A. (2007) 'A closer look at serial growth rate correlation', *Review of Industrial
    Organization*, 31: 69–82.
Cohen, W. and Levinthal, D. (1990) 'Absorptive capacity: A new perspective on learning
    and innovation', *Administrative Science Quarterly*, 35: 128–52.
David, P.A. (1994) 'Why are institutions the "carriers of history"? Path dependence and
    the evolution of conventions, organizations and institutions', *Structural Change and
    Economic Dynamics*, 5: 205–20.
de Wit, G. (2005) 'Firm size distributions: An overview of steady-state distributions
    resulting from firm dynamics models', *International Journal of Industrial Organiza-
    tion*, 23, 423–50.
Dosi, G. and Marengo, L. (2007) 'On the evolutionary and behavioral theories of organi-
    zations: A tentative roadmap', *Organization Science*, 18: 491–502.
Dunne, P. and Hughes, A. (1994) 'Age, size, growth and survival: UK companies in the
    1980s', *Journal of Industrial Economics*, 42: 115–40.
Dunne, T., Roberts, M.J. and Samuelson, L. (1989) 'The growth and failure of U.S. man-
    ufacturing plants', *Quarterly Journal of Economics*, 104: 671–98.
Evans, D.S. (1987a) 'The relationship between firm growth, size, and age: Estimates for
    100 manufacturing industries', *Journal of Industrial Economics*, 35: 567–81.

—— (1987b) 'Tests of alternative theories of firm growth', *Journal of Political Economy*, 95: 657–74.

Fagiolo, G. and Luzzi, A. (2006) 'Do liquidity constraints matter in explaining firm size and growth? Some evidence from the Italian manufacturing firms', *Industrial and Corporate Change*, 15: 1–39.

Fu, D., Pammolli, F., Buldyrev, S.V., Riccaboni, M., Matia, K., Yamasaki, K. and Stanley, H.E. (2005) 'The growth of business firms: Theoretical framework and empirical evidence', *Proceedings of the National Academy of Science*, 102: 18,801–6.

Gavetti, G. and Levinthal, D. (2000) 'Looking forward and looking backward: Cognitive and experiential search', *Administrative Science Quarterly*, 45: 113–37.

Geroski, P.A. (2000) 'The growth of firms in theory and in practice', in N. Foss and V. Manke (eds.), *Competence, Governance and Entrepreneurship*, Oxford: Oxford University Press.

—— (2005) 'Understanding the implications of empirical work on corporate growth rates', *Managerial and Decision Economics*, 26: 129–38.

—— and Jacquemin, A. (1988) 'The persistence of profits: A European comparison', *Economic Journal*, 98: 375–89.

—— and Mueller, D.C. (1990) 'The persistence of profits in perspective', in D.C. Mueller (ed.), *The Dynamics of Company Profits: An International Comparison*, Cambridge: Cambridge University Press.

Gibrat, R. (1931) *Les Inégalités Economiques*, Paris: Sirey.

Goddard, J.A. and Wilson, J.O.S. (1999) 'The persistence of profits: A new empirical interpretation', *International Journal of Industrial Organization*, 17: 663–87.

Growiec, J., Pammolli, F., Riccaboni, M. and Stanley, H.E. (2008) 'On the size distribution of business firms', *Economics Letters*, 98, 207–12.

Hall, B.H. (1987) 'The relationship between firm size and firm growth in the US manufacturing sector', *Journal of Industrial Economics*, 3: 583–606.

Hart, P.E. and Oulton, N. (1996) 'Growth and size of firms', *Economic Journal*, 106: 1242–52.

Hart, P.E. and Prais, S.J. (1956) 'The analysis of business concentration: A statistical approach', *Journal of the Royal Statistical Society, Series A (General)*, 119: 150–91.

Hawawini, G., Subramanian, V. and Verdin, P. (2003) 'Is performance driver by industry – or firm-specific factors? A new look at the evidence', *Strategic Management Journal*, 24: 1–16.

Heiner, R.A. (1983) 'The origin of predictable behavior', *American Economic Review*, 73: 560–95.

Hymer, S. and Pashigian, P. (1962) 'Firm size and rate of growth', *Journal of Political Economy*, 70: 556–69.

Ijiri, Y. and Simon, H.A. (1977) *Skew Distributions and the Sizes of Business Firms*, Amsterdam: North-Holland.

Kauffman, S.A. (1993) *The Origins of Order: Organization and Selection in Evolution*, Oxford: Oxford University Press.

Kumar, M.S. (1985) 'Growth, acquisition activity and firm size: Evidence from the United Kingdom', *Journal of Industrial Economics*, 33: 327–38.

McGahan, A.M. and Porter, M.E. (2002) 'What do we know about variance in accounting profitability?', *Management Science*, 48: 834–51.

Mansfield, D.E. (1962) 'Entry, Gibrat's law, innovation, and growth of the firms', *American Economic Review*, 52: 1024–51.

March, J.G. (1994) *A Primer on Decision Making: How Decisions Happen*, New York: The Free Press.

Misangyi, V.F., Elms, H., Greckhamer, T. and Lepine, J.A. (2006) 'A new perspective on a fundamental debate: A multilevel approach to industry, corporate, and business unit effects', *Strategic Management Journal*, 27: 571–90.

Mueller, D.C. (1977) 'The persistence of profits above the norm', *Economica*, 44: 369–80.

—— (1990) *The Dynamics of Company Profits: An International Comparison*, Cambridge: Cambridge University Press.

Nelson, R.R. (1991) 'Why firms differ, and how does it matter?', *Strategic Management Journal*, 12: 61–74.

Palestrini, A. (2007) 'Analysis of industrial dynamics: A note on the relationship between firms' size and growth rate', *Economics Letters*, 94: 367–71.

Pavitt, K. (1998) 'Technologies, products and organization in the innovating firm: What Adam Smith tells us and Joseph Schumpeter doesn't', *Industrial and Corporate Change*, 7: 433–52.

Reichstein, T. and Jensen, M.B. (2005) 'Firm size and firm growth rate distributions: The case of Denmark', *Industrial and Corporate Change*, 14: 1145–66.

Rumelt, R.P. (1991) 'How much does industry matter?', *Strategic Management Journal*, 12: 167–85.

Schmalensee, R. (1985) 'Do markets differ much?', *American Economic Review*, 75: 341–51.

—— (1989) 'Inter-industry studies of structure and performance', in R. Schmalensee and R. Willig (eds), *Handbook of Industrial Organization*, vol. 2, Amsterdam: North-Holland.

Simon, H.A. (1996) *The Sciences of the Artificial*, Cambridge, MA: The MIT Press.

—— and Bonini, C.P. (1958) 'The size distribution of business firms', *American Economic Review*, 58: 607–17.

Singh, A. and Whittington, G. (1975) 'The size and growth of firms', *Review of Economic Studies*, 42: 15–26.

Stanley, M.H.R., Buldyrev, S.V., Havlin, S., Mantegna, R.N., Salinger, M.A. and Stanley, H.E. (1995) 'Zipf plots and the size distribution of firms', *Economics Letters*,49: 453–57.

Stanley, M.H.R., Amaral, L.A., Buldyrev, S.V., Havlin, S., Leschhorn, H., Maass, P., Salinger, M.A. and Stanley, H.E. (1996) 'Scaling behaviour in the growth of companies', *Nature*, 379: 804–6.

Sutton, J. (1997) 'Gibrat's legacy', *Journal of Economic Literature*, 35: 40–59.

—— (1998) *Technology and Market Structure*, Cambridge, MA and London, UK: The MIT Press.

Teece, D.J. (2007) 'Explicating dynamic capabilities: The nature and microfoundations of (sustainable) enterprise performance', *Strategic Management Journal*, 28: 1319–50.

Thompson, J.D. (1967) *Organizations in Action: Social Science Bases of Administrative Theory*, New York: McGraw-Hill.

Waring, G.F. (1996) 'Industry differences in the persistence of industry specific returns', *American Economic Review*, 86: 1253–65.

Wiggins, R.R. and Ruefli, T.W. (2002) 'Sustained competitive advantage: Temporal dynamics and the incidence and persistence of superior economic performance', *Organization Science*, 13: 82–105.

Woodward, J. (1965) *Industrial Organization: Theory and Practice*, London: Oxford University Press.

Part VIII
Finale

29 The most difficult questions

A brief reflection inspired by
K. Vela Velupillai's contributions in
computable economics, evolution and
complexity

Cassey Lee

The most interesting questions tend to be also the most difficult ones to answer. In any discipline, such questions might be those that pertain not only to the subject matter of the discipline but have wider implications for other disciplines. This also means that to answer such questions often requires some knowledge of other fields of study. After all, each discipline is a study of only a limited aspect of our very complex reality. In trying to gain this knowledge of reality, we all hope that, while we may never gain the full knowledge of reality, we may at least be a little bit 'wiser' about what we don't know and perhaps more importantly, something about ourselves. The body of knowledge that is the lifetime work of K. Vela Velupillai takes us on a journey of discovery of such kind.[1] Where do we begin?

My own impression of the ultimate value of Vela's work is in its contributions to the broadening of our understanding of the discourse in economics by placing it within a wider universe of knowledge. Most of us would like to think of economics as a well-defined discipline – one amenable to mathematical theorizing, empirical verification and policy recommendations. This is done, most of the time, with the rigorous tools of trade that we accumulate over time and often use with complete ignorance of where they came from. The consequence of such lack of exposure and appreciation of the history of economic theory with regards to our use of such tools condemns the discipline to paths that eventually leads to intellectual dead ends. Over the years, Vela has carefully and eloquently written about the manner in which economic theory was mathematized and its consequence.[2] This history is that of the axiomatization of economic theory in the Hilbert tradition. It is a history about how economics adopted tools from a certain mathematical tradition (classical real analysis) while ignoring others and, worse, remained ignorant of subsequent developments that shattered the 'completeness' of the former (read Gödel).

The dire consequence of the path taken in mathematizing economics is the demonstration, using an alternative mathematical tradition such as recursion theory, that most of the solutions or equilibrium (including their existence) derived using classical real analysis cannot be obtained in reality from a computational point of view. This has important implications for economics as almost all (if not all) economic problems are posed as optimization problems which would imply the use of some algorithms or procedures to obtain the attendant solutions. What then would be a more appropriate way to mathematize economic theory?

The choice of an appropriate 'mathematical language' to theorize about reality may require a deeper understanding of the nature of reality, i.e. impermanence, nature as a process. This is a view that finds resonance not only in the physical and natural sciences (evolution, thermodynamics) but also in ancient philosophy and religion (Parmenides, Buddha). This, I believe, is very much a view embraced by Vela (2005b) in his unpublished little essay. In this essay, we find a glimpse of the holistic and integrative nature of Vela's thinking where there is no boundary between views on economics and on life.

Moving forward with this line of thinking, we can then argue that the issue at hand is about the nature of the different types of mathematics and whether they lead to structures or systems that can or cannot capture reality. This is not an easy question to answer because 'reality as process' also implies that there is no 'closure' in reality, i.e. the universe does not stand still for us to capture (even here, we are trapped by a non-Einsteinian notion of time!). Perhaps, this is also related to the ineffectiveness of reductionist methods in making sense of emergence phenomena, where a computable perspective may yield deeper insights into reality – namely, an emergent system is 'open' in the sense of being universally computational and that finiteness in itself is an essential element of emergence. These insights are reminiscent of holistic views in older metaphysical traditions (e.g. Tao?) where one's limitation(s) (e.g. bounded rationality) is an inextricable ingredient of our complex existence.

Where do we go from here then? If we use a more 'appropriate' mathematical language, one that has process/computation as part of its nature (e.g. recursion theory), and show that we cannot obtain such and such a solution – does it mean that the chosen language has once again failed us or, more intriguingly, has it has captured the essence of reality, namely its impermanence (masquerading perhaps as incompleteness at a point in time) or that the future cannot indeed be known by any finite means and beings? These are deep questions and much of Vela's writings inspire and prompt us to think beyond the narrow confines of our normal economic mind.

Morning dew,
Leaving no traces
On a leaf...

Notes

1 I first encountered Vela more than ten years ago in a footnote. Searching for an area for my doctoral studies, what sparked the initial contact was Axel Leijonhufvud's 1993 essay that contained an intriguing acknowledgment which read: 'I am particularly grateful to my colleague Kumaraswamy Velupillai, who has taught me all I know about computability, complexity and related matters. That I do not know more than I do is not his fault!' Exactly my sentiments today.
2 See Velupillai (1996, 2000, 2005a and 2007).

References

Leijonhufvud, A. (1993) 'Towards a not-too-rational macroeconomics', *Southern Economic Journal*, 60:(1): 1–13.

Velupillai, K. (1996) 'The computable alternative in the formalization of economics: A counterfactual essay', *Kyklos*, 49(3): 252–72.

—— (2000) *Computable Economics*, Oxford: Oxford University Press.

—— (2005a) 'The unreasonable ineffectiveness of mathematics in economics', *Cambridge Journal of Economics*, 29(6): 849–72.

—— (2005b) 'Buddhism and the ZEITGEIST', Mimeo.

—— (2007) 'Variations on the theme of conning in mathematical economics', *Journal of Economic Surveys*, 21(3): 466–505.

30 A homage to my father

Viveka Velupillai

I can't begin to thank all the contributors for the efforts they have put into this volume. Not only because I am grateful for a Festschrift in honour of my father, whom I consider the most lovable grump imaginable, but also because a lot of pieces about him fell into place for me while going through the various chapters when helping out with the editing process. My father is, as anyone who has met him will know, a mosaic of superlatives, and as with all mosaics, there is nothing linear about the pattern of his intellectual development. Of course growing up, I had a very vague notion indeed of what he was doing all these years. As far as I was concerned, he spent his time reading excruciatingly boring books instead of devoting himself to sensible literature, such as Winnie the Pooh. But there you go, was my philosophy, that's Daddies for you.

I myself grew up to stay in academia, the world of my father, but as I ended up in Linguistics, I can tell you very little about my father's achievements in his field. I can, however, give you some of the origins of them, a few of the trampolines of his various leaps and bounds that then ended up paving the way for his intellectual odyssey.

Let me start out by showing how it was inevitable that my father would end up in macroeconomics in the first place. As a boy in the Sri Lanka of the 1950s my father was doing well in school but tended to be a bit on the wild side on the playground. On one occasion, when he was embroiled in a fist fight against a boy who had been bullying another boy, some American Peace Corps soldiers intervened and suggested a proper boxing match instead, where the winner would get an *entire* crate of Coca Cola. As the other boy was much bigger than my father, the odds were that my father would lose. He didn't. With this the yellow brick road for the fascination of probabilities (winning against a much bigger boy) in, as well as in relation to, the world market (as manifested by the crate of Coca Cola) against the backdrop of dynamic optimization (the soldiers setting up the game) was paved. In fact, I would propose that

$$\left(\sum_{r=1}^{n} \Pr(q_r|H)\Pr(p|q_r,H) \right)^{-1}$$

where H is that the other boy was much bigger and q_1 is losing the match (and thus the Coke), q_2 is winning it (and the Coke), q_3 is a tie (nobody gets the Coke), q_4 the prize is something else than Coke ... q_n, while p is my father ending up in macroeconomics.

I will have you notice, by the way, that my father ended up in that fight in the first place by defending another boy. And here is another piece of the mosaic of superlatives: my father's generosity. Although I think few would argue with me if I claim that my father is one of the most stubborn mules that you ever came across, he is, at the same time, a most caring and considerate mule. Being his daughter meant (and still means) that you got nothing by half measure, be it story telling, messing about or the never ending gifts and surprises. Having imbued the essence of kindness from his own father, my *Paata* ('grandfather' in Tamil), his anchor in this turbulent world, he has done his outmost to impart that unfettered and unconditional caring to us, his children. And, as far as I'm concerned, he has, in turn, succeeded in providing us with a supportive anchor.

I learnt so much beauty from my father. I grew up surrounded by music, delicious food, splendid surroundings. Like I said, my father does nothing by half measure, which goes for his cooking too. Seeing my father cook – *if* you're allowed to remain in the kitchen – is a symphony of meditational delight. His concentration as he delves into the selection, peeling, cutting, stirring and general pottering about with the ingredients is so intense it is almost tangible. And here we have, I am convinced, the origins of his *Computable Economics* (Velupillai 2000). As with Bela Bartók's unparalleled compositions, my father's cooking is an equation of delicacy. And I don't mean simply for the palate. When he cooks, my father cooks in "recursively enumerable but not recursive sets" (ibid.: 29) of ingredients, in the same manner as Bela Bartók plays around with his notes. With the rational choice of a register k of ingredients and their adaptive behaviour, depending on the state s of the stove, the dish i will be modified, depending on what piece of music my father will be listening to (α_s, β_t, γ_s, δ_t respectively), into a new state t which can be shaped by setting

$$f_s(x) = g_s\left[\left(\frac{x-s}{n}\right)(x-s)\gamma_s + \delta_t\right] + \left[1 - g_s\left(\frac{x-s}{n}\right)\right][(x-s)\alpha_s + \beta_t]$$

where

$$f(x) = \sum_{s=1}^{n-1} h_s(x)f_s(x).$$

What we have, of course, is nothing but a culinary Turing machine.

There were, however, certain aspects about my father that always remained elusive to me. For instance, he is able to drink from a bottle of water while lying down. I always admired that and was never able to do it myself. In fact, I remember in vivid detail how I, like the cocky four-year old I was, tried to follow suit, only to splash a fountain all over my face and soak my pillow. Choking, cursing and coughing, I vowed to never try and copy my father again. Presumably that's why I ended up in Linguistics. Or the cricket business, this holiest of holy, best savoured from a horizontal position on the sofa. I truly did want to understand what all those fellows in their v-necked sweaters were up to for days on end, but he always refused to explain it to me. "It can't be explained; you either understand it or you don't", was the answer. Try and argue with that.

But I must say, growing up with my father, with his insatiable appetite for epistemology and philosophy of science, by necessity sharpens your intellect and hones your capacity for argumentative retort. I remember, for instance, the time my father was, under grumbling protest, cutting the yew bush outside our front door. When he puffingly announced that he was done, Aruna, my sister, who shares Idefix's love for all trees and bushes, was furious at my father for having cut the bush all skewed, and shouted at him that he had ruined the whole thing. To which he shouted back that this cult for symmetry was nothing but a manifestation of western hegemonial arrogance!

However, there was one character in my childhood that actually measured up to my father's superlative stubbornness: our neighbour Axel, a wonderfully obstinate old sailor. He was very fond of us, and especially enjoyed chatting with my father. Now, the concept of "chatting" with my father is a fantastic contradiction in terms, pure and simple. And our neighbour, needless to say, usually managed to choose the most inconvenient times to pop over for a – usually lengthy – "chat". On one occasion my father was at his desk and spotted Axel's ominous approach, and as my father was at that moment in the middle of writing, his capacity to ride out a chit-chat was at nil. But, being my father, he was also much too polite to actually let Axel know that the timing was bad. So, assuming, as usual, that his more or less subtle hints would be understood, he hurriedly took off to the bathroom and told us to let Axel know that he (my father) was taking a bath. Which we duly did. "Oh, that's OK", says Axel magnanimously and makes himself comfortable in the kitchen. *Two solid hours* later, when my father was so thoroughly chilled he just couldn't stand it anymore, he comes out of the bathroom, his face the most menacing thunderstorm you've ever seen. His shoulders were literally hunched up above the ears, and the famous Jutting Jaw – which everybody knows is an acute warning to get out of the way or face the consequences – was as far out as physically possible. Axel had won the waiting game, and with that catapulted my father straight into the Hopf bifurcation theorem. This, I am convinced, is the origin of my father's various disequilibrium models (e.g. Velupillai 2006).

These are, of course, merely a few scattered examples of the glittering mosaic that is my father. How to give a summary on someone who has the curiosity of Nikola Tesla, the humbleness of Niels Bohr and the depth of the *Tirukkural*? My father has the memory of an elephant and his associative capacities are as quick and mobile as a dragonfly's dance. He will have connected the dots before the rest of us have even registered the existence of any dots. My father will make up his mind and then actively go deaf to any counter argument. He will be snoring with the radio on next to him, instantly wake up if you switch it off, claiming with a frown that he "was listening to that!" and turn his head in a huff only to immediately go back to sleep. My father might seem like a no-nonsense kind of guy, but squirrels hop up to him and munch goodies straight from his hand. So, in short: here's to you, my dearest Appa. Stay the way you are.

Postscript

In reality, some of the details described in the Coca Cola incident happened on a separate occasion. However, in the interest of fluidity, I allowed myself a pinch of poetic freedom and glommed them into one event.

References

Velupillai, K. (2000) *Computable Economics*, Oxford: Oxford University Press.
—— (2006) 'A disequilibrium macrodynamic model of fluctuations', *Journal of Macro-economics*, 28: 752–67.

Author index

Subject index

For Product Safety Concerns and Information please contact our EU
representative GPSR@taylorandfrancis.com
Taylor & Francis Verlag GmbH, Kaufingerstraße 24, 80331 München, Germany